W9-AZV-260

# Organizational Behavior

A MANAGEMENT CHALLENGE

# Organizational Behavior

## A MANAGEMENT CHALLENGE

**Gregory B. Northcraft**
*University of Arizona*

**Margaret A. Neale**
*Northwestern University*

THE DRYDEN PRESS

Chicago   Fort Worth   San Francisco   Philadelphia
Montreal   Toronto   London   Sydney   Tokyo

Acquisitions Editor:   Robert Gemin
Developmental Editor:   Penny Gaffney
Project Editor:   Paula Dempsey
Production Manager:   Barb Bahnsen
Permissions Editor:   Doris Milligan
Director of Editing, Design, and Production:   Jane Perkins

Text and Cover Designer:   Rebecca Lemna
Cover Photographer:   Pete Johnsen/Midwest Studio Association
Copy Editor:   JoAnn Learman
Indexer:   Leoni McVey
Compositor:   The Clarinda Company
Text Type:   10/12 ITC New Baskerville

**Library of Congress Cataloging-in-Publication Data**

Northcraft, Gregory B.
     Organizational behavior : a management challenge / Gregory B.
  Northcraft, Margaret A. Neale.
        p.   cm.
     Includes bibliographical references and index.
     ISBN 0-03-020539-5
     1. Organizational behavior.   2. Management.   I. Neale, Margaret
  Ann.   II. Title.
  HD58.7.N68   1990                                        89-12061
  658—dc20                                                     CIP

Printed in the United States of America
901-032-987654321
Copyright © 1990 by The Dryden Press, a division of Holt,
Rinehart and Winston, Inc.

Address orders:
The Dryden Press
Orlando, Florida 32887

Address editorial correspondence:
The Dryden Press
908 N. Elm St.
Hinsdale, IL 60521

The Dryden Press
Holt, Rinehart and Winston
Saunders College Publishing

*To Natasha, Galen, C.J., and Al,*
*for their consistent and enthusiastic support of our efforts and us.*

# The Dryden Press Series in Management

Bartlett
**Cases in Strategic Management for Business**

Bedeian
**Management**
*Second Edition*

Bedeian
**Organizations: Theory and Analysis, Text and Cases**
*Second Edition*

Boone and Kurtz
**Contemporary Business**
*Sixth Edition*

Bowman and Branchaw
**Business Communication: From Process to Product**

Bowman and Branchaw
**Business Report Writing**
*Second Edition*

Cullinan
**Business English for Industry and the Professions**

Czinkota, Rivoli, and Ronkainen
**International Business**

Daft
**Management**

Efendioglu and Montanari
**The Advantage Ski Company: A Strategic Simulation**

Gaither
**Production and Operations Management: A Problem-Solving and Decision-Making Approach**
*Fourth Edition*

Forgionne
**Quantitative Management**

Gatewood and Feild
**Human Resource Selection**
*Second Edition*

Greenhaus
**Career Management**

Higgins
**Strategy: Formulation, Implementation, and Control**

Higgins and Vincze
**Strategic Management: Text and Cases**
*Fourth Edition*

Hills
**Compensation Decision Making**

Hodgetts
**Modern Human Relations at Work**
*Fourth Edition*

Holley and Jennings
**The Labor Relations Process**
*Third Edition*

Holley and Jennings
**Personnel/Human Resource Management: Contributions and Activities**
*Second Edition*

Huseman, Lahiff, and Penrose
**Business Communication: Strategies and Skills**
*Third Edition*

Jauch, Coltrin, and Bedeian
**The Managerial Experience: Cases, Exercises, and Readings**
*Fifth Edition*

Kemper
**Experiencing Strategic Management**

Kuehl and Lambing
**Small Business: Planning and Management**
*Second Edition*

Kuratko and Hodgetts
**Entrepreneurship: A Contemporary Approach**

Lee
**Introduction to Management Science**
*Second Edition*

Luthans and Hodgetts
**Business**

Montanari, Morgan, and Bracker
**Strategic Management: A Choice Approach**

Northcraft and Neale
**Organizational Behavior: A Management Challenge**

Tombari
**Business and Society: Strategies for the Environment and Public Policy**

Varner
**Contemporary Business Report Writing**

Vecchio
**Organizational Behavior**

Weekly and Aggarwal
**International Business: Operating in the Global Economy**

Wolters and Holley
**Labor Relations: An Experiential and Case Approach**

Zikmund
**Business Research Methods**
*Second Edition*

# Preface

A book, like a large corporation, can't just be thrown together—it must be *organized*. And as with the organization of a large corporation, the organization of a book says something about the people who created it, what they believe is important, and what they are trying to accomplish. This book is organized around two themes: a subtle undercurrent and an explicit focus.

The subtle undercurrent of this book is its emphasis on understanding organizational behavior by understanding what goes on in the minds of managers and employees when they interact in organizations. Organization is, after all, in the eye of the beholder, and the real challenge of organizational behavior lies in managing the uncertainty, conflict, and complexities of organizational life that we each experience. This undercurrent probably reflects the rise of social cognition in the 1970s and 1980s as a central intellectual force in our parent fields of social psychology and organizational behavior.

The explicit focus of this book is making the wisdom and insights of organizational behavior research not just available but *accessible*—easy to learn—for students. Accessibility of material is important because it's what makes education both a rewarding activity for students and a manageable task for instructors. Naturally, this means that this book includes many special features that help both the student and the instructor. But accessibility, like quality, cannot be added on; it must be built in. So the text of this book has been written with accessibility in mind.

To that end, this book (while certainly comprehensive in coverage) is not an encyclopedia of organizational behavior. The table of contents is not a laundry list of what's out there in the field, nor are the individual chapters laundry lists within major topics. Instead, we have made a conscious attempt to build a book with a conceptual "flow." Instead of 18 distinct mini-books on organizational behavior, chapters and topics are carefully sequenced and integrated to build on each other. Further, there are no "special topics" that end up as stand-alone chapters; instead, the presentation of this material has been integrated into the mainstream of organizational behavior theory. Communication, for instance, is introduced with perception as a conceptual foundation. Stress is presented in the context of organizational conflict. And culture and socialization are presented as part and parcel of organizational entry. A particularly good example of this integration is the handling of international issues; they are integrated within each chapter of the book.

An important issue in making the wisdom and insights of organizational behavior accessible to students is the delicate marriage of scholarly explication and concrete application. Alone, neither is particularly useful. We have merged these tasks by continually interweaving the presentation of concepts and theory with both formal and informal examples. The formal examples are drawn from traditional work organizations; the informal examples are taken from non-work organizations such as clubs, study groups, and even families, with which students are particularly familiar. The book's many annotated color photographs capture slices of organizational life to enhance the balance of theory and practice.

## ORGANIZATION OF THE TEXT

The five parts of the book also have a structure and logic. Part 1 defines the challenge of managing behavior in organizations and reviews past attempts to meet this challenge. Part 1 represents both the core of the book and the core of the field. It frames in the mind of the student an answer to the question, "Why organizational behavior?" Parts 2 and 3 provide foundation knowledge for meeting the challenge of organizational behavior. For most employees, the individuals and small groups they interact with each day *are* their organization, so the foundation knowledge of organizational behavior is Part 2, "Individual Behavior," and Part 3, "Behavior in Groups." Part 4 provides explicit integrated applications of this foundation knowledge to three primary issues in managing behavior in organizations: getting employees into organizations (Organizational Entry), putting them to work (Job Design), and helping them succeed (Managing for Performance). Finally, Part 5 examines the larger context of organizational behavior. We all know that somewhere beyond these day-to-day interactions of everyday work life is a larger sense of organizations, including the environment, the structure of organizations, and the changes that organizations must endure. These are the focus of Part 5.

## SPECIAL FEATURES

Our goal of making the wisdom and insights of organizational behavior more accessible to students has been aided by the full-color photos and artwork provided in the text. The captions that accompany both the photos and the figures create a parallel text—a second chance for the book to teach and the student to learn. The photos and figures also provide vivid and concrete referents for the major concepts presented in the text.

## "FOCUS ON" BOXED ITEMS

Formal examples of organizational behavior are presented in **"FOCUS ON"** boxed features sprinkled throughout the text and the brief cases that begin each chapter. These examples are drawn from a broad spectrum of both international and U.S. firms, the private and public sectors, and large and small organizations. The variety of examples provided encourages the student to see and understand the pervasiveness of organizational behavior in everyday life. Every chapter contains an **"INTERNATIONAL FOCUS ON"** boxed item, which should help ingrain in students an appreciation for the global marketplace in which they will be working.

END-OF-CHAPTER
LEARNING AIDS

**"On Your Own"** experiential exercises appear at the end of each chapter. These exercises are designed to be completed individually by students and can also be used as the basis for class discussion. The exercises allow students to gain knowledge while reflecting on their own aptitudes and abilities.

 **"The Manager's Memo"** represents a different slant on the typical end-of-chapter case and is another example of the book's integration. Each memo presents a management problem that the student must solve by applying concepts learned in the chapter. The cases are designed to be used either as discussion material or as assignments in which students respond to the memo in writing.

 Under the heading **"If You Want to Know More,"** each chapter contains a list of classic and contemporary readings on chapter topics. This list of readings can provide extra stimulation for ambitious students, or supplementary paper assignments, or even a way to get a better handle on "The Manager's Memo" closing case.

 Each chapter ends with a glossary of **Key Terms,** and the **Discussion Questions** can be used as a basis for discussion or a chance for students to test their learning.

 Again, in keeping with the explicit focus of the book, each part ends with both a group exercise and a comprehensive case. The part-closing exercises have been chosen for their appropriateness regardless of class size. These part-closing cases and exercises further encourage students to integrate their understanding and application of material across the chapters of each part.

UNIQUE CHAPTERS

Finally, there are several unique chapters in this book. Chapter 2, "Facing the Challenge: Historical Perspectives," and Chapter 15, "Technology," represent the old and the new in organizational behavior. The history of organizational behavior is useful for understanding what has happened. Understanding technology in organizational behavior will be useful for understanding the future. Because of the book's emphasis on the importance of cognitions, expanded coverage has been provided on decision-making processes: Chapter 5, "Individual Decision Making," and Chapter 9, "Group Decision Making."

ANCILLARY
PACKAGE

A comprehensive set of ancillaries for students and instructors has been prepared to accompany *Organizational Behavior: A Management Challenge*.

FOR THE STUDENT

A *Study Guide/Exercise Manual,* prepared by Barry A. Gold of Pace University, includes a detailed summary, key-terms quiz, and a self-help test of multiple choice and true/false questions for each chapter. Additionally, each chapter concludes with two individual experiential exercises.

FOR THE
INSTRUCTOR

The following items are available for adopters.

**Instructor's Manual with Transparency Masters**   The *Instructor's Manual* contains detailed chapter outlines, suggested answers to the discussion questions and "The Manager's Memo" cases, and instructions for using the "On Your Own" exercises. The manual includes one additional case and group exercise for each part of the book. A special topic also has been identified for each chapter and supplementary lecture material developed by Debra Arvanites at Villanova University and Dennis Duchon at the University of Texas at San Antonio. A special feature of the manual is the inclusion of teaching notes and suggested class discussion questions for each of the transparency acetates. Finally, 50 transparency masters are provided.

**Test Bank**   The *Test Bank,* written by Calvin Kellogg of The University of Mississippi, contains multiple choice questions, true/false items, mini-cases, and essay questions for each chapter. Each question is identified as either factual or application, its level of difficulty is indicated, and text page where the material is covered is given. A computerized version of the *Test Bank* is available in both IBM and Apple versions.

**Transparency Acetates**   A total of 72 color acetates that further enhance the text material in a visual format have been developed. Teaching notes for each of the acetates are included in the *Instructor's Manual.*

ACKNOWLEDGMENTS

We subtitled this book "A Management Challenge" because we believe that uncertainty, conflict, and complexity make managing behavior in organizations a difficult—even potentially hazardous—enterprise. The same could be said for writing a book on this topic.

Not surprisingly, we have been reminded many times in the past two years that a major undertaking on this scale requires the coordination and cooperation of a great many people. We would like to acknowledge their efforts and thank them for their contributions. We owe a great debt to our project team at The Dryden Press for indulging our incessant (and perhaps naive) insistence that everything be absolutely perfect, and then helping make sure that it was. We are also indebted to our colleagues, students, and administrators in the Department of Management and Policy at the University of Arizona, in the Department of Organization Behavior at the J. L. Kellogg Graduate School of Management at Northwestern University, and in the Amos Tuck School of Business Administration at Dartmouth College for gamely indulging our efforts. We would especially like to thank Mary Fischer for being the person most responsible for getting us "knee deep in the big muddy" of this project and Alfred C. Lindahl for keeping our goals clearly in focus and continually reminding us why we had to finish what we'd started, and soon.

We also are indebted to those active participants in this project whose thoughtful feedback provided through focus groups and manuscript reviews helped raise our own understanding of organizational behavior to new heights, including: Royce Abrahamson, Southwest Texas State University; Aaron Andreasan, University of Montana; Jack W. Brittain, University of Texas at Dallas; Gene E. Burton, California State University, Fresno; Brian Boyd, University of Southern California; Dennis L. Dossett, University of Missouri—St. Louis; Robert Fisher, Henderson State University; Cynthia V. Fukami, University of Denver; Bruce Garrison, Houston Baptist University; Barry Gold, Pace University; Scott Hammond, Brigham Young University; Eileen A. Hogan, George Mason University; John Hollenbeck, Michigan State University; Ralph Katerberg, University of Cincinnati; Calvin Kellogg, The University of Mississippi; Mary Kernan, Kent State University; Jeff Mello, Northeastern University; Herff Moore, University of Central Arkansas; Edward J. Morrison, University of Colorado—Boulder; Brian Niehoff, Kansas State University; Suzyn Ornstein, Suffolk University; Dennis Patzig, James Madison University; Karen Paul, Bowling Green State University; Bob Renn, Georgia State University; Peter Richardson, Southwest Missouri State University; Janice Rouiller, University of Maryland; Sue Schafer, North Texas State University; Ronald R. Sims, College of William and Mary; Sim B. Sitkin, The University of Texas at Austin; Linda K. Trevino, Penn State University; Robert J. Vandenberg, Georgia State University; and Kelly A. Vaverek, Texas Christian University.

There is an old saying that "Life is a great adventure—or nothing." For us, this book has been a great adventure in writing. We trust it also proves to be a great adventure in learning for students and instructors.

Gregory B. Northcraft
Margaret A. Neale

*August 1989*

# About the Authors

**Gregory B. Northcraft** is Associate Professor of Management and Policy at the Karl Eller Graduate School of Management at the University of Arizona. He received bachelor's degrees in psychology and Russian language and literature from Dartmouth College, and in psychology and philosophy from Oxford University. Professor Northcraft received his master's degree and Ph.D. in social psychology from Stanford University. His major research interests include behavioral decision theory, conflict management, employee motivation, and job design, particularly in high-technology manufacturing settings. Professor Northcraft has authored or coauthored more than 40 articles and book chapters on these topics and has conducted management development programs in conflict management, human resource management, negotiation, and the management of change. Professor Northcraft also has interned for several major federal agencies and has held visiting professorships at the Amos Tuck School of Business Administration (Dartmouth College) and the Guangzhou Institute of Foreign Trade (People's Republic of China).

**Margaret A. Neale** is Associate Professor of Organization Behavior at the J. L. Kellogg Graduate School of Management at Northwestern University. She received her bachelor's degree in pharmacy from Northeast Louisiana University, her master's degrees from the Medical College of Virginia and Virginia Commonwealth University, and her Ph.D. in business administration from the University of Texas. Prior to her joining the faculty at Northwestern University, Professor Neale was on the faculty of the Eller Graduate School of Management at the University of Arizona. Professor Neale's major research interests include bargaining and negotiation, third-party dispute intervention, behavioral decision theory, performance appraisal, and organizational justice. She is the author of more than 30 articles on these topics and is a coauthor with Max H. Bazerman on an upcoming book, *Cognitive Perspectives on Negotiation*. She has conducted executive seminars and management development programs throughout the United States and abroad for public agencies, trade associations, small businesses, and *Fortune* 500 corporations in the areas of negotiating skills, performance appraisal systems, employee commitment, work force demographics, and employee participation.

# Contents in Brief

# Contents

APPENDIX A        # The Scientific Method                              A1

# PART

# 1

# Introduction

CHAPTER

# Organizational Behavior: A Management Challenge

**Organizational Behavior: A Prescriptive View**
Effectiveness
Efficiency
Management Functions

**Organizational Behavior: Alternative Perspectives**
Conflict
*Focus on Politics and Conflict: Turmoil in the Tour de France*
Uncertainty
*Focus on Uncertainty: Tragedies in the Persian Gulf*
*Focus on Changes in Work-Force Values: Why More Temporary Employees?*
Complexity
*International Focus on Complexity: Do American Management Theories Apply Abroad?*
Related Fields

**About This Book**

## Shuttle Probe Throws Shower of Sparks

The investigation into the explosion of the space shuttle Challenger became deeper, wider, and more embarrassing almost overnight as threats of subpoenas and talk of cover-ups ricocheted through Washington. The search for the cause of the January 28 disaster yielded shocking disclosures that abruptly shifted the focus from technical failure to human error. Testimony and documents appeared to point to critical gaps in the chain of command at the National Aeronautics and Space Administration (NASA).

Pronouncing himself both "surprised and appalled" at a decision-making process that may have been flawed, presidential commission Chairman William Rogers issued directives that heightened the suspicion: All NASA personnel involved in the decision to launch Challenger were removed from the space agency's own internal probe. . . .

Among commission members, there remained little question that a technical failure caused the fatal explosion. . . . Still, there were increased fears that NASA officials may have overridden strong objections from engineers—who were concerned by potentially lethal faults in the O-ring seals of the booster rockets—and ordered an over-hasty launch of Challenger. Some even hinted that NASA may have tried to mask any chain-of-command error in the decision to press ahead with the launch.

The most damning testimony yet came from engineers at Morton Thiokol, manufacturers of the solid rockets that power the shuttle during its first 2 minutes and 8 seconds of flight. In interviews, Thiokol engineers told of trying to talk their superiors out of giving an "all clear" for the launch amid an unusual Florida cold snap, yet watching as NASA "bullied" company officials into giving a "go" for the launch.

"I fought like hell to stop that launch," one engineer told National Public Radio. "I'm so torn up inside I can hardly talk about it." Another said he was so worried

3

about the O-rings that on the eve of the launch, "I kept having fantasies that at the moment of ignition, the shuttle would blow up instantly."

In talks with Lawrence Mulloy, chief of the solid-rocket-booster program at the Marshall Space Flight Center in Alabama, Thiokol engineers angrily insisted that NASA wait until temperatures climbed into the 50s before launching. They told NPR that Mulloy responded: "My God, Thiokol, when do you want me to launch? Next April?" After hours of discussion, top Morton Thiokol officials overruled their engineers and signed a launch approval.

NASA has not revealed details of the launch discussions, except to confirm that the three highest-ranking NASA officials were not informed about the debate over the low temperatures.

NASA itself began what some observers called a classic response of a bureaucracy under fire: It reorganized. A respected 20-year agency veteran, general manager Phil Culbertson, was fired by NASA chief William Graham. . . .

NASA's Houston center, meanwhile, brought in a psychologist to help employees deal with their worries about an agency suddenly adrift. Declared former astronaut Joe Allen, now with Space Industries, Inc., in Houston: "Any government agency in difficult times needs real strong leadership. These are very difficult times. The fact of the matter is, it isn't clear who is running the agency."

Source: *US News & World Report,* March 3, 1986, pp. 6–7.

---

## INTRODUCTION

This book is about people. People think and plan. Some people work hard and succeed, while others get discouraged, give up, and fail. And people dream. People have built monuments to civilization, including the tall buildings that dominate our cities' skylines, the factories that supply our daily needs and desires, and the libraries that house civilization's accumulated knowledge for future generations. People even have built the spaceships that carried astronauts to the moon.

None of these achievements, however, is the product of one person. In fact, none of these achievements would have been possible if only one person had worked toward their completion. Can you imagine the experience, knowledge, and effort of only one person building the Empire State Building or a Saturn V rocket? It seems unlikely. Instead, these achievements are made possible because people work together.

When people come together to combine their talents and efforts, they form **organizations.** A good working definition for the word *organization* is provided by J. D. Mooney in his book, *The Principles of Organization:*

Organization is the form of every human association for the attainment of a common purpose . . . the framework of every group moving toward a common objective . . . It refers to the complete body, with all its correlated functions . . . It refers to the coordination of all these [functions] as they cooperate for the common purpose.[1]

Mooney emphasized that organizations are "pure process," not buildings or machines or anything tangible. Organizations instead are practices, procedures, and relationships entered into to coordinate human talents and efforts toward common goals. This book is also about organizations.

Our lives are taken up participating in an endless series of organizations including families, schools, clubs, and the firms and corporations for which we work. Some organizations succeed in combining the talents and efforts of their members to produce major accomplishments (like putting astronauts on the moon) while other organizations never produce much of anything. A quick scan of the daily newspaper reveals both the latest discoveries and breakthroughs achieved by organizations *and* the latest fiascoes and bankruptcies. Some workers are fiercely loyal to and proud of the organizations to which they belong. Some organizations are plagued by high absenteeism, turnover, and even sabotage from within. Why are some organizations successful while others fail? This is the challenge of understanding how and why people work together in organizations. This is the challenge of organizational behavior.

Before discussing the specifics of how and why people behave the ways they do in organizations, it is important to have an overall sense of behavior in organizations. In this opening chapter, we will consider two different views of the meaning of behavior in organizations. The first is a *prescriptive* view of organizations. It prescribes what organizations are supposed to accomplish and how they are supposed to do it. The second, alternative view of behavior in organizations is *descriptive*. It describes what actually happens in organizations. In doing so, this descriptive view provides an introduction to the field of organizational behavior. Organizational behavior is the description and explanation of how people actually behave in organizations.

## ORGANIZATIONAL BEHAVIOR: A PRESCRIPTIVE VIEW

From the viewpoint of someone joining an organization for the first time, perhaps a newly graduated business major, the meaning of behavior in organizations probably seems straightforward. Everyone knows that people come together and form organizations because organizations can accomplish things that are beyond the reach of individuals. People come together to accomplish what none of them could accomplish alone. The meaning of behavior in organizations, therefore, revolves around managing behavior to take advantage of the performance benefits of groups over individuals.

[1]J. D. Mooney, *The Principles of Organization* (New York: Harper and Brothers, 1939), 3.

**FIGURE 1-1**      Two Reasons for Organizing

1. **Effectiveness** The ability of an organization to accomplish an important goal, purpose, or mission. Organizations combine the efforts and talents of many individuals and thereby bring into reach objectives that would be out of reach for individuals.

2. **Efficiency** The ability of an organization to maximize productivity per unit of resources (labor and capital). Organizations allow individuals to specialize. Each individual can accomplish a few tasks more quickly and with fewer mistakes than if that individual had many more responsibilities.

There are two ways in which organizations provide opportunities for accomplishments that are beyond the reach of individuals. These two reasons for organizing, shown in Figure 1-1, are effectiveness and efficiency.

EFFECTIVENESS

**Effectiveness** is the ability of an organization to accomplish an important goal, purpose, or mission. A 24-hour dry cleaning service is effective if it can dry clean its customers' clothes in 24 hours or less. A full-service stock brokerage house is effective if it can provide customers a full range of promised financial services. A university instructor is effective if students learn the subject matter of the course.

People can achieve some goals and objectives only by combining their talents or coordinating their efforts. A full-service stock brokerage house, for instance, tries to provide its clients a dizzying array of financial services. Included would be information and purchasing arrangements for stocks, bonds, options, futures, commodities (like wheat and corn), and retirement accounts. To be effective—that is, to deliver *all* of these financial services to its customers—the stock brokerage house must have a source of expertise for each of its offered services. The amount of expertise and up-to-date knowledge needed to deliver all six services is beyond the capacity of a single individual. However, an organization provides the opportunity for specialists. A specialist is a person who works only on a limited number of tasks. To provide the six mentioned services, a full-service brokerage house would need six different specialists, one for each of the six offered financial services. The full-service brokerage house example demonstrates that effectiveness often can be attained only by combining the talents of multiple individuals. No individual alone can be a full-service financier, but an organization of specialists can provide a full range of services.

EFFICIENCY

**Efficiency** is a second reason why people come together in organizations. Efficiency has to do with the amount of effort required to deliver a promised good or service. Organizations have opportunities to increase

Tribal clans probably formed the first primitive organizations because survival was more likely if many individuals combined their talents and efforts. The nonindustrial group shown here has organized for the difficult task of building a stone structure—a task that would be impossible for an individual working alone.

efficiency as well as effectiveness through specialization. Specialization increases efficiency because specialists are extremely familiar with their tasks and therefore can accomplish more work per hour than they could if their efforts were not so focused.

Organizations also may have access to more efficient production technologies than those available to individuals. In production circles, this is known as an *economy of scale*. When a lot of something is needed, organizations can use more efficient production technologies to produce it. A cobbler is effective in making shoes for his customers, but a large corporation can be more efficient. A corporation like Nike Shoes can purchase machinery to make shoes very quickly and at much lower cost than the cobbler.

The fact that organizations can achieve greater effectiveness and efficiency than individuals no doubt provided the foundation for the first and most basic form of organization—the clan. Primitive men and women may have tried to go it alone, perhaps distrusting the intentions of their fellow primitives. If so, the survivors no doubt were those men and women who first realized that everyone eventually has to sleep. Thus, individuals could obtain round-the-clock protection from the ravages of the wild only by combining their talents and efforts into an organization.

Efficiency and effectiveness, though tied together as the twin justifications for organizing the talents and efforts of individuals, are not always achieved hand in hand. An organization can be effective (that is, provide a highly desired good or service) without doing so efficiently. On the other hand, an organization may succeed in producing a good or service very efficiently only to find that no customer wants it. Since both effectiveness and efficiency are critical to the survival of an organization,

Fayol's functional approach to management focuses on the tasks that management *should* do—planning, organizing, staffing, and controlling—to manage behavior in organizations. The planning meeting shown here is one way of following Fayol's prescriptions to allow the organization to outperform individuals.

maintaining a healthy balance between them is another important challenge in managing behavior in organizations.

## MANAGEMENT FUNCTIONS

The importance of managing behavior in organizations to achieve effectiveness and efficiency has led researchers to identify primary managerial functions. Managers must accomplish these functions if their organizations are to outperform individuals. Henri Fayol is credited with first identifying these **managerial functions** in 1916.[2] As shown in Figure 1–2, Fayol's four functions include planning, organizing, staffing, and controlling.

**Planning**  The thinking that precedes action in an organization is planning. **Planning** takes place on at least two levels. The first level is concerned with the purpose, mission, or goals of the organization. What is the good or service that this organization will produce and market? Who and where are the potential consumers of this good or service? What characteristics must the good or service have to satisfy the needs of its potential consumers? These all are questions management must answer for an organization to be effective. The missions or purposes of an organization are often abstract, long-term objectives, such as becoming the biggest or best supplier in an industry. Goals are the concrete stepping-stones that the organization must achieve along the way to ensure that the mission is fulfilled.

 The second level of planning is concerned with how the organization will produce or provide the good or service that is its mission. We might think of this as planning the strategies and tactics that will allow the organization to attain its goals and fulfill its mission efficiently. What resources (including people) are necessary to produce or provide the goods or services central to the organization's mission? How will these resources be obtained?

[2]H. Fayol, *General and Industrial Management* (London: Pitman, 1961).

**FIGURE 1–2**        Fayol's Management Functions

Fayol's four management functions represent a prescription for managing behavior in organizations.

| | |
|---|---|
| **Planning** | Thinking before taking action |
| **Organizing** | Setting up the policies and procedures that govern worker behavior |
| **Staffing** | Supplying a work force |
| **Controlling** | Motivating, directing, and adjusting the efforts of the work force in its pursuit of the organization's plans |

**Organizing**  Creating a structure through which the members can produce the organization's central goods or services is **organizing.** We can think of this structure as having several distinct components. First, there is the structuring of individual job responsibilities and duties. Who will do what and how will they do it? Next is the structuring of relationships among the individual jobs. What are the reporting relationships in the organization to be like? Who will be supervising whom? What kinds of departments will be necessary? How will these departments interact with each other? Finally, there is the physical structuring of the facility. Given the nature of individual jobs and the desired departmental structures and reporting relationships, what is the best way to arrange everyone physically? Should there be walls between desks to provide privacy, or should supervision be "line-of-sight"? If there is production machinery, where and how should it fit into the physical layout? All three of these organizing structures—individual, group, and physical—represent the first concrete stage of implementing the organization's action plan.

**Staffing**  Once the organization's action plan is in hand and the structures needed to implement it have been identified or put in place, staffing becomes a primary concern. **Staffing** is the process of supplying a work force (people) to fill the organization's designed structures. Staffing consists of three components. First, a selection procedure must be designed and implemented to fill job descriptions identified in the organizing function. Second, those hired must be trained and socialized so that they can contribute to the organization's attainment of its goals and accomplishment of its mission. Third, an employee support system (including a wages-and-benefits package) that satisfies at least the minimum requirements and needs of the work force must be put in place. In concert, these three staffing activities provide the organization its human resources.

**Controlling**  Once the operating structures have been put in place and the work force has been hired to make the operating structures go, what is left for the manager is to control the work force's execution of the work. **Controlling** includes directing and motivating the work force, often by generating direction and enthusiasm for work through leadership. Incentive systems or rewards and discipline or punishment procedures also can be used to both motivate and direct the behaviors of the work force.

Controlling also implies monitoring the progress of the organization toward its stated goals and mission. Monitoring progress requires measuring organizational performance, comparing performance against standards, and taking corrective action when performance turns out to be substandard. Corrective actions may include those taken to get the work force back on track (such as changes in leadership patterns or incentive systems). Corrective actions also may be directed toward revising the organization's action plan, thereby giving rise to consequent changes at the levels of organizing and staffing.

## ORGANIZATIONAL BEHAVIOR: ALTERNATIVE PERSPECTIVES

Defining life in organizations in terms of effectiveness, efficiency, and the four managerial functions used to pursue them—planning, organizing, staffing, and controlling—paints a picture of the organization as a production system. This picture of organizational life suggests that managers calmly consider all the relevant inputs; formulate plans; design and put in place people and systems to execute the plans; give a few pep talks; and fine-tune the people, systems, and even the plan itself if outcomes are less than optimal. The image is one of calm, deliberate, and thoughtful pursuit of organizational effectiveness and efficiency.

This idealized picture of life in organizations is misleading in several important ways. First, it is misleading because it *underestimates* the disjointedness of organizational life. Life in organizations is hardly an orderly progression of activities, each following logically from the one preceding it. Second, defining organizational life in terms of the four managerial functions is misleading because it *overestimates* the extent to which organizational life consists of deliberate, planned activities focused on production efficiency and effectiveness.

Crisis and adversity (like the Challenger space-shuttle disaster) reveal most clearly the differences between the manager's ideal (calm, deliberate, and thoughtful pursuit of efficiency and effectiveness) and what actually goes on in organizations. Over the years, the National Aeronautics and Space Administration (NASA) developed a solid reputation in the eyes of the general public for both effectiveness and efficiency. Timetables for the successful completion of projects (such as astronauts orbiting the earth or walking on the moon) had been met and even exceeded with numbing regularity. Further, the pictures beamed out over national television during launches have provided a very distinct image of NASA. From the Houston "ground control" nerve center for launches, television coverage routinely shows rows and rows of computers and monitors calmly manned by serious, scientific-looking personnel. The image is one of calm and deliberate planning and execution, with everyone working together toward a common goal.

In the wake of the Challenger disaster, the public has seen a different view of organizational behavior at NASA. The decision to launch the Challenger cost seven astronauts' lives and billions of dollars and appears in retrospect to have been indefensible. What happened at NASA leading up to the launch hardly could be characterized as deliberate and thoughtful planning and execution. The technical problems that led to the shuttle's explosion apparently were known about prior to the launch, yet the shuttle was launched anyway. Further, the tarnished portrait of NASA now includes cover-ups, name-calling, and internal bickering.

How could this have happened? Clearly there must be more to organizational life than thoughtful, orderly, and deliberate planning and execution. A realistic portrait of behavior in organizations includes three additional components: conflict, uncertainty, and complexity.

## CONFLICT

The functional approach to managing behavior in organizations assumes that all members share identical perceptions, beliefs, and goals. This assumption is problematic. As noted by Stanford political scientist James March, we should not expect agreement among organizational members. We should expect **conflict:** differences among the perceptions, beliefs, and goals of organization members.[3]

The inevitability of conflict in organizations suggests that organizations are more than just production systems. Organizations also are political systems. A **political system** is a collection of individuals or groups that must work together and speak with one voice even though each has a private agenda to pursue. The "Focus on: Politics and Conflict" notes that even sports teams often are plagued by political problems.

The U.S. Senate is a more classic example of a political system. Each member of the Senate has a constituency (home state). The constituency has goals that it wants its senator to pursue. Each senator also has personal goals to pursue. And the United States (as an organization) has goals that it would like the Senate to pursue as well. Yet with all of these goals to balance, the Senate must speak with one voice by passing only one law for any issue. How does the Senate, given these multiple goals, ever come to a decision?

In a political system like the U.S. Senate, actions are a function of power. In its simplest form, **power** is the ability to influence the behaviors of others, usually through the control of resources. (Power and its use will be discussed in detail in Chapter 8.) In a political system, an individual with more power can impose his or her will on an individual

[3]J. G. March, "Business Firm as Political Coalition," *Journal of Politics* 24 (1962): 662–678.

# FOCUS ON:

## Politics and Conflict

**Turmoil in the Tour de France**

Politics and political conflict normally are associated with large bureaucratic organizations, such as the U.S. government. In reality, however, politics—the settlement of goal disagreements by coalition formation and power plays—can be a part of any organization, even a professional bicycle team. And if not managed well, political conflict can destroy an organization—even a successful one like La Vie Claire, the French professional bicycle team.

Americans Andy Hampsten and Greg LeMond were teammates on La Vie Claire for the 1986 Tour de France, the world's most prestigious bicycle race. Hampsten played a supporting role during LeMond's historic Tour victory, the first ever by an American. But LeMond's victory was a stormy one, and Hampsten barely endured the emotional rigors of his role.

At the center of the turmoil were LeMond and Frenchman Bernard Hinault. LeMond had dutifully played a supporting role during the 1985 Tour by sacrificing his own chance to win so that Hinault could capture a record-tying fifth victory. In return, LeMond understood that the 1986 Tour would be his and that all of La Vie Claire's resources (including Hinault) would be marshalled on his behalf. By the summer of 1986, however, it was clear that Hinault had other ideas—namely, winning a sixth Tour for himself.

The struggle for control on La Vie Claire was a bitter one. LeMond felt betrayed, and with most of La Vie Claire and all of France aligned against him he enlisted teammate and fellow-American Andy Hampsten to support his cause. LeMond triumphed, but the struggle between LeMond and Hinault had long-term repercussions. Said Andy Hampsten, "I'd been on the inside of one of the ugliest things I'd ever seen."

La Vie Claire paid a huge price for the poor management of its internal politics. In the summer of 1987, La Vie Claire began to prepare for the upcoming Tour de France with the world's best cyclist of that year missing from its ranks. The new king of the cycling world—Andy Hampsten—had left La Vie Claire for the relative serenity of the American 7-Eleven team.

Source: A. Wolf, "A Wheeler But No Dealer," *Sports Illustrated*, June 29, 1987, pp. 58–64.

with less power. That means that when goals conflict in a political system, which goals get pursued are a function of who has the power in the system.

Often, goal inconsistencies and incompatibilities remain unresolved within an organization. Rather than foster conflict by confronting them, managers make plans and decisions on an issue-by-issue basis. This strategy of considering issues *serially* and ignoring their long-term implications or interrelationships avoids conflict *in the short run*. However, it also renders meaningless any sense of legitimate overall goals for the organization.

Because organizations are collections of individuals with inconsistent or even conflicting goals, decisions are often made and actions taken according to who has power or who can best use power. Not surprisingly, decisions and actions often are terrible compromises. Individuals and groups bargain away what is important in exchange for being able to keep what they cannot live without.

Again, the case of NASA and the Challenger is revealing. In a major launch, many different groups and individuals have many different goals and differing amounts of power. Some people saw the Challenger's space mission as an important public relations tool for NASA's public image and funding, and for their personal career advancement, but *only* if the launch proceeded on schedule! Others working on the project saw the possibility of danger, but also the possibility of losing their jobs if they pushed the matter too far and were wrong. The action eventually taken—the unfortunate launch of the Challenger—could not fulfill all the conflicting goals of the individuals and groups working on the project. Instead, the decision represented the underlying power realities of those working with NASA on the launch. Apparently those wanting the launch to proceed had more power (or made better use of what power they had) than those who did not want the launch to proceed. In retrospect, it appears that the decision was less a function of what was the right thing to do than a function of which group or individual had the power to decide which goals to pursue.

The idea that organizations are political systems emphasizes the importance of interpersonal relationships and the behavior of individuals in groups (which will be discussed in Chapter 7). It also identifies two critical tasks in managing organizational behavior. First, because organizations consist of groups and individuals with inconsistent and conflicting goals, it is important that managers see conflict management as an important organizational task. (Conflict management will be discussed in Chapter 6.) Along these lines, one study of manager behaviors[4] found that managers spend a substantial part of each day discussing apparently irrelevant topics with their superiors, subordinates, and coworkers. The researchers labeled this activity "socializing and politicking," thereby suggesting that its purpose was building rapport, relationships, and allegiances to weather the storms of later conflicts. Second, political decision-making processes hold the potential of undermining organizational efficiency and effectiveness. Leadership is important in keeping all organizational members focused on organizational survival through maintaining acceptable levels of efficiency and effectiveness. (Leadership will be the focus of Chapter 10.)

[4]J. P. Kotter, *The General Managers* (New York: Free Press, 1982).

UNCERTAINTY                One of the subtle assumptions of Fayol's managerial functions is that there is enough information available for orderly and deliberate planning to take place. But is this a good assumption? In reality, organizations are plagued by uncertainty that makes planning a very difficult enterprise.[5]

Uncertainty is not knowing for sure. Would a better motivated work force make a difference? Would new incentive or training programs help? What values will interest any particular work-force member? History or research may *suggest* answers to these questions, but in practice their answers can be known only by trial and error. Managing this uncertainty is another key component of the challenge of managing organizational behavior. As shown in Figure 1–3, uncertainty comes from a variety of internal and external sources.

**Internal Sources of Uncertainty**   Much of the uncertainty faced by individuals both in and outside of organizations arises from perception—the collecting of information from the environment. (The perception process will be the focus of Chapter 3.) The behaviors of fellow workers can be a constant source of confusion. Was that friendly greeting by my supervisor a sign that I have been doing a good job? Or did my supervisor just have a good time at the company party last night? Is he being nice to me because he's about to give me an awful work assignment? Or is he grooming me to take over his position when he leaves? The inputs we receive from the environment are just inputs. They come to have meaning only by the interpretations we assign to them. In many cases we must act on the interpretations we make. As noted in the "Focus on: Uncertainty," if we have made the wrong interpretations, our actions will be wrong as well.

**FIGURE 1–3**          Sources of Uncertainty

**Internal**

Individual:               Perceptions
                          Goals/motivations

Organizational:           Means-ends relationships
                          Organizational goals
                          Responsibility/authority

**External**

Constant changes:         In the work force
                          In values and expectations
                          In technology
                          In the legal environment

[5]R. M. Cyert and J. G. March, *A Behavioral Theory of the Firm* (Englewood Cliffs, N.J.: Prentice-Hall, 1963).

## FOCUS ON:
Uncertainty

**Tragedies in the Persian Gulf**

Uncertainty is not having information that is critical to making an informed decision and taking appropriate action. On May 17, 1987, an Iraqi jet fighter was cruising the skies over the Persian Gulf when the pilot noticed a ship on his radar screen. Was it an Iranian tanker? That would be a prime target for the fighter. Unsure, the pilot noticed that the ship *seemed* to be in the war zone of the Gulf, where no "friendly" ships would be traveling, and launched a missile attack.

On board the U.S.S. *Stark,* radar had picked up the approaching plane. Was it attacking? Radar suggested that the plane was Iraqi and therefore not hostile. No defensive action was taken. The aftermath of this incident included the deaths of 37 American sailors, substantial damage to a $180 million American warship, and profuse apologies from the Iraqi government for a most regrettable accident.

A little more than a year later, another U.S. warship in the Persian Gulf, the U.S.S. *Vincennes,* played out the mirror image of this disaster. While under attack from Iranian gun-boats, the *Vincennes* picked up a blip on its radar screen. Was it an attacking Iranian jet fighter? The *Vincennes* radar team tracking the blip's approach concluded that it was. The *Vincennes* launched two computer-guided missiles and destroyed the approaching plane. The plane, however, turned out to be not an attacking Iranian fighter but a scheduled commercial airliner carrying 290 civilian passengers.

How could these tragic mistakes have happened? Actions were taken on the basis of educated guesses, as in many cases actions must be. Uncertainty is not having all the information necessary to know for sure what to do. Uncertainty is simply a fact of life. In these cases, the role of uncertainty may have been particularly consequential. Naval analyst Norman Polmar summed it up best in his comments about the tragedy of the U.S.S. *Stark:* "The problem was the unclear circumstances of the *Stark's* mission. The captain didn't know whether he was at war or peace." That may be the ultimate uncertainty.

Sources: J. V. Lamar, Jr. "Why Did This Happen?" *Time,* June 1, 1987, pp. 17–19; G. J. Church, "High-Tech Horror," *Time,* July 18, 1988, pp. 14–17.

Uncertainty also exists in the understanding of means-ends relationships. A means-ends relationship is the probability that an outcome (the end) will occur if an action (the means) is taken. For example, if we replace all our typewriters with word processors, will the productivity of our work force go up or down? Will our employees be more or less satisfied with their jobs? Means-ends relationships are filled with uncertainty. Past experiences may tell us what to expect, but they can never tell us *for sure* what will happen. Taking action, then, always contains an element of rolling the dice and holding your breath.

Once again, the case of the Challenger space shuttle is revealing. No one would have launched the Challenger knowing *for certain* that it would blow up. But then on one *ever* knows for certain that something is going to happen. A few engineers thought there might be a major problem, but was that likelihood enough to abort the launch? What probability of disaster could be assigned to their concerns? And what actions *should* have been taken based on these probability estimates? Is a 50 percent chance of an accident enough to warrant aborting the launch? How about 10 percent? And how would you know if the probability were closer to 50 percent or 10 percent?

Within an organization, goals also may be uncertain. Individuals may not know what they want out of their jobs, or what they want may change from day to day. (Individual uncertainty in motivation will be discussed in more detail in Chapter 4.) Similarly, different members of an organization may have quite different ideas of the organization's goals. Or the goals may have to be changed when changes occur in the organization's environment. Imagine how difficult planning must be if organizational goals are not stable or agreed upon!

Not all personal or organizational uncertainty is unintentional. Some decisions are pleasant or useful to make (for example, staffing or budget decisions) and others onerous (budget or staffing *cuts*). Therefore it could be in the interests of managers to generate enough confusion to allow themselves a "palace coup"—the seizing of responsibility—if desired, as well as easy escape routes from unpopular decisions. Similarly, a manager whose goals and loyalties remain ambiguous retains the luxury of both joining the winning side of a dispute *after* the smoke has cleared *and* claiming to have favored that side from the beginning. Thus, intentional uncertainty can have its benefits.

**External Sources of Uncertainty**   A lot of uncertainty faced by managers is external to their organizations. It comes from the constantly changing and evolving environment in which the organization must function. While the role of the environment will be discussed in much greater detail in Chapter 14, there are several primary sources of environmental uncertainty that the modern manager must keep in mind.

*Changes in the Work Force*   As if the management of organizational behavior were not already complex enough, the manager must deal with changes in the kinds of people who become employees. The modern work force, for example, is more educated than it has ever been. By 1981, the average amount of education in the U.S. work force exceeded 12 years. Of those aged 25 to 64, about 40 percent were high-school graduates, and more than 20 percent had college degrees.[6] Rising levels of education mean worker demands for more challenging and involving jobs.

---

[6]A. D. Young, "Educational Attainment of Workers, March 1981," *Monthly Labor Review* 105 (1982): 52.

While managerial work can be very complex, lower-level workers in organizations often find that their work is not complex enough, resulting in worker boredom and alienation. The letter sorters shown here find little to interest or involve them in their highly mechanized task.

Other significant characteristics of the modern work force also are changing. For instance, women have been entering the U.S. work force in recent years at a much faster pace than males. In 1960, only 33 percent of the work force was female. By 1982, the number was 43 percent.[7] Further, in 1960 only 19 percent of all mothers of children under six worked outside the home; by 1986, fully 55 percent were employed.[8]

*Changes in Worker Values and Expectations*   As the face of the U.S. work force and its educational level have changed, so too have workers' values and expectations. First, modern workers are more likely to want work to be meaningful and involving, rather than just a way to get a paycheck. Management has had to respond with job enrichment programs that provide workers more opportunities to get involved in work. (These problems will be discussed in Chapter 12.)

Second, workers now seem more interested in fitting work into a larger sense of their lives than in devoting their lives to the organization. As noted in the "FOCUS ON: Changes in Work-Force Values," interest in the flexibility of *temporary* employment has reached an all-time high and promises to continue growing.[9] Also, the mobility boom of the 1950s and 1960s is drawing to a close. Young executives no longer are ready and willing to uproot a family in the name of career advancement. Dual-career marriages and housing costs are encouraging more sedentary life-styles, even on the corporate fast-track.[10]

[7]R. W. Bednarzik, M. A. Hewson, and M. A. Urqubart, "The Employment Situation in 1981: New Recession Takes Its Toll," *Monthly Labor Review* 105 (1982): 13.

[8]C. Wallis, "The Child Care Dilemma," *Time*, June 22, 1987, 54–60.

[9]P. Hall, "Temporary Services: Lasting Success?" *Financial World* 154, March 6, 1985, 89–91.

[10]"America's New Immobile Society," *Business Week*, July 27, 1981, 58–62.

FOCUS ON:

Changing in Work-Force Values

**Why More Temporary Employees?** The days when temporary workers were used mostly as occasional fill-ins for vacationing secretaries or receptionists are ending at a growing number of companies. Although 60 percent of the booming temporary-services market still consists of office clerical help, employer demand for nonpermanent workers with a vast range of other skills is increasing rapidly. Technical and professional help such as accountants, bookkeepers, engineers, architects, and computer programmers now represent 19.5 percent of the market demand for temporaries, according to the 400-member National Association of Temporary Services. An additional 11.5 percent are nurses, lab technicians, and other health-care specialists.

"The technical end of the industry is surging," says Sam Sacco, the association's executive vice-president. "It's one of the fastest-growing areas of the business."

Behind much of the boom, say experts, is a burgeoning commitment by business to lean, year-round, permanent staffing that can be supplemented with temporaries as work loads expand. "Companies are increasingly reluctant to add to fixed expense," says John Fanning, president of Uniforce Temporary Services. "They want to better synchronize work flow and personnel needs."

Many of the most skilled temporaries say they wouldn't work any other way, at least not in the foreseeable future. They do it by choice, not because they can't find permanent jobs. Roger Lightowler, 34, a computer data-base specialist in Kingston, N.H., has earned up to $90,000 in a year since he began free-lancing through temporary-help agencies in 1980. Though he frequently is contacted by headhunters trying to lure him to permanent jobs with clients, Lightowler continues to refuse them.

"I like the freedom I have," Lightowler says. "I can choose the projects I work on. I'm able to avoid office politics, and when I'm finished, I can take off for two or three months to refresh myself. That kind of flexibility just isn't available with permanent employment."

Source: *U.S. News & World Report,* February 25, 1985, pp. 76, 79 (Reported by C. W. English).

Along with changing values, the modern work force also has changing expectations. Gone are the days when employees felt some sense of gratitude for the opportunity to work. In its place is a new feeling, the "entitlement" mindset. Employees in the modern work force see themselves as entitled to certain rights, such as privacy, fair treatment, and even interesting work.[11]

*Changes in Technology*   In 1967, computers were bulky boxes of poorly understood electronic hardware. More than 20 years later, it is probably

[11]R. A. Katzell, "Changing Attitudes toward Work," in *Work in America: The Decade Ahead,* eds. C. Kerr and J. Rosow (New York: Van Nostrand, 1979): 35–57.

Changes in the work force provide tremendous uncertainty for managers in organizations. Most recently, rapid changes in technology are making it possible for workers to "dial in" to work from almost anywhere. This man has hooked a FAX machine to a public pay phone and turned a phone booth into an impromptu office.

hard for managers and clerical staff in many sectors of American industry to remember what it was like to work without computers. The advent of the age of computers serves as a striking reminder that the possibility of technological change is a critical source of uncertainty for organizations. (The importance of technology to the management of organizational behavior will be addressed in more detail in Chapter 15.)

Advances in computer networking are even threatening to make the nine-to-five job at the office obsolete. Instead workers may be "dialing in" to work and doing their work over a telephone computer link.[12] Technological developments of this magnitude can have profound effects on the best-laid organizational plans. Thus, if managers hope to keep on top of their organization's efficiency and effectiveness goals, they must keep an eye on the most recent changes in available technologies.

*Changes in the Law*   Many of the rights to which employees now feel entitled, such as the right to form unions for the purpose of collective bargaining, have been codified into law. The legal environment in which organizations must function represents another source of uncertainty. Laws that influence the day-to-day workings of organizations include those affecting hiring (the Equal Employment Opportunities Act), compensation (the Equal Pay Act), and maintenance (the Occupational Safety and Health Act). As our society has become increasingly litigious, greater emphasis has been placed on the development of laws that protect employee rights. Since 1900, the legal environment in which

[12]P. Mandell, "Change in the Corporate Workplace: Telecommuting Takes Workers Home," *PC Week* 4 (March 3, 1987): 45–48.

organizations must function has evolved from an emphasis on the rights of management, to an emphasis on the rights of unions, to an emphasis on the rights of the individual employee. Further, ethical standards have changed and also have found their way into the laws that govern the behavior of organizations and their members (such as the laws against insider trading).[13]

All of these evolving elements in the organization's external environment combine with the internal sources of uncertainty described earlier to create an organizational environment in which nothing seems very certain. All this uncertainty often leads to managers behaving in ways that do not much resemble Fayol's portrait of deliberate and orderly planning and execution.[14]

## COMPLEXITY

With all this conflict and uncertainty that managers must face, it should not be surprising that complexity is also a defining feature of life in organizations. **Complexity** refers to the overwhelming number of concerns that managers must keep track of and manage. Part of this complexity arises in the fact that in any organization there are really two organizations: the formal and the informal. As shown in Figure 1–4, the formal organization consists of the procedures and structures suggested by the functional approach to managing behavior in organizations. In effect, the formal organization represents the organization's perceptions, beliefs, and goals. Yet it is only the "tip of the iceberg."

The informal organization represents the rest of the organizational iceberg. The **informal organization** encompasses the interpersonal realities of an organization (such as employees' personal goals, perceptions, and beliefs), realities that typically are *not* part of the organization's action plan and yet are very much a part of the organization. These characteristics of the organization's members must be taken into account in managing their behavior to achieve organizational efficiency and effectiveness.

The complexity of organizational life has been captured and documented by several studies of what managers actually do on a minute-to-minute basis during the course of their workdays. Perhaps the best-known study describing the lives of managers in organizations was conducted by Henry Mintzberg.[15] Mintzberg was concerned that while the functional approach to managing behavior in organizations might be an ideal to which managers and organizations aspired, it did not describe what actually happened in organizations. Mintzberg carefully observed several weeks in the lives of five upper-level managers. The distribution

---

[13]V. Cahan, "What Is Insider Trading? An Answer May Be on the Way," *Business Week*, June 29, 1987, 28.

[14]Cyert and March, *A Behavioral Theory of the Firm.*

[15]H. Mintzberg, *The Nature of Managerial Work* (New York: Harper & Row, 1973).

**FIGURE 1–4**                    The Organizational "Iceberg"

In any organization there are really two organizations: (1) the formal organization, consisting of the formal reporting relationships, rules, and procedures, and (2) the informal organization, consisting of what really goes on in the organization, including beliefs and social relationships.

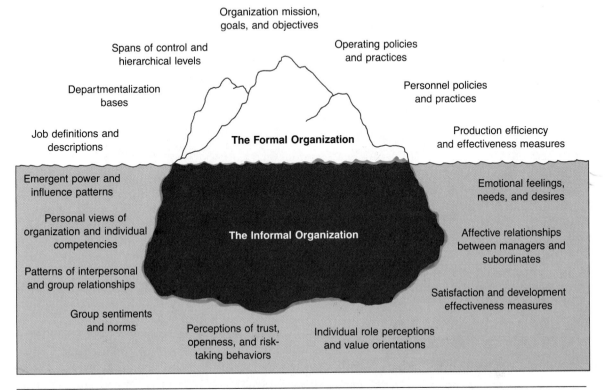

Source: R. J. Selfridge and S. L. Sokolik, "A Comprehensive View of Organizational Development," *MSU Business Topics* (1975): 47.

of the managers' time at work across different types of activities is shown in Figure 1–5.

Mintzberg's conclusions about managerial work stand in stark contrast to the calm and orderly portrait of organizational behavior provided by Fayol's managerial functions. Mintzberg found that his managers' workdays were characterized by variety, brevity, and fragmentation. Mintzberg's five managers worked on many different things during a typical working day and worked on each only briefly. Many of the activities they worked on had little apparent connection to each other. Telephone calls were short and to the point, lasting on the average only 6 minutes. Desk work and unscheduled meetings were similarly brief, each lasting less than 15 minutes on the average.

## FIGURE 1–5          Managers' Activities

Mintzberg's study of executive managers revealed that managerial work is best characterized by variety, brevity, and fragmentation: many different tasks and little time to spend on each.

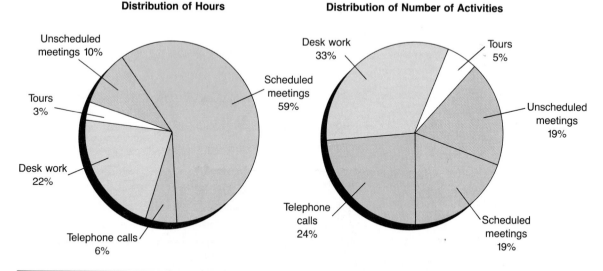

Note: Based on five weeks of observation of chief executives' work.
Source: From *The Nature of Managerial Work* by H. Mintzberg. Copyright © 1973 by Henry Mintzberg. Reprinted by permission of Harper & Row, Publishers, Inc.

Mintzberg found that his upper-level managers spent 78 percent of their time engaged in verbal communication. Other studies have estimated that managers spend anywhere from 66 percent to 80 percent of their time in verbal communication activities.[16] For Mintzberg's managers, more than 90 percent of these verbal contacts were arranged on an ad hoc basis.

The portrait of managerial activity provided by Mintzberg's study suggests that organizational behavior can be quite chaotic. Half of the activities engaged in by Mintzberg's executive managers lasted less than five minutes and only 10 percent lasted more than an hour. Further, many of these activities were terminated by the managers themselves so that they could push on to more pressing job demands.

Other studies of the work lives of managers found similar results. One study of 50 foremen in the United States found that they averaged 583 distinct activities per 8-hour shift—about one new activity every 48 seconds.[17] Another study of 160 British managers found that only about

[16]T. Burns, "The Directions of Activity and Communication in a Departmental Executive Group," *Human Relations* 7 (1954): 73+.

[17]R. H. Guest, "Of Time and the Foreman," *Personnel* 32 (1956): 478–486.

once every two days did the managers work uninterrupted for more than one half hour.[18] In a more recent U.S. study,[19] the American Telephone and Telegraph Company (AT&T) examined the behaviors of 60,000 of its middle and 170,000 of its first-line managers. As shown in Figure 1–6 on page 25, the results of this study support Mintzberg's claim that managerial life is extremely complex and fragmented.

The intense and fragmented complexity of managerial life is perhaps best captured in a quote by Columbia Business School professor Leonard Sayles, a noted authority on managerial behavior:

> [The manager] is like a symphony orchestra conductor, endeavoring to maintain a melodious performance in which the contributions of the various instruments are coordinated and sequenced, patterned and paced, while the orchestra members are having various personal difficulties, stagehands are moving music stands, alternating excessive heat and cold are creating audience and instrument problems, and the sponsor of the concert is insisting on irrational changes in the program.[20]

Sayle's quote again emphasizes the disjointed complexity of managerial behavior. Managers are like jugglers, trying to keep many balls in the air at once. As noted in the "INTERNATIONAL FOCUS ON: Complexity," the increasing internationalization of business is adding another dimension, foreign cultures, to the complexity of managing. Managing the complexity of organizational behavior is an important component of the management challenge.

---

## INTERNATIONAL FOCUS ON: Complexity

**Do American Management Theories Apply Abroad?** During the twentieth century, the United States has been the world's largest producer and exporter of theories of management. But will theories based on experiences in American culture apply in other countries and cultures? Culture can be thought of as the collective mental programming of an entire group of people—for example, a country. The natives of many countries share a "national character" that is apparent to foreign visitors. This national character represents the cultural mental programming that the people of that country have in common. This does not mean that every person in the country has all the traits of the national character. But it does mean that a country's culture plays an important role in determining how its people act.

Geert Hofstede, a director of human resources in the Netherlands, was concerned that cultural mental programming might make management theories developed in one country invalid in other countries. After all, management theories are premised

*(Continued)*

---

[18]R. Stewart, *Managers and Their Jobs* (London: Macmillan, 1967).

[19]C. MacDonald, *Performance Based Supervisory Development* (Amherst, Mass.: Human Resources Development, 1983).

[20]L. R. Sayles, *Managerial Behavior* (New York: McGraw-Hill, 1964).

*International Focus On (Continued)*

on the way people are likely to act. Theories based on the way people are likely to act in one culture might be useless in a culture where people act completely differently. To examine this problem, Hofstede compared the beliefs and values of employees working for a single multinational corporation with subsidiaries in 40 different countries.

Hofstede examined four dimensions of the employees: power distance, uncertainty avoidance, masculinity, and individualism. Power distance is the belief that inequalities in social relationships are legitimate and inevitable. Uncertainty avoidance refers to a concern that formal rules, procedures, and structures are important for maintaining stability and predictability in social interactions. Masculinity is a preference for assertiveness and acquisition of things as primary values, rather than caring for others and quality of life. Individualism is a focus on self-reliance and independence, rather than on social relationships and community. He found that American workers were relatively low on power distance (15th out of the 40 countries), very low on uncertainty avoidance (9th out of 40), well above average on masculinity (28th out of 40), and higher than *any other country* on individualism (40th out of 40).

Are these differences important? Hofstede has argued that they have important implications for management practice. For example, managers in many companies throughout the world are now interested in making work more interesting for their workers. But given national differences in character, what is interesting to workers may vary substantially from country to country. Not surprisingly, the movement to make work more interesting in the United States has focused on restructuring *individual* jobs, thereby satisfying the needs of American workers for individual achievement. In other countries like Norway and Sweden, the movement to make work more interesting has concentrated instead on developing work groups and a "team" orientation—an approach more consistent with their cultures' emphasis on interpersonal relationships over individual achievement. It is perhaps most telling that Hofstede found in his research that the word *achievement* could not even be translated into many languages.

Differences in cultures are extremely important for multinational corporations. Management practices that work well at home could turn out to be hopelessly inappropriate abroad. Even within a country, regional differences in culture and character come into play. A theory of organizational behavior that explains the motivations of inner-city factory workers may not apply to farmers in a developing Third-World country, or even to rural factory workers in the same country! Managers need to understand the limitations of the theories they attempt to apply at work. The careful and systematic recording and replication of results employed in the scientific method provide the basis for understanding where theories came from and therefore where they will apply.

Source: G. Hofstede, "Motivation, Leadership, and Organization: Do American Theories Apply Abroad?" *Organizational Dynamics,* Summer 1980, pp. 42–63.

**FIGURE 1–6**    Principal Duties of First-Line and Middle Managers

AT&T's study of 60,000 middle managers and 170,000 first-line supervisors supported Mintzberg's claim that managerial work is extremely complex and fragmented.

| Rank Order | Duty | Percentage of Manager's Time | Frequency of Performance |
|---|---|---|---|
| **First-Line Managers** | | | |
| 1 | Controlling (work activities) | 15 | Every day |
| 2 | Solving problems | 12 | Every day |
| 3 | Planning (work activities) | 11 | Every day |
| 4 | Communicating informally and orally | 11 | Every day |
| 5 | Communicating with superiors | 11 | Every day |
| 6 | Providing performance feedback to subordinates | 10 | Every day |
| 7 | Coaching subordinates | 10 | Every day |
| 8 | Writing letters and memos | 6 | Every day |
| 9 | Creating and maintaining a motivating atmosphere | 5 | Every day |
| 10 | Managing time | 3 | Every day |
| 11 | Attending meetings | 3 | Twice monthly |
| 12 | Reading and other self-development activities | 1 | Weekly |
| 13 | Career counseling with a subordinate | 1 | Bimonthly |
| 14 | Representing the company | 1 | Monthly |
| **Middle Managers** | | | |
| 1 | Controlling | 21 | Every day |
| 2 | Developing subordinates | 14 | Every day |
| 3 | Planning | 14 | Every day |
| 4 | Managing time | 10 | Every day |
| 5 | Attending meetings | 8 | Every day |
| 6 | Making decisions | 5 | Every day |
| 7 | Reading and other self-development activities | 5 | Every day |
| 8 | Providing performance feedback to subordinates | 4 | Every day |
| 9 | Writing letters and memos | 4 | Every day |
| 10 | Creating a motivating atmosphere | 3 | Every day |
| 11 | Communicating upward | 3 | Every day |
| 12 | Performing community-relations activities | 3 | Bimonthly |
| 13 | Communicating downward | 3 | Every day |
| 14 | Communicating with peers | 3 | Every day |

Source: Charles McDonald, *Performance Based Supervisory Development*, (Amherst, Mass.: HRD Press, 1982). As appeared in Don Hellriegel and John W. Slocum, Jr., *Management*, 5th ed. (Reading, Mass.: Addison-Wesley, 1989), 20.

RELATED FIELDS

Much of the conflict, uncertainty, and complexity that characterize life in organizations arises precisely because organizations are collections of people. Understanding the behaviors of the people in organizations, therefore, is critical to good management. The study of people's behavior in organizations—organizational behavior—is one of a family of scientific areas of study known as the behavioral sciences. The behavioral sciences all share both a scientific orientation *and* a focus on human behavior as the object of scientific study. (A brief discussion of the scientific orientation or "scientific method" is provided in Appendix A.) This focus on human behavior differentiates the behavioral sciences from "hard" sciences (such as geology and astronomy) that study physical processes and objects (such as rocks and stars).

Several behavioral sciences figure prominently in the study of organizational behavior. Included are psychology, the study of individual behavior; sociology, the study of group behavior; political science, the study of social power and social conflict; and anthropology, the study of the evolution of man. Within the broad field of psychology, experimental psychology in particular is concerned with learning, perception, and other processes through which individuals interact with their environment. Social psychology focuses both on group influences on individual behaviors and on the individual thought processes that control individual behavior in groups. Cultural anthropology studies ways in which symbols are used to create and maintain belief systems.

Since organizations are made up of individuals and groups, knowledge from psychology, sociology, political science, and anthropology should be useful in understanding their behavior. Organizational behavior differs from these related fields, however, in its focus not just on individual or group behavior but specifically on individual and group behavior *in organizations*. Again, this is the challenge of organizational behavior—not just understanding individual and group behavior, but understanding individual and group behavior as they relate to the smooth running of organizations.

Management is also a field related to organizational behavior. Management has been defined as getting things done through people. The relationship between organizational behavior and management is one of knowledge base and application. Organizational behavior provides a knowledge base for understanding and predicting the behavior of individuals and groups in organizations. The field of management is comprised of a series of skills and techniques (such as designing work systems and compensation plans) for managing the behaviors of individuals and groups. Hopefully, the skills and techniques of management reflect the accumulated knowledge base provided by the field of organizational behavior. Thus, management is the application of organizational behavior knowledge to the challenge of managing behavior in organizations.

**FIGURE 1–7**  Organization of the Text

At the core of this book—and the field of organizational behavior—is the challenge of managing behavior in organizations. To meet that challenge, management for performance must reflect an understanding of individual and group behavior. It also must reflect the larger context in which organizational behavior occurs, including organizational structure and the environment.

**ABOUT THIS BOOK**

As shown in Figure 1–7, this book divides the study of organizational behavior into five parts. Part 1 (Chapters 1 and 2) defines the challenge of managing behavior in organizations. Chapter 1 has introduced the topic of organizational behavior and presented a description of life in organizations that highlights the importance for managers of understanding human behavior. Chapter 2 provides a historical perspective on organizational behavior. Several classic theories and studies in management are presented and their roles in the development of the field of organizational behavior are discussed.

Part 2, Individual Behavior, and Part 3, Behavior in Groups, represent the foundation knowledge of organizational behavior. Part 2 (Chapters 3 through 6) explores the individual behavior processes of perception and communication, learning and motivation, conflict, and individual decision making. Part 3 (Chapters 7 through 10) focuses on the behaviors of individuals when they behave in groups. The topics of Part 3 include group dynamics, power, group decision making, and leadership.

Part 4, Managing for Performance, applies the foundation knowledge of organizational behavior to the challenge of managing in organizations. Chapter 11 (Organizational Entry) examines how individuals are brought into organizations and how organizations welcome and socialize new members. Chapter 12 (Job Design) explores how task assignments in an organization can be arranged to reflect our understanding of individual and group behavior. Finally, Chapter 13 (Maintaining Performance) addresses the issue of maintaining workers' motivation and performance on the job, primarily through performance appraisals and programs such as goal setting.

The scope of any individual's focus in an organization is his or her personal behavior and the behaviors of those in the immediate work group. But individual and work-group behaviors occur in the larger context of entire organizations. Part 5 explores the larger context of organizations and its implications for our understanding of behavior in organizations. Chapters 14 and 15 look at the environment and technology as primary *external* influences on behavior in organizations. Chapter 16 examines the influence of organizational structure and design (such as formalization and departmentalization) on organizational behavior. Chapter 17 focuses on the critical issue of change in organizations and how it can best be managed from a human standpoint. Finally, Chapter 18 looks beyond the present to see what lies ahead for organizations and organizational behavior.

An implicit concern in this book is the importance of understanding organizations and organizational behavior in everyday life. Organizational behavior is not just the study of *work* organizations. Organizational behavior refers to behavior in all organizations, including social clubs, families, and even study groups at school. To that end, the practical examples of organizational behavior contained in this book are drawn from a variety of different organizations, and even a variety of different countries. Each chapter also ends with some additional suggestions for readings, in case you want to know more about what you have read. A sound understanding of organizational behavior is useful for managing your life at work, but it is also useful for managing your life outside work.

## SUMMARY: THE CHALLENGE OF ORGANIZATIONAL BEHAVIOR

The portrait of organizational behavior painted in this chapter stands in stark contrast to a functional view of managerial life as deliberate and orderly planning and execution. Probably the truth falls somewhere between the two. A functional approach to organizational behavior may tell us what a manager should be doing to manage behavior in the best of all possible organizations. Unfortunately, no manager manages in the best of all possible organizations.

Instead this chapter has suggested that managers manage in organizations made highly complex by people and their behaviors, in which conflict is inevitable, and in which the only certainties that a manager can depend on are that nothing is certain and everything is changing. Managing an organization's human resources to achieve effectiveness and efficiency in the face of complexity, conflict, and uncertainty and constant change is the challenge of organizational behavior. Preparing you to meet that challenge is the goal of this book.

KEY TERMS

**Complexity**  Overabundance of inputs that managers must keep track of, consider, and manage.

**Conflict**  Differences among the perceptions, beliefs, and goals of organization members.

**Controlling**  Management function of directing and motivating the work force, often by generating direction and enthusiasm for work through leadership.

**Effectiveness**  Ability of an organization to accomplish an important goal, purpose, or mission.

**Efficiency**  Amount of effort required to deliver a promised good or service; can be increased through specialization and economies of scale.

**Informal organization**  Interpersonal realities of an organization, such as employees' personal goals, perceptions, and beliefs, that are not part of the organization's formal goals and plans but that must be taken into account to achieve organizational efficiency and effectiveness.

**Managerial functions**  Activities that must be performed for organizations to outperform individuals, including planning, organizing, staffing, and controlling.

**Organization**  Form of human association for the attainment of a common purpose by combining the talents and efforts of its members.

**Organizing**  Management function of creating a structure through which members can produce the organization's central goods or services.

**Planning**  Management thought processes that precede action in an organization.

**Political system**  Collection of individuals or groups that must work together and speak with one voice even though each has a private agenda to pursue.

**Power**  Ability to influence the attitudes or behavior of others, usually through the control of resources.

**Staffing**  Management function of supplying a work force (people) to fill the organization's designed structures.

**Uncertainty**  Not knowing for sure; may include future actions or events, or relationships between actions and consequences.

DISCUSSION
QUESTIONS

1. What is an organization? Why do people become members of organizations? Think of some organizations to which you belong. Why did you join these organizations? Think of an organization of which you are *no longer* a member. Why did you leave it?

2. Differentiate between efficiency and effectiveness. Why are Fayol's managerial functions an inadequate description of how organizations pursue these goals?

3. How would you characterize the life of a manager? How does your description fit in with the three defining characteristics of organizations (conflict, uncertainty, and complexity) presented in this chapter?

4. Consider your class as an organization. What sources of uncertainty exist for you as a student? What sources exist for your instructor? What goals do you and your instructor share? What goals might you and your instructor have that are incompatible?

IF YOU
WANT TO
KNOW
MORE

A summary of Henry Mintzberg's study of executive behavior patterns is provided in his article, "The Manager's Job: Folklore and Fact," published in the *Harvard Business Review* 53 (1975). Studs Terkel also has put together a collection of interviews of workers at all levels and types of American work organizations. The book is entitled *Working* (New York: Pantheon Books, 1974).

Though Henri Fayol first proposed the functional approach to management in 1916, his book on the topic *(General and Industrial Management)* was not translated from French into English until 1949 (London: Pitman Press). A more contemporary discussion of traditional approaches to management is contained in Peter Drucker's book, *Management: Tasks, Responsibilities, and Practices* (New York: Harper & Row, 1974).

The two alternative perspectives on managing behavior in organizations described in this chapter are discussed at length in Graham Allison's book, *The Essence of Decision* (Boston: Little, Brown, 1971). Allison uses the alternative perspectives to explain the U.S. foreign policy decisions preceding both the Bay of Pigs fiasco and the Cuban Missile Crisis. These two alternative perspectives on life in organizations also are discussed along with several others in Gareth Morgan's book, *Images of Organization* (Beverly Hills, Calif.: Sage, 1986). The political perspective is discussed in detail in Roger Hilsman's book, *To Move a Nation* (Garden City, N.Y.: Doubleday, 1967). Hilsman uses the political perspective to analyze U.S. government decision making under the Kennedy administration. The effects of uncertainty and politics on effectiveness are discussed in an article by Richard Hall, "Goals and Effectiveness," in B. Staw's volume, *Psychological Foundations of Organizational Behavior* (Glenview, Ill.: Scott, Foresman, 1983).

Two best-sellers detail possible sources of uncertainty and change in America that would profoundly influence life in work organizations. John Naisbitt's book, Megatrends (New York: Warner Books, 1982), outlines ten major sources of change in American society. Alvin Toffler's book, *The Third Wave* (New York: Bantam Books, 1980), takes an historical perspective, examines two previous major waves of change in America, and predicts a third one.

Jean Auel's *The Clan of the Cave Bear* (New York: Bantam Books, 1980) is an entertaining novel about life in a primitive clan. Her descriptions of how the clan deals with both crises and daily routines provide valuable insights into the workings and justifications of organizations.

**ON YOUR OWN**

**The Organizational Behavior IQ Test**   Please fill out the following questionnaire. Your instructor will provide you with information about the meaning of your responses.

On the following pages are 24 pairs of statements. For each pair, circle the letter preceding the statement that you think is most accurate. Circle *one* and *only one* letter in each pair.

After you have circled the letter, indicate how certain you are of your choice by writing 1, 2, 3, or 4 on the line in front of each item according to the following procedure.

Place a "1" if you are *very uncertain* that your choice is correct.
Place a "2" if you are *somewhat uncertain* that your choice is correct.
Place a "3" if you are *somewhat certain* that your choice is correct.
Place a "4" if you are *very certain* that your choice is correct.

Do not skip any pairs.

_____ 1. a. A supervisor is well advised to treat, as much as possible, all members of his/her group exactly the same way.

b. A supervisor is well advised to adjust his/her behavior according to the unique characteristics of the members of his/her group.

_____ 2. a. Generally speaking, individual motivation is greatest if the person has set goals for himself/herself which are *difficult* to achieve.

b. Generally speaking, individual motivation is greatest if the person has set goals for himself/herself which are *easy* to achieve.

_____ 3. a. A major reason why organizations are not so productive as they could be these days is that managers are too concerned with managing the work group rather than the individual.

b. A major reason why organizations are not so productive as they could be these days is that managers are too concerned with managing the individual rather than the work group.

Source: R. Weinberg and W. Nord, "Coping with 'It's All Common Sense'," *Exchange: The Organizational Behavior Teaching Journal* 7(2), (1982): 29–33.

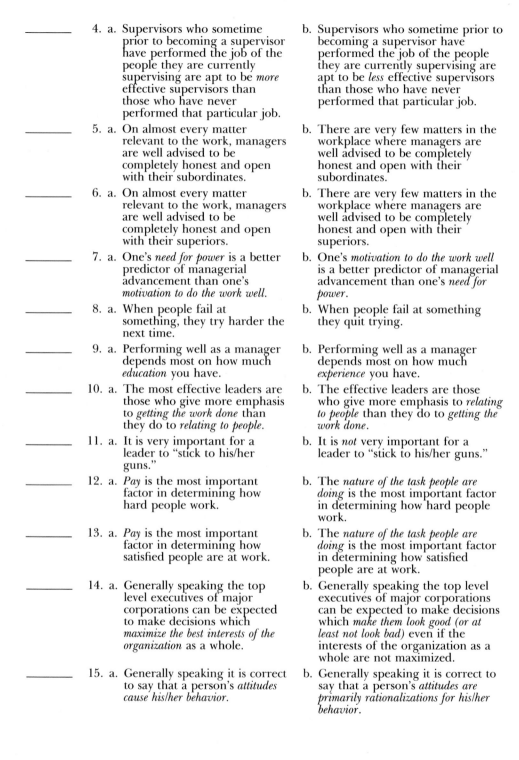

———————   4. a. Supervisors who sometime prior to becoming a supervisor have performed the job of the people they are currently supervising are apt to be *more* effective supervisors than those who have never performed that particular job.

b. Supervisors who sometime prior to becoming a supervisor have performed the job of the people they are currently supervising are apt to be *less* effective supervisors than those who have never performed that particular job.

———————   5. a. On almost every matter relevant to the work, managers are well advised to be completely honest and open with their subordinates.

b. There are very few matters in the workplace where managers are well advised to be completely honest and open with their subordinates.

———————   6. a. On almost every matter relevant to the work, managers are well advised to be completely honest and open with their superiors.

b. There are very few matters in the workplace where managers are well advised to be completely honest and open with their superiors.

———————   7. a. One's *need for power* is a better predictor of managerial advancement than one's *motivation to do the work well.*

b. One's *motivation to do the work well* is a better predictor of managerial advancement than one's *need for power.*

———————   8. a. When people fail at something, they try harder the next time.

b. When people fail at something they quit trying.

———————   9. a. Performing well as a manager depends most on how much *education* you have.

b. Performing well as a manager depends most on how much *experience* you have.

———————   10. a. The most effective leaders are those who give more emphasis to *getting the work done* than they do to *relating to people.*

b. The effective leaders are those who give more emphasis to *relating to people* than they do to *getting the work done.*

———————   11. a. It is very important for a leader to "stick to his/her guns."

b. It is *not* very important for a leader to "stick to his/her guns."

———————   12. a. *Pay* is the most important factor in determining how hard people work.

b. The *nature of the task people are doing* is the most important factor in determining how hard people work.

———————   13. a. *Pay* is the most important factor in determining how satisfied people are at work.

b. The *nature of the task people are doing* is the most important factor in determining how satisfied people are at work.

———————   14. a. Generally speaking the top level executives of major corporations can be expected to make decisions which *maximize the best interests of the organization* as a whole.

b. Generally speaking the top level executives of major corporations can be expected to make decisions which *make them look good (or at least not look bad)* even if the interests of the organization as a whole are not maximized.

———————   15. a. Generally speaking it is correct to say that a person's *attitudes cause his/her behavior.*

b. Generally speaking it is correct to say that a person's *attitudes are primarily rationalizations for his/her behavior.*

_____ 16. a. Satisfied workers produce *more* than workers who are not satisfied.     b. Satisfied workers produce *no more* than workers who are not satisfied.

_____ 17. a. Generally speaking the *structure* of an organization determines the *technology it uses*.     b. Generally speaking the *technology* of an organization determines its structure.

_____ 18. a. The statement, "A manager's authority needs to be commensurate with his/her responsibility" is practically speaking a *very meaningful statement*.     b. The statement, "A manager's authority needs to be commensurate with his/her responsibility" is practically speaking a *basically meaningless statement*.

_____ 19. a. A major reason for the relative decline in American productivity is that the division of labor and job specialization *have gone too far*.     b. A major reason for the relative decline in American productivity is that the division of labor and job specialization *have not been carried far enough*.

_____ 20. a. The notion that most semiskilled workers desire work which is interesting and meaningful is most likely *incorrect*.     b. The notion that most semiskilled workers desire work which is interesting and meaningful is most likely *correct*.

_____ 21. a. People welcome change for the better.     b. Even if change is for the better, people will resist it.

_____ 22. a. Leaders are born, not made.     b. Leaders are made, not born.

_____ 23. a. Groups make better decisions than individuals.     b. Individuals make better decisions than groups.

_____ 24. a. Generally speaking the largest corporations would be more efficient if they were *larger*.     b. Generally speaking the largest corporations would be more efficient if they were *smaller*.

CLOSING CASE
FOR CHAPTER 1

## THE MANAGER'S MEMO

FROM: J. Cox, Executive Vice President

TO:      M. Berger, Manager, Swimwear Division

RE:      Second Quarter Performance

In reviewing each division's performance for the second quarter, I note that our new Swimwear Division is failing to meet its planned goals. Sales are well below targeted levels. I understand from the sales department that our swimsuits have failed to incorporate the most recent fashion innovations introduced by our major competitors. In addition, we have been receiving complaints that the legholes of our swimsuits are often sewn shut.

How can you explain these problems? As I recall, when you started up the division last year you had prepared an impressively detailed plan and had organized the division for maximum efficiency. Can it be that the division's fashion designers are poorly qualified or that the production work force is not cooperating with your goals?

None of this really fits the orderly management of organizations I was led to expect in business school. Am I being naive about the realities of organizational life?

CASE DISCUSSION
QUESTIONS

Based upon what you have learned about organizational behavior, assume you are the manager of the Swimsuit Division and respond to this memo. What are some possible causes of the division's problems?

# Facing the Challenge: Historical Perspectives

**Traditional Views**
Bureaucracy
Scientific Management

**The Hawthorne Studies**
The Illumination Studies
The Bank Wiring Room Study
*FOCUS ON The Hawthorne Studies: Legacy of the Legend*

**Human Relations**
Maslow's Need Hierarchy
*The Man on the Assembly Line*
Theory Y
*FOCUS ON Theory Y: Interdependence*
System 4

**The Satisfaction-Performance Controversy**

**Beyond Human Relations**
Worker Participation in Europe
*INTERNATIONAL FOCUS ON Worker Participation in Europe: Yugoslavian Workers in Control*
The Japanese Experience
In Search of Solutions

**Open Systems Theory**

## They Practiced What They Preached

Frank and Lillian Gilbreth, two of America's earliest and best-known efficiency experts, pioneered the use of motion pictures in the early 1900s to identify efficient production techniques. Their photographic time-and-motion studies were used to identify the basic component motions of work tasks. They called these basic components "therbligs" (which is very nearly *Gilbreth* spelled backwards), and sought to simplify work tasks by eliminating unnecessary motions. Included in their successes were: (1) the simplification of a bricklaying task from 18 to 5 basic motions, yielding an increase in output from 120 to 350 bricks per hour and a net *decrease* in worker fatigue; and (2) the simplification of a cotton cloth-folding task from more than 20 basic motions to 12 or less, yielding an increase in output of 167 percent with no net increase in worker fatigue. The Gilbreths opposed the views of their more famous contemporary Frederick Taylor. Taylor believed that efficiency would be maximized only if workers followed orders with no back talk. The Gilbreths, on the other hand, encouraged worker suggestions and participation in their attempts to improve productivity scientifically.

For Frank and Lillian Gilbreth, improving efficiency was more than just a way to make a living. It was a way of life. Two of their children, Frank, Jr., and Ernestine, popularized their parents' attempts to apply scientific management to life at home through the book, *Cheaper by the Dozen*. The Gilbreths' exploits proved so entertaining that the book was made into a feature-length motion picture. In one particularly revealing description of life at the Gilbreths', the children noted that:

> . . . Our house at Montclair, New Jersey, was a sort of school for scientific management and the elimination of wasted motions—or "motion study," as Dad and Mother named it. Dad took moving pictures of us children washing dishes, so that he could figure out how we could

37

reduce our motions and thus hurry through the task. . . .

Yes, at home or on the job, Dad was always the efficiency expert. He buttoned his vest from the bottom up, instead of from the top down, because the bottom-to-top process took him only 3 seconds, while the top-to-bottom took 7. He even used two shaving brushes to lather his face, because he found that by so doing he could cut 17 seconds off his shaving time. For a while he tried shaving with two razors, but he finally gave that up.

"I can save forty-four seconds," he grumbled, "but I wasted two minutes this morning putting this bandage on my throat."

It wasn't the slashed throat that really bothered him. It was the two minutes.

The Gilbreths' refinements of time-and-motion studies have not been lost on contemporary American businesses. Faced with increasing competition in the fast-food industry, management at Burger King has used time-and-motion studies to increase productivity. For instance, the Drive-through Task Force at Burger King observed that order takers needed 11 seconds to react when cars drove over the bell hose. Moving the bell hose back ten feet meant that order takers would be in position by the time a car had braked and was ready to order, and no sooner. With this and some other changes accomplished by careful time-and-motion analysis, the Drive-through Task Force helped Burger King handle an extra 30 cars each hour.

Sources: F. B. Gilbreth, Jr., and E. G. Carey, *Cheaper by the Dozen* (New York: Thomas Cromwell, 1948), pp. 2–3; E. Meadows, "How Three Companies Increased Their Productivity," *FORTUNE*, March 10, 1980, pp. 92–101; F. B. Gilbreth and L. M. Gilbreth, *Applied Motion Study* (New York: Sturgis & Walton, 1917).

## INTRODUCTION

To understand organizational behavior as a field of scientific inquiry one must first look back on the history of management thought and theory. Organizational behavior found its roots in the shortcomings of classical theories (such as Fayol's functional approach to management) to explain behavior in organizations. These shortcomings in turn found their roots in a management vision of rank-and-file workers that failed to capture their essential humanity. This chapter traces the origins and history of the field of organizational behavior by examining the evolution of management thought and theory up to the present day.

## TRADITIONAL VIEWS

In the beginning there was the Arsenal. The Arsenal was not the *very* beginning, of course, but it could easily have been the beginning of modern management. The Arsenal, opened in 1436, was the shipyard of

| FIGURE 2–1 | Characteristics of a Bureaucracy |
|---|---|

1.  Each office has fixed official duties.
2.  Conduct is governed by impersonal rules and regulations.
3.  Effort is coordinated through a hierarchy of levels of authority.
4.  Order and reliability are maintained through written communication and files.
5.  Employment is a full-time occupation for members of the organization.
6.  Appointment to office is made by superiors.
7.  Promotion is based upon merit (that is, who does the best job).

Source: M. Weber, *Essays in Sociology* (New York: Oxford University Press, 1946).

Venice, Italy. By 1400, Venice had become a thriving center of commerce. To protect its fleet of commercial ships, the city of Venice set up its own shipyard to build, repair, and outfit war galleys. By 1500, the Arsenal shipyard employed almost 2,000 workers and covered more than 60 acres of the Venice waterfront. This shipyard was the forerunner of the modern industrial organization.[1]

The Arsenal was the first modern assembly line. A series of Arsenal warehouses were arranged along a Venice canal, each corresponding to a different set of tasks in the building, repair, and outfitting of warships. The galleys were towed up the canal, from warehouse to warehouse, until required work was completed. When a galley reached a particular warehouse, needed parts and equipment were passed out windows onto the galley.

**BUREAUCRACY**

The Arsenal was a bureaucratic organization. The defining characteristics of a bureaucratic organization are presented in Figure 2–1. In a bureaucratic organization (or **bureaucracy**), there are clearly defined lines of authority and responsibility for employees. Behavior is tightly controlled by rules, policies, and job assignments. In the Arsenal, the warehouses had been sequenced carefully so that no backtracking in the "assembly line" would be needed. Standardization of parts, specialization of labor, and accounting and inventory control all were used to keep a tight rein on the Arsenal's production process.

Bureaucratic organizations like the Arsenal function like machines. In a machine, every part has a specific, well-defined role which it performs in perfect concert with all other parts of the machine. There are no extra parts, nor are there parts which function independently from the rest of the machine.

[1]F. Lane, *Venetian Ships and Shipbuilders of the Renaissance* (Baltimore: Johns Hopkins Press, 1934).

Max Weber, a German sociologist, was a great admirer of the bureaucratic model of organizations and wrote extensively on its characteristics during the latter nineteenth and early twentieth centuries. As shown in the following passage from *Legitimate Authority and Bureaucracy,* Weber believed that bureaucratic organizations represented something of an *ideal* organizational form for proper management:

> Experience tends universally to show that the purely bureaucratic type of administrative organization . . . is, from a purely technical point of view, capable of attaining the highest degree of efficiency and is in this sense formally the most rational known means of carrying out imperative control over human beings. It is superior to any other form in precision, in stability, in the stringency of discipline, and in its reliability. It thus makes possible a particularly high degree of calculability of results for the heads of the organization and for those acting in relation to it. It is finally superior both in intensive efficiency and in the scope of its operations.[2]

To Weber's way of thinking, bureaucracy provided the ideal means of impersonal control, and thereby the surest path to organizational efficiency. Bureaucratic control enhances efficiency by ensuring that all worker effort is properly channeled toward the accomplishment of organizational goals.

*Impersonal* control in a bureaucracy means control that is achieved by closely governing organizational life through rules, regulations, and job descriptions that clearly dictate proper conduct in the organization. This impersonal control stands in contrast to *personal* means of control, such as charisma or social persuasion. From the bureaucratic perspective, personal means of organizational control are far too dependent upon individuals for getting things done, and therefore are far too unreliable. In a bureaucracy, control is a function of the *system* (the rules and regulations) rather than of the people in the system. Control occurs because of authority vested in a position by the rules and regulations. By implication this means that the system should be able to survive changes in personnel with no loss in efficiency. This is highly desirable from the viewpoint of reliability. It also means that the personalities and personal motivations of officeholders should be largely irrelevant to understanding behavior in a bureaucracy.

The prevailing view of workers in bureaucratic organizations is mechanical or mechanistic. Management views each worker as a collection of skills and abilities—a cog in the machine with performance potential. Management uses pay to fuel the cog's contributions to the functioning of the machine. In a bureaucracy, management pays little if any attention to the fact that workers might be *thinking* about the work they are doing. It seems revealing that it is a defining characteristic of bureaucracy that employment is viewed as a *full-time career* for members

---

[2]M. Weber, *Essays in Sociology* (New York: Oxford University Press, 1946).

of the organization. Once again, this implies a limited view of employee motivation in which the employee's life revolves around a role in the organization.

Despite the enormous efficiency advantages available through the use of bureaucratic organization, the organization model provided by the Arsenal shipyard was not widely adopted until the invention of the steam engine. When the steam engine was introduced in England, it became possible for the first time to design highly efficient, large-scale production technologies. In place of craftsmen working at home in cottage industries, large factories were built to house the new machines and the armies of workers necessary to run them. The Industrial Revolution had arrived.

## SCIENTIFIC MANAGEMENT

With the Industrial Revolution came the acceptance of large industrial factories and bureaucratic organizations as appropriate approaches to doing business. How to run these factories and organizations and take advantage of their tremendous efficiency potential remained something of a mystery, however. After all, workers were familiar primarily with "craftsman" models of production in which skilled individuals worked independently. Large industrial factories used greater job specialization, required increased standardization of work, and were structured around a differentiation between labor and levels of management. These new arrangements were unexpected and unfamiliar and required a new way of thinking about getting work done.

That new way of thinking was a theory of management. The functional approach detailed the essence of this new way of thinking for managers and supervisors. For managers and supervisors in these new, large industrial organizations, the new game was planning, organizing, staffing, and controlling. Frederick Taylor translated this new way of thinking into prescriptions for changing the behaviors of workers at the level of the shop floor. Taylor's approach to planning, organizing, staffing, and controlling work on the shop floor became known as scientific management. **Scientific management** took its name from the careful and systematic observational techniques it used to design jobs and arrange work for the rank-and-file factory worker.

While employed as a manager at the Midvale Steel Works in Philadelphia, Taylor became disgusted with the gross inefficiency and waste he found on the factory shop floor. At the heart of factory labor management at the time was a piecework compensation plan. That is, workers were paid a fixed amount for every correctly produced item. Unfortunately, Taylor observed that workers were ill-equipped, inadequately trained, and poorly supervised. Moreover, it was obvious that workers were restricting their output *intentionally* to keep management's productivity expectations low and piece rates high. Taylor suspected that with a more careful and systematic approach to labor management,

**FIGURE 2–2**     Features of Scientific Management

1. *Time-and-motion studies.* Using a clipboard and stopwatch, Taylor calculated the speed of different approaches to a task. Taylor also conducted experiments in which he varied approaches to a task to see which was the most efficient.

2. *Work standards.* A "fair day's work" was the amount of production that could be expected of an industrious worker who followed Taylor's directions for completing a task efficiently.

3. *Selection and training.* Taylor emphasized that the selection of qualified workers and their careful training were essential to the achievement of highly efficient production.

4. *Wages.* Taylor believed that workers should share in the production gains attained by their highly efficient work. Taylor pioneered the use of wage differentials, which paid a worker extra for production beyond "a fair day's work."

worker productivity could be increased dramatically, perhaps more than tripled.

Taylor's attempts to correct the problems he found took the four related directions shown in Figure 2–2. First, Taylor popularized **time-and-motion studies.** Using a clipboard and stopwatch, Taylor observed different workers' ways of accomplishing the same task. He would time each worker's attempts and use the results to determine which methods were the most efficient. Taylor also conducted experiments. In an experiment, Taylor would instruct a worker to try different methods for accomplishing a task while Taylor watched, timed, and recorded observations. For instance, when trying to identify the most efficient method for shoveling coal, Taylor systematically manipulated such factors as the size of the shovel, the amount of coal in the shovel, the number of shovels between rest breaks, and the length of the rest breaks. Taylor's time-and-motion experiments identified the most efficient means for accomplishing a work task.[3] Some applications of Taylor's time-and-motion studies were provided in "They Practiced What They Preached," at the beginning of this chapter.

Second, when the time-and-motion study of a work task had been completed, Taylor used this information to establish work standards. **Work standards** included specific instructions to workers for doing a work task, expected time to complete a task, and expected volume of output. Taylor used these standards to establish scientifically what he called "a fair day's work." "A fair day's work" was defined as the amount of production that could be expected from a worker who followed Taylor's directions and worked diligently throughout the entire work-

[3]F. W. Taylor, "The Principles of Scientific Management," *The Bulletin of the Taylor Society* (December 1916): 13–23.

day. The standards Taylor provided made it clearer to workers what was expected of them both in quantity and method.

Third, Taylor emphasized the importance of the systematic selection and training of workers. Having identified (using time-and-motion studies) the most efficient method for completing a task, Taylor thought it critical to select workers capable of working according to the identified instructions. Then, careful training of those workers would ensure that they knew the correct method for accomplishing the work task.

Finally, Taylor firmly believed that, "What workermen want most from their employers beyond anything else is high wages."[4] As noted earlier, Taylor felt that workers intentionally restricted output to keep management productivity expectations low and piece rates high. To reverse this trend, Taylor offered workers a piece-rate differential. Whenever the daily output of a worker exceeded the calculated "fair day's work," the piece rate received by the worker would be higher. For example, a worker whose output exceeded the calculated "fair day's work" might receive 6¢ per piece produced instead of 5¢. Further, this higher piece rate would be paid for *all* the pieces the worker produced during the day in which the "fair day's work" was exceeded. Because Taylor believed that money was the only important motivator of workers on the job, he felt this incentive would be far too attractive to pass up and workers would work hard to obtain it.

Using these four techniques—time-and-motion studies and experiments, work standards, systematic selection and training, and piece-rate differentials—Taylor's applications of scientific management at Bethlehem Steel apparently produced stunning increases in efficiency. In some recorded cases, Taylor increased worker output from 12½ to 47 tons of pig iron loaded in a ten-hour day, even though his instructions had workers resting 57 percent of the time. Taylor is credited with saving Bethlehem Steel as much as $80,000 per year in pig-iron handling costs while simultaneously increasing workers' wages by more than 50 percent.[5]

Later research has questioned the accuracy of Taylor's reported successes using scientific management at Bethlehem Steel.[6] Nevertheless, scientific management caught on big. In 1914, the Ford Motor Company raised basic wages to $5 per day—an unheard-of sum that Ford attributed to the successes of its scientific management cost-cutting programs.[7]

Taylor's pioneering principles of systematic observation and analysis of work tasks using time-and-motion studies and the scientific arrange-

---

[4]F. W. Taylor, *Shop Management* (New York: Harper and Brothers, 1911).

[5]W. J. Duncan, *Management.* (New York: Random House, 1983).

[6]C. Wrege and A. Perroni, "Taylor's Pig-Tale: An Historical Analysis of Frederick W. Taylor's Pig-Iron Experiments," *Academy of Management Journal* 17 (1974): 6–27.

[7]Duncan, *Management*, p. 19.

Frederick Taylor used the principles of scientific management (including time-and-motion studies, work standards, careful selection and training, and a piece-rate differential wage package) to dramatically increase the productivity of workers such as these employees of Bethlehem Steel.

ment of work functions can be found today in the fields of operations management and human factors psychology. Operations management is a sister field of organizational behavior within the larger discipline of management. While organizational behavior is concerned with management of an organization's *human* resources, operations management focuses on management of the organization's *technical* resources (such as machinery, raw materials, and plant layout). Typical topics of study in operations management include purchase and storage of materials, work-flow and delivery scheduling, and quality-control issues. Human factors psychology is concerned with the importance of human characteristics and limitations in the design of training programs, work environments, and technologies.

Careful employee selection and training, standard setting, and financial incentives all remain powerful tools in today's management repertoire.[8] Scientific management did fall out of vogue, however. While the productivity gains it achieved were impressive, some were concerned that they represented a subtle form of worker exploitation. Further, the application of Taylor's techniques often resulted in labor-force reductions, making scientific management at times unpopular in local communities.

Scientific management also lost popularity, though, because Taylor built his theory of management around the assumption that money was the only important motivator of worker behavior. As noted earlier, Taylor's work also acknowledged the role of noneconomic factors in work settings. In particular, Taylor reported the existence of worker

[8]E. A. Locke, "The Ideas of Frederick W. Taylor: An Evaluation," *Academy of Management Review* 7 (1982): 14–24.

norms to restrict output intentionally. However, Taylor believed that these social concerns (and other noneconomic worker motivations) were relatively unimportant and would be overwhelmed by financial incentives. The inadequacies of this view of worker motivation were brought to light by a series of studies conducted at the Hawthorne plant of the Western Electric Company. A different view of worker motivation emerged from these studies and provided the seeds from which the field of organizational behavior has grown.

## THE HAWTHORNE STUDIES

Elton Mayo is not always credited with ending the reign of scientific management in American industry. Nevertheless, it probably is accurate to say that Mayo was one of the first management theorists to see beyond scientific management's simplified economic assumptions about the American factory worker. Mayo, a professor at Harvard University, headed up a research team investigating high turnover in a Philadelphia textile mill. The year was 1923. After careful study, Mayo's research team reorganized the work schedule to include more rest pauses—a procedure not unfamiliar to the scientific management practitioners of Mayo's era. The major effects of adding rest pauses were to reduce turnover greatly while substantially increasing worker morale.[9]

While the reduction in turnover was expected, the changes in morale were a surprise. The unexpected worker morale increases that occurred as part and parcel of the work rearrangements suggested to Mayo that purely economic characterizations of the American worker were missing something important. Mayo left the textile mills with a new sensitivity to the viewpoint of the worker. He did not have to wait long to apply his new insight. His Harvard research group had been asked to help unravel a perplexing mystery then unfolding at the Hawthorne plant of Western Electric.

## THE ILLUMINATION STUDIES

Before Mayo and his colleagues arrived, an initial study at the Hawthorne plant had explored the effects of workplace illumination levels on worker productivity. Tungsten-filament electric lamps recently had been invented and quickly were displacing gas lamps as the lighting source of choice in industrial plants. Electric companies, fearing substantial revenue losses from the highly efficient tungsten bulbs, wanted to encourage industrial electricity usage by suggesting that higher levels of illumination would increase worker productivity on the shop floor (and yield higher electric bills as well!).

To test this "illumination" hypothesis, researchers selected two groups of about six female workers each from the shop floor. One group of six

[9]E. Mayo, *The Social Problems of an Industrial Civilization* (Boston: Harvard University Press, 1945).

The Hawthorne studies are an important part of the history of organizational behavior. While their scientific validity remains in doubt even today, there is little doubt that the results of these studies forced management theorists to reexamine their assumptions about human motivation.

subjects (the control group) was placed in a test room where the illumination level remained constant throughout the study. The other group of six subjects (the experimental group) was placed in a test room where the amount of work-area illumination was varied systematically.

If the design of this study was in keeping with the best traditions of scientific management, the results certainly were not. In the test room where illumination levels were varied systematically, worker productivity increased when work-area illumination increased. This was expected. However, productivity also increased for this group when work-area illumination *decreased,* even to the level of moonlight intensity. Furthermore, the productivity increases achieved by the experimental group were matched by the *control* group, even though the control group illumination levels remained constant throughout the study!

Elton Mayo and his Harvard colleagues were brought in to help solve this mystery. Immediately they noticed a subtle but important parallel with their findings in the Philadelphia textile mills. In both cases, simple economic and mechanistic views of the rank-and-file factory worker— consistent with the dominant orientation of scientific management— were unable to explain the results. These failures of scientific management at Hawthorne led Mayo and his colleagues to a new understanding of the rank-and-file factory worker that encompassed more human attributes.

Mayo and his colleagues pursued his new vision of the factory worker through additional research at Hawthorne. By 1932, when research at Hawthorne ended, seven studies had taken place and more than 20,000

Western Electric employees had participated as subjects. Next to the illumination studies, the most provocative research results came from a study of workers wiring telephone connection terminals (or "banks").

**THE BANK WIRING ROOM STUDY**

The bank wiring room study began with careful observation of the productivity of the bank wiring workers. According to the results of a time-and-motion analysis of bank wiring, industrial engineers had arrived at a standard of 7,312 connections per day per worker. This corresponded to a standard of two and one-half completely wired telephone connection terminals per day per worker. In fact, the workers produced on the average only two completed terminals per day.

Following in the footsteps of the illumination studies, the bank wiring group was moved into a special test room for further observation. In contrast to the results of the illumination studies, however, this special treatment did *not* produce any changes in the group's productivity. Average output remained at two completed terminals per day. In light of the results of the illumination studies and the output expected from the time-and-motion analysis of the bank wiring task, attention was focused on why the group's average output was only two completed terminals per day.

The workers in the bank wiring room offered several explanations for their "restriction of output." First, management seemed to be satisfied with the current level of productivity. After all, no one had been fired and the group had not been reprimanded for its performance. Second, the workers were afraid that productivity increases would result in the eventual reduction of the work group size. If management was satisfied with the current level of output, it stood to reason that higher productivity would mean that fewer workers would be needed to achieve it. Finally, higher productivity probably would just raise management's expectations, which would lead to higher work standards, which would just make work life harder for everyone in the group.

None of these explanations for the group's output restriction was particularly novel or noteworthy. What did command the researchers' attention was the manner in which output restriction was being achieved. Members of the bank wiring group were friendly both on and off the job. Apparently they were a tight *social* group, in addition to a work group. There seemed to be an unstated conviction that *all* members of the group had family responsibilities and needed to remain employed. So the slower workers were protected by the work group—no one outproduced the slowest workers enough to get them in trouble.

Protection of the slower workers was achieved by group members applying social pressure on the "rate busters." Group members might tease or ridicule a particularly fast worker who seemed to be on the verge of violating the group's informal production norm of only two completed terminals per day. If a fast worker's productivity really got out of hand, the group members might resort to "binging." "Binging" was a game in which one worker would punch the rate buster, setting off a chain reaction of returned punches. While the punching was all in good fun, "binging" did serve to distract fast workers from the task at hand and to convey the message that an important group expectation (productivity level) was being violated.

What did Elton Mayo and the management community learn from the Hawthorne studies? They learned that mechanistic and economic visions of worker motivation were inadequate for understanding human behavior in organizations. The results of the illumination studies demonstrated that mechanistic views of worker motivation do not take into account the human complexities that drive worker behavior. Mechanistic views of worker behavior could explain why productivity would go up when work area illumination was increased, but not why productivity would go up when illumination was *decreased* or *remained unchanged*. Perhaps of greater importance, the bank wiring group study demonstrated the power of the informal social structure of a work group. The bank wiring group workers were paid on an individual piece-rate plan. Nevertheless, social pressures proved quite effective in restricting output of the work group's members.

As the years have passed, the scientific quality of the Hawthorne studies has come under attack. The celebrated Hawthorne effect, a concept learned in all introductory psychology classes and detailed in the "Focus on: The Hawthorne Studies," is now believed to be a misinterpretation of the original findings. Several of the studies produced important contradictions that apparently were ignored by researchers for many years. And, in some instances, workers in experimental groups were replaced for not producing adequately. These worker replacements completely undermine the studies' scientific value. In retrospect, even Fritz Roethlisberger, one of the central research figures in the studies, admits that some of the Hawthorne study conclusions are questionable because they were based on "testing for the effect of a single variable in a situation where there were so many uncontrolled variables."[10] Nevertheless, the Hawthorne studies played a major role in shifting the emphasis of management theory away from simple mechanistic and economic views of worker motivation.

# Human Relations

By demonstrating the power of social relationships in work settings, the Hawthorne studies created a need for new ways of thinking about management. Judging from the behavior of the workers in the bank wiring group at Hawthorne, social relationships could be even stronger

[10]F. J. Roethlisberger, *The Elusive Phenomena* (Cambridge, Mass.: Harvard University Press, 1977).

motivators than management's economic incentives. Approaches to managing behavior in organizations now had to incorporate a more complex, and indeed more *human,* vision of the American worker. The new approach to management that emerged emphasized the importance of workers' personal and social needs. It came to be known as **human relations.**

---

FOCUS ON:

The Hawthorne Studies

**Legacy of the Legend**   "It looked as if the workers were reacting more to the positive concern of the experimenters about their working conditions than to the actual physical changes in illumination." With these words, Fritz Roethlisberger summarized a widely held belief about the importance of the Hawthorne studies at Western Electric. While this explanation of the findings of the Hawthorne studies has fallen into disrepute over the years, its message remains critical to the practice of behavioral science research. Subjects in experiments do not always act like workers on the job. This change in the behavior of subjects who know that an experiment is taking place is called *the Hawthorne effect.*

A. H. Pierce first noted this effect in 1908, when he wrote that subjects who know they are involved in experiments often take on a "cheerful willingness to assist the investigator in every possible way by reporting to him those very things which he is most eager to find." This willingness of subjects to help out or please the researcher was dramatically demonstrated in a series of studies conducted by Martin Orne. Orne asked subjects to perform serial additions of adjacent rows on sheets of paper filled with rows of random numbers. To complete just one sheet would require 224 separate additions. After completing a page, the subject was "to tear up the sheet of paper which you have just completed into a minimum of thirty-two pieces and go on to the next sheet of paper."

Orne was looking for a particularly objectionable task to use in some other research he was pursuing. He expected that subjects would quit when they realized that the sheets were identical and that each finished sheet had to be destroyed—in short, when they realized that the task was meaningless. Instead subjects persevered at this task for *several hours,* showing no signs of hostility. Apparently subjects feel there is an implicit contract with the experimenter that they are duty-bound to honor.

Outside of the behavioral science laboratory, it seems inconceivable that an adult human being would put up with such nonsense. That it happens even in a behavioral science laboratory provides a testament to the power of Hawthorne effects—and a caution about interpreting the results of experiments that are clearly defined as such to their subjects.

Sources: M. Orne, "On the Social Psychology of the Psychology Experiment: With Particular Reference to Demand Characteristics and Their Implications," *American Psychologist* 17 (1962): pp. 776–783; F. J. Roethlisberger, *The Elusive Phenomenon* (Cambridge, Mass: Harvard University Press, 1977).

At the center of this new way of thinking was a big problem for managers. The application of high-efficiency management techniques often resulted in jobs that were efficient but not very interesting or involving for the workers. Insufficiently stimulated by their work, workers turned to social fulfillment in the workplace. Managers needed to direct worker attention and effort toward the job. And this meant that the real problem was how to keep workers' search for noneconomic fulfillment from interfering with their accomplishment of the organization's objectives.

Human relations management offered some solutions to these problems. The human relations approach took two things that had been ignored in previous theories about worker behavior in organizations and put them front and center. First, human relations embraced a broader concept of human needs and desires. Gone forever were purely economic approaches to understanding worker behavior. Human relations also accepted informal organizational structures (such as social networks and group memberships) as critical components of organizational life. Human relations viewed bureaucratic models of organizational life, which ignored the humanity of workers, as inadequate. From the perspective of the human relations movement, the worker had social, personal, *and* economic motivations, and the organization was a complex network of work *and* social relationships. The business of managing for effective and efficient productivity had some new elements to consider.

The new emphasis on human relations in management was reflected in several other developments: (1) Abraham Maslow's identification of a need hierarchy, (2) Walker and Guest's research concerning organizational life for *The Man on the Assembly Line,* (3) Douglas McGregor's Theory Y, and (4) Rensis Likert's System 4 theory of management.

## MASLOW'S NEED HIERARCHY

One important message of the Hawthorne studies was that traditional economic models of worker motivation could not explain organizational behavior. Worker motivations went beyond money.

Abraham Maslow offered a view of human motivation radically different from the classic economic one. While Maslow's theory will be discussed in detail in Chapter 4, it is worth noting here that his views of human motivation reflected an emerging trend. A psychologist at Brandeis University, Maslow was not interested in understanding organizational behavior. Instead, his theory was simply the most prominent of many reactions to economic and mechanistic theories of motivation that then dominated the field of psychology.

Maslow suggested that there was a **hierarchy of human needs,**[11] consisting of at least five distinct classes (physiological, safety/security, affiliation, esteem, and self-actualization). This meant that much more

[11]A. H. Maslow, *Motivation and Personality* (New York: Harper and Row, 1954).

than just economic needs were driving worker behavior in organizations, so much more than just economic needs had to be included in theories of organizational behavior.

Maslow's need hierarchy theory had two other important implications. First, at any point in time *different people have different needs*. If there are different kinds of needs, at any point in time what is important to one worker (what *drives* that worker's behavior) may not be important to another worker. Second, *people's needs change*. What motivates a worker today may not motivate that same worker tomorrow. Traditional theories of management may have recognized that the same amount of money might influence a worker differently on different days. However, only after the introduction of need hierarchy theories did it become accepted that on some days, factors other than money might be foremost in the minds of workers. Maslow also believed that worker needs changed predictably over time. In fact, Maslow used the term "hierarchy" to refer to the idea that some needs would become important to a worker only after other needs (those *lower* in the "hierarchy") had been fulfilled.

## THE MAN ON THE ASSEMBLY LINE

One highly visible research effort that came out of the new focus on human relations in the workplace was a series of studies conducted by Charles Walker and Robert Guest entitled *The Man on the Assembly Line*.[12] These studies became the forerunners of all current research on *job design* (a topic that will receive more attention in Chapter 12 of this book).

Walker and Guest's studies differed from virtually all previous management research. Following the lead of the Hawthorne studies before them, Walker and Guest focused their research on discovering which aspects of the organizational context made workers interested and involved. Walker and Guest interviewed 180 workers at an American automobile assembly plant that was considered one of the most modern and technologically sophisticated in the world.

Walker and Guest studied many of the same job aspects as scientific management practitioners. However, they also looked at what they called the total job situation. The **total job situation** included the seven characteristics shown in Figure 2–3. The influence of the Hawthorne studies should be apparent in this list of research topics. A primary emphasis of human relations management was the inclusion of worker *social relationships* (for instance, with other workers and with the union) in a theory of worker behavior in organizations.

The role of social relationships in organizational behavior was only one important emphasis of the research conducted by Walker and Guest. They also were interested in worker alienation. *Alienation* refers to a

[12]C. R. Walker and R. H. Guest, *The Man on the Assembly Line* (Cambridge, Mass.: Harvard University Press, 1952).

**FIGURE 2–3**          Features of the Total Job Situation

The human relations movement brought with it a broader sense of a job that went beyond work tasks. In their study of assembly-line jobs, for example, Walker and Guest defined the "total job situation" in terms of seven characteristics, which included social relationships on the job.

1.   The worker's immediate job
2.   The worker's relation to fellow workers
3.   The worker's relation to supervisors
4.   The worker's relation to the union
5.   Pay and job security
6.   Promotion and transfer
7.   Working conditions in the plant

Source: C. R. Walker and R. H. Guest, *The Man on the Assembly Line* (Cambridge, Mass.: Harvard University Press, 1952).

worker's feelings of boredom and underutilization of mental capacity. Walker and Guest were convinced that alienation occurred when workers were assigned highly specialized, highly routinized, and highly repetitive tasks—the very kinds of tasks designed into assembly lines by scientific management practitioners to achieve efficiency advantages. Walker and Guest also felt that at the root of alienation were workers' beliefs that management saw them only as production labor. Many workers apparently felt that the regimentation of their jobs made it possible for management to replace any worker any time. It was, after all, the *system* rather than the workers that produced the cars. Walker and Guest found that jobs that scored high on alienating characteristics (for instance, assembly-line jobs) typically suffered *twice as much* turnover and absenteeism.

Walker and Guest interpreted their findings as a mandate for management to increase the mental role of workers in production. In fact, they came out clearly in favor of allowing workers some say in the arrangement and pacing of their work. They suspected that "gains in quality and a drop in turnover or absenteeism may balance some decrease in output, if it occurs."[13] The issue of worker participation in decision making on the shop floor provides a strong contrast between human relations and scientific management; Frederick Taylor had maintained that, "all possible brain work should be removed from the shop and centered in the planning or lay-out department. . . . The time during which the [worker] stops to think is part of the time that he is not productive."[14]

[13]Ibid., p. 151.
[14]F. W. Taylor, *Scientific Management* (New York: Harper & Row, 1947), pp. 98–99, 262.

Walker and Guest's studies of assembly-line workers in the 1950s (like these Magneto assemblers) led them to conclude that workers became alienated when they were assigned specialized, routinized, and repetitive tasks—the very kinds of tasks recommended by the principles of scientific management.

A second, parallel set of studies of manufacturing workers confirmed many of Walker and Guest's conclusions. In 1944 and 1945, Donald Roy worked as a radial drill operator for the Geer Company.[15] His observations and the descriptions of his work there have provided valuable insights for students of organizational behavior. Twenty years later, Michael Buroway returned to the same company to see if organizational behavior, as described by Roy, had changed much over the years.[16] While the manufacturing technology used in the Geer Company had changed dramatically (and the Geer Company had changed its name!), Roy's most important insights about worker behavior remained true.

Both Roy and Buroway found that while the pace of work for the typical rank-and-file laborer was fast, psychologically the work was not involving. The highly repetitive, routinized, and specialized jobs characteristic of high-efficiency manufacturing companies apparently are *not* difficult enough to challenge the intellectual capabilities of many manufacturing laborers. Absenteeism, turnover, and a general sense of alienation result. As one well-known job design expert has noted in

[15]D. Roy, "Banana Time: Job Satisfaction and Informal Interaction," *Human Organization* 18 (1958): 1960.

[16]M. Buroway, *Manufacturing Consent* (Chicago: University of Chicago Press, 1979).

describing this situation, most American workers are "underutilized and underchallenged at work."[17]

Both Roy and Buroway found that because work on the shop floor did not sufficiently tax the intellectual capacities of the workers, the workers would devise games and rituals or ceremonies to pass the time and make the draining repetitiveness of their jobs more bearable. Roy and Buroway agreed that these games and rituals generally were counterproductive from the viewpoint of the organization's effectiveness and efficiency goals. They concluded that there exists in every worker an untapped reservoir of intellectual energy. If the manager cannot usefully harness this energy, it will be turned to counterproductive purposes.

It is interesting to note that neither Roy nor Buroway concluded that American factory workers are lazy. On the contrary, they both believed that the reservoir of intellectual energy in the American worker is a potential source of heightened productivity just waiting to be tapped. This conclusion is consistent with the results of surveys of American workers. Surveys have shown both that American workers report not working as hard as they might, and that they would be willing to work harder if their jobs were more interesting and involving.[18]

THEORY Y

Maslow's need hierarchy and Walker and Guest's research represent only a sampling of work at the time of the human relations movement. Together these developments represented a fundamental shift in the focus of managing organizational behavior. This shift found its strongest voice in the writings of two management theorists: Douglas McGregor and Rensis Likert.

Douglas McGregor was the executive director of industrial relations at the Massachusetts Institute of Technology during the 1940s and later became the president of Antioch College. McGregor was a big fan of Maslow's views of worker motivation and felt that productivity problems in American manufacturing were largely due to management not providing workers the opportunity to fulfill any but their economic needs. He believed that managers did not provide opportunities to fulfill these other needs because they operated on the wrong *assumptions* about human nature. In the preface to *The Human Side of Enterprise*, McGregor noted that successful management of behavior in organizations is to a very large degree:

> . . . the result of management's conception of the nature of its task and all the policies and practices which are constructed to implement this conception. The way a business is managed determines to a very large extent what people are perceived to have "potential" and how they

---

[17]R. J. Hackman, "The Design of Work in the 1980s," *Organizational Dynamics* (Summer 1978): 2–17.

[18]"Most Workers Really Want to Work Harder," *Nation's Business* (June 1980): 18.

**FIGURE 2–4**                    Assumptions of Theory X and Theory Y

McGregor offered Theory X and Theory Y as two different approaches to the business of management. McGregor felt that a flexible but not permissive style like that represented by Theory Y was necessary to fully develop employees as organizational resources.

**Theory X:**

1.  Management is responsible for organizing the elements of productive enterprise—money, materials, equipment, people—in the interest of economic ends.

2.  With respect to people, management must direct their efforts, motivate them, control their actions, and modify their behavior to fit the needs of the organization.

3.  Without this active intervention by management, people would be indifferent—even resistant—to organizational needs. They must therefore be persuaded, rewarded, punished, and controlled.

4.  The average worker is by nature indolent—he works as little as possible. He lacks ambition, dislikes responsibility, prefers to be led. He is inherently self-centered, indifferent to organizational needs. He is by nature resistant to change. He is gullible, not very bright, the ready dupe of the charlatan and the demagogue.

**Theory Y:**

1.  The expenditure of physical and mental effort in work is as natural as play or rest.

2.  External control and the threat of punishment are not the only means for bringing about effort toward organizational objectives. Man will exercise self-direction and self-control in the service of objectives to which he or she is committed.

3.  Commitment to objectives is a function of rewards associated with their achievement. The most significant of such rewards . . . can be the direct products of effort directed toward organizational objectives.

4.  The average human being learns under proper conditions not only to accept but to seek responsibility.

5.  The capacity to exercise a relatively high degree of imagination, ingenuity, and creativity in the solution of organizational problems is widely, not narrowly, distributed in the population.

6.  Under the conditions of modern industrial life, the intellectual potential of the average human being is only partially utilized.

Source: D. McGregor, "The Human Side of Enterprise," *Management Review* 46 (1957):22–28, 88–92.

develop. . . . The blunt fact is that we are a long way from realizing the potential represented by the human resources we now recruit into industry.[19]

McGregor called management's traditional view of the worker Theory X. As shown in Figure 2–4, **Theory X** consists of a set of assumptions about what drives the behavior of the rank-and-file worker, such as his

[19]D. McGregor, *The Human Side of Enterprise* (New York: McGraw-Hill, 1960), p. iv.

motive to avoid hard work. McGregor believed that these assumptions were not only incorrect but "unnecessarily limiting." He felt that by accepting such a limited view of workers' human potential, management constructed systems to control organizational behavior that made the realization of human potential impossible. A worker believed by management to be inherently lazy and averse to taking responsibility never will be given it and never will flourish as an employee.

McGregor also believed that by accepting Theory X assumptions about the worker, management defined its role in the organization as the director and controller of labor through the exercise of authority. Having authority in an organization simply means having a position that confers the right to give orders to other workers and to punish workers who don't obey. The use of authority as a way of getting things done will be discussed in detail in Chapter 8.

As noted in the "Focus on: Theory Y," McGregor felt that getting work done through authority was exceptionally short-sighted. After all, authority will force action only when (1) workers have no choice but to go along, and (2) failure to obey can be detected and punished effectively (for instance, through dismissal). On the question of workers having no choice but to go along with orders (or get punished or fired), McGregor felt that perhaps Theory X assumptions simply were out of date. By 1940, legislation had begun to protect worker rights and the union movement in America was growing in strength. As a result, management was just beginning to realize that it depended on workers for productivity just as much as workers depended on management for jobs.

## FOCUS ON:
## Theory Y

**Interdependence**   In *The Human Side of Enterprise,* Douglas McGregor provides anecdotal evidence of the importance of interdependence in management-labor relations:

An agent of the Textile Workers Union of America likes to tell the story of the occasion when a new manager appeared in the mill where he was working. The manager came into the weave room the day he arrived. He walked directly over to the agent and said, "Are you Belloc?" The agent acknowledged that he was. The manager said, "I am the new manager here. When I manage a mill, I run it. Do you understand?" The agent nodded, and then waved his hand. The workers, intently watching this encounter, shut down every loom in the room immediately. The agent turned to the manager and said, "All right, go ahead and run it."

For McGregor this was dramatic proof of the limits of authority, and consequently the limits of Theory X. Theory X is destined to fail if it relies on threats and punishment because interdependence (management and labor's mutual dependence on each other) ultimately renders them ineffective.

On the enforcement side, McGregor noted that continual observation of an organization's entire work force is out of the question. Compliance in the open might be followed by foot-dragging or even sabotage when the supervisor is out of sight. Further, it is possible for workers to go along with the *letter* of an order without fulfilling the *spirit* of what was intended. Worker compliance with orders is not really what management wants; management wants productivity. Cracking the whip is likely just to bring out the worst in the work force instead.

McGregor felt that this vicious cycle could be broken only with a more flexible management philosophy. To get the most out of workers, McGregor believed it was necessary for managers to assume that there was a lot there to get out. McGregor provided an example of a more flexible set of assumptions in his Theory Y. As shown in Figure 2–4, **Theory Y** differed from Theory X primarily in being much more *optimistic* about human nature. A manager with a Theory Y view of his work force would be likely to give his workers opportunities to succeed and flourish, and thereby discover untapped potential. In contrast, a manager with a Theory X view of his workers never would trust his workers enough to give them a chance.

Under the Theory Y view of the worker, McGregor saw the role of management as integration. **Integration** means "the creation of conditions such that members of the organization can achieve their own goals *best* by directing their efforts toward the success of the enterprise."[20] Integration removes the necessity for punishment by management when workers ignore management's orders. If work is arranged so that the worker's goals are achieved when the organization's goals are achieved, failure to achieve the organization's goals will mean failure to achieve the worker's goals, which already should be punishment enough for the worker.

McGregor went to great lengths to point out that the distinction between Theory X and Theory Y was not like that between "hard" and "soft" approaches to administration. For McGregor, "hard" approaches to management were those in which managers maintained *control* over agendas and decision making; "soft" approaches to management were those in which control was delegated or even abdicated. McGregor was openly critical of "soft" management styles such as "industrial democracy" that turned decision making over to the workers. McGregor placed the blame for the 1957–1958 recession squarely on the shoulders of such *permissive* approaches to management. Theory Y represents an abdication of neither the right nor the obligation to manage. McGregor felt that management needed to retain control, but not through authority, threats, and punishment, as suggested by Theory X. Rather, Theory Y suggested that control was a matter of aligning manager and

[20]Ibid., p. 49.

worker goals. If workers could get what they wanted by accomplishing what the organization needed, they would work hard and everyone would prosper.

Douglas McGregor intended his Theory Y to be speculative, and it was never scientifically tested or validated. Nevertheless, McGregor's work had a significant impact on management thinking in the United States, and several of his recommendations concerning job enlargement, delegation, the use of performance appraisal, and worker participation in organizational decision making today remain part of the fabric of American management theory.

## SYSTEM 4

While McGregor's Theory Y was mostly speculation, Rensis Likert's System 4 theory of management was instead heavily anchored in behavioral science research. Likert was a social psychologist and the director of the Institute for Social Research at the University of Michigan. Likert had uncovered important differences between the behaviors of superior and mediocre or inferior managers. He characterized the work units managed by superior managers as coordinated, motivated, and cooperative social systems with the following features:

1. a favorable climate, with lots of mutual confidence and trust among workers and supervisors
2. management attention to multiple motivations of workers
3. highly cohesive and participative work groups
4. the availability of performance feedback for worker self-guidance.[21]

Likert proposed that the two common threads linking all superior work units were an optimistic, supportive, and humanistic view of workers by management and the use of work groups. Likert thought it was particularly important for every worker to belong to a highly cohesive and participative work group with high performance goals and expectations. His System 4 ("group-participative") theory of management emphasized these characteristics. System 1 and System 2 referred to punitive and benevolent authoritarian management; System 3 was consultative management, in which management consulted with workers but retained its decision-making responsibility.

In a review of 20 years of research and several hundred studies concerning System 4 management, Likert found substantial support for his views, including higher productivity and production quality, higher levels of employee satisfaction and health, better labor relations, and lower absenteeism and turnover.[22] With Likert's System 4, management

---

[21]R. Likert, *New Patterns of Management* (New York: McGraw-Hill, 1961).

[22]R. Likert, "Retrospective Comment," in *The Great Writings in Management and Organizational Behavior*, eds. L. Boone and D. Bowen (Tulsa, Okla.: Penwell Books, 1980), p. 249.

theory had come full circle from the Hawthorne studies. ~~At Hawthorne, Elton Mayo had discovered that social relationships were an impediment to traditional management practice; in his System 4, Rensis Likert made those same social relationships the centerpiece of management theory~~.

**THE SATISFACTION-PERFORMANCE CONTROVERSY**

These four influential themes in management theory—Maslow's need hierarchy, Walker and Guest's *Man on the Assembly Line* study, McGregor's writing on Theory Y, and Likert's System 4—provided a glimpse of the new climate of human relations. Gone were mechanistic and purely economic visions of worker motivation. What remained in their place was somewhat unclear, however.

One by-product of the human relations movement that reflected current management beliefs about worker motivation was a confusion about the relationship between worker performance and satisfaction. Did satisfaction lead to superior work performance? Did superior work performance make workers satisfied? Or was there perhaps something else that made workers both satisfied and productive? ~~Human relations management practice seemed to be based on the idea that satisfied employees would be productive *because* they were satisfied~~. At issue, of course, was the task of the manager. ~~The "satisfaction-causes-performance" view maintained that the manager's role was to make organizational life satisfying for workers in the hopes of eliciting superior worker performance~~. The logic of this belief was compelling:

> . . . the degree of job satisfaction felt by an employee determines his performance, that is, satisfaction causes performance. This proposition has theoretical roots, but it also reflects the popular belief that "a happy worker is a productive worker" and the notion that "all good things go together." It is far more pleasant to increase an employee's happiness than to deal directly with his performance whenever a performance problem exists. Therefore, acceptance of the satisfaction-causes-performance proposition as a solution makes good sense, particularly for the manager because it represents the path of least resistance. Furthermore, high job satisfaction and high performance are both good, and, therefore, they ought to be related to one another.[23]

The findings of the Hawthorne studies did nothing to discourage this view. The female workers reported increased job satisfaction when moved into the test room for the "illumination" experiments. This is hardly surprising. After all, the test room was quieter, the participants in the study had a strong sense of being part of some grand, important research project, and they were flattered with the attention. They seemed very satisfied with their new employment situation, and their

[23]C. H. Greene, "The Satisfaction/Performance Controversy," *Business Horizons* 15 (1972): 31–41.

satisfaction was reflected in higher productivity regardless of illumination level. It also should not be surprising that some researchers have argued that the higher productivity of test group members in the initial Hawthorne study was a *direct consequence* of their satisfaction, almost as if the workers were repaying the compliment of being treated so well in the study.

One explanation for the belief that worker satisfaction *causes* superior performance is exchange theory.[24] According to exchange theory, life is a series of transactions. The values of the things being traded (for example, flattery for the favors of an attractive companion) may not be easily compared, but everyone tries to keep score. If someone gives you something of value, you are obligated by the unwritten rules of social interaction to give something of comparable value in return. If an organization treats a worker well and the worker is satisfied, the worker is likewise obligated to return comparable value in the form of hard work and productivity.

The Hawthorne studies and exchange theory were not alone in suggesting a link between worker satisfaction and performance. An early review of 23 studies of the relationship between worker satisfaction and performance revealed *only one study* in which satisfaction and performance were not positively related to each other.[25] On the other hand, the relationships found between satisfaction and performance, while consistently positive, rarely have been strong. This, too, is not surprising. There are *lots* of unproductive or even *counterproductive* ways for workers to find satisfaction in work. Donald Roy and Michael Buroway detailed the unproductive games that workers play on the assembly line. These games are a way of making uninteresting work interesting—a way of gaining satisfaction *on* the job when satisfaction *with* the job is not available. This sentiment is echoed in one writer's comments concerning his own experiences in the blue-collar labor force:

> At first I was surprised at how skillful people were in using up the time of day and yet producing so little. I have now become intrigued with the notion that most of us want a job with security, as in the military; we want good pay and maximum benefits, tenure and seniority, but there seems to be a powerful inclination to do as little work as possible. If we have job security and basic needs are being met, do we lose our motivation to work? My experience has given rise to serious doubts regarding humans' intrinsic desire to work at all.[26]

Research does support the importance of job satisfaction to the management of organizations. Job satisfaction has been shown to be

[24]A. W. Gouldner, "A Norm of Reciprocity: A Preliminary Statement," *American Sociological Review* 25 (1960): 161–178.

[25]V. H. Vroom, Work and Motivation (New York: Wiley and Sons, 1964).

[26]R. Schrank, *Ten Thousand Working Days* (Cambridge, Mass: MIT Press, 1978).

strongly related to worker turnover and absenteeism. Both of these are critical considerations for managers because of the costs they entail. An absent worker cannot be a productive one, and a worker who leaves the organization—whether voluntarily or not—must be replaced, resulting in lost productivity and selection and training costs for the replacement. Thus, even though greater job satisfaction may not *cause* better performance, job satisfaction certainly has an *indirect* effect on organizational performance.

One current view of the relationship between job satisfaction and performance is that when superior performance leads to desired rewards, the receipt of those rewards results in worker satisfaction.[27] This view of the relationship between satisfaction and performance means that the task of the manager is to encourage superior worker performance and reward it when it occurs. Superior worker performance then leads to rewards and thereby to job satisfaction, low turnover, and low absenteeism—not to mention organizational efficiency and effectiveness. This view suggests an important alteration of McGregor's Theory Y. It is not hard work that is natural to workers. What is natural to workers is the dogged pursuit of satisfaction. In that dogged pursuit the worker may become all the things that McGregor hoped for—creative, industrious, and accepting if not desirous of responsibility. It is the task of the manager to arrange work so that the surest path to a worker's satisfaction runs through actions that are productive for the organization.

## BEYOND HUMAN RELATIONS

While the human relations movement treated participation primarily as a way to satisfy workers, that view was soon to change. As noted by Reinhard Bendix in *Work and Authority in Industry,* the rallying cry of human relations was that "failure to treat workers as human beings [was] the cause of low morale, poor craftsmanship, unresponsiveness, and confusion."[28] Workers had become something more than mere bundles of skills and strength. Workers needed to be respected and to feel useful to the organization. By consulting with workers on decisions such as the distribution of tasks within work groups, work group leadership, and even production method design and scheduling, managers believed they were providing their workers a sense of being useful and important.

In its early stages, worker participation was meant only to advise and not replace management's decisions. In its most cynical form, human relations cast worker participation as the "lubricant which oils away resistance to formal authority."[29] This comment implies that managers

---

[27]E. E. Lawler and L. W. Porter, "The Effect of Performance on Job Satisfaction," *Industrial Relations* 7 (1967): 20–28.

[28]R. Bendix, *Work and Authority in Industry* (New York: Wiley and Sons, 1956), p. 294.

[29]R. E. Miles, "Human Relations or Human Resources?" *Harvard Business Review* (July/August 1965): 148–163.

may have believed it to be easier and better to make decisions *without* worker input. Nevertheless, workers were involved to boost morale and ensure their later cooperation. As noted by one management theorist, this is not a complimentary view of the workers' capacity to contribute something useful through participation:

> The manager "buys" worker cooperation by letting his subordinates in on departmental information and allowing them to discuss and state their opinions on various departmental problems. He "pays a price" for allowing his subordinates the privilege of participation in certain decisions and exercising some self-direction. In return, he hopes to obtain their cooperation in carrying out these and other decisions for the accomplishment of departmental objectives.[30]

From the human relations perspective, then, worker participation had become a way to satisfy workers and thereby secure their cooperation and compliance. Outside the United States, however, worker participation in organizational decision making was taking on a different flavor altogether.

## WORKER PARTICIPATION IN EUROPE

In European management circles, worker participation in organizational decision making became the centerpiece of the policy of codetermination. **Codetermination** refers to allowing workers a say in major organization policy decisions—not just minor or trivial operational decisions. It gives workers the chance to codetermine with management the direction taken by a company.

Perhaps owing to the strength of the socialist labor movement in Europe (which campaigns for power for the rank-and-file worker), worker participation in European industry has for some time been considered a *right* of workers rather than a bone that management might throw them. In Germany, worker participation in policy decisions even was institutionalized and *legally guaranteed* through the Codetermination Law of 1951. According to this law (designed only for organizations of more than 2,000 employees), corporate employees and shareholders have an indirect influence over corporate governance. As shown in Figure 2–5, shareholder and employee groups each separately elect representatives to a board of supervisors. The board of supervisors in turn elects a board of management. The board of management assumes responsibility for day-to-day operations of the corporation, subject to review by the board of supervisors. The board of supervisors also must be kept continually informed of the current and projected state of the corporation. Thus, the employees indirectly maintain a voice in corporate governance through their elected representation on the board of

[30]Ibid.

Industrial democracy in Europe has taken the human resources philosophy far beyond participative management practices in the United States. In Europe, laws often require management to give employees a say in organizational decision making.

supervisors.[31] As noted in the "INTERNATIONAL FOCUS ON: Worker Participation in Europe," other countries have experimented with even more direct forms of corporate management by employees.

The European experience suggests that as a need satisfier, worker participation may not always live up to its billing. In keeping with the intent of codetermination policies in countries such as Norway, rank-and-file workers (or their union representatives) have been given seats on boards of directors. Where rank-and-file workers have so served, work force productivity has not increased and work force alienation has not decreased.[32]

## THE JAPANESE EXPERIENCE

If worker need satisfaction had been the only impetus for management's turning to worker participation, participation's role in the history of organizational behavior might have been minor and short-lived. However, worker need satisfaction gave way to *organization* need satisfaction as the justification for allowing worker participation when organizations began to realize the instrumental value of worker participation. Worker participation could be more than a way for managers to keep workers satisfied and therefore productive. Worker participation could be a tool used by management to *improve* the organization's decisions and plans. With this insight, human relations management gave way to a new view of managing organizational behavior—the human resources view.

[31]K. E. Agathe, "Mitbestimmung: Report on a Social Experiment," *Business Horizons* 20 (1977): 5–14.

[32]"Work in America: Report of a Special Task Force to the Secretary of Health, Education, and Welfare" (Cambridge, Mass.: MIT Press, 1973).

**FIGURE 2–5**     A Model for Industrial Democracy in Germany

Worker participation in organizational decision making has been taken much further in European management circles than in the United States. In the model for industrial democracy in Germany, workers have a say in electing the board of supervisors, which in turn elects a board of management to manage the company.

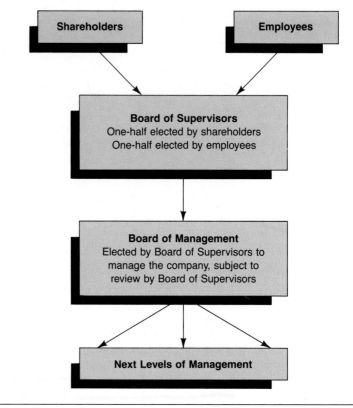

Source: K. E. Agathe, "Mitbestimmung: Report on a Social Experiment," *Business Horizons* 20 (1977): 5–14.

**Human resources** differs from human relations management in its emphasis on participation as a means to productivity improvement through better, more informed organizational planning and decision making. Human resources sees the workers' mental capabilities as *key resources* in the constant battle to improve organizational efficiency and effectiveness. Rank-and-file workers are closest to the work and possess much useful information—useful, that is, if only they are given a chance to share it. A summary of the differences between the human relations and human resources viewpoints is provided in Figure 2–6 on page 66.

The human resources orientation found strong support in the experiences of Japan. In 1950, Edward Deming and a delegation of industrial engineers were sent to Japan to teach statistical quality control to the Japanese. Statistical quality control is a method for assessing whether a production system is performing correctly or needs to be adjusted. The delegation was charged with helping to modernize and

INTERNATIONAL
FOCUS ON:

Worker
Participation
in Europe

**Yugoslavian Workers in Control**

Hastily launched in 1950 as Marshal Tito's alternative to the sternly centralized communism of the Stalinist era, Yugoslavia's "self-management" has evolved into a pervasive way of life. The ramifications go far beyond this independent Communist country, because Yugoslavia provides an extreme example of just how far the idea of "worker control" being broached today in the West can go—for better or for worse.

In theory, the system couldn't be simpler: The people who know the most about any business are its workers, so they ought to be in charge. Thus, legal control rests with the employees of each economic unit, known under the 1974 constitution as a "basic organization of associated labor," or BOAL.

The sizes vary widely, but the BOAL structure is standard. Each "complete" economic function forms its own BOAL. So a single factory would have separate BOALs for various types of production workers, its marketing staff, and its administrative staff. One BOAL, say of 600 people, has a 21-member workers' council. Council members are elected by secret ballot for a maximum of two consecutive two-year terms, staggered so that about half are elected each year. The council hires the top executives, whose major proposals can't take effect unless the council and the total membership agree.

Western diplomats here strongly reject any notion that the system may be only an elaborate facade. "This is not a shell game, this is an extremely decentralized economic and political system," one embassy man says.

"There's a degree of laissez-faire here that hasn't applied in England since the beginning of this century," another diplomat adds.

As far as outsiders can tell, many Yugoslavs are content with their system. "I participate directly in all decision making in my organization," happily declares Mrs. Dusanka Pjevac, a Belgrade seamstress. Hoopla aside, however, the system does have its problems. Among these is managing the flow of paper when *everyone* has a hand in organizational decision making. One Belgrade metalworking firm produced over 800,000 pages of reports in 1987—about 1.5 kilograms of paper for each of its 2,900 employees. Enterprise leaders find that the time demands of truly democratic decision making can be enormous, to the point of seriously undermining efficiency. Further, laws constrain enterprises from absolute "self-management" when it comes to disposal of enterprise income. While this was meant to ensure that enterprises acted in the public interest, the lack of freedom has encouraged enterprise leaders to rely on political favors to work the system. In some circles, the critics have dubbed this "feudal socialism."

A new generation of reforms of the unwieldy aspects of self-management already is under way. Some feel that a high degree of democracy may be appropriate in an enterprise's initial stages of planning and strategizing, but that more streamlined execution should occur in day-to-day operations. Whether the right balance between participation and efficiency can be achieved in Yugoslavia's industrial democracy remains to be seen.

Sources: R. F. Janssen, "Yugoslavia's System of Letting Employees Manage Business Works Surprisingly Well," *The Wall Street Journal,* October 8, 1975, p. 38; N. Stanic, "Yugoslavia's Self-Managed Crisis," *International Management,* January 1988, pp. 65–67.

**FIGURE 2–6**     ## Human Relations versus Human Resources

The human resources approach to managing organizational behavior represents a revision of the human relations approach. Both affirm the ability and desire of workers to contribute more on the job. Human resources casts worker satisfaction more as a consequence of increased worker productivity than as a means to achieve it.

| **Human Relations** | **Human Resources** |
|---|---|
| **Attitudes toward People** | |
| 1. People in our culture share a common set of needs—to belong, to be liked, to be respected. | 1. In addition to sharing common needs for belonging and respect, most people in our culture desire to contribute effectively and creatively to the accomplishment of worthwhile objectives. |
| 2. They desire individual recognition but, more than this, they want to feel a useful part of the company and their own work group or department. | 2. The majority of our work force is capable of exercising far more initiative, responsibility, and creativity than their present jobs require or allow. |
| 3. They will tend to cooperate willingly and comply with organizational goals if these important needs are fulfilled. | 3. These capabilities represent untapped resources which are presently being wasted. |
| **Kind and Amount of Participation** | |
| 1. The manager's basic task is to make each worker believe that he or she is a useful and important part of the department "team." | 1. The manager's basic task is to create an environment in which subordinates can contribute their full range of talents to the accomplishment of organizational goals. He or she must attempt to uncover and tap subordinates' creative resources. |
| 2. The manager should be willing to explain decisions and to discuss subordinates' objections to plans. On routine matters, he or she should encourage subordinates to participate in planning and choosing among alternative solutions to problems. | 2. The manager should allow and encourage subordinates to participate not only in routine decisions but in important matters as well. In fact, the more important a decision is to the manager's department, the greater should be the effort to tap the department's resources. |
| 3. Within narrow limits, the work group or individual subordinates should be allowed to exercise self-direction and self-control in carrying out plans. | 3. The manager should attempt to continually expand the areas over which subordinates exercise self-direction and self-control as they develop and demonstrate greater insight and ability. |

**FIGURE 2—6** (*Continued*)

### Expectations

1. Sharing information with subordinates and involving them in departmental decision making will help satisfy their basic needs for belonging and for individual recognition.

2. Satisfying these needs will improve subordinate morale and reduce resistance to formal authority.

3. High employee morale and reduced resistance to formal authority may lead to improved departmental performance. They should at least reduce intradepartment friction and thus make the manager's job easier.

1. The overall quality of decision making and performance will improve as the manager makes use of the full range of experience, insight, and creative ability in the department.

2. Subordinates will exercise responsible self-direction and self-control in the accomplishment of worthwhile objectives that they understand and have helped establish.

3. Subordinate satisfaction will increase as a by-product of improved performance and the opportunity to contribute creatively to this improvement.

Source: R. E. Miles, "Human Relations or Human Resources?" *Harvard Business Review* (July/August 1965): 148–163.

westernize Japan's industrial base, which had been largely destroyed at the conclusion of World War II. Deming's lessons on statistical quality control were eagerly absorbed by the Japanese, no doubt because America in the 1950s was without question the most industrially advanced nation in the world. If statistical quality control was part of the American success story, they reasoned, it should become the foundation for similar successes by Japanese industry.[33]

The Japanese took statistical quality control ideas further, however, than even Deming might have imagined. Statistical quality control, as practiced in America at the time, was a procedure performed by specialists for the exclusive consumption of managerial personnel. The Japanese reasoned that if it was useful for managers to have statistical quality control information, it made sense for *everyone* to be collecting, interpreting, and applying it. Soon worker groups, called "quality circles," began appearing in a few of Japan's industrial enterprises. In a quality circle, rank-and-file workers would get together to discuss their collected quality control statistics and their implications for manufacturing practice. Worker participation had come to Japan.

[33]A. Gabor, "The Man Who Changed the World of Quality," *International Management* (March 1988): 42–46.

**FIGURE 2–7**            Theory J: Japanese Labor Practices

The human resources approach to managing organizational behavior has found strong support in the management practices of major Japanese corporations. Worker involvement in Japan, however, is just one aspect of the well-publicized Japanese management package, and this approach is used by only about 1 percent of Japanese corporations.

- Lifetime employment
- Consensual decision making
- Collective responsibility
- Slow evaluation and promotion
- Implicit and informal means of control
- Nonspecialized career paths
- Wholistic concern for the employee's welfare

Source: W. G. Ouchi and A. M. Jaeger, "Type Z Organization: A Corporate Alternative to Village Life," *Stanford Alumni Bulletin* (1977): 13–32.

It should be emphasized that training rank-and-file workers in statistical quality control techniques and providing them an arena for using the information was but one feature of the new Japanese orientation toward workers. A summary of the Japanese management package is provided in Figure 2–7. In reality, these practices are used by only 1 percent of Japanese companies, so it would be misleading to attribute Japan's recent enormous industrial success to them alone.[34] Nevertheless, the advent of these labor practices in Japan coincided with substantial gains in Japanese industrial productivity. By some estimates, productivity gains in Japan have been more than twice those in the United States in the past two decades.[35]

As Japan has gained strength as an industrial power, it has threatened U.S. dominance of international and even domestic markets. Not surprisingly, the Japanese threat has focused the attention of U.S. companies on the management practices that helped Japan gain its position, and has encouraged many U.S. manufacturers to look for better ways to exploit the enthusiasm and expertise hidden in the lower levels of the work force. Some U.S. companies even have successfully imported Japanese techniques to manage their own companies. Lockheed, for instance, tried quality circles. With only 30 circles in place, estimated savings exceeded $3 million and defects were down by two-

[34]T. K. Oh, "Japanese Management: A Critical Review," *Academy of Management Review* 1 (1976): 14–25.

[35]E. E. Lawler III, *High-Involvement Management* (San Francisco: Jossey-Bass, 1986), p. 33.

**FIGURE 2–8**          Review of Studies Using Participative Management

Studies of participative management suggest that it is no panacea. The literature review summarized here found that worker productivity was just as likely to fall as rise when a participative management program was implemented. Worker satisfaction increases more reliably.

|  | **Positive Effects** | **No Effects** | **Negative Effects** |
|---|---|---|---|
| Laboratory studies |  |  |  |
| Productivity | 4 | 6 | 4 |
| Satisfaction | 5 | 0 | 2 |
| Field studies |  |  |  |
| Productivity | 6 | 20 | 6 |
| Satisfaction | 21 | 13 | 2 |
| Combined Findings |  |  |  |
| Productivity | 22% | 56% | 22% |
| Satisfaction | 60% | 30% | 9% |

Source: E. A. Locke and D. M. Schweiger, "Participation in Decision Making: One More Look," in *Research in Organizational Behavior*, vol. 1, ed. B. Staw (Greenwich, Conn.: JAI Press, 1979).

thirds.[36] Others have attempted to mold the Japanese human resources philosophy to fit the needs and character of U.S. workers.[37]

**IN SEARCH OF SOLUTIONS**

The themes of this latest wave of management theory—the human resources wave—have found highly vocal support in the writings of management evangelists Tom Peters and Bob Waterman.[38] Their 1982 best-seller, *In Search of Excellence,* sold over five million copies and was arguably the most-quoted management book of the 1980s. The book details a survey of 43 of the "best" U.S. companies and concludes that employee involvement and participation programs are a prominent feature in the best of the best. The proof that Peters and Waterman offer for their views is largely anecdotal, however, and their findings have been questioned because of their survey's lack of systematic observation and analysis.[39]

Scientific attempts to ascertain the value of worker participation programs have proven less supportive. The results of one comprehensive analysis of 89 studies examining the value of participative management techniques are shown in Figure 2–8. Fully 80 percent of the

[36]R. E. Cole, "Made in Japan—Quality Control Circles," *Across the Board* 16 (1979): 72–78.
[37]W. G. Ouchi and A. M. Jaeger, "Type Z Organization: A Corporate Alternative to Village Life," *Stanford Alumni Bulletin* (1977): 13–32.
[38]T. J. Peters and R. H. Waterman, *In Search of Excellence* (New York: Harper and Row, 1982).
[39]M. A. Hitt and R. D. Ireland, "Peters and Waterman Revisited: The Unended Quest for Excellence," *Academy of Management Executive* 1 (1987): 91–98.

studies included in this analysis found no effects or negative effects of participation programs on productivity. Over 60 percent of the studies did report positive effects on worker satisfaction, however.

What conclusions should be drawn from these findings? Perhaps the safest summary comment on the human resources approach to management would be the same as appropriate summary comments about human relations and scientific management: It provides no final solution but sometimes it works very well. The uncertainty about the value of any of these approaches has led to yet another approach to management—contingency theory. According to **contingency theory,** which management technique is appropriate depends on the particular situation. Each of the approaches we have reviewed—scientific management, human relations, and human resources—can be quite valuable, but under different circumstances. A contingency framework for understanding when participative management techniques would be appropriate will be presented in Chapter 9.

## OPEN SYSTEMS THEORY

More than just management's image of the rank-and-file worker has evolved during the twentieth century. Also changing has been management's image of the organization in which these rank-and-file workers do their labors. For much of the twentieth century, theories about organizational behavior have focused on the challenge of managing worker behavior *within* organizations to achieve efficiency and effectiveness. It has become apparent, however, that the enormity and complexity of changes in the environment in which organizations function have a direct impact on behavior *within* organizations. This insight has sensitized organizational theorists to the importance of understanding the relationship between organizations and their environments. Our current understanding of this relationship is encompassed in open systems theory.

**Open systems theory,** as described by Katz and Kahn in *The Social Psychology of Organizations,*[40] is focused on two assumptions. First, organizations are social systems, meaning that changes in one part of the organization necessarily are reflected in changes in other parts. The system perspective differs from a traditional *mechanistic* view of organizations, which likens organizations to machines. In a machine, failure by one part *stops* the machine. Thus, all parts of the machine are equally essential to the machine's functioning. In a system, failure in any part (or subsystem) of the system *perturbs* the system, forcing a reaction. However, only rarely does subsystem failure stop a system. Instead, the system adjusts to accommodate the failure and continues to function, though it probably will never be the same again.

[40]D. Katz and R. L. Kahn, *The Social Psychology of Organizations* (New York: Wiley and Sons, 1966).

Imagine, for instance, that a firm's marketing director suddenly resigns to start a new company. Business at the firm does not grind to a halt. The firm adjusts to the loss and continues on. An acting director is appointed to keep things going, a search is initiated to find a permanent replacement, and precautions are taken to decrease the impact of such a loss should it recur. The loss perturbs the system; the system adjusts and continues functioning.

The system notion also implies a hierarchy of importance to an organization's levels of subsystems. Not all of a system's parts are equally essential, hence changes or failures at higher levels of the organization's subsystem hierarchy will have a greater impact on the system and will necessitate greater adjustments. For instance, the resignation of a janitor or student intern is unlikely to have the same impact as the marketing director's departure.

Second, organizations are systems open to influence from the environment. An organization's reason for being comes from the needs of the environment, and its ability to meet those needs derives from the environment's supply of resources. McDonald's Hamburgers would be nowhere if Americans didn't want hamburgers, or if McDonald's couldn't find the beef, the buns, or the brawn to make them.

The open systems perspective is important to the understanding and management of organizational behavior because of the contingent character of social systems. The environment cannot be assumed to be a constant or dependable source of inputs. Thus, the turbulence of the environment, and the effects of this turbulence on organizational behavior, are critical areas of study.[41] The implications of open systems theory for organizational behavior and the contingent character of organizations it implies provide the focus for Part 4 of this book.

## SUMMARY

Most written histories share several important characteristics. First, they are incomplete. They contain only a *selection* of the facts about only *some* of the events and people of the past. This chapter's history of management thought and theory is no exception. It has presented only the most striking attempts to face the management challenge of organizational behavior up to and into the twentieth century. The remainder of this book will elaborate on these major themes, and in doing so will fill in the important gaps in the story.

Second, written histories make events appear in retrospect to have been much more of a *sensible and orderly progression* than they ever were in fact. As with music and clothing, fads and fashions come and go in the field of organizational behavior. Ideas explode into prominence and then disappear just as quickly. Some are rebirths and rediscoveries of old themes; some are too new and revolution-

[41]Ibid., p. 3.

ary for the field to accept. Most never command the field's attention, but many nevertheless have an influence. Histories are an attempt to make sense of these many ebbs and flows of people and events. In retrospect, it is the overall directions that are remembered. So it has been with management thought and theory.

Finally, the selective recall of written histories is generally committed in the service of a message. In the case of management thought and theory, the message concerns two major changes in the twentieth century. The first change has occurred in management's image of the rank-and-file worker. Gone is the one-dimensional, economic view of worker motivation. In its place are human relations and human resources—two philosophies about

human nature that are optimistic about workers' capacity to contribute meaningfully to organizational efficiency and effectiveness. Moreover, the definition of management's task has taken a subtle but significant turn. Managers must now manage workers as a *mental* resource as well as a physical resource.

The second change has occurred in management's image of the organization itself. Bureaucratic views of the organization focused attention on internal aspects of the management challenge. Open systems theory casts the organization as a ship adrift in a sea of external influence. Keeping it afloat means extending the management challenge—and our knowledge of organizational behavior—beyond the boundaries of the organization itself.

KEY TERMS

**Bureaucracy**   Form of organization in which there are clearly defined lines of authority and responsibility for members, and behavior is tightly controlled by rules, policies, and job assignments.

**Codetermination**   Policy of allowing workers a say in major organizational decisions, not just minor operational decisions.

**Contingency theory**   Approach to organizational behavior stating that choice of appropriate management technique is dependent on the particular situation.

**Hierarchy of human needs**
Abraham Maslow's theory of five

distinct classes of human needs—physiological, safety, social, esteem, and self-actualization—some of which ("higher" needs) become important to a worker only after "lower" needs have been fulfilled.

**Human resources**   View of workers' mental capabilities as key resources in organizational efficiency and effectiveness; emphasizes worker participation for more informed organizational planning and decision making.

**Integration**   Role of management defined by D. McGregor as the creation of conditions such that members of the organization can best achieve their own goals by directing their efforts toward the success of the enterprise.

**Open systems theory**   Management theory proposed by D. Katz and R. Kahn, which focuses on the assumptions that organizations are (1) social systems in which changes in one part are reflected by changes in other parts, and (2) open to influence from the environment.

**Scientific management**   Frederick Taylor's theory of careful and systematic observations and prescriptive techniques for designing jobs and incentive pay schemes for rank-and-file factory workers.

**System 4**   Management theory of Rensis Likert proposing that in superior work units management has an optimistic, supportive, and humanistic view of workers, and every worker belongs to a highly cohesive and participative work group with high performance goals and expectations.

**Theory X**   Management's traditional view of workers, including the assumptions that workers are naturally lazy, self-centered, and resistant to change and will avoid

responsibility, and management must direct, motivate, and control them.

**Theory Y**   View of workers as naturally motivated to work as much as to rest or play; workers will exercise self-direction and self-control in the service of objectives to which they are committed.

**Time-and-motion studies**   Scientific management technique of timed observations and experiments to identify the most efficient means for accomplishing a task.

**Total job situation**   Seven characteristics of a job derived by C. R. Walker and R. H. Guest, including the worker's immediate job, relation to fellow workers, relation to supervisors, relation to the union, pay and job security, promotion and transfer prospects, and working conditions in the plant.

**Work standards**   Scientific management technique of providing specific instructions to workers for doing a task, including expected time for completion and expected volume of output.

DISCUSSION QUESTIONS

1.  What is a bureaucracy? Why did Max Weber believe that bureaucracies were the ideal organizational form?

2.  What is scientific about "scientific management"? What assumptions does scientific management make about rank-and-file workers and how to manage them?

3.  What were the contributions of the Hawthorne studies? In what ways did they alter current thinking about managing organizational behavior?

4.  What did studies of rank-and-file workers in the 1950s reveal about worker motivation?

5. Distinguish between the human relations and human resources approaches to managing organizational behavior. What differing assumptions does each approach make about the relationship between worker satisfaction and performance?

6. Describe McGregor's Theory Y and Likert's System 4 approaches to management. What assumptions do their views make about worker motivation?

7. In what ways are the worker democracy movement in Europe and Japanese management examples of human resources approaches to management?

8. Describe the fundamental assumptions underlying open systems theory. How does the open systems theory approach to understanding organizations differ from Weber's notion of the bureaucratic organization?

**IF YOU WANT TO KNOW MORE**

Excerpts from the writings of the traditional theorists including Taylor (on scientific management) and Weber (on bureaucracy) are contained in the volume, *The Great Writings in Management and Organizational Behavior* (Tulsa, Okla.: Penn Well Books, 1980). Each reading includes retrospective comments by contemporary researchers in organizational behavior. Wrege and Perroni provide a hard look at Taylor's pioneering efficiency studies in their article, "Taylor's Pig Tale: A Historical Analysis of Frederick W. Taylor's Pig-Iron Experiments" (*Academy of Management Journal* 17 (1974): 6–27).

An excellent review of the Hawthorne studies, the origins of the human relations movement, and the beginning of the field of organizational behavior are provided in Fritz Roethlisberger's autobiography, *The Elusive Phenomena* (Cambridge, Mass.: Harvard University Press, 1977), which reads much more like a novel than a textbook. A latter-day critique of the scientific value of the Hawthorne studies appears in the *Psychology Today* article, "The Hawthorne Defect: Persistence of a Flawed Theory," by B. Rice (February 1982).

A condensed version of McGregor's views on Theory X and Theory Y is provided in his article, "The Human Side of Enterprise," which appeared in *Management Review* (November 1957). An attempt to test the assumptions of Theory Y and its implications for management is described by Byron Fiman in his article, "An Investigation of the Relationships among Supervisory Attitudes, Behaviors, and Outputs: An Examination of McGregor's Theory Y," which appeared in *Personnel Psychology* (26, Spring 1973). A field test of Theory Y is detailed in Erwin Malone's article, "The Non-Linear Systems Experiment in Participative Management," which appeared in the *Journal of Business* (48, January 1975).

A review of evidence concerning the relationship between satisfaction and performance is detailed in Greene's article, "The Satisfaction-Performance Controversy," which appeared in *Business Horizons* (Vol. 15, 1972).

Ray Miles, in his July/August 1965 *Harvard Business Review* article, "Human Relations or Human Resources?," summarizes the features that distinguish between these two schools of management thought. A more contemporary look at the profusion of management techniques emanating from human relations and human resources is provided in John Byrne's *Business Week* cover story, "Business Fads: What's In and What's Out?" (January 20, 1986, pp. 52–61). This article also is a good source for additional readings about human resources approaches to managing organizational behavior.

An excellent review of open systems theory is provided in Chapter 6 of John Miner's volume, *Theories of Organizational Structure and Process* (Hinsdale, Ill.: Dryden Press, 1982). An application of this theory in an organizational setting is detailed in Ned Rosen's article, "Open Systems Theory in an Organizational Subsystem: A Field Experiment" (Organizational Behavior and Human Performance 5 (1970): 245–265).

ON YOUR OWN

**Management Practices Questionnaire**   Complete the following questionnaire. Indicate your agreement or disagreement with each of the eight statements by circling the number on the scale below each statement. Determine the appropriate score by noting the points for the response you made to each statement. For example, if your response to Question 1 was strongly agree, you would give yourself five points; disagree is worth two points; and so on. Add the eight scores together.

1. The average human being prefers to be directed, wishes to avoid responsibility, and has relatively little ambition.

| (5) | (4) | (3) | (2) | (1) |
|---|---|---|---|---|
| Strongly Agree | Agree | Undecided | Disagree | Strongly Disagree |

2. Most people can acquire leadership skills regardless of their particular inborn traits and abilities.

| (5) | (4) | (3) | (2) | (1) |
|---|---|---|---|---|
| Strongly Agree | Agree | Undecided | Disagree | Strongly Disagree |

3. The use of rewards (for example, pay and promotion) and punishment (for example, failure to promote) is the best way to get subordinates to do their work.

| (5) | (4) | (3) | (2) | (1) |
|---|---|---|---|---|
| Strongly Agree | Agree | Undecided | Disagree | Strongly Disagree |

4. In a work situation, if the subordinates can influence you, you lose some influence over them.

| (5) | (4) | (3) | (2) | (1) |
|---|---|---|---|---|
| Strongly Agree | Agree | Undecided | Disagree | Strongly Disagree |

Source: Adapted from M. Haire, E. Ghiselli, and L. Porter, *Managerial Thinking: An International Study*, Appendix A. Copyright © 1966 by John Wiley & Sons, Inc. Reprinted with permission of John Wiley & Sons, Inc.

5. A good leader gives detailed and complete instructions to subordinates rather than giving them merely general directions and depending on their initiative to work out the details.

| (5) | (4) | (3) | (2) | (1) |
|---|---|---|---|---|
| Strongly Agree | Agree | Undecided | Disagree | Strongly Disagree |

6. Individual goal setting offers advantages that cannot be obtained by group goal setting, because groups do not set high goals.

| (5) | (4) | (3) | (2) | (1) |
|---|---|---|---|---|
| Strongly Agree | Agree | Undecided | Disagree | Strongly Disagree |

7. A superior should give subordinates only the information necessary for them to do their immediate tasks.

| (5) | (4) | (3) | (2) | (1) |
|---|---|---|---|---|
| Strongly Agree | Agree | Undecided | Disagree | Strongly Disagree |

8. The superior's influence over subordinates in an organization is primarily economic.

| (5) | (4) | (3) | (2) | (1) |
|---|---|---|---|---|
| Strongly Agree | Agree | Undecided | Disagree | Strongly Disagree |

☐ Total Score

*Scoring Key:* A score of greater than 32 points indicates a tendency to manage others according to the principles in Theory X. A score of less than 16 points indicates a tendency to manage others according to the principles in Theory Y. A score somewhere between 16 and 32 indicates flexibility in the management of others.

CLOSING CASE
FOR CHAPTER 2

## THE MANAGER'S MEMO

FROM: R. Wolferman, Manager, Water Sports Department

TO:   F. Crane, Line Supervisor, Canoe Production

RE:   Worker Performance and Turnover

Congratulations! You have met this year's goal of a 15 percent increase in canoe production using the same number of worker-hours as you did last year. It appears that your ideas for production efficiency have paid off in a big way—specifically, a $780,000 increase in the value of goods produced for the year.

Nevertheless, a review of our financial performance for the past year does raise some concerns. I see that we spent $1.2 million for hiring and training last year, an $800,000 increase over the year before. According to the personnel department, this increase does not reflect a new training program, but rather the fact that turnover among canoe production workers tripled last year.

Could there be a link between the efficiency effort and the increased employee turnover? As I recall, your plans included making tasks more routine and specialized, as well as training workers to accomplish each task more quickly. While I know you put in many lonely hours developing these efficiencies, I wonder whether some workers have left as a result of them.

You have every right to be proud of the efforts that led to accomplishing the goal of higher output, and achievement of this goal will be reflected in your annual bonus. However, for next year, I would like to develop a goal of reducing the cost of employee turnover while attempting to maintain at least some of the gain in worker output. To that end, please recommend some ways in which we can reduce next year's hiring and training costs. We'll discuss those ideas at our next meeting.

CASE DISCUSSION
QUESTIONS

Assume you are the line supervisor, and write a response to the department manager's memo. Consider the management theories described in this chapter, and look for ways in which each can shed light on the circumstances of the memo. Can the supervisor maintain the increased efficiency while improving employee turnover? If so, how? If not, how can he or she strike a balance between these two concerns?

EXERCISE FOR
PART 1:
Bridge Building

For this exercise, your instructor will divide the class into groups of about 8 to 10 students. One group will act as observers; the remaining groups will be "bridge builders."

The task of the bridge-building groups will be to build a bridge spanning two desks in your classroom. Your instructor will give each bridge-building group a package of "construction materials." This package will contain:

- 5 straws
- 1 newspaper
- 2 pencils
- 1 blue felt-tip pen
- 5 rubber bands
- 1 box of paper clips
- 1 red felt-tip pen
- 1 pad of "Post-it" notes

Additionally, your instructor will have a pair of scissors, a roll of tape, and a stapler that the bridge-building groups will have to share.

The bridge-building groups will have about 15 minutes to construct their bridges. At the end of the allotted construction time, all bridge builders will leave the classroom so that the observer group can evaluate the constructed bridges. Using the scoring sheet on the following page, the observer group will evaluate the bridges on the basis of five criteria: length, width, height, strength, and beauty.

The observer group will also have responsibility for observing the **processes of group interaction** that occur as the bridge-building groups build their bridges. Your instructor will provide the observer group members with an "Observation Checklist" for that purpose.

## Evaluation Form: Bridge Building

Evaluate each bridge on the following criteria (circle a number):

**1. Length:**
(1)    (2)    (3)    (4)    (5)    (6)    (7)    (8)    (9)    (10)
Very Poor                                                    Outstanding

**2. Width:**
(1)    (2)    (3)    (4)    (5)    (6)    (7)    (8)    (9)    (10)
Very Poor                                                    Outstanding

**3. Height:**
(1)    (2)    (3)    (4)    (5)    (6)    (7)    (8)    (9)    (10)
Very Poor                                                    Outstanding

**4. Strength:**
(1)    (2)    (3)    (4)    (5)    (6)    (7)    (8)    (9)    (10)
Very Poor                                                    Outstanding

**5. Beauty:**
(1)    (2)    (3)    (4)    (5)    (6)    (7)    (8)    (9)    (10)
Very Poor                                                    Outstanding

CASE FOR
PART 1:
The Ultimate
Frisbee Team's
Dilemma

Harry, Jere, George, and Bob L. were students at Centerville University who enjoyed playing Ultimate Frisbee, a game requiring two teams of seven. Since it was hard to round up 14 players every time they wished to play, they decided to start a regular frisbee team. Their hopes were to get some potentially good frisbee players together and teach them how to play Ultimate. They realized they would need to publicize the team. One of them, Jere, spoke to a reporter from the school newspaper, and a short article appeared about the team (see Exhibit 1). In the interview, Jere stated, "The team is open to all students, especially girls." Any of the four could have spoken to the reporter, but Jere took the initiative. Jere also announced a practice through the newspaper. Eleven people came to that initial practice: Jere, Fred, Roger (Fred's roommate), Jim H., Jean, Bob L., George, Pete C., Pete R., Paul, and Harry. Jere took their names, addresses, and telephone numbers and announced that practices would be held at 4 P.M. on Tuesdays and Thursdays (at a time that was convenient for Jere). It wasn't clear why Jere should be the one to decide this, but since Jere was taking names, he was the one asked by the newcomers.

At the second practice some new people showed up: Chas, Alex, Bert, Gene (all of whom lived together), Bob M., Linda, Sharon, and Jack. However, some people from the first practice didn't come because they had conflicting classes. Jere took these new people's names and toyed with the idea of taking attendance, but nothing came of it because, as he said to his roommate, "I didn't want to turn people off or make them feel they had to come." However, many players made a mental note of who was there and who wasn't. Different people came and went like this at each practice thereafter.

**EXHIBIT 1**

### The *Centerville News*, March 1, 1984

#### "Ultimate Frisbee" Arrives with Spring
#### By Janice M. Dupre

Springtime is just around the corner, and for frisbee lovers it's time to warm up the old throwing arm.

This spring a group of frisbee enthusiasts are trying to get together a frisbee team at Centerville University (CU). Originator of the team is Jere Harris.

Many people are familiar with the frisbee as simply a plastic disc used for throwing around on a beach.

But there is an official game played with a frisbee. It's called Ultimate Frisbee, and it's like soccer in many ways.

"In Ultimate Frisbee there are seven players per team on the field. There is a kickoff, but you can't run with the frisbee in your hand," explains Harris. "It's an extremely fast game with two 24-minute halfs."

*(Continued)*

Source: A. Cohen, S. Fink, H. Gadon, and R. Willits, eds., *Effective Behavior in Organizations*, 4th Edition (Homewood, Ill.: Irwin, 1988), 910–915. Reprinted with permission.

According to Harris, a Middle States Frisbee League is now being formed by a student from Amenon College. Colleges that already have teams and will hopefully be joining the league include: Western Reserve, Ohio Wesleyan, Wayne University, and Clarke. One of the best frisbee teams in the area is the New Hampton College team.

In past years individuals from CU have gotten together to play other schools, but there never has been an official team. "I've been playing frisbee all my life, but I never heard of Ultimate Frisbee until a friend of mine told me about the game last year. It's really a fast-moving game with lots of collisions because the frisbee is always in the air with everyone diving for it," said Harris, a junior hospital administration major.

Ultimate Frisbee is by no means a gentle game. At this moment Bob LaPointe, future cocaptain of the forming CU team has a dislocated shoulder from a frisbee game he recently played in.

The friend that introduced the game to Jere Harris last year was a graduate of Columbia High School in New Jersey. It was at Columbia where the first game was played.

"The Columbia-High team can beat any team in the nation," said Harris. "They won over 30 games at the national tournament held in Michigan last year. Columbia High School also publishes the Ultimate Frisbee rulebook."

Each year a national frisbee tournament is held at Copperhopper, Michigan. Hundreds of Ultimate Frisbee teams from the United States and Canada come to take part in the tournament. The game of Frisbee is not confined to North America; it's very popular overseas and according to Harris is just being introduced to Red China.

So far the CU Frisbee team comprises about 10 members. Harris is hoping to get the team off the ground and start practicing soon. He is planning to announce practices as soon as he can arrange a time in the indoor track and as soon as the weather is nice.

"Frisbee is open to women," stresses Harris. "To play you don't have to be a super frisbee thrower; you just have to be able to throw and catch the frisbee and to run."

Along with all the food, energy, and political crises there is also a frisbee crisis. Frisbees are made with plastics, and since there is a plastic shortage the frisbees are an endangered species. Harris said that the major frisbee companies such as Whamo are urging people to buy their frisbees now because soon they will be hard to come by.

But until that time comes, frisbees will continue to fly in the sky on warm spring days at Centerville.

---

Jere and several others knew how to play Ultimate and spent the first few practices teaching the others. Jere dominated the direction of these early practices, but after a short time the rest of the players were as good and some even better. Everyone had a lot of fun learning and playing. Jack and Chas were two players who stood out at practice. Jack (a grad student) was calm and collected, never became angry, and always played fairly. Chas had been the captain of his high-school football team and always organized the team he was on, deciding who should play and who should sit out.

Jere dealt with much of the administrative work such as announcing to the school radio and newspaper where and when practices would be held. No one asked Jere to do this, but attendance was sporadic and he hoped to get new people to fill the gaps at practice. However, response to the newspaper and radio announcements was minimal; consequently Jere felt there should be an organizational meeting at night that hopefully would generate interest and attract more players. At the next practice Jere announced the meeting and explained that it was also to set up officers, dues, and so forth. Jack had 200 fliers printed up and he and Chas posted them around campus.

Jere came to the meeting late and found that strong opposition had developed against dues and against organization in general. Jere tried to explain that in order to receive funding from the university or to use university vehicles, the team must be organized with officers and a constitution, saying that the sports director for the university had told him this. A vote on dues barely passed whereupon several members left the meeting vowing they had quit. Jere followed them into the hall pleading with them to be sensible but could overhear two other members saying, "So what, we don't need them anyway." A debate ensued for a few minutes, and Jere called an end to the meeting, putting off a vote on a captain because he feared it would create further division among the team, since either Jere, Jack, or Chas might have made a good captain. Many new people who had shown up to the meeting explained they couldn't make practices as currently scheduled. Jere shrugged and said he'd try to set up alternative practices; however, this was never done.

A new group of players arrived after about 10 practices: Stan, Reggie, Mark, Bill T., and Howie. They always came and left together and often played on the same team. They were good players and talked about the coming games and their anticipated role in them. Reggie asked Jere at his first practice. "Do you think I'll start the first game?" Jere just shrugged.

By this time over 20 people had come out for the team, including 3 women (see Exhibit 2). The players fell into five friendship groups as shown in Exhibit 3. As practices continued, they became hard and competitive, and a lot of the fun which had been evident in the beginning seemed to disappear. One day Jere enraged Sharon by taking the frisbee away from her and throwing it himself. She started to walk off the field, but Jere called her back and the two had an argument right out in the middle of the field where everyone could see and hear it. She stayed at practice but was silent the rest of the day.

As the date for the first game drew near, all of the dues money was used to rent a 15-seat bus for the 50-mile trip to the other school. The day before the game about 12 people attended a meeting to discuss travel plans. Jack brought a letter written by Sharon. It was addressed to the team, but started:

> Dear Jack:
>
> The incident at this afternoon's practice was the last straw, but, I would like to impress, it was far from the only one. I'm writing this to you because you are the only one on the team who ever gave me any encouragement or made me feel like a real live person and not a bumbling incompetent.
>
> I joined the frisbee team because I enjoy playing vigorous frisbee in the comradeship of others, and to develop my own skill and confidence; but none of these is achievable under the present conditions.

**EXHIBIT 2**

| Name | Attendance[a] | Initial Appearance | Ability[a] | Age | Class | Showed Up for Bus |
|------|------------|--------------------|---------|-----|-------|-------------------|
| Jack | regular | 2nd practice | A | 23 | Grad. | XX |
| Fred | regular | 1st practice | A | 19 | Fresh. | XX |
| Jere[b] | regular | 1st practice | B | 20 | Jr. | XX |
| Jean | regular | 1st practice | C | 19 | Soph. | XX |
| Harry[b] | regular | 1st practice | A | 21 | Sr. | XX |
| Roger | sporadic | 1st practice | B | 21 | Sr. | XX |
| Reggie | regular | 10th practice | A | 18 | Fresh. | XX |
| Mark | regular | 10th practice | A | 18 | Fresh. | XX |
| Howie | regular | 10th practice | A | 18 | Fresh. | XX |
| Stan | regular | 10th practice | A | 19 | Fresh. | XX |
| Paul | sporadic | 1st practice | B | 19 | Soph. | XX |
| Jim H. | regular | 1st practice | A | 19 | Jr. | XX |
| Chas | regular | 2nd practice | A | 20 | Soph. | XX |
| Gene | sporadic | 2nd practice | B | 20 | Soph. | XX |
| Bert | sporadic | 2nd practice | B | 19 | Soph. | XX |
| Sharon | regular | 2nd practice | C | 20 | Jr. | XX |
| Linda | sporadic | 2nd practice | C | 18 | Fresh. | XX |
| George[b] | regular | 1st practice | A | 19 | Soph. | XX |
| Bob L. | sporadic | 1st practice | B | 19 | Soph. | XX |
| Bob M.[b] | sporadic | 2nd practice | B | 20 | Jr. | XX |
| Pete C. | sporadic | 1st practice | B | 19 | Fresh. | XX |
| Bill T. | regular | 10th practice | C | 19 | Soph. | XX |
| Alex | sporadic | 2nd practice | C | 19 | Soph. | |
| Pete R. | sporadic | 1st practice | C | 18 | Fresh. | XX |

[a]Based on Jere's "mental notes."
[b]Founders of the team.

How can I enjoy and concentrate on the game, when not a minute goes by that I must force myself to ignore and rise above degrading and humiliating sexist treatment? It's often said that a female, be it a filly race horse or me on the frisbee team, must be three times as good as a male in order to be considered equal. Nothing truer has ever been said. Even Jere, who's practiced with me so much and encouraged my progress, turns overtly sexist in the presence of his teammates. Certainly the issues are not completely imagined in my mind—ask the other female players.

I am not against competitiveness as long as the competition element stimulates constant improvement. But when point-making takes priority over the freedom to make mistakes or try new things, then I think something is wrong. Maybe, if anyone cares you could let them in on this. . . .

**EXHIBIT 3**  Subgroups (with spokesperson listed first)

Group A: Jere, Harry, Bob L., George
Group B: Chas, Gene, Alex, Bert
Group C: Jack, Jean, Linda, Sharon, Jim H.
Group D: Stan, Reggie, Mark, Howie, Bill T.
Group E: Fred, Roger, Pete C., Paul

All the rest are independents, coming under no group.

With this Sharon announced her resignation from the team. The letter was received with much debate by the team, and some players refused to read the letter. Jack sided with the opinions stated in the letter and was joined in this opinion by many of the original members, including the two remaining women. Jere remained silent, unable to side with one view or the other.

Obviously some choice had to be made as to who would go on the bus. Group D insisted on "sending down the best 15," in which case all of them would go. Group C said, "Take those who have come to the most practices." Jere felt that this was the fairest solution, but it was hard to implement since no one was sure as to who had attended how many practices.

Jere, Jack, and Stan sat down and wrote up several lists of 15 (see Exhibit 4), but none was acceptable to all of the groups. Jere put off making any decision; several people got quite sore. Jere felt caught in the

**EXHIBIT 4**  Comparative Lists: Who Should Go to the Game

| Jack's List | Group D's List |
|---|---|
| Jere | Reggie |
| Jack | Mark |
| Fred | Howie |
| Jean | Stan |
| Roger | Paul |
| Jim H. | Jere |
| Sharon | Jack |
| Linda | Fred |
| Bob L. | Roger |
| George | Jim H. |
| Harry | Chas |
| Paul | Gene |
| Pete R. | Bert |
| Chas | George |
| Gene | Harry |

middle, and it was not something he could shrug off. He tried to act as the moderator of the dispute but kept saying, "Does anyone have any ideas?" Argument continued and people began to leave very upset with no decision reached. Jere felt that he had been responsible for letting the scene get out of hand.

The day of the game came, and 19 people stood outside near the bus. Everyone wondered what to do. Some expressed the opinion that a captain should be elected to make the decision.

### Questions for Discussion

1. Why has the Ultimate Frisbee Team had so much trouble getting organized?
2. Think about the traditional management functions of planning, organizing, staffing, and controlling. Has the Ultimate Frisbee team failed to do any or all of these?
3. How have uncertainty, conflict, and complexity contributed to the Ultimate Frisbee team's dilemma?

CHAPTER

# Perception and Communication

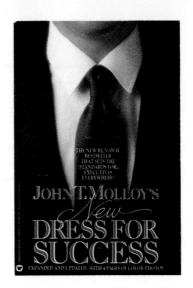

## WARDROBE PASSAGES

In 1975, John Molloy published his landmark book, *Dress for Success*. Molloy's central message was that "the clothes make the man" (or woman); the first image communicated by a businessperson is through his or her clothing. Molloy believed that the image presented by clothing affects the attitudes and confidence of the person wearing the clothes: the better you dress, the better you feel about yourself and the better you perform.

*Dress for Success* sold four million copies, and Molloy's *New Dress for Success* was published in 1988. In 1977, Molloy wrote *The Woman's Dress for Success Book*, which focused on the importance of clothing to would-be executive women. The message was that if a woman wanted to succeed in a man's world (that is, the business world), she would have to dress like a man. As a result, women's business fashions turned toward blue and gray suits.

There is evidence that in the mid-1980s the tide turned again. In a 1985 article for *Working Woman*, Heather Twidale noted that as women have achieved the rarefied atmosphere of the executive suite the basic blue and gray suits have given way to self-assured elegance in fashion—though not completely. One successful female executive Twidale interviewed suggested that the corporate uniform—white shirt and blue suit—may be necessary at first to be taken seriously and to gain credibility and legitimacy. Beyond initial successes, however, cultivating some individual style can be crucial. Blue suits may send the appropriate message when a new executive is starting out, but leaders have a style all their own. The way you should dress depends on the message you want to send.

Sources: J. T. Molloy, *Dress for Success* (New York: P. H. Wyden, 1975); J. T. Molloy, *The Woman's Dress for Success Book* (Chicago: Follet Publications, 1977); H. Twidale, "The Triumph of Executive Chic," *Working Woman*, November 1985, pp. 138–140.

INTRODUCTION

**Perception** is an individual's window to the world. When you look at this book, you *perceive* the words written in it. When you start a fire in the fireplace, you *perceive* the warmth the fire gives off. When you interact with someone, you *perceive* the kind of person that individual is, and you *perceive* the causes of his or her actions. Perception is the process by which we come to know the world so that we may act upon it.

The world comes to us through the firing of our nerve endings—a process called **sensation.** When you put your hand on a hot stove or someone calls your name, your nervous system comes alive and your nerve endings send inputs back to your brain. But there is no meaning attached to the firing of nerve endings. As William James noted in 1909, at the level of sensation the world must appear as something of a "buzzin', blooming confusion."[1] Perception is the process of making sense of the firing of our nerve endings by attaching meaning to sensations. As noted in Chapter 1, uncertainty is a defining feature of organizational behavior. More is always going on in an organization than any one person can digest, and much of what happens is ambiguous. If managing the uncertainty and confusion of the world around us is a central challenge of organizational behavior, perception is the first step in facing that challenge.

Psychologist Jerome Bruner is largely responsible for our current views of the perception process. In the 1940s and 1950s, Bruner and his colleagues wrote several articles concerning the "new look" in perception.[2] This "new look" ended the view of perception as a passive process in which the observer simply receives inputs from the environment. Instead it emphasized that perception is an *active* process—the perceiver plays an important role in determining what view of the world is provided by sensory inputs. This active view of perception also led researchers to look for new ways of understanding differences in perception among individuals.

The remainder of this chapter is divided into two parts. First, a model that explains the role of three component processes of perception will be presented. Second, the implications of this model of perception will be applied to the challenge of managing and understanding organizational behavior.

THE PROCESS OF PERCEPTION

The best way to understand perception is to remember that the act of perceiving is like painting a picture of the world with canvas and paints. Painting is a stylized activity, one in which the personal and unique style of the painter plays an active and important role. The painter selects which aspects of the event to include in the painting. Usually not all

[1]W. James, *The Principles of Psychology* (New York: Henry Holt and Company, 1925).
[2]J. S. Bruner, "On Perceptual Readiness," *Psychological Review* 64 (1957): 123–152.

FIGURE 3-1 Processes of Perception

Perception is an active process in which the perceiver plays an important role. The perceiver selectively attends to sensory inputs, constructs a representation of the inputs, and interprets the meaning of the construction. These three processes each can be influenced by both the perceiver and the source of the sensory inputs—either the object of perception or the context in which perception occurs. Perceptions then become the inputs to subsequent actions of the perceiver.

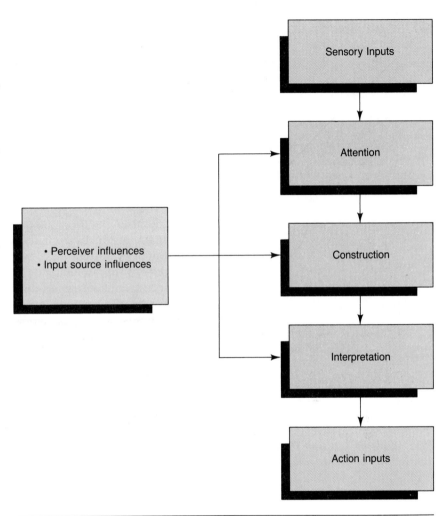

aspects are included—only those that the painter sees as central to constructing a representation of the event. The painter's representation of an event is not a true recording of that event. It is an interpretation of the event through the eyes of the painter. This is the essence of the perception process: perception is the selective construction of an interpretation of the world. The roles of each of these three component perception processes—attention, construction, and interpretation of sensory inputs—are captured in the model of perception shown in Figure 3-1.

ATTENTION

It is easy to forget that our sensory systems are constantly bombarded with potential inputs. Walking down the street, we are exposed to signs, people, buildings, and cars. In the work setting, there are any number of potential inputs, including bosses, subordinates, pieces of furniture, reports, newspapers, and production machines. The fact is that **attention**—where we choose to direct our sensory input system—is a scarce resource that we direct and ration.

Psychological research repeatedly has demonstrated the limitations of our sensory input system. Imagine yourself walking along the street. A car drives by. You are in a position to notice the license plate, features of the car, and characteristics of the driver. But do you perceive these things? While we are exposed to an infinite number of sensory inputs, only a limited number can be processed by our perceptual system. We can attend to only a limited selection—a sample—of all the available inputs, and hope we get a sample that is representative of the inputs we could *not* consider. Some of the directing and rationing of our attention comes from within; for instance, from our expectations and agendas. Some of the directing of our attention comes from characteristics of the sources of sensory inputs themselves.

The most important selection procedure for choosing among the infinite number of available sensory inputs is called accommodation. Accommodation occurs when a perceiver ignores a sensory input because the input is *not changing.* A sensory input that is not changing is not providing new information, so it can be ignored. For example, as long as the temperature does not change, our temperature sensory system is "on hold," monitoring changes at a level below conscious awareness. Temperature messages are being sent by our nerve endings, but as long as the messages don't change, we ignore them. Similarly, we all accommodate the habits and eccentricities of our coworkers, including the clothing they typically wear. Only when something out of the ordinary occurs—a particularly nasty coworker acts pleasant, or the boss comes to the office in shorts—are we likely to take notice.

With so many sensory inputs to choose from, the inputs that don't provide new information usually are the first to be ignored. Accommodation, however, is only one of several processes that determine which sensory inputs are processed.

**Perceiver Influences**   What a perceiver attends to can be influenced tremendously by theories that the perceiver harbors about the way the world works. Consider Sylvia Pichois's selection decision presented in the "Focus on: Perceiver Influences on Attention." Of all the available sensory inputs Sylvia Pichois could have used to form an impression of the job candidate, she chose to focus her attention on the candidate's use of the dessert fork. Apparently Pichois has a theory (a set of beliefs) about sophistication in using a dessert fork and its relationship to

FOCUS ON:

Perceiver
Influences on
Attention

**Little Things Mean a Lot**  Imagine you are being interviewed for a high-level executive position. Naturally, you would expect a critical examination of your qualifications. In a short interview, however, it is impossible for an evaluator to learn everything about you. So what would you expect your evaluator to focus on? If your evaluator were Sylvia Pichois, she would observe how you used a dessert fork:

Sylvia Pichois, the president of a major firm, was considering promoting one of the upper-level managers, Clare Allen, to a top position in the firm. She invited the prospective candidate to her home for dinner. During the dessert course, Allen made the mistake of putting the tines of the fork straight into the point of the pie instead of using the side of the fork. Pichois rejected Allen because of her lack of sophistication, and she told the Personnel Department that anyone so naive

in her approach to such a simple matter as eating pie could not be trusted to make important corporatewide decisions.

Pichois apparently had a theory (a set of beliefs) that linked pie-eating behavior to corporate competence. Whether that theory was correct or not, it allowed Pichois to predict important characteristics of job applicants from seemingly meaningless behaviors. In a similar vein, legend has it that Henry Ford evaluated people by watching whether they salted their food before tasting it. His theory: Those who salt before tasting are likely to make judgments without first considering all the facts at hand.

Beliefs about the relationships between personal characteristics and behaviors are at the core of the perception process. They direct our attention and can lead us to draw big conclusions from small bits of information.

Source: D. Hellriegel, John W. Slocum, and R. W. Woodman, *Organizational Behavior* (St. Paul, Minn.: West, 1983), p. 73.

sophistication in making on-the-job decisions. This theory directed Sylvia's attention to the candidate's use of the dessert fork. Other evaluators probably would have looked at completely different characteristics of the candidate and thereby constructed completely different evaluations of the candidate's job suitability.

The needs and motivations of a perceiver can have a similar influence on the rationing of attention. A hungry individual entering a dining room probably will notice what kinds of foods are available. A single and lonely young male more likely would notice the number and location of attractive females in the room. Needs and motivations also can lead a perceiver to look more carefully at objects or events, carefully enough to pick up fine nuances or distinctions that otherwise would be missed. An expert skier, for example, can differentiate among many different snow conditions, partly because the expert skier needs to and partly because that need leads the expert to attend to features of snow conditions that the casual observer or weekend skier would look at but not see. Similarly, an aspiring junior executive likely will pay extra attention to the boss's actions (and perhaps thereby gain some important insights into the boss's behavior) in the hopes of gleaning some hints about how to get promoted.

Are these perceiver influences on attention problematic? Certainly they can be. An interviewer whose implicit theories focus attention on unimportant characteristics of job candidates may miss critical information that could predict the job success or failure of the candidate. However, such influences also are unavoidable and even necessary. Because we all are exposed to an unlimited number of sensory inputs, we must have a way to decide which inputs to attend to and which to ignore. Sylvia Pichois's theory may be the wrong theory, but it is impossible to conduct a selection interview without *some* theory to direct the information collection process. The perception process has to start with a rule for selecting which of the infinite number of available sensory inputs will be attended to. This means that good perceptions of the world begin with good theories of the world. Only with good theories are we likely to attend to the most valuable available sensory inputs.

**Input Source Influences**    Sometimes a perceiver's attempts to direct attention with theories about what to look for are upstaged by characteristics of the source objects or events, or **input source influences.** An object or event that is particularly eye-catching is said to be salient: It commands a perceiver's attention. Several characteristics of objects or events will make them more likely to command attention.

Motion is a contributor to salience. Advertisers long ago realized that movement in a billboard or neon sign will make the sign more likely to be noticed and its information processed. Magicians take advantage of the attention-capturing quality of motion. Motion with one hand often is used to distract an observer's attention and thereby mask movement by the magician's other hand.

Distinctiveness and novelty also contribute to the salience of an object or event. Distinctiveness and novelty are the flip side of accommodation. The expected often is ignored or overlooked; new and novel sensory inputs demand attention. The first black executive in a company, the first female worker on a construction site, and the first male nurse in a hospital each command more than their fair share of attention. They are different from those around them—or at least novel in their positions—so they stand out more in the eyes of their beholders.

Interestingly, novelty also can refer to the unexpected absence of a sensory input. Most everyone has heard of someone who awakened suddenly from a deep sleep one night because the local train didn't go by on schedule. Similarly, Sherlock Holmes solved the mystery of *Silver*

No doubt your eye was
drawn to this picture
when you first turned the
page. The picture's vivid
colors and distinctive patterns make it particularly
salient, or eye-catching.
Without the correct per-
ceptual set, however, it
would take you a few sec-
onds to arrive at a correct
perception of the picture.
It's the S&P 500 Index
trading pit on the floor of
the Chicago Mercantile
Exchange.

*Blaze* because his attention was drawn to the fact that the dogs in the
story did *not* bark when they should have.[3]

Vividness also contributes to the salience of an object or event.
Vividness has to do with the visual intensity of an object of the
perception process. An object or image may be particularly vivid,
meaning that the colors are bright and memorable and our eyes are
drawn to the image. In a written report, wording also may be vivid in that
it calls forth vivid images. Vividness commands the attention and
information processing of a perceiver.

Personal perspective also can profoundly influence which sensory
inputs are considered. An individual's own contributions to something
(such as a task force report) are much more salient than the contributions

[3]A. C. Doyle, *The Memoirs of Sherlock Holmes* (London: John Murray and Jonathan Cape,
1974).

of others. That's because you never miss what you yourself contribute, but you may miss what others contribute. It is not surprising, then, that group members asked to evaluate the percentage of their contribution to a joint project routinely provide answers that sum to more than 100 percent. We all think we do more than our fair share because our share is more salient to us than others' contributions.

Personal perspective also is responsible for the false consensus effect.[4] False consensus occurs when an individual assumes that everyone else shares his or her beliefs or biases. False consensus happens because an individual's perspective often makes a belief very compelling; the perceiver feels that the "facts" leave no room for alternative beliefs. What the perceiver fails to realize is that not everyone shares his or her perspective. No one else will have the same sensory inputs, so for no one else may the belief seem as compelling.

Source characteristics have their greatest influence on attention under conditions of information overload. **Information overload** occurs when there are too many attention-grabbing sensory inputs. In familiar surroundings, where many features of the environment are well-known and need little attention, plenty of attention is available for new or unusual objects or events. In novel situations, where a perceiver has few theories about where to direct attention and receives many unusual inputs, characteristics of objects and events that command attention (for instance, motion or vividness) will play a major role in what information gets attended to and processed.

CONSTRUCTION

Once sensory inputs have been selected for further processing, the perceiver uses them to construct a representation of the event or object being attended to. The **construction** process organizes and edits the sensory inputs in a way that makes them potentially meaningful. The construction process also is subject to both input source and perceiver influences.

**Perceiver Influences**   At the most basic level of perceptual construction are perceptual grouping principles. **Perceptual grouping** is the tendency to organize sensory inputs into familiar and potentially meaningful patterns. Consider the patterns of shapes shown in Figure 3–2. Most people see these 19 spots as a horse and rider. This is an example of the perceptual grouping principle of closure. Closure occurs when we can perceive an object or event even when *only part* of it is evident. Our

[4]L. Ross, D. Greene, and P. House, "The False Consensus Phenomenon: An Attributional Bias in Self-Perception and Social Perception Processes," *Journal of Experimental Social Psychology* 13 (1977): 279–301.

**FIGURE 3–2**          Closure

Closure is important to
constructing an accurate
perception when some
elements are absent. In
this picture, only parts of
the horse and rider are
provided, but most peo-
ple "see" a horse and
rider. Closure and conti-
nuity both help us use
limited inputs to see ap-
parent problems as famil-
iar situations we are prepared to handle.

Source: Dennis Coon, *Introduction to Psychology: Explorations and Applications* (St. Paul, Minn.: West, 1977).

perceptual system takes the available sensory inputs and constructs a meaningful understanding of what we are looking at.

Another perceptual grouping principle is continuity. Continuity occurs when two or more sensations are assumed to be part of one whole because they are close in time or space. The human visual system cannot "see" shapes or objects. Instead, it senses many dots of light of various shades and colors. The perceptual system automatically assumes adjoining dots of light of the same shade and color are part of the same whole object. Generally we do not need to figure out where one object ends and another begins: our perceptual system constructs those judgments automatically. Similarly, sensory inputs that follow each other in time are perceived as being related.

Perceptual grouping principles such as closure and continuity play an important role in dealing with the potentially infinite pool of available sensory inputs. By organizing sensory inputs into plausibly appropriate and familiar patterns, perceptual grouping principles immediately reduce the number of inputs bombarding the perceptual system. In the example provided in Figure 3–2, each of the spots is made up of many points of color, and the background is made up of many points of white. Seeing each spot as a continuous shape and the white background as a

**FIGURE 3–3**          The Young Woman and the Old Woman

Expectations can lead us to perceive what we expect. In these pictures, most people who first see the young woman in the middle see another young woman in the large, ambiguous picture. In work organizations, training and socialization create important expectations that help workers perceive apparently novel and insoluble problems as familiar situations they are well prepared to handle. Expectations can be dangerous if they lead us to perceive what really isn't there.

Source: R. Leeper, "A Study of a Neglected Portion of the Field of Learning—The Development of Sensory Organization," *Journal of Genetic Psychology* 46 (1935): 41–75.

continuous background reduces our sensory load from an innumerable number of points of white and color to 19 spots on a continuous background of white. Grouping the 19 spots into the construction "horse and rider" further reduces cognitive processing demands by 18 sensory inputs—from 19 spots to 1 horse and rider. Grouping principles such as closure and continuity also help us recognize the familiar in new situations by allowing us to "fill in" the missing elements and "see" something familiar.

The perceptual construction process also can be influenced tremendously by perceptual set. **Perceptual set** refers to the expectations that a perceiver brings to the perception task. What a perceiver expects or wants to see plays a major role in the perception he or/she constructs.

A visual demonstration of perceptual set is provided in Figure 3–3. If you were led to expect to see an old woman in the large picture, you would see an old woman. If you were told to expect to see a young woman, you would see a young woman. In fact, this picture can be seen as *either* an old woman or a young woman. The expectation determines which construction a perceiver makes from the same sensory inputs.

Experiences can be the source of perceptual sets. If an individual were shown the drawing in the middle before seeing the large "old woman/young woman" picture, a young woman would be likely to emerge from it. But if an individual were shown the drawing on the left before seeing the large "old woman/young woman" picture, an old woman likely would emerge from it. In this case there is no "right" answer. The picture can be seen as either an old woman or a young woman. What is important is that the perceiver's prior experience (seeing the unambiguous old woman or young woman picture) creates a perceptual set; the perceptual set in turn determines which subsequent perceptions are likely to be constructed.

Nobel Prize winner Herbert Simon describes a graphic example of the effects of perceptual set in the book *Administrative Behavior*.[5] Executives from different departments of major companies read a case study. The case study described the problems faced by the chief executive officer (CEO) of a major corporation. After they had read the case, the executives were asked to analyze the cause of the CEO's problems. Not surprisingly, each executive perceived the cause of the CEO's problems to be within his or her own specialty. For example, the marketing executives saw a marketing problem, the finance executives saw a finance problem, and so on. Each executive brought to the perception task a perceptual set—his or her own business specialty—which in turn determined the perception of the CEO's problems that each executive constructed. Another example of the influence of perceptual set on perceptual constructions, in the domain of college sports, is shown in the "FOCUS ON: Perceiver Influences on Construction."

Prejudice represents a particularly dangerous form of perceptual set influences on construction. Prejudice refers to the tendency of an individual to prejudge the actions of another individual according to a set of beliefs. For instance, if a male executive believes that women make poor managers, he will be likely to perceive all attempts to manage by women as inappropriate. As we shall see later, two forms of prejudicial perceptual sets (stereotypes and implicit personality theories) influence not only perceptual constructions, but also the meanings people attach to these constructions.

**Input Source Influences**   Characteristics of the source of sensory inputs—the object or event being perceived—also can influence the perceptual construction process. Three examples of input source influences on perceptual construction are contrast, anchoring-and-adjustment, and "halo" effects. All three arise when one sensory input influences the construction of perceptions of other sensory inputs.

**Contrast effects** occur when an individual sees something as larger or smaller than it really is because of a comparison to a very small or very large reference point. Think about how you would feel about a $3,000 increase in your annual salary. If your last salary increase was only $1,000, this raise would seem generous *in contrast*. If you learned that a coworker had received a $10,000 increase, your $3,000 would seem pretty paltry. Of course, $3,000 is $3,000. It's the contrast with either $1,000 or $10,000 that makes it seem big or small.

**Anchoring-and-adjustment effects** are the flip side of contrast effects. Contrast effects occur when our perceptual system constructs two

[5]H. Simon, *Administrative Behavior* (New York: MacMillan, 1945).

Focus on:

Perceiver
Influences on
Construction

**They Saw a Game**　The role of perceiver motivations in constructing perceptions is regularly on display when a perceiver's self-image is on the line. For example, if a perceiver *identifies* with a sports team—takes pride in the team's wins and wallows in misery when the team loses—the perceiver has a *vested interest* in the team's actions being right and good. This vested interest dramatically affects constructed perceptions about the team's actions, as demonstrated in the following study of fan reactions to a football game:

　　Anyone who has observed the spectators at athletic events can't help noticing that two apparently reasonable people can experience a play in football or basketball in very different ways as a function of having been "tuned" by different expectations and purposes. This fact of experience was illustrated by a case study of a football game. It so happened that Dartmouth and Princeton played each other in football one November afternoon. The game

turned out to be very rough, and tempers flared both during and after the game. Immediately following the game, partisans for both schools made accusations that the other school had played rough and dirty football. The school papers, the school alumni magazines, and a number of the metropolitan newspapers highly publicized the whole affair. There was clearly a very real disagreement as to what had actually happened during the game. What is of special interest . . . were the results of showing a movie of the game to a group of Dartmouth students and a group of Princeton students. Keeping in mind that an identical movie was shown to both groups of students, it is interesting to [note] the number of infractions perceived in the same film by two groups of people with different loyalties and different expectations. Students . . . tended to see the team from the other university as having committed the most infractions.

Source: D. J. Schneider, A. H. Hastorf, and P. C. Ellsworth, *Person Perception* (Reading, Mass.: Addison-Wesley, 1979).

sensory inputs to be more dissimilar than they really are; anchoring-and-adjustment effects occur when our perceptual system constructs two sensory inputs to be even more *similar* than they really are. Imagine you are trying to assign a value to something—for instance, how much a particular employee should be paid. A friend suggests that you pay the new employee $50,000, which you reject as too high. This "suggestion," even though you rejected it, nevertheless has an effect. Knowing the suggestion to be too high, you would *adjust* away from it (lower) in formulating your perception of what would be fair. However, research repeatedly has demonstrated that adjustments of this sort are almost always *insufficient*. In this case, insufficient adjustment down from the $50,000 suggestion would result in a higher salary actually assigned to the new employee. The $50,000 suggestion anchors your perception of what would be a fair wage for the new employee, even though the suggestion itself is obviously inappropriate. If the suggestion had been $5,000, you would have rejected it as well and adjusted upward. Again, however, the adjustment would be insufficient, producing a bias now to perceive a *lower* salary as fair.

Interestingly, the ability of an "anchor" (such as a suggested salary) to influence perceptual construction does not seem to depend on its being a sensible clue to the correct answer. In one study of anchoring-and-adjustment effects, students were asked to estimate the proportion of African countries in the United Nations. Before making their estimates, however, each student was given a number to consider from one spin of a "wheel of fortune." Obviously this random number obtained from a spin of the wheel could not be a useful clue in deciding the correct proportion of African countries in the United Nations. Nevertheless, the numbers obtained from the spin of the wheel clearly influenced the students' estimates.[6]

**Halo effects** are a form of anchoring-and-adjustments effects across dimensions. In anchoring and adjustment, a suggested value for one dimension influences estimates of that same dimension; a suggested salary influences salary assignments; a suggested proportion influences proportion estimates. In "halo" effects, the perception of an object or event on one dimension influences the construction of perceptions of that object or event on other dimensions. A physically attractive individual, for instance, may be perceived as more competent than another worker who is less physically attractive. Why? Physical attractiveness is positive, so it creates a positive "halo." Other traits of the attractive individual (such as ability or accomplishments) are perceived as more positive because of the positive "halo." Perception of the individual on one dimension (physical attractiveness) influences the perception of the individual on other dimensions (such as ability or accomplishment). Unfortunately, "halo" effects also probably are responsible for people thinking that their friends can do no wrong. Friendship creates a positive "halo" that can seriously compromise an individual's evaluations of a friend's actions.

Contrast, anchoring-and-adjustment, and "halo" effects all are examples of the influence of one sensory input on the constructed perception of another. These effects arise, of course, as a reaction to uncertainty. Your perception of your own age is not likely to be influenced by anchoring and adjustment. Nor is your perception of your own physical attractiveness likely to influence your perception of your own age. But your own age is something you *know*. Most things you cannot know; you can only construct perceptions of them. The perceptual construction

[6]A. Tversky and D. Kahneman, "Judgment under Uncertainty: Heuristics and Biases," *Science* 185 (1974): 1124–1131.

process is an uncertain one, because you never know if you are seeing things the way they really are. It is this uncertainty that makes perceptual construction vulnerable to influence.

INTERPRETATION

The selection and construction processes provide the perceiver with only a representation of what object or event has occurred in the world. A final stage in the perception process is **interpretation** of the representation, to assign meaning to what the perceiver has perceived.

One process people use to assign meaning to actions and their outcomes is attribution. **Attribution** is the process of perceiving the *causes* of actions and outcomes. When a foreman yells at a worker, what caused the yelling behavior? Was it something the worker did? Something the worker didn't do? Something the foreman ate? Perhaps the foreman just likes to yell at everyone. These are important distinctions because they help us determine the meaning of the yelling. Should the worker take yelling as important criticism, write it off as a bad day for the foreman, or believe that yelling is something everyone on this job needs to learn to live with? Determining whether the foreman is yelling (as opposed to talking normally) is a matter of attention and construction. Yelling in and of itself is not an important sensory input. The *meaning* of the yelling is what counts.

Attributions are particularly useful because they provide models of how the people around us function, what their motives are, and what determines their behavior. These models in turn reduce our uncertainty in social interaction. If we understand how others are likely to behave and why, we can use this knowledge to achieve our goals. Attributions help us understand cause-and-effect relationships, such as what caused the foreman to yell and therefore when he is likely to yell again. Attributions allow us to predict the future behavior of others based upon our understanding of the causes of their past and present behavior. Attributions then are critical to formulating action plans for the future.

**Processes of Attribution**   The central principle of attribution is co-variation. Psychologist Harold Kelley, the founding father of the theory of attribution, explained covariation by noting that "an effect is attributed to that condition which is present when the effect is present and absent when the effect is absent."[7] In other words, if a condition is present when an effect occurs but absent when the effect fails to occur, the condition is said to *covary* with the effect. Conditions that covary with an effect will be perceived to *cause* the effect. To take a concrete example, if a worker's performance is good (the effect) when the worker is supervised (the condition) but poor when the worker isn't supervised,

[7]H. H. Kelley, "Attribution Theory in Social Psychology" in *Nebraska Symposium on Motivation* 15, ed. D. Levine (Lincoln, Neb.: University of Nebraska Press, 1967).

then supervision will be perceived as the cause of good performance. People judge covariation three ways: via distinctiveness, consensus, and consistency.

Imagine that your boss has just complimented you (the effect) on a report that you recently submitted. You are wondering what to make of this compliment. What *meaning* should you attach to your boss's remark, and what implications does that meaning hold for your future behavior? Was the quality of your report the *cause* of your boss's compliment? To sort out this uncertainty, first you would want to note whether the compliment was *distinctive:* Does your boss compliment people all the time or is this a rare event? If an effect occurs all the time (for instance, if everyone compliments everyone else in this company all the time just as a matter of politeness), then it is pointless to look for causes of the effect. Attribution is a worthwhile activity only if an effect occurs some but not all of the time. Then situations in which the effect occurs are distinctive (they differ from other situations), and it is useful to ask what *causes* the effect to occur sometimes but not others.

*Consensus* has to do with whether the condition produces the effect for other people. Assume for the moment that your boss's compliment was distinctive and therefore merits further search for a cause. If other people read the report and also compliment it, that would be evidence of covariation of the report and the compliment *across people*—a consensus that the quality of the report (the condition) causes the compliment (the effect).

Finally, you might look at the *consistency* of your boss's compliments across time and across situations. Does your boss compliment all your reports, or did she single out this report in particular? Has she similarly complimented other reports on this same topic? Has she similarly complimented other reports written in this same style? These questions all attempt to isolate the cause of the boss's compliment by finding consistencies between appearance of the effect and plausible causes.

Attributions are important because different attributions for actions or events merit different responses. Figure 3–4 provides a framework for the different types of attributions you might arrive at for a subordinate's performance. This framework has two dimensions: location of the cause and stability of the cause. Location can be internal (the individual) or external (outside the individual); stability can be permanent or temporary. As shown in Figure 3–4, these two dimensions yield four different types of causes for behaviors: luck, effort, task characteristics, and ability/personality. Each type of cause carries with it a different recommendation for action.

Consider a worker whose performance is disappointing. Before a supervisor can decide what to do to correct the poor performance, the supervisor must determine its cause. If through observation the supervisor determined that other workers handled this task well, the supervisor would make an internal attribution—decide that the worker's

**FIGURE 3–4**          Attributions

The attributions we make for the causes of events (actions and their outcomes) are critical to our responses to those events. This table provides a framework for our attributions and the responses those attributions will occasion. For example, we are likely to punish an employee who failed if we think he or she didn't make an effort. On the other hand, we may be likely to help an employee who failed if we think he or she doesn't have the ability.

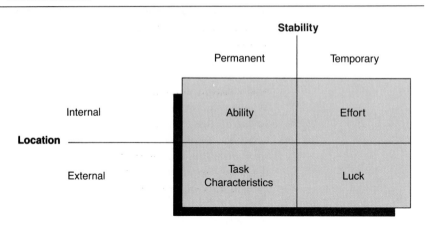

Source: B. Weiner, *Achievement Motivation and Attribution Theory* (Morristown, N.J.: General Learning Press, 1975).

failure was due to either lack of effort or lack of ability. If the worker did fine at other tasks, lack of effort could be ruled out as an explanation. Having determined lack of ability to be the cause of the poor performance, the supervisor could reassign the worker to a task more suitable to the worker's abilities.

If on the other hand the supervisor noted that the worker had done fine on this job in the past but *only recently* had performed poorly, the supervisor would have to conclude that the cause of the performance failure was unstable. The supervisor then might see if other workers recently had experienced similar difficulties, or if only *this* worker was having trouble. If only this worker was having trouble, that would suggest that perhaps something was temporarily causing the worker not to give as much effort as before. A new assignment would not be necessary: a personal pep talk would be more appropriate.

Finally, what if further investigation by the supervisor revealed consensus—that lots of workers were having similar performance problems? That would suggest an external cause of poor performance. Perhaps the design of the task might be at fault, or training for the entire work force might be inadequate.

That attribution is a *perception* process should be obvious from this example. The sensory input is the same in all cases: the employee's performance is disappointing. What varies is the interpretation of this performance. Is the cause of the performance failure internal or external to the individual, and is the cause permanent or only temporary? Each attribution carries with it a different prescription for resolving the performance problem.

The framework of possible attributions also suggests how we come to understand the personality of another individual. Personality refers to the tendency of an individual to behave consistently across situations and across time. We attribute an individual's behaviors to stable internal causes when that individual behaves similarly across situations and across time, and unlike other people. In effect, personality is the cause assigned to consistent behavior that cannot be explained otherwise. (The process of perceiving others will be discussed in greater detail later in this chapter.)

*Perceiver Effects*   Attribution is not the discovery of true causes of behavior, merely an individual's interpretation of the likely causes of behaviors and outcomes. Attribution represents the attempts of an individual to make causal sense of the world. Unfortunately, like the perceptual processes of attention and construction, attribution is subject to influences.

One important source of attributional influence is personal perspective. When we observe the behaviors of another individual, the most salient plausible cause of that individual's behaviors is that individual. That other individual is always front and center stage in the production of his or her own behaviors. When we ourselves act, our own persona is *not* a salient component of the visual landscape. In fact, most of us rarely see ourselves behaving at all. Instead, we see only the environment to which we are responding.

Furthermore, we see our own behaviors in a variety of different settings—at home, at work, at play. Many of the other individuals with whom we interact we see only in a considerably more limited number of circumstances. Some, for instance, we may see only at work. As a result, the diversity of circumstances in which we observe their behaviors will be quite limited. We may mistakenly see their behavior as very consistent across circumstances when in fact their behavior is consistent only over an extremely limited set of circumstances.

These consequences of personal perspective—greater visual salience of others as plausible causes of their behaviors and limited diversity of circumstances in which to view others' behaviors—give rise to an important perceptual bias known as the fundamental attribution error.[8] The **fundamental attribution error** is the tendency of a perceiver to see others' behaviors as caused primarily by stable, internal characteristics (such as personality) while seeing his or her own behavior primarily as a response to environmental circumstances. The fundamental attribution error suggests that explanations for actions typically will take the form, "*I* did it because the circumstances demanded it; *he* did it because that's the kind of person he is."

[8]E. E. Jones and R. E. Nisbett, "The Actor and the Observer: Divergent Perceptions of the Causes of Behavior" in *Attribution: Perceiving the Causes of Behavior*, eds. E. E. Jones et al. (Morristown, N.J.: General Learning Press, 1972).

The fundamental attribution error is important because of the role (described earlier) that a supervisor's attributions play in evaluating employee behaviors. Supervisors are likely to conclude that a subordinate's behaviors reveal something about the subordinate, and therefore are worthy of blame or praise. The subordinate is instead likely to believe that those same behaviors are simply sensible reactions to environmental cues—what anyone would have done under the same circumstances.

*Input Source Influences*   Sometimes we forget that *other people* represent a significant feature of the perceptual field in which actions and consequences occur. Because others often are present when we are trying to interpret ambiguous sensory inputs, actions of others also can influence our perceptions. If a classmate says that a test the two of you just took was difficult, you may also be disposed to see the test as having been difficult—especially if you weren't sure what to think. In effect, the comments and opinions of others can anchor our perceptions and judgments.

This process of having one's perceptions influenced by the comments and perceptions of others is called **social comparison.** Social comparison will be discussed in greater detail in Chapter 7.

## SELF-PERCEPTION

The perceptual process described here applies to more than just the perception of the behaviors of others. Perceptual selection, construction, and interpretation also are applied to a perceiver's understanding of the meanings of his or her *own* actions (why did I just do that? What led me to do that?). Perceptual processes also play a key role in constructing explanations for the *consequences* of actions—including our own.

Perceivers have shown self-serving biases when, for instance, interpreting the causes of their own behaviors and their consequences. A **self-serving bias** is the tendency of individuals to attribute the causes of actions or their outcomes in a way that reflects well on them or absolves them from responsibility for poor outcomes. Self-serving attributions take one or two forms: (1) they explain an action as a sensible response to situational demands or constraints (thereby excusing the outcome), or (2) they explain the outcome as the result of causes external to the individual (such as the interfering behaviors of others). These two forms of self-serving bias differ in that the first form admits that the action taken was wrong, but excuses it as a sensible reaction to the situation; the second form suggests that the action taken might even have been *correct* and that it didn't produce a good outcome for reasons beyond the individual's control.

In one demonstration of self-serving attribution bias, several groups of students played a game in which they were responsible for governing a fictitious nation torn by revolution. Many decisions were required during the game, and the researcher arranged for each group of

One of the most important aspects of success, whether in athletics or business, is being able to build on it, and that requires being able to correctly attribute the cause of the success. Was Florence Griffin-Joyner's success a function of a good strategy? A supreme effort? Subpar competitors? Or just dumb luck? The right attribution represents an accurate understanding of the cause of the success, which is the first step on the road to the next success.

students to meet with some significant successes and some significant disasters. The researchers found that students tended to place blame for the failures on situational circumstances, but claimed responsibility for the successes.[9] Similar self-serving attributional biases have been demonstrated by teachers who credit their high-quality instruction for their students' successes but blame the students' lack of effort for their failures.[10] Research also has shown that in their annual reports to stockholders, unstable corporations often attribute their past successes and failures in ways that emphasize management's ability to control corporate performance and therefore improve it in the future.[11]

Self-perception also comes into play when an individual acts quickly and only later reflects back on why the action was taken. If we engage in actions that are to ourselves mysterious (for instance, because we do not wish to own up to our subconscious motives), we will look around for circumstances that may have led us to the actions. If there are environmental forces (such as incentives or requests by powerful others) that could have "caused" our behaviors, we will be unlikely to attribute the actions to our own motives.

Personal perspective is an important source of differences in our self-perceptions and the perceptions other individuals have of our behaviors. Self-perception biases arising from personal perspective differences can be alleviated by forcing an actor to see his or her actions as others would, with the actor in the center of the visual landscape.

**Objective Self-Awareness**   Making an actor more aware of his or her own role in causing actions or their consequences means making the actor more aware that the actions or their consequences are the product of personal motivations and preferences rather than simple reactions to environmental demands. An actor's awareness of his or her own role in causing behaviors and their consequences is called **objective self-awareness**.[12] Studies have shown, for instance, that without objective self-awareness individuals will make more *situational* attributions for their actions and consequences (as discussed in the fundamental attribution error). What happens, however, when individuals instead are given feedback that highlights their own roles in the actions? What happens, for example, when individuals view videotapes of their behavior? It turns

[9]S. Streufert and S. C. Streufert, "Effect of Conceptual Structure, Failure, and Success on Attribution of Causality and Interpersonal Attitude," *Journal of Personality and Social Psychology* 11 (1969): 138–147.

[10]T. J. Johnson, R. Feigenbaum, and M. Weiby, "Some Determinants and Consequences of the Teacher's Perception of Causality," *Journal of Educational Psychology* 55 (1964): 237–246.

[11]G. R. Salancik and J. R. Meindl, "Corporate Attributions as Strategic Illusions of Management Control," *Administrative Sciences Quarterly* 29 (1984): 238–254.

[12]R. A. Wicklund, "Objective Self-Awareness," in *Advances in Experimental Social Psychology* 8, ed. L. Berkowitz (New York: Academic Press, 1975).

out that individuals then attribute more of their behaviors and consequences to themselves—to internal motivations and preferences—just
as an impartial observer would. Decreasing differences in personal
perspective by helping an individual see him- or herself at the center of
the action effectively eliminates a major source of differences between
processes of perception applied to the self and to others.

## PERCEPTION IN ORGANIZATIONAL BEHAVIOR

A summary of internal and external sources of influence on the three
component processes of perception is represented in Figure 3–5. The
remainder of this chapter will consider the contributing role of
perception in three central organizational phenomena: conflict, person
perception, and communication.

## CONFLICT

Conflict often occurs when differing viewpoints or beliefs about how to
make decisions or divide scarce resources clash. If two people want
different things, these differences in goals or motivations will result in
differing views about how to make decisions or divide up resources. But
what if members have *common* goals? Is this enough to ensure an absence
of organizational conflict?

The answer is no. Even if two people have exactly the same goals, they
may have very different views about how best to accomplish those goals.
These differences in beliefs can provide an important source of conflict
if they must be reconciled to produce a single decision or action. These
differences in beliefs also can be a function of differences in perception.

Consider as an example the assassination of presidential candidate
Senator Robert Kennedy in Los Angeles in 1971. On hand at the time
was a crowd of eyewitnesses who saw the entire event unfold before
them. Further, this event was one witnesses would be unlikely to
forget—an event so vivid and shocking that it likely would remain

**FIGURE 3–5**       Influences on Perception

|  | Perceiver Influences | Input Source Influences |
|---|---|---|
| Attention | Accommodation<br>Theories<br>Needs and motivations | Motion<br>Distinctiveness<br>Vividness<br>Perspective |
| Construction | Grouping<br>Closure<br>Continuity<br>Set and expectations<br>Prejudice | Contrast effects<br>Anchoring-and-adjustment effects<br>"Halo" effects |
| Interpretation | Attribution | Social comparison |

indelibly inscribed in their minds' eyes forevermore. How do the witnesses' accounts of the event compare? Two researchers who spent three years studying witness testimony concerning the circumstances of the assassination provide the following report:

> The eyewitnesses, many of them standing next to each other, saw—or remembered they saw—very different things. Against the recollections of the assistant maitre d'hotel, who says that he was holding Kennedy's hand and leading him along—toward [the assassin] Sirhan—one can place the recollections of at least four other people who testified that Kennedy was turning to his left at the time Sirhan fired in order to shake hands with one of the waiters. Frank J. Burns, a friend of Kennedy's, was standing off Kennedy's right shoulder when the shots were fired, and he testified at Sirhan's trial that Kennedy had turned "almost ninety degrees" at the time and therefore was not facing Sirhan's gun muzzle but indeed presenting his right and hinder side to it. It is difficult to find witnesses—apart from the maitre d'hotel—who directly contradict his recollections and those of many others, such as Edward Minasian, Martin Petrusky, Jesus Perez, and Vincent Di Perro, all employed in the Ambassador's kitchen.
>
> It is, however, impossible to find witnesses who directly corroborate the autopsy evidence that the gun was practically touching Kennedy's head. Their estimates vary wildly. Pete Hamill, the columnist, put Sirhan seven feet from Kennedy. Juan Romero, a busboy who had just shaken hands with Kennedy, estimated "approximately one yard." Valerie Schulte, a college student, said at the trial that "Sirhan's arms and gun" were "approximately three yards, something like that, from the senator." Edward Minasian, who was walking about a yard in front of Kennedy, thought the barrel of Sirhan's gun was "approximately three feet" from Kennedy. The closest to Kennedy that one can place the gun muzzle, going on these recollections, is about two feet—a distance calculated from one recollection that Sirhan was "three or four" feet away from Kennedy.[13]

The unreliability of eyewitness testimony demonstrated in the Kennedy assassination trial is hardly an isolated event. In cases where crimes have been carefully staged to test the ability of eyewitnesses to recall critical information, witnesses often are incapable of reproducing the sequence of events as they occurred. In one study, only 14 percent of witnesses were able to pick an assailant out of a police lineup.[14]

That eyewitness accounts of memorable events would be hopelessly incomparable is at once both surprising and understandable. It is surprising because we would like to think of perception as a faithful recording of events and people. It is understandable because this "recording" process is *stylized* process that involves attention, construction, and interpretation and often reflects as much about the perceiver as about the event or person being perceived.

[13]B. Langman and A. Cockburn, "Sirhan's Gun," *Harper's* 250, January 1975, 16–27.
[14]R. Buckhout et al., "Determinants of Eyewitness Performance in a Lineup," *Bulletin of the Psychonomic Society* 4 (1974): 191–192.

Many conflicts in organizations arise because of differences in perception. Even if two disputants share identical goals, they may not share the same rules for attention, construction, and interpretation of events around them. They can find themselves in conflict over differences in perceptions of what has happened or is happening, and therefore what they should do next.

The processes of attention, construction, and interpretation are like a set of *rules* for getting a perceiver from the sensory inputs of an event to a recording of that event in the mind's eye. Unfortunately, personal perspective in perception virtually guarantees that the sensory inputs to which different perceivers attend will be different. The sensory inputs may be different only in minor ways, but they will be different nevertheless.

Even if the sensory inputs were identical, it is unlikely that every perceiver would apply the construction and interpretation "rules" in the same way. Sexual harassment conflicts in organizations often occur not because disputants disagree about what happened, but because they assign different interpretations to the same events. For instance, women are three times as likely as men to interpret a man eyeing a woman up and down as sexual harassment; men are twice as likely as women to agree that claims of sexual harassment are exaggerated.[15] Apparently male and female beliefs about what behaviors constitute sexual harassment differ dramatically.

Differences in belief structures also play an important role in understanding the conflicting attributions made by perceivers for actions and their consequences. A perceiver who believes that money is the strongest of motivators may be likely to look for monetary explanations of behaviors. On the other hand, another perceiver who believes that social motives (such as wanting to have friends or feel like a "part of the group") are a critical determinant of behavior will more likely formulate social explanations for actions. The catalogue of possible cause-and-effect relationships that perceivers carry around in their heads cannot help but influence the kinds of attributions they are willing to make. Different interpretations stemming from different beliefs help explain, for instance, why two individuals might interview a job candidate together, observe the same behaviors, and still reach quite different conclusions about the candidate's suitability. Different beliefs lead to different attributions for the candidate's actions, and therefore different conclusions about the candidate.

The key to minimizing conflicts among perceivers that arise from differences in their perceptions is process sharing—talking about the *process*, including relevant beliefs and assumptions, by which the differing perceptions arose. If two supervisors have differing views about the competence of a particular worker, they should look at all three components of the perception process to see where the differences arose. Did they draw their conclusions based on different samples of the worker's performance? What are the assumptions or "rules" by which they constructed and interpreted a perception of the worker?

Consider the differences in perceptions among supervisors and subordinates catalogued in Figure 3–6. Some of these perceptual

[15]E. G. C. Collins and E. B. Blodgett, "Sexual Harassment: Some See It . . . Some Won't," *Harvard Business Review*, March/April 1981, 76–95.

**FIGURE 3–6**  Differences in Perception between
Supervisors and Subordinates

Supervisors and subordinates have different needs, different expectations, and
different personal perspectives, so it's no surprise that their perceptions differ in
important ways. Reconciling these differences in perception—for instance, by
openly discussing them—can help supervisors avoid conflicts with their subordinates.

| Types of Recognition | Frequency with Which *Supervisors* Say They Give Various Types of Recognition for Good Performance | Frequency with Which *Subordinates* Say Supervisors Give Various Types of Recognition for Good Performance |
|---|---|---|
| Gives privileges | 52% | 14% |
| Gives more responsibility | 48 | 10 |
| Gives a pat on the back | 82 | 13 |
| Gives sincere and thorough praise | 80 | 14 |
| Trains for better jobs | 64 | 9 |
| Gives more interesting work | 51 | 5 |

Source: Adapted from R. Likert, *New Patterns in Management* (New York: McGraw-Hill,
1961), p. 91.

differences no doubt arise from differences in what supervisors and
subordinates are willing to call "privileges," "praise," and "interesting"
work. Personal perspective also may be influencing what the supervisors
and subordinates are likely to focus attention on. No doubt such large
differences in perception could be the focus of considerable friction
between supervisors and subordinates. And no doubt this friction could
be avoided if both sides better understood the rules the other side was
using to build its perceptions.

It seems unlikely that two perceivers working from the same pieces of
evidence and using the same perception "rules" would arrive at different
perceptions. Yet wildly divergent perceptions are not uncommon
sources of conflict in organizations. Examining the source of a perception disagreement—differences in information samples, or differences
in the construction and interpretation of the meaning of those samples—provides an opportunity to settle the disagreement and minimize
the conflict that might otherwise arise. The topic of conflict will be
considered in greater detail in Chapter 6.

PERSON
PERCEPTION

Because organizations are groups of people, getting to know other
people is a primary perceptual task for all members of organizations.
Where do our impressions of other organizational members come from?
The answer is that we build perceptions of others from both (a) evidence

we gather about the person and (b) beliefs we have about the evidence we gather. Often this "building" process involves stereotypes.

**Stereotypes**   A **stereotype** is a complex set of expectations and beliefs associated with specific personal characteristics, such as sex, race, or occupation. As noted in the "Focus on: Person Perception," there is a stereotype associated with having a master's degree in business administration (MBA). If you know just this one characteristic of an individual, it brings forth an entire set of beliefs and expectations about him or her. Knowing that an individual has an MBA may suggest to you that the individual is arrogant, impatient, self-centered, and highly focused on money.

## FOCUS ON:
### Person Perception

**MBAs in the Press**  In a recent article about graduates of MBA programs, Meryl Reis Louis noted that there are very strong stereotypes about what MBAs are like and that these stereotypes are, for the most part, inaccurate:

It has become fashionable to discuss MBAs as a class of people with a set of common characteristics. They are arrogant, competitive, single-minded, and motivated by money in their pursuit of the fastest track to the executive suite. The fact that the group encompasses a half million diverse individuals who at some time during the past several decades earned an MBA degree from one of 500 different schools is forgotten when the label "MBA" is applied. It is a little like looking for similarities among adults who sang in church choirs as children.*

Louis goes on to note that MBA programs differ tremendously across schools and even across the years at the same schools. Nevertheless, the popular press commonly portrays MBAs as "inexperienced, arrogant, highly individualistic operators with no patience for team effort . . . MBAs want too much too soon."** Louis concludes that since these negative stereotypes persist despite their inaccuracy, they must serve a purpose. Most likely, these stereotypes are a form of *scapegoating*—a way for older or less well-trained workers to voice their frustrations with the successes of the new generation of businessmen and businesswomen.

*M. R. Louis, "MBAs in the Press: Stereotypes and Unscientific Samples, Wharton Magazine 6 (1981): 12–18.
**O. Friedrich, "The Money Chase," *Time*, May 4, 1981, pp. 58–69.

Where do stereotypes come from? Some may come from experience, from having met a few MBAs who were self-centered, for example. Stereotypes also come from other people. You may be told that MBAs are arrogant and impatient by your friends. The accuracy of stereotypes is always problematic. Obviously, not *all* MBAs are arrogant, impatient, self-centered, and money-focused. Further, having a stereotype will lead us to see things in individuals (through the stereotype's influence on attention, construction, and interpretation) that are not really there. So why do we have stereotypes at all? There are two reasons: uncertainty and projection.

*Uncertainty*   When you meet a new member of the organization for the first time, you have no idea how that person will act. Will the new worker be trustworthy? Will the new worker be responsible? Will the new worker be fun to work with? You cannot *know* these things until you have worked with the new person for a while and gotten to know him or her better.

But what do you do in the meantime? Getting to know someone means working together and sharing experiences. To do this, you must make some assumptions about how the person is likely to act. What does this person—say, a young man—consider to be "forward" behavior? Would you be perceived as "obnoxiously aggressive" if you asked him out to lunch his first day on the job? If you act too friendly will he think you want to borrow money from him? To interact with the individual at all, you have to make some inferences about him based on whatever small amount of information you have about him. The question is not *whether* you should assume anything about the new person, but *how much* you should assume.

Stereotypes assume a lot. But having a stereotype doesn't necessarily mean *acting* on the beliefs it dictates. For many of us stereotypes serve as hypotheses or speculations we can test about what kind of person the new person *might* be. If the new worker has an MBA, we might watch at lunch and see if he is impatient with the waiter or obsessed about the bill. In effect, stereotypes provide a way to learn about another person by providing a series of hypotheses to test.

*Self-Fulfilling Prophecies*   The problem with having hypotheses about a person is that we cannot test them objectively. Hypotheses about how a person is likely to act, even innocent and tentative ones, give rise to self-fulfilling prophecies.[16] A **self-fulfilling prophecy** occurs when an expectation about how someone is likely to act *causes* that person to confirm the hypothesis or fulfill the expectation. Self-fulfilling prophecies were popularized by a stage play called *Pygmalion*. In the play, a bet was made (and won) by an English lord that a common servant girl would blossom into a beautiful and sophisticated princess *if only she were treated as one.*

There are two kinds of self-fulfilling prophecies: passive and active. In a passive self-fulfilling prophecy, the perceiver's expectations do not actually change the "target" individual's behaviors, but only the perceiv-

[16]R. Rosenthal and L. Jacobson, *Pygmalion in the Classroom* (New York: Holt, Rinehart and Winston, 1968).

er's perceptions of that behavior. If a perceiver expects MBAs to be arrogant and meets an MBA, the perceiver's attention will be biased to search for evidence of arrogance, and the perceiver will be more likely to construct and interpret ambiguous actions as arrogance. The expectation of arrogance will likely be fulfilled because the expectation will *drive* the attention, construction, and interpretation processes. And not coincidentally, confirmation of the "arrogant MBAs" expectation should strengthen this passive self-fulfilling prophecy and make it *even more likely* to be confirmed in the future.

In a passive self-fulfilling prophecy, the perceiver and the perceiver's expectations are somehow insulated from the real world. The expectations do not influence another's actions, but only the perceiver's perceptions of those actions. Active self-fulfilling prophecies, on the other hand, are more dynamic. In an active self-fulfilling prophecy, the expectations of the perceiver actually *change* the behaviors of the "target" individual so that they fulfill the perceiver's expectations.

Consider what happens when a supervisor has a high opinion of a new worker. The supervisor acts friendly toward the new worker, gives the new worker opportunities to assume responsibility, and checks on the new worker to see if things are going well or if the new worker needs some assistance. If the new worker fouls something up, the supervisor will see the failure as a learning experience and urge the new worker to shrug it off. In fact, failures by the new worker are likely to be seen as not the new worker's fault—or not even failures!—by the supervisor. In short, positive expectations lead the supervisor to provide the new worker with a supportive climate that includes every possible opportunity to succeed. No doubt such a supportive climate would not be lost on the new worker, and that is how expectations become *actively* self-fulfilling. If treatment of the new worker makes a difference (for instance, confidence leads to better performance), then the supportive climate provided by the supervisor with high expectations will yield a performance that fulfills the supervisor's high expectations.

Compare this scenario to what happens if the supervisor has *low* expectations for the new worker. If the supervisor doesn't trust the new worker to do a good job, the supervisor probably will watch the new worker constantly. All this attention may make the new worker nervous, and thereby more likely to fail on the job. The new worker's behavior will fulfill the supervisor's low expectations. Douglas McGregor summed up the problem of self-fulfilling prophecies succinctly in his comment that in our attitudes toward our subordinates "we may be caught in a web of our own weaving."[17]

Self-fulfilling prophecies highlight the importance of *first impressions* in person perception. The first information received about an individual may evoke expectations (for instance, a stereotype) that lead (through

[17]D. McGregor, *The Human Side of Enterprise* (New York: McGraw-Hill, 1960), 42.

**FIGURE 3–7**                    Favorable Perceptions

Organizations use image
advertising to create a
favorable perceptual set
that will influence attention, construction, and
interpretation of perceivers' sensory inputs about
them. In this ad, the
Navy encourages young
people to think about ca-
reers in the Navy through
the perceptual set "adventure."

Source: *Sports Illustrated,* February 10, 1986, p. 177.

self-fulfilling prophecies) to their own confirmation. It should not be
surprising, then, that corporations are willing to spend millions of dollars
annually on image advertising. Image advertising (such as the advertise-
ment shown in Figure 3–7) tries to convey a positive image of an
organization—for example, that the company is friendly and helpful or
likes children. This image acts as an expectation that leads customers into
positive self-fulfilling prophecies (or so the organization hopes) when
they interact with the organization or read about it in the news.

The potency of first impressions also explains why so much attention
in corporate circles is accorded to clothing. John Molloy's dictum that
"the clothes make the man" forced people to realize that clothing is an
important component of any first impression. One of the first things
most people learn about a new member of an organization is the way the
person dresses. When a new person first enters the hallowed halls of the
organization, how the person is dressed is immediately salient—perhaps
as salient as the person's sex or race, and certainly more salient than

educational background or work experience. Blue three-piece suits convey a certain image—of power, knowledge, seriousness—that can significantly influence later perceptions of and actions toward a new organizational member. While the dictates of fashion may change as executives move up the corporate ladder (see "Wardrobe Passages" at the beginning of this chapter for an example), the role of clothing in those important first impressions remains a constant. Clothing is one way to manage the uncertainty of first impression formation.

*Projection*   In addition to helping sort out how to deal with a new person, stereotypes also serve symbolic purposes. Stereotypes can symbolize how one group of people *feels* about another group of people; that is, what the first group would *like* to think is true about the second group, rather than what *is* true. For example, as noted in the "Focus on: Person Perception," unfavorable stereotypes about new MBAs in an organization may symbolize the feelings of the organization's "old guard" toward the organization's new generation of managers. If the older workers are jealous of the successes of the new MBAs, envious of their higher salaries, upset that the new MBAs didn't have to "work their way up from the shop floor," these feelings may surface in negative stereotypes. The older workers are projecting their negative feelings into their image of the new MBAs in the organization. In this example, the older workers' negative stereotypes do not represent actual characteristics of the new MBAs (though, through self-fulfilling prophecies, they certainly could!). The negative stereotypes instead represent the older workers' feelings about the new MBAs in the organization.

It is important to realize that symbolic stereotypes do not always translate into prejudicial public behavior. In 1937, when sentiment against Asian-Americans was running high in the United States, one adventurous researcher decided to test the relationship between stereotypes and action. The researcher had a Chinese couple visit 250 restaurants and hotels in the western United States. The researcher also contacted each establishment to ask if it would provide service to Asian-Americans. While 90 percent of the responding proprietors reported that they would refuse to serve Asian-Americans, only once was the couple actually refused service in person. Apparently stereotype beliefs and behaviors don't always match.[18]

If stereotypes serve symbolic functions, mismatches between behaviors and (apparent) beliefs should not be surprising. The negative stereotype may represent people's attempt to let off steam in a way that they would never direct at any individual. Another possibility is that negative stereotypes often present such horrible images that actual individuals provide a stark contrast. The new person then can be treated as an *exception* to the stereotype—an MBA who is "one of the guys," for

[18]R. T. LaPiere, "Attitudes and Action," *Social Forces* 13 (1934): 230–237.

example. This allows the stereotype to remain intact and continue to fulfill its symbolic function while the new worker gets treated according to beliefs about his or her *other* characteristics.

Unfortunately, the failure of women and blacks to attain positions of corporate leadership in the 1960s and 1970s suggests that unfavorable stereotypes can have damaging consequences as well. Further, unfavorable stereotypes always claim more victims than just those individuals discriminated against. The organizations that allow stereotypes to be the basis of their personnel decisions are also casualties, as they forgo the valuable contributions of the individuals they erroneously reject.

## COMMUNICATION

The model of perception offered in this chapter also provides an important foundation for understanding communication processes in organizations. **Communication** is the transmitting of information and understanding by one organization member to another through the use of symbols.[19] The effectiveness of communication processes in organizations — how quickly and accurately information is transmitted — can be affected dramatically by the perceptual processes of attention, construction, and interpretation. The importance of perception to effective communication is particularly apparent in the use of nonverbal communication.

As shown in Figure 3–8, communication between two individuals (the sender and the receiver) involves six steps. Intended meaning is the thought or idea that the sender would like to convey to the receiver. In order to transmit this intended meaning, the sender must encode it. **Encoding** is the process of creating a message for the receiver to receive.

Encoding is a three-part process. First, the sender must select some contents of the intended meaning to transmit. To do this, the sender must decide what the receiver knows, what the receiver will assume, and what else must be conveyed. Second, the sender must select a communication medium and channel (or channels) through which to transmit the intended meaning. For instance, will the communication be verbal or written? If verbal, will other channels (nonverbal gestures or voice inflections, for instance) be used? The importance of communication medium and channel selection was immortalized forever by Marshall McLuhan's pronouncement that "the medium is the message."[20] McLuhan's comment serves as a reminder that medium and channel selections themselves convey information. Sending a memo communicates something different from a personal phone call or a face-to-face discussion, even if the words are the same. Finally, the sender must translate the contents selected for the message into symbols. Communication symbols

---

[19]J. M. Ivancevich and M. T. Matteson, *Organizational Behavior and Management* (Plano, Tex.: BPI, 1987), 632.

[20]M. McLuhan, *The Medium Is the Message* (New York: Random House, 1967).

FIGURE 3–8        Communications Model

Communication is essentially a perceptual process. The sender must encode intended meaning to create messages. The receiver then decodes the messages to obtain perceived meaning. Effective communication depends on the sender and receiver sharing an understanding of the rules used to encode meaning into messages. Feedback can be used to help sender and receiver fine-tune that shared understanding.

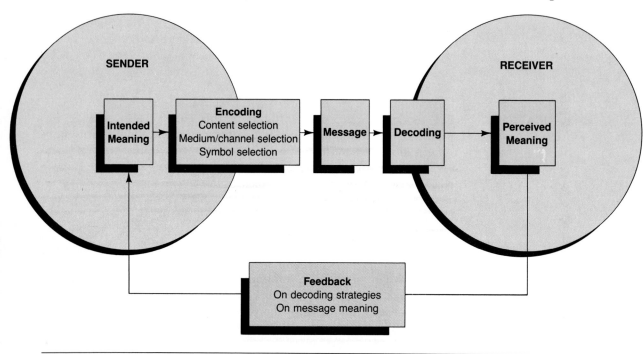

are agreed-upon representations of meaning in a communication medium. Spoken words, for instance, are appropriate symbols for verbal communication.

Once the message is sent, the receiver must decode it. **Decoding** is an attempt by the receiver to reverse the encoding process and extract meaning from a message. Decoding is a perception process. The receiver must select symbols and correctly construct and interpret them. The success of decoding is dependent on the sender and receiver agreeing on the meanings of communication symbols. The perceived meaning that the receiver extracts from a message will not much resemble the sender's intended meaning if the symbols used have different meanings for the sender and receiver.

The sixth and final stage of communication is feedback. Communication is action taken by the sender, and feedback is the receiver's reaction to the sender's message and the perceived meaning of that message. Feedback is critical to communication effectiveness.

BARRIERS TO COMMUNICATION

Communication is essentially a perceptual process. Receivers must attend to, construct, and interpret communication symbols to arrive at a meaning for a message. Many communication failures can be explained as problems of perception. We will consider two examples of communication problems here: problems with attention and problems with interpretation.

**Attention and Information Overload** One of the biggest barriers to effective communication is information overload. As noted earlier, information overload occurs when there is more information available than the receiver can decode. In perceptual terms, this is a problem of limited attention. Managers are buried under an avalanche of information transmitted to them daily from a variety of sources: subordinates, superiors, outside mail, and newspapers, to name a few. The problem is deciding what to attend to. As noted in the beginning of this chapter, attention is a scarce resource. Much of the communication directed at a manager may be "noise." It may be unimportant or redundant information of little or no value to the manager. No manager can attend to all of the available information in order to decide what is important and what is not. The manager must select which messages to decode. Given that uncertainty is a defining characteristic of organizations, the receiver will not always know which messages are the most important. Therefore, the first barrier to effective communication is that any single message may not even be received.

Anything that can increase the salience of a message will make it more likely to be received. For instance, unusual formats or colors often are used in resumes to set them apart from the sea of look-alike resumes submitted for job openings. Motivations of the receiver—the individual for whom the communication is intended—also play a role. Communication attempts from above usually are attended to more carefully than those from below.

**Interpretation and Decoding** Figure 3–9 suggests that attention to (and even appropriate construction of) a message is not sufficient to ensure effective communication. As noted earlier in the chapter, the interpretation process in perception attaches meaning to sensory inputs. For information to be communicated accurately, the "rules" behind the encoding of the message must be shared by the information decoder. The receiver must share the sender's views about what aspects of the intended message need to be transmitted, and the receiver must share the sender's beliefs about the meanings attached to communication symbols and channels. In the communication failure shown in Figure

**FIGURE 3–9**          Encoding/Decoding

In communication, a per-
ceiver can construct a correct representation of incoming sensory inputs
but still miss the message
by not making the correct
interpretation, as the pictured scientists have
done. Perceivers often
need to "read between
the lines"—interpret
meaning beyond what is
explicitly said, perhaps
based on nonverbal cues.
A shared set of rules and
expectations is essential if
this type of communica-
tion is to be effective.

"Matthews ... we're getting another one of
those strange 'aw blah es span yol' sounds."

3–9, the scientists have attended to and built appropriate constructions
of the dolphins' messages. However, the scientists do not know the rules
for decoding the message: they have not figured out that the dolphins
are speaking Spanish. The scientists have attended to the correct symbols
and constructed a correct representation, but they cannot accurately
decode the dolphins' communication attempts.

When two communicators literally are not speaking the same
language, the importance of shared encoding/decoding rules seems
obvious. The importance of sharing rules may be less obvious, however,
when two people *seem* to be speaking the same language but really are
not. There is a story about a plumber who wrote to the government to
find out if it was safe to use hydrochloric acid to unclog drains. The
government responded that, "The efficacy of hydrochloric acid is
indisputable, but the corrosive residue is incompatible with metallic

permanence." What the government meant, of course, was that hydro-chloric acid "eats the hell out of pipes"—a message that would have been significantly more understandable to a relatively uneducated plumber.[21]

Every occupation or profession—in fact, every group of people—uses special words or attaches special meanings to common words. These special words or common words used with special meanings are called jargon. **Jargon** summarizes a group's common experiences and history and allows the simple communication of complex meanings by group members. Unfortunately, jargon also requires shared understanding and shared experiences to be interpreted correctly.

Effective communication goes beyond knowing how to say what you want to say. Sometimes you also have to know *when* to say it. As noted in the "INTERNATIONAL FOCUS ON: Communication," cultural norms determine when and how certain communications can take place. Unless you know when a communication is appropriate, even the right words won't get the message across.

## IMPROVING COMMUNICATION EFFECTIVENESS

Because communication is essentially a perceptual process, communication can be improved by increasing the probability that the receiver will accurately perceive (that is, attend to and decode) a sender's communication attempt. Two keys to improving the receiver's perceptual accuracy are sender empathy and active listening.

**Sender Empathy**   For communication to be effective, the sender must empathize with the receiver. **Empathy** is the ability of one individual to appreciate another's perspective. Obviously, if the receiver speaks only Spanish, a message in English is unlikely to convey the intended meaning. Even within the same language, however, empathy can help a sender ensure that the intended meaning is the one received. Which channels is the receiver likely to attend to? What meaning will the receiver attach to the choice of a particular communication medium? Will the receiver attach the same meanings to our symbols as we do?

Senders often fail to realize that subtle shades of meaning can be quite group-specific and embedded in personal experience. Does "participative management" have the same meaning for employees at Hewlett-Packard and at General Motors? Since their companies' participative management programs are different, the term will have different meanings for employees of these two companies. Consequently, use of the term *participative management* in a message to an employee of either company will require some clarification. And the clarifications are likely to be different, depending on which company the receiver is from.

[21]K. N. Wexley and G. A. Yukl, *Organizational Behavior and Personnel Psychology* (Home-wood, Ill.: Irwin, 1977).

INTERNATIONAL
FOCUS ON:
Communication

**Courting the Japanese** Despite seemingly overwhelming cultural differences, by 1988 more than 1,000 foreign companies (including 600 American ones) had found ways to bridge the cultural gap between East and West, and to tap Japan's wealth and technology. Essentially, they have found that doing business with the Japanese is like conducting a courtship. As in most courtships, attaining matrimony takes time, patience, and a lot of give and take. Even when the language barrier is bridged, foreign executives find themselves mired in fine detail and the subtlety of Japanese communication and negotiation.

Because Japan is a very private society, establishing personal contacts is the first step in building successful business relationships. Unlike in America, where correspondence is an accepted method for making introductions, letter writing doesn't cut it in Japan. Correspondence is considered too formal.

An American electronics firm discovered the importance of personal contacts, but only after much frustration and near failure. The American company sent several letters of introduction to appropriate Japanese firms that went unanswered. The firm then sent a top executive to Japan to try a more personal approach. This too ended in failure. A chance encounter in a Tokyo bar, however, turned the situation around. The American firm's representative met an English-language teacher who had been employed by a large Japanese electronics distributor. The teacher offered to speak with his former employer on behalf of the American, and before long the American had found a business partner.

Once contact is made with a Japanese firm, it is essential to engage the services of an interpreter. Unlike the English language, Japanese can be extremely ambiguous, a tongue not really suited for doing business "the American way." For example, the

Effective communication requires that the sender realize and adjust to how a receiver is likely to decode messages. Effective communication requires that the sender appreciate the receiver's perspective and tailor messages to fit the receiver's ability to decode them.

**Active Listening** Active listening is the mirror image of sender empathy. Sender empathy means the sender accepts responsibility for ensuring proper transmission of intended meaning. **Active listening** involves the receiver accepting responsibility for ensuring proper transmission of intended meaning.

The term *active listening* originated in the counseling professions.[22] Counselors often find their clients saying one thing but perhaps meaning something else. In such situations, the role of the counselor goes beyond

[22]C. R. Rogers and R. E. Farson, "Active Listening," in *Organizational Psychology: Readings on Human Behavior in Organizations*, eds. D. Kolb, I. Rubin, and J. McIntyre (Englewood Cliffs, N.J.: Prentice-Hall, 1984), 255–267.

words *nozomu* and *kitai-suru* can be translated to mean "expect" and "look forward to," or "hope for" or "desire." Mistranslation of these two words caused quite a bit of friction between the United States and Japan's Ministry of International Trade and Industry (MITI). A congressional subcommittee conducted an investigation of the business practices of Japan's aluminum industry. During the first round of talks, replies were translated to imply that MITI expected or looked forward to the aluminum industry's undertaking certain policies and actions. In reality, MITI said only that it hoped these events might take place. During the second round, the subcommittee members made critical accusations based on answers received in the first round. Fortunately, a well-qualified and observant translator noticed that there had been a slight mistranslation of meaning in the original round of answers.

Relations between a Japanese footwear retailer and its American business partner were nearly jeopardized by lack of translation. Correspondence sent to the Japanese was written in English. Executives at the Japanese firm were embarrassed to admit that they could not quickly and accurately translate it. Meanwhile, executives at the American firm feared that the increasing delays and sometimes total lack of response from the Japanese signaled a swelling dissatisfaction with the relationship. Fortunately, the idea of producing manuals in Japanese was already on the back burner. When the suggestion was made, the Japanese were overwhelmingly enthusiastic. Today, relations between the two firms are better than ever. Some Japanese companies are perfectly capable of understanding written English, but offering them material in Japanese is essential in building smooth relations.

Source: Ko Shioya, "Courting the Japanese," *Management Review* 3 (1988): pp. 54–55.

just listening carefully. The counselor must use feedback to actively assist the sender in clarifying the meaning of the message.

A receiver's active assistance in clarifying the meaning of a message can take two forms. First, a receiver can use feedback to check the appropriateness of decoding strategies even as a message is transmitted. For instance, if a sender uses a symbol whose meaning is ambiguous, the receiver can request more information about the sender's use of the term. ("By participative management, did you have in mind something like suggestion boxes or employee committees?") Second, a receiver can help clarify the meaning of a message by reflecting the received meaning back to the sender. ("It seems like you're very angry about what's happened. Is that right?") Feedback about received meaning gives the sender a chance to try again if a message was not received as the sender intended. Of course, feedback is itself another message and therefore also susceptible to lost meaning when the sender (now acting as a receiver) decodes it.

Impressions are created from a variety of inputs, including the clothes people wear and the cars they drive. Expensive cars may convey status by suggesting that their owners are people of importance. Of course, status is in the eyes of the perceiver. A car suggests that its owner is important only if the perceiver shares that interpretation of cars.

Active listening represents a form of **two-way communication:** communication in which receivers can return messages to senders. Research has shown that one-way communication, in which the receiver cannot return messages to the sender, is more efficient and less threatening for the sender. However, it is also less effective and more frustrating for the receiver.[23] Communication is about transmitting meaning, and two-way communication provides the best opportunity for the sender's intended meaning to be the one perceived by the receiver.

**Nonverbal Communication**   Nowhere is the importance of perception to communication more apparent than in understanding nonverbal communication. **Nonverbal communication** refers to any communication channel other than formal verbal language. It typically includes facial cues, hand or arm gestures, and body positioning. Clothing can be used to send nonverbal signals as well—for example, when a male colleague buttons up his shirt and tightens his tie to signal that a meeting is all business. People also surround themselves with objects (such as fancy cars, walnut desks, and corner offices) that communicate who they are—or who they would like to be.

[23]H. J. Leavitt and R. A. H. Mueller, "Some Effects of Feedback on Communications," *Human Relations* (November 1951):401–410.

Nonverbal communication channels often are used to supplement verbal communication by highlighting or reinforcing parts of a verbal message. Verbal messages have two advantages over nonverbal messages. First, verbal communication is an accepted and expected channel for transmitting information. Therefore, it is likely to be attended to. Second, verbal communication in the form of language has codified rules of interpretation, so that basic meanings of verbal messages should be readily accessible to perceivers.

Nonverbal communication is generally more uncertain, both in meaning and in likelihood of receipt. Some perceivers may not attend to nonverbal communication attempts or may completely misunderstand them. What is the meaning of a wink at the end of a sentence? What does it mean if a speaker turns away when sending a message? Or, as noted in the "Focus on: Nonverbal Communication," when is a kiss just a kiss?

The meaning of nonverbal communication is particularly ambiguous when it is *inconsistent* with a simultaneously transmitted verbal message. A subordinate may turn away, for instance, while complimenting a superior, thus betraying other (and not so positive!) feelings. The verbal communication channel usually is easy for a sender to control. Nonverbal channels (such as facial expressions) may be less controllable and thereby provide more direct access to a sender's real feelings. But of course, that is only if the receiver knows the "rules" for decoding nonverbal messages.

---

## Focus on:
### Nonverbal Communication

**A Kiss Instead of a Handshake?** It happens in a split second: You've been kissed by a business associate. Social kissing—the peck on the cheek—has become so widespread that it's spilling over into the business world. In certain corporate circles, at company parties and even in offices, some people who barely know each other exchange kisses as freely as handshakes.

Yet many people find corporate kissing awkward and confusing. Both men and women say they are often unsure about just whom to kiss, and under what circumstances. And recipients of corporate kisses often are horrified. Indeed, etiquette gurus say corporate kissing is usually a faux pas unless the participants are close friends outside the workplace.

But when two people aren't close friends, the recipient of a corporate smooch often feels uncomfortable. Part of the problem is that those who have been kissed are suspicious of the kisser's motives; are they trying to sell something, ingratiate themselves, or impress others? Many kissers say they do it because it puts people at ease.

As the practice spreads, businesspeople increasingly face the dilemma of whether to kiss. Steve Hayden, chief creative officer of the advertising agency BBDO/Los Angeles, says deciding can be hard because there are "about 17 variables"—including the

*(Continued)*

city, business, ages, and ranks of the two people—to consider before kissing, while a kiss happens in an instant.

People who move in many different corporate circles may become especially confused. Hayden says he is unsure whether to kiss in business relationships about 10 percent of the time. "We go from a Japanese meeting to a meeting with passionate movie people to a meeting with staid New Yorkers. You start getting your signals mixed up."

He recently met with a female executive from a big Chicago-based company about a new business pitch and gave her a buss on the cheek. "I had just gotten out of a meeting where that was the behavior. I was in a kissing mode," Hayden recalls. But halfway into the kiss he started to regret it, remembering that the woman "had already expressed some concern that we were a bunch of L.A. hot-tub types." The executive wasn't pleased. "Her eyes kind of widened and she drew back. She was a bit shocked. Then she smiled a little bit,

as if to say, 'This is how they act in Los Angeles.'" BBDO/Los Angeles didn't get that account. "It was all the wrong kiss," Hayden says with a sigh.

There are also geographical differences. Some Bostonians, for instance, won't even *talk* about kissing. Others just dismiss it. George Lodge, a professor of comparative government–business relations at Harvard, says: "I don't recall any instances of kissing at Harvard Business School."

In Los Angeles, a fear of contagious diseases has boosted the popularity of the "air kiss," in which two people put their cheeks in close proximity without touching. Sometimes they just make kissing sounds, and sometimes they just say, "Kiss, kiss." Still, Los Angeles may well be the nation's kissing capital. "Sometimes people purse their lips and come running at you," says Thomas D. Tannenbaum, president of Viacom Productions, Inc. "If someone puts their face up to be kissed, you can't just let them hang there."

Source: K. A. Hughes, "Kissing in the Workplace Poses Dilemma," *Wall Street Journal*, July 6, 1988, 27.

## SUMMARY

Perception is the prelude to action in organizations. Before we can act—before we even can decide what action to take—we must perceive what is going on around us.

Perception is an active process. Perceptions are the product of selection, construction, and interpretation activities by the perceiver. First, the perceiver must sample inputs from the infinitely complex "buzzin', blooming confusion" that is reality. After a manageable set of inputs has been selected, a representation of what is going on must be constructed. Finally, this representation must be interpreted to give it meaning. The meaningful representations of reality that become the output of the perceptual process become the inputs to our decisions and actions.

Because perception is an active process, it is susceptible to influence. Perceiver theories, beliefs, and expectations necessarily influence (and sometimes bias) all three components of the perception process. In fact, without some preconceptions on the part of perceivers, perception could not occur at all. Characteristics of the objects of perception, as well as the context in which perception occurs, also influence the perceptual outcome.

Perception is an important part of organizational behavior. Attribution—a perceptual interpretation activity—is a primary source of our understanding of cause-and-effect relationships. Differences in perception arising from differential selection, construction, or interpretation are at the base of much organizational conflict. Perception is the process by which we come to know and understand other people and their actions in organizations. It is the foundation of organizational communication.

## KEY TERMS

**Active listening**   Receiver accepting responsibility for ensuring proper transmission of the intended message.

**Anchoring-and-adjustment effect**   Tendency of individual perceptions or judgments to be similar to a reference point even when the reference point is arbitrary or irrelevant.

**Attention**   Individuals' choice of where to direct and how to ration their limited sensory input system.

**Attribution**   Process of perceiving the causes of actions and outcomes; provides models of how other people function, what their motives are, and what determines their behaviors.

**Communication**   Transmission of information and understanding from one organization member to another through the use of symbols.

**Construction**   Process of perceiver organizing and editing sensory inputs in a way that makes them potentially meaningful; subject to both input source and perceiver influences.

**Contrast effect**   Tendency of individual perceptions or judgments to be seen as very different from an extreme reference point.

**Covariation**   Central principle of attribution theory, stating that behaviors are attributed to causes that are present when the behaviors are present and absent when the behaviors are absent; covariation is judged by distinctiveness, consensus, and consistency.

**Decoding**   Attempts by receivers to extract meaning from messages.

**Empathy**   Ability of one individual to appreciate another's perspective.

**Encoding**   Three-part process of creating a message for the receiver to receive: selecting contents of the intended meaning, selecting a communication medium and channel, and translating the contents into communication symbols.

**Fundamental attribution error**
Tendency of individuals to perceive others' behaviors as caused primarily by stable, internal characteristics (such as personality) and to perceive their own behavior as primarily a response to environmental characteristics.

**Halo effect**   Tendency for an individual's perception of an input on one dimension to influence his or her perceptions of that input on other dimensions.

**Information overload**   State of perceivers when their sensory input systems are overwhelmed with new, unusual, attention-grabbing inputs.

**Input source influences**   Characteristics of a source object or event that affect perceivers' attempts to direct their attention, including motion, distinctiveness, novelty, vividness, contrast effect, anchoring-and-adjustment effect, and halo effect.

**Interpretation**   In perception, the process of assigning meaning to a constructed representation of an object or event.

**Jargon**   Special words or common words used with special meaning that summarize a group's common experiences and history and allow simple communication of complex meanings.

**Nonverbal communication**   Use of any communication channel other than formal language, such as facial expressions, eye contact, body language, and the use of physical objects and space.

**Objective self-awareness**   Individuals' perceptions of their own roles in causing behaviors and their consequences.

**Perception**   Process by which individuals receive and interpret sensations from the environment so they may act upon it.

**Perceptual grouping**   Tendency of the perceiver to organize sensory inputs into familiar and potentially meaningful patterns by the principles of closure and continuity.

**Perceptual set**   Expectations that a perceiver brings to the perception task, based on suggestions, beliefs, or previous experiences.

**Self-fulfilling prophecy**   Expectation about how someone is likely to act that actually causes the person to meet the expectation.

**Self-serving bias**   Tendency of perceivers to attribute the causes of actions or their outcomes in a way that reflects well on the perceivers or absolves the perceivers from responsibility for poor outcomes.

**Sensation**   Process of nerve endings sending inputs to the brain with no meaning attached.

**Social comparison**   Process of having one's perceptions influenced by the comments and perceptions of others.

**Stereotype**   Complex set of expectations and beliefs associated with specific personal characteristics, such as sex, race, or occupation.

**Two-way communication**   Communication in which receivers can return messages to senders.

DISCUSSION
QUESTIONS

1. In what ways is perception an *active* rather than passive process?

2. Why are good theories about reality a necessary prerequisite to accurate perceptions of reality?

3. Which of the following statements is more defensible, given the view of perception developed in this chapter: "A little knowledge is a dangerous thing," or "A little knowledge is a necessary thing"?

4. Drawing only on your understanding of the perceptual process, provide three explanations for the phrase, "There's no accounting for taste."

5. In what way might the attributions we make about the consequences of our behaviors be more important than the consequences themselves?

6. What suggestions for settling disputes in organizations are implied by the model of perception developed in this chapter?

7. How are our perceptions of our own actions different from our perceptions of the actions of others?

8. Why is it important for managers to have confidence in and expect a lot from their subordinates?

9. In what ways is communication essentially a perceptual process?

IF YOU
WANT TO
KNOW
MORE

A classic article on influences on attention and input selection is provided by Bruner and Goodman, "Value and Need as Organizing Factors in Perception" (*Journal of Abnormal and Social Psychology* 42, 1947: 33–34).

Allport's article, "Prejudice, a Problem in Psychological and Social Causation" (*Journal of Social Issues* 4, 1950), provides a good foundation for understanding the role of stereotypes in person perception. Lord and Kernan provide a similar foundation for understanding the role of scripts in action perception in their article, "Scripts as Determinants of Purposeful Behavior in Organizations" (*Academy of Management Review* 12, 1987: 265–277).

The role of attributions in organizational perception is discussed in an article by Bartunek entitled, "Why Did You Do That? Attribution Theory in Organizations" (*Business Horizons* 24, 1981: 66–71). Pettigrew provides some interesting insights into what happens when attributional processes are driven by stereotypes in, "The Ultimate Attribution Error: Extending Allport's Cognitive Analysis of Prejudice" (*Personality and Social Psychology Bulletin* 5, 1979: 461–476).

A particularly good example of self-fulfilling prophecies at work in organizations is provided by Word, Zanna, and Cooper in their article, "The Nonverbal Mediation of Self-fulfilling Prophecies in Interracial Interaction" (*Journal of Experimental Social Psychology* 10, 1974: 109–120). The role of attributional processes in fueling self-fulfilling prophecies is described in detail by Storms and McCaul in, "Attribution Processes and Emotional Exacerbation of Dysfunctional Behavior" (in Harvey, Ickes, and Kidd, eds., *New Directions in Attribution Research,* Hillsdale, N.J.: L. Erlbaum Associates, 1976).

Goffman's classic, *The Presentation of Self in Everyday Life* (Edinburgh University Press, 1956), offers some interesting insights into the application of perception to the process of impression management. A good book about the face as a source of nonverbal communication is Ekman and Friesen's *Unmasking the Face* (Englewood Cliffs, N.J.: Prentice-Hall, 1975). A good general introduction to communication in business is Mary Munter's

*Business Communication: Strategy and Skill* (Englewood Cliffs, N.J.: Prentice-Hall, 1987).

The tenets of self-perception processes are laid out by Bem in "Self-Perception Theory" (in Berkowitz, *Advances in Experimental Social Psychology* 6, 1972). A summary of some of the relevant research studies on this topic appears in Wicklund and Frey's "When the Self Makes a Difference" (in Wegner and Vallacher, *The Self in Social Psychology,* Oxford University Press, 1980).

While this chapter has touched on the role of perception in language, Whorf develops the controversial belief that language drives perception in his *Language, Thought, and Feeling* (Cambridge: MIT Press, 1956).

ON YOUR
OWN

**Perceiver Influences**    Take a long look at the following picture, and then write a paragraph explaining who this woman is and what she is doing in the picture. Would you want this woman to be your boss? One of your trusted subordinates? Why or why not?

When you have completed your paragraph, think about the story you have written. How much of the story reflects what you see and how much represents construction; that is, goes *beyond* what is presented in the picture? Using the scoring sheet below, try to analyze your story to see what kinds of information you have attended to and what assumptions you have made. Take three statements you have made about the woman and see how much of each comes from the picture and how much comes from your own construction:

1.   Statement about the woman:_____

_____

_____

_____

Facts in the picture that led to this:_____

_____

_____

_____

Assumptions you have made:_____

_____

_____

_____

2.   Statement about the woman:_____

_____

_____

_____

Facts in the picture that led to this:_____

_____

_____

_____

Assumptions you have made:_____

_____

_____

_____

3.   Statement about the woman:_____

_____

_____

_____

Facts in the picture that led to this:_____

_____

_____

_____

Assumptions you have made:_____

_____

_____

_____

CLOSING CASE
FOR CHAPTER 3

# THE MANAGER'S MEMO

FROM: P. Clydesdale, President

TO:     A. Jablonski, Comptroller

RE:      Reports from the Finance Department

I am getting tired of being bombarded with incomprehensible reports from the Finance Department. Your hotshot MBAs may think they are impressing me with their fancy words and long columns of numbers, but they are just telling me they are too big for their britches.

Just last week, I received five more reports from different members of your staff. One report was 23 pages long. When do these people think I have time to read this stuff?

Long as the reports are, they are woefully short on policy ideas. So what if gross margin return on investment is up 3 percent over the last quarter? What does that tell us about our business of selling fire-fighting equipment? Believe me, having started this business from scratch, I could tell your pinstriped people a lot about fire-fighting equipment!

Please establish some guidelines to stem this tidal wave of paper, and then let me know what you've done.

CASE DISCUSSION
QUESTIONS

Assume you are the comptroller, and respond to the president's memo. In setting guidelines that will meet the president's needs, consider what you have learned about perception and communication. In writing your response, try to follow any relevant guidelines you have set for your staff members to follow in *their* writing.

# Learning and Motivation

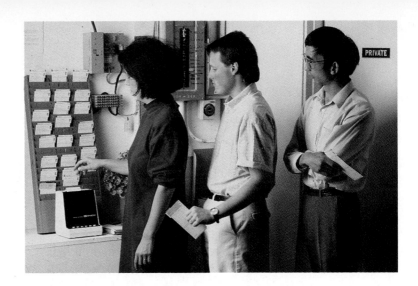

## Bonuses for Just Showing Up

Sick pay is one of those necessary and sensible corporate institutions that is often abused. If employees are hung over or simply don't feel like working because it is a lovely day, they can call in with a feigned case of the blahs. That escape hatch from work is threatened by a newfangled idea aimed at dedicated malingerers: well pay.

Now being tried in several small and medium-size companies on the West Coast, well pay rewards people for doing what they are supposed to do: go to work regularly and on time. Some results have been impressive. Reports James Parsons, 59, president of Parsons Pine Products of Ashland, Oregon, maker of nearly 80 percent of the nation's wooden mousetrap bases: "Our absenteeism has dropped 30 percent, and our tardiness is almost zero." Par-

sons' incentive: an extra day's pay at the end of every month to workers who are punctual. Reichhold Chemicals' fiberglass manufacturing division in Irwindale, California, offers half an hour's extra pay for each week a worker completes a full shift without illness or absence. The bonuses are called "sweet pay" (for "Stay at Work, Earn Extra Pay").

Most employees like the idea, but some workers and union leaders seem skeptical. Says Mildred Corriveau, a vocational nurse at one of the 151 nursing homes owned by Pasadena's Beverly Enterprises, whose employees get 5-percent bonuses each month for showing up on time: "It's not enough money to persuade a person to come to work." For some folks, no reward can match the luxury of loafing.

Source: *Time*, August 7, 1978, p. 67.

## THE MEANING OF MOTIVATION

For a manager in an organization, the challenge of managing employee behavior is more than just providing work for employees to do. The manager also must motivate the employees to do the work. Learning and motivation are the processes of directing and energizing behavior at work.

Motivation presents a particularly complex challenge for the modern manager. To begin with, no two employees—not even two employees working the same job—are alike. At any point in time, different employees will have different needs and different desires. What turns one employee on to work may not turn on another employee at all. Further, as highlighted in the "Focus on: Changing Motivations," employees are always changing. What works for an employee today—what motivates that employee to do his or her work and do it well—may not "turn on" that same employee next year, next week, or even next hour! Motivating employee behavior is a process fraught with uncertainty.

Motivating employee behavior also is a process filled with promise. A survey of worker attitudes in the late 1970s revealed that most American workers could work harder if they really wanted to do so.[1] They just don't want to. Instead, workers often play the kinds of counterproductive games described by Donald Roy and Michael Buroway in their studies of American industry, discussed briefly in Chapter 2.

What happens if employees do work hard? When managers properly motivate their workers, worker performance and satisfaction can both improve dramatically. Everyone benefits. At Parsons Pine Products, described in this chapter's opening vignette, a motivational intervention by management dropped absenteeism by 30 percent. Management at Union National Bank also has discovered the power of properly motivating its work force. In 1985, Union's wide variety of individualized motivational programs paid workers $1 million in incentives, while increasing productivity between 200 and 300 percent.[2]

This chapter explores two pieces of the employee motivation puzzle. First, motivating employees means that employees must feel they will gain something personally through their actions. It is not enough that accomplishment of a task is important for the welfare of the organization. To energize an employee, managers must make the accomplishment of work tasks contribute to the welfare of the employee as well. This is the realm of content theories of motivation. **Content theories of motivation** outline what workers want and need and therefore what tools managers can use to energize their subordinates' behaviors.

Second, motivating employees means that their actions must be properly *directed*. This implies that the employees have learned what

---

[1] R. A. Katzell, "Changing Attitudes toward Work," in *Work in America: The Decade Ahead*, eds. C. Kerr and J. Rosow (New York: Van Nostrand Reinhold, 1979): 35–37.

[2] W. Dierks and K. A. McNally, "Incentives You Can Bank On," *Personnel Administrator* (March 1987): 60–65.

FOCUS ON:
Changing
Motivations of
the American
Work Force

**The New Look of the New Generation** During the business ebbs and flows of the 1980s, at least one consistent trend emerged: America's celebrated generation of young, upwardly mobile professionals no longer was taking its show on the road. U.S. Census Bureau statistics have revealed a steady decline in the proportion of the working population changing addresses each year.

Many companies have found the new reality of executive *nonrelocation* to be a problem. The Norton Company, a large New England manufacturing concern, saw refusals of corporate transfers double to over 30 percent in just a few years. Other companies have run into similar problems.

Why the change? Dual-career marriages are one of the chief causes. The number of dual-career marriages has been rising steadily. Perhaps of more importance is the fact that many working women today have careers that they take just as seriously as their husbands; not just jobs that can be started or stopped according to the career fortunes of their spouses. Even nonworking wives today are less willing to "grin and bear" corporate uprooting.

"Quality of life" concerns—family, recreation, and community activities—also have fueled the change. A survey of 200 new college graduates at AT&T in 1980 revealed a decreased interest in accepting the sacrifices necessary to scale the corporate ladder. The "other" interests apparently have gained equal time in career decisions. Noted Pearl Meyer, a management-consulting firm executive, "Nowadays a manager will decide he just plain likes it where he is. He likes the town, he likes the fishing, he likes coaching Little League, and it's all worth more to him than bigger bucks or a bigger job."

The result of these changes may be accelerated decentralization in American industry. If the talent won't come to the companies, the companies will have to go to the talent. New advances in information-processing technologies have threatened to make organizations of the 1990s nothing more than networks of home phone lines. Several U.S. electronics companies have started down that road already.

Source: "America's New Immobile Society," *Business Week,* July 27, 1981, pp. 58–62.

needs to be done, and how and when to do it. Directing behavior is the realm of process theories of motivation. **Process theories of motivation** describe how managers can use knowledge of subordinates' needs and desires to direct subordinate behavior appropriately.

ENERGIZING
BEHAVIOR:
CONTENT
THEORIES

Motives, needs, wishes, and desires are all terms used (for the most part interchangeably) to describe the reasons behind worker behaviors. In some cases these terms refer to physiological necessities (such as the need for food and water); in other cases they refer to outcomes that individuals would like to have but certainly could live without (such as power and achievement).

Content theories of human motivation summarize the kinds of motives that energize worker behaviors. Since different people seem to have different needs, wishes, and desires that are constantly changing, managers need to have a framework for understanding what motives people are likely to act upon and how those motives are likely to evolve over time. These issues are within the realm of content theories of motivation. There are a number of content theories. We will examine three in this chapter: Maslow's need hierarchy, Herzberg's two-factor theory, and McClelland's learned needs. We will examine the basic tenets of each theory, its shortcomings, and its unique contribution to our understanding of human motivation.

## MASLOW'S NEED HIERARCHY

In Chapter 2, Maslow's need hierarchy was introduced as an important component of the human relations movement. Maslow's views of human motivation were based on several assumptions. First, Maslow proposed five principal categories of human wants and needs.[3]

1.  *Basic physiological needs.* These include hunger, thirst, and sex drives.
2.  *Safety needs.* Concern about protection from physical sources of harm, including shelter from the weather.
3.  *Belonging/affiliation needs.* The need for interpersonal relationships with others that include personal liking, affection, care, and support.
4.  *Esteem needs.* The need for respect, positive regard, status, and recognition from others.
5.  *Self-actualization needs.* The need to fulfill one's potential—to be all that one can be.

Second, as shown in Figure 4–1, Maslow believed that there was a specific order in which individuals would pursue the fulfillment of these needs. For instance, since the basic physiological needs are the most primary needs, attention will be focused first on their fulfillment. Only after these basic physiological needs have been met will an individual's attention turn to the fulfillment of needs higher up on the need hierarchy. From Maslow's perspective, then, self-actualization is a need that individuals will pursue only after *all* their other needs have been met. These rules for attention to and fulfillment of needs in the hierarchy are known as the satisfaction-progression hypothesis: unfulfilled lower-order needs take precedence over unfulfilled higher-order needs, and fulfillment of lower-order needs leads to a progression of attention up the hierarchy to higher-order needs. A literary example of what happens to motivation when basic needs are unfulfilled is provided in the "Focus on: The Hierarchy of Needs."

While many of us rely on money as a primary motivator, content theories suggest that workers want or need a variety of things on the job, including a sense of belonging or accomplishment.

[3]A. H. Maslow, "A Theory of Human Motivation," *Psychological Review* (July 1943): 370–396.

**FIGURE 4–1**                    Maslow's Hierarchy of Needs

Maslow's need hierarchy
helps explain differences
in needs among employ-
ees and across time. Ac-
cording to Maslow's the-
ory, employees turn their
attention to higher-order
needs only when lower-
order needs have been
fulfilled.

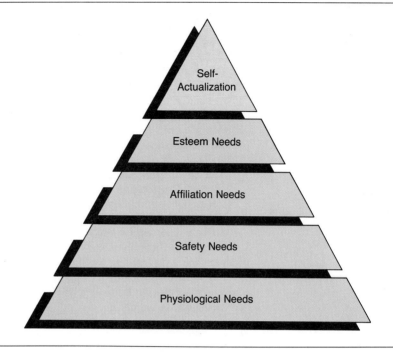

Maslow's need hierarchy was the prototype of *hierarchical* theories of human motivation. It represented a significant departure from economic theories of worker motivation. As a result, the theory had an important impact in three ways. First, Maslow's need hierarchy presented an entire array of noneconomic worker needs. If an employee doesn't respond to economic incentives, managers have alternative sources of employee motivation to consider. Second, Maslow's hierarchy provided an impor-tant explanation for the changing motivations of workers over time. When a new employee first starts on the job, needs lower on the hierarchy—physiological or safety needs—are likely to command the most attention. Later, as these needs are fulfilled, the employee's attention will turn to the fulfillment of higher-order needs, such as gaining the acceptance and respect of coworkers. Finally, Maslow's need hierarchy explained the motivational differences among employees. Though the need hierarchy is the same for all individuals, at any point in time individuals are likely to be at different levels of the hierarchy, depending upon which of their needs have been fulfilled and which have not.

Research has not been kind to Maslow's need hierarchy theory. A general review of need hierarchy studies revealed no consistent support for Maslow's five need categories or for Maslow's satisfaction-progression

FOCUS ON:

The Hierarchy
of Needs

**One Day in the Life**  One of the reasons that need hierarchy theories may be so appealing is that it is easy to believe that certain types of needs are more "basic" than others, and that they will command our full attention when left unfulfilled. A classic example of what happens when basic needs are unfulfilled is provided in a novel by Alexander Solzhenitsyn, *One Day in the Life of Ivan Denisovich.*

Ivan Denisovich Shukhov, the title character of the story, is a victim of the Stalinist post–World War II purges. Ivan is no one special; he is just an ordinary soldier whom fate has relegated to a Siberian concentration camp. There, in his fight for survival, Ivan's focus on basic needs becomes painfully apparent in his description of a typical day in the camp:

> Shukhov went to sleep fully content. He'd had many strokes

of luck that day; they hadn't put him in the cells; they hadn't sent his squad to [hard labor]; he'd swiped a bowl of kasha at dinner; the squad leader had fixed the rates well; he'd built a wall and enjoyed doing it; he'd smuggled that bit of hacksaw blade through; he'd earned a favor from [a friend]; he'd bought that tobacco. And he hadn't fallen ill. He'd got over it.

A day without a dark cloud. Almost a happy day.

It is easy to see the need hierarchy in Ivan's description of a day in his life at the camp. The focus of the description is on basic needs. This is not a day that a Fortune 500 executive would be fully content with. But then, an executive's daily struggle is for achievement and recognition. Ivan's struggle is for survival.

Source: A. Solzhenitsyn, *One Day in the Life of Ivan Denisovich* (New York: Bantam Books, 1984), p. 159.

rule.[4] These studies suggest that workers can distinguish only between broad categories of lower-order and higher-order needs. Within these broad categories, there seems to be little relationship between fulfillment of one need and attention to another.

A modification of Maslow's need hierarchy was proposed by Clay Alderfer. Alderfer's views on motivation arose from the results of questionnaires he gave to over 100 employees at several levels of responsibility in a bank.[5] Alderfer's work led him to propose that there are *three* (rather than Maslow's five) primary categories of human needs. These categories are:

 *Existence.* The basic physiological needs (hunger and thirst) and protection from physical danger.

[4] M. A. Wahba and L. G. Bridwell, "Maslow Reconsidered: A Review of the Research on the Need Hierarchy Theory," *Organizational Behavior and Human Performance* 15 (1976): 212–240.

[5] C. P. Alderfer, "An Empirical Test of a New Theory of Human Needs," *Organizational Behavior and Human Performance* 4 (1969): 141–175.

2. *Relatedness.* Social and affiliation needs, and the need for respect and positive regard from others.
3. *Growth.* The need to develop and realize one's potential.

By establishing these broader categories of human needs, Alderfer retained the idea of a hierarchy of needs, but offered a less rigid version of Maslow's "satisfaction-progression" hypothesis. For example, since Maslow's social and esteem needs are together in Alderfer's ERG model under the umbrella of "relatedness" needs, neither takes fulfillment precedence over the other.

Unlike Maslow's, Alderfer's model also proposes a frustration-regression hypothesis. If fulfillment of a higher-order need is blocked—if something prevents the higher-order need from being fulfilled—an individual's attention will *regress* back toward further fulfillment of needs lower in the hierarchy. For instance, if relatedness needs are relatively fulfilled but growth-need fulfillment is blocked, an individual's attention will return to fulfillment of relatedness needs. Finally, Alderfer's ERG model also assumes that growth needs become *more* rather than less important as they become fulfilled.

Research on Alderfer's modifications to Maslow's theory has been supportive. Both laboratory and field studies have generated support for Alderfer's three categories and their hierarchical fulfillment relationship.[6] Other studies have supported Alderfer's seemingly paradoxical contention that need strength will increase when a need is either very satisfied or very unsatisfied.[7]

## HERZBERG'S TWO-FACTOR THEORY

A second major content theory of motivation is the **two-factor theory.** The two-factor theory traces its origins to Frederick Herzberg's study of 200 white-collar engineers and accountants.[8] Unlike other content theories of motivation, the two-factor theory is framed in terms of factors that affect work satisfaction (rather than needs). The two categories of factors proposed in the two-factor theory are:

1. *Hygiene factors.* A broad category of working conditions, including safety and amount of pay, quality of supervision, and the social environment of work.
2. *Motivators.* Factors associated with the performance of work, such as recognition for a job well done, achievement, autonomy, and responsibility.

[6]J. P. Wanous and A. Zwany, "A Cross-Sectional Test of Need Hierarchy Theory," *Organizational Behavior and Human Performance* 18 (1977): 78–97.

[7]C. P. Alderfer, R. E. Kaplan, and K. K. Smith, "The Effect of Variations in Relatedness Need Satisfaction on Relatedness Desires," *Administrative Sciences Quarterly* 19 (1974): 507–532.

[8]F. Herzberg, *Work and the Nature of Man* (Cleveland: World, 1966).

**FIGURE 4–2**         A Summary of Factors Affecting Job
                       Satisfaction and Dissatisfaction

Herzberg's research suggests that job dissatisfaction and job satisfaction are caused by different aspects of the work setting. Job dissatisfaction is high when hygiene factors (like work conditions and supervision) are inadequate. Job satisfaction is high when motivators (like achievement and recognition) are present.

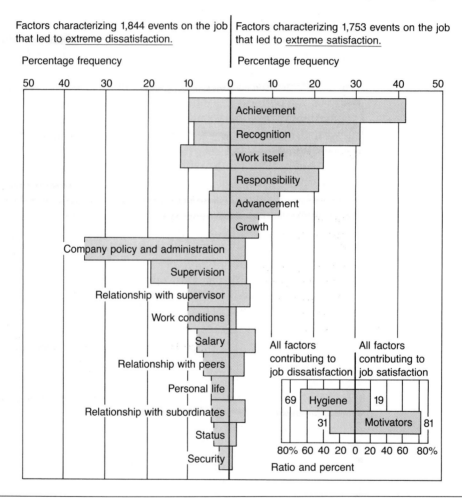

Source: Frederick Herzberg, "One More Time: How Do You Motivate Employees?" *Harvard Business Review* (January/February 1968), 57.

The two-factor theory of needs specifically applies to understanding job satisfaction in work settings. As shown in Figure 4–2, the two-factor theory proposes that the determinants of job satisfaction and job dissatisfaction are not the same. According to the theory, dissatisfaction results when the work setting does not fulfill the worker's basic needs—the **hygiene factors** in the terms of the theory. A worker who is worried about safety on the job, or basic pay, cannot devote attention to the task at hand and therefore cannot do a good job. However, fulfillment of these hygiene needs *does not* satisfy workers. Rather, fulfillment of these basic needs simply *prevents* dissatisfaction. Satisfaction depends on a second set of factors, **motivators,** which include the opportunity for achievement, responsibility, and recognition through work.

Like Maslow's need hierarchy and Alderfer's ERG model, the two-factor theory subscribes to a form of the "satisfaction-progression" hypothesis. In the two-factor theory, hygiene factors are *preconditions* for job satisfaction. Management cannot satisfy workers by fulfilling worker hygiene needs, but unfulfilled hygiene needs can prevent workers from being satisfied. Motivators, on the other hand, satisfy workers, but only when management has also fulfilled their hygiene needs.

Herzberg's two-factor theory has come under fire for a variety of reasons.[9] The studies on which it is based have been challenged on methodological grounds. For instance, the two-factor theory may be the result of an attributional bias. People may want to perceive and blame features of the work setting as the causes of their job dissatisfaction, even if this is not true. Further, Herzberg's separation of factors affecting dissatisfaction and satisfaction has not stood up to empirical scrutiny. Studies have shown that achievement and recognition—two motivators related to satisfaction according to the theory—also influence job dissatisfaction. Finally, the importance of the two-factor theory revolves around the idea that job satisfaction and dissatisfaction are critically related to work motivation and performance. As discussed in Chapter 2, this is at best a tenuous assumption.

## McCLELLAND'S LEARNED NEEDS

David McClelland's work on **learned needs** provides a final content theory of motivation. McClelland's work focused on three categories of needs:

1. *Need for affiliation.* Concern for establishing and maintaining social relationships.
2. *Need for power.* Concern for reputation, responsibility, influence, and impact.
3. *Need for achievement.* Concern for establishing and maintaining high levels of performance quality.

McClelland's approach to motivation differs from that of the other content theories discussed. McClelland emphasizes that affiliation,

---

[9]R. J. House and L. A. Wigdor, "Herzberg's Dual-Factor Theory of Job Satisfaction and Motivation: A Review of the Evidence and a Criticism," *Personnel Psychology* 20 (1967): 369–390.

power, and achievement are *learned* needs rather than instinctive desires. In a dramatic demonstration that needs can be learned, McClelland attempted to improve the economic climate of Kakinada, India, by training 50 of its businessmen to have greater needs for achievement. Training was accomplished by encouraging the training group to imagine positive outcomes of aggressive investment strategies, to imagine how these strategies would fulfill their personal needs, and to set goals. Follow-up studies several years later revealed that the "trained" businessmen had invested more money in local business ventures, started more new businesses, participated in more community development activities, and created more new jobs in the community than their untrained counterparts.[10]

Because the needs for affiliation, power, and achievement are learned, McClelland contends that they fit into no static hierarchical ordering. Instead, different individuals feel different needs in differing degrees. Thus, there are no "satisfaction-progression" or "frustration-regression" relationships among the needs.

McClelland's learned needs have received considerable support. In his book, *The Achieving Society*,[11] McClelland presents evidence for a relationship between the current state of economic development of countries and measured levels of need for achievement in those countries. Studies also have demonstrated that individuals with strong needs for affiliation have better attendance records and respond best to performance feedback that is personally supportive rather than task-related. Finally, research has shown individuals with strong needs for power to be superior performers, more likely to occupy supervisory positions, and to be rated higher in leadership by coworkers.[12]

McClelland's views do not address basic physiological needs such as Maslow's physiological and safety/security needs or Herzberg's hygiene needs. It is unlikely that McClelland believed that such needs did not exist. Instead, McClelland's is a theory of *learned* needs rather than the basic needs instinctive to the human condition.

| | |
|---|---|
| IMPLICATIONS OF CONTENT THEORIES | To a student new to the field of organizational behavior, the three content theories of motivation we have discussed—need hierarchies, the two-factor theory, and learned needs—probably seem like two theories too many. Is one of these content theories more correct than the others? |

---

[10]D. C. McClelland and D. G. Winter, *Motivating Economic Achievement* (New York: Free Press, 1971).

[11]D. C. McClelland, *The Achieving Society* (Princeton, N.J.: Van Nostrand, 1961).

[12]R. M. Steers and N. D. Braunstein, "A Behaviorally Based Measure of Manifest Needs in Work Settings," *Journal of Vocational Behavior* 9 (1976): 251–266; E. French, "Some Characteristics of Achievement Motivation," *Journal of Experimental Psychology* 50 (1955): 232–236.

## FIGURE 4–3          A Comparison of Four Content Theories of Motivation

There are a variety of content theories of motivation, but the sources of motivation proposed by each bear many similarities. All theories propose self-development needs and social affiliation needs. Only McClelland's "learned" needs do not posit any basic physiological needs, perhaps because they do not need to be learned.

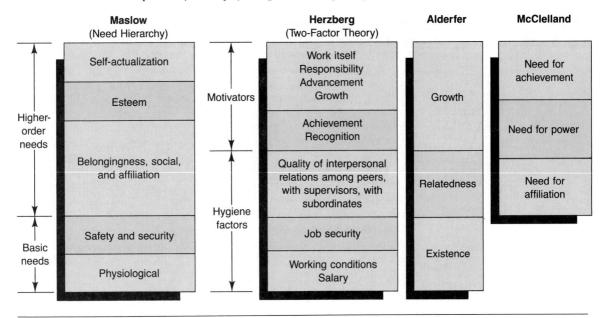

Source: James L. Gibson, John M. Ivancevich, and James H. Donnelly, Jr., *Organizations: Behavior, Structure, Processes*, 6th ed. (Plano, Tex.: BPI, 1988), p. 127.

To begin with, there are important similarities in the *types* of needs proposed by these theories. As shown in Figure 4–3, these theories propose similar types of needs, but divide them into slightly different categories. Only McClelland's theory of learned needs does not hypothesize any hierarchical ordering of needs. However, in modern industrial America, fulfillment of physiological, safety, and security needs is virtually guaranteed by government legislation. It is therefore plausible that these needs simply did not surface in McClelland's work precisely because they are generally fulfilled.

In all fairness to the theories, each has served an important function in the evolution of management theories of work motivation. Need-hierarchy theories highlighted the importance of noneconomic needs—such as Maslow's self-esteem needs or Alderfer's relatedness needs—in motivating workers. Although it hasn't enjoyed widespread support, Herzberg's two-factor theory raised in managers' minds an important distinction between extrinsic (work context) and intrinsic (inherent in the work) sources of motivation. Finally, McClelland's theory drove home the idea that some needs are learned. As noted in the "INTERNATIONAL FOCUS ON: Energizing Behavior," McClelland's view that some needs are

INTERNATIONAL
FOCUS ON:
Energizing
Behavior

**A Cure for Workaholics?** Employees of Isetan Co., a Japanese retailer that caters to the mink-and-Mercedes trade, average fewer than 37 hours a week behind the counter. They work five days a week and must use all of their paid vacation. To make sure they do, each department posts a schedule of all staff holidays six months in advance. Isetan is a pacesetter in Japan's newborn drive to adopt a Western-style, five-day working week. Workaholism is out of fashion. Increasing leisure time was a common plank in the platforms of all three men who tried to succeed Yasuhiro Nakasone as prime minister when his term expired in October 1988.

The change will not happen overnight. Starting in 1988, the workweek was cut to 46 hours, with a further reduction to 44 hours to come in 1991. A 40-hour week probably won't become the norm at major corporations before the mid-1990s. Small companies will take much longer to fall into line. Still, says University of Tokyo law professor Kazuo Sugeno, "It's a turning point for Japanese society."

The growing and widespread support for a shorter week reflects a pervasive feeling in the country that Japan has come of age. "After World War II, people worked very hard to reconstruct the country," notes Koichi Sato, director of research for Domei, the Japanese labor confederation.

"But as the economy of Japan becomes stronger, people start to wonder if the living standard is really as enjoyable as it should be."

The awesome task of rebuilding Japan made long hours' toil an integral part of post–World War II Japanese culture. "The ethic for my generation was 'work hard and be dedicated to a company'," says Sugeno, who was born in 1943. That's still the watchword of most of Japan's salaried employees. Although they are entitled to 15 paid holidays a year, they actually take only half that number, and few take more than four days off at a time. Peer pressure and fear of burdening coworkers are the main reasons.

Younger Japanese are leading the assault on workaholism. While their parents save compulsively and toil long hours without complaining, young people are free spenders out to have a good time. They crowd into expensive health clubs and discos after work, and they flee their offices at 6 p.m. on Fridays in winter to catch a train to ski slopes in the mountains. Many spend their holidays touring Europe or windsurfing in Hawaii.

"Young people today are a completely different species," says Sugeno. "My 18-year-old son can enjoy music, plays, art, novels, and so on. He knows how to use his vacation time. I don't."

Source: "Japan Seeks a Cure for Workaholics," *International Management,* January 1988, pp. 32–33.

learned also explains a few important differences among cultures and allows room for hope if a culture's motivational focus seems problematic.

Taken together, all three content theories emphasize the variety of possible worker needs. This has two important implications for the challenge of managing behavior in organizations. First, these theories remind managers that there is no such thing as an ideal job design. While our later discussions of job design will focus on how to make jobs more enlarged, more enriched, and more involving, it should always be remembered that more of any of these job features is only better for a worker who wants or needs more. This conclusion has led some management theorists to suggest that an important part of selecting a new employee is finding one whose needs fit what the job has to offer.[13]

A second implication of content theories for management practice is the need to tailor compensation schemes to different individual needs. Cafeteria benefit plans, which allow workers to individually tailor their mix of fringe benefits, and incentive schemes that allow workers to choose their own rewards both acknowledge this important contribution of content theories of motivation.[14] These issues will be discussed in greater detail in Chapter 13.

**DIRECTING BEHAVIOR: PROCESS THEORIES**

Once a manager has identified the needs that will energize subordinates' behavior on the job, the next challenge is to use that knowledge to *direct* worker actions appropriately. An employee with needs surely will act to fulfill them. It is up to the manager to make sure that worker need fulfillment is in concert with fulfillment of the organization's needs. Process theories describe how managers can use knowledge about their subordinates' needs to direct subordinates' behaviors. Process theories also provide the foundation for many of the specific management techniques (such as goal setting and job design) that will be the focus of Part 4.

The challenge of directing worker behavior really boils down to two forms of learning. Many on-the-job tasks require behaviors that are already within a worker's repertoire or require only minimal instruction. For example, having a subordinate make marks on a check sheet for each unit produced is a simple behavior that requires minimal instruction. The learning that must take place in these cases occurs when the employee learns which simple behaviors will accomplish the organization's goals and therefore will be rewarded. This type of learning is called **conditioning.**

A second kind of learning occurs when on-the-job tasks require complex behaviors that are not in the worker's behavioral repertoire. Interviewing, for example, requires a variety of verbal and nonverbal skills that a new interviewer has not yet acquired. The **complex learning** that must take place in these cases is the acquisition of a new behavior.

[13]E. E. Lawler III, "For a More Effective Organization—Match the Job to the Man," *Organizational Dynamics* 3 (Summer 1974).

[14]A. Brown, "Today's Employees Choose Their Own Recognition Awards," *Personnel Administrator* 31 (1986): 51–58.

**CONDITIONING**

As noted above, conditioning is concerned with eliciting appropriate work behaviors. In simpler terms, conditioning amounts to building good habits in workers. A habit is an automatic or routine behavior, such as brushing your teeth before you go to bed or cleaning a machine at the beginning of a work shift. In many cases, appropriate work behaviors are inconvenient and do not produce short-term personal benefits. However, they will produce long-term benefits for the organization. Therefore, the manager needs to strengthen the appropriate behaviors in the worker. The manager needs to create good worker habits.

**The "Law of Effect"**   How are good work habits created? The primary principle for building good work habits is Thorndike's "law of effect." The law of effect states that:

> Of several responses to the same situation, those that are accompanied or closely followed by satisfaction . . . will be more likely to recur; those which are accompanied or closely followed by discomfort . . . will be less likely to occur.[15]

The two central concepts of the law of effect are **contingency** and **consequences.** If good consequences are contingent upon (follow) a behavior, the probability of that behavior occurring again will be strengthened: it will become a habit or routine. If bad consequences are contingent upon (follow) a behavior, the probability of that behavior occurring again will be weakened: the behavior will be avoided and will not become habitual. Simply stated, the law of effect says that worker behaviors are a function of the consequences they produce.

In practice, there are two different contingencies. First, there is a contingency between performance and consequences. What level of performance is required to merit desired consequences? Second, there is a contingency between behavior and performance. Which behavior will produce the level of performance required?

An important qualification of the law of effect is satiation. The law of effect assumes that if the consequences of a behavior are desirable, the worker will perform the behavior again in order to obtain more of the consequences. However, if the consequences fulfill the need completely, the worker is said to be *satiated*. The need disappears and will not motivate further behavior to fulfill it.

The law of effect became the basis for J. B. Watson's theory of "behaviorism" in the 1920s.[16] **Behaviorism** is a radical view of human motivation that contends that *all* behavior can be understood by examining only contingencies and consequences. According to behaviorism, thoughts and beliefs are irrelevant to understanding behavior.

---

[15]E. L. Thorndike, *Animal Intelligence* (New York: Macmillan, 1911), 244.

[16]J. B. Watson, *Psychology, From the Standpoint of a Behaviorist* (Philadelphia: Lippincott 1919).

Recognition awards (such as plaques or certificates) increase the probability of appropriate work behaviors only if the awards are desired by employees and are awarded to correctly behaving employees. If employees desire recognition and accomplishment, any acknowledgment of their contribution may be greatly prized.

Behaviorism was popularized by B. F. Skinner in the 1960s through his book, *Walden II,* which described a fictional experimental community run according to the principles of behaviorism.[17] *Walden II* offered readers new insights into the importance of the law of effect in understanding and controlling everyday behavior.

*Walden II* also touched off a storm of controversy. Behaviorism, some said, presented a degrading view of the human condition. The argument was that if human behavior was controlled exclusively by contingencies and consequences, there was no such thing as free choice: all behavior was controlled. Without free choice, there in turn could be no dignity or humanity, since they existed only when an individual *freely chose* to be moral in the face of immoral temptation. In another of Skinner's popular books of the 1960s, *Beyond Freedom and Dignity,* Skinner responded to this critique of behaviorism.[18] He argued persuasively that there was no question that human behavior was controlled by contingencies and consequences, only whether behavior was controlled well or poorly.

**Reinforcement Theory**   How can the law of effect be put into practice to direct worker behavior? The answer is simple: a manager should reinforce appropriate worker behaviors and not reinforce (or even punish) inappropriate behaviors. **Reinforcement** occurs when a manager gives a worker something the worker wants or needs (or takes away something the worker dislikes) when the worker behaves appropriately. This makes the appropriate behavior more likely to occur in the future. Providing approval or recognition to a worker with a high need for achievement will increase the probability that the worker will repeat the desired behavior. Similarly, if a worker has a high need for safety, removing a potential hazard in the workplace following appropriate

[17]B. F. Skinner, *Walden II* (New York: Macmillan, 1948).
[18]B. F. Skinner, *Beyond Freedom and Dignity* (New York: Knopf, 1971).

work behavior reinforces that behavior. This chapter began with an example of how reinforcement was used to decrease absenteeism in two major companies. The "Focus on: Reinforcement Theory" describes the difficulty of using reinforcement theory correctly—and the costs of using it incorrectly.

**Punishment** occurs when a manager gives a worker something the worker dislikes (for example, a suspension or a punch in the nose) in response to *inappropriate* work behaviors. A worker with a high need for affiliation could be punished by isolation—removal from social contacts. The use of punishment will be discussed in more detail later in this chapter.

In applying Thorndike's law of effect to managing behavior in organizations, it is critical to distinguish among several different kinds of consequences of individual work behaviors:

1. Consequences of individual work behaviors for the organization (for example, efficiency, effectiveness, productivity)
2. Consequences of individual work behaviors provided by the organization for the individual (such as wages or promotions)
3. Consequences of individual work behaviors provided informally by coworkers (such as praise or criticism)
4. Consequences of individual work behaviors that occur as part of the behaviors (such as fatigue and social interaction).

What makes an appropriate behavior appropriate is that it produces good consequences. If you brush your teeth, you are less likely to get cavities (a good consequence). If you thank a coworker (a good consequence) for doing something nice, the coworker is more likely to do something nice again. Some behaviors are even intrinsically rewarding— they are their own reward. (These **intrinsic rewards** are what Herzberg's two-factor content theory called "motivators.") For example, the worker pictured in Figure 4–4 (page 150) enjoys making noise and can't help but do so when using his jackhammer.

Whether that worker is tearing up the *correct* road with his jackhammer is, of course, a different matter altogether. What makes an appropriate *work* behavior appropriate is that it produces good consequences *for the organization.* Unfortunately, the individual work behaviors that produce consequences needed and desired by the organization often are not the same as the behaviors that produce consequences needed and desired by employees. If they were, employees would be called players instead of workers. What makes work work is that usually it is not enjoyable. The intrinsic consequences of work behaviors (such as fatigue) typically are not desired by the worker. This has important implications for managers.

Managers need to ensure that appropriate work behaviors will be followed by consequences desirable to the workers, so that these behaviors will be more likely to be repeated. This means finding out what

FOCUS ON:

Reinforcement Theory

**Rewarding A and Hoping for B**

Thorndike's "law of effect" seems a very obvious principle of behavior. Yet it also may be the most widely ignored.

Virtually everyone knows at least one parent who is despondent over a teenager's unwillingness to accept the mantle of adult responsibilities. Or one friend whose love affair has gone sour. What is a typical response to these tragic circumstances? Far too often, the strategy is to give, give, give. The disappointed parent feeds, clothes, shelters, and generally supports the recalcitrant teenager, hoping to get him or her back on the right track; the disappointed lover showers the standoffish partner with gifts and affection, trying to convince the partner of the error of breaking up. While at first blush these actions seem natural and appropriate, the consequences they give rise to are, predictably, disastrous. The teenager *learns* to be a bit more lazy every day; the lover's partner *learns* to pout.

The problem, of course, lies in ignoring the relevant contingencies. Reward children for being a disappointment and they will learn to be a disappointment. Reward a lover for being distant and the lover will learn to be distant. This is the law of effect in its simplest form.

In his article, "The Folly of Rewarding A, While Hoping for B," Steven Kerr has documented examples of this backwards treatment of contingencies in organizations. Two examples he mentions are budget allocations and worker cooperation. When allocating financial resources, most corporations hope for sensible and frugal spending. Yet new annual allocations often are made on the basis of the amount spent during the previous year. Divisions therefore are rewarded with budget increases for doing exactly what no one in the company wants them to do—overspend. Similarly, managers often bemoan the failures of their work force to work together like a team. Yet the basis of most corporate compensation systems is *individual* effort. If individual effort is what the organization rewards, is it really any surprise that individual effort—rather than workgroup cooperation—is what the organization gets?

Thorndike's law of effect is easy to understand. For some reason, it is not always so easy to follow.

Source: S. Kerr, "On the Folly of Rewarding A, While Hoping for B," *Academy of Management Journal* 18 (1975), pp. 769–783.

workers want or need and making fulfillment of those wants or needs contingent on appropriate on-the-job behaviors. If John likes lottery tickets, his manager could give John a lottery ticket when he shows up on time for work.

While this strategy may look good on paper, overall it is terribly impractical. No manager can reinforce the appropriate behaviors of *all* his or her employees *every time* they occur. There just isn't that much time in the day. That is why conditioning is important. The manager must use reinforcement and the law of effect to condition good work habits into the workers. As noted earlier, a habit is a routine behavior. You don't ask

**FIGURE 4–4**

The rewards for work behaviors can be either extrinsic or intrinsic to the actual performance of the task. Wages and compliments are two forms of extrinsic rewards: rewards the organization gives employees in exchange for appropriate work behaviors. The employee in this picture also has found some intrinsic rewards: rewards he receives as part of performing his job, such as exercise and "the opportunity to make lots of noise."

"I FIND THIS WORK TRULY FULFILLING IN MANY WAYS — THERE'S THE EXERCISE, THE SENSE OF ACCOMPLISHMENT, AND, MOST IMPORTANT THE OPPORTUNITY TO MAKE LOTS OF NOISE."

Source: © 1990 by Sidney Harris.

whether there will be good consequences every time you brush your teeth; brushing your teeth is a habit. That means you do it whether it is immediately followed by good consequences or not.

Habits are developed through partial reinforcement. **Partial reinforcement** means that an appropriate behavior is followed by a reinforcer only *part* of the time. This is in contrast to continuous reinforcement, in which *every* occurrence of appropriate behavior is reinforced. If managers had the time and resources to observe and reinforce *every* appropriate worker behavior, habits would be unnecessary. Habits—the tendency of workers to behave appropriately without hope of immediate reward—take the place of continuous reinforcement. Habits keep workers behaving appropriately even when the boss isn't around to observe and immediately reinforce appropriate behavior.

Partial reinforcement can be provided on a variety of reinforcement schedules. Reinforcement can be provided on a fixed or variable ratio of appropriate behaviors (for instance, after every fifth appropriate behavior) or following the first appropriate behavior after a fixed or variable

**FIGURE 4–5**          Reinforcement Schedules and Their Effects on Behavior

Different schedules of reinforcement have dramatically different effects on behavior. Continuous reinforcement means rewarding a subordinate after every correct behavior and is the fastest way to teach someone a new behavior. Variable reinforcement schedules (variable ratio or variable interval) reward correct behaviors only occasionally and promote their persistence even when rewards are not available.

| Schedule | Description | When Applied to Individual | When Removed by Manager | Organizational Example |
|---|---|---|---|---|
| Continuous | Reinforcer follows every response | Fastest method for establishing new behavior | Fastest method to cause extinction of new behavior | Praise after every response, immediate recognition of every response |
| Fixed interval | Response after specific time period is reinforced | Some inconsistency in response frequencies | Faster extinction of motivated behavior than variable schedules | Weekly, bimonthly, monthly paycheck |
| Variable interval | Response after varying period of time (an average) is reinforced | Produces high rate of steady responses | Slower extinction of motivated behavior than fixed schedules | Transfers, promotions, recognition |
| Fixed ratio | A fixed number of responses must occur before reinforcement | Some inconsistency in response frequencies | Faster extinction of motivated behavior than variable schedules | Piece rate, commission on units sold |
| Variable ratio | A varying number (average) of responses must occur before reinforcement | Can produce high rate of response that is steady and resists extinction | Slower extinction of motivated behavior than fixed schedules | Bonus, award, time off |

Source; O. Behling, C. Schnesheim, and J. Tolliver, "Present Theories and New Directions in Theories of Work Effort," *Journal of Supplement Abstract Service of the American Psychological Association*, 1974, p. 57.

interval of time (for instance, the first appropriate behavior after five minutes). These different types of reinforcement schedules have different effects on worker behaviors, as summarized in Figure 4–5.

No form of partial reinforcement is as effective as continuous reinforcement for getting a behavior to occur initially. Every reinforcement of an appropriate work behavior increases the likelihood that the behavior will occur again. Similarly, every occurrence of the appropriate behavior that is *not* reinforced decreases the likelihood that the appropriate behavior will occur again. Continuous reinforcement is useful for initially building up the probability of occurrence of the appropriate behavior. Then, gradually, reinforcement can be given less and less often, just often enough to keep the habit in place.

Consider how you might handle a worker in your organization who is habitually late. You might start out with continuous reinforcement. You could find out what the worker needs or desires and provide it every time the worker is on time. If the worker wants recognition, you might stop by the worker's work station and provide praise each day the worker shows up on time. After a while, the worker's habit of showing up on time should be strong. You could gradually decrease the frequency of reinforcement, reinforcing only once every few times the worker showed up on time. Eventually you might be able to maintain his or her punctual behavior by praising punctuality only during scheduled performance reviews, once every several months. This is partial reinforcement and the law of effect at work.

**Punishment**   On the other hand, you might start out by punishing your tardy worker every time the worker showed up late for work. What would be the likely consequences of this conditioning strategy? **Punishment** means administering an unpleasant consequence (for example, docking a worker's pay) when an undesirable behavior occurs. Punishment has several undesirable effects. First, the point of punishment is to stop inappropriate behavior. But that is *not* the goal of the organization. The goal of the organization is to increase the probability of appropriate behavior. Two possible outcomes of punishing tardiness are that the worker will simply not show up at all or will show up on time but drunk. In both instances, punishment has stopped the original behavior, showing up sober but late, but the behavior that has occurred instead is equally (if not more) inappropriate.

These unfortunate and equally inappropriate new behaviors are not so unlikely, either. One side effect of punishment is to generate resentment that surfaces as "acting out." If a worker feels humiliated for being punished, the worker may act out resentment through different but equally inappropriate behaviors (such as showing up on time but drunk or not showing up at all). Worse yet, the worker may decide to get even with the punisher through subtle forms of interpersonal or organizational sabotage.

Punishment also tends to build an interpersonal wall between the punisher and the worker. The punished worker will be less likely to discuss work with the punisher. Other problems that might have been prevented may blossom into full-fledged crises.

One problem with punishment is that it creates the wrong kind of choice for the worker. As we noted in the beginning of this chapter, behaviors occur for a reason. If a worker is always late for work, the worker must be getting some benefit out of being late (for example, a little more sleep). Punishing this inappropriate behavior means lateness now is *both* punished and reinforced, giving it an expected value of zero—and *a lower value than it had before.* The worker has lost value, leading to resentment and acting out.

Now consider the outcomes of counterconditioning: reinforcing the appropriate behavior (rather than punishing the inappropriate behavior) in the hopes of substituting appropriate behaviors for inappropriate ones. This is the strategy used so successfully by Parsons Pine Products, as described in the opening vignette for this chapter. Reinforcing appropriate behavior (punctuality) creates a different choice for the worker. From the worker's perspective, counterconditioning substitutes the reinforcement of appropriate behavior for the foregone reinforcement of inappropriate behavior. The net expected values of appropriate and inappropriate behavior now are equally positive for the worker, so the worker might as well come to work on time. From the perspective of the organization, counterconditioning substitutes appropriate for inappropriate worker behavior. The probability of appropriate worker behavior is increased *without* risking the undesirable consequences of punishment.

This is not to suggest that punishment does not have its uses. It does suggest, however, that punishment alone is not a complete strategy for managing subordinate behavior. Punishment is sometimes used by clinical psychologists when a patient's counterproductive behaviors must be stopped before any productive behaviors can be learned. In organizations, punishment is most appropriate when a manager can use it to immediately stop counterproductive behaviors—for example, by suspending an employee who shows up for work drunk. Unfortunately, managers cannot immediately punish inappropriate behaviors they don't witness, and punishment becomes ineffective when it is delayed. Further, as noted earlier, the use of punishment still begs the question of what motivated the inappropriate behavior in the first place. If a worker is sabotaging the assembly line because sabotage is more interesting than the job, punishment of the sabotage isn't going to make the job more interesting. At the least, punishment should be used together with counterconditioning, thereby giving the subordinate a greater incentive to perform appropriate work behaviors than already exists for inappropriate ones.

**OB–Mod** The systematic application of simple conditioning and reinforcement theory principles to the management of organizational behavior is known as **organizational behavior modification (OB–Mod)**. OB–Mod encompasses the important aspects of conditioning and reinforcement theory in a simple framework that a manager can apply to any behavioral problem. Five steps are used to establish an OB–Mod behavioral-change program:[19]

1. *Define the target behavior.* This must be a clear and unequivocal statement of the desired behavior. For example, "at work on time" would be defined explicitly: "checked in, work smock on, at your workbench, and ready to begin work when the plant time clock

[19]F. Luthans and R. Kreitner, *Organizational Behavior Modification* (Glenview, Ill.: Scott, Foresman, 1975).

reads 8:00 a.m." This means that a manager must be able to state desired performance in terms of precise events. After all, if the manager can't decide what the desired behavior is supposed to be, how should a subordinate know?

2. *Measure the frequency of behavior.* The success of a change effort needs to be measured against a baseline of normal performance. This is important so that both management and the worker will be able to tell whether progress is being made, and they will know when to reinforce the behavior.

3. *Set reasonable performance goals.* If the subordinate's behavior is to be changed, a goal will give the employee something to think about and shoot for. (The importance of goals in motivating work behavior will be discussed in detail in Chapter 13.)

4. *Monitor behavior.* Keep track of the frequency of occurrence of the appropriate behavior. Requiring the subordinate to collect this information will help maintain the subordinate's involvement in the behavior change effort.

5. *Administer rewards.* Since OB–Mod is based on conditioning and reinforcement theory, the final and most important step is to reward appropriate behaviors. The manager must reward acceptable progress toward or achievement of the performance goals. This increases the likelihood that these desired behaviors will become habits.

Has OB–Mod proven successful? Two researchers identified ten organizations that have used OB–Mod approaches to deal with behavioral problems; in nine of the ten organizations, OB–Mod was successful. Interestingly, in many of the organizations where OB–Mod had been successfully implemented, social rewards (such as praise) were commonly used instead of money to reinforce appropriate behaviors.[20]

**COMPLEX LEARNING**

Complex behaviors are behaviors unlikely to occur naturally or without substantial training and practice. Complex behaviors present a problem for managers because they cannot be simply conditioned. As an example of a complex behavior, consider the golf swing. How would you condition someone to swing a golf club correctly? You could punish poor swings and reinforce good swings, hoping to increase the probability of good-swing recurrence. Unfortunately, a good golf swing is sufficiently complex that you might wait *forever* for a good swing—especially if you were training someone who was just learning to play golf. So what might you do instead? Two options are considered here: **successive approximation** and **vicarious learning.**

---

[20]W. C. Hamner and E. P. Hamner, "Behavior Modification on the Bottom Line," *Organizational Dynamics* 4 (1976): 3–21.

**Successive Approximation** Conditioning and the law of effect also can be used to help workers acquire complex behaviors required on the job. Since the appropriate behavior is unlikely to occur at first, it is conditioned by reinforcing successively better approximations of the final desired behavior.

One variant of reinforcing successively better approximations of the final desired behavior is *shaping*. In shaping, the entire desired behavior is reinforced or not reinforced, but the requirements for reinforcement become more stringent over time. Shaping a golf swing, for instance, would entail at first reinforcing almost any swing, then only reasonable approximations of the final correct swing, then only good approximations of the final swing, and finally only the correct swing. As the reinforcement criteria become more stringent, the behavior of the learner is being "fine-tuned" to more closely approximate the final desired behavior.

Another form of successive-approximation conditioning is *chaining*. In chaining, the desired complex behavior is broken down into component behaviors; successively more complete demonstrations of the desired behavior chain then are reinforced until the final desired behavior is acquired. A golf swing, for instance, could be broken down into five parts: the address, the take-away, the backswing, the downswing, and the follow-through. To chain a correct golf swing, you would start by reinforcing only a good address; then a good address and take-away; then a good address, take-away, and back swing; and so on, until you were reinforcing only good examples of the *entire* chain.

In practice, chaining and shaping often are used together. Extremely complex work behaviors can be broken down into components and (using chaining) acquired one component at a time. Within the process of learning each component, shaping may be used to encourage acquisition.

**Vicarious Learning** Largely ignored to this point in our discussion of work motivation is the role of workers' cognitions (thoughts) in acquiring and performing appropriate work behaviors. The image of learning offered by conditioning, reinforcement theory, and behaviorism is "learning by doing" or learning by "trial-and-error." The worker tries behaviors; appropriate work behaviors are acquired when workers are reinforced for trying them. A major criticism of behaviorist approaches to learning is that they ignore the fact that workers learn many behaviors without ever doing them, just by observing others engaged in these behaviors. This criticism has been voiced by psychologist Albert Bandura, a noted expert in behavior modification:

> . . . It is doubtful if many classes of responses would ever be acquired if [learning] proceeded solely by the method of successive approximations through differential reinforcement of emitted responses. The technique of

Complex work behaviors often are acquired by observation of other workers. Placing new workers next to good role models may increase the speed with which they learn appropriate work behaviors. Vicarious or social learning may help these air-traffic controllers pick up an initial approximation of their complicated task, which is later reinforced with conditioning.

reinforced shaping requires a subject to perform some approximation of the terminal response before he can learn it. In instances where a behavioral pattern contains a highly unusual combination of elements . . . the probability of occurrence of the desired response, or even one that has some remote resemblance to it, will be zero. . . . In cases involving intricate patterns of behavior, modeling is an indispensable aspect of learning.[21]

Learning by observing others is called vicarious learning. Vicarious learning can refer either to acquiring complex behaviors (such as a golf swing) or to learning which behaviors (simple or complex) will be reinforced and which will not. Vicarious learning also is called *social learning* because it always involves observing behaviors modeled by others.

Behavior acquisition through modeling must be different from behavior acquisition through conditioning. Acquisition of appropriate behaviors through conditioning can occur through what is essentially "muscle memory." Imagine that you engage in an appropriate behavior and the behavior is reinforced. The reinforcement strengthens the probability that you will repeat the same component motions of the reinforced behavior the next time you get a chance. With modeling, someone else has engaged in the reinforced behavior, so the appropriate motions cannot be stored in your muscles.

Learning from modeling involves symbolic storage of the appropriate behavior. Symbolic storage of an action is storage of a representation of the behavior, rather than storage of the behavior's component motions themselves. If you observe someone else engaging in the appropriate

[21]A. Bandura, *Principles of Behavior Modification* (New York: Holt, Rinehart, & Winston, 1969), 143–144.

behavior, the observation creates an image in your mind that you retain. If you think or talk about this image or the behavior itself, the words you think or speak also are retained as verbal representations of the behavior. These verbal representations and images of behaviors then serve as templates (road maps or instructions) to later help you correctly engage in the appropriate behavior yourself.

These two different forms of behavior storage—"muscle memory" and symbolic storage—explain why occasionally an individual can do something quite complex without being able to describe how. For instance, can you describe how to maintain your balance? Probably not. Yet, maintaining your balance is quite easy. Maintaining balance is a habit that we learn from doing—from trial-and-error—and we have "muscle memory" for engaging in the appropriate motions. We do not have good symbolic representations of this behavior, however, so we can do it much better than we can explain it.

Vicarious learning and conditioning are complementary forms of learning. As Bandura noted, it is inconceivable that certain complex behaviors could be learned by trial-and-error conditioning. Vicarious learning explains how initial approximations of complex behaviors occur. Reinforcement then can make correct initial approximations more likely to recur.

Vicarious learning is also limited, however. Watching another individual engage in a complex behavior provides a symbolic representation of a gross approximation of the appropriate behavior. However, symbolic representations are exactly that—gross. The subtle nuances of an appropriate behavior often cannot be observed easily. Observation may provide a good first approximation; reinforcement of successively better approximations is required to fine-tune the appropriate component motions.

Interestingly, the sequence of these two types of learning—vicarious learning first, conditioning later—can be reversed to further fine-tune complex behaviors. Some work behaviors are so foreign to new workers that even after a cycle of symbolic acquisition followed by conditioned fine-tuning, the behaviors remain only grossly acquired. In these circumstances, further vicarious observation of others *or even of oneself* (for instance, by videotape) can be helpful in fine-tuning the symbolic representation of the appropriate behavior. Observation of one's own behavior at this point also may reveal differences between actual and intended implementation of the behavioral template. In such cases, vicarious learning and conditioning truly become complementary components of complex behavior acquisition.

## COGNITIVE QUALIFICATIONS

From the view of a behaviorist, contingencies and consequences are all there is to understanding work motivation. If a manager knows what workers need and makes the fulfillment of those needs contingent on appropriate behaviors, appropriate behaviors *will* occur. As noted in some further comments by Bandura, however, this is far too simple a view of human behavior:

> A valid criticism of extreme behaviorism is that . . . it has neglected determinants of behavior arising from cognitive functioning. . . . A theory that denies that thoughts can regulate actions does not lend itself readily to the explanation of human behavior. Although cognitive activities are disavowed in the [behaviorist] framework, their role in causal sequences cannot be eliminated.[22]

Vicarious learning presents undeniable proof that **cognitions (beliefs and thoughts)** are critical to understanding worker motivation and performance. Having thus opened the Pandora's box of cognition, we must examine its further role in determining behavior. In particular, if appropriate work behaviors have been acquired by the worker and outcomes desired by the worker have been made contingent upon their execution, can worker thoughts and beliefs *prevent* the appropriate behavior from occurring? The answer is yes. Two such worker cognitions will be considered in the remainder of this chapter: expectancy and equity.

## EXPECTANCY

The basic principles of **expectancy theory** are presented in an early statement of the theory:

> If a worker sees high productivity as a path leading to the attainment of one or more of his personal goals, he will tend to be a high producer. Conversely, if he sees low productivity as a path to the achievement of his goals he will tend to be a low producer.[23]

The contrast between this expectancy view of worker motivation and the law of effect discussed earlier is both subtle and striking. The law of effect states that if managers make desired consequences contingent upon appropriate work behavior, appropriate behaviors will occur. Expectancy theory instead proposes that if workers *believe* that a consequence they believe they need is contingent upon appropriate work behavior, they will engage in appropriate work behavior. The key difference between these two perspectives is the central role of beliefs in expectancy theory. According to expectancy theory, it is not sufficient to motivate a worker that desired consequences are contingent upon appropriate behavior; the worker must *believe* that the consequences are desirable and *believe* that the behavior will produce them.

The differences between behaviorist and expectancy theories of work motivation are outlined in Figure 4–6. The red and blue boxes in the figure present a simple behaviorist model of worker motivation. If

[22]A. Bandura, *Social Learning Theory* (Englewood Cliffs, N.J.: Prentice-Hall, 1977), 10.

[23]B. S. Georgopoulos, G. M. Mahoney, and N. W. Jones, "A Path-Goal Approach to Productivity," *Journal of Applied Psychology* 41 (1957): 346.

**FIGURE 4–6**    Expectancy Theory

Expectancy theory captures the importance of cognitions (beliefs and thoughts) to motivation. A worker may be capable of superior performance and superior performance may be rewarded. But if the worker does not *believe* that he or she can do the work, or that the work will be rewarded, he or she will not be motivated.

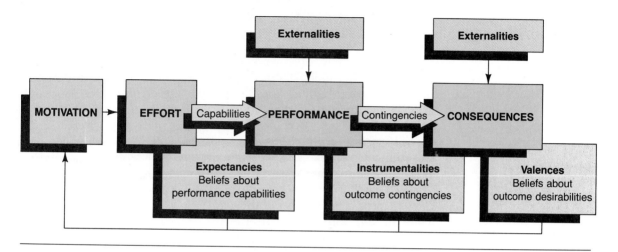

contingent consequences are desired, they will reinforce the worker's behavior, making the behavior (short of satiation) more likely to occur again. Each experience of the contingency also adds to the worker's learning ("muscle" or symbolic memory) about the contingency.

The green boxes in the figure present an expectancy model of worker motivation. The expectancy model adds three "belief" components to the behaviorist model: valence, instrumentality, and expectancy. **Valence** refers to the value of a behavior's consequences, as perceived by the worker. What workers really need is only as important to determining behavior as what workers *think* they need. What people actually need—help, for instance—is often quite different from what they think they need. For better or worse, what people think they need is what they are willing to work for.

Expectancy refers to the worker's belief that his or her own efforts are capable of producing the required levels of performance. **Instrumentality** refers to the worker's belief that attaining the required levels of performance will produce desired personal outcomes (such as monetary rewards or praise). If the worker believes that performance is not really contingent on effort, or that the desired rewards are not really contingent on performance, the worker will not be motivated to engage in the behavior, even if it really would produce the desired consequences. The worker's *beliefs* about contingencies are more important than the contingencies themselves.

What influences the roles of beliefs in motivating worker behaviors? Externalities have a big impact on expectancy and instrumentality beliefs. As noted in Figure 4–5, **externalities** are the causes of a worker's behaviors or the consequences of those behaviors that are beyond the worker's control, such as the behaviors of another worker or the reliability of a machine. Imagine that you work as a salesperson and a performance bonus is available, contingent upon the sales volume of the entire sales force reaching a predetermined level. You cannot achieve the bonus through your own behaviors alone. Instead, you are dependent upon other members of the sales force working hard and making their own contributions to the group's sales volume. What would expectancy theory predict about sales force motivation with this kind of bonus?

Externalities decrease worker motivation because they introduce uncertainty into the perceived causal relationship between individual behavior and attainment of desired consequences. If the bonus will be awarded based upon group performance, it is possible for one individual to work very hard and get nothing if the rest of the sales force doesn't come through with an equally effective effort. On the other hand, if the rest of the sales force does come through with a big effort, an individual could not work hard at all and still end up receiving the bonus. These externalities both decrease the probability that appropriate work behaviors will occur simply because they decrease the perceived strength of the contingency.

Externalities surface in other ways as well. Consider the difference between performance bonuses based upon profit sharing and performance bonuses based upon cost savings. With profit sharing, the receipt of a bonus not only depends on the behaviors of immediate coworkers. It also depends on the (uncertain) behaviors of other parts of the organization, other competitors in the field, and customers or clients. If the marketing department chooses a poor marketing strategy, for example, profits may disappear (and any profit-sharing bonus with them!) even while the production workers are producing at record efficiency. A cost-savings bonus, on the other hand, is a matter of production efficiency alone and reduces a production worker's perceived dependency on a host of other organizational actors.

The inhibiting effects of externalities on worker motivation can be decreased in two ways. First, if management can identify individual contributions to work outcomes, workers will be able to tell who in the work group is pulling their weight and who is not. The work group then can bring pressure to bear on poor contributors. Workers also then can calculate better the likely impact of their own effort on the group's performance.

Second, if individual contributions to the group effort can be measured, managers can separately reinforce them. If workers really are dependent on each other, however, it will not make sense to do away

with group incentives. Reinforcing only individual performance predictably trains workers to be concerned only with individual accomplishments, even at the expense of group accomplishments. Maintaining both
individual and group-based reward systems encourages both individual
effort and group collaboration.

Attributions also play a major role in instrumentality beliefs. Instrumentality beliefs are perceptual constructions of the causal relationship
between individual behaviors and desired consequences. And there is
enough uncertainty in the behavior-performance-consequences chain
that hopelessly incorrect attributions are always possible. For example,
**superstitious behavior** occurs when a worker believes a behavior will be
rewarded even though that behavior is in fact irrelevant. A worker may
engage in a behavior (such as saying, "Have a nice day!" to the boss first
thing in the morning) while *also* engaging in the appropriate behavior.
Since both behaviors are paired with the reinforcement, the probability
of both increases, even though one is completely irrelevant. Attributions
can lead to two other forms of instrumentality beliefs—self-efficacy and
learned helplessness—that are critical to a worker's willingness to
activate appropriate work behaviors.

**Self-Efficacy**  Self-efficacy is a worker's belief that he or she can
produce required levels of performance by engaging in appropriate
work behaviors. **Self-efficacy** beliefs arise in workers' observations of
their work behaviors and the attributions they make about their role in
controlling levels of performance. Workers with high self-efficacy
believe that (1) they have the ability needed, (2) they are capable of the
effort necessary to produce a required level of performance, and (3) no
outside causes will prevent their behavior from attaining the required
performance level. If workers have low self-efficacy, they believe that no
matter how hard they try, something (insufficient ability, inadequate
effort, or outside interference) ultimately will prevent them from
reaching their performance goal.

As perceptions, self-efficacy beliefs can be incorrect. Even if a worker
achieves the required performance, he or she may attribute the
accomplishment to causes other than personal efforts or abilities—
"beginner's luck" or ease of the task, for example. On the other hand,
even if the worker fails to reach the required level of performance, he or
she may find causes for the failure (such as interference from other
workers, lack of time, or even lack of personal effort) that excuse the
failure and allow the worker to continue to believe that the required
performance level is well within reach.

In either case, the worker will have arrived at a self-efficacy belief that
is in stark contrast to the latest consequences received. If correct, such
attributions are tremendously useful. High self-efficacy will encourage a
worker to persevere in the face of failure, and even to continue with a
successful strategy that accidentally has produced poor performance.

Similarly, accurate low self-efficacy beliefs should force a worker to reevaluate his or her approach to a problem, find ways to exert greater effort, or perhaps just convince the worker that assistance (perhaps in the form of additional training) is necessary.

Inaccurate self-efficacy beliefs can be a nightmare for a manager. There is almost nothing worse than subordinates or coworkers who believe that their behaviors are appropriate to obtain the required level of performance—who believe that they have the correct strategy for the task at hand and are exerting the necessary effort—and are *wrong*. As we noted in the chapter on perception, inaccurate constructions by the workers of their role in producing required levels of performance could arise from defensiveness or from personal perspective. Regardless of their origin, in such circumstances workers will not entertain proposals to alter their task strategy, exert more effort, or seek assistance. The performance failures that have occurred will occur again and again because the workers have neutralized the law of effect with their cognitive rationalizations. For a manager, there could be only one worse motivational headache: workers whose attributions cause them to give up when in fact required performance levels are well within reach.

**Learned Helplessness**   When workers believe that they are incapable of producing the required performance, or that the required performance (even if produced) would not lead to desired consequences, motivation to engage in appropriate work behaviors will be low. When work motivation is low enough that workers give up—don't even bother to try—**learned helplessness** has occurred.[24]

Learned helplessness is more tragic than inappropriately high self-efficacy. Repeated failures eventually should lead even the most confident incompetent to see the error of his or her ways. And the confident incompetent at least is trying, so a manager always retains the hope (however dim) that accidentally appropriate behaviors will change everything (performance and expectancies) for the better. Workers who are suffering from learned helplessness never try, however, or try only hard enough to confirm their suspicions, and so never find out that they are capable or with some assistance could be. Learned helplessness thus takes on all the characteristics of a classic self-fulfilling prophecy, and the kind of self-fulfilling prophecy that every manager should be desperate to avoid.

How can overly optimistic self-efficacy beliefs and overly pessimistic learned helplessness beliefs be avoided? Not surprisingly, there are two answers: one behavioral and one cognitive. The behavioral answer is that self-efficacy and learned helplessness beliefs are based on individuals' perceptions of their own behaviors. A manager can help a subordinate

[24]M. E. P. Seligman, *Helplessness* (San Francisco: W. H. Freeman, 1975).

alter inaccurate perceptions by altering what the individual sees. If a subordinate's expectancies are inflated, the subordinate will not be as careful or try as hard as possible. Encouraging the subordinate to carefully keep track of performance can lead to a more realistic perception of his or her accomplishments. On the other hand, if an individual feels unable to do anything well and seems to have given up, a few easy tasks (with perhaps a little extra supervision) may be just the way to get the worker's expectancies back on the road to recovery.

The cognitive answer to inappropriate expectancies is communication. Managers should encourage their subordinates to share their perceptions of the causal factors at work. At the very least the manager should make sure that subordinates understand the contingencies as management sees them and as the organization has laid them out. What behaviors are likely to produce the required performance? What levels of performance are going to be rewarded and how? Misperceptions of work contingencies often are a function of uncertainty. As noted in the "Focus on: Cognitive Qualifications," a little information can go a long way in curing these misperceptions.

Problems arising from self-efficacy and learned helplessness also highlight the importance of performance appraisal as a managerial tool. While performance appraisal often is viewed primarily as a means of assigning compensation, it also can play a major role in diagnosing the causes of and correcting performance deficiencies. Performance appraisal provides the manager a tremendous opportunity to help a worker who is spiraling into learned helplessness to rethink the way to successful new task strategies. Performance appraisal also provides the manager a chance to help the overconfident incompetent face the reality of failures. These motivational aspects of performance appraisal will be discussed in detail in Chapter 13.

EQUITY

Expectancy deals with how workers answer the questions: "Can I obtain the outcomes I want at work? What do I really think the contingencies are? And do I want what I can get?" **Equity** deals instead with the questions: "If I can get the outcomes I want, will they be worth the price I pay? Do I really want them?" As noted in the opening vignette, just because a reward is desired does not mean it is desired at the *cost* of the behavior demanded—such as foregoing a day off on "sick leave."

Animal psychologist Edward Tolman's experiments with monkeys in the 1930s provided a first glimpse at the importance of equity to the motivation of behavior.[25] Tolman was interested in the ability of monkeys to recognize symbols. He would put different symbols on each of several cups. Then, over many trials, he would consistently put

[25]E. C. Tolman, *Purposive Behavior in Animals and Men* (New York: Century, 1932).

Focus on:
Cognitive
Qualifications

**Bringing Discontent to the Surface**
In the late 1970s, Houston-based Geosource Inc. was having trouble. One unit of welders in the company had become extremely dissatisfied. It was found that these welders had seen ads in the Houston papers offering welding jobs for "up to $7.84 per hour"—more than the average wage Geosource welders were making. In fact, Geosource was paying competitive wages and the ad was somewhat misleading: the $7.84 figure was the absolute top wage for the offered jobs. When the unit manager straightened out the misunderstanding, work-force dissatisfaction disappeared.

How did Geosource Inc. discover its problem? It used an employee opinion survey. Many company management teams have adopted the practice of asking employees once a year to tell the bosses what's going on in the company—and how the bosses are doing. Management teams see the employee opinion survey as a source of invaluable feedback about their own practices. Some consulting firms even have data banks that allow companies to compare the results of their own surveys with those of other companies.

The experience of Geosource Inc. suggests that an important function of the employee opinion survey is to identify employee misconceptions that can disrupt worker motivation. Geosource apparently headed off a crisis by assuring employees that they were being treated equitably. Other companies have had similar experiences. General Electric found that more than 50 percent of its work force was unhappy with opportunities for advancement in the company—a serious self-efficacy problem. When the work force was provided a clearer picture of promotion opportunities, the number of unhappy employees dropped to only 20 percent, without any changes in the promotion policy. Apparently just having a better understanding made the difference.

Source: "A Productive Way to Vent Employee Gripes," *Business Week*, October 16, 1978, pp. 168–170.

bananas under the cup with a particular symbol and observe whether the monkey could use the symbol to find the banana.

As the story goes, one day Tolman tried to substitute "monkey chow" for the banana under the cup. Monkeys like "monkey chow," but monkeys *love* bananas. So what happened when Tolman's clever monkey picked the correct symbol and turned over the cup, only to find "monkey chow" instead of a banana? Just like any self-respecting human being under the same circumstances, the monkey got hysterical, threw a temper tantrum, and refused to play Tolman's game any more.

Why was this outcome so upsetting for the monkey? Why would it be upsetting if it happened to you? The consequences were desirable, and the contingencies were not violated. The problem was that the outcome wasn't fair. The monkey had been led to believe he *deserved* a banana for the difficult task of identifying the correct symbol. When you deserve a banana, getting paid off in "monkey chow" just isn't fair.

Equity has to do with fairness judgments and how they influence a worker's willingness to activate appropriate work behavior. Equity theory is an exchange perspective, a perspective that views behavior as a process in which workers exchange appropriate work behaviors for desired consequences. This means workers are aware of more than just which behaviors are appropriate and which desired consequences they will merit. It means that workers also are aware of the *relationship* between appropriate behaviors and desired consequences, of just how much need fulfillment they receive in exchange for how much appropriate behavior.

J. Stacey Adams first developed and tested the ideas underlying equity theory while working as a researcher with the General Electric Company in Crotonville, New York. His research led Adams to conclude that equity is an important component of work motivation. Workers strive to maintain equity in their exchange relationships at work; when they perceive inequity, workers will strive to reestablish equitable exchange arrangements.[26]

**Judging Equity** Equity is a function of the perceived ratio between the inputs a worker puts into the job and the outputs (consequences) he or she receives in exchange. A list of possible work inputs and outputs is provided in Figure 4–7. It should be understood that this is not meant to be a complete list, nor does any worker necessarily think of all these inputs and outputs when deciding if the offered contingencies are equitable. This list does, however, provide some idea of the inputs and outputs that typically are considered by workers in equity calculations.

One key concern in worker equity calculations is how a worker decides whether a particular inputs/outputs exchange ratio is or is not fair. The answer is comparisons: a worker decides whether an inputs/outputs exchange ratio is fair by comparing it to other exchange ratios. Several comparisons are likely: to personal or absolute standards, to the ratios of other workers in the organization, and to the ratios of other workers outside the organization. Personal standards might include an individual's actual living costs; a full-time job that cannot cover living expenses will be perceived as inequitably compensated. Absolute standards would include the federally established minimum wage. When equity comparisons are made either within an organization or to those of workers in other organizations, an individual might compare input/output ratios with those of other workers who have the same or similar jobs, have equal seniority, or have jobs with similar selection requirements.

[26]J. S. Adams, "Toward an Understanding of Inequity," *Journal of Abnormal and Social Psychology* 67 (1963): 422–436.

**FIGURE 4–7**         Possible Inputs and Outputs Considered
in Equity Calculations

An individual decides whether the consequences contingent upon work behaviors are equitable by comparing work inputs (what the worker brings to or puts into the job) to work outputs (the rewards received from the work). Work outputs include both those extrinsic rewards provided by the organization, such as wages, and rewards intrinsic to the job, such as the possibility of personal growth and development.

**Inputs**

| | |
|---|---|
| Quality of work performed | Adaptability-versatility |
| Reliability | Judgment |
| Acceptance of responsibility | Intelligence |
| Job knowledge | Experience |
| Cooperation with others | Personal appearance |
| Self-improvement | Oral communication skills |
| Attitude | Education |
| Quantity of work performed | Written communication skills |
| Initiative | Personal involvement with work |

**Outputs**

| | |
|---|---|
| Job security | Adequate planning/management |
| Pay | Adequate personnel policies |
| Competent supervisor | Amount of work |
| Possibility of growth | Responsibility |
| Fair supervisor | Advancement |
| Recognition | Routine work |
| Adequate working conditions | Status |
| Interpersonal relations with | Difficult work |
| ■   Supervisor | Personal life |
| ■   Peers | |

Source: D. W. Belcher and T. J. Atchison, "Equity Theory and Compensation Policy," *Personnel Administration* 33 (3) (1970): 28; Belcher and Atchison, "Equity, Rewards, and Compensation Administration," *Personnel Administration* 34 (2) (1971): 34.

Most likely, equity comparisons are made on the basis of salience and availability. If another worker's input/output ratio for some reason becomes salient (for example, because salary is mentioned in conversation), an equity comparison is likely to be made. If workers feel that their input/output ratio is out of line, comparisons are likely to be made using the most available comparison ratios—those of the workers' acquaintances within and without the organization.

Regardless of the basis for comparison, it is important to remember that equity judgments are based on perceptions of inputs and outputs and therefore are susceptible to error. As noted in Chapter 3, workers generally *overestimate* their own contributions at work relative to other workers; because of personal perspective, workers see more of what they themselves accomplish and less of what others do. This should encourage judgments of inequitable treatment.

Many organizations have attempted to prevent judgments of inequitable compensation from occurring by keeping compensation levels secret. Maintaining pay secrecy will render equity judgments difficult, since the outputs received by coworkers can only be estimated. Unfortunately, keeping pay levels secret only makes matters worse. When pay is secret, workers tend to *overestimate* compensation levels received by other workers, fostering perceptions of inequity.[27] If an organization is compensating its employees equitably, its best defense against inequity perceptions should be information. A performance-review system that leads workers to an accurate perception of their work contributions and publicized rules about the relationship between work contributions and compensation should reduce the probability of inaccurate equity perceptions.

**Restoring Equity** How do workers react to perceived inequities in the workplace? They will strive to restore equity, to get their personal input/output ratio more in line with the ratios of relevant others. Exactly how equity is restored depends on whether the inequity comes from overreward or underreward.

Overreward means that a worker believes he or she is receiving *more* compensation than that deserved for services rendered (inputs). Perhaps surprisingly, overreward is distressing to workers because it leads to "insecure nonreliance upon the continuance of earnings, provokes fear of rivalry in others who are not favored, and stimulates an anxious and selfish desire further to improve the favored position."[28] Several research studies have demonstrated that workers often react to overreward by increasing their work inputs. For example, if workers believe they are being paid too much per completed unit on a piecework compensation schedule, they will increase the *quality* of the units produced. By raising the quality of the completed units, the workers are increasing personal work contributions and thereby justifying the overpayment.

Because equity judgments are perceptions of work contributions and of the value of consequences received, overreward also may be justified simply by adjusting perceptions. If workers think they are overpaid, the easiest path to reconciling this inequity is to become convinced that either (1) their work contributions were more substantial than earlier believed, or (2) the consequences received were not (upon reflection) nearly as valuable as initially suspected. In sum, workers often sort out overreward inequities by convincing themselves that their work merited the extra compensation after all.

Inequity judgments arising from *underreward* pose a more serious threat. Workers' feelings of inequity stemming from perceived underre-

[27]E. E. Lawler, *Pay and Organizational Effectiveness: A Psychological View* (New York: McGraw-Hill, 1971).

[28]E. Jaques, *Equitable Payment* (New York: Wiley, 1961), 142–143.

ward have been linked with absenteeism and turnover, either of which could prove disastrously expensive for the organization. How a worker resolves underreward inequity depends upon the financial incentives available for the work force. If workers are paid on an hourly basis, underreward leads to decreased quantity of production. This decreases the worker's perceived contributions and thereby lowers the inputs/outputs ratio.

If workers are paid on a piece-rate basis, underreward inequity is resolved a little differently. From the perspective of the workers, lowering their production output would be personally counterproductive. On a piece-rate compensation schedule, lowered production means lower wages at the end of the pay period. For reasons of self-interest, then, lowering production quantity is an unlikely equity-resolving path for workers paid by units completed. Instead, under piece-rate compensation schedules, production *quantity* is maintained while unit *quality* quietly erodes. As unit quality slips, perceived inputs decrease and equity ratios fall to acceptable levels.

## SUMMARY

Motivation is the process of energizing and directing worker behavior. Content theories of motivation provide an understanding of what types of needs and desires are likely to energize behavior in organizations. Behaviorism and reinforcement theory provide a model for directing worker energies toward the fulfillment of organizational needs through appropriate work behaviors. Workers will pursue organizational objectives when personal need fulfillment is contingent upon appropriate work behaviors.

Unfortunately, contingencies and consequences present far too simplistic a view of the challenge of motivating worker performance in organizations. Expectancy concerns qualify behaviorist theories of energizing and directing behavior. Contingencies between desired consequences and appropriate behaviors will energize appropriate work behaviors only if the worker believes they will lead to personal need fulfillment. Equity concerns provide a qualification to energizing behavior. A desired consequence will be pursued by a worker only if the price (worker inputs) is equitable. Expectancy and equity concerns both are perceptions of motivational arrangements at work. These perceptions play an important role in a worker's decision to engage in appropriate work behaviors.

## KEY TERMS

**Behaviorism**  View of human motivation that all behavior can be understood by examining only contingencies and consequences.

**Cognitions**  Beliefs and thoughts; the information processing that goes on inside an individual's head.

**Complex learning** Form of learning requiring acquisition of new behaviors not yet available in a worker's behavioral repertoire.

**Conditioning** The use of reinforcement and punishment to create habits.

**Consequences** A central concept of the law of effect: the good or bad results following from a behavior.

**Content theories of motivation** Theories that focus on the factors within people that motivate them to perform; for example, the theories of Maslow, Herzberg, and McClelland.

**Contingency** A central concept of the law of effect: the relationships between actions and their outcomes.

**Equity** Workers' judgments of fairness based on the ratio of work inputs to work outputs.

**Expectancies** Workers' cognitions concerning the likely consequence of their actions.

**Expectancy theory** Theory stating that worker behaviors are a function of workers' *beliefs* about consequences and contingencies.

**Externalities** Causes of a worker's behaviors or the consequences of those behaviors that are beyond the worker's control.

**Hygiene factors** In two-factor theory, workers' basic needs of pay, safety on the job, quality of supervision, and social environment, fulfillment of which prevents dissatisfaction.

**Instrumentality** Worker's belief that attaining the required levels of performance will produce desired personal outcomes.

**Intrinsic rewards** Rewards that occur naturally as the product of engaging in a behavior.

**Learned helplessness** Workers' beliefs that they are incapable of producing a required performance or that the required performance, even if produced, would not lead to desired consequences; causes the worker to stop trying.

**Learned needs** Content theory of motivation proposing that three categories of needs—affiliation, power, and achievement—are learned, not innate, desires.

**Motivators** In two-factor theory, factors that provide worker satisfaction, such as the opportunity for achievement, responsibility, and recognition through work.

**Organizational behavior modification (OB–Mod)** Systematic application of simple conditioning and reinforcement theory principles to the management of organizational behavior.

**Partial reinforcement** Rewarding an appropriate behavior in a noncontinuous or variable manner, serving to develop desirable work habits that are more resistant to extinction than those acquired under continuous reinforcement.

**Process theories of motivation**
Theories that focus on the process by which rewards direct behavior; for example, expectancy, equity, and reinforcement theories.

**Punishment**   Administering an unpleasant consequence (for example, docking a worker's pay) in response to inappropriate work behaviors.

**Reinforcement**   Reward for a behavior that increases the probability that the behavior will be repeated.

**Self-efficacy**   Workers' beliefs that they can produce required levels of performance by engaging in appropriate work behaviors.

**Successive approximation**
Reinforcing increasingly better attempts at a final desired behavior; may include shaping or chaining.

**Superstitious behavior**   Belief that a behavior will be rewarded even though the behavior is in fact irrelevant.

**Two-factor theory**   Content theory of motivation framed in terms of factors that affect work dissatisfaction and satisfaction: hygiene factors and motivators.

**Valence**   The perceived value of a behavior's consequences.

**Vicarious learning**   Acquiring desirable behaviors by observing the behaviors of other people; also called *social learning*.

DISCUSSION
QUESTIONS

1.  Think about the phrase, "Spare the rod and spoil the child." Given your understanding of the principles of motivation, does this sound like a sensible approach to raising children? Does it sound like a sensible approach to directing workers?

2.  Is compassion incompatible with the principles of motivation?

3.  In what way might behaviorism be thought to be dehumanizing? Does adding the expectancy and equity qualifications to behaviorism produce a theory of worker motivation that is *less* dehumanizing?

4.  One criticism of behaviorism in particular (and of the application of reinforcement theory to motivating workers in general) is that behaviorism is "manipulative." Are the tenets of behaviorism incompatible with free will and freedom of choice?

5.  Compare and contrast the assumptions underlying the content theories of motivation discussed in this chapter. Why hasn't one of these theories simply "won out" as the best theory?

6.  Why is conditioning (or behaviorism) an inadequate explanation of the acquisition of complex behaviors?

7. Why is it difficult to predict whether a worker's performance of appropriate work behaviors will be undermined by equity or expectancy concerns? How can a manager prevent equity and expectancy concerns from undermining appropriate work behavior?

8. Why is it important to avoid the use of punishment as a means of directing work behaviors?

**IF YOU WANT TO KNOW MORE**

Many reviews of each of the content theories of motivation are available. Wahba and Bridwell provide a critical analysis of Maslow's need hierarchy perspective in their article, "Maslow Reconsidered: A Review of Research on the Need Hierarchy Theory" (*Organizational Behavior and Human Performance* 15 [1976]: 212–240). Herzberg's theory is reviewed and critiqued in House and Wigdor's piece, "Herzberg's Dual-Factor Theory of Job Satisfaction and Motivation: A Review of the Evidence and a Criticism" (*Personnel Psychology* 20 [4] [1967]: 369–380). A more general review and critique of content theories of motivation and their role in understanding work motivation is provided by Salancik and Pfeffer in, "An Examination of Need-Satisfaction Models of Job Attitudes" (*Administrative Science Quarterly* 22 [3] [1977]: 427–456).

The general principles of action direction discussed in this chapter are summarized in two books by Albert Bandura. *Principles of Behavior Modification* (New York: Holt, Rinehart and Winston, 1969) provides excellent discussions of the basic behaviorist principles of reinforcement theory. *Social Learning Theory* (Englewood Cliffs, N.J.: Prentice-Hall, 1977) provides a concise summary of research and theory on vicarious forms of learning and motivation. An application of reinforcement theory principles in an organization setting is detailed in an article by Fred Luthans and Jason Schweizer, "OB Mod in a Small Factory: How Behavior Modification Techniques Can Improve Total Organizational Effectiveness," in *Management Review* (September 1979): 43–50.

The tenets of expectancy theory are developed by Vic Vroom in his book, *Work and Motivation* (New York: Wiley, 1964), and updated in Chapter 7 of Craig Pinder's book, *Work Motivation* (Glenview, Ill.: Scott-Foresman, 1984). An interesting application of the theory to life in organizations is provided by P. J. Andrisani in his article, "Internal and External Attitudes, Personal Initiative, and the Labor Market Experiences of Black and White Men" (*Journal of Human Resources* 12 [1977]: 308–388). The article discusses the relationship between self-efficacy and earning potential in males.

An update on the latest developments in equity theory is provided in an article by Huseman, Hatfield, and Miles, "A New Perspective on Equity Theory: The Equity Sensitivity Construct" (*Academy of Management Review* 12 [1987]: 235–249).

ON YOUR
OWN

**Assessing Your Work Motivation** This exercise will give you two different ways to assess your own work needs and motivations. First, fill out the following questionnaire. Scoring instructions will be provided by your instructor. Next, take a look at the woman in the photograph. Is she relaxing, worrying, daydreaming? Just what is going through her mind? Write a one-paragraph description of what you think is going on in this picture.

This picture is an example of a projective test, in which the respondent *projects* his or her inner feelings into the description of the picture. There is no right answer to the question, "What is going through the young woman's mind?" The picture is intended to be ambiguous, so that the respondent's answer will reflect what is at the forefront of his or her mind. Projective tests have been used extensively to assess affiliation, power, and achievement motives.

**Motivation Questionnaire** You are to indicate how important each characteristic is to you. Answer according to your feelings about the most recent job you had or about the job you currently hold. Circle the number on the scale that represents your feeling— 1 (very unimportant) to 7 (very important).

1. The feeling of self-esteem a person gets from being in that job

   1  2  3  4  5  6  7

2. The opportunity for personal growth and development in that job

   1  2  3  4  5  6  7

3. The prestige of the job inside the company (that is, regard received from others in the company)

   1  2  3  4  5  6  7

4. The opportunity for independent thought and action in that job

   1  2  3  4  5  6  7

5. The feeling of security in that job

   1  2  3  4  5  6  7

6. The feeling of self-fulfillment a person gets from being in that position (that is, the feeling of being able to use one's own unique capabilities, realizing one's potential)

   1  2  3  4  5  6  7

7. The prestige of the job outside the company (that is, the regard received from others not in the company)

   1  2  3  4  5  6  7

8. The feeling of worthwhile accomplishment in that job

   1  2  3  4  5  6  7

9. The opportunity in that job to give help to other people

   1  2  3  4  5  6  7

Source: Lyman W. Porter, *Organizational Patterns of Managerial Job Attitudes* (New York: American Foundation for Management Research, 1964), pp. 17, 19.

| | | | | | | | | | |
|---|---|---|---|---|---|---|---|---|---|
| 10. The opportunity in that job for participation in the setting of goals | 1 | 2 | 3 | 4 | 5 | 6 | 7 |
| 11. The opportunity in that job for participation in the determination of methods and procedures | 1 | 2 | 3 | 4 | 5 | 6 | 7 |
| 12. The authority connected with the job | 1 | 2 | 3 | 4 | 5 | 6 | 7 |
| 13. The opportunity to develop close friendships in the job | 1 | 2 | 3 | 4 | 5 | 6 | 7 |

Now that you have completed the questionnaire, score it as follows:

Rating for question 5 = ____. Divide by 1 = ____ security.
Rating for questions 9 and 13 = ____. Divide by 2 = ____ social.
Rating for questions 1, 3, and 7 = ____. Divide by 3 = ____ esteem.
Rating for questions 4, 10, 11, and 12 = ____. Divide by 4 = ____ autonomy.
Rating for questions 2, 6, and 8 = ____. Divide by 3= ____ self-actualization.

The instructor has national norm scores for presidents, vice-presidents, and upper middle-level, lower middle-level, and lower-level managers with which you can compare your *mean* importance scores. How do your scores compare with the scores of managers working in organizations?

**CLOSING CASE
FOR CHAPTER 4**

## THE MANAGER'S MEMO

FROM: R. Prince, Manager, Word-Processing Center

TO:      E. Switzer-Greer, Manager, Personnel Department

RE:      Department Policies

Unfortunately, some members of my staff are less than conscientious
when it comes to arriving on time in the morning and after their lunch
break. In addition, some of the word-processing staff are not very
motivated to do their best.

I think that the most effective way to reduce this problem would be a
clear, simple, understandable policy to motivate the employees. I have
developed the following guidelines for punctuality and output:

- All employees are to be punctual. At 8:30, which is starting time, I
  will patrol the word-processing department and make a note of
  anyone who is late. Anyone who is late three times will be laid off.
- All employees are to let me know when they go to lunch. They must
  be back at their desks within one hour. Anyone who is late three
  times will be laid off.
- Based on five years' experience with this department, a reasonable
  quantity of work is 15 pages a day of original typing or 30 pages of
  revisions. Employee's annual raises will be based on whether they
  exceed, meet, or fall below this level of output.
- Raises will be computed as follows: An employee who exceeds the
  standard level will receive a 6 percent raise. An employee who meets
  the standard level will receive a 3 percent raise. An employee who
  falls below the standard level will receive no raise for the year.

I believe this four-point policy is easy to remember and understand.
Please let me know whether you think the policy will be effective in
motivating employees to be on time and to work diligently while they
are here. Also, I'm interested in seeing any suggestions you have for
improving this policy.

CASE DISCUSSION
QUESTIONS

Assume you are the manager of the personnel department, and write a response to this memo. To support your position, refer to the motivation theories and research described in the chapter. In phrasing your response, keep in mind that you can benefit by reinforcing certain behaviors of the word-processing manager (such as seeking good policies and consulting you).

# Individual Decision Making

## Following the Leader

When E. F. Hutton speaks, its slogan claims, people listen. But in 1985, E. F. Hutton found itself deep in trouble because no one in Hutton was speaking or listening. What was not spoken about—or at least not questioned—was check kiting by Hutton's money managers. And what no one listened to was the voice of conscience whispering misgivings about an unethical and illegal practice.

The scheme was simple. A branch of E. F. Hutton would have, say, $70,000 on deposit in a small bank in Ohio. The Hutton branch would request a cash transfer from the account for $1 million. The bank, not wanting to lose Hutton's valuable business, would advance the money, and a day later Hutton would replace it. Hutton got the free use of $1 million of the bank's money for 24 hours.

While substantial account overdrafts occur from time to time in business banking, Hutton made a practice of them. On any given day, the firm overdrew its bank accounts to the tune of millions of dollars. The interest on that money became a major source of revenue for Hutton. When the U.S. Justice Department finally investigated, E. F. Hutton was cited on 2,000 counts of mail and wire fraud, received a $2 million fine, and had to set up a multimillion-dollar fund to reimburse banks for lost interest payments.

Few employees at E. F. Hutton seem to have questioned the practice before the federal investigation; once established among Hutton executive echelons, it was taken for granted. In fact, an internal memo from the corporate department in charge of cash management advised, rather blandly, "If an office is overdrafting their ledger balance consistently, it is probably best not to request an account analysis." In other words, the memo said they would rather not know about it—and rather the bank not notice, either.

Source: Daniel Goleman, "Following the Leader: Sometimes It's Folly to Go Along with the Boss," *Science '85* (October): pp. 18–19.

## FIGURE 5–1     Organizational Decision Making

Organizational decision making is cyclical. Individuals (1) think and (2) choose. Individual choices add up to (3) organizational choices, which invite (4) environmental responses. These responses in turn influence individual thought.

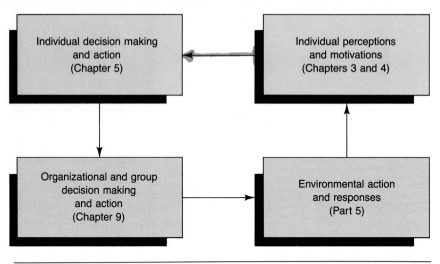

INTRODUCTION

E. F. Hutton's practice of intentionally overdrawing bank accounts was at worst illegal and at best unethical, and it provides a graphic example of organizational decision making gone haywire. Employees at E. F. Hutton were making decisions on a daily basis that could not have been consistent with the long-term interests and goals of the company. How could this have happened? This chapter provides answers to such questions by examining the processes of individual choice and decision making and the way decisions are made in organizations.

The complete cycle of organizational decision making is illustrated in Figure 5–1. Individual decision making is one component of the larger context of organizational decision making. The four components of organizational decision making can be described as follows:

1.  Decision making begins when individuals perceive a discrepancy between how their organization could or should be and how it actually is. This perceived difference between what is and what could or should be precipitates decision making and action.
2.  Individuals respond to these perceived discrepancies by making decisions and taking actions. This chapter focuses on the nature and importance of these individual decisions in the larger organizational context.
3.  The process through which individuals' choices and actions come together to produce group or organizational choices and actions—group decision making, for instance—is the focus of Part 3. It should be noted that at the group or organizational level, good

decisions do not always produce good actions. When there are lots of people involved, even good decisions can be implemented incorrectly.

4.  Finally, the larger environment in which the organization functions responds to behavioral changes. The importance of the environment and its responses to and influences on organizations is the focus of Part 5. These responses by the environment provide inputs that lead individuals to new perceptions, choices, and actions.

## MAKING DECISIONS

The focus of this chapter is the individual decision-making component of organizational decision making. Decisions are responses to problems—differences between what is and what could or should be. Problems may vary in importance from figuring out which job you should accept after graduation to deciding which brand of toothpaste you should buy.

## FIVE STEPS OF DECISION MAKING

**Recognition and Definition of the Problem**  Perceiving a discrepancy between what is and what could or should be is problem recognition, and provides the foundation for all individual decision making. Problem recognition requires the decision maker to: (1) understand goals and objectives (either of the organization or of the individual), (2) monitor accomplishment of those goals (performance discrepancies), and (3) evaluate the importance of the discrepancy. Problem recognition is a critical aspect of individual decision making. If a manager identifies the wrong problem or erroneously evaluates its importance, then the final decision will not address the real concerns of the organization.

Defining the problem correctly is critical to successful decision making. Because problem recognition is a *perceptual* process, managers may not come up with accurate assessments of the problems at hand, which gets decision making off on the wrong foot. Managers often make poor decisions because: (1) they allow available solutions to define the problem, (2) they focus on aspects of problems they know they can solve and ignore the larger, more difficult issues confronting them, or (3) they diagnose problems in terms of the most obvious symptoms.[1] In other words, decision makers often get sidetracked by tangential aspects of the real problem and by their beliefs about what problems they know they can solve.

**Information Search**  If a perceived discrepancy is important, then the decision maker will implement a second stage of the decision-making

---

[1]G. Huber, *Managerial Decision Making* (Glenview, Ill.: Scott, Foresman, 1980).

process: determining why the problem occurred. The decision maker must gather information about the problem or discrepancy and possible ways to solve it. At this point, the decision maker should have a clear understanding of the problem and have collected sufficient information to begin the third phase of the decision-making process.

**Alternative Generation**   The third phase of individual decision making is developing or identifying potential courses of action. This phase requires that the information previously gathered be transformed into a set of alternatives. Identifying alternatives is a difficult task; it requires a considerable amount of creativity and mental flexibility. Often managers spend too little time on this phase because they are willing to choose among alternatives before they have generated a diverse range of options. Theoretically, managers should continue to generate alternatives until the potential for improving on them is too small to justify the added expense. More often than not, managers are willing to stop generating alternatives at the first sign of a potentially acceptable solution.

**Evaluation and Choice**   When a sufficient number of alternatives have been identified, the decision maker must evaluate them and make a choice. This evaluation can be accomplished in one of two ways. The decision maker can compare each alternative to every other alternative, or the decision maker can compare each alternative to the desired goal. While both methods have their strong points, the more clearly defined the problem and its antecedents (or causes) and the more specific the alternatives, the better the eventual choice.

**Implementation and Assessment**   Once a choice has been made, the decision maker must implement the decision. While the choice process is important, decisions are worthless unless implemented. Individual decision makers are remiss if they do nothing to implement a decision after having devoted time, energy, and organizational resources to identifying an appropriate course of action. However, decision makers also may be remiss if they make no attempt to assess the appropriateness of the chosen course of action. After implementing the choice, the decision maker can monitor the outcomes to determine what changes have occurred. Did the discrepancy between desired and actual states disappear? If not, perhaps the real problem was not solved. The problem information may have been incomplete, or the wrong alternative was selected. Do changes need to be made in how alternatives are evaluated? Perhaps the decision was not correctly implemented. Regardless of the cause, if the decision does not resolve the discrepancy, then the process will begin again. Figure 5–2 illustrates this complete cycle of individual decision making.

**FIGURE 5–2** Individual Decision-Making Process

Individual decision making, like organizational decision making, can be represented as a feedback cycle. The individual defines the problem and collects information to generate alternatives. When a choice is made and implemented, the outcome provides feedback about whether the problem was defined correctly, and whether it was solved or needs further attention.

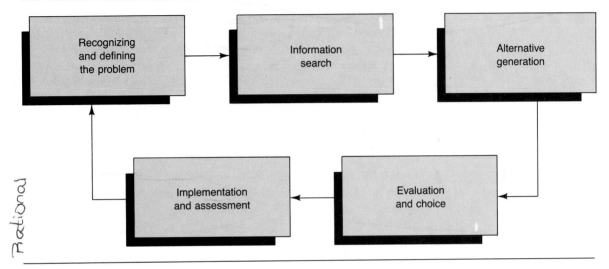

RATIONALITY AND BOUNDED RATIONALITY

The five-phase cycle of individual decision making is often referred to as the "rational model." **Rationality** suggests that a decision has been based on the careful and calculated understanding of action alternatives and their consequences. In Western society, the term *rationality* also suggests high-quality decision making uninfluenced by irrelevant considerations.

While this five-phase rational decision-making process represents an ideal to which decision makers aspire, it is also a difficult (if not impossible) ideal to achieve. In order to be a rational decision maker, a manager would have to compile a complete listing of all alternatives and their consequences. The manager would have to know how the world (or at least the organization and its environment) would be affected by each alternative. Even for apparently simple decisions of the organization, this places substantial demands on the information collection, storage, and integration powers of individual decision makers—such great demands that the information-processing requirements of rationality exceed the capabilities of the human mind. Thus, while rationality is an attractive ideal, actual decision making typically falls short of rationality in a number of ways:[2]

[2]J. G. March and H. A. Simon, *Organizations* (New York: John Wiley & Sons, 1958).

1. The rational ideal requires complete knowledge and anticipation of the consequences that will follow each choice. In practice, knowledge is always incomplete.

2. Since the consequences of actions occur in the future, they can only be imagined. In attaching preference or value to a particular outcome, then, decision makers must rely on imagination rather than experience. The attractiveness of a consequence can be anticipated only imperfectly through imagination. Only by actually experiencing the consequence can we know our preference for that consequence.

3. Rationality requires a choice among all possible alternatives. But the number of alternative actions in any situation is unlimited. In practice, decision makers have the time to consider only a few of the infinite possibilities.

4. Human decision makers can retain only a relatively small amount of information in memory.

5. Limited human information-processing capabilities constrain the ability of decision makers to perform the necessary calculations (even given all the necessary information) to determine the best alternative.

6. Rationality assumes that decision makers have a stable, specifiable, and consistent hierarchy of needs and motivations. As noted in Chapter 4, however, human needs and goals change over time, and individuals and organizations often simultaneously pursue apparently incompatible objectives.

Given these limitations on any decision maker's abilities, it should not be surprising that actual decision making often falls far short of the rational ideal. However, because rationality is such an attractive goal, individuals are hesitant to give up their perceptions of themselves as rational decision makers. Much of research on managers as decision makers has been based on managers' self-reports of how they claim to make decisions. Managers typically describe the process by which they make decisions as closely following the five-phase rational cycle of individual decision making.

When actual managerial decision behavior has been systematically observed, quite a different picture has emerged. In contrast with the perception that managers sit in their offices, carefully consider information and alternatives, and make calculated choices, observation indicates that managers' decision-making processes are hardly ideal. One study found that in making decisions managers tend to avoid hard (systematic, analytical) data and to rely on softer forms of information, such as gossip or speculation.[3] Since managers make hundreds of decisions daily, it

[3]H. Mintzberg, "The Manager's Job: Folklore and Fact," *Harvard Business Review* (July–August 1975): 49–61.

seems likely that even approximating the systematic and time-consuming demands of rational decision making is beyond reach. A different decision-making model is required to capture the actual decision behavior of managers.

The rational model of decision making really defines how a decision should be made, rather than describing how managers actually make decisions. In his Nobel Prize–winning work, economist Herbert Simon suggested that individual decision making is bounded in its ability to approach rationality by the limits of the human information-processing apparatus. Given these limitations, Simon argued that prescriptions for how decisions should be made (such as the five-step rational ideal pictured in Figure 5–2) are not nearly so useful for understanding and predicting individual decision behavior as are descriptions of how decisions are made.[4] Simon's notion of **bounded rationality** is a descriptive model of individual decision making. Bounded rationality diverges from the rational ideal in four important ways. Bounded rationality characterizes actual individual decision-making behavior as based on a limited perspective, the sequential evaluation of alternatives, satisficing, and the use of judgmental heuristics.

**Limited Perspective**  First, bounded rationality assumes that the information-processing demands of actual decision makers are managed by limiting the scope of decisions. Not all alternatives are considered, and not all goals are accommodated. Instead, the focus of the choice is limited to a manageable subset of goals, alternatives, and consequences. For example, bounded rationality assumes that a decision maker may simultaneously pursue multiple and conflicting goals. To reconcile the different goals, decision making is compartmentalized. Decisions at one point in time may attempt to achieve one goal; a second decision at some other point in time may help to achieve another, mutually exclusive, goal.

Consider, for example, a department head who issues a travel policy at the beginning of the fiscal year. The policy states that reimbursement for all company-sponsored travel will be limited to $500. The policy is designed to promote departmental budgetary goals. However, two weeks after the policy is put in place, an employee known for his "squeaky wheel" behavior requests reimbursement of $650 for a trip. After three meetings with the employee, the department head approves the $650 request. The decision satisfies the decision maker's need to limit further interactions with the troublesome employee—an important goal—but at the cost of violating the first goal of careful fiscal management. Limited-scope decision making reduces information search and processing demands and makes decision making manageable. But it has its costs.

[4]H. A. Simon, *Administrative Behavior* (New York: MacMillan, 1957).

**Sequential Alternative Evaluation**   The second way in which bounded rationality deviates from the normative model of decision making is in evaluation of alternatives. Rather than simultaneously considering all possible alternatives and their consequences and choosing the best possible alternative, decision makers evaluate alternatives sequentially. For example, two alternatives are considered and the better one is chosen. That alternative may then be compared to another alternative. This "pair-wise" comparison requires considerably less mental activity than comparing a number of alternatives simultaneously. In fact, a recent study of personnel-selection decision making found that individuals who evaluated candidates in a sequential manner took significantly less time than those who evaluated the same number of candidates simultaneously.[5]

**Satisficing**   Theoretically, a decision maker could continue making pair-wise comparisons of all possible alternatives until the optimal solution emerged. However, given the number of decisions that need to be made and the amount of time that would be consumed in such extended comparisons, another goal—taking timely action—must take precedence. Since the costs of finding an optimal course of action are too dear, decision makers must be willing to forego the best solution in favor of one that is acceptable or reasonable. That is, decision makers **satisfice**. They do not examine all possible alternatives. They look at a small number of familiar or likely solutions and choose one that produces a "good enough" outcome.

**Judgmental Heuristics and Biases**   The fourth way in which bounded rationality differs from the rational ideal is its use of judgmental heuristics. **Judgmental heuristics** are rules of thumb, or shortcuts, that reduce the information-processing demands for decision makers. Judgmental heuristics summarize past experiences and provide an easy method to evaluate the present. Judgmental heuristics facilitate individual decision making by substituting rules or "standard operating procedures" for complex information collection and calculation. For the most part, heuristics save considerable mental activity. However, in certain situations, using these cognitive heuristics can result in systematically biased outcomes. To distinguish this misapplication of cognitive heuristics from their appropriate use, we will use the term *cognitive bias* to refer to the inappropriate use of cognitive heuristics that results in systematically biased decisions. Two examples of judgmental heuristics (or biases) are availability and representativeness.

---

[5]V. L. Huber, M. A. Neale, and G. B. Northcraft, "Decision Bias and Personnel Selection Strategies," *Organizational Behavior and Human Decision Processes* 40 (1987): 136–147.

*Availability*   Decision makers often assess the frequency or likelihood of an event's occurrence by how easily they can remember it.[6] This "rule" is based on the notion that frequently occurring events are familiar to us, and, thus, are easy to recall. This heuristic is useful because familiar events often are more easily recalled than less frequent events. However, biased outcomes result from dependence on this rule when the ease of memory recall is influenced by factors unrelated to the frequency of an event's occurrence. If an event evokes emotions, is vivid, easily imagined, or specific and concrete, it will be more "available" from memory than will equally occurring events that are unemotional, bland, vague, or difficult to imagine.

Problems 1, 3, and 4 in Figure 5–3 all provide examples of the use of the **availability bias.** For all three of these problems, most people chose option A. B is really the correct choice, however. The corporations represented by answer B in Problem 1 have over twice the sales volume of the companies listed in answer A. Because the first group contains consumer firms, they are more likely to be familiar to us as consumers. The second (B) group contains industrial firms or holding companies that are less familiar to us. If the availability bias did not influence us, our exposure to these two groups of companies would not alter our judgments.

For Problem 3, driving a car on a 400-mile trip is actually much riskier than flying 400 miles on a commercial airliner. However, media attention to airplane crashes has made them quite vivid in our memories. Little attention is given to automobile accidents, probably because they are so common.

The common response to Problem 4 is that more words in the English language begin with "r" than have "r" as the third letter. In fact, we can draw up a rather extensive list of words that begin with the letter "r." However, considerably more words have "r" as their third letter. In deciding how to answer this question, you probably tried to come up with a list of words that begin with the letter "r" and another list that have "r" as the third letter. Because of the way in which we store information in memory, it is much easier to generate examples of words beginning with "r." If we think of our memory as analogous to a card catalogue in the library, it is very easy to come up with all sorts of "r" words (just as it would be easy to generate from the card catalogue listing authors whose last name was "Woolf"). The card catalogue would be of little use to us in trying to identify words with "r" as the third letter, just as it would not help in trying to find authors whose first name was Virginia. Neither the catalogue nor our memories is designed to store and retrieve information in that way.

[6]A. Tversky and D. Kahneman, "Judgment under Uncertainty: Heuristics and Biases," *Science* 185 (1974): 453–463.

**FIGURE 5–3**                    Decision-Making Quiz

1.  The following 10 corporations were ranked by *Fortune* magazine to be among the 500 largest United States–based firms, according to sales volume for 1982:

    *Group A:* American Motors, Wang Laboratories, Lever Brothers, Kellogg, Scott Paper
    *Group B:* Costal, Signal Companies, Dresser Industries, Agway, McDermott

    Which group (A or B) had the largest total sales for the five organizations listed?

2.  The best student in the graduate organizational-behavior class writes poetry and is rather shy and small in stature. What was the student's undergraduate major: (a) Chinese studies or (b) psychology?

3.  Which is riskier: (a) flying in a commercial airliner on a 400-mile trip or (b) driving a car on a 400-mile trip?

4.  Are there more words in the English language that (a) begin with the letter "r" or (b) have "r" as the third letter?

5.  On one day in a large metropolitan hospital, eight births were recorded by gender in the order of their arrival. Which of the following orders of births (B = boy, G = girl) was most likely to be reported?
    a.  BBBBBBBB
    b.  BBBBGGGG
    c.  BGBBGGGB

6.  A large car manufacturer has recently been hit with a number of economic difficulties, and it appears as if three plants need to be closed and 6,000 employees laid off. The vice-president of production has been exploring ways to avoid this crisis. She has developed two plans:
    a.  Plan A will save one of the three plants and 2,000 jobs.
    b.  Plan B has a one-third probability of saving all three plants and all 6,000 jobs, but it has a two-thirds probability of saving no plants and no jobs.

    Which plan would you select?

Source: M. H. Bazerman, *Judgment in Managerial Decision Making* (New York: Wiley, 1989).

*Representativeness*   In Problem 2 in Figure 5–3, the most common response is that the undergraduate major of the student was Chinese studies. However, the correct response is that the individual majored in psychology. In selecting the first option, important base-rate information has been ignored. A base-rate probability is an overall probability that something will occur, all other things being equal. In this case, the base-rate probability that any MBA student is a psychology major is higher than the probability that the student is a Chinese studies major simply because overall there are a lot more psychology than Chinese studies majors. Thus, the rational choice is psychology because it so dominates Chinese studies. However, individuals who write poetry and are short in stature, studious, and shy more closely resemble our stereotypes of a Chinese person or the type of person who would be likely to major in Chinese studies. That individual, then, is representative of our stereotype. Thus, we decide that Chinese studies must be the major of the best student, regardless of the fact that there are many more psychology majors than Chinese studies majors.

Problem 5 provides another example of the **representativeness** bias. The most common response to this problem is that option c is the most likely birth order to be observed. The common reason given for this choice is that the third option looks random. The first and second options are too ordered and, thus, seem highly unlikely to occur. The correct response is that all three of the options are equally likely to occur. The problem here is that we believe that a sequence of independent events (such as eight births) generated from a random process should resemble the essential characteristics of a random process, even when the sequence is too short for that process to express itself statistically. This is referred to as the "law of small numbers." Decision makers expect a few examples of a random event to behave in the same way as large numbers of the event.

In large samples of births, the births of girls and boys occur about equally. However, there is no reason why one should not expect a run of eight boy births or four boy births followed by four girl births in a small sample. The premise that randomness has some specific order (or specific lack of order) requires the assumption that there is some relationship or dependence between one occurrence and the next. Yet the gender of Mother A's baby has no effect on the gender of Mother B's.

This belief that events have some sort of memory is rampant in the bias known as the *gambler's fallacy*. Assuming a fair (untampered with) roulette wheel, if the ball landed on a red number ten times in a row, how would you bet (red or black) on the next spin of the wheel? Many decision makers would bet on a black number, feeling that a black number was due. Since there are an equal number of black and red numbers, the objective probability of the ball's landing on a red or black number must be exactly the same. The ball does not remember where it has landed in the past. While you may remember where the ball landed on the last spin of the wheel, from the ball's perspective each event is completely independent from the next. When examined in detail, the gambler's fallacy is obviously wrong, but it does have considerable intuitive appeal.

**DECISION MAKING UNDER UNCERTAINTY**

In addition to the information-processing demands it places on decision makers, rationality also assumes a complete understanding of means-ends relationships—what consequences occur as a result of actions. "Bounded rationality" shows that decision makers cannot possibly consider, evaluate, and integrate all means-ends information into decisions. Uncertainty raises an additional problem for decision makers: knowledge about means-ends relationships is often only fuzzy at best.

For some decisions, the amount of risk and uncertainty are well defined. The probability of being dealt a particular hand in cards, for instance, can be determined exactly ahead of time. The probability that a new product line will be successful cannot be determined exactly.

In Chapter 1, uncertainty was defined as "not knowing for sure." The terms **uncertainty** and **risk** both suggest that the consequences of an action can be known only in terms of a perceived likelihood of occurrence. A particular action may produce a desired consequence, but at the risk of other consequences. The consequences of the action are uncertain. Most decisions must incorporate this notion of risk or uncertainty. The number of certain means-ends relationships is very small.

Although individuals may wish their lives were filled with certainty, most of us are constantly faced with decisions among risky alternatives. Without complete knowledge, then, even the best plans and decisions are implemented at the risk of poor outcomes. Though we may try to ignore the risk inherent in our daily decisions, we often express our uncertainty about outcomes, saying "Chances are," "It seems likely that," "I think," and "I bet." A more formal way to express our uncertainty is through probabilities.

**Probability** (a statistical term) is a measure of the likelihood that a particular event will occur. Our confidence in a particular probability can be very high. For example, with a fair coin, most people would agree that there is a 50 percent probability of a tossed coin coming up heads. However, few people would agree on the probability that the Dow-Jones Industrial Average will be above 3100 on March 30, 1991. The difference between these two situations is that for the Dow-Jones

**FIGURE 5–4**            Chances of Being Dealt Different Poker Hands

In poker, the probability of being dealt a pair (two of the same card—for instance, two kings) is one in 2.5, or 40 percent. If you were offered $1 if you could deal yourself one pair, your expected value would be ($1 × .4) + ($0 × .6) = $.40.

| | | |
|---|---|---|
| Straight flush | 1 in | 64,974 |
| Four of a kind | 1 in | 4,165 |
| Full house | 1 in | 694 |
| Flush | 1 in | 509 |
| Straight | 1 in | 256 |
| Three of a kind | 1 in | 48 |
| Two pair | 1 in | 21 |
| One pair | 1 in | 2.5 |
| No pair | 1 in | 2 |

Source: O. Jacoby, *Oswald Jacoby on Poker* (New York: Doubleday, 1940), p. 114.

average, we are forecasting the future without being able to understand or specify everything that could happen to affect it. When dealing with cards, coins, gambling, and games, it is much easier to produce accurate probabilities of an event's occurrence because we can identify all possible outcomes and all the processes that should affect them. The probability of a particular event's occurrence may be low, but it is knowable. For example, the probabilities of being dealt certain hands in a poker game are illustrated in Figure 5–4.

**Reactions to Risk**  Decision makers' reactions to risk and uncertainty often do not reflect careful consideration of the consequences of alternatives. The rational ideal for decision making under uncertainty is to select the alternative with the highest expected value. The **expected value** of an action is the value assigned to each possible consequence of the action, multiplied by the probabilities that each of these possible consequences will occur.

As an example of expected value, imagine that you are deciding whether to insure your computer against theft. The insurance company's brochure indicates that the company will reimburse you for the full replacement cost of your computer less a $50 deductible charge if it is stolen. The cost of this insurance is $50 per year. If someone steals your computer and you have insurance, you lose $100. (The insurance company will replace your computer, but you will still be out the $50 deductible and the $50 cost of the insurance.) If someone steals your computer and you have no insurance, you will lose $3,500 (the cost of replacing the computer). If you buy the insurance and no one steals your computer, you will lose $50 (the insurance premium). If no one steals your computer and you are not insured, you lose nothing. Should you

**FIGURE 5–5**          Payoff Matrix for Computer Insurance Purchase

Insurance is a way of minimizing risk when outcomes are uncertain and stakes
are high. As shown in this figure, a person who buys insurance spends a little to
avoid losing a lot.

|  | **Outcomes** | |
| --- | --- | --- |
| **Choices** | **Stolen** | **Not Stolen** |
| Buy insurance | −$100 | −$50 |
| Do not buy insurance | −$3,500 | 0 |

purchase the insurance for your new $3,500 computer? The payoff
matrix for this decision is presented in Figure 5–5.

At this point, you still do not have sufficient information to answer the
question. What is missing is information concerning the probability that
your computer will be stolen. After doing a little research, you discover
that there is a 1-in-100 chance that your computer will be stolen. Armed
with this information, you can calculate the expected value of buying and
not buying insurance:

$$\text{Expected Value } (EV)_{(buy)}$$

$$= P_{(stolen)} \times \text{Net loss}_{(stolen)} + P_{(not\ stolen)} \times \text{Loss}_{(not\ stolen)}$$

$$= (.01)(-\$100) + (.99)(-\$50)$$

$$= -\$50.50$$

$$EV_{(do\ not\ buy)}$$

$$= P_{(stolen)} \times \text{Loss}_{(stolen)} + P_{(not\ stolen)} \times \text{Loss}_{(not\ stolen)}$$

$$= (.01)(-\$3,500) + (.99)(\$0)$$

$$= -\$35.$$

Based upon these calculations and the rule of choosing the option with
the greatest expected value, you should not buy the insurance. In the
long run (which may include losing an occasional computer to thieves),
you will come out ahead by not buying the insurance.

Do decision makers rely on expected-value calculations when they
make decisions? For the decision presented in Figure 5–6, the "rational"
decision is to select the alternative with the highest expected value. For
option A, the expected value (or $EV$) of taking the $10 million is the
outcome ($10 million) multiplied by the probability of that outcome
(100%), or $10 million. For option B, the expected value is the sum of
the two possible outcomes ($22 million and $0 million) each multiplied
by the probability of their occurrence (50% and 50%), or:

**FIGURE 5–6**                    Framing the Decision

---

Some choices bring out our aversion to risk; others, our attraction to it. When we have sure gains to protect (as in scenario 1), we are likely to avoid risks. When we are facing possible losses (as in scenario 2), we are likely to take chances to avoid these losses or break even.

1. You can (A) have $10 million for sure ($EV$ = $10 million) or (B) flip a fair coin and receive $22 million if heads appears and nothing if tails appears ($EV$ = $11 million). The simple decision rule would select the "B" option. What would you do?

2. You are being sued for $5,000 and estimate a 50 percent chance of losing the case ($EV$ = −$2,500). The other side, however, is willing to accept an out-of-court settlement of $2,400 ($EV$ = $2,400). Ignoring attorney fees, court costs, aggravation, and such, would you (A) fight the case or (B) settle out of court? The simple decision rule would lead you to settle out of court.

---

Source: M. H. Bazerman, *Judgment in Managerial Decision Making* (New York: Wiley, 1986).

$$EV = (\$22 \text{ million} \times 50\%) + (\$0 \text{ million} \times 50\%) = \$11 \text{ million.}$$

Surprisingly, the most common response to this choice is the A option, even though A results in a smaller expected value. One explanation for this is that the typical decision maker is not **risk neutral.** Choosing the option with the highest expected value is a risk-neutral decision—it assumes that the decision maker is indifferent between risky and certain outcomes if they have the same expected value. However, in many situations, **risk averse** decision makers ignore the expected-value solution and choose the option in which there is less risk. The decision maker is willing to pay a premium (the $1 million difference in the first situation) to avoid the risk of the $22 million gamble. Paying such a premium to avoid risk is a common practice. The enormous size of the insurance industry is evidence of our willingness to pay money to avoid risks.[7]

**Risk-seeking** behavior is just the opposite. That is, a decision maker is risk seeking when he or she pays a premium to experience risk. Participating in gambling activities in Las Vegas is an example of risk-seeking behavior. Since objectively the odds of winning money are in favor of the "house," the risk-neutral (or expected-value) decision would be not to play. Given the odds and the risk inherent in the situation, the risk-averse decision would also be not to play. However, a visit to any of the casinos there reveals a large number of individuals who have made the risk-seeking choice to play. In making decisions, the risk or

---

[7]C. Holloway, *Decision Making under Uncertainty: Models and Choices* (Englewood Cliffs, N.J.: Prentice-Hall, 1979).

uncertainty that accompanies decision options influences the final selection. In fact, we all know people we would categorize as risk seeking or risk averse. However, it is much more difficult to know whether we ourselves are risk seeking or risk averse. That is, we can think of situations in which we take risks and situations in which we avoid risks. We may operate hang gliders and fly airplanes as hobbies yet religiously wear automobile seat belts and pay our life, health, liability, dental, pet, and credit-card insurance premiums.

Attempts to identify a personality characteristic that predicts risk attitude have met with little success.[8] In general, more intelligent decision makers tend to have more consistent risk attitudes. In general, however, risk taking seems to be influenced more by a decision maker's situation than by the personality of the individual.

What is an appropriate level of risk taking within an organization? Different constituency groups in an organization may lobby for different risk attitudes on the part of the manager. Stockholders or owners of the company may have their own view of appropriate levels of risk. Lower-level managers generally are more risk averse than upper-level managers. Further, managers indicate that their risk strategies mirror their best interests rather than the best interests of the company.[9] The credit department of an organization may be more risk seeking than the manufacturing department.

How, then, can an organization influence the risk strategies of its managers in the direction of the company's best interests? It may be that managers take risks inconsistent with the company's risk attitude because they are unaware of the organization's risk policy. In such cases, communicating the level of acceptable risk to the employees may generate a more consistent risk policy within the organization.

Second, managers may accept levels of risk that are in their own best interest (and not the company's) because of the incentive structure of the organization. If incentives are based on the individual's success and not the company's success, then it is little wonder that individuals make decisions consistent with their own best interests. The task here is to make the best interests of the organization and the best interests of the individual consistent. Chapter 13 will consider in detail the importance and impact of incentive systems on organizational performance.

*Framing*   One judgmental heuristic that decision makers use to deal with risk is **framing.** In Problem 6 in Figure 5–3, the typical response is to select Plan A. However, let's reconsider the problem, replacing the two original choices with the following choices:

[8]P. Slovic, "Information Processing, Situation Specificity, and the Generality of Risk Taking Behavior," *Journal of Personality and Social Psychology* 22 (1972): 128–134.

[9]R. O. Swalm, "Utility Theory—Insights into Risk Taking," *Harvard Business Review* 44 (1966): 123–136.

C. Plan C will result in the loss of two of the three plants and 4,000 jobs.
D. Plan D has a two-thirds probability of resulting in the loss of all three plants and all 6,000 jobs but has a one-third probability of losing no plants and no jobs.

Which plan would you select? If you closely compare plans A and B to plans C and D, you will discover that they are *exactly* the same. Plans A and C both result in the loss of two plants (and 4,000 jobs) and the saving of one plant (and 2,000 jobs). Plans B and D both represent a gamble—a 1-in-3 chance that all the plants and jobs will be saved and a 2-in-3 chance that all the plants and jobs will be lost. Yet, when individuals see only Plans C and D, they typically choose Plan D. Although both sets of plans represent exactly the same two options, changing the descriptions from potential gains (jobs and plants saved) to potential losses (jobs and plants lost) is sufficient to alter the average plan selection from the risk-averse choice of Plan A to the risky choice of Plan D. Why?

There is a fundamental difference in decision makers' responses to gains and losses. When we are confronted with the choice of losing $10 for certain or taking a gamble with an equal expected value, we are likely to take the gamble rather than incur the pain of losing for certain. (After all, we may get lucky and lose nothing at all.) Gains, however, are a different story. When we must choose between that $10 for certain or a gamble with an equivalent expected value, we will typically choose the certain $10. Consistent with the old adage that "a bird in the hand is worth two in the bush," we prefer choices that are certain (risk averse) when we can gain. Having that bird safely under control is worth more to us than the potential of twice as many birds. Further, it seems the pain associated with losing, say, $10 is greater than the pleasure associated with gaining that $10. Thus, as the potential losses get larger, we are likely to become more and more risky in our behavior. Conversely, as the potential gains get larger, we are likely to forego more and more of them for the comfort of certainty.

*Escalation* The impact of framing can be quite costly to organizations, as demonstrated in the following example.[10]

You are a bank loan officer. A seemingly good credit risk comes to you and asks for a $50,000 business start-up loan. After careful review of the application, you personally make the decision to grant the loan. Six months later, the same applicant shows up in your office and says, "I have bad news and I have good news. The bad news is that the company is having problems. In fact, without additional help, we are going under and you will lose the $50,000. The good news is that I am quite confident

---

[10]M. H. Bazerman, *Judgment in Managerial Decision Making* (New York: John Wiley & Sons, 1989).

Decision escalation commonly causes owners of old cars to pour more and more money into repairs. A "rational" decision maker recognizes that the sunk costs of past repairs are immaterial to the current decision. Only the future costs and benefits of repairing versus buying a new car should be considered.

that if you lend us an additional $50,000, we can turn the whole thing around." Do you lend him an additional $50,000?

In this situation, the odds are that you will seriously consider the additional $50,000 loan. Why? One way to look at this situation is from the perspective of a negative frame. In this case, the loan officer is likely to view the situation as a choice between two options: (1) not loaning the additional money and losing the $50,000 for certain, or (2) loaning a second $50,000 to the business in hopes that it will survive to repay the loan and the interest. Viewing this scenario as a choice between (1) a loss for certain and (2) a gamble in which you may not lose is likely to induce you to make the second loan. Committing additional resources to failing causes based on the (slim) hope that there will be a dramatic change is called **escalation.**[11] Thus, escalation is continuing a commitment to a previous decision, when a "rational" decision maker would withdraw.

Examples of this sort of behavior are commonplace. Do you put more money into the repair of your old car? How long do you wait once you have been put on "hold"? How long do you wait for an elevator? How long do you persist in getting a degree once you realize there is no hope of getting a job after graduation? How many more resources (buying a house, having a baby) do you commit to a failing marriage? How many more soldiers was President Johnson willing to commit to what was obviously the losing proposition of the Vietnam War?

For escalation to exist, there must have been a previous commitment of resources. Because these resources were committed in the past, they

[11]B. M. Staw, "Knee-Deep in the Big Muddy: A Study of Escalating Commitment to a Chosen Course of Action," *Organizational Behavior and Human Performance* 16 (1976): 27–44.

are unrecoverable and should be ignored. That is, they are "sunk," or historical, costs. Objectively, a decision maker should be concerned only with the future costs and benefits associated with a particular course of action. Thus, it does not matter if you have invested 10 years in your current relationship; the primary consideration should be the future costs versus the future benefits of remaining in the relationship. This future-oriented perspective is likely to lead to a more optimal outcome.

In accounting, one of the major prescriptions is to ignore sunk costs. While we are involved in accounting tasks, it is quite easy to implement this rule. However, when we are confronted with similar unrecoverable costs in our daily lives, we tend to include them in our mental calculations. In avoiding a certain loss, a decision maker may discount the negative information received in an attempt to justify the initial decision. In committing additional resources, the decision maker may believe that the downturn is temporary—that contributing more resources increases the chance that the initial decision will be proved correct. But such rationalizations may be very risky to the health of an organization.

An example of escalation is provided in the "FOCUS ON: Escalation." At Merrill Lynch, Howard Rubin fell victim to the phenomenon of escalation. If he had not viewed his options as a choice between certain losses and breaking even, but rather had paid attention to the opportunity costs his decisions incurred, he may well have made a different decision. Victims of escalation do not include opportunity costs in their mental arithmetic. Opportunity costs are the costs of inefficient use of resources. Unlike out-of-pocket costs, which are very vivid and salient in nature, opportunity costs are passive and abstract. These costs are incurred by the passage of time. Ignoring them makes the option of continuing a failing project appear more positive and the option of abandoning the project appear more negative.[12]

While escalation is a very insidious process, the following recommendations can reduce its influence:[13]

1. Set limits on your involvement and commitment in advance, and stick to those limits.
2. Avoid looking to other people to see what you should do, since they are likely to be escalating their commitment inappropriately.
3. Actively reevaluate why you are continuing your commitment (escalation is often a function of impression management—we want other people to think that we know what we are doing).
4. Remind yourself of the costs involved; the opportunity costs or the costs of continuing are often ignored.

[12]G. B. Northcraft and M. A. Neale, "Opportunity Costs and the Framing of Resource Allocation Decisions," *Organizational Behavior and Human Decision Processes* (1986): 28–38.

[13]J. Z. Rubin, "Experimental Research on Third Party Intervention in Conflict: Toward Some Generalizations," *Psychological Bulletin* 87 (1980): 379–391.

**Merrill Lynch Takes a Bath**

Howard Rubin knew his stuff. Merrill Lynch & Co. hired him away from Salomon Brothers in 1985 and put him in charge of trading for its burgeoning mortgage-securities operation. But in May 1987, Merrill said Rubin also knew more than he was telling his bosses. His unauthorized trading in mortgage-backed securities, the firm charged, was a major factor in a whopping $250 million trading loss that the firm suffered in just one week. The unprecedented bath left Merrill thoroughly chastised. "It's poor supervision; we know that," said a spokesman for the firm. "We'll do something about it."

The losses stemmed from a wrinkle in the trading of securities that were backed by pools of mortgages: interest only/principal only (IOPO) instruments. Bond traders buy mortgage-backed instruments and "strip" them; that is, divide them into two parts— one entitles the owners to collect all the interest due on the mortgages, the other entitles other owners to all the principal. Rubin had sold the interest-bearing portion of the bonds he stripped and kept the principal-only paper. He thought the interest rates were going to fall and the value of his investment would rise.

But the market went against him. Trying to recoup his losses, says a Merrill source, he amassed still more principal-only investments. When the market continued to drop, he piled up still more. His supervisors had approved his general strategy but had placed a limit on his risk taking. Merrill says Rubin ignored the strictures. By the time he was found out, the IOPO market had sunk so low that the firm was saddled with huge losses. Merrill said $165 million of the losses came from authorized trades, $85 million from Rubin's allegedly unauthorized trading. Rubin was fired and refused comment.

Source: D. Pauly and P. Wang, "Merrill Lynch Takes a Bath: A $250 Million Loss," *Newsweek*, May 11, 1987, p. 53.

## TYPES OF DECISIONS

If rationality is only an unattainable dream of decision makers, what determines how carefully a decision maker attempts to follow the rational model, versus when (for instance) heuristics are used? What determines just how "bounded" a decision maker's efforts are likely to be?

Individual decisions cover a wide range of issues of varying importance to the organization. At one extreme, decisions can be made quickly—almost without the appearance of conscious thought. At the other extreme, decisions can involve many groups and considerable organizational resources. What influences the amount of cognitive and organizational resources allocated to making a decision? The time and effort put into the decision-making process are directly related to the importance of that decision for the individual and the organization.

The amount of time and resources spent on any decision-making process is a function of three factors: problem significance, solution irreversibility, and decision-maker accountability.[14] The more important the decision to the individual or the organization, the more irreversible the solution once implemented, and the greater the responsibility of the decision maker for the actual decision, the more organized, analytic, and purposeful the decision maker is in making a choice. Decisions that are trivial or easily reversible result in less well-organized decision-making strategies.

The familiarity of a decision also will influence the resources devoted to it. The routine problems that face organization decision makers allow the use of standard operating procedures, rules, and policies as substitutes for comprehensive decision making. If the same problem recurs regularly (for example, how much travel money to allow for any business trip), a policy can be established that makes the decision itself. Rather than confronting the problem anew each time it surfaces, the "automatic" decision greatly reduces information-processing demands for the decision maker. Without standard operating procedures, rules, and policies to direct the daily activity of organizational actors, it is unlikely that managers could ever cope with the minute-to-minute demands for decisions necessary to produce the goods or services demanded by the organization's customers.

## AIDING DECISION MAKING

Certain types of choices may lead decision makers to expend more time and energy approximating the rational ideal, but individual decision making also can be improved by using decision analysis, linear models, and even computerized decision aids.

## DECISION ANALYSIS

Expected-value calculations are an integral part of decision analysis. **Decision analysis** refers to separating the decision process into its components prior to making the decision. One common method of decision analysis used by managers is the **decision tree.** The decision maker needs only four types of information to construct a decision tree:

1. What are the possible courses of action?
2. What are the events that might follow from those actions?
3. What is the likelihood of each event?
4. What is the value of each event to me?

[14]D. W. McAllister, T. R. Mitchell, and L. R. Beach, "The Contingency Model for the Selection of Decision Strategies: An Empirical Test of the Effects of Significance, Accountability, and Reversibility," *Organizational Behavior and Human Performance* 24 (1979): 228–244.

**FIGURE 5–7**        A Decision-Tree Analysis of Whether
                     to Buy Computer Insurance

Decision trees graphically capture the risk inherent in an uncertain choice. The branches specify the possible outcomes and their probabilities of occurrence and thus make it easy to calculate expected values.

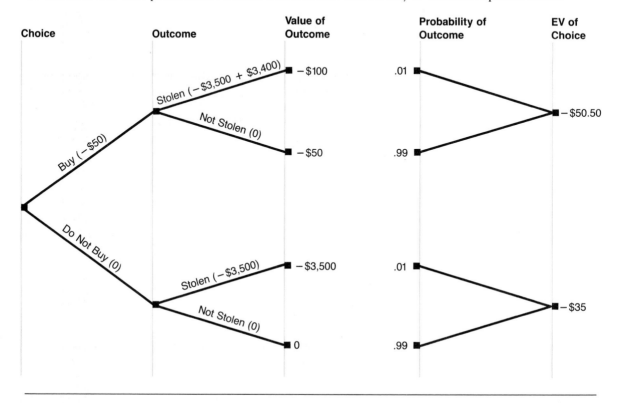

Figure 5–7 illustrates the decision tree used to decide whether or not to purchase computer insurance. The decision tree is an excellent decision aid. As long as the four types of information are available, any decision can be analyzed by such a tree. It forces the decision maker to explicitly consider the bases for the decision. Simply generating the four different types of information may require the decision maker to be more organized than he or she would be otherwise.[15] The obvious problems with this process are that sometimes the information is not available and that values and probabilities are difficult to assess.

While the usefulness of the decision tree hinges on the accuracy of the estimates, it can also be used to see how sensitive the dominant solution

[15]H. R. Arkes and K. R. Hammond, *Judgment and Decision Making: An Interdisciplinary Reader* (Cambridge: Cambridge University Press, 1986).

(buy or do not buy) ~~is to changes in the numbers (values and probabilities) initially assigned~~. Say, for example, that there is really a 5 percent chance that a computer will be stolen rather than the 1 percent chance upon which the initial calculations were based. Running these modified probabilities through the decision tree indicates that now the best solution is to buy the insurance ($EV_{(buy)} = -\$50.25$ and $EV_{(do\ not\ buy)} = -\$175$). Given a change in the probabilities, the decision changes. In this case, a small change in the probability of theft resulted in a different "best" solution. The "best" original solution was very sensitive and thus not very robust. Even if the theft probability were only 2 percent rather than 1 percent, the decision would still change to "buy."

## LINEAR MODELS

~~Linear models are combinations of important variables that predict outcomes of interest~~. Suppose, for example, you were a member of a selection committee for the MBA program. How would you go about choosing who would be admitted to your program? You might consider an applicant's undergraduate grade-point average, letters of recommendation from faculty members, scores on standardized tests such as the Graduate Management Admissions Test (GMAT), outside activities while a student, and the quality of the applicant's undergraduate institution.

If you had all of this information for each applicant, how would you decide who to admit? Would you admit only those who scored well on the GMAT? What about those individuals who did poorly on the GMAT but went to a very selective undergraduate institution and had an outstanding undergraduate GPA? Or what about the applicant who had excellent letters of recommendation but only an above-average undergraduate GPA? What if you had to make these decisions over the course of four to six months? How confident would you be that your decisions were good and your evaluations consistent across applicants?

A linear model (or a consistent way of combining information) may help. In fact, considerable research supports the premise that linear models are superior to experts (the faculty sitting on the selection committee) in predicting outcomes (success in graduate school). The reason for the superior performance of linear models is that the experts are much better at selecting and evaluating information than they are at integrating the information they have collected. The linear model excels at integrating information.[16]

Consider the problems of National Airlines during the gasoline crisis of the early 1970s. For a description of the problem and its eventual solution, see the "Focus on: Linear Models."

---

[16]R. M. Dawes, "The Robust Beauty of Improper Linear Models," *American Psychologist* 34 (1979): 571–582.

FOCUS ON:
Linear Models

**The Fuel Crisis and National Airlines**  The gasoline crisis in the early 1970s had a considerable impact on the airline industry. In four months, prices for aviation fuel soared from an average of $.14 to $.22 per gallon. The federal government also limited the amount of fuel available to an individual airline, based on a percentage of its 1972 fuel consumption.

The resulting difficulties faced by all airlines were staggering. Vendors were often unable to supply fuel at certain cities. There were excess allocations to some cities and shortages in others. The airlines did not plan their consumption of fuel judiciously, and many times their monthly allocations were gone by the middle of the month. With no fuel available, there was a significant increase in cancelled flights and exhorbitant fees were charged for emergency purchases of fuel. Because of these problems, most airlines experienced major increases in operating costs (of which fuel costs were the major contributor).

National Airlines decided that it had to bring fuel costs under control. In deciding how to purchase and allocate fuel, a number of factors had to be considered:

- *Aircraft rotation,* or the chain of flights or legs that each aircraft follows. For example, one plane may leave Seattle as Flight 1413, arrive in Los Angeles, and then leave Los Angeles as Flight 5 going to Chicago. After a few days, the same aircraft may return to Seattle and become Flight 1413 again. Of course, since this is a daily flight, other planes must also be following this schedule.
- *Price, availability, and vendor allocations of fuel.*
- *Quantity of fuel carried by each aircraft.* Extra fuel adds weight to the plane, which causes extra fuel to be burned.
- *Maximum landing weight allowed at a particular airport.*
- *Fuel consumption patterns of different planes.* An aircraft's fuel consumption is a function of its weight, flight altitude, etc.

In solving this problem, National Airlines had to consider 2,400 different variables with 800 constraints (limits) for a flight schedule of 350 legs with 50 vendor combinations and several different types of aircraft. Without a linear program this would be virtually impossible. Using linear programming to determine how, when, and where to buy fuel immediately improved fuel availability and reduced fuel costs. The first month that National used this approach, in June 1974, fuel costs dropped to an average of $.144 per gallon, compared to an average of $.225 per gallon for ten other airlines (including American, United, and Transworld).

In addition, during price negotiations with various vendors, the linear programming model allowed National to determine the effects of proposed price and supply changes on the total system. It also allowed the company to analyze alternative flight schedules quickly to determine their impact on current fuel use.

Source: D. Darnell and C. Loflin, "National Airlines Fuel Management Allocation Model," *Interfaces* (February 1977): pp. 1–16.

Linear models can never completely replace experts. People must decide what to look for in reaching a decision. However, after experts identify the important variables, linear models can combine the information and reach better and more consistent solutions than those of the experts. Yet even though there is overwhelming proof that linear models make superior decisions (unlike humans, they do not get grumpy, angry, tired, or sleepy), there has been considerable resistance to using them in such situations as determining guilt or innocence in criminal trials, evaluating psychiatric admissions, and making personnel-selection decisions or graduate-admission decisions. Resistance to the use of linear models can be traced to a number of causes:

- Our ready memory of successful exceptions to whatever rule was used ("I knew someone once who . . .").
- Self-fulfilling prophecy (a member of the faculty selection committee may believe his or her judgment is vindicated when the candidate does well, regardless of the fact that much of the candidate's success may be due to the positive expectations of the selection committee).
- Fear of loss of control (it may be that what we want from the decision maker is not the best decision, but a decision in our favor; as such, the importance of interpersonal influence cannot be ignored).

For these reasons, the use of linear models is not commonplace in making predictive decisions. Their lack of use, however, has not dampened the interest in finding ways to improve human decision making. Given the increasing use of computers in the workplace, providing the decision maker with computerized decision support systems seems a logical next step.

**COMPUTERIZED DECISION AIDS**

Evidence suggests that even simple decision aids such as worksheets are useful in improving decision making.[17] More sophisticated and appealing than paper-and-pencil worksheets, computerized decision aids may compensate for the frailties and limitations of human decision making. The most sophisticated approach among various computerized decision aids is the use of expert systems.[18] An expert system is a programmed computational rule or algorithm used to generate a decision. The appropriate considerations (that is, variables to be considered), weighted by importance, are programmed in, along with a scheme for integrating them and a series of decision rules. The up-front specification of how the

---

[17]Northcraft and Neale, "Opportunity Costs."

[18]G. A. Gorry and R. B. Krumland, "Artificial Intelligence Research and Decision Support Systems," in J. Bennett (ed.), *Building Decision Support Systems* (Reading, Mass.: Addison-Wesley, 1983).

Computers offer tremendous potential as decision aids. Information can be stored and accessed quickly. Ultimately, of course, computer-aided decisions are only as good as the information the decision maker puts into the computer. The doctors shown here bring the crucial medical judgment to the decision-making process, whereas the computer contributes only the data sorting and calculating capacity.

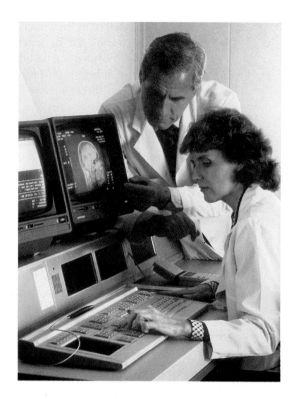

decisions are made allows public scrutiny of this process. This increases the likelihood that faulty assumptions and incorrect calculation strategies can be exposed and corrected. The expert system can, at least, provide a comparison for decisions made by human information processors.

Comparing decisions to those selected by an expert system or a linear program can help human decision makers evaluate the success of their decision process. Determining what is a good decision is often very tricky. Decision makers are constantly faced with making choices in an uncertain environment. An individual may make an excellent decision, based on a careful and objective analysis of the data available, that still results in a bad outcome. Factors beyond an individual's control may turn even the best decision into abject failure.

If we cannot or should not determine the "goodness" of a decision based on the ultimate outcome, then how do we evaluate decisions? While an individual's decision-making process can be evaluated in many ways, we will focus our attention on using ethical standards as the benchmark for judging decision propriety. That is, what are the ethical implications of decision options for the individual, the organization, and society at large?

ETHICAL
DECISIONS

To this point in this chapter, we have approached decision making from the perspective of self-interest. We have examined how an individual decision maker can generate consequences that are good for that decision maker. But what happens when the self-interest of one decision maker interferes with the self-interest or even human rights of another, or the rights of society as a whole? This is the issue of ethics.

The concept of self-interest as the basis for action has been justified by many scholars. One of the earliest was Adam Smith. As evidenced in the "FOCUS ON: Self-Interest," Smith believed that the general welfare of the society is promoted as a side-effect of people's self-interest. People will work harder for their own self-interests than if they are made to contribute directly to society.[19]

---

FOCUS ON:
Self-Interest

**Adam Smith** As the following comments show, Adam Smith believed that people promoted the general welfare only as a side-effect of promoting their own self-interest.

As every individual, therefore endeavors as much as he can both to employ his capital in the support of domestic industry, and so to direct that industry that its produce may be of the greatest value; every individual necessarily labors to render the annual revenue of society as great as he can. He generally, indeed, neither intends to promote the public interest, nor knows how much he is promoting it. By preferring the support of domestic to that of foreign industry, he intends only his own security; and by directing that industry in such a manner as its produce may be of the greatest value, he intends only his own gain, and he is in this, as in many other cases, led by an invisible hand to promote an end which was no part of his intention. Nor is it always the worse for the society that it was no part of it. By pursuing his own interest, he frequently promotes that of the society more effectually than when he really intends to promote it.

Source: A. Smith, *The Wealth of Nations* (New York: Modern Library, 1937), p. 43.

---

The justification of decisions in light of self-interest is compelling. First, it is unlikely that our capitalist system would function if individuals were truly altruistic and pursued the interests of others to the detriment of their own. Second, people are likely to be more highly motivated if they are encouraged to pursue their own self-interests. However, a distinction needs to be made between short-term, or immediate, self-interest and long-term, or enlightened, self-interest. When Adam Smith describes self-interest, he is referring to the long-term view of

[19]R. Buccholz, *Isn't It All a Matter of Self-Interest?* Business Ethics series, Vol. V (Chicago, Ill.: Loyola Marymount, 1986).

**FIGURE 5–8**    The Tragedy of the Commons

A common grazing area is used freely by a town's dairy farmers. Increasing the number of cattle grazed in the area is obviously in the best interest of any particular farmer. However, if all the farmers keep increasing their herds, they will eventually overgraze the commons. Ultimately, they will kill the grass and diminish the collective interest; that is, they will reduce the value of the commons to the group as a whole as well as to themselves as individuals. What should (will) the individual farmer do?

Source: G. R. Hardin, "The Tragedy of the Commons," *Science*, 162 (1968): pp. 1243–1248.

self-interest.[20] The conflict between these two perspectives is often referred to as a social dilemma. That is, when will the best long-term interests of the individual (and, simultaneously, the society) be served when they conflict with the immediate interests of the individual?

A common example of a social dilemma is provided in Figure 5–8, "The Tragedy of the Commons." Obviously it is in the best interest of the individual to graze as many dairy cattle as possible. However, with this strategy, the land quickly becomes unusable for the entire village.

The tragedy of the commons is not an unusual problem. Consider the typical experience in group projects. It is probably in the short-term self-interest of any individual not to contribute his or her fair share in group efforts, especially if the individual effort of each participant cannot be identified. In fact, people who exhibit this unwillingness to contribute to the larger good are termed **free riders.** Free riders are a common problem in work groups.

However, while a free-rider solution is initially attractive, let's consider some of the outcomes that may result from such a choice. First, if all the group members chose that option, then thousands of students in hundreds of colleges would receive poor grades and miss out on a useful learning experience. Alternatively, the individual who chooses this option may enjoy the benefits of receiving a grade without incurring the cost of contributing, but what happens if this person's behavior becomes public knowledge? The free-rider may end up without a group to share the burden of future group projects.

Given these facts, why is it that some individuals will opt for short-term gain to the exclusion of long-term benefits? Why are short-term benefits chosen even in the face of considerable long-term costs? Three factors promote our selection of short-term gains or benefits. First, referring to our earlier discussion of the availability heuristic, immediate benefits are more likely to be vivid and salient to the individual. Time-delayed costs or benefits are likely to be less available to the decision maker. Thus, when deciding the likely outcome of a choice,

[20]A. Smith, *The Wealth of Nations* (New York: Modern Library, 1937).

decision makers may discount the probability of incurring those long-term costs or benefits. Therefore, decision makers will evaluate the short-term benefits as more attractive than the long-term rewards or costs.[21]

Second, choices that maximize short-term gain may be selected because of ignorance or limited cognitive capabilities. That is, from the bounded-rationality perspective, the information search may not have been sufficient for the decision maker to choose the "enlightened" alternative. For example, a fish swimming into a baited net does not know he cannot get out. The decision maker may not possess the cognitive capabilities to make the what-if analyses needed to maximize the long-term value of a complex decision.

Finally, short-term benefits may be very rewarding early on. However, these reinforcers may become less and less rewarding over time until they are eventually punishing. Examples of these sliding reinforcers might include drug and alcohol use/abuse, extramarital affairs, and excessive consumption of natural resources.[22]

If these difficulties are going to plague individual decision makers, then it becomes imperative at an organizational and societal level to institutionalize ethical standards and rules.

## MANAGING ORGANIZATIONAL ETHICS

. . . institutionalizing ethics may sound ponderous, but its meaning is straightforward. It means getting ethics formally and explicitly into daily business life. It means getting ethics into company policy formation at the board and top management levels and through a formal code, getting ethics into all daily decision making and work practices down the line, at all levels of employment. It means grafting a new branch on the corporate decision tree—a branch that reads "right/wrong."[23]

When asked to list factors that might lead to unethical decisions, respondents in a *Harvard Business Review* poll identified the behavior of their superiors as most influential. Other highly ranked factors included lack of a formal policy, the behavior of one's peers, society's moral climate, one's personal financial need, and even (as shown in Figure 5–9) the general ethical climate of the industry.[24]

[21]M. A. Neale, "The Effect of Negotiation and Arbitration Cost Salience on Bargainer Behavior: The Role of Arbitrator and Constituency in Negotiator Judgment," *Organizational Behavior and Human Performance* 36 (1984): 97–111; J. Platt, "Social Traps," *American Psychologist* (August 1973): 641–651.

[22]J. Platt, "Social Traps."

[23]T. V. Purcell and J. Wever, *Institutionalizing Corporate Ethics: A Case History*, Special Study No. 71 (New York: The Presidents Association of American Management Associations, 1979).

[24]S. N. Brenner and E. A. Molander, "Is the Ethics of Business Changing?" *Harvard Business Review* (January-February 1977): 64–68.

**FIGURE 5–9**

For some decision makers, ethics provides absolute standards against which behaviors are judged. As noted in this cartoon, for others, ethics is just another input to the decision-making process.

Since the United States is a cultural "melting pot," it is increasingly important for organizations to specify their ethical standards and expectations of conduct. Given the increasingly frequent occurrences of blatantly unethical and often illegal behavior within large and highly respected organizations, it is critical for managers and firms to promote the ethical conduct of business—that is, the institutionalization of ethics.

**INSTITUTION-ALIZING ETHICS**

Within organizations, ethical principles can be institutionalized in a variety of ways. The goal of such activities is to ensure that ethical concerns are considered in the same routine manner in which legal, financial, and marketing concerns are addressed.

In some corporations, permanent board-level committees are created to monitor the ethical behavior of the organization. These committees, often called "social responsibility" or "public policy" committees, serve two functions within an organization. First, they lend legitimacy to the consideration of an ethics agenda at the highest level of organizational decision making. Second, they symbolically communicate to the employees and external stakeholders of the organization its commitment to ethical principles in conducting business.

A second mechanism for institutionalizing ethics within an organization is the use of a **code of ethics.** Within an organization, this code

Courts protect individuals from illegal acts, but they often cannot prohibit all unethical behavior. Codes of ethics identify acceptable and unacceptable behavior in organizations, much as laws do for society at large. In 1989, Congress rejected President Bush's appointment of John Tower as Secretary of Defense based on allegations of unethical lobbying activities and questionable personal behavior.

describes the general value system of the organization, defines the organization's purpose, and provides guidelines for decision making consistent with these principles. Examples of behaviors routinely prohibited by typical ethics codes are described in Figure 5–10.

A third method which has gained in popularity in recent years is the implementation of ethics training programs. Of 279 large companies responding to a 1985 survey conducted by the Center for Business Ethics at Bentley College in Waltham, Massachusetts, 20 percent said they were using seminars or workshops to reinforce good ethics.[25] Interestingly enough, the most visible companies in the ethics business are those struggling to repair their damaged reputations. Because of the check-kiting behavior illustrated in the opening vignette, E. F. Hutton is one of those. General Dynamics developed an ethics program so that it could remain eligible for its Navy contracts after allegations about improper contracting procedures surfaced. Corporations that have not been guilty of wrongdoing have recently initiated formal ethics programs in an effort to avoid public-relations problems, raise employee morale and productivity, and make their organizations more honest.

When we broaden our perspective on institutionalizing ethics from the organization to the larger society, an interesting cycle is evident. Ethical issues for the organization or the individual are those for which society has not established clear-cut mandates. For example, the domain of ethics is completely separate from the legal domain. Business ethics, then, represent concepts of appropriate and inappropriate behavior that reflect how society views business practices that are not covered by legal principles.

[25]P. Richter, "Big Business Puts Ethics in Spotlight," *Los Angeles Times*, June 19, 1986.

**FIGURE 5–10**    Percentage of Firms with Codes of Ethics Prohibiting
Specific Employee Behaviors

A corporate code of ethics captures the value system of an organization. It also
may increase the probability of ethical behavior by providing guidelines for
individual decision making.

| Prohibited Behavior | Percentage of Firms |
|---|---|
| Extortion, gifts, and kickbacks | 67% |
| Conflict of interests | 65 |
| Illegal political payments | 59 |
| Violation of laws in general | 57 |
| Use of insider information | 43 |
| Bribery | 37 |
| Falsification of corporate accounts | 28 |
| Violation of antitrust laws | 25 |
| Moonlighting | 25 |
| Legal payments abroad | 23 |
| Revealing company secrets | 22 |
| Ignorance of work-related laws | 22 |
| Fraud, deception | 11 |
| Justifying illegal behavior that serves the company | 10 |

Source: R. Chatov, "What Corporate Ethics Statements Say," *California Management Review*
21 (1980): p. 22.

Further, what composes the domain of ethical issues seems to change
in decade-long cycles. Typically, what is part of an ethical agenda at one
time becomes the focus of law in subsequent years. For example,
protection of the environment was an ethical and moral issue beginning
in the 1950s. The first major environmental legislation was passed in the
1960s. Concern about unethical behavior on the part of U.S. firms
operating in foreign countries was an ethical issue in the 1960s, and the
Foreign Corrupt Practices Act was passed by Congress in the 1970s.
Issues of workplace safety and employment discrimination were ethical
problems in the 1960s that resulted in major legislation in the 1970s.
Concerns with sexual harassment in the workplace in the 1970s led to the
implementation of laws in the 1980s.

Apparently, once ethical concerns gain sufficient attention, they
become codified into law. However, this is not to suggest that one should
ignore such dilemmas until they become law. Rather, this evolution is the
process of individuals, organizations, and society at large forming a
consensus about the appropriate form of conduct. Because the laws
reflect many of society's attitudes, current ethical concerns will become
the grist for future lawmakers. Each individual, then, has a responsibility
to examine his or her behavior within the workplace and the community

INTERNATIONAL
FOCUS ON:
South Africa

**Ethics, Social Responsibility, and South African Investments** A major example of the impact of ethics on decision making can be observed in the controversy over American investments in South Africa. In supporting investments in South Africa, a number of financial managers question whether they are, indeed, supporting apartheid. In attempting to resolve this thorny ethical issue, Leon H. Sullivan, a Baptist minister from Philadelphia, Pennsylvania, developed a code of behavior for companies still involved in South Africa.

1. Nonsegregation of races in all eating, comfort, locker-room, and work facilities.
2. Equal and fair employment practices for all employees.
3. Equal pay for all employees doing equal or comparable work for the same period of time.
4. Initiation and development of training programs that will prepare substantial numbers of blacks, coloreds, and Asians for supervisory, administrative, clerical, and technical jobs.
5. Increasing the number of blacks, coloreds, and Asians in management and supervisory positions.
6. Improving the quality of employees' lives outside the work environment in such areas as housing, transportation, schooling, recreation, and health facilities.

These principles have created a great deal of controversy. Some people argue that what is needed is for all American companies to leave South Africa. The basis for this argument is that without American business, the South African economy would shut down. Economic failure would result in removing the current government from power and allowing another, more liberal, government to be established.

Those who disagree with this position suggest that the resulting economic depression would hurt most those already suffering under apartheid. If the economic conditions in South Africa worsen, the likely response of the Afrikaners would be to impose more stringent segregation policies. In addition, complete U.S. divestiture would cripple the black unions. Many observers believe that it is the black unions that will allow blacks to have a greater voice in the country's decisions. From this perspective, American companies may have more of an impact by staying than by leaving. Until about 1986, even Reverend Sullivan supported the latter perspective in suggesting that companies stay in South Africa and use their influence to bring about peaceful change. Now, because of mounting political pressure, Sullivan and other leaders are supporting the exodus of U.S. companies from South Africa.

Source: "Pull Out Parade," *Time,* November 3, 1986, pp. 32–34; Stratford P. Sherman, "Scoring Corporate Conduct in South Africa," *Fortune,* July 9, 1984, pp. 168–172.

and incorporate ethical concerns into the decision-making process. An example of the use of ethical concerns in the behavior of individuals and organizations is illustrated in the "INTERNATIONAL FOCUS ON: South Africa."

CREATIVITY

A final aspect of individual decision making is the individualistic, novel, idea-generating process known as **creativity.** In the past, most people believed that creativity was something you were born with. Recent research, however, suggests otherwise. Creativity now is viewed as a process of mental gymnastics. The creative process draws on all parts of the brain, from knowledge, logic, imagination, and intuition to the ability to see relationships between ideas and things.[26]

The notion that creativity can be learned has not been ignored by corporate America. A 1983 study of 25 major companies found that a majority had undertaken some sort of formal training in creativity within the last two years.[27] While a number of different methods are used to teach creativity, four prescriptions are common to most creativity training programs:

1. First, make sure you thoroughly understand the problem you are trying to solve. Sometimes problems elude solutions because they are poorly defined.
2. Relax. Stress reduces creative ability.
3. Try to think in terms of analogies or metaphors. For example, how is this problem similar to problems you have solved previously? If that doesn't help, try thinking about the problem as a paradox and find an analogy that solves it. In general, the idea here is to break out of rigid thinking patterns that may block new ideas. Some examples of creative ideas born of analogies and paradoxical thinking are described in the "FOCUS ON: Creativity."

[26]E. T. Smith, S. Yanchiniski, M. Sabin, and P. E. Simmons, "Are You Creative?" *Business Week,* September 30, 1985, pp. 80–84.

[27]Reported in W. Kiechel, "Getting Creative," *Fortune,* July 25, 1983, pp. 109–114.

FOCUS ON:
Creativity

**From Cats to Spoiled Beer**  One way to think creatively is to use analogies and paradoxes. Some successful users of these techniques include Eli Whitney, Sister Tabatha Babbett, and Adolph Coors Co. Eli Whitney conjured up the idea of the cotton gin by watching a cat try to catch a chicken through a fence—just the thing to comb seeds out of cotton bolls. Sister Babbett, while watching two men saw wood with a straight saw as she worked at her spinning wheel, figured that the job would be much easier if teeth were cut into the edge of a wheel—hence the development of the circular saw.

Paradox was the method by which the Adolph Coors Co. solved the problem of paying to dispose of gallons of spoiled beer. Inspired by the scene in *Tom Sawyer* in which Tom talks his friends into helping him whitewash the fence, Coors now sells its spoiled beer to the Japanese to be used as feed for their beef cattle.

Source: "Are You Creative?" *Business Week,* September 30, 1985, p. 84.

4. Pay attention to daydreams. Try to put together an image or piece of information that is outside the problem. Reconciling the two can force the mind to make new connections. Try, for example, consulting the dictionary. This worked for a greeting-card company. Combining the word *shrink* and the business (greeting cards) led to the development of business card–sized greetings that could be slipped into lunch boxes and shirt pockets.

Creativity can be cultivated. To do so, a decision maker must look at things in new and different ways. Creativity is a form of decision making that requires heuristics rather than logical, comprehensive calculation.

## SUMMARY

Because human beings make thousands of decisions every day, the process of decision making appears deceptively simple. Upon closer examination, however, it is clear that making a good decision is often difficult and time-consuming. While individuals would like to perceive their decision process as rational, we are unable to meet the cognitive and information demands necessary to reach the optimal solution.

Although the demands of rationality exceed the capabilities of human decision makers, we still strive to make rational decisions. Decision makers adapt to their limitations by four means: conducting local rather than comprehensive alternative searches, evaluating alternatives sequentially rather than simultaneously, satisficing rather than optimizing, and using judgmental heuristics to reduce information-processing demands.

Attempts to improve our decision-making skills are made more difficult by the uncertain nature of our environment. Not knowing for certain what outcome will result from a particular decision alternative, we are forced to include elements of risk in our mental calculations. Expected value models and decision trees are useful mechanisms when probabilities are clear and outcomes can be assigned different values or utilities. However, many decision processes are not so clear. Even when a dominant solution can be identified by expected-value calculations or the decision tree, that option is not always selected. To understand how decisions are made, other factors, such as the risk preferences of decision makers—in addition to probabilities and preferences—need to be considered.

Given the inevitability of flawed decision making, how can we make better decisions? We can develop linear models and computerized decision support systems. The use of these "crutches" does not guarantee great outcomes. We must also consider the ethical implications of decisions at the individual, organizational, and societal level.

Attempts to ensure that ethical considerations be a routine part of organizational decision making have led to different organizational interventions. Some organizations have instituted board-level committees to tackle ethical issues, adopted official codes of ethics, and implemented ethics training for employees. In addition to these organizational efforts, society, through legislation, provides a final mechanism for reinforcing ethical decision making, removing the decision from the voluntary domain of ethics to the regulated area of law.

Improving the general process of our decision making is a continuing process. With the advent of computers with high-speed calculation capabilities, some of the cognitive limitations of the human information-processing system can be overcome. However, the decision maker must have both access to the machines and a willingness to trust their programming and generated solutions. As these decision support systems become more flexible and people become more comfortable with them, the quality of human decision making is likely to improve considerably.

## KEY TERMS

**Availability bias**   Assessing the frequency or likelihood of an event's occurrence by how easily it is remembered, even though memory recall is influenced by factors unrelated to the frequency of an event.

**Bounded rationality**   A model of individual decision making that diverges from the rational ideal in being based on a limited perspective, the sequential evaluation of alternatives, satisficing, and the use of judgmental heuristics.

**Code of ethics**   Mechanism for institutionalizing ethics within an organization that describes the general value system of the organization, its purpose, and guidelines for decision making consistent with these principles.

**Creativity**   Individualistic, novel, idea-generating process.

**Decision analysis**   Separating the decision to be made into its components before making a decision.

**Decision tree**   A common type of decision aid using four types of information: possible courses of action, events that might follow from these actions, likelihood of each event, and value of each event.

**Escalation**   Committing additional resources to failing causes based on the slim hope that there will be a dramatic change.

**Expected value**   Value of an option, determined by summing the values assigned to each possible consequence of an action, multiplied by the probabilities that each of these possible consequences will occur.

**Framing**   Judgmental heuristic that decision makers use to deal with risk in which they become increasingly likely to take risks when confronting potential losses and increasingly likely to avoid risks when confronting possible gains.

**Free rider** Person who accepts the benefits of being a member of a group but is unwilling to contribute to the good of the group.

**Judgmental heuristics** Rules of thumb, or shortcuts, that reduce the information-processing demands on decision makers.

**Rationality** Basing a decision on careful and calculated action alternatives and their consequences.

**Representativeness** Decision heuristic based on the belief that an outcome should resemble its cause.

**Risk** Amount of uncertainty associated with a particular decision alternative or choice.

**Risk averse** Willingness of a decision maker to pay a premium

to avoid risk, ignoring the expected-value solution.

**Risk neutral** Indifference of a decision maker between risky and certain outcomes if they have the same expected value.

**Risk seeking** Willingness of a decision maker to pay a premium to experience risk.

**Satisficing** Foregoing the optimal solution in favor of one that is acceptable or reasonable in order to save the time and effort needed for extended comparisons.

**Uncertainty** Consequences of an action can be known only in terms of a perceived likelihood of occurrence.

DISCUSSION
QUESTIONS

1. Think about your general strategies for making a decision. How do they change when you make a decision about your choice of breakfast foods, compared to what computer you will purchase? What are some of the critical differences in these very different decisions?

2. Even if we did have the cognitive mechanisms necessary to make optimal choices, why might we choose not to engage in a rational decision strategy?

3. What are the three ways in which an individual can achieve a "great" outcome? What differentiates the expert

from the novice, if both can achieve "great" outcomes?

4. What is your general attitude toward risk? List some situations in which you are willing to take risks. List some situations in which you are not willing to take risks. In what general ways do these two groups of situations differ?

5. Ethical dilemmas can occur at all levels of organizations. Why is it difficult for individuals who are low in the organizational hierarchy to confront such issues? Why is it difficult for individuals who are highly placed in the organization to address these ethical concerns?

6. Linear models of decision making have consistently outperformed the experts who developed the models. How can this be true? What factors would lead a computer model (or a linear model) to outperform the expert on whose judgment the model was based? List some of the reasons why there is so little acceptance of linear models as substitutes for human judgment. Would you be willing to have your application to graduate school evaluated by a linear model? Why or why not?

7. Consider the following poem:

I am not free
Nor want to be.
I produce my claim to humanity
Through my willingness to accept
The unjustified demands
Of duty.*

What approach to decision making is implied by this poem? What are the implications for a manager? Would you want this person working for you?

8. Why might it be important for people to believe that they take action on the basis of rational decisions?

*J. G. March, *Academic Notes* (London: Poets' and Painters' Press, 1974).

**IF YOU WANT TO KNOW MORE**

The study of individual decision making is currently enjoying great popularity in both the popular and academic press. Recent articles such as "Decisions, Decisions" by Kevin McKean, which appeared in the June 1985 issue of *Discover* magazine, focus on identifying the cognitive biases to which human decision makers are subject. Understanding risk was the basis for an article entitled "The Compleat Worrier: Staying Alive in the 20th Century" by William Allman, published in the October issue of *Science '85*. An interesting but older article on escalation entitled "Psychological Traps," by Jeffrey Rubin, appeared in the March 1981 issue of *Psychology Today*.

These articles provide excellent overviews of cognitive biases, risk, and escalation. However, for a more indepth examination, one of the earlier (1957) books by Simon entitled *Administrative Behavior* certainly merits attention. More recent books on the topic of individual decision making include Bazerman's *Judgment in Managerial Decision Making* (Wiley, 1989); Kahneman's, Slovic's, and Tversky's reader *Judgment under Uncertainty: Heuristics and Biases* (Cambridge University Press, 1982); and Hogarth's *Judgment and Choice* (Wiley, 1981).

For a more detailed exploration of ethics and ethical decision making within organizations, you may wish to read Blanchard's and Peale's *The Power of Ethical Management: You Don't Have to Cheat to Win* (Morrow, 1987); Mark Pastin's latest book, *The Hard Problems of Management: Gaining the Ethics Edge* (Jossey, Bass, 1986); or *The Way We Do Things around Here: Managers Talk Ethics* (Wiley, 1986) by Barbara Ley Toffler.

ON YOUR
OWN

In a recent article in the *Harvard Business Review,* Laura Nash suggests that there are 12 questions that "draw upon the traditional philosophical frameworks [of ethics], but avoid the level of abstractions normally associated with formal moral reasoning." These are practical questions which, if answered honestly, may give you a general indication of the ethical nature of your decision.

1. Have you defined the problem accurately?
2. How would you define the problem if you stood on the other side of the fence?
3. How did this situation occur in the first place?
4. To whom or to what do you give your loyalty as a person and a member of the corporation?
5. What is your intention in making this decision?
6. How does this intention compare with the probable results?
7. Whom could your decision or action injure?
8. Can you discuss the problem with the affected parties before you make your decision?
9. Are you confident that your position will be as valid over a long period of time as it seems now?
10. Could you disclose without qualm your decision or action to your boss, your CEO, the board of directors, your family, or society as a whole?
11. What is the symbolic potential of your action if understood? If misunderstood?
12. Under what conditions would you allow exceptions to your stand?

The twelve questions are a way to articulate an idea of the responsibilities involved and to lay them open for examination. Whether or not a final policy emerges from this process, the process is useful for the following reasons:

■ The process encourages talk in a group on a subject that traditionally has been reserved for one's conscience.
■ It is a way of determining the values and goals of a company.
■ It provides a mechanism for sharing information within an organization.
■ It may uncover dramatic differences between values and the practicality of their implementation.
■ It helps improve the nature and range of alternatives.
■ It is cathartic.

Source: L. Nash, "Ethics without the Sermon," *Harvard Business Review* (November/ December 1981): pp. 78–90.

CLOSING CASE
FOR CHAPTER 5

## THE MANAGER'S MEMO

FROM: P. Dawson, Purchasing Manager

TO:    F. Baumgartner, Vice President, Small-Car Division

RE:    Alternative Supplier of Seat Belts

The representative of a potential supplier has informed me that his
company can supply us with seat belts made of a new material. The
primary advantage of using this supplier is that the new material is less
expensive. At our present rate of production, switching to this
manufacturer could save our company $3 million a year.

According to the sales rep, the new seat belts are like the standard
ones in every way except that they are slightly less strong. In crash tests,
the seat belts tear apart in one in 10,000 tests. This seems like a minor
risk, although the standard seat belts never tear apart in crash tests. (As
an aside, I checked with the legal department and learned that the
average settlement for a death of a driver of one of our cars when we
were held liable is $1 million.)

Considering the competitive pressure we are under, this alternative
supplier may be a wise choice. I am, of course, aware that the company
is considering closing the Mill City plant in order to cut costs. Perhaps
the savings from this alternative supplier would enable us to keep the
plant open, saving 500 to 1,000 jobs.

Please let me know whether you want to try the new seat belts in
your division's cars.

CASE DISCUSSION
QUESTIONS

Based on what you have learned about individual decision making,
assume that you are the vice president of the Small-Car Division, and
write a memo describing your decision. Consider whether your decision
is a rational one and, if not, why it is not.

CHAPTER

# 6

# Conflict in Organizations

TENSION AND
INFIGHTING AT
THE FIRST
NATIONAL BANK
OF CHICAGO

In early May 1980, Robert Abboud was fired as chairman of the First National Bank of Chicago by its board of directors. The response on Wall Street and among the bank's employees was surprisingly positive. Employees were quoted as saying "people were singing 'Ding-dong, the witch is gone',", and bank executives and spouses were reportedly celebrating Abboud's dismissal with "steaks and champagne."

Such glee at the chairman's departure was predictable, for he had been abrasive, autocratic, and unpopular since being named to that position in 1975. When he was selected, two of the other three candidates for the position and more than two hundred bank officers resigned.

In his defense, the conflict did not begin with Mr. Abboud's tenure; rather, his selection as chairman may have exacerbated an already existing condition. One middle-level bank officer indicated that the tendency since 1972 was to take sides and take "swipes" at the

other team. Individuals were defined based upon their affiliation with a particular "side." A rumor, since proved false, indicated that the First National Bank of Chicago's poor performance (a 47 percent drop in operating net income in the fourth quarter of 1979) was directly attributable to Edwin H. Yeo III, the top financial executive. The bank officer recalls, "I don't remember where I heard it, and I had no idea if any of it was true, but I passed it on anyway. Yeo was the enemy." (This particular employee was reported to be a supporter of Abboud.)

A few days before Yeo resigned, an unsigned memo was circulated which detailed complaints about Yeo's management style. No one knew who wrote the memo or how it got circulated; it was assumed to be written by a senior-level executive. Its wide circulation and implied legitimacy resulted in the perception that the accusations were, indeed, true.

Some observers suggested that the conflict evident at the First

National Bank of Chicago was the result of Abboud's choice of talented but ambitious outsiders for inner-circle positions. Others believed that Abboud's style was perceived as abrasive only by those who "didn't like to go in and face him because they felt they might be asked a question they couldn't answer."

Regardless of the basis of the conflict, the friction within the bank was regarded by many observers as so severe that it had seriously affected operations. While Abboud is given credit for strengthening the balance sheet and stabilizing the loan portfolio after the 1973–1975 recession, many employees contend that he intensified the conflict by playing executives off one another and criticizing subordinates in public. Because of this environment, the bank's top managers may have been so immersed in political infighting that they ignored the larger organizational issues. It was

reported that, because of the organizational climate, bank executives refused to confront some of the bank's major problems. Instead, managers preferred to blame "bad data" or assume that the bank would "grow out of the problem." As a result, the bank's holding company had a reduction in net operating income of 12 percent in 1979 and 44 percent in the first quarter of 1980.

Although fired by the directors of the First National Bank of Chicago in 1980, Robert Abboud was selected to head the struggling First City Bancorp of Texas in the second biggest bank bailout in U.S. history. His management style of personally approving almost every commercial loan considered by the bank, which irked many of his department heads, may be just what First City needs. His associates say Abboud believes righting the woes of First City would be the ultimate vindication for his 1980 ouster.

Sources: Lawrence Roet, "Bank Politics: First Chicago with or without Abboud Is a Place of Tension," *The Wall Street Journal,* May 13, 1980; Todd Vogel, "Abboud Gets His Bank," *Business Week,* May 2, 1988, 38.

## THE NATURE OF CONFLICT IN ORGANIZATIONS

As evidenced in the description of the First National Bank of Chicago, **resource conflict** is a critical consideration in both individual and organizational performance. Employees at the bank avoided or played down the importance of problems the bank was facing. No one seemed willing to bear the costs inflicted by the enormous level of conflict within this organization. What happened at the First National Bank of Chicago illustrates the destructive nature of uncontrolled conflict. However, as noted in Chapter 1, conflict is not only a common organizational experience, but a defining characteristic of behavior in organizations.

Conflict—the result of individuals having separate but incompatible interests—becomes a critical determinant of organizational behavior in the face of perceived or real **resource scarcity.** That is, conflicts become important when there are not enough resources (food, love, attention, cars, clothes, opportunities, and so on) for all to accomplish their goals. Consequently, individuals must compete with others for a share of those scarce resources. Competition can occur between family members and friends, among social groups, and within organizations. It should be noted that conflict does not always lead to competition, unless resources are scarce. If two marketing executives have conflicting ideas about how to sell a new product and the marketing budget can accommodate both ideas, the conflict generates no competition. For two individuals (or groups) to compete, they must perceive their goals to be mutually exclusive (that is, if one party gets what he or she wants, the other cannot). In the case of the First National Bank of Chicago, conflicting goals and opinions within management's inner circle apparently could not be satisfied under Abboud's leadership.

While managers may be guilty of creating conflict, they are more often associated with managing conflict. Of the ten managerial roles identified by Mintzberg, three specifically relate to conflict management duties.[1] Managers deal directly with organizational conflict in the roles of disturbance handler, negotiator, and resource allocator. In fact, if you ask managers how they spend each day, they will report that on average over 20 percent of each working day is spent in some form of conflict-management activity.[2]

The importance of conflict to organizational behavior was first highlighted in the 1920s by early management theorist Mary Parker Follett. In contrast to the mechanistic perspectives of her more famous contemporaries (such as Frederick Taylor), who focused on ways to structure organizations to avoid conflict, Follett believed that conflict was inherent and necessary for effective organizational performance. Much of her theorizing now serves as the basis for current perspectives on managing conflict in the workplace. An overview of her views and work is presented in the "Focus on: The Nature of Conflict."

It is important to remember that while all organizational members are destined to be involved in a variety of conflicts and competitions, individual interests are not all incompatible nor is conflict uniformly bad or unwanted. As noted in Chapter 1, conflict occurs when individuals have differing perceptions, beliefs, and goals. Such differences are both inevitable and healthy. Multiple and conflicting perspectives on a problem, when effectively managed, can reveal creative solutions and insights. Conflict, as with many other human conditions, is destructive in the extreme. When conflict is poorly managed and leads to hostility and infighting—as at the First National Bank of Chicago—it becomes

[1]H. Mintzberg, *The Nature of Managerial Work* (New York: Harper and Row, 1973).

[2]K. Thomas and W. Schmidt, "A Survey of Managerial Interests with Respect to Conflict," *Academy of Management Journal* 19 (1976): 315–318.

**FOCUS ON:**

The Nature
of Conflict

**Mary Parker Follett**    The view that conflict can have a positive influence on organizational performance is usually considered a rather modern invention. Early management theorists tended to endorse the perception that conflict resulted in poor organizational performance. In fact, scientific management focused on reducing the amount of interaction and interdependence (and, thus, opportunities for conflict) among workers.

One management theorist provided a stark contrast to the prevailing view of conflict in the 1920s. Mary Parker Follett (1868–1933) believed that conflict provided management with an opportunity for creativity. She was one of the first management theorists to break away from the tenets of scientific management and to focus instead on developing philosophical and psychological foundations of management.

Follett defined conflict simply as difference. She noted, "As conflict— difference—is here in the world, as we cannot avoid it, we should, I think, use it. Instead of condemning it, we should set it to work for us." From Follett's perspective, conflict was neither good nor bad. She compared conflict to the necessary friction between the wheel of a locomotive and its track, suggesting that conflict was a critical component of organizational life.

The influence of her thinking is found in the work of many modern conflict-management theorists. She first introduced the concept of "integration" as her preferred method for dealing with conflict. Integration, she wrote, produced outcomes in which the desires of both parties are recognized and neither side has had to sacrifice. Such a strategy was compared to the other two forms of conflict management: domination and compromise. While her theorizing is consistent with more modern views of conflict, it is interesting to speculate why her work received so little attention for so long.

Source: M. P. Follett, "Constructive Conflict," in *Dynamic Administration: The Collected Papers of Mary Parker Follett*, eds. E. M. Fox and L. Urwick (New York: Hippocrene, 1982), pp. 1–20.

destructive. However, too little apparent conflict often signals serious organizational or group problems as well.

Consider, for example, two married couples: one constantly fights and bickers, another never fights. Both couples are likely to be having problems. The apparent absence of inevitable conflict often means that important differences between individuals are being suppressed or covered up. This does not mean that fighting is a good thing. It does mean that differences in perceptions, beliefs, and goals are inevitable and can be useful—but only if these conflicts are expressed so that they can be managed properly.

Examples of too much conflict are common in our society. Examples of too little conflict are much more difficult to identify. In his book *Groupthink*, Irving Janis suggests that disastrous foreign policy decisions often result when too little conflict is expressed within important

Organizational conflict is not only inevitable but healthy when managed well. At Iowa Beef Processing (IBP), management and the United Food and Commercial Workers International Union (UFCW) worked together to decrease safety hazards in the packinghouse, which benefited both the employees and the company. At the podium are UFCW President William H. Wynn (left) and IBP Executive Vice President Maurice McGill. Seated at left is Robert Harbrant, president of the AFL-CIO's Food and Allied Service Trades Department, who helped negotiate the agreement.

decision-making bodies.[3] In a special task force, for instance, too little expressed conflict usually means that either inevitable conflicts are being suppressed or there are not enough diverse perspectives to generate insightful, high-quality decisions. Thus, moderate levels of conflict within organizations and between individuals are desirable if managed appropriately. Figure 6–1 illustrates the relationship between levels of conflict and organizational outcomes.

Too much conflict can be detrimental to organizations when it arouses anxiety in individuals, lowers job satisfaction levels, decreases productivity, increases turnover, and reduces the amount of information sharing and creative risk taking among employees. It may create a climate of mistrust or defeat. Too little apparent conflict hampers organizational functioning when it results from the suppression of critical (and useful) differences among organizational actors or the withdrawal of active involvement or commitment by organizational participants. Both suppression and withdrawal are likely to result in poorer organizational performance because of inadequate information sharing, ignorance of critical interdependencies and critical differences, reduced participation, and low employee commitment to organizational goals and activities.

Conflict is useful to organizations in a variety of ways. Effectively managed, conflict promotes creative problem solving and the search for new ways of doing business. It increases employee interest and clarifies individual decisions and perceptions. In addition to its motivating and involving aspects, conflict can point up problem areas and signal the need for change within an organization. It allows a variety of perspectives to be brought to bear in finding new solutions to problems and identifying new directions for the organization. Thus, the successful manager is not the one who eliminates conflict in the organization.

[3]I. Janis, *Groupthink: Psychological Studies of Policy Decisions and Fiascoes* (Boston: Houghton-Mifflin, 1982).

**FIGURE 6–1**                  Conflict Intensity and Organizational Outcomes

Conflict occurs because people differ in their perceptions, beliefs, and goals. Some conflict in organizations is not just inevitable, but useful and healthy, if managed appropriately.

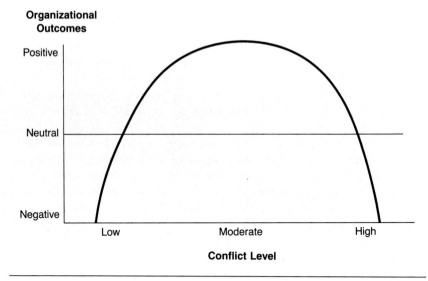

Source: L. D. Brown, *Managing Conflict at Organizational Interfaces* (Reading, Mass.: Addison-Wesley, 1983).

Rather, the successful manager is the one who manages moderate levels of conflict to achieve individual and organizational goals.

## TYPES AND LEVELS OF CONFLICT

### THE JOHNSONS' FOUR TYPES OF CONFLICT

As noted earlier, conflict becomes important because of scarce resources. However, scarce resources and decisions about how they are to be allocated can take many forms in organizations. Two researchers, David and Robert Johnson, have suggested that whenever individuals with wide ranges of skills and expertise come together to make decisions, managing the resulting conflict and information exchange is an essential component of successful management.[4] Critical to the Johnsons' perspective is how the conflict surfaces—the process or procedure by which the conflict occurs. The Johnsons have identified four types of conflict that surface when individuals or groups come together to decide which of several courses of action should be taken to reach the organization's goals and objectives. The four types of conflict are **controversy, debate, concurrence seeking,** and **individualistic decision making.**

Controversy exists when one person's (or group's) ideas, information, perspective, or opinions are in conflict with another's and the two seek to understand and resolve these differences. Consider a policy group determining whether more or less regulation is needed to manage the disposal of hazardous wastes. Because only one policy statement (the

[4]D. W. Johnson and R. Johnson, *Learning Together and Alone: Cooperation, Competition, and Individualizations,* 2d ed. (Englewood Cliffs, N.J.: Prentice-Hall, 1987).

scarce resource in this case) concerning hazardous waste management is expected from this group, the potential for controversy exists because the competing perspectives within the group must eventually be resolved. One or both parties must change their perceptions, beliefs, or goals, or the parties must produce a policy statement that accommodates their differences. In effect, the larger decision-making body is divided into subgroups, each advocating a particular perspective; information is exchanged and evaluated; and differences are resolved. Whenever multiple alternatives are being considered, there is a potential for controversy.

Debate stands in contrast to controversy. Debate involves both the individuals (or groups) who argue for incompatible alternatives and a judge who makes the decision based upon the relative merits of both sides' arguments. In a debate, both parties to the conflict compete to present the best argument, and there is no attempt to understand or resolve differences.

Concurrence seeking occurs when group members suppress conflict to seek agreement. The problem of groupthink presented in Chapter 9 is an example of extreme concurrence seeking. New information that could upset the perceived consensus is ignored. There is little information search and, thus, the potential for high-quality decisions is low. Often the underlying goal of concurrence seeking (and groupthink) is to preserve the harmony of the group rather than to reach the best decision.

Individualistic decision making occurs when each member of the group independently selects his or her most preferred alternative without interacting with other group members. These members are therefore unaware of the others' differing perspectives and expertise. Because each person has already reached a conclusion, the motivation to learn and interact with other group members is minimal. Of course, individualistic decision making is not possible when organizational resources are too scarce to implement all individual decisions. Even when possible, it is not healthy if the management of conflicting perspectives would enhance decision quality. Figure 6–2 summarizes these four types of conflict.

In their work, the Johnsons suggest that controversy is the healthiest type of conflict in organizational settings. It is the type of conflict that will, in the long run, result in better decisions and improved organizational interaction. The likelihood that controversy will be the process by which a particular conflict is managed is improved when the participants follow a five-step process. These steps and the rules necessary for successful controversy are described in Figure 6–3.

In examining these different types of organizational conflict, one should bear in mind that conflict can occur at a variety of levels in an organization: within individuals, between individuals, between organizational groups, and among organizations. We will consider each of these levels separately.

**FIGURE 6–2**    Process of Controversy, Debate, Concurrence Seeking, and Individualistic Decision Making

Controversy, debate, concurrence seeking, and individualistic decision making represent four different ways in which conflict surfaces in organizations. Controversy is the healthiest because disputants share their ideas and perspectives. This fosters better understanding of differences in beliefs, perceptions, and goals and can lead to new and creative allocations of organizational resources.

| Controversy | Debate | Concurrence Seeking | Individualistic Decision Making |
|---|---|---|---|
| Active exchange of information and elaboration of position | Active exchange of information and elaboration of position | Active restatement of group's position | No formal statement of position or active exchange of information |
| Challenged by opposing views | Challenged by opposing views | Quick compromise to a single view | Considers only one perspective |
| Uncertain as to the correctness of a position; cognitive conflict | Uncertain as to correctness of position; cognitive conflict | Certain as to "correct" action | Certain as to "correct" action |
| Arouses curiosity about alternative views | Arouses curiosity about alternative views | Arouses no curiosity about alternatives | Arouses no curiosity about alternative perspectives |
| Requires high reconceptualization | Requires moderate reconceptualization | Requires no reconceptualization | Requires no reconceptualization |
| High-quality outcomes | Moderate-quality outcomes | Potential for poor-quality outcomes | Potential for poor-quality outcomes |
| Positive regard for competing other | Moderate regard for competing other | Indifferent with respect to other | Indifferent with respect to other |

Source: D. W. Johnson, R. T. Johnson, and K. Smith, "Choosing among Alternatives: Controversy within Decision-Making Situations," *Managing Conflict: An Interdisciplinary Approach*, ed. M. A. Rahim. (Praeger Publishers, New York, a division of Greenwood Press, Inc., 1989), pp. 251–64. Copyright © 1989 by M. Afzalur Rahim. Used with permission.

## INDIVIDUAL-LEVEL CONFLICT

**Intrapersonal Conflict**    When conflict exists at an individual level, it can take the form of intrapersonal conflict (conflict within an individual) or interpersonal conflict (conflict between individuals). In the case of intrapersonal conflict, choosing one goal and selecting the appropriate alternative to maximize this goal removes other alternatives from consideration. For example, in deciding to go to graduate school, an applicant must eventually make a choice for one particular program, thus eliminating the other schools from consideration. The amount of conflict that surfaces in these decisions depends upon the attractiveness of each choice. Three common types of intrapersonal goal conflict have

**FIGURE 6–3**                       Successfully Dealing with Controversy

For conflict to be healthy, it must be managed well. These five steps are a prescription for controversy: the healthy sharing and resolving of differences. The accompanying "rules" offer a frame of mind that will help make controversy productive.

To deal with controversy, the following five-step procedure is recommended:

1. **Preparing positions:** Meet with others who hold your perspective on the issue and plan how to argue effectively for your position. Make sure your group has mastered as many of the arguments as possible.

2. **Presenting positions:** Be forceful and persuasive in presenting your positions. Take notes and clarify anything you do not understand when the opposing pair present their position.

3. **Discussing the issues:** Present as many facts as you can to support your point of view. Critically listen to the opposing position, asking for facts that support that position. Work together as a group to get all the facts out. Make sure each side understands the facts that support each perspective.

4. **Reversing perspectives:** Reverse the roles by arguing the opposing position. In arguing for this position, be as forceful and persuasive as you can. Elaborate the opposing position.

5. **Reaching a decision:** Come to a decision to which all parties can agree. Summarize the best arguments for each position. Detail the facts supporting each position. Develop a position statement that details your arguments and the basis for your group's decision.

### Rules

In conducting a "controversy," certain rules and behavioral assumptions should be observed when arguing your position:

1. I am critical of ideas, not people. I challenge and refute the ideas of the opposing group but I do not challenge or reject the individuals presenting the ideas or arguments.

2. I will focus on attaining the best decision possible, not on winning.

3. I encourage everyone to participate and understand the relevant information.

4. I listen to opposing ideas, even if I am not in agreement.

5. I restate what I have heard if it is not clear.

6 I first try to bring out all the ideas and facts supporting both sides, and then I try to integrate them in a way that makes sense.

7. I try to understand both sides of the issue.

8. I change my mind when the evidence clearly indicates that I should do so.

---

been identified, each representing different levels of attractiveness among options.

**Approach-approach conflict** occurs when an individual must choose between two equally attractive alternatives, such as two outstanding job offers. On first blush, this may seem to be an ideal situation. However, if both alternatives are equally attractive, then the choice between them may be difficult. Fortunately, this type of conflict is not long lasting because often we are able to find reasons why one choice dominates—if only just by a little bit. Once this happens, then the slightly preferred option is chosen.

Unfortunately, approach-approach conflict does not always end there. Often, once the choice is made, "decision regret"[5] may occur. The option not chosen now becomes more attractive, simply because it was not chosen. Decision regret may lead decision makers to reconsider the positive aspects of the chosen option and give them more weight to justify and validate the decision made.

**Avoidance-avoidance conflict** is created when we are faced with two equally unattractive choices, both with negative outcomes. For example, an employee may be faced with choosing between increased company-related travel time or a demotion. As with approach-approach conflict, this is difficult to resolve because it represents a choice between unattractive outcomes.

**Approach-avoidance conflict** is the most common type of intrapersonal conflict and is based upon having to choose an option with both good and bad outcomes. For example, one may have to choose between one's current job and a great position in a bad location. The intensity of the approach-avoidance conflict increases as (1) the number of alternatives increase, (2) the attraction/aversion of the outcomes remains about equal, and (3) the issues increase in importance. If the conflict becomes too extreme, individuals may remove themselves from the conflict by refusing to make a decision. This sort of response to conflict probably is not very functional, but is quite common.

Being confronted with these types of choices is difficult. The more such choices we experience, the greater the intrapersonal conflict we may have to manage. One of the primary indicators of intrapersonal conflict is stress. **Stress** has been defined in a number of ways.[6] A common understanding of the term is that stress refers to experiencing something unpleasant. However, more formal definitions of stress are based upon the factors identified as stress originators. The stimulus definitions of stress suggest that stress is an external force, such as imminent deadlines, acting on a person. This suggests that what is stressful to one person is equally stressful to another.

The second perspective on stress suggests that it is a physiological or psychological response of an individual to environmental demands. These demands are known as stressors. Hans Seyle, often referred to as originator of the concept of stress, suggests that stress is "the rate of all the wear and tear caused by life."[7]

[5]D. Bell, "Regret in Decision Making under Uncertainty," working paper, Harvard University, Boston, Mass.

[6]J. M. Ivancevich and M. E. Matteson, *Stress and Work: A Managerial Perspective* (Glenview, Ill.: Scott, Foresman, & Co., 1980).

[7]H. Seyle, *The Stress of Life*, rev. ed. (New York: McGraw-Hill, 1976), p. 54.

| FIGURE 6–4 | The Demand-Response Imbalance |
|---|---|

Optimal individual performance occurs when there is a balance between the demands placed on an individual and that individual's ability to cope with those demands. Performance deteriorates not only when demands greatly exceed coping skills but also when coping skills greatly exceed the demands placed upon the individual.

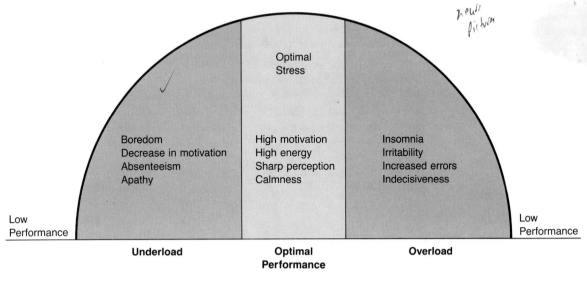

Source: Don Hellriegel, John W. Slocum, and Richard B. Woodman, *Organizational Behavior*, 4th ed. (St. Paul, Minn.: West, 1986), 529.

A third point of view attempts to combine both the stimulus and the response view by suggesting that any attempt to partition what is environment and what is an individual's response to the environment is arbitrary. From this perspective, stress is a mismatch between a person's skills, abilities, and job demands and his or her needs. Stress does not exist in isolation in the environment or in the individual, but rather in the interaction of the two. What is stressful for one person may not be stressful for another. Stress then can be seen as the psychological and physiological response to a substantial imbalance between environmental demands and the individual's ability to cope with them.[8] It is important to note that this imbalance can arise from too many environmental demands as well as too few. Figure 6–4 illustrates the consequences of the demand-response imbalance.

**Sources of Stress** As suggested by the above definitions, stress can be induced by a variety of factors. They include organizational, social, and

[8]J. E. McGrath, "Stress and Behavior in Organizations," in *Handbook of Industrial and Organizational Psychology*, ed. M. Dunnette (Chicago: Rand McNally, 1976).

**FIGURE 6–5**                    Sources of Work Stress

Conflict is only one
source of stress in life. All
of the stressors pictured
here fit into one of two
families: stress from un-
certainty or stress from
lack of control.

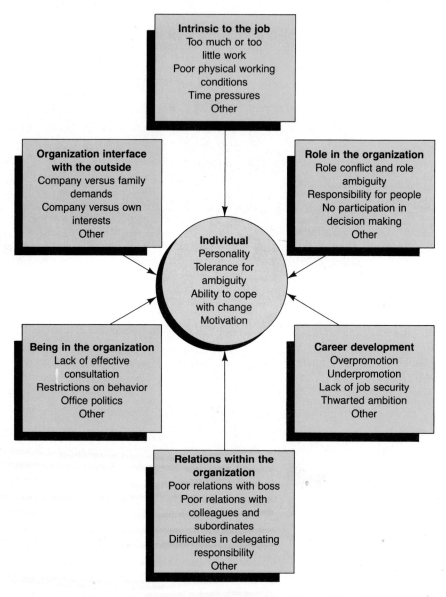

family demands and specific predispositions to the stress response, such
as an individual's health and personality.

Figure 6–5 specifies sources of stress that are related to an individual's
involvement with an organization. It should be noted that the frustration
inherent in conflict is not the only source of stress. We can categorize
each of these potential stressors as one of two major forms of

frustration—frustration from lack of control and frustration from uncertainty. Thus, the greater an individual's frustration from lack of control and uncertainty, the more potential for stress. Reexamining Figure 6–5 provides support for this point of view. Frustration arising from lack of control (the inability to do what you want to do) can be manifested in lack of consultation, restrictions on behavior, too much or too little work, time pressures, lack of participation in decision making, competing individual and family demands, overpromotion, underpromotion, and poor relations with colleagues, subordinates, and superiors. Frustration from uncertainty centers around the inability to predict future events. The changing nature of office politics, job insecurity, role ambiguity, concerns about delegating (what will happen if . . . ?), and responsibility for future outcomes are all potential sources of uncertainty frustration. An example of the impact of uncertainty on stress and job performance is highlighted in the "Focus on: Stress."

# Focus on:
## Stress

**Stress and Job Security** As all employees who depend on a regular paycheck know, job security is paramount when it comes to maintaining financial well-being. What they may not know is that security affects their physical and mental health as well.

Psychologist Karl W. Kuhnert surveyed more than 200 employees in two similar manufacturing companies to see if attitudes toward job satisfaction, job security, and work involvement were predictive of employee health. They were asked to agree or disagree with statements such as "I can keep my job for as long as I want it," "Everything is an effort for me," and "I experience chest pains."

Kuhnert found a strong relationship between perceived job security and health. The more permanent the employees thought their position was, the greater their physical and mental well-being. Surprisingly, perceived job security was found to be a better predictor of employees' health than any other factor.

Further, the study showed that the workers' assessment of their own job performance was tied directly to their belief about how secure their job was. In other words, the higher workers perceived the quality of their work to be, the more permanent they saw their position, regardless of their actual job performance.

It is no secret that organizations suffer financially as a result of employee stress and ill health. With skyrocketing medical costs, rising insurance claims, and worker-compensation laws, it's in employers' best interest to keep their employees happy and healthy, Kuhnert says.

He also suggests that companies can combat the problem of worker insecurity by letting their employees know how well they're doing. "Since employees believe that if they do good work, they'll be able to keep their jobs, and a key feature in job security is not knowing where you stand, organizations can help their employees by giving them regular feedback."

Source: Mindy Schanback, "Stress and Job Security," *Psychology Today,* May 1987. Reprinted with permission from *Psychology Today* Magazine. Copyright © 1987 (PT Partners, L.P.).

**FIGURE 6–6**     Common Type A Behaviors

One individual characteristic that has been implicated in stress-prone people is a Type A personality. One clinical study has shown that Type A personalities run twice the risk of premature coronary artery disease.

| | |
|---|---|
| Explosive, accelerated speech | Dissatisfaction with life |
| A heightened pace of living | A tendency to compete, regardless of the situation |
| Impatience with slowness | |
| Concentration on multiple activities simultaneously | Free-floating hostility |
| Preoccupation with personal concerns | A tendency to evaluate one's accomplishments in numerical terms |

Source: K. A. Matthews, "Psychological Perspectives on the Type A Behavior Pattern," *Psychological Bulletin* 91 (1982): pp. 293–323.

**Stress Moderators**   Other factors moderate the level of stress an individual will experience within an organization. Remember that, according to the stimulus-response definition of stress, stress results from interaction of the individual and the environment. What is it about some individuals that makes them more prone to the negative effects of stress?

One characteristic found in many stress-prone people is a **Type A personality.**[9] People with the trait are involved in a continuous struggle to accomplish more and more in less and less time. They express a chronic sense of urgency, have very short tempers, and are impatient with any impediments to their successful performance of a task. Figure 6–6 lists the behaviors common to Type A personalities.

In contrast is the **Type B personality.** While Type A personalities seem to be obsessed with the clock, Type B personalities are considerably more relaxed and less agitated. This is not to suggest they are lazy or unproductive. Rather, they are more likely to work at a consistent pace.

Our current organizational and academic environments appear to reinforce Type A behavior. In general, Type A men and women attain a higher educational level, occupational status, and income. Type A students achieve more academic honors and Type A women are more likely to be employed and less likely to be homemakers.[10] However, in a longitudinal study of several thousand males, those categorized as Type A personalities were found to run at least twice the risk of premature coronary artery disease.[11]

[9]M. Friedman and R. H. Rosenman, *Type A Behavior and Your Heart* (New York: Fawcett Crest, 1974).

[10]O. Behling and A. L. Darrow, "Managing Work-Related Stress," in *Modules in Management,* eds. J. E. Rosenzweig and F. E. Kast (Chicago: Science Research Associates, 1984).

[11]Freidman and Rosenman, *Type A Behavior.*

Stress often arises because of major changes in our lives. Even apparently positive changes such as moving to a larger home can create stress by forcing us to think about things (such as new drapes or new furniture purchases) that previously had not demanded our attention.

The amount of change or upheaval one has experienced may also play a significant role in how one is affected by environmental demands. Figure 6–7 shows the Social Readjustment Rating Scale.[12] The scale points, which range from 11 (minor violations of the law) to 100 (death of a spouse), correlate roughly with the degree of adjustment demanded by the particular change. To determine the point value of recent life changes (both positive and negative), the points associated with each life change were summed. Individuals with more than 200 points in a single year had a 50 percent chance of a serious health problem occurring in the following year. If point totals exceeded 300, then the risk factor rose to over 75 percent. This research suggests that adaptation to positive and negative change is stressful, and takes a physiological toll on the body. Excessive adaptation may drain resources necessary for continued health, thus increasing the body's vulnerability to attack by disease.

While stress in its various forms can be elicited by conflict at any level—intrapersonal, interpersonal, group, or organizational—it remains an intrapersonal phenomenon. Coping with the stress that results from intrapersonal conflict is the basis for intrapersonal conflict management, a topic to be discussed later in this chapter.

**INTERPERSONAL CONFLICT**

Interpersonal conflict arises because of incompatible goals, ideas, feelings, or behaviors among two or more people. The most common form of interpersonal conflict is mixed-motive conflict. Mixed-motive conflict occurs when the participants have multiple interests at stake,

[12]R. H. Holmes and R. H. Rahe, "The Social Readjustment Rating Scale," *Journal of Psychosomatic Medicine* 11, (1967): 213–218.

**FIGURE 6–7**    The Social Readjustment Rating Scale

Certain events in life can provide shocks to an individual's system that create stress. These shocks come from major life changes, such as those listed here.

| Life Event | Mean Value |
|---|---|
| 1. Death of Spouse | 100 |
| 2. Divorce | 73 |
| 3. Marital Separation | 65 |
| 4. Jail Term | 63 |
| 5. Death of Close Family Member | 63 |
| 6. Personal Injury or Illness | 53 |
| 7. Marriage | 50 |
| 8. Fired at Work | 47 |
| 9. Marital Reconciliation | 45 |
| 10. Retirement | 45 |
| 11. Change in Health of Family Member | 44 |
| 12. Pregnancy | 40 |
| 13. Sex Difficulties | 39 |
| 14. Gain of New Family Member | 39 |
| 15. Business Readjustment | 39 |
| 16. Change in Financial State | 38 |
| 17. Death of Close Friend | 37 |
| 18. Change to Different Line of Work | 36 |
| 19. Change in Number of Arguments with Spouse | 35 |
| 20. Mortgage over $10,000 | 31 |
| 21. Foreclosure of Mortgage or Loan | 30 |

some of which are best served by competitive behavior and others, by cooperative behavior. A common example of a mixed-motive situation is the prisoner's dilemma.[13] A description of the prisoner's dilemma is presented on page 236 in the "FOCUS ON: Interpersonal Conflict."

In the prisoner's dilemma, two prisoners are faced with a choice to cooperate with their accomplice or to compete. Each prisoner must decide whether to (1) cooperate by remaining silent, thereby risking minor punishment if the accomplice also remains silent or major punishment if the accomplice confesses, or (2) compete (confess and earn either a minimal sentence if the accomplice "holds out" or a larger sentence if both confess). This situation illustrates two basic points about interpersonal conflict. First, the parties to a dispute are often interdependent—that is, the choices one makes influence the outcomes and

[13]A. Rapaport and A. Chammah, *Prisoner's Dilemma: A Study in Conflict and Cooperation* (Ann Arbor, Mich.: University of Michigan Press, 1965).

| Life Event | Mean Value |
|---|---|
| 22. Change in Responsibilities at Work | 29 |
| 23. Son or Daughter Leaving Home | 29 |
| 24. Trouble with In-laws | 29 |
| 25. Outstanding Personal Achievement | 28 |
| 26. Wife Begin or Stop Work | 26 |
| 27. Begin or End School | 26 |
| 28. Change in Living Conditions | 25 |
| 29. Revision of Personal Habits | 24 |
| 30. Trouble with Boss | 23 |
| 31. Change in Work Hours or Conditions | 20 |
| 32. Change in Residence | 20 |
| 33. Change in Schools | 20 |
| 34. Change in Recreation | 19 |
| 35. Change in Church Activities | 19 |
| 36. Change in Social Activities | 18 |
| 37. Mortgage or Loan Less than $10,000 | 17 |
| 38. Change in Sleeping Habits | 16 |
| 39. Change in Number of Family Get-togethers | 15 |
| 40. Change in Eating Habits | 15 |
| 41. Vacation | 13 |
| 42. Christmas | 12 |
| 43. Minor Violations of the Law | 11 |

Source: Reprinted by permission from "The Social Readjustment Rating Scale," by T. H. Holmes and R. H. Rahe, *Journal of Psychosomatic Medicine* 11, pp. 213–218. Copyright © 1967, Pergamon Press.

choices of the other. Second, separate individual and joint outcomes may be mutually exclusive. The dominant (best) individual outcome results when the individual confesses. The dominant joint outcome occurs when both parties remain silent. Thus, whether to maximize the individual or the joint outcome is the nature of the prisoner's dilemma.

GROUP CONFLICT

It would be simple if we could take what we know about intrapersonal and interpersonal conflict and apply it directly to groups. While much of what we know about dyadic (two-person) conflict can be applied to groups, group conflict involves more than just summing the conflicts and motives of the individual actors. Although we will go into considerably more detail about groups in Chapters 7 and 9, it is important to consider the added dimensions that groups bring to the management of conflict.

Group conflict can occur within the group (intragroup) or between groups (intergroup). In day-to-day activities, it is often difficult to

FOCUS ON:

Interpersonal
Conflict

**The Prisoner's Dilemma** Two suspects are taken into custody and separated. The district attorney (D.A.) is certain they are guilty of a specific crime but does not have sufficient evidence to convict them. She points out the alternatives to both prisoners—to confess to the crime that the police are sure they committed or not to confess. If both do not confess, then the D.A. will prosecute them on a minor charge for which they will both receive minor punishments. If they both confess, they will be prosecuted, but she will recommend less than the most severe sentence. If one turns "state's evidence" and confesses and the other does not, the confessor will receive a small sentence but the other will receive the maximum sentence. (The possible outcomes are shown below. Each prisoner must make his decision *without* knowing what the other is doing.)

|  | | A | |
|---|---|---|---|
| | | **Keep Quiet** | **Confess** |
| **Keep Quiet** | | $-1, -1$ | $-15, -3$ |
| B | | | |
| **Confess** | | $-3, -15$ | $-10, -10$ |

separate the effects of each of these forms of conflict, since one group rarely exists in isolation. Intragroup conflict occurs primarily because groups exert considerable influence on individual members. This influence usually takes the form of shaping the individual's behavior into a form acceptable to the group. Individual members may resist, resulting in conflicting goals (What is the nature or focus of our group?), ideas (What does this group stand for? What does it mean for me to be a part of the group?), emotions (How do I feel about being a part of this group?), and behaviors (How are we to accomplish our goals?). The more intragroup conflict, the less coordination, communication, and productivity.[14]

Intergroup conflict can also alter what is occurring within a particular group. In a study of interactions within and between groups, Sherif found that when two groups found themselves in conflict, behaviors within the groups changed in the following predictable ways:[15]

- Group cohesiveness increased.
- Task orientation increased.

[14]M. Deutsch, "An Experimental Study of the Effects of Cooperation and Competition upon Group Process," *Human Relations* 2 (1949): 199–232.

[15]M. Sherif, *Intergroup Conflict and Cooperation* (Norman, Okla.: University Book Exchange, 1977).

- Loyalty to the group increased.
- Acceptance of autocratic leadership increased.

In short, conflict with another group tends to coalesce or unify a group and make it better able to cope with external threats. Additionally, Sherif noted that conflict between groups often produces a "we/they" mentality that reveals itself in:

- Distorted perceptions and goals
- Negative stereotypes about the other group
- Reduced communication

Sherif and his colleagues collected much of their data on group conflict at a summer camp that they conducted. Known as the Robber's Cave experiments, Sherif's summer camp studies provide the basis for much of what we know about competition between groups. These experiments are described in more detail in the "FOCUS ON: Group-Level Conflict."

# FOCUS ON:

## Group-Level Conflict

**The Robber's Cave Experiments** Set up specifically for these experiments, the Robber's Cave boys' camp recruited participants from different schools (to eliminate previous acquaintances) and screened for both physical and psychological health. During the first days of camp, the boys were allowed to develop friends spontaneously through a variety of camp-wide activities. The boys were then housed in two cabins. The population of each cabin was designed so that approximately two-thirds of an individual's best friends were in the other cabin. Within a few days, the pattern of interaction shifted dramatically. The boys tended to interact almost exclusively with their cabinmates and shared norms about group activities began to develop.

The researchers then arranged a series of competitive activities (such as football, baseball, and tug-of-war) in which the two cabins were pitted against each other. To increase the conflict, prizes were awarded to the winning team. During this time, the researchers noted that campers were developing hostility towards and stereotyped the behavior of members of the other cabin; they even planned ambushes and raids. New leaders emerged who were effective in combat, and intragroup solidarity increased dramatically.

The researchers devised situations specifically to promote conflict between the groups. At a campwide party, one group (the Red Devils) was allowed to arrive considerably earlier than the other group (the Bulldogs). The refreshments for the party consisted of two very different kinds of food. Half of the food was very fresh and appealing; the other half was old, ugly, and unappetizing. Because of the general level of competition that existed between the groups, the Red Devils consumed most of the attractive food, leaving the damaged food for their adversaries. When the Bulldogs arrived, they were so annoyed that the incipient conflict escalated from name-calling to a full-scale food fight.

Source: M. Sherif, *Intergroup Conflict and Cooperation* (Norman, Okla.: University Book Exchange, 1977).

## ORGANIZATIONAL CONFLICT

Organizational conflict embodies aspects of both group and individual conflict. The organization provides an arena for conflict to occur, as well as defines relationships and interdependencies among the disputants. However, conflict can occur in a number of patterns—between two individuals, between an individual and a group, between two groups, or between to or more groups. Further, this conflict can occur in the same level of the organization's hierarchy (between two equal-status disputants), or it can occur across different levels of the organization (between supervisor and subordinate, for example).

**Vertical conflict** refers to conflict between people at different levels in an organization. The primary basis for this conflict is the differences in power across levels in the organization. For example, senior managers are likely to have very different personal and organizational expectations from assembly-line workers in the same organization. These expectations can color their experiences, beliefs, and interests, making them appear to be incompatible.

**Horizontal conflict** refers to conflict occurring at similar organizational levels. The more organizational units come into contact with each other, the more dependent they are on each other, and the smaller the amount of available resources, the greater the probability for horizontal conflict.[16] Three different types of group interdependence have been identified: pooled, sequential, and reciprocal interdependence.

**Pooled interdependence** exists when each department or unit contributes to the larger good but is not dependent upon the other. **Sequential interdependence** exists when the outputs of one unit become the inputs of another unit. The second unit is, then, quite dependent upon the first unit. **Reciprocal interdependence** exists when the outputs of one department become the inputs of a second; and the outputs of that second unit become the inputs for the first. Thus, both units are mutually dependent. As you might expect, reciprocal interdependence is likely to produce more conflict than sequential interdependence, and sequential interdependence is likely to produce more conflict than pooled interdependence.

**Line-staff conflict** is also a common organizational occurrence. Line employees are those directly involved in some aspect of producing the organization's product. Staff employees provide technical and advisory assistance to the line. As such, both groups have very different perspectives, goals, and statuses.

Traditionally, staff members tend to be more educated, better trained, and younger than line managers. Staff members tend to be professional, and as such have primary loyalty to their profession rather than to the organization. Staff members tend to be in lower organizational positions

---

[16]K. Thomas, "Conflict and Conflict Management," in *Handbook of Industrial and Organizational Psychology,* ed. M. Dunnette (Chicago: Rand McNally, 1976): 889–936.

than the line managers they advise. Further, because the staff member is technically trained, he or she is familiar with a critical body of knowledge necessary for the effective functioning of the line manager. Thus, there is a large gap between the line manager's authority to produce the product and the staff member's skill or knowledge necessary to produce the product.

It is easy to see the basis for this conflict. As organizational technologies become more complex, the demand for technically sophisticated staff members also will increase. Thus, the potential for conflict between line and staff members can only become more intense in the future.

**Role conflict** is a special form of organizational conflict. A role is a set of activities associated with a particular position. These activities are determined by the expectations of other organizational members (usually supervisors and coworkers), who make up the role set. When two or more role-specific activities are incompatible, then role conflict occurs.[17] In such cases, any attempt to comply with one set of expectations makes it impossible or difficult to comply with the other set of expectations. Unlike other forms of conflict, this form of conflict is organizationally based. That is, role conflict exists because expectations for job performance (as defined by the role set) do not coincide with the perception of appropriate job-related activities of either the role occupant or other members of the role set.

## MANAGING CONFLICT

By now it should be obvious that conflict is a common experience, regardless of whether we are by ourselves, with friends and relatives, or in work groups. What is important from both a personal and managerial perspective is how to manage it effectively. At the individual level, we need to know how to handle internal conflict as well as that between individuals with incompatible interests. In addition, we also need to know how to handle conflict within the groups and organizations to which we belong.

## INTRAPERSONAL CONFLICT MANAGEMENT

While a great deal of attention has been paid to the development of interpersonal and organizational responses to conflict, the success of these strategies depends largely upon the effective functioning of the individual experiencing the conflict. It is important, therefore, that the individual be able to handle the psychological and physiological demands of conflict situations. Because one of the more common consequences of conflict is stress, a major factor in managing intrapersonal conflict is learning to cope successfully with the resulting stress.

[17]D. Katz and R. L. Kahn, *The Social Psychology of Organizations* (New York: Wiley and Sons, 1978).

**Stress Management**   Stress and stress-related illnesses are very expensive for American companies. It has been estimated that businesses have lost as much as $15 billion in foregone productivity because of employees' personal problems. The costs of executive stress include $2.9 billion for lost workdays, $.2 billion for hospitalization, $.1 billion for outpatient care, and $16.5 billion for mortality.[18] These numbers represent only the quantifiable costs of stress. We must consider also the cost in human potential of the nonquantifiable costs induced by stress.

An individual or organization can attempt to manage stress in a variety of ways. The following section will describe some of these methods. For a more detailed examination of these topics, consult the references provided at the end of the chapter.

Individual strategies for managing stress are quite varied. Physical exercise (jogging, walking, swimming, bicycling, aerobic exercise, and other such activities) is an excellent way of relieving stress and tension. In fact, many organizations are routinely adding on-site exercise facilities and developing incentive plans to foster their use by organizational members. Other stress-management activities include the use of relaxation techniques such as meditation and biofeedback. Another, rather novel approach to stress management is illustrated in the "Focus on: Managing Stress."

A second way individuals can reduce their vulnerability to potentially stressful situations is through the use of time-management skills. Individuals skilled in time management are able to identify and set daily priorities so that sufficient time is allocated to their more important tasks. The advantage of successful time management is that it returns to the individual a sense of control over his or her life and workday. It can also reduce role overload and role conflict.[19]

The third method for reducing stress at the individual level is to create a strong social support system. Interacting with our social support systems—our spouses, relatives, and friends—enables us to discuss our problems from a different frame of reference, put work into better perspective, and keep from becoming too involved with our day-to-day work activities. In fact, a recent study suggests that persons with few close friends are two to three times more likely to die than those with many close friends, even controlling for preexisting illnesses, smoking, and a number of other factors.[20]

Stress also can be managed at the level of organizational activities. Since our definition of stress focuses on an imbalance between the

[18]Behling and Darrow, "Managing Work-Related Stress."

[19]A. Lakein, *How to Get Control of Your Time and Your Life* (New York: Peter H. Wyden, 1973).

[20]P. J. Rosch, "Stress and Illness," *Journal of the American Medical Association* 242 (1979): 427–428.

FOCUS ON:

Managing Stress

**Laughter: The Best Medicine for Burnout?** Lighten up a little. You'll feel better. More important, you'll be healthier, more creative, and more productive. That's the message 1,000 people paid $200 each to hear at the fifth annual conference on "The Power of Laughter and Play."

Speakers at the three-day conference said there is a growing awareness that workers do best when their jobs are fun and rewarding. Conversely, they burn out and incur higher medical bills when they are thrust into a humorless, corporate pressure cooker day after day.

"We've learned that lesson the hard way," said Erin Sommerville, a staff member with the Palo Alto–based Institute for the Advancement of Human Behavior, sponsor of the conference. "Now we're learning that reducing stress really helps employee relations and helps productivity."

Nevertheless, few companies have taken concrete steps to bring any laughter, let alone play, to the workplace, according to several humor consultants who addressed the conference. Matt Weinstein, founder of the Berkeley-based consulting company called Playfair, encouraged those at the conference to help their coworkers take themselves a bit less seriously and to realize "that their lives are more important than their jobs." He recommends, for example, that employees bring a Walkman and a comedy tape to work each day and "force yourself to take at least three or four laugh breaks."

Joel Goodman, director of the Humor Project in Saratoga Springs, N.Y., said he tells his corporate clients to invest in a humor "first-aid kit" containing joke books and tapes, which can be checked out by stressed-out employees.

Most of the speakers said there is a direct connection between playfulness and creativity. If people are intimidated in the office and are afraid to make mistakes, they'll never make "the creative leap that really characterizes growth companies," Weinstein said.

In addition to sparking creativity, fun can be just plain healthy, most speakers said. They pointed out that the body releases T-cells, the ones that battle disease, when one indulges in a good, hearty laugh. There's some evidence that endorphins, the body's natural painkillers, are also stimulated through laughter.

"It's not only OK to laugh and have a good time," Sommerville said. "It's beneficial." She added, "If you take yourself too seriously, you're liable to get seriously ill."

Speakers at the conference said several companies have made positive steps to lighten things up in the workplace. Weinstein told of one executive in Philadelphia who routinely includes cheery notes in the material he gives to his secretary for typing. The same executive went a bit further when he learned that his secretary enjoyed dancing. One day, he buzzed her into his office, asked her to shut the door, then turned on a cassette tape and started dancing madly with her for one minute. "It totally changed the way she felt about the job," Weinstein said.

Source: "Laughter: The Best Medicine for Burnout?" *Arizona Daily Star,* March 22, 1987, p. A–5.

individual and his or her organizational demands, it is important that the person and the position are matched. The correct person-job fit can be attained in two different ways. First, the person recruited for the position can be carefully screened to ensure a balance between the individual's tolerance for stress and the position's stress level. A second and more promising solution is to alter the position to reduce or increase its **stress quotient,** or the amount of stress the position is likely to generate in the jobholder. Chapter 12 includes an extensive discussion of job design that describes how a position can be enriched. However, it should be noted that too much job enrichment is also stressful.

In decreasing the stress quotient of a position, one should pay special attention to reducing the amount of role ambiguity, role conflict, and role overload. Role ambiguity may be reduced by developing detailed job descriptions, discussing job expectations with subordinates, and promoting a clear understanding of the nature and intent of the performance evaluation system. Role conflict also can be reduced by discussions with superiors and other members of the role set to outline common expectations of performance. Role overload may be monitored through periodic evaluation of the changing capabilities of the employee over time.[21]

A second stress-reduction mechanism that can be instituted at the organizational level is **employee assistance programs.** Many organizations, such as IBM, Equitable Life, and B. F. Goodrich, have programs that diagnose and treat a variety of stress-related problems, such as drug and alcohol abuse and other emotional and psychological problems.

## INTERPERSONAL CONFLICT STRATEGIES

A number of interpersonal conflict strategies can be brought to bear on disputes between individuals. Figure 6–8 illustrates five common strategies for resolving or managing conflict. The five strategies are competing, avoiding, accommodating, collaborating, and compromising. Notice that these five strategies are based upon differing levels of concern with maximizing your needs and maximizing the needs of the other party. Which conflict-management strategy you select depends upon where in the figure's two-dimensional space your interests lie.

If you are primarily concerned with getting what you want out of the exchange, then two strategies are likely to be most useful: competing and collaborating. If you are unconcerned with the other party's needs, **competing** may be the appropriate strategy. Other situations when you might need a competing strategy include when you are involved in an emergency or critical situation, when the other party is untrustworthy, or when you are sure of the correct solution.

If it is just as important that the other party's concerns be considered as that yours be considered, then **collaborating** may be a better strategic

[21]Behling and Darrow, "Managing Work-Related Stress."

**FIGURE 6–8** √A Two-Dimensional Model of Conflict Behavior

The approach to inter-personal conflict can be characterized by individuals' concern with their own needs or concern for others' needs. Variations along these dimensions can give rise to five distinct conflict-resolution styles.

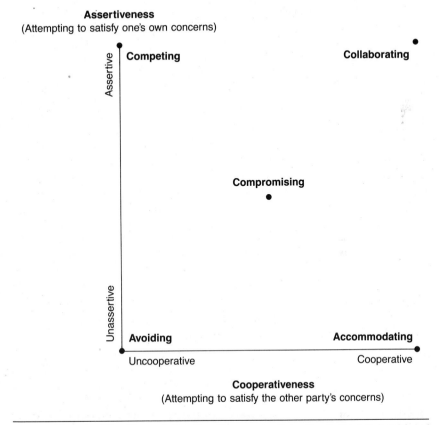

Source: Thomas, "Conflict and Conflict Management," in *Handbook of Industrial and Organizational Psychology,* ed. M. D. Dunnette (Santa Monica, Calif.: Goodyear Publishing Company, 1976), 900.

choice. Collaborating is a particularly useful alternative when the issue is too important to compromise, when you are trying to engender commitment among the parties to the dispute, or when you are trying to gain insight.

If you have little concern for your position or the position and desires of the other party, then it may be best to implement an **avoiding** strategy. If the issue at conflict is trivial or you are seriously outmatched by your opponent, you may choose not to confront the conflict at all. Avoidance may be the wisest course of action if (1) others can better handle the problem, (2) time is needed to let people cool down and regain perspective, or (3) the potential disruption that may occur from confronting the problem is greater than the potential benefit from solving it.

There are likely to be occasions when the other party's issues have priority. If you find out that the position you have been arguing is wrong or you wish to minimize a losing position, you may choose to give in. Perhaps by **accommodating** the other party's desires, you can earn "social credits" for your next interaction ("You have convinced me on this one, but just remember that you owe me one.").

Finally, if both sets of goals are important, but not worth the potential disruption of more aggressive strategies, then a **compromising** strategy may be most effective. If a quick, temporary solution is needed or nothing else seems to be working, then a simple compromise may be what is needed. Compromising—a solution that "splits the difference" between the disputants—is probably the strategy with which we have the most experience. The classic compromise is a strategy used by many parents in trying to solve the "last-piece-of-pie-and-two-children-want-it" dilemma. The obvious solution: one child cuts the pie into two pieces, the other child selects the first piece.

Conflict and conflict management represent very broad categories of behavior—so broad that it is often difficult to grasp exactly how to implement a particular strategy. To understand the usefulness of the five strategies we presented, it is important to place them in a specific context. An individual might view conflict resolution in a variety of ways. Given the nature of organizations and western society, negotiation is a particularly fruitful mechanism for resolving conflict.

**Negotiation**    Negotiation is a widely used conflict-management technique. **Negotiation** is the process whereby two or more parties decide what each will give and take in an exchange between them.[22] This definition of negotiation highlights (1) its interpersonal nature, (2) the dependency of the parties, and (3) its allocation of resources.

Negotiation can be distinguished from other conflict-management techniques in that it involves two or more parties to a dispute who are in approximately equal power positions. Further, negotiation involves the division of tangible and intangible resources through a sequential evaluation of alternatives. In an attempt to manage conflict through negotiation, both parties (either explicitly or implicitly) prefer to search for a mutually acceptable solution rather than to fight openly, give in, break off interaction, or have their dispute resolved by a higher authority.[23]

Depending upon the desires of the parties, negotiation can incorporate all of the conflict-management tactics previously described. One may choose to avoid certain issues or provocations, one can give in on certain issues (usually with the expectation that the other party will be

---

[22]J. Z. Rubin and B. R. Brown, *The Social Psychology of Bargaining and Negotiation* (New York: Academic Press, 1975).

[23]R. J. Lewicki and J. R. Litterer, *Negotiation* (Homewood, Ill.: R. D. Irwin, 1985).

Negotiation is a process in which parties decide what each will give and take in an exchange. Bartering in an open-air market provides an explicit example of negotiating. Many negotiations are much more subtle and involve intangible resources.

accommodating on other issues), or one can state one's position and resist conceding. These strategies are part and parcel of the two dominant conflict-management strategies used in negotiation—compromise (distributive negotiating) and collaboration (integrative negotiating).

**Distributive negotiation** is the most commonly used negotiation strategy, and it is what most of us imagine negotiation to be. In distributive negotiation, the parties decide how to allocate a fixed amount of resources. The perception of a fixed pie of resources leads negotiators to behave in a competitive, contentious manner. The assumption is that every time one party wins, the other must give up something. As a result, the other party is seen as an adversary and as the origin of the problem—"it's me against you." Both must concede or compromise their initial positions. As such, neither wins completely, but then again, neither loses everything.

As suggested by our earlier description of the compromise strategy, distributive negotiation is a style of conflict management best implemented under the following conditions:

1. No ongoing relationship or potential for one exists—the interaction is a one-shot deal.
2. A quick, simple solution to the conflict is needed.
3. The parties have mutually incompatible goals.

What about conflict between supervisors and subordinates, coworkers, spouses, friends, and family groups? Many of these interactions are characterized by the potential for or the existence of long-term relationships, compatible goals, and longer time horizons for discovering solutions. When these conditions exist, distributive negotiation is an

# FIGURE 6-9

Integrative agreements arise when two parties find their needs and resources are *complementary*. In this cartoon, a single ice-cream bar provides dessert for two: the ice cream for the man and the wooden stick for the beaver. Both seem to want the ice-cream bar, but they really want different parts of the treat.

FRANK AND ERNEST ©by Bob Thaves

WHEN YOU'RE DONE, MAY I HAVE THE STICK?

THAVES 6-1
© 1987 by NEA, Inc.

Source: Reprinted by permission of NEA, Inc.

inappropriate technique. Rather than an adversarial perspective, one might wish to assume an advocacy, or cooperative, orientation.

**Integrative bargaining** is a more cooperative negotiation strategy. It assumes that there can be an expanding pot of resources for the parties to divide. Thus, one can gain without the other having to lose. If the resources can be expanded through creative problem solving, then the parties need not compete with each other. Since, in this case, one is not the enemy or adversary of the other, the disputants may be more willing to share concerns, ideas, and expectations. An example of an integrative division of resources is illustrated in Figure 6-9.

However, integrative bargaining also has its own unique set of demands. For integrative bargaining to succeed, both participants must have high aspirations or goals (for the attainment of the "right" solution), a problem-solving orientation (it's both parties against the problem), and a sufficient level of trust so that information can be shared.[24]

Integrative bargaining has much to commend it. While it is the more difficult technique to implement, its benefits are considerable. Agreements reached integratively are more stable and strengthen the relationship between the parties. They also may be the only way to get an agreement between individuals who have high aspirations and resist conceding on these important issues.[25] Figure 6-10 illustrates the differences between distributive and integrative bargaining.

Each of us has a great deal of experience with and skill in distributive negotiation. It is easy to envision an opponent as the source of the conflict. It is much more difficult to develop and maintain the level of

[24]D. G. Pruitt, "Integrative Agreements: Nature and Consequences," *Negotiating in Organizations*, eds. M. H. Bazerman and R. J. Lewicki (Beverly Hills, Calif.: Sage Publishing, 1983).

[25]Ibid.

**FIGURE 6–10**                    Types of Bargaining

Integrative agreements—those that seek out complementary needs and resources—can be difficult to find. However, they tend to be more stable and strengthen the long-term relationship between the disputing parties.

|  | **Distributive** | **Integrative** |
|---|---|---|
| **Payoff Structure** | Fixed amount of resources to be divided | Variable amount of resources to be divided |
| **Primary Motivation** | To gain at the expense of the other | To maximize joint outcomes |
| **Interests** | Diametrically opposed | Convergent or congruent |
| **Relationships** | Short-term relationship | Long-term relationship |

trust required to view the other party as a collaborator (with whom information should be freely shared) and the dispute as the enemy. An all-too-common response is to view all negotiations as adversarial processes. Thus it is important to learn how to "reframe" negotiations from a distributive to an integrative perspective.

It is difficult to transform a conflict with distributive potential into one with integrative potential. Five suggested tactics are described below:[26]

1. **Superordinate goals.** A primary difference between distributive and integrative bargaining is that, in the latter, the relationship between the parties is important. It is therefore much easier to develop goals that supercede the short-term conflict the parties may be experiencing. Organizational members have an explicit superordinate goal—resolving the conflict in the organization's best interest. Acknowledging such goals can enhance the parties' perception that they are aligned in achieving the superordinate goal—that they are advocates rather than adversaries.

2. **Separate the people from the problem.** It is very difficult not to personalize a problem or conflict. As suggested earlier, one of the critical differences between integrative and distributive negotiation is the perception of the other party. To see the other party as an advocate rather than an adversary is critical to developing the trust needed to achieve integrative agreements.

3. **Focus on interests, not on positions.** Positions are demands the negotiator makes. Interests are what underlie demands or

[26]R. Fischer and W. Ury, *Getting to Yes* (New York: Houghton-Mifflin, 1981).

positions. While positions may be one-dimensional, individuals typically have multiple interests. Often shared and different (although not incompatible) interests underlie incompatible positions. Consider the typically distributive, adversarial relationship between landlord and tenant. It is not difficult to identify their common and different interests. Both want stability (a permanent address and a stable tenant); a well-maintained apartment; and a good relationship (a tenant who pays his rent regularly and a landlord responsive to repair requests). Their interests differ in that the landlord values the rent more than living in the apartment, and the tenant values living in the apartment more than the rent.

4. **Invent options for mutual gain.** This is the basis for expanding the resource pie. All too often, however, individuals ignore the opportunity for mutual gain because they assume the resource pie is fixed. To invent options for mutual gain, participants must be willing to think creatively. They must separate the act of creating alternatives (brainstorming) from judging those alternatives. They must go beyond the obvious issues or positions and look for broader solutions. In the search for mutual gain, the task is to get the other side to make the decision you want. Thus, you need to make it as easy as possible for them to agree. Understand their perspective, search for precedents, and develop proposals to which they can respond with a single word: yes.

5. **Use objective criteria.** No matter how integrative each party may be, they are likely to have some incompatible interests. Rather than seeing these disagreements as contests of will, a more productive tactic may be to focus on what is fair. Framing your disagreements as searches for fair standards is likely to be much more fruitful than focusing on who will win. Deciding what is fair requires both parties to understand the criteria for judging fairness. Each party must be reasonable and open. In our landlord-tenant interaction, both parties may wish the apartment repainted. The landlord might prefer that the tenant buy the paint and repaint the apartment in a suitable color. In contrast, the tenant would certainly prefer to have the apartment's owner assume responsibility for the painting of the apartment. In determining what is fair, the parties may agree that the landlord will reimburse the tenant for the purchase of the paint and reduce the rent to compensate the tenant for the work.

Even with the best of intentions, even when the negotiated settlement is in both parties' best interests, it is sometimes difficult to reach agreement. A host of factors can cripple even the most well-intentioned set of negotiators. The "INTERNATIONAL FOCUS ON: Negotiations" illustrates the impact of two of these factors, inexperience and cultural

INTERNATIONAL
FOCUS ON:
Negotiations

**Negotiating with the Japanese**
When the plane landed in Tokyo for the 14-day negotiation, I was the first passenger to trot down the ramp, raring to go. At the bottom of the ramp two Japanese gentlemen awaited me, bowing politely. I liked that.

The two Japanese helped me through customs, then escorted me to a large limousine. I reclined comfortably on the plush seat at the rear of the limousine, and they sat stiffly on two fold-up stools. I said expansively, "Why don't you people join me? There's plenty of room back here."

They replied, "Oh, no. You're an important person. You obviously need your rest." I liked that, too.

As the limousine rolled along, one of my hosts asked, "By the way, do you know the language?"

I replied, "You mean Japanese?"

He said, "Right, that's what we speak in Japan."

I said, "Well, no. But I hope to learn a few expressions. I've brought a dictionary with me."

His companion asked, "Are you concerned about getting back to your plane on time?" (Up until that moment, I had not been concerned.) "We can schedule this limousine to transport you back to the airport."

I thought to myself, "How considerate."

Reaching into my pocket, I handed them my return flight ticket, so the limousine would know when to get me. I didn't realize it then, but they knew my deadline, whereas I didn't know theirs.

Instead of beginning negotiations right away, they first had me experience Japanese hospitality and culture. For more than a week, I toured the country, from the Imperial Palace to the shrines of Kyoto. They even enrolled me in an English-language course in Zen to study their religion.

Every evening for four-and-a-half hours, they had me sit on a cushion on a hardwood floor for a traditional dinner and entertainment. Can you imagine what it's like sitting on a hardwood floor for all those hours? If I didn't get hemorrhoids as a result, I'll probably never get them. Whenever I inquired about the start of negotiations, they'd murmur, "Plenty of time! Plenty of time!"

At last, on the twelfth day, we began the negotiations, finishing early so we could play golf. On the thirteenth day, we met again, and ended early because of a farewell dinner. Finally, on the morning of the fourteenth day, we resumed our negotiations in earnest. Just as we were getting to the crux of things, the limousine pulled up to take me to the airport. We all piled in and continued hashing out the terms. Just as the limousine's brakes were applied at the terminal, we consummated the deal.

How well do you think I did in that negotiation? For many years, my superiors referred to it as "the first great Japanese victory since Pearl Harbor."

Source: Herb Cohen, *You Can Negotiate Anything* (New York: Bantam Books, 1982), pp. 93–95.

differences, which resulted in a very poorly negotiated outcome. The next section examines the ways in which the cognitions of negotiators can sabotage potential agreements.

**Cognitive Biases and Negotiation** In Chapter 5, we identified a number of heuristics, or cognitive shortcuts, which, when used inappropriately, result in systematically biased decisions. In recent years, considerable research has demonstrated the impact of some of the cognitive biases—framing, anchoring and adjustment, and availability—on negotiator behavior.

As you may recall, the framing heuristic is associated with the risk inherent in an individual's decisions.[27] That is, when a decision is framed in terms of potential gains, the decision maker is more likely to choose the risk-averse option. When the decision is framed in terms of potential losses, the decision maker is likely to choose the riskier option. In negotiation, this tendency can be translated into an increased willingness to reach agreement in the former case and a resistance to agreement in the latter case.

Any potential agreement can be valued in two different ways. That is, a negotiator can consider what is being gained from the new agreement (how much better it is than the old agreement, for example) or what is being given up to get the new agreement. Researchers have shown that individuals who perceived the outcome of a negotiation in terms of what they had to gain were more willing to reach agreement than those who perceived it in terms of potential losses. For example, individuals who were told to maximize profits (gains) in their negotiation reached agreements more easily than those who were told to minimize expenses (losses).[28] Thus, simply altering how the negotiation is presented can significantly influence how the negotiators behave.

The second bias that has been examined in the context of negotiation is anchoring-and-adjustment effect, which was discussed in Chapter 3 as a building block of the perception process. This heuristic suggests that people will use a piece of information as a basis upon which to make a judgment or decision, but will insufficiently adjust from that informational base to the correct answer. This is the basis for research suggesting that the level of the initial offer is highly correlated with the level of the final agreement. The more extreme the initial offer, the more extreme the final agreement. For example, when real estate agents were asked to assess a piece of residential property, their estimate of the value of the property was significantly influenced by the seller's listing price. The higher the seller's listing price, the higher the perceived value of the property by the real estate agents.[29] This was true whether the property

[27]D. Kahneman and A. Tversky, "Prospect Theory: An Analysis of Decisions under Risk," *Econometrica* 47 (1979): 263–291.

[28]M. H. Bazerman, T. Magliozzi, and M. A. Neale, "The Acquisition of an Integrative Response in a Competitive Market," *Organizational Behavior and Human Decision Processes* 35 (1985): 294–313.

[29]G. B. Northcraft and M. A. Neale, "Experts, Amateurs, and Real Estate: An Anchoring-and-Adjustment Perspective on Property Pricing Decisions," *Organizational Behavior and Human Decision Processes* 39 (1987): 84–97.

was listed above or below its actual appraised value. The results of this research suggest that negotiators are influenced by the anchor of the party's initial offer—so much so that it can color the final valuation of the negotiated commodity or product.

The availability heuristic occurs when individuals attempt to judge the likelihood of an event's occurrence. The rule here is "that which is most easily remembered occurs most frequently."[30] While it is true that frequently occurring events are familiar to us, it is not always true that familiar events occur frequently. Consider the negotiator who is representing a constituency. The consequences of not meeting the constituency's expectations may be very clear to the negotiator (loss of status or position, evaluation anxiety, and so forth). In determining the strategy to be used in the subsequent interaction, the negotiator is likely to overestimate the probability that those costs will be incurred. The costs are more vivid to the negotiator because they are costs he or she would personally bear. The more overestimated the probability of these costs occurring, the more likely the negotiator is to behave in a competitive manner and to be unwilling to concede on issues for fear of his or her constituency's response.[31]

Many more heuristics can systematically bias a negotiator's behavior and subsequent agreements. However, this sampling illustrates how important it is that negotiators give serious consideration to the ways in which they may be crippling their own attempts to reach high-quality negotiated agreements. The barriers to good negotiated agreements are many, and the organizational and individual costs of reaching poor agreements can be quite high. It is in the best interest of the individual to commit the time to prenegotiation planning and strategy that so serious an interaction warrants.

## ORGANIZATIONAL CONFLICT MANAGEMENT

In the previous two sections, we have focused on individual methods for reducing or managing conflict. In this section we will focus on ways in which organizations can be structured to alleviate conflict. Two types will be discussed—formal organizational structures and informal organizational structures. Formal organizational structures include liaisons, organizational slack, and ombudsmen or employee/client/customer representatives, whose task is to resolve conflict at both internal and external organizational boundaries. Informal organizational structures to resolve conflict focus primarily on the manager as a dispute resolver. Within such an arena, a manager's task often requires considerable conflict-resolution skill.

[30]A. Tversky and D. Kahneman, "Availability: A Heuristic for Judging Frequency and Probability," *Cognitive Psychology* 5 (1973): 207–232.

[31]M. A. Neale, "The Effects of Negotiation and Arbitration Cost Salience on Bargainer Behavior: The Role of Arbitrator and Constituency on Negotiator Judgment," *Organizational Behavior and Human Performance* 34 (1984): 97–111.

**Formal Organizational Roles**   Since conflict is commonly associated with scarce resources and interdependencies, an organization can reduce the potential for conflict by reducing the interaction among groups and the competition for resources. This can be accomplished through the use of slack resources and buffers. **Slack,** or excess, resources can minimize conflict because they reduce the amount of necessary interaction. For example, if two departments are sequentially interdependent, having excess inventory of A's output (slack) insulates or buffers B from the inconsistencies of A. **Buffers** need not be only excess inventory or product. Individuals or groups of individuals may serve the same function. A liaison or linking pin is an individual assigned to integrate the activities of two interdependent organizational units or groups. Within a matrix organization (a form of organizational structure described in Chapter 16), the project manager often serves this function.

A different form of linking-pin role is that of the **organizational ombudsman.** While linking pins generally integrate the activities of two interdependent organizational units, the ombudsman may focus on conflict at the employee/organizational boundary. The ombudsman provides a formal mechanism for employee grievances to be aired. In different institutions, the ombudsman may offer a means for clients or customers to make their dissatisfactions known.[32] The duties of an ombudsman usually cover interpreting policy, counseling, resolving disputes, and providing feedback and identifying potential problem areas to senior management.[33] For example, ombudsmen at McDonnell Aircraft in St. Louis, Missouri, and Douglas Aircraft in Long Beach, California, have found that most of their cases concern corporate housekeeping matters: conflicts with supervisors, arguments over promotions and transfers, or misunderstandings over benefits. Most such problems can be sorted out by a direct call to the department head involved, without invoking higher authority. A few cases, however, deal with whistle-blowing on the safety of a product design or the billing of a defense contract. Another example of the corporate ombudsman's work can be found in the "Focus on: Corporate Ombudsmen."

**Informal Organizational Roles**   The ombudsman has a formal role as dispute resolver. This formal designation does not, however, limit the role that others play in reducing or managing conflict in organizational settings. Because conflict is so common in group and organizational life, formal structures or procedures often do not adequately meet the

---

[32]D. M. Kolb, "Who Are Organizational Third Parties and What Do They Do?" in *Research on Negotiation in Organizations,* eds. R. J. Lewicki, B. Sheppard, and M. H. Bazerman (Greenwich, Conn.: JAI Press, 1987).

[33]I. Silver, "The Corporate Ombudsman," *Harvard Business Review* 45 (May–June 1967): 77–87; M. P. Rowe, "The Non-Union Complaint System at MIT: An Upward-Feedback Model," *Alternatives to the High Cost of Litigation* 2 (1984): 10–18.

FOCUS ON:

Corporate
Ombudsmen

**Resolving Disputes within Organizations** Making sure that bad news gets passed up the chain of command is a topic receiving a lot of attention in executive suites these days. In the past few years, dozens of major companies have set up formal ombudsman systems in which a senior executive operating outside the normal chain of command is permanently available to deal with employee grievances and alarms on a confidential basis.

Companies that have put these systems into place say that they are worth their modest cost. The sheer number of calls logged—over 3,000 in 1986 at General Dynamics—suggests that workers like and trust ombudsmen. By monitoring the complaints, companies can pinpoint plants, programs, or managers causing serious morale problems. At AT&T's Bell Labs, ombudsman Martha Maselko says that the costs of

recruiting and training a skilled engineer are so high that simply keeping three employees a year from quitting is enough to cover the $200,000 yearly cost of her office.

Not everyone is a fan of the ombudsman system. Former Du Pont chairman Irving Shapiro thinks an extensive personal grapevine is a top executive's best protection against nasty surprises; his own version of management by wandering around, he notes, was "doing a lot of business in the men's room." In a company where everyone knows the boss wants to hear about things (and where all the employees have access to the boss and the men's room), Shapiro's method may work. However, in corporations that have not traditionally fostered upward communication, such methods may not work. A company-wide number to an executive can go a long way in encouraging troubled employees to speak out.

Source: Michael Brody, "Listen to Your Whistle-Blower," *Fortune*, November 24, 1986, pp. 77–78.

demand for conflict resolution. As a result, a variety of individuals assume the role of dispute resolver or intervenor. The manager is an excellent organizational example of someone who spends a great deal of time managing conflict,[34] even though conflict resolution is not usually considered a formal aspect of his or her job description. A complete list of potential third-party intervenors is presented in Figure 6–11.

Managers often serve as third parties to a conflict. Being a third party means that the manager is indirectly involved in the conflict. He or she is not one of the disputants. **Third-party intervention** in conflict is not limited to managers acting within organizations. The legal system is a common example of a formal third-party intervention system. Judges resolve conflicts between private parties in civil courts or between

[34]Mintzberg, *The Nature of Managerial Work;* Thomas and Schmidt, "A Survey of Managerial Interests."

**FIGURE 6–11**          Individuals Engaged in Informal Dispute Resolution

Many roles in society contain a large conflict-resolution component. Managers also spend a lot of their time informally resolving conflict, perhaps without realizing how central conflict-resolving activities are to their role.

| | |
|---|---|
| Go-betweens (messengers) | Matchmakers |
| Lawyers | Brokers |
| Auditors | Agents (insurance agents, |
| Managerial consultants | real estate agents) |
| Marriage counselors | Umpires |
| Psychotherapists | Parents |
| Special envoys | Dictators |
| Priests, rabbis | Law enforcement officials |
| Village elders | International monitors |
| Elected representatives | Regulatory agencies |
| Auctioneers | International courts of law |

Source: S. Kaufman and G. T. Duncan, "Third-Party Intervention: A Theoretical Framework," in *Managing Conflict: An Interdisciplinary Approach*, ed. A. Rahim (New York: Praeger Press, 1988).

representatives of public and private parties in criminal courts. Within the context of industrial relations, third parties may resolve differences between labor and management through mediation, arbitration, or factfinding. Consumer complaints, property-settlement and child-custody issues in divorce proceedings, landlord-tenant disputes, and neighborhood disagreements are often resolved through the use of mediators.

Each of these types of third-party intervention solves disputes in specific ways. **Arbitration** is similar to the American judicial system. An arbitrator is a neutral third party who, after hearing both sides of the dispute, determines a final, binding outcome. **Mediation** occurs when a neutral third party encourages interaction between the disputants but has no authority to force a solution upon them. **Factfinding** occurs when a neutral third party, based upon the evidence presented by the parties, determines a reasonable solution to the dispute. As in mediation, the parties are not bound to follow the recommendation of the fact finder.

Unlike formal third parties or organizational ombudsmen who have prescribed ways of interacting with the disputants, the manager has considerably more leeway in choosing how to handle a dispute. Managers differ from formal third-party intervenors in many ways. Figure 6–12 describes these differences.

**FIGURE 6–12**          Differences between Managerial
                        and Institutional Third-Party Roles

| Dimension | Institutional Third Parties | Managers as Third Parties |
|---|---|---|
| **Dispute Characteristics** | | |
| 1. Construal of disputes | Disputes exist and involve parties with competing claims. Often with basis in law or prior agreement. | Conflict is a problem of misunderstanding that demands a rational solution. |
| 2. Boundaries of dispute | Dispute well demarcated and isolated from other activities of parties. | Dispute embedded in ongoing stream of activity. |
| 3. Point of intervention | Third party sought, often as a last effort at dispute resolution. | Intervention frequently early, at the initiative of the manager. |
| **Third-Party Role** | | |
| 1. Involvement in dispute | Disinterested third party. Principal concern for resolution. | Frequently a part of the problem with concern, for own and organization's best interests. |
| 2. Authority | Limited authority circumscribed by role as mediator or arbitrator. | Wide range of authority without clear demarcation of third-party role. |
| 3. Cultural expectations | Expected to act as conflict solver involved in recognized conflicts of interest. | Expected to act as decision maker involved in differences of opinions over best direction for organization. |
| 4. Frequency of exposure | Limited exposure to parties, typically only once. | Frequent interaction with parties within many roles. Often dealt with similar problem in past. |

While formal third parties are usually restricted to acting as mediators, fact finders, or arbitrators, managers tend to intervene in organizational disputes as inquisitors, judges (arbitrators), mediators, delegators, avoiders, or providers of impetus. Each of these types of intervention is described below.

1. **Judges** exert high degrees of control over the outcome of the conflict but not the process by which it is resolved. Judges typically allow both sides to present whatever facts, evidence, or arguments they desire, then decide the outcome of the conflict. They have the power to enforce that decision on the disputants.

2. **Inquisitors** exert high degrees of control over both the outcome and the process of conflict resolution. They direct the presentation of evidence, ask questions, act as referees, and call for evidence

not willingly offered. As judges do, inquisitors decide the outcome of the conflict and enforce that decision on the disputants.

3. Mediators exert high degrees of control over the process of conflict resolution, but not its outcome. A mediator may separate the parties, interview them, and bring them back together. A mediator may also separate the parties and ferry proposals back and forth between them to help them forge their own solution.

4. Avoiders, delegators, and the "providing impetus" tactic exert low degrees of control over either the process or the outcome. Avoiders prefer to find ways to ignore the conflict or minimize its importance. Delegators recognize that the conflict exists, but try to return responsibility for its solution to the disputants or get someone else to accept it. The "providing impetus" tactic (also known as the kick-in-the-pants style) delegates the conflict back to the parties with a threat—"Either resolve this yourselves or the manager will resolve the problem, and nobody will like that solution!"

To categorize these forms of intervention, it is useful to consider whether the manager attempts to control the outcome, the process of arriving at a solution, both, or neither. In working with a variety of disputes managers were found to use the inquisitorial style most often, followed by the judging and "providing impetus" styles. Managers reported that they use mediation frequently, but in fact seldom give the disputants any real control over the outcome. They were more likely to use strategies that controlled outcomes when (1) there were time pressures, (2) the disputants were not likely to work together in the future, and (3) the settlement had broad implications for the resolution of other disputes.[35]

Researchers may understand what managers do in conflict situations, but they do not suggest that these are the correct or optimal responses. Describing managers' behavior does not mean endorsing it as the optimal or correct behavior.[36] Lewicki, Sheppard, and their colleagues have proposed and tested a contingency model of managerial intervention. Based upon their research results, they believe that choice of managerial intervention strategy should be based upon what the manager wishes to accomplish in addition to resolving the dispute. Is the objective of the intervention that:

1. the conflict be resolved quickly (efficiency)?
2. the optimal solution be chosen (effectiveness)?
3. the disputants be satisfied with the outcome (satisfaction)?
4. the outcome be perceived as just by the disputants (fairness)?

[35]R. J. Lewicki and B. Sheppard, "Choosing How to Intervene: Factors Affecting the Use of Process and Outcome Control in Third-Party Dispute Intervention," *Journal of Occupational Behavior* 6 (1985): 49–64.

[36]Mintzberg, *The Nature of Managerial Work.*

**FIGURE 6–13**            Managerial Dispute Intervention Outcomes

**Efficiency:** to solve the problem with a minimum expenditure of resources—third-party time, disputant time, capital outlay, etc. Solving the problem quickly would be an example of procedural efficiency.

**Effectiveness:** to solve the problem so it is solved well and stays solved. Making sure that the third party listens to all parties who have a relevant perspective on the conflict is an example of procedural effectiveness; brainstorming to invent the best possible solution—one that will *work* or one that will not bring the parties back to the manager with the same dispute—is an example of outcome effectiveness.

**Participant satisfaction:** to solve the problem so that the parties are satisfied with the solution. Giving all sides an opportunity to present their case or having the disputants play a critical role in the development of the actual solution are examples of procedures that enhance participant satisfaction.

**Fairness:** to solve the problem so that the parties believe the outcome is fair (by some specific standard—equality, equity, etc.). Hearing both sides, applying rules consistently, and treating both disputants in a similar manner are mechanisms that promote the perception of fairness.

Figure 6–13 describes these four outcomes in more detail.

Whether or not the manager attempts to control the outcome of the conflict or the manner in which the conflict is resolved determines which intervention objective will result. Figure 6–14 illustrates the relationship between concern with process or outcome control and the four intervention objectives. If the manager cares most about simply getting a solution, any solution, then the focus on efficiency suggests that the manager should use an inquisitorial style if he or she wishes to have

**FIGURE 6–14**            Strengths of Intervention Strategies

Conflict intervention strategies differ in the extent to which they exert control over the process and outcomes of the dispute. These differences, in turn, result in maximizing a variety of conflict-resolution goals such as participant satisfaction.

|  |  | **Third Party Controls the Outcome** | |
|---|---|---|---|
|  |  | Yes | No |
| **Third Party Controls the Process** | Yes | Efficiency<br>Effectiveness | Satisfaction<br>Fairness |
|  | No | Fairness<br>Effectiveness | Efficiency |

control over how the outcome is reached. If the manager does not want control over either the process or the outcome of the conflict resolution, then the appropriate strategy would be a choice among avoiding, delegating, or providing impetus.

If getting the best or optimal solution to the conflict (effectiveness) is the primary objective of the manager's intervention, then the choice is between using the style of an inquisitor or a judge. If how the solution is determined is at issue, then the inquisitorial style is more appropriate. If a manager has little concern with controlling the conflict-resolving process, then the strategic choice should probably be to act like a judge.

When a manager is most concerned that the disputants are satisfied with the resolution, mediation is the only correct choice of intervention strategy. Disputant satisfaction may be important when commitment to the solution is critical for its successful implementation.

Finally, if the manager wishes to ensure that the solution is perceived by the disputants as fair, then he or she has a choice of strategies available. If the manager's goal is to control the solution, then intervening as a judge is the best choice. This strategy has the additional benefit of being associated with effective solutions. Alternatively, if the manager is not concerned with the exact nature of the final solution, then a mediating strategy is an appropriate choice. Because mediation promotes both participant satisfaction and perceived fairness, it is the form of intervention most desired by disputants. It allows them the greatest control over the actual solution, while providing them with some incentive to reach agreement (via the involvement of the mediating manager).

Managers seem to understand the attractiveness of this strategy to subordinates, since they report using mediation to a greater extent than observations of their actual behavior suggest. However, giving up control over the solution is difficult for managers. In fact, a recent study of managers indicated that lower-level managers were more likely to use intervention strategies that stressed control over outcome. The higher the manager was in the organization, the more likely he or she was to use mediation as an intervention strategy.[37]

## ALTERNATIVE DISPUTE RESOLUTION

Up until this point, we have been focusing on conflict intervention within an organization. However, considerable conflicts occur between organizations and between organizations and individuals with whom they interact. In an effort to reduce the extraordinary amount of such conflict (and the resulting financial and time costs), a revolution of sorts has been

[37]M. A. Neale and J. W. Brittain, "Managerial Third-Party Dispute Resolution: The Effects of Intervenor Status, Issue Importance, and Level of Conflict," working paper, Northwestern University, Evanston, Ill.

FOCUS ON:

Alternative Dispute Resolution

**Managing Conflicts between Organizations** Space Communications Company (SPACECOM) had been selected as the contractor to build and design a new tracking and data relay system for the National Aeronautics and Space Administration (NASA). A disagreement between these two agencies erupted that led to SPACE-COM's filing a claim with NASA's Board of Contract Appeals. After two years of pretrial work and over a million dollars in costs with the realistic expectation that the project would be delayed indefinitely, it was suggested that both parties participate in a mini-hearing (an abbreviated trial of the case before the principals to the dispute). The principals heard both parties' positions over the course of five hours. After failing to reach a solution in a meeting on the next day, the principals were able to reach an agreement not only on the issues for which the claim was filed but also on four other, unrelated disputes. Parker, the lawyer suggesting the ADR, said, "The mini-hearing created a momentum and psychology to settle."

The net savings to NASA was at least one year spent in litigation and a quarter of a million dollars. For SPACECOM, the savings was estimated to be at least one million dollars. The first launch of the new system was scheduled less than a year after the completion of the mini-hearing.

Source: "How NASA Aborted a Legal Wrangle," *Business Week*, August 23, 1982.

Alternative dispute resolution combines a series of techniques designed to manage or resolve disputes *prior to* the involvement of the courts. The use of ADR "mini-hearings" by NASA and one of its subcontractors kept a major project on schedule and saved both sides more than $1 million.

occurring. Alternatives are being sought and disputes managed rather than automatically litigated.

**Alternative dispute resolution (ADR)** combines a series of techniques designed to manage or resolve disputes before they reach the courts. One of the benefits of ADR is that the disputants are often the ones charged with coming up with the solution. Thus, they do not have to give up control of the outcome to a judge, arbitrator, or other formal decision maker. One of the most popular ADR procedures is that of the "minitrial," in which senior executives from both disputing organizations get to play both judge and juror. The assumption is that, in most cases, if both parties can be forced to listen to the other side's position and consider its merits, the dispute can be settled. One successful example of the minitrial technique occurred between the National Aeronautics and Space Administration (NASA) and Space Communications Company (SPACECOM). A detailed description of the dispute and its resolution is presented in the "FOCUS ON: Alternative Dispute Resolution."

As with all techniques of dispute resolution, ADR does not provide a panacea for avoiding litigation. Cases in which the facts are disputed or legal precedent is at issue are likely to be resolved through formal litigation. However, ADR does provide another tool in the organization's arsenal for managing conflict.

SUMMARY

Conflict is an organizational reality. Managers and other organizational members are constantly involved in competition for scarce resources. The task of an effective manager is to maintain an optimal level of conflict, given the unique characteristics of the organization and the individuals who compose it.

Ability to cope with conflict is based upon a variety of factors. Of primary concern is a person's ability to deal with stress. Because conflict is stressful, the optimal amount of conflict is a function of the individual's ability to handle it. That ability is influenced by personality and past history. Developing the skills to resolve conflict successfully is an essential aspect of controlling one's environment. Understanding conflict and its impact on individuals and groups increases a person's ability to predict its outcomes and make interventions when appropriate. Further, once conflict is viewed as a common organizational process rather than an aberration, its presence becomes that much less stressful. The more conflict management is viewed as an appropri-

ate managerial skill, the more structural alternatives will be implemented to address organizational conflict.

Structural forms of conflict management are likely to be found primarily in organizations that exist in constantly changing and unpredictable environments and have high intraorganizational interdependencies. Thus, a typical source of conflict management is the manager. Managers are likely to, on the average, spend one-fifth of each working day on some form of conflict-related activity. Given the extensive time crunch all managers experience, increasing their effectiveness in managing conflict can allow more time to be spent on producing the product for which the organization exists. But increasing one's skills means more than simply finding a way (any way) to resolve a dispute for now. Rather, it requires an understanding of the nature of the conflict and the manager's objective in resolving the conflict. Identifying the objectives or goals of the conflict intervention allows the manager to choose the intervention style that will best achieve those goals.

KEY TERMS

**Accommodating**   Strategy for interpersonal conflict that maximizes the other party's concerns or outcomes.

**Alternative dispute resolution (ADR)**   Series of techniques for avoiding litigation between organizations, usually by encouraging the disputants to arrive at a mutually agreeable solution through the use of specific techniques such as mock juries, minitrials, and so on.

**Approach-approach conflict** Occurs when an individual must choose between two equally attractive options, both with positive outcomes.

**Approach-avoidance conflict** Occurs when an individual must choose among options with both positive and negative outcomes.

**Arbitration**   Resolution of a conflict by a neutral third party who, after hearing both sides of a dispute, determines a final, binding outcome.

**Avoidance-avoidance conflict** Occurs when an individual must choose between two equally unattractive options, both with negative outcomes.

**Avoiding** Strategy for interpersonal conflict that is suitable when the positions of both parties are trivial or when one party is seriously outmatched by the other party.

**Buffer** Mechanism that reduces the environmental shocks or interdepartmental conflict to allow an organizational unit to complete its task more smoothly.

**Collaborating** Strategy for interpersonal conflict that is suitable when both your own and the other party's concerns are equally important, when the issue is too important to compromise, when trying to engender commitment among the parties, or when trying to gain insight.

**Competing** Strategy for interpersonal conflict that is suitable when the individual is concerned about his or her own needs, issues, or outcomes, such as when in an emergency or critical situation, when the other party is untrustworthy, or when the individual or group is sure of the correct solution.

**Compromising** Strategy for interpersonal conflict that is suitable when both sets of goals are important but not worth the potential disruption of more aggressive strategies.

**Concurrence seeking** Suppression of conflict by group members to seek agreement.

**Controversy** When one person's (or group's) ideas, information, perspective, or opinions are in conflict with another's and the two seek to understand and resolve these differences.

**Debate** Involves two individuals or groups who argue for incompatible alternatives and a judge who makes a decision based on the relative merits of both sides' arguments.

**Distributive negotiation** Common negotiation strategy in which parties decide only how to allocate a fixed amount of resources.

**Employee assistance programs** Typically in-house or contractual programs that diagnose and treat a variety of stress-related problems, such as drug and alcohol abuse and other emotional and psychological problems.

**Factfinding** Form of third-party intervention in which a neutral third party determines a reasonable solution based on evidence presented by the parties, who are not bound to follow the recommendation.

**Horizontal conflict** Conflict between people at similar organizational levels.

**Individualistic decision making** Each member of the group independently selects his or her most preferred alternative without interacting with other group members.

**Inquisitor** Informal third-party role in a dispute in which a manager exerts a high degree of control over both the outcome and the process of conflict resolution.

**Integrative bargaining**   A more cooperative negotiation strategy that assumes there can be an expanding amount of resources for the parties to divide.

**Judge**   Informal third-party role in a dispute in which a manager exerts a high degree of control over the outcome of a dispute but not the process by which it is resolved.

**Line-staff conflict**   Conflict between employees involved directly in some aspect of producing the organization's product and employees who provide technical and advisory assistance to the line.

**Mediation**   Resolution of a conflict by a neutral third party who can control the interaction between the disputants but has no authority to force a solution on them.

**Negotiation**   The process whereby two or more parties decide what each will give and take in an exchange between them.

**Organizational ombudsman**   An individual whose responsibility it is to interpret policy, counsel disputing parties, resolve disputes, and provide feedback and identify potential problem areas for senior management.

**Pooled interdependence**   Exists when each department or unit contributes to the larger good but is not dependent on the others.

**Resource conflict**   Individuals having separate and incompatible interests.

**Resource scarcity**   Not having enough of a particular commodity (for example, food, love, attention, cars, clothes, opportunities, etc.) for all to accomplish their goals.

**Reciprocal interdependence**   Exists when the outputs of one department become the inputs of a second, and the outputs of that second unit become the inputs for the first.

**Role conflict**   Occurs when two or more role-specific activities, or expectations of other organizational members, are incompatible.

**Sequential interdependence**   Exists when the outputs of one unit become the inputs of another unit.

**Slack**   Excess resources that can minimize conflict because they reduce the amount of necessary interaction.

**Stress quotient**   The amount of stress a job is likely to generate in the job holder.

**Third-party intervention**   Involvement in a conflict of someone not directly concerned, such as arbitration, mediation, and factfinding.

**Type A personality**   Set of personality characteristics found in many stress-prone people, such as impatience, competitiveness, and the drive to succeed.

**Type B personality**   Classification of behaviors found in less stress-prone people, such as a relaxed, easy-going, noncompetitive attitude toward work and life.

**Vertical conflict**   Conflict between people at different levels in an organization.

DISCUSSION
QUESTIONS

1. In common usage, the term *conflict* has a negative connotation. Within an organizational setting, however, conflict is a necessary and even critical resource of the successful manager. What is it about conflict that makes it so useful to organizations while being perceived as negative by the general public?

2. What indicators might warn a personnel director in a large organization that excessive, nonfunctional conflict exists?

3. Managers are often required to intervene in conflict within and between their departments and other organizational entities. What specific skills would a manager need to accomplish this role successfully?

4. While managers report using mediation techniques extensively, direct observations of managerial interventions indicate that they rely more upon controlling strategies. What is it about mediation that makes it attractive but not often implemented by managers (except possibly at the higher organizational levels)?

5. How might an organization respond to reduce excessive levels of stress?

6. What effects does intergroup conflict have on the groups themselves?

7. What are some examples of organizational slack? How do these examples "buffer" the organization from conflict?

8. What are the major advantages of alternative dispute resolution (ADR) procedures? Some have called this form of dispute resolution "poor man's justice." Do you agree? Why or why not?

IF YOU
WANT TO
KNOW
MORE

The study of conflict and conflict management has received a great deal of attention in both the popular and scholarly press in recent years. Roger Fischer and Bill Ury have written the book *Getting to Yes* (Houghton-Mifflin, 1981), which provides an excellent description of principled, integrative bargaining. Eminently readable, this book is quite popular with practicing managers as well as professional negotiators. David Lax and James Sebinius have recently published a book (*Manager as Negotiator*, Free Press, 1986) that examines in detail the manager's role in dispute intervention. A third book, Howard Raiffa's *The Art and Science of Negotiation* (Belknap, 1982), focuses on a prescriptive model for effective negotiating.

For a different perspective, those interested in negotiating might also wish to read Herb Cohen's *You Can Negotiate Anything* (Bantam Books, 1980) or Gerald Nierenberg's *Fundamentals of Negotiating* (Hawthorne/Dutton, 1973). These books introduce and develop negotiating skills for the practicing manager.

Stress and stress management are common topics in the popular press. Many magazines such as *Ms., Inc., Working Women, Time, Business Week,* and *Psychology Today* often have articles on this topic. A number of very useful books also have been published on this subject. For example, John Ivancevich and Michael Matteson have written a book called *Stress and Work: A Manage-* *rial Perspective* (Scott, Foresman, 1980). Finally, an interesting book entitled *Is It Worth Dying For?* was written by Robert Eliot and Dennis Breo (Bantam Books).

ON YOUR OWN

**Conflict Questionnaire**   *Directions:* Consider situations in which you find your wishes differing from those of another person. For each of the following statements, think how likely you are to respond in that way. Check the rating that best corresponds to your response.

|  | Very Unlikely | Unlikely | Likely | Very Likely |
|---|---|---|---|---|
| 1. I am usually firm in pursuing my goals. | _____ | _____ | _____ | _____ |
| 2. I try to make my position win. | _____ | _____ | _____ | _____ |
| 3. I give up some points in exchange for others. | _____ | _____ | _____ | _____ |
| 4. I feel that differences are not always worth worrying about. | _____ | _____ | _____ | _____ |
| 5. I try to find a position that is between the other person's and mine. | _____ | _____ | _____ | _____ |
| 6. In approaching negotiation, I try to consider the other person's wishes. | _____ | _____ | _____ | _____ |
| 7. I try to show the logic and benefits of my position. | _____ | _____ | _____ | _____ |
| 8. I always lean toward a direct discussion of the problem. | _____ | _____ | _____ | _____ |
| 9. I try to find a fair combination of gains and losses for both of us. | _____ | _____ | _____ | _____ |
| 10. I attempt to work through our differences immediately. | _____ | _____ | _____ | _____ |
| 11. I try to avoid creating unpleasantness for myself. | _____ | _____ | _____ | _____ |
| 12. I might try to soothe the other's feelings and preserve our relationship. | _____ | _____ | _____ | _____ |
| 13. I attempt to get all concerns and issues immediately out. | _____ | _____ | _____ | _____ |
| 14. I sometimes avoid taking positions that create controversy. | _____ | _____ | _____ | _____ |
| 15. I try not to hurt the other's feelings. | _____ | _____ | _____ | _____ |

SCORING: Very Unlikely = 1; Unlikely = 2; Likely = 3; Very Likely = 4.

Source: Kenneth W. Thomas, "Toward Multi-Dimensional Values in Teaching: The Example of Conflict Behaviors," *Academy of Management Review* 2 (1977): p. 487, Table 1. Used with permission.

| Competing: | Item 1 _____ | Item 2 _____ | Item 7 _____ | TOTAL _____ |
|---|---|---|---|---|
| Collaborating: | 8 _____ | 10 _____ | 13 _____ | TOTAL _____ |
| Compromising: | 3 _____ | 5 _____ | 9 _____ | TOTAL _____ |
| Avoiding: | 4 _____ | 11 _____ | 14 _____ | TOTAL _____ |
| Accommodating: | 6 _____ | 12 _____ | 15 _____ | TOTAL _____ |

| Conflict-Handling Modes | Appropriate Situations |
|---|---|
| Competing | 1. When quick, decisive action is vital—emergencies.<br>2. On important issues where unpopular actions need implementation—cost cutting, discipline.<br>3. On issues vital to organizational welfare when you know you are right.<br>4. Against people who take advantage of noncompetitive situations. |
| Collaborating | 1. To find an integrative solution when both sets of concerns are too important to compromise.<br>2. When your objective is to learn.<br>3. To merge insights from people with different perspectives.<br>4. To gain commitment by incorporating concerns into a consensus.<br>5. To work through feelings that have interfered with a relationship. |
| Compromising | 1. When goals are important, but not worth the effort or potential disruption of more assertive modes.<br>2. When opponents with equal power are committed to mutually exclusive goals.<br>3. To achieve temporary settlement of complex issues.<br>4. To arrive at expedient solutions under time pressures.<br>5. As a backup when collaboration or competition is unsuccessful. |
| Avoiding | 1. When an issue is trivial, or more important issues are pressing.<br>2. When you perceive no chance of satisfying your concerns.<br>3. When potential disruption outweighs the benefits of resolution.<br>4. To let people cool down and regain perspective.<br>5. When gathering information supersedes an immediate decision.<br>6. When others can resolve the conflict more effectively.<br>7. When issues seem tangential or symptomatic of other issues. |
| Accommodating | 1. When you find you are wrong—to allow a better position to be heard, to learn, and to show your reasonableness.<br>2. When issues are more important to others than yourself—to satisfy others and maintain cooperation.<br>3. To build social credits for later issues.<br>4. To minimize a loss when you are outmatched and losing.<br>5. When harmony and stability are especially important.<br>6. To allow subordinates to develop by learning from mistakes. |

CLOSING CASE
FOR CHAPTER 6

## THE MANAGER'S MEMO

FROM: F. Cunningham, Manager, Cookie Sales Force

TO:     P. Rodriguez, Vice President, Cookie Division

RE:     Problems with Engineering

I think we have a problem with the division's Chief Manufacturing Engineer, Bill Lee. It seems to have started in the meeting where we launched our new novelty-shaped graham crackers, TeleGrahams.

At the meeting, Angela Boskin, who is in charge of sales for this product, was excited about our expectation that we can exceed our initial sales projections by 200 percent. This would involve opening a second production facility in the southeast within three months.

As Angela was explaining the favorable results of our test marketing, Bill said, "When are we going to talk about the bugs in the production process that are causing us to burn 25 percent of the product?" Well, as Angela explained, consumers in the test markets have been satisfied with the product as it is, so we can go ahead with launching the product and work out the bugs later. But Bill just stormed out of the room, shouting something about how we always expect Production to work miracles.

I don't see what his problem is; you'd think he'd be excited about doubling production. I guess he's just a typical engineer—more concerned about his machinery than he is about the big picture.

I tried to call Bill today to smooth things over, but he was out sick. Maybe you can talk to him. Or maybe if we just ignore him, he'll get over his attitude problem. What, if anything, do you think I should do?

CASE DISCUSSION
QUESTIONS

Assume you are the vice president, and respond to the sales manager's memo. Try to infer the real nature of this conflict, and determine your goals for intervention. Use those goals as the basis for choosing an intervention style and phrasing your response. If you think it will help you achieve your goals for resolving this conflict, also write a memo to Bill Lee, the Chief Manufacturing Engineer.

Exercise for
Part 2:
Carter Racing (A)

WHAT SHOULD
WE DO?

John Carter was not sure, but his brother and partner, Fred Carter, was on the phone and needed a decision. Should they run in the race or not? It had been a successful season so far, but the Pocono race was important because of the prize money and TV exposure it promised. This first year had been hard because the team was trying to make a name for itself. They had run a lot of small races to get this shot at the big time. A successful outing could mean more sponsors, a chance to start making some profits for a change, and the luxury of racing only the major events. But if they suffered another engine failure on national television . . .

Just thinking about the team's engine problems made John wince. They had blown the engine seven times in twenty-four outings this season with various degrees of damage to the engine and car. No one could figure out why. It took a lot of sponsor money to replace a $20,000 racing engine, and the wasted entry fees were no small matter either. John and Fred had everything they owned riding on Carter Racing. This season had to be a success.

Paul Edwards, the engine mechanic, was guessing the engine problem was related to ambient air temperature. He argued that when it was cold the different expansion rates for the head and block were damaging the head gasket and causing the engine failures. It was below freezing last night, which meant a cold morning for starting the race.

Tom Burns, the chief mechanic, did not agree with Paul's "gut feeling" and had data to support his position (see Exhibit 1). He pointed out that gasket failures had occurred at all temperatures, which meant temperature was not the issue. Tom has been racing for twenty years and believed that luck was an important element in success. He had argued this view when he and John discussed the problem last week: "In racing, you are pushing the limits of what is known. You cannot expect to have everything under control. If you want to win, you have to take risks. Everybody in racing knows it. The drivers have their lives on the line, I have a career that hangs on every race, and you guys have got every dime tied up in the business. That's the thrill, beating the odds and winning." Last night over dinner he had added to this argument forcefully with what he called Burns' First Law of Racing: "Nobody ever won a race sitting in the pits."

John, Fred and Tom had discussed Carter Racing's situation the previous evening. This first season was a success from a racing standpoint, with the team's car finishing in the top five in 12 of the 15 races it completed. As a result, the sponsorship offers critical to the team's business success were starting to come in. A big break had come two weeks ago after the Dunham race, where the team scored its fourth first-place finish. Goodstone Tire had finally decided Carter Racing

Source: Copyright 1986 by Jack W. Brittain and Sim B. Sitkin. Entered into The Stanford Case System by permission of the authors.

**EXHIBIT 1**          Note from Tom Burns

John,

I got the data on the gasket failures from Paul. We have run 24 races this season with temperatures at race time ranging from 53 to 82 degrees. Paul had a good idea in suggesting we look into this, but as you can see, this is not our problem. I tested the data for a correlation between temperature and gasket failures and found no relationship.

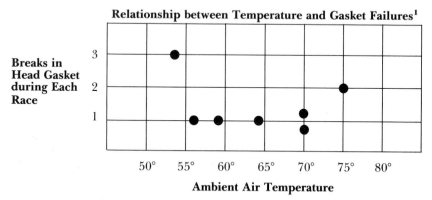

**Relationship between Temperature and Gasket Failures[1]**

**Breaks in Head Gasket during Each Race**

**Ambient Air Temperature**

In comparison with some of the other teams, we have done extremely well this season. We have finished 62.5 percent of the races, and when we finished we were in the top five 80 percent of the time. I am not happy with the engine problems, but I will take the four first-place finishes and 50 percent rate of finishing in the money[2] over seven engines any day. If we continue to run like this, we will have our pick of sponsors.

                              Tom

---

[1]Each point is for a single race. A gasket can have multiple breaks, any of which may produce an engine failure.

[2]The top five finishers in a race are "in the money."

deserved its sponsorship at Pocono—worth a much needed $40,000—and was considering a full season contract for next year if the team's car finished in the top five in this race. The Goodstone sponsorship was for a million a year, plus incentives. John and Fred had gotten a favorable response from Goodstone's racing program director last week when they presented their plans for next season, but it was clear that his support depended on the visibility they generated in this race.

"John, we only have another hour to decide," Fred said over the phone. "If we withdraw now , we can get back half the $15,000 entry and try to recoup some of our losses next season. We will lose Goodstone, they'll want $25,000 of their money back, and we end up the season $50,000 in the hole. If we run and finish in the top five, we have Goodstone in our pocket and can add another car next season. You know as well as I do, however, that if we run and lose another engine, we are back at square one next season. We will lose the tire sponsorship and a blown engine is going to lose us the oil contract. No oil company wants a national TV audience to see a smoker being dragged off the track with its name plastered all over it. The oil sponsorship is $500,000 that we cannot live without. Think about it—call Paul and Tom if you want—but I need a decision in an hour.

John hung up the phone and looked out the window at the crisp, fall sky. The temperature sign across the street flashed "40 DEGREES AT 9:23 AM."

## Carter Racing (B)

"Get Paul Edwards for me." John was calling to get his engine mechanic's opinion on whether they should run. The data Tom put together indicated that temperature was not the problem, but John wanted to get Paul's direct assessment.

Paul Edwards was a classic "gas station mechanic." His fingernails were permanently blackened by grease and his coveralls never stayed clean for more than two minutes on Saturday mornings. He had been knocking around the professional circuit for ten years after dropping out of school at sixteen to follow drag racing. He lacked the sophisticated engineering training that was getting more common in racing, but he did know racing engines.

John had discussed the gasket problem with Paul two days ago. As he waited for Paul to come to the phone, he reflected on their previous conversation. Paul was a man of few words and was not given to overstatement. "The way I see it, the turbo pressure during warm-up—in conjunction with the different expansion rates for the head and block—is doing a number on us," was about the extent of what he had to say on the problem. It was his personal opinion on the cause of the engine failures; he would never represent it as anything else.

It was the same story John had heard twenty times, but it did not match Tom's data. "Paul, we have chewed this over before. How do you know this is the problem? When we ran at Riverside the temperature was 75 degrees, and we still lost the gasket and engine."

"I am not sure what happened at Riverside," Paul had replied. "I am not sure that temperature is the problem, but it is the only thing I can figure out. It is definitely the gaskets that are blowing out and causing the engine to go."

Part of Carter Racing's success was due to a unique turbo-charging system that Tom and John had developed. They had come up with a new head design that allowed them to get more turbo pressure to the engine while maintaining fuel consumption at a fairly constant level. By casting the head and turbo bodies in a high-strength aircraft alloy, they had also saved almost fifty pounds of weight. The alloy they were using was not as temperature sensitive as the material in the engine block, but the head gasket should be able to handle the different expansion rates.

John could hear the sounds of race day in the background as Paul approached the phone. "Hello John," he said, obviously excited. "The Goodstone coveralls just got here. We are talking some fine threads. No sew-on patches from these guys. The logo on the back and our names are stitched right into the material. I guess this means we get to keep 'em. Course, I got some grease on mine already, so they probably won't want 'em back anyway."

"I'm glad you like them," John said. "I need to get some information from you. What are we doing about the gasket failure business?"

"The car is set to go. We have been using a different seating procedure since Slippery Rock and had no problems for two races. Tom says the Goodstone deal is set as long as we finish in the money today. The guys in the shop want this bad. Goodstone is a class act. They can make us the number one team on the circuit if they decide to take us on."

CASE FOR
PART 2:
The Case of the
Disputed Arches

A complex, technical description of a yieldable arch roof support is not required. Suffice to say that long before Christ, the Greeks knew that the more pressure put on a keystone the stronger it became. The concept has found numerous applications, including, in this instance, as mine haulage roof supports. I had worked five years as a union miner and acquired a mining engineering degree. Nobody was going to bullshit *me* about yieldable arches.

Joe Bond was a motorman. He was henpecked, cuckolded, and discontented in ways only he could understand. Worst of all he was smarter than his job required. In short, he was a troublemaker. Nobody could bullshit me about Joe Bond either.

I was twenty-four years old and had just become superintendent of the Bunker Mine. The average age of the union employees at Bunker was 46. I had just been left a note that Bond, who worked midnight shift, had complained about the condition of the arches at the 1,200 block on the haulage. He demanded that the arches be replaced. Rumor was that he would "cause trouble" if they were not replaced. Fact was, I was being tested.

James Franklin, the mine foreman of twenty-seven years and a man much respected by the union, looked at the arches. Frank Randall, the federal mine inspector, looked at the arches. I looked at the arches. We all agreed: even though they showed signs of taking pressure, the arches were safe. Furthermore, replacing the arches would require closing the haulage, and therefore the mine, for about four days.

I left a polite note for Joe Bond, to be given him by the midnight shift foreman. I thanked Joe for his suggestion, his attention to matters of safety, and his wisdom in reporting these matters to management. However, the arches in question did appear to be perfectly safe. I would continue to watch them and perhaps change them out at the first convenient opportunity, thank you very much anyway.

The midnight shift foreman called to tell me that Joe had received the note, had promptly gone into the waiting room and announced that management was trying to get him killed. Then he went home. The rest of the shift had followed close behind. The mine was on strike.

I hurriedly phoned the union safety committee and met them at the mine at 2:30 a.m. The safety committee asked me to show them the arches in question. I had a better idea, I said. If these arches were as unsafe as claimed, that fact should be immediately obvious to so well-trained and experienced a group as the safety committee. I would accompany them down the entire length of the haulage, and *they* could tell *me* where the bad arches were.

This case was prepared by G. R. Spindler, under the supervision of David L. Bradford, as the basis for class discussion rather than to illustrate either effective or ineffective handling of an administrative situation. Reprinted with permission of Stanford University Graduate School of Business. © 1980 by the Board of Trustees of the Leland Stanford Junior University.

Two trips up and down the haulage produced half-a-dozen wrong guesses. At the end of the second trip one member of the safety committee told me to cut the crap and just show them the arches in question. Another member suggested that the two of us step into a cross-cut and settle the whole matter man-to-man.

Finally the exact cause of Joe Bond's complaint was pointed out to the committee. They reluctantly admitted that the arches didn't look too bad to them. They indicated they would take the matter under advisement and let me know their recommendation.

Day shift worked, much to the disgust of the men on midnight shift. There was an unwritten union rule that no one could work until the shift that initiated a strike decided to return. Afternoon shift would be the problem. The youngest, most volatile employees were on afternoon shift and I felt that their inclination would be to rekindle the strike. To forestall this, James Franklin and I went into the waiting room to talk to the men on afternoon shift as they arrived. I decided to let James do the talking, relying on his excellent reputation to add weight to his words.

James haltingly explained the situation to the men in terms couched with caution. He refused to definitely disclaim any hazard, saying only that while he didn't believe there was, he couldn't guarantee anything and there was no substitute for a man's own best judgment in these matters. I finally lost patience with him and declared that I could guarantee that there was no hazard, and furthermore, I could see no point in anyone else losing a day's pay because of the troublemaker, Joe Bond.

After talking among themselves, the afternoon shift finally decided to continue the strike. This established a two-to-one vote and guaranteed that tomorrow, day shift also would not work.

At this point I had my first consultation with my supervisor, Mike Beanch. Mike was well-known for giving in to union pressure, so much so that even the union lacked respect for him. After a lengthy conversation, I convinced Mike that we should "hang tough" and resist the demands to replace the arches.

Thus began what promised to be a long strike. Every day I met with the safety committee in an attempt to prove the safety of the arches and find some way to get the men back to work. Every day I was encouraged and congratulated by the line foremen who worked under me for finally standing up to the union and restoring dignity to management. Every day Mike got more and more nervous.

During one meeting with the safety committee, when Joe Bond was present, I was asked if I had referred to Joe as a troublemaker. I replied that I certainly had, and furthermore, that I had every belief that even Joe didn't think any hazard existed, that he simply did not want to work and chose to penalize everyone else's paycheck along with his.

Halfway through the second week of the strike, Mike called me up. "We have a new wrinkle in the union's demands," he said. "They've backed down. They no longer insist the arches be replaced. I've just finished talking to the safety committee on the phone."

I was a little miffed that the safety committee was talking to Mike directly, bypassing me, but I ignored this for the present.

"They are coming back to work, then," I said.

"No," Mike replied. "Now they won't come back to work until you are fired."

### Questions for Discussion

1. How would you characterize the motivations of the case writer? What are Joe Bond's motivations in this case? Do any of these motivations change over the course of the case?

2. What is really in dispute in this case? Does it change from the beginning to the end of the case? How have the case writer's attempts to resolve this conflict made it worse?

3. Are there some important differences in perception in this case? How are they contributing to the problem?

CHAPTER

# Group Dynamics

# The Macdifference at Apple Computers

The youthful exuberance at Apple Computers seems a long way from the starched and staid halls of many *Fortune* 500 companies in America. Nevertheless, Apple has remained a giant among computer producers (annual sales of more than $1 billion) despite its relatively small size (only 6,000 employees, compared to more than 300,000 at IBM).

Apple's initial successes came from an industry first—the introduction of the Apple personal computer. When IBM later introduced its own personal computer—the PC—industry analysts foresaw the day when Apple (like many other small IBM competitors) would be forced out. But Apple decided to fight back.

Apple's management knew it needed something different to survive the IBM threat. The vision it settled on was the Macintosh—an inexpensive, easy-to-use personal computer as powerful and sophisticated as IBM's PC, but playful enough to make it attractive to young professionals. How does a major corporation generate something this radical?

Apple Computers pursued this vision by encouraging the Macintosh project team to break all the rules. During the project, a Jolly Roger flag flew over the Macintosh project building, reminding the team members that management wanted them to behave like pirates—beyond the constraints of corporate rules and regulations. Even the building that housed the Macintosh project team was completely separate from the rest of Apple's headquarters facility.

Apple's renegade approach extended beyond design of the new computer to its manufacturing. The assembly line constructed for the Macintosh was state-of-the-art and virtually completely automated. After bringing in two seasoned professional managers to handle this radical production facility and firing them both, Apple decided to break all the rules again. Apple hired Debbie Coleman, a financial analyst on the Macintosh design team who had *no*

277

previous manufacturing experience, to run the assembly plant.

Apple's pirate tactics have paid large dividends. First-quarter sales of the Macintosh exceeded expectations by 44 percent, and Macintosh now accounts for almost half of Apple's annual sales. The history of the Macintosh has been people breaking all the rules. And for Apple Computers, macdifferent really has been macbetter.

Source: Adapted from the PBS program, "In Search of Excellence," 1983.

---

## THE NATURE OF GROUPS

Groups are the building blocks of organizations and of social life. Individuals may come into and leave this world alone, but in between they interact with lots of other people. Groups provide the settings in which many of these interactions take place. And when people get together in groups, things happen. The challenge of group dynamics is learning how to manage the energy of groups. Well-managed groups (like the Macintosh group at Apple Computers) are positive and productive both for their individual members and for the larger organizations and societies in which they exist.

What is a group? A **group** is "an organized system of two or more individuals who are interrelated so that the system performs some function, has a standard set of role relationships among its members, and has a set of norms that regulate the function of the group and each of its members."[1]

There are two important features to this definition. First, groups have a function—they serve a purpose. People do not simply come together to come together. People come together to accomplish something. Second, groups have structure. Groups must be organized to pursue their functions effectively. Some groups, such as task forces, have formal structures. These groups exist as legitimate, documented subunits of larger organizations. Their structures exist on paper in the form of charters or handbooks. Other groups, such as study groups, are informal. These groups exist only in the minds of their members, and their structures may be known only implicitly by the members. In either case, there must be rules that govern the conduct of group members, and each member of the group must have some tasks or duties to perform in the service of the group's function.

## GROUP FUNCTIONS

The social philosopher Thomas Hobbes outlined the essential paradox of groups in his book *The Leviathan*.[2] Hobbes argued that human nature consists of a primary drive for *individual* preservation and betterment.

[1] J. W. McDavid and M. Harari, *Social Psychology: Individuals, Groups, and Societies* (New York: Harper & Row, 1968), 237.

[2] T. Hobbes, *Leviathan, or the Matter, Forme, and Power of a Common-wealth Ecclesiasticall and Civill* (London: Andrew Crooke, 1651).

He believed that the natural passions of men and women include selfishness, pride, and revenge, and that the pursuit of these natural passions leads mankind into a perpetual state of unproductive conflict:

> In such conditions, there is no place for Industry; because the fruit thereof is uncertain: and consequently no Culture of the Earth; no Navigation, nor use of the commodities that may be imported by Sea; no commodious Building; no Instruments of moving, and removing such things as require much force; no Knowledge of the face of the Earth; no account of time; no Arts; no Letters; no Society; and which is worst of all, continuall feare [sic], and danger of violent death; And the life of man, solitary, poore, nasty, brutish, and short.[3]

Hobbes's statements contain two important claims. First, if we all did exactly as we pleased all the time, everyone constantly would be engaged in unproductive conflict. Second, the tremendous benefits of civilization are accessible only when individuals subordinate their personal passions to the pursuit of group goals. The paradox here is the "free rider" problem described in Chapter 5. Any one individual benefits most when all others subordinate their personal interests to the group and the one individual does not. For Hobbes, this analysis justified the necessity of government, or "common-wealths." Common-wealths meant a social covenant (an agreement on rules of conduct) backed by the power of enforcement. This power (the Leviathan) prevents anyone (through threat of punishment) from pursuing private agendas that are detrimental to the greater good of the group. Thus, for Hobbes groups are a tenuous compromise. Groups arise only when individuals reluctantly and begrudgingly forgo their selfish pursuits to avoid perpetual conflict among themselves and gain the otherwise inaccessible benefits of cooperative behavior.

As an analysis of group dynamics, Hobbes's arguments are deficient in several important ways. Primarily, Hobbes failed to grasp the powerful attraction of individuals to groups. Hobbes proposed the need for a Leviathan because he believed that group members would willingly forfeit their independence to the governing covenants of a group only because groups are important to survival. This ignores the *rewards* inherent in group interaction, such as being accepted and respected by the group. These rewards create tremendous drive in individuals to obey the rules of a group simply to maintain membership. Even if an individual could otherwise gain all the practical advantages of group effectiveness and efficiency, life without groups would nevertheless remain "nasty, brutish, and short" in its lack of social companionship.

Second, Hobbes certainly was correct in emphasizing the necessity of a **social covenant:** a set of rules that constrain and structure social interaction. What he failed to realize was that group members' willingness (if not eagerness) to accept the dictates of social covenants might

[3]Ibid.

Rules and roles provide structure for group interaction. Rules and roles help this sailboat racing team work together effectively to achieve more than each member as an individual could ever hope to. Each team member can rely on the others to perform the appropriate task at the correct time to maximize the speed of the boat and maintain safety because of the agreed-upon rules and roles established long before the race.

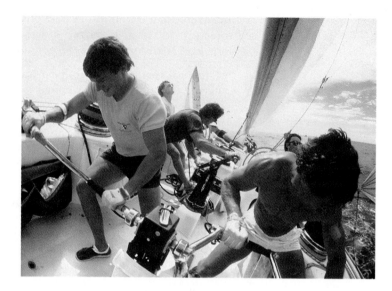

*Why people join group*

release a "dark side" of human nature. Social covenants structure group interaction, and it is this structure which makes the benefits of group interaction possible. As we shall see later in this chapter, however, the structural features of groups that make group interaction possible have undesirable effects as well.

So why do people join groups? What are individuals hoping to obtain through groups that they could not obtain alone? Our analysis of Hobbes's social philosophy of group interaction suggests two general categories of reasons why people join groups: groups as means and groups as ends.

**Means**   As we noted in the introductory chapter of this book, one important reason why people come together and form groups (and join those groups into organizations) is that groups can be an important means to accomplishing desired outcomes. In particular, groups can enhance individual effectiveness and efficiency. This can be good for each of the individual members of the group, and also for any larger organization of which the group is a part. A neighborhood watch will form because no one individual can police an entire neighborhood alone. A carpool will form because it's more efficient to have only one person drive to work each day. Groups allow individuals to pool their resources and increase their individual productivities by taking advantage of economies of scale.

**Ends**   Individuals also join groups because group interactions can be desirable outcomes themselves. Someone may join a carpool because it saves gasoline and time, but that carpool also provides companionship and interesting conversation. A student may join a study group to improve grades, but the interaction of the study group also provides an intimate social circle with whom to commiserate when the demands of the classroom become overwhelming. The processes of group interaction represent more to group members than just the means to accomplishing difficult tasks. Group interaction itself provides important rewards.

College football teams provide a particularly good illustration of the differences between groups as means and groups as ends. Many big-time college athletes play football because football is a *means* to career success. If a college player develops professional-level abilities, a professional team will offer a lucrative professional contract. This in turn could lead to product-promotion contracts and personal-appearance income. Even if the athlete plays football only in college, the scholarship he receives for doing so will underwrite the cost of his education and launch him on a successful career outside of sports. Further, the exposure the player receives while playing and the personal contacts he makes as a player provide valuable networking that also can enhance later career opportunities inside or outside sports.

These are all examples of college athletics as a means to career success. For many college athletes, however, the experience of simply being a member of a successful team offers tremendous benefits; it is an important *end* in itself. Camaraderie develops, lifelong friendships are established, and team members feel a sense of belonging. The successful coordination of team efforts on the playing field, with all members of the team working together like a well-oiled machine, can be tremendously satisfying and rewarding if team efforts lead to achievement.

## THE STRUCTURING OF GROUP INTERACTION

Whether as means or ends, groups are useful only if the interaction of group members produces something greater than the sum of all the individual efforts. Thomas Hobbes's arguments make it clear that social covenants are needed to structure group interaction so group members will coordinate their actions in the cooperative pursuit of both individual and group objectives. The structure of group interaction is apparent in the rules and roles that define acceptable behavior in the group.

**Rules**    Group **rules** that define the boundaries of acceptable and expected behavior in the group can be formal or informal. Some groups have formal policies. Formal policies are rules explicitly agreed upon by the group members and even written down — for example, how often or what time of day the group will meet. Many groups structure their meetings according to Robert's Rules of Order. These well-known rules specify in writing who may talk and when, and how disagreements will be settled by discussion and vote.

Informal, unstated rules that govern and regulate group behavior are called **norms.** Groups may have norms about what is appropriate to wear to meetings of the group. Groups often have norms about lateness or absence. It may be the norm, for instance, for group members to call ahead to warn the group if they are going to be more than 10 minutes late for a meeting.

Groups also may have norms prohibiting criticism of group decisions to "outsiders"—people who are not members of the group. This type of norm demonstrates an important difference between norms and explicit group policies. A group might feel uneasy about adopting an explicit rule against airing group dissension outside the group. Nevertheless, an informal rule of this sort may be necessary for group members to feel free to voice dissenting or controversial positions during group discussions, or if it is important for the group to appear united in its opinions to outsiders.

Formal policies and norms also differ in terms of enforcement. Formal policies often specify punishments if rules are breached. For example, a breakfast club may fine members for missing meetings. Because norms are only implicit rules, norms are enforced instead by group disapproval or rejection of the offending group member. This is not to suggest that norms constitute a weaker form of group structure than formal policies. In fact, in some cases norms may have more regulatory power over group members precisely because they are implicit. An explicit policy always can be challenged, reconsidered, and altered through open group discussion. Because norms are unstated agreements about conduct, it may be difficult for group members to question or reconsider a norm's appropriateness or challenge its punishment openly. An unfair norm therefore may be harder to fight than an unfair policy.

Knowing a group's rules for social interaction and playing by them often is critical if a newcomer wants to make good first impressions and establish healthy long-term relationships with members of the group. Nowhere is this more apparent than when managers take their business abroad. As noted in the "INTERNATIONAL FOCUS ON: Rules and Norms," the rules that govern social interaction in other countries often are very different. Managers traveling abroad are well-advised to learn the local rules of social interaction, in order to avoid accidentally insulting their foreign hosts.

The formal and informal rules that structure a group's interaction derive from a variety of sources. Some rules are established by formal consideration and decision. To select a meeting time, for instance, group members might identify potential times and potential conflicts until they finally arrive at a decision. (The process of group decision making of this sort will be discussed in greater detail in Chapter 9.)

Not all rules are arrived at so formally, however. Group members may *import* rules of conduct from other groups. Perhaps a group member has found Robert's Rules of Order to be a useful mechanism for structuring group meetings in the past and suggests that the group adopt them.

INTERNATIONAL
FOCUS ON:
Rules and Norms

*Norms*

**Strangers in Strange Lands** Rules and norms can facilitate smooth and productive social interaction only when individuals are aware of them. Within a country there may be subtle differences in social conventions among regions, or even among organizations within a region. But these differences pale in comparison to the differences across countries. Consider some of the rules for social interaction in the Arab Middle East.

The Arab concept of privacy is quite different from that held by most Americans. Americans new to the Middle East may schedule a confidential meeting to discuss classified company business, only to find their Arab host's office filled with friends, relatives, and professional associates at the appointed hour. Of course, finding *anything* in the Middle East at the appointed hour is no small triumph because of the Arab sense of time. Arabs view time as a continuous flow of events in which past, present, and future blur together. If unanticipated events prevent an Arab from meeting agreed-upon deadlines, it's the immutable will of Allah. As one frustrated U.S. oil company executive put it, "Arab clocks have no hands."

Hospitality is also an important aspect of Arab social interaction rules.

To ancient bedouins, from whom modern Arabs take many cultural cues, the purpose of hospitality was to strengthen group ties, vital to security in a tenuous nomadic existence in the harsh desert. Today, Arab hospitality is still a two-way street: a show of mutual respect, reciprocity, and delicately balanced obligations between host and guest who will then, in a future situation, become guest and host. Not only do Arabs feel obligated to be generous to their guests, but for a guest to *refuse* such generosity is an insult, a rejection of bonding to the group with which the host is aligned. When the situation is reversed, the former guest is expected to play the host with equal, but not greater, hospitality, so as not to create an imbalance in the relationship.

When you're offered something by an Arab colleague—be it coffee, tea, nuts or dates, an invitation to dinner, even a gift—Arab rules of politeness dictate that you should accept it. Whether or not you want it is irrelevant. It's the symbolic meaning of the offer and your acceptance that matters, not the content of the offer or your desire to receive it. And it's your playing by the rules in a foreign country that matters when it comes to their acceptance of you.

Source: N. Chesanow, "A Thousand and One Arabian Nights," *The World-Class Executive* (New York: Rawson Associates, 1985), 110–147.

*Primacy*—what is done first—also may determine rules for group interaction. If everyone comes to the first meeting of a group dressed formally (dresses or suits for the women, jacket and tie for the men), that could establish a group norm for being "dressed up" at the group's meetings. Interestingly, primacy may lead to the establishment of some rather silly norms. For instance, even if it is only by coincidence that everyone comes to the first meeting of a group "dressed up," all group members might conclude that all other group members came dressed that way intentionally. Thus, the norm for being "dressed up" could be established through primacy even though everyone in the group would rather be dressed casually at the meetings.

Importation and primacy are especially useful for establishing rules of conduct when it is important to have some rule, but any rule will do. For example, to have free-flowing discussion, it is probably important that all group members be dressed similarly. *How* everyone is dressed (whether dressy or casually) may be less important. Importation or primacy may settle this issue without the group devoting time to its resolution.

**Critical incidents** also establish rules of conduct, either informally or formally. Policies and norms typically do not cover all possible behaviors of group members or the group. New behaviors outside the coverage of the group's policies and norms therefore are always possible. When new behaviors are tried, particularly successful or unsuccessful outcomes — the critical incidents — may lead to the establishment of group policies or norms to incorporate a successful behavior or prevent recurrences of past disasters. A group may have no rules regulating romantic attachments among group members, for instance, until two group members become attached romantically. If the romance is successful (in terms of improving or not interfering with group functioning), further such romantic attachments may be encouraged—or at least tolerated or not discouraged—by the group. On the other hand, if the relationship is a disaster from the viewpoint of group functioning, norms may arise or formal policies even may be established to prevent similar disruption of the group in the future.

**Roles**     While rules delineate the proper behaviors of all members in a group, **roles** define the set of behaviors appropriate to particular *positions* occupied by individuals in a group. Roles also specify the authority relationships within a group, including who has the right to call meetings, set agendas, and assign tasks to group members. Social psychologist Erving Goffman contends that roles (like rules) smooth interaction in groups.[4] Roles allow us to know what we should be doing and what to expect from others. Like rules, the roles that structure the interaction of group members can be formal or informal.

In work organizations, formal roles are specified by job descriptions. **Job descriptions** are written documents that specify what duties individuals must perform, to whom they must report, what goals they must attain—in short, their role in the organization. Job descriptions are very useful because they decrease an individual's uncertainty about what to do to fulfill the group's needs and expectations.

Many groups (especially informal ones) do not have job descriptions. Roles instead evolve or are negotiated informally as the group develops. Some role assignments evolve during group development as particular

---

[4]E. Goffman, *The Presentation of Self in Everyday Life* (New York: Doubleday Anchor, 1959).

Informal tailgate conferences like this one at New England Electric can provide an important arena for workers to share ideas and solve problems. For many employees, informal group interaction like this also fulfills affiliation needs and provides a sense of belonging or contribution.

strengths and talents of group members are revealed. As we shall see in Chapter 10, most groups have at least two leadership roles: a task leader (who focuses on getting the group's goals accomplished) and a socioemotional (relations-oriented) leader (who focuses on maintaining harmony and good working relationships within the group). While task leadership often is arrived at formally (for example, by vote of the group members or appointment from a higher source), socioemotional (relations-oriented) leadership emerges (and even changes) as the group develops and matures. A selection of typical roles occupied by group members is shown in Figure 7–1.

Roles are specific to particular positions within particular groups. The role an individual occupies in one group may be completely different from the role that same individual occupies in other groups. Figure 7–2 identifies a variety of roles that one individual might assume in a variety of different groups and relationships. Because all of us simultaneously occupy different roles, *role conflict* is always a potential problem. Role conflict occurs when the behaviors dictated by one role conflict with the behaviors dictated by another. The coach of a company softball team may find himself in a quandary about how to address his boss if his boss tries out for the softball team. Is the boss still "Ms. Perkins" on the softball field (as she is in the office), or "Janet"? And if she's "Janet" on the softball field, is she now "Janet" in the office? This role conflict can become acute if social or even romantic interaction is tolerated or encouraged among softball-team members but discouraged between supervisors and subordinates in the company.

An important component of most roles is status. **Status** refers to the position of a role in a social hierarchy. The amount of status that a role

**FIGURE 7–1** √ Typical Roles Occupied by Group Members

### Task-Oriented Roles

The task-oriented role facilitates and coordinates decision-making activities. It can be broken down into the following subroles:

- *Initiators* offer new ideas or modified ways of considering group problems or goals as well as suggest solutions to group difficulties, including new group procedures or a new group organization.

- *Information seekers* try to clarify suggestions and obtain authoritative information and pertinent facts.

- *Information givers* offer facts or generalizations that are authoritative or relate experiences that are pertinent to the group problem.

- *Coordinators* clarify relationships among ideas and suggestions, pull ideas and suggestions together, and try to coordinate activities of members of subgroups.

- *Evaluators* assess the group's functioning; they may evaluate or question the practicality, logic, or facts of suggestions by other members.

### Relations-Oriented Roles

The relations-oriented role builds group-centered activities, sentiments, and viewpoints. It may be broken down into the following subroles:

- *Encouragers* praise, agree with, and accept the ideas of others; they indicate warmth and solidarity toward other members.

- *Harmonizers* mediate intragroup conflicts and relieve tension.

- *Gatekeepers* encourage participation of others by using such expressions as, "Let's hear from Sue," "Why not limit the length of contributions so all can react to the problem?" and "Bill, do you agree?"

- *Standard setters* express standards for the group to achieve or apply in evaluating the quality of group processes, raise questions of group goals and purpose, and assess group movement in light of these objectives.

- *Followers* go along passively and serve as friendly members.

- *Group observers* tend to stay out of the group process and give feedback on the group as if they were detached evaluators.

### Self-Oriented Roles

The self-oriented role focuses only on members' individual needs, often at the expense of the group. This role may be broken into the following subroles:

- *Blockers* are negative, stubborn, and unreasoningly resistant; for example, they may try to bring back an issue the group intentionally rejected or bypassed.

- *Recognition seekers* try to call attention to themselves; they may boast, report on personal achievements, and, in unusual ways, struggle to avoid being placed in an inferior position.

- *Dominators* try to assert authority by manipulating the group or certain individuals in the group; they may use flattery or assertion of their superior status or right to attention; and they may interrupt contributions of others.

- *Avoiders* maintain distance from others; these passive resisters try to remain insulated from interaction.

Source: Reprinted by permission from *Organizational Behavior*, 5th ed. by Don Hellriegel, John W. Slocum, and Richard W. Woodman, pgs. 212–213. Copyright © 1989 by West Publishing Company. All rights reserved.

**FIGURE 7–2**          One Person = Many Roles

Every person assumes many different roles. At home, an individual might be a parent or spouse, at work a supervisor or subordinate (or both). Each of these roles carries with it prescriptions for behaviors and expectations on the part of others. For example, your boss expects you to obey, while your spouse expects you to be supportive and affectionate. These roles help us know what to do—and help others know what to expect from us.

Source: Lawrence S. Wrightsman, *Social Psychology*, 2d ed. (Monterey, Calif.: Brooks/Cole, 1977), p. 17.

commands is the amount of personal worth, respect, prestige, and deference that the role provides *any* individual occupying that role. Status is a source of power for a role-holder. High-status individuals can influence the behaviors of a group because of their revered positions. High-status individuals also are looked to by other group members as opinion leaders.

These forms of power of high-status individuals over low-status group members are sensible when status reflects ability or expertise. For example, senior students at a university (high-status role-holders) are likely to be extremely knowledgeable and thereby worthy of the deference freshman students accord them. The role of university professor carries even more status, though this status may be less deserved if the professor has been on campus only a few days and is therefore ignorant of campus policies, norms, and procedures.

Interestingly, undeserved status may be no less powerful than earned status. In courtroom trials, jurors from high-status occupations disproportionately influence final jury decisions, even though a high-status occupation may make an individual no more capable of rendering a just verdict.[5]

**Maintaining Group Adaptability**    Rules and roles are important for coordinating and regulating group interaction. After all, in their absence there is chaos and a low probability of effective group functioning. This does not mean, however, that rules and roles are universally good for a group. Rules and roles improve the effectiveness of group functioning precisely because they constrain the behaviors of group members, thereby allowing predictability and coordination of group behavior. While a little constraint is not only good but *necessary*, too much constraint can prove disruptive to the effective functioning of a group.

In an article entitled "The Technology of Foolishness," political scientist Jim March has suggested that rules and roles can constrain the creativity and flexibility of a group.[6] This constraint in turn can hinder the group's adaptability to changing demands and opportunities. Norms and roles represent prescriptions for behavior—prescriptions that summarize past learning about how the group can best function. For example, a norm previously may have been established for group members to bring food to meetings. The food makes it possible for the group to work during the lunch hour without anyone missing lunch. The food also informalizes the meetings, thereby encouraging open discussion. Having a norm about bringing food to meetings allows these advantages to occur at every meeting without members having to figure out anew how to accomplish them. What the norm also does, however, is to discourage anyone from figuring out a *better* way of accomplishing these same (and admittedly valuable) benefits. This can prove extremely important if circumstances change so that rules that were appropriate for regulating group behavior in the past are no longer appropriate. Once a norm has been established, group members will hesitate to break the norm and risk sanctions by the group.

March suggests that it is important that group members occasionally "act out" and violate group rules and roles. Violating group rules and

[5]F. L. Strodtbeck, R. M. James, and D. Hawkins, "Social Status in Jury Deliberations," *American Journal of Sociology* 22 (1957): 713–719.
[6]J. G. March, "The Technology of Foolishness," *Civil o konomen* 18 (4) (1971).

roles seems foolish. After all, the group's rules and roles summarize past learning about how to structure group interaction appropriately. In most cases, then, violating a group's rules and roles will result in poor outcomes for the group. However, sometimes the violation of group rules and roles will reveal that a norm or policy was ill-advised in the first place, that circumstances have changed, or that there simply is a better way of doing things. Only violation of a rule or role can show why the rule or role is still appropriate, if in fact it still is. Unfortunately, unless one group member is willing to risk sanctions by the group, violations of the group's rules and roles will not occur. Thus, while rules and roles capture past learning about effective group functioning, they also may stand in the way of continual learning and adaptation by the group. The opening vignette for this chapter demonstrates the role of "foolish" rule breaking in fostering creativity at companies like Apple Computers.

**Idiosyncrasy credits** provide groups a way to be creative within the necessary constraints of rules and roles. Idiosyncrasy credits are allowances given to group members to violate group rules and roles.[7] If someone has proven to be a good group member—has in the past largely gone along with the behavioral prescriptions of the group's rules and roles—that individual will be *allowed* to violate the group's rules and norms without incurring extreme sanctions. If an individual has been a good group member (that is, played by the rules) for a long period of time, that individual's actions in breaking the group's rules or roles are unlikely to be seen on balance as a threat to the group. In contrast, an individual new to the group or one who has consistently violated rules and roles in the past is likely to be seen by group members as a threat to the rules and roles. Since the rules and roles are important to maintaining the group's coordination and stability, these violations are unlikely to be tolerated. Thus, group members accumulate idiosyncrasy credits by demonstrating their loyalty to the group's rules and roles. This makes later occasional violations less likely to be seen as revolutionary or destructive. Idiosyncrasy credits provide the mechanism by which the continuing appropriateness of group rules and roles can be challenged and reaffirmed by group members.

Rules and roles also can be problematic to group functioning when they define a reality or morality within the group that is inappropriate and inconsistent with reality or morality outside the group. A famous study at Stanford University provided a graphic demonstration of this tyranny of group rules and roles by simulating life in prisons.[8] In the study, the students participating as guards became extremely brutal and

[7]E. P. Hollander, "Conformity, Status, and Idiosyncrasy Credits," *Psychological Review* 65 (1958): 117–127.

[8]C. Haney, C. Banks, and P. G. Zimbardo, "A Study of Prisoners and Guards in a Simulated Prison," in *Readings about the Social Animal*, ed. E. Aronson (New York: W. H. Freeman, 1984).

inhumane. There was nothing different about these students that should have led them to commit reprehensible acts. Their own morality simply was swallowed up by the prescriptions of their roles as prison guards.

Any time the rule and role enforcement mechanisms at work in a group lead the group members to engage in behaviors that violate or suspend the larger rules and roles of society, the group's effectiveness and even survival are threatened. This problem was in evidence in the E. F. Hutton check-kiting scam discussed in Chapter 5. The earlier discussion of check kiting at E. F. Hutton focused on how this practice might have begun; the additional question of how group norms and roles at E. F. Hutton supported the practice and allowed it to continue seems equally important. A more subtle example of how groups can create a dangerously distorted view of reality for their members will be presented in the discussion concerning groupthink in Chapter 9. How a group's invaluable processes of rule and role formation can be distorted in this way is the focus of the next section.

## STAGES OF GROUP DEVELOPMENT

The rules and roles that structure group interaction do not simply exist. They must evolve and develop over time. As described in Figure 7–3, there are four distinct stages in the development of groups: formation, differentiation, integration, and maturity.

**Formation**   When groups first come together, the members must get acquainted. Formation includes learning the traits and strengths of each potential member. If participation in the group is voluntary, potential members might be trying to decide during formation if membership is necessary, or whether this group is likely to fulfill their needs. Preliminary identification of a leader usually occurs at this stage as well.

**Differentiation**   Once group members have had a chance to assess the human resources available in a group, several battles of **differentiation** must be fought within the group. First, the group must decide what its goals and priorities will be. Is a study group there only to study, or does it fulfill an important social function as well? If there is a social function as well, how can these two goals be reconciled? And are there other functions for the group? Can the group fulfill its functions without creating problems for its members? The second battle arises because the group must structure its interaction to ensure effective group functioning. Who will fulfill which roles becomes an important question. Disagreements that are not handled now typically force the group back to this stage again later in its development.

**Integration**   Once group functions have been (at least tentatively) decided upon and roles have been assigned, the tone of group interaction changes. Group members now identify with a common purpose, and the group has identified the human resources it needs to

**FIGURE 7–3** ✓ Stages of Work-Group Development

Groups and teams tend to go through four predictable developmental stages. Each of these stages serves a slightly different purpose for the group, and therefore is characterized by a slightly different set of objectives. The early stages of group development—formation, differentiation, and integration—are necessary prerequisites to effective group functioning once a group or team reaches maturity.

| Stage | Description |
|---|---|
| **Formation** | ■ Members get acquainted and size up the new territory<br>■ Initial task definition and identification of simple group processes<br>■ First attempts to clarify member roles and authority/responsibility relationship<br>■ Members try to determine how their skills will fit the group task and how the group activity will help group members<br>■ Tentative decision on leadership and behavioral norms |
| **Differentiation** | ■ Progress on identifying roles and norms<br>■ Better feel for group task and for composition of groups<br>■ Formation of coalitions within the group to promote certain views and interests<br>■ Emergence of interpersonal and intercoalition conflicts<br>■ Working through of conflicts<br>■ Emergence of competing values and norms for guiding behavior |
| **Integration** | ■ Stage of balance in the life of a group<br>■ Norms operating to obtain conformity<br>■ Procedures for coping with deviations from norms established<br>■ Work flow handled easily<br>■ Development of cohesiveness among group members<br>■ Danger of "groupthink," where loyalty to the group becomes a powerful group norm; "fat and sassy" attitude<br>■ Members perceive themselves as a group |
| **Maturity** | ■ Appreciation of group's need for stable norms, roles, goals, leadership, and work processes<br>■ Appreciation of group's need to be flexible about changing demands on group<br>■ Members' awareness of each other's strengths and weaknesses<br>■ Acceptance of individual differences<br>■ Efficient and effective group processes<br>■ Tolerance of conflict or over task-related issues; positive approach to conflict management<br>■ Minimal intermember conflict |

Source: Robert Albanese and David D. Van Fleet, *Organizational Behavior: A Managerial Viewpoint* (Hinsdale, Ill.: Dryden, 1983), 259.

fulfill that purpose. In **integration** the group members must define a set of rules and roles to coordinate group interaction and make pursuit of the goals effective.

**Maturity**    Once a group has identified its rules and roles, it has a structure within which to pursue its goals and the group has reached **maturity.** If further conflicts surface among members, the structure (roles and rules) put in place should lead to nondisruptive resolution of the conflicts.

Some time after a group has reached maturity, it may make sense for the group to disband. Perhaps all the goals of the group have been met. Or perhaps circumstances—the loss of critical members, for example—conspire to render the group incapable of fulfilling its goals. Sometimes groups that remain effective may disband simply because they no longer fulfill the nontask goals of group members, such as friendship or companionship.

Two important points should be kept in mind when considering the stages of group development. First, during their development groups may find themselves moving back and forth among these stages. As noted earlier, it is not unusual for a group to find that all of its conflicts were not settled initially. In such cases, a second or even third phase of differentiation may occur, until all conflicts are ironed out. Second, while virtually all groups pass through these stages of development, the transitions may not be obvious to the group members themselves. In fact, much of the negotiation of the group's roles and rules may be quite implicit.

Nevertheless, once a structure for group interaction is in place, the group can begin to influence the thoughts and behaviors of its members. These influences are the subject of the next section of this chapter.

# GROUP INFLUENCES ON INDIVIDUALS

An important part of understanding the role that groups play in organizations is understanding how and why individuals behave differently in groups than they behave when alone. These differences go beyond the constraints and prescriptions on behaviors created by roles and rules of group interaction. The previous chapters of this book that have discussed perception (Chapter 3) and motivation (Chapter 4) carefully outlined the impact of contextual factors on individual behavior. In a group, *other group members* are the most salient and powerful contextual influences on individual behavior. The group influences the judgments (or perceptions or beliefs) of its group members, which in turn influences their behaviors. The group also often directly influences the behavior of its members. As shown on pages 294–295 in the "Focus on: Group Influence," in the extreme, group forces can tremendously distort the beliefs and actions of group members. In work organizations these powerful influences may be even more dangerous precisely because they can be so subtle and difficult to detect.

GROUP
INFLUENCES
ON JUDGMENT

Most of what is known about group influences on individual judgment falls under a single heading, **social comparison theory**.[9] Social comparison theory, discussed briefly in Chapter 3, simply says that *the opinions and actions of other people* are a major input to our perceptions (selecting, constructing, and interpreting) of the world around us. When we construct a perception or judgment or belief about the world, we check its accuracy by comparing it to the perceptions and judgments constructed by others around us. If our perceptions and judgments match those of others around us, everything is fine. But what happens when we construct beliefs, perceptions, and judgments that *differ* from those of others? The following fictional account demonstrates the acquisition of a work group norm:

> You are a newly hired worker on the assembly line at Mega Manufacturing. Your supervisor spends the morning introducing you around and explaining your new job to you—how to work the machinery at your work station, where to get raw materials when you run out, when you can take breaks, and so on. She winds up the morning by noting that she would like you to think about shooting for 50 complete units per day as a performance goal. Then she sends you off to lunch with your assembly-line coworkers.
>
> At lunch some of the old hands on the assembly line seem friendly enough and ask if you have any questions about the job. You mention that you are wondering about keeping up with the daily quota of 50 units suggested by your supervisor. At this point the old hands laugh. They reassure you that it's the job of the supervisor to talk about completing 50 units per day, but that no one really *expects* you to do that much. They claim that the supervisor usually seems pleased with 40. One of the old hands even notes that if you did make 50, it would make some of the older workers (for whom even 35 units is a challenge) look bad.
>
> Late in the afternoon, your supervisor stops by to see how you are doing and asks whether, in your judgment, you think you will be able to keep up a 50-units-per-day pace.

As suggested in this story, work group norms often dictate more than just which behaviors are appropriate. Work group norms also may dictate which *thoughts* are appropriate—which perceptions, beliefs, or judgments about possible performance levels are allowed. In the story, what would you say to the supervisor at this point about your ability to keep up a 50-unit-per-day pace? And how would your coworkers' comments at lunch influence your answer?

**Social Evidence**   One possibility is that you might treat the comments of your coworkers as evidence. If you have worked the assembly line a couple of hours before the supervisor comes around, you already could have a good idea of what is possible and what is not. Let's say you think 50 units per day is possible. In the back of your mind, of course, are the

[9]L. Festinger, "A Theory of Social Comparison," *Human Relations* 7 (1954): 117–140.

FOCUS ON:
Group Influence

**The Lesson of Jonestown**   How strong is the influence of groups over individual behavior? Consider the case of Jonestown.

Jonestown, the jungle enclave of the People's Temple, was meant to be heaven on earth. The Reverend Jim Jones had founded the People's Temple in Indiana in the 1950s as a religious group with a distinct socialist flavor. Jones's preaching stressed the need for racial brotherhood, and his group helped to feed the poor and elderly and find them jobs. Jones relocated his headquarters to northern California in 1965, and the People's Church movement began to gain momentum. In 1977, the Temple membership emigrated to an outpost in Guyana that came to be known as Jonestown.

At Jonestown the People's Temple struggled to begin a new and better life. As one writer would later describe Jonestown:

. . . no outsider visiting Jonestown for the first time could fail to be impressed by the physical site itself. The people, through sheer hard work and perseverance, had converted three hundred acres of dense jungle into a neatly laid out, administered, and maintained town of nearly a thousand people. One need only to walk the boardwalks to see the pride that had gone into constructing the colony—the row upon row of weeded crops on either side of the long road into Jonestown and around the cottages and dormitories, the vegetable beds and citrus groves planted in and around the settlement. . . . Most new arrivals felt a special sense of adventure. They also felt their experiment was significant: that they were building a model for socialism.*

*T. Reiterman, *Raven: The Untold Story of the Rev. Jim Jones and His People* (New York: Dutton, 1982).

old hands' comments that 40 is really the normal target for the work group. At this point you might think to yourself, "These coworkers of mine are reasonable people, and while their perceptions may not be entirely accurate, mine may not be entirely accurate either." In the end, you would adjust your own estimate to reflect the old hands' input and report to your supervisor that you will shoot for 46.

Using others' opinions as **social evidence** for your own beliefs is the simplest form of social comparison. In this case, you have formed your own judgment or belief about the correct answer, yet you also acknowledge that others' opinions are valid and useful inputs. If others are formulating judgments reasonably and in good faith, differences among judgments may reflect important differences in perspective, assumptions, or background knowledge. Just like sensory inputs, other people are a source of information about the state of the environment that must be considered. The complexity of organizational life also adds the feeling that perhaps you have missed something that others have not missed.

Even U.S. Congressman Leo Ryan, visiting Jonestown on a fact-finding mission, noted in a speech to the assembled membership that "by the few conversations I've had with some of the folks . . . there are some people who believe this is the best thing that ever happened in their whole lives."**

Unfortunately, there was more to Jonestown than a socialist paradise in the jungle. Congressman Ryan had come to Jonestown accompanied by journalists to investigate allegations that members of the Temple were being held in Jonestown against their will. What Ryan's conclusions or recommendations might have been will never be known. As Ryan and his entourage tried to leave Guyana with several of the malcontents in tow, the entire party was ambushed by gunmen from the Temple. Five members of Ryan's group—including the Congressman—were killed.

What followed next still seems unbelievable. While the attack on the Congressman was taking place, Reverend Jones gathered his flock and informed them that the dream of Jonestown was over and that they should end their lives. A poison of potassium cyanide and grape drink was prepared. In the name of the People's Temple the residents of Jonestown drank the poison or gave it to their children and committed mass suicide together. Altogether more than 900 died.

How could such a tragedy occur? The lesson of Jonestown is the tremendous power that groups have over individual behavior. Can there be any greater power over people than the power to convince them to take their own lives in the name of the group? The lesson of Jonestown was not a pretty one, but it was both memorable and important.

**C. Krause, *Guyana Massacre* (New York: Berkeley, 1978).

---

Other individuals' opinions become a particularly compelling source of information when those individuals are quite similar to us. It is not unusual to find that someone voices different judgments or beliefs if that someone has a different background, makes different assumptions, or entertains different motivations as the basis for perceptual or judgmental construction. In fact, if you can find reasonable explanations for differences between your judgments and those of others, the differences will exert little influence on your conclusions. Thus, when the older workers suggest that 50 isn't possible, you may think that for them 50 really isn't possible, even if it is for you! When an individual can find no obvious basis for differences in opinion, however, these differences can be quite alarming and demand adjustment of the judgment.

**Social Anchoring** The previous discussion assumes that an individual is capable of arriving at a judgment independently. But what if there is so much uncertainty that individuals have no faith in their own judgment? What if the worker in our example, after several hours on the assembly line, still has no idea of what a reasonable production target would be? What roles do the opinions of others play in that case?

When the perception or judgment process is extremely uncertain, opinions of others can strongly anchor judgment, even subconsciously. The **social anchoring** of judgment was convincingly demonstrated by a series of studies concerned with **bystander apathy**—why observers fail to lend assistance in emergency situations. The scenario for a typical bystander apathy study is described below:

> You have been asked to participate in a research study at your university. You report as requested. The experimenter seats you in a small room at a desk, gives you a short background questionnaire to complete, and leaves the room while you fill it out. After working on the questionnaire for about five minutes, you notice that some wisps of smoke seem to be coming out of a vent in the room. What do you do?[10]

It seems obvious if you are alone in the room that you should get up to investigate the smoke. Perhaps you would leave the room to sound the alarm or seek assistance. But what happens if there are *other subjects* in the room with you, also filling out the questionnaire?

The key to understanding human reactions to this situation is that the meaning of the smoke is *highly uncertain.* It could be an emergency, but then maybe it's just dust blowing out of an air-conditioning vent or something equally harmless. The fact is that you really *don't know,* just as when you join a new organization, you really *don't know* what behaviors are regulated by the organization's rules and roles. Under conditions of high uncertainty, we allow others to anchor our judgments, often without even knowing we are doing so! In the study described above, most subjects (75 percent) *when alone in the room* judge the smoke to be a potential emergency and investigate. However, if there are other subjects in the room *who have been told to ignore the smoke,* the real subject gets up to investigate the smoke only 10 percent of the time. The unresponsiveness of the other subjects anchors the uncertain judgment of the real subject.

The difference between evidence and anchoring effects of social comparison is a subtle but important one. When you use someone else as evidence for a judgment, you are aware of your *own* opinion and are attempting to reconcile the differences between your judgments, beliefs, or perceptions and those of others you trust. There is a conscious awareness of the differences in judgment, and you feel the need to understand the origins of those differences. In contrast, anchoring effects often catch us unawares. The real subjects in the bystander-apathy study probably didn't realize the extent to which their judgments

[10]B. Latane and J. Darley, *The Unresponsive Bystander: Why Doesn't He Help?* (New York: Appleton-Century-Crofts, 1970).

When the world seems too complex or uncertain, we fall back on the actions and opinions of co-workers—often without realizing it—as the basis for forming our own beliefs. Occasionally we will go along with the opinions of others not because we believe those opinions but simply to avoid conflict.

were being influenced. They experienced a situation that they perceived as *not an emergency.*

Returning to the example of our assembly-line worker, uncertainty would increase the extent to which the production target he provides his supervisor reflects anchoring by the opinions of the old hands. Using their opinions as evidence, he would judge 50 units to be possible but hedge his estimate to 46 in deference to the possibility that they knew something he didn't. If he is really uncertain about what is possible, the opinions of the old hands would anchor his judgment: he would report that 40 units was about right, and honestly believe that it was.

As a final thought on group influences on judgment, remember that evidential and anchoring influences both have important roles in ensuring *appropriate* group functioning. A group's roles and rules summarize the group's past learning. The roles and rules allow newcomers to produce high-quality behaviors and judgments for the group immediately without "reinventing the wheel" through a lot of unnecessary trial-and-error learning. Evidence and anchoring influences both are important mechanisms by which the group teaches the newcomer what the group has learned. If the group has learned well, everyone benefits when newcomers fall in line with the old hands, and a little social influence will be a good thing. If the group has learned poorly, a little "foolishness" (ignoring the old hands) can be a good thing, too.

## GROUP INFLUENCES ON BEHAVIOR

Group influences on judgment provide an *indirect* path by which other people (namely, group members) influence an individual's behavior. It is natural to expect that the group's influence over an individual's thoughts (perceptions, judgments, and beliefs) will be reflected in the individual's behaviors. This influence may be particularly indirect when, as in the case of social anchoring, the individual is not even aware of the influence. However, groups also can *directly* influence the behavior of their members. Two kinds of direct influence will be considered here: social inhibition and social facilitation.

**Social Inhibition**    The presence of a group may directly decrease the amount of task effort its members are willing to contribute. Three ways in which this **social inhibition** of performance might occur are social loafing, self-handicapping, and conformity.

*Social loafing* occurs when individuals decrease the amount of effort they put into a task—loaf—while doing that task with other people. The important word here is "with." Social loafing occurs when several people are working on the same task *together* so that it is difficult (if not impossible) to tell who is doing how much of the work. A behavioral scientist named Ringlemann first discovered social loafing. He noticed that in strength tasks like "tug-o-war" the effort exerted by the team never added up to the sum of the amounts of effort that each individual was capable of exerting alone.[11] He later demonstrated the social loafing effect over a variety of tasks. In one study the researchers told a group of subjects each to scream into their own microphones as loud as possible: first one at a time, then together. By hooking sensors up to each of the individual microphones, the researchers were able to show that the subjects each screamed much louder when screaming alone than when screaming as a group.[12]

Social loafing is thought to occur because of **diffusion of responsibility in groups.** When group members work together on a single task and it is difficult to determine who is working hard and who is not, the responsibility for the outcome is diffused—shared—over the entire group. Whether the outcome is a success or a failure, credit is shared relatively equally among group members. This decreases the incentive for any individual to work hard because there is only a loose connection between effort and the outcome for the group or the individual. Extra effort may have little or no effect on the final outcome for the group and will have *absolutely* no effect on the share of the group outcome received by the individual (as long as the individual *appears* to be trying hard). The result again is the kind of free rider problem noted earlier. Each individual slacks off a little bit and in the end the performance of the entire group suffers.

[11]From Ringlemann, cited in D. R. Forsyth, *An Introduction to Group Dynamics* (Monterey, Calif.: Brooks-Cole, 1983), 152.

[12]B. Latane, K. Williams, and S. Harkins, "Many Hands Make Light the Work: The Causes and Consequences of Social Loafing," *Journal of Personality and Social Psychology* 37 (1979): 822–832.

*Self-handicapping* is a way that groups socially inhibit individual performance even when an individual is working alone. Self-handicapping occurs when an individual *chooses* a course of action that publicly makes failure a very likely outcome. Examples include individuals who knowingly take on impossible tasks, or who take on more assignments than anyone could possibly handle simultaneously. In either case (an impossible task or an impossible number of possible tasks) failure appears almost certain.

Why would group members intentionally choose a course of action that is obviously likely to fail? Curiously enough, the answer probably is "to protect their self-image." Imagine you are a member of a group and you want the group to think highly of you. If you accept an assignment from the group that seems within your capabilities *and fail in the assignment,* you will be disgraced. If, on the other hand, you accept an assignment that is impossible, or if you accept more assignments than the number anyone reasonably could expect you to complete, you have a built-in *excuse* for failure. The point, of course, is that failure is not a disgrace when you have a good excuse for failing, so that the failure is not your fault.

Self-handicapping constructs an attributional defense for an individual's self-image. In Chapter 3 we stated that attributions are how we make sense of the world by inferring the causes of outcomes. If a member of our group fails, we will judge the person not only by the failure but by the cause to which we attribute the failure. If an obvious explanation for the failure is that anyone would have failed under the same circumstances, the failure is unlikely to reflect badly on the failing individual. Self-handicapping is an attempt by a group member to accept a high probability of poor performance in exchange for an equally high probability that the poor performance will not count against him or her. Unfortunately, from the viewpoint of accomplishing group goals, self-handicapping simply means a high probability of poor performance.

**Conformity** is a form of social inhibition that often masquerades as a social influence on judgment. Evidential use of others' opinions seems a reasonable form of social influence, while judgmental anchoring is an unfortunate one because we are often unaware of its powerful influence. However, conformity has tragic potential. Conformity occurs when a group member engages in a behavior or professes to a belief encouraged by the group even though the group member believes it is incorrect or inappropriate. Conformity occurs *not* because the judgments of others are good evidence and *not* because the group member's own judgment is uncertain, but simply because the member wants *to go along with the group to avoid conflict with the group.* What is socially inhibited in conformity is constructive dissent. An individual group member who is concerned that the course of action selected by the group is hopelessly inappropriate fails to say so.

The psychological experiment described below, known as the Asch study, provides a classic example of conformity effects:[13]

> You are invited to participate in a research study. You report at the appointed hour and are ushered into a room with six other participants. The seven of you are seated in a row (you occupy the last chair in the row), and you are told that this will be a study of your ability to make visual judgments of size. For each judgment, a machine will project four lines on the wall. One line will be the target line, and you must judge which of the test lines (A, B, or C) best matches the target (see Figure 7–4).
>
> The experiment seems quite boring. For the first six trials, it seems obvious which test line matches the target and there is no disagreement at all among the participants. The seventh target line is just like the one shown in Figure 7–4 and just as easy to match as the others have been, so you are quite surprised when the first subject responds "C"—an *obvious* wrong answer. Before you can even ponder why this has occurred, however, the other five participants each give their responses—*also* "C" and *also* obviously wrong! At this point it is your turn to respond. The other six all have agreed on "C," but you *know* the correct answer is "B." How do you respond?

The key to understanding the importance of the Asch study is to realize that there is *little or no uncertainty* about the right answer in the minds of subjects. Subjects *know* that "B" is the correct answer. When presented the target and test lines in the absence of other respondents, subjects virtually never make mistakes. What that seventh subject in the experiment doesn't know, of course, is that the first six respondents have been told to answer "C" on the seventh trial of the study, even though the correct answer obviously is "B." How does that seventh subject respond in the face of a unanimous but obviously incorrect majority? About *one-third of the time* the seventh subject *goes along with the group* and says that "C" is the correct answer.

Despite its obvious behavioral similarities to evidential and anchoring effects on judgment and behavior, conformity is a different kind of group influence. In using others' opinions as *evidence*, an individual has a good idea of what is correct, but is willing to consider and incorporate the opinions of more experienced others. In using others' opinions as *anchors*, an individual really doesn't know what's correct and is open to influence (perhaps without knowing it) from the opinions of more experienced others. In the case of conformity, the individual knows what is correct but doesn't voice that opinion and acts as if in agreement with the group. The individual *conforms* to the group.

What causes conformity? Why do people "go along with the group" when they *know* the group is wrong? In our hypothetical example of the assembly-line worker, why would the new worker report to his or her supervisor that 40 units seems like a reasonable target, while knowing

[13]S. E. Asch, "Studies of Independence and Conformity: A Minority of One against a Unanimous Majority," *Psychological Monographs* 70 (1956): Whole #16.

**FIGURE 7–4** | The Asch Study: Which Test Line Matches the Target?

The Asch experiment demonstrated the power of group influence. In this figure, it seems obvious that test line B is the best match for the target line. However, if several of your friends all claimed that test line C was the closest match to the target line, what would go through your mind? Would you begin to doubt your judgment? Would you perhaps "go along" with them to avoid looking foolish if they just happened to be right?

| Target Line | Test Lines | | |
| --- | --- | --- | --- |
| | A | B | C |

full well that 50 units would be more appropriate? There are several possible explanations.

First, the individual may wish to avoid conflict with the group. In the case of the new assembly-line worker, it has been made clear to him or her that 40 units is the agreed-upon norm for a production target. Violating this norm by reporting a target of 50 units would risk the wrath of the group members, perhaps by exposing their collusive attempts to keep down management's performance expectations and protect the less able workers. Second, by disagreeing with the majority, the individual risks being labeled a deviant. Depending on the individual's reasons for joining the group, being accepted may be more valuable than being right. Disagreement may not be the fastest path to making new friends, especially if it is seen as an attempt to show up the rest of the group. Most of all, disagreement quite simply risks rejection by the group—no doubt in part for being a deviant troublemaker.

Normally we think of mistakes in judgment as incurring formal sanctions from the organization. A poor hiring decision, a bad investment, or a sloppy report will be punished formally by the organization. Conformity raises the specter of an informal, even intangible, set of sanctions within work groups that quietly and implicitly enforce work-group norms. It is worth noting that in the Asch subject group, acceptance or rejection by the group should not have been a big concern for subjects. Nevertheless, the power of the group over the individual was apparent.

This power becomes tragic when the norms implicitly enforced by the work group run contrary to the best interests of the organization as a whole, and therefore even prove contrary to the long-term interests of the work group. The assembly-line workers who promote the illusion for management that 40 units per day is the maximum possible may one day find that 40 units per day is not enough to justify keeping the plant open. Perhaps more to the point, the silencing effects of conformity beg the question of how many imaginative and useful ideas never are voiced by workers and therefore never taken advantage of either by the organization as a whole or by the work group itself. How many great innovations never have been discovered because workers believed there was only one way to do something—the company's way?

It should be obvious now why idiosyncrasy credits are so critical to organizational growth and survival, and why March was so concerned that organizations develop a "technology of foolishness." Idiosyncrasy credits allow a way for new ideas to be voiced without risking rejection by the group. Once group members have proven their loyalty to the group, their questioning of the group's roles and rules can be seen as constructive and appropriate by the group. March believes that organizations need to *institutionalize* a process by which norms regularly are challenged or broken—foolishness—and thereby regularly are tested for continuing appropriateness. This ensures that new workers are conforming to appropriate and effective behaviors rather than just conforming to traditions.

**Social Facilitation**   When the mere presence of other individuals (for instance, other group members) spurs an individual on to greater efforts, **social facilitation** has occurred. As discussed in the "Focus on: Social Facilitation," Norman Triplett was first credited with exploring social facilitation in 1897. Triplett noticed that world records in sports such as cycling always are set during events when many riders are competing against each other, and almost never when athletes are competing only against themselves or the clock. Triplett concluded that world-class athletes derive extra energy from the mere presence of competitors.

Where does this extra energy come from? One possibility is that the mere presence of other individuals arouses fears of failing and then being evaluated negatively by the other group members who are watching.[14] According to this explanation, the extra energy provided by the mere presence of others is a form of arousal that comes from fear or anxiety. Another possibility is that the presence of others is a distraction for an individual who is working on a task. If the other people are working on the same task, their actions might provide clues for the individual about how to improve performance. If the other people are just observing the individual, their facial expressions provide valuable feedback about how well the individual is doing. The individual feels

[14]N. B. Cottrell, D. L. Wack, G. S. Sekerak, and R. H. Rittle, "Social Facilitation of Dominant Responses by the Presence of an Audience and the Mere Exposure of Others," *Journal of Personality and Social Psychology* 9 (1968): 245–250.

FOCUS ON:
Social Facilitation

**The Dynamogenic Factors** Norman Triplett's interest in the effects of groups on individual effort began with his study of bicycle racers. Triplett studied the results of three kinds of races:

> The unpaced race against time is an effort by a single individual to lower the established record. No pacemaker is used; the only stimulation of the rider being the idea of reducing his own or some other man's former time. The paced race against time is also a single effort to make a record. It differs only in the fact that a swift multicycle, such as a tandem or "quad," "makes the pace" for the rider. . . . The third or paced competition race is a real race. Here, besides keeping up with the pacemaker, is the added element of beating the other contestants. . . . The fact may be mentioned, too, that wheelmen themselves generally regard the value of a pace to be from 20 to 30 seconds in the mile.

Triplett's research showed that the presence of a pacer improved racers' times on the average by 22.9 percent. Competition improved racers' times an additional 3.5 percent. Triplett later reproduced these social facilitation effects in well-controlled laboratory experiments. Triplett attributed his findings to what he called "dynamogenic" factors:

> This theory of competition holds that the bodily presence of another rider is a stimulus to the racer in arousing the competitive instinct; that another can thus be the means of releasing or freeing nervous energy for him that he cannot of himself release; and, further, that the sight of movement in that other by perhaps suggesting a higher rate of speed, is also an inspiration to greater effort.

Interestingly, even in these early studies Triplett noticed that, for some of his subjects, social stimulation brought on an apparent loss of control that led to substantial *decrements* in performance.

Source: N. Triplett, "The Dynamogenic Factors in Pacemaking and Competition," *American Journal of Psychology* 9 (1898): 507–533.

conflict because on the one hand he wants to concentrate on the task, while on the other hand he wants to look at the other people. This internal conflict becomes a source of arousal from which the individual derives extra energy.[15]

*Social facilitation* refers to increases in an individual's supply of *energy*—not necessarily to improvement of performance. Research on social facilitation has shown that the extra arousal derived from the mere presence of others will improve performance only if the behaviors

[15]G. S. Sanders, "Driven by Distraction: An Integrative Review of Social Facilitation Theory and Research," *Journal of Experimental Social Psychology* 17 (1981): 227–251; R. S. Baron, "Distraction-Conflict Theory: Progress and Problems," in *Advances in Experimental Social Psychology,* ed. L. Berkowitz (San Francisco: Academic Press, 1985).

necessary for high-quality performance are well learned or the task is very simple.[16] Arousal increases the probability of dominant responses. If the task is well learned or simple, high-quality responses are likely to be dominant and social facilitation simply will increase their probability, leading to enhanced performance. If the task is difficult or unfamiliar, correct responses are not likely to be dominant. Arousal from social facilitation therefore may only increase the probability of *incorrect* behaviors, thereby leading to worse performance. Social facilitation thus is a "sword that cuts both ways." The presence of others increases an individual's arousal level; whether this arousal level improves or hurts performance depends upon how difficult or unfamiliar the task is.

**Deindividuation**    Behavior reflecting a dark side of human nature also may be encouraged by the presence of other group members. Social loafing (described earlier) is one example of what happens when the actions of one individual are not easily distinguished from the actions of the group. In such circumstances the group is said to take collective action. Social loafing is collective action because it is not possible to distinguish the actions, effort, or impact of any one member of the group from those of any other member of the group. All members of the group share equally in the success or failure of—and therefore the praise or blame for—the group's actions. This is so because when lots of people are working together on one task, it is not possible to tell who really is working hard and who isn't. There is another circumstance, however, in which group members are working alone but still do not feel publicly responsible for their actions. This other circumstance is known as deindividuation.

**Deindividuation** occurs when the personal identities of group members—and therefore the responsibility they feel for their actions—are submerged in the identity of the group. Consider an important difference between the "tug-o-war" game mentioned earlier and an infamous incident during the Vietnam War: the My Lai massacre described in the "Focus on: Deindividuation." If someone in the "tug-o-war" game isn't working as hard as possible, no one would know because the collective action is made up of many smaller individual behaviors that cannot be examined separately. There is only one action, the pulling of the rope by the group. In the My Lai massacre of the civilian population of a small village in Vietnam, the collective action (the massacre) was made up of many individual actions. Hypothetically, the death of each My Lai villager was an individual action that could have been attributed to an individual soldier. But in practice this did not happen. In reality, no one knew anything more than that it was American soldiers who massacred the villagers, and to any observer of the incident any soldier would have looked pretty much like any other

[16]R. B. Zajonc, "Social Facilitation," *Science* 149 (1965): 269–274.

# Focus on:
## Deindividuation

**Tales from the Dark Side** In March of 1968, the following events occurred:

> U.S. Army troops of the American Division massacred a large number of noncombatants (comprised almost exclusively of old men, women, and children) in two hamlets of Son My Village (known as My Lai), Vietnam. The precise number of Vietnamese killed was at least 175, and may exceed 400.
>
> A part of the crimes visited on the inhabitants . . . included individual and group acts of murder, rape, sodomy, maiming, and assault on noncombatants and the mistreatment and killing of [prisoners]. They further included the killing of livestock, destruction of crops, closing of wells and the burning of dwellings within several subhamlets.*

This is a passage from the official report on the My Lai massacre. The real question is how do incidents like this occur? One analyst has suggested that:

> In mortal danger, numerous soldiers enter into a dazed condition in which all sharpness of consciousness is lost. When in this state, they can be caught up into the fire of communal ecstasy and forget about death by losing their individuality, or they can function like cells in a military organism, doing what is expected of them because it has become automatic.**

This statement explains some of the power of groups over the individual. Individuals may lose their identities in the group, and with them any sense of personal responsibility. Or individuals may simply surrender their morality to the dictates of their roles in the group. Certainly these claims were part of one soldier's defense to the charges that he was responsible for crimes at My Lai.

The actions of deindividuated group members often are rationalized through the stereotyping of their victims. In war, soldiers come up with nicknames—the enemy were "gooks" in Vietnam—to dehumanize their victims. Dehumanizing the victims allows group members to feel less reticent about violating society's larger rules about social interaction. Society's rules and morality don't apply because the victims aren't really people.

In the end it must be remembered that My Lai does not represent the actions of fanatics or homicidal maniacs. In fact, during the later public recriminations, participants in the massacre mostly maintained that they were just doing their jobs. Regardless of why it occurred, My Lai stands as a testament to a dark side of human nature lurking within—a dark side that apparently can be released in groups.

*J. Goldstein, B. Marshall, and J. Schwartz, *The My Lai Massacre and Its Cover-up* (New York: Free Press, 1976), 1.

**J. G. Gray, *The Warriors* (New York: Harcourt Brace Jovanovich, 1959), 102.

soldier. There were no individuals involved in the massacre, only group members each acting *not as individuals* but as members of the group.

Anonymity is an important part of the deindividuation process. Mobs often engage in behaviors that no individual alone would ever consider, such as lynching an untried suspect. In a mob, there are no individuals and therefore no individual actions and no individual responsibility for actions. There is only the mob and the mob's actions. If the mob's actions are bad, that is certainly not felt to be the fault of any individual. Obviously, diffusion of responsibility is an important part of deindividuation.

What causes deindividuation? Anything that decreases the individual identity of a group's members contributes to deindividuation. This is one reason why lynch mobs lynch at night. The darkness masks the identity of any individual in the mob. *Uniforms* also promote submergence of individual identity into the identity of the group. A soldier can know that any observer will not see *him* killing the enemy, but simply a soldier—a member of the group—killing the enemy. It is the role and not the person committing the act. Feelings of responsibility for actions are suspended within the reality or morality defined by the group.

Notice that the uniform serves two purposes in this context. On the one hand it masks individual identity (to some extent), making it less likely that any inappropriate actions can be attributed to particular individuals. The uniform also makes it salient to group members that, while wearing the uniform, their actions are the actions not of an individual, but of a member of the group. The uniform thus deindividuates group members both for outsiders and for the group members themselves.

Is deindividuation universally bad? Some would claim that there are necessary tasks in our organizations for which no individual wants to accept responsibility. Deindividuation makes it possible for these tasks to be accomplished. The deindividuation of an army's soldiers accomplished through their training and clothing may be necessary to get soldiers to do some of the things they do, such as killing other soldiers. Similarly, juries are acting collectively when they convict a criminal. The jury renders only one conviction, not twelve individual ones. Juries provide a healthy twelve different perspectives on a criminal case; juries also make sure that no one individual feels responsible for the verdict. So deindividuation may help get the job done in an organization when the job is a dirty one but someone has to do it. On the other hand, one has to wonder about the advisability of fostering group actions for which no member of the group would want to accept individual responsibility.

## BUILDING EFFECTIVE GROUPS

It should be apparent that groups present both tremendous opportunities and tremendous dangers for organizations. Individuals can work harder and smarter together than alone, and group interaction can fulfill the affiliation needs that individuals simply cannot satisfy working in isolation. These are the potential benefits available through the use of groups in organizations. On the other hand, the attractiveness of group interaction makes it possible for groups to hold hostage the thoughts of their members. Individuals can be seduced by the illusory morality of a group, and individuals can avoid taking responsibility for their actions by hiding behind a group's roles and rules.

Hobbes believed that individuals possess great potential but have a dark side that must be controlled. So it is with groups. The challenge of managing groups in organizations is getting group members to go along with good rules and roles, to question openly the bad ones, and to consider carefully the questions about rules and roles offered by their fellow group members.

The remainder of this chapter briefly explores this important challenge in two ways. First, a model that details the characteristics of effective groups will be presented. Second, a technique used in organizations specifically to improve group functioning will be described.

## CHARACTERISTICS OF SUCCESSFUL GROUPS

What makes a group successful? What makes a group able to harness its dark side and put its energies to constructive use? Successful groups typically share five characteristics: group objectives, role differentiation, rule clarity, membership, and communication.

**Group Objectives**   The goals, purposes, and functions that a group is trying to achieve are **group objectives**. For a group to be successful, its goals must be specific. From vague goals are born vague attempts to pursue them. Specific goals get everyone working in the same direction and sharing the same priorities.

Group objectives also should be shared by the entire group membership. It is no help to group functioning if two members of the same group have specific *but different* beliefs about where the group is headed and why. All group members should have in mind the *same* goals for the group, even if some of the members don't completely agree with those publicly stated objectives.

Finally, very successful groups figure out ways to *integrate* individual and group goals. When group and individual goals are integrated, group actions become more than just the price individuals must pay for access to fulfillment of individual goals. Group actions themselves become a path to individual goal fulfillment. As noted by Susan Kare, Macintosh artist at Apple Computers, "There's nothing like a group effort toward a common goal to unite people."

A demonstration of the importance of individual and group goal integration was provided by the "jigsaw classroom" in Austin, Texas. The jigsaw classroom is a grade-school instructional technique based upon building cooperative student learning teams:

> In a jigsaw classroom, small student-directed groups replace the teacher-dominated lecture method; students serve as the principal sources of information and reinforcement for one another. Students are placed in small groups of five or six for about an hour each day. The day's lesson is divided up into as many segments as there are group members and each student is given a unique part. Each member is then responsible for learning the assigned segment well enough to teach it to the others. Since group members can only learn a lesson in its entirety by pooling all their knowledge, interdependence is established.[17]

The jigsaw classroom was devised to combat racial prejudice during desegregation efforts in Texas. Grading systems in U.S. elementary schools typically reward individual achievement. In a jigsaw classroom, cooperation—and thereby group achievement—is the only effective path to individual achievement. Jigsaw classroom students in Austin learned their classroom lessons better *and* they learned the value of teamwork and coordinated group efforts toward shared goals. The jigsaw classroom also enhanced students' abilities to understand other students' perspectives, leading to decreased racial prejudice and misunderstanding in the schools.

**Role Differentiation**   Members of successful groups know more than just what the group is trying to accomplish. Each group member also has a role that specifies the individual's contribution. Appropriate **role differentiation** occurs in two ways. First, all group members should have a clear idea of their own roles—their own duties and responsibilities in the organization and how they contribute to the realization of the group's goals. Second, the roles assigned to each member of the organization should reflect individual strengths and interests. It is not enough that each member of the group have a role and know what it is. As much as possible, the roles assigned to group members should maximize each individual's opportunities to contribute to fulfillment of group, organizational, *and individual* objectives.

**Rule Clarity**   The formal rules and informal norms that structure interactions within the group also should be agreed upon and shared by all members of the group. These rules and norms include authority (task assignment) and reporting relationships. As we discussed earlier in the chapter, rules are critical to the coordination of group member activities. If appropriate rules are not agreed upon or not known, their ability to control and direct group interaction is nonexistent.

[17]E. Aronson and S. Yates, "Cooperation in the Classroom: The Impact of the Jigsaw Method on Interethnic Relations, Classroom Performance, and Self-Esteem," in *Small Groups and Social Interaction* 1, eds. H. Blumberg, A. Hare, V. Kent, and M. Davies (New York: John Wiley and Sons, 1983).

Team development activities come in many shapes and forms. At Motorola's headquarters, volleyball games like the one pictured here are used to foster effective cooperation and communication.

**Membership**  Successful groups strike an appropriate balance among similarities and differences of their members' values and backgrounds. A certain amount of variety in member perspectives is important for providing a healthy background of controversy and conflict in the group. Too much controversy and conflict can lead to hostility and the eventual breakup of the group. Rules for membership and participation in group activities also should be clear.

**Communication**  Finally, all successful groups have in place adequate channels of communication. Good communication is any group's first line of defense against threats to its survival, whether from external or internal sources. No matter how well objectives might be selected and shared, rules and roles made clear, and membership constructed, circumstances are bound to change. Good channels of communication in the group are important if the group is to adapt to new challenges and remain successful over time.

This chapter began by noting that groups are essentially collections of individuals whose interactions are structured to fulfill functions. The five characteristics of successful groups we have outlined reflect a group with a good understanding of its functions (objectives) and an appropriate structure (in the form of role differentiation, rule clarity, membership, and communication) for achieving them. How do groups come to possess these five important characteristics? Some groups achieve them through natural evolution. Other groups get a helping hand from team development activities.

## TEAM DEVELOPMENT

**Team development** is defined as "an inward look by the team at its own performance, behavior, and culture for the purposes of dropping out dysfunctional behaviors and strengthening functional ones."[18] The desired outcome of team development is a *team*—a highly effective group of individuals who work well together. Team-development activities teach team members valuable skills in working and getting along with others. These skills become the foundation for team effectiveness. As noted in the "FOCUS ON: Team Development," the skills developed for team interaction often have tremendous value beyond the boundaries of the team as well. All team-development (or "team-building") activities share the following important functions:

**Diagnosis**    Team development always includes activities that focus on identifying functional and dysfunctional aspects of group interaction. Typically, roles and rules for group interaction will be examined and their appropriateness openly questioned. Often group members will be asked to complete questionnaires like the one shown in Figure 7–5. The results of the questionnaire then can be fed back to the group and used to stimulate awareness and discussion of problems concerning any of the five dimensions (group objectives, role differentiation, role clarity, membership, and communication) of effective group interaction.

**Change**    Once a group has identified its problems, the group must work together to remove impediments to effective group functioning. Naturally, change attempts will prove successful only if diagnosis has been careful and thorough. Many times team development efforts fail because groups accept only surface definitions of group interaction problems. For instance, if a leader is ineffective, changing the leader's behavior may be only part of the solution. Have the behaviors of other group members been reinforcing the previous ineffective behaviors of the group leader? If so, the behaviors of these other group members also must be altered. The immediate identification of obvious behavior problems rarely provides a complete diagnosis of group interaction deficiencies. The "maintaining conditions" that have allowed this problem to persist or grow in the group also must be examined and questioned.

Many groups find it useful to draw up change plans in the form of a contract. The contract specifies what is going to be changed and by whom. Just as role clarity is necessary for successful day-to-day group functioning, specifying the role of each group member in the agreed-upon team development changes should help ensure their successful implementation.

**Development**    Successful group development goes beyond identifying and repairing group interaction dysfunctions. The need for group

[18]W. French and C. Bell, *Organizational Development: Behavioral Science Interventions for Organizational Improvement* (Englewood Cliffs, N.J.: Prentice Hall, 1978).

FOCUS ON:

Team
Development

**Banking on the Benefits of Team Building**   Imagine you are the CEO of a bank, and you are trying to convert the Mortgage Division of your company to a new generation of electronic data processing. Your wise and experienced "old-line" managers are fond of and familiar with the old system and seem to be stonewalling the changes. Your younger managers are fed up with the bank's apparent reluctance to keep pace with technological developments and quietly are leaving the company at an alarming rate. Moreover, these two warring factions appear unwilling to talk out their differences. Finally, imagine you already have tried to solve your problem using consultants, opinion surveys, and even management education efforts. What do you do now?

What one major East Coast bank decided to do was team building. It formed a team consisting of three managers from the data processing group and six managers (representing both factions) from the Mortgage Division. The team was given two tasks by the CEO: (1) become an effective problem-solving group, and (2) find a way to resolve the problems surrounding implementation of the new data processing system.

A process consultant was brought in to help develop the team. He began by asking each member of the team to submit *anonymously* a list of all the obstacles to the team's working effectively together or the bank functioning effectively. These anonymous lists became the focus of discussions during the team's first meeting—a week-end retreat. Thanks to the lists, the simmering discontents within the group were out on the table where they could be discussed and resolved or accommodated. By the end of the weekend, the group had laid out the rules necessary for effective group interaction. Task forces were set up to address the major issues identified by the group. Within a year the group had disbanded—because its mission had been accomplished!

Close inspection of the effects of this team-building effort reveals stunning results. The creation and development of this team led to increased productivity in the Mortgage Division and to decreased turnover and absenteeism. The Mortgage Division effected a smooth transition to the new data processing system, and several other divisions of the bank soon followed suit.

Perhaps of more importance, the team building had some unanticipated effects for *other* work groups in the bank. The team had developed rules for its meetings and interactions to minimize disruptive conflict, and these rules apparently incorporated some valuable insights of the managers who participated on the team. The team members brought these new insights back to their own work groups, and six years later the team's rules had become part of the rules for work group interaction throughout the bank. At the bank, team building led to more than just development of one team: it provided team members lessons in effective work group dynamics that were not soon forgotten.

Source: R. Beckhard and D. G. Lake, "Short- and Long-Range Effects of a Team Development Effort," in H. Hornstein et al. (eds.), *Social Interventions: A Behavioral Science Approach* (New York: Free Press, 1971).

**FIGURE 7–5**                  Rating Group Effectiveness

Diagnosis—finding out what a group is doing well and what it is doing poorly—is a critical first step in improving the quality of group interaction. Groups can use questionnaires like this one to identify for themselves areas where group functioning needs to be improved. Sometimes simply identifying the problem is enough to get the group working toward better functioning.

### A: Goals

| Poor | 1 | 2 | 3 | 4 | 5 | 6 | 7 | 8 | 9 | 10 | Good |
|------|---|---|---|---|---|---|---|---|---|----|------|

Confused; diverse; conflicting; indifferent; little interest

Clear to all; shared by all; all care about the goals, feel involved

### B: Participation

| Poor | 1 | 2 | 3 | 4 | 5 | 6 | 7 | 8 | 9 | 10 | Good |
|------|---|---|---|---|---|---|---|---|---|----|------|

Few dominate; some passive; some not listened to; several talk at once or interrupt

All get in; all are really listened to

### C: Feelings

| Poor | 1 | 2 | 3 | 4 | 5 | 6 | 7 | 8 | 9 | 10 | Good |
|------|---|---|---|---|---|---|---|---|---|----|------|

Unexpected; ignored or criticized

Freely expressed; empathic responses

### D: Diagnosis of Group Problems

| Poor | 1 | 2 | 3 | 4 | 5 | 6 | 7 | 8 | 9 | 10 | Good |
|------|---|---|---|---|---|---|---|---|---|----|------|

Jump directly to remedial proposals; treat symptoms rather than basic causes

Problems carefully diagnosed before action proposed; remedies attack basic causes

### E: Leadership

| Poor | 1 | 2 | 3 | 4 | 5 | 6 | 7 | 8 | 9 | 10 | Good |
|------|---|---|---|---|---|---|---|---|---|----|------|

Group needs for leadership not met; group depends too much on single person or on a few persons

Needs for leadership met by various members as they arise ("distributed leadership"); all feel free to volunteer as they see a group need

development activities in the first place suggests that a group is not adequately self-diagnostic. The group's interaction patterns do not include effective problem identification and problem solving. Successful group development therefore does more than just solve group interaction problems. It also creates a system for identifying and resolving *future* group interaction problems.

   **Role therapy** is one example of a group-development activity. Role therapy is a training technique in which someone from outside the group

**F: Decisions**

| Poor | 1 | 2 | 3 | 4 | 5 | 6 | 7 | 8 | 9 | 10 | Good |
|------|---|---|---|---|---|---|---|---|---|----|------|
| Needed decisions unmade; decisions made by part of group; others uncommitted | | | | | | | | | | | Consensus sought and tested; deviates appreciated and used to improve decision; decisions when made are fully supported |

**G: Trust**

| Poor | 1 | 2 | 3 | 4 | 5 | 6 | 7 | 8 | 9 | 10 | Good |
|------|---|---|---|---|---|---|---|---|---|----|------|
| Distrust among members; they are polite, careful, closed, guarded; they listen superficially but inwardly reject what others say; they are afraid to criticize or to be criticized | | | | | | | | | | | Trust among members; they reveal to group what they would be reluctant to expose to others; they respect and use the responses they get; they can freely express negative reactions without fearing reprisal |

**H: Creativity and Growth**

| Poor | 1 | 2 | 3 | 4 | 5 | 6 | 7 | 8 | 9 | 10 | Good |
|------|---|---|---|---|---|---|---|---|---|----|------|
| Members and group in a rut; operate routinely, persons stereotyped and rigid in their roles; no progress. | | | | | | | | | | | Group flexible; seeks new and better ways; individuals changing and growing; creative; individually supported. |

Source: Reproduced by permission of the publisher from E. Schein, *Process Consultation* (Reading, Mass.: Addison-Wesley, 1969), pp. 2–43.

(a group process consultant) comes into the group temporarily to act as a catalyst to improve the effectiveness of group interaction. A group engages in role therapy to ensure that role differentiation has been accomplished appropriately. The focus of role therapy is the definition of individual roles in the group. Nevertheless, the process of negotiating any member's role in the group also creates opportunities to clarify the group's overall objectives and rules, and to enhance channels of communication within the group.

Role therapy develops a group's self-diagnostic skills through analysis, modeling, and coaching. The process consultant talks with each group member to understand each member's role, how the roles all are meant to function together, and where the problems in the role structure arise. At first, these inquiries by the process consultant are done privately with each group member. Later, the process consultant will convene a meeting of the group and publicly solicit information from group members about role definitions and possible sources of role problems, thereby *modeling* the diagnostic techniques for group members. Finally, the process consultant will encourage group members to take over ownership of the diagnostic process and will only *coach* group members' attempts to engage in appropriate diagnostic behaviors.

Through this intervention cycle of analysis, modeling, and coaching by the process consultant, role therapy achieves two important objectives. First, sources of role problems are identified publicly so that the group can begin to work toward their resolution. Second, group communication processes are improved so that future role problems can be identified, acknowledged, and resolved by the group on its own. Role therapy is one of a variety of techniques that organizations use to develop more effective group functioning. Several more of these techniques will be discussed in Chapter 17.

## SUMMARY

Groups are the building blocks of organizations. People come together in groups because groups provide the means to desired ends and because group interaction is a desired end in itself. Group behavior is governed by roles and rules that evolve as groups move through the stages of group development.

Groups have value because they can profoundly influence the thoughts and behaviors of their members. It is these social influence processes that allow groups to perform better than just a collection of individuals. Groups can influence group members' thoughts by presenting evidence that different opinions exist and by anchoring group member thinking under uncertainty. Groups can influence group members' behaviors through the processes of social facilitation and social inhibition.

Social influence processes in groups must be carefully managed. While social anchoring and social facilitation provide the means to decrease learning time in groups and increase group member task effort, conformity and deindividuation represent potentially dangerous outcomes of group interaction. Team development activities such as role therapy improve the quality of group roles and rules, so that the benefits of group interaction can be realized.

KEY TERMS

**Bystander apathy**  Failure of observers to lend assistance in emergency situations; an example of the results of social anchoring effects on judgment.

**Conformity**  Form of social inhibition in which a group member engages in a behavior or professes a belief that is encouraged by the group even though the member believes it is incorrect or inappropriate.

**Critical incidents**  Particularly successful or disastrous new behaviors that lead to the establishment of new group policies or norms.

**Deindividuation**  Submersion of personal identities and personal responsibility of group members in the identity of the group.

**Differentiation**  Second stage of group development, in which the group decides what its goals and priorities will be and structures its interaction to ensure effective group functioning.

**Diffusion of responsibility**  Sharing the credit or blame for the outcomes of a group's actions over the entire group.

**Formation**  First stage of group development, in which group members decide whether membership is necessary, learn the traits and strengths of other members, and identify a leader.

**Group**  Organized system of two or more individuals who are interrelated so that the system performs some function, has a standard set of role relationships among its members, and has a set of norms that regulate the function of the group and each of its members.

**Group development**  Process of identifying and resolving present and future group interaction problems.

**Group objectives**  Goals, purposes, and functions that a group is trying to achieve.

**Idiosyncrasy credits**  Allowances given to group members to violate group rules and norms because of consistent past adherence to those rules and norms.

**Integration**  Third stage of group development, in which group members define a set of rules and roles to coordinate group interaction and make pursuit of the goals effective.

**Job description**  Written document that specifies an individual's role in a work organization: duties to be performed, to whom the person must report, and the goals he or she must attain.

**Maturity**  Final stage of group development, in which group members work within its structure to pursue its goals.

**Norm**  Informal, unstated rule that governs and regulates group behavior.

**Role**  Formal or informal definition of the set of behaviors appropriate to a particular position occupied by a member of a group.

**Role differentiation**  Establishment of clear concepts for group members of their specific duties and responsibilities to the group, based on their individual strengths and weaknesses, and how these duties and responsibilities contribute to the realization of the group's goals.

**Role therapy**   Training technique in which someone from outside the group comes in temporarily to act as a catalyst to improve the effectiveness of group interaction by ensuring that role differentiation has been accomplished appropriately.

**Rule**   Formal policy or informal norm that defines the boundaries of acceptable and expected behavior in the group.

**Social anchoring**   Forming perceptions or judgments in an extremely uncertain situation by relying on the opinions of others.

**Social evidence**   Using the opinions of other people as an input to individual beliefs.

**Social facilitation**   Tendency for the presence of others to enhance an individual's energy level.

**Social inhibition**   Tendency for the presence of others to impair an individual's performance, including social loafing, self-handicapping, and conformity.

**Status**   Position of a role in the social hierarchy.

**Social covenant**   Set of rules that constrains and structures group interaction.

**Team development**   An inward look by the team at its own performance, behavior, and culture for the purposes of correcting dysfunctional behaviors and strengthening functional ones.

DISCUSSION QUESTIONS

1.  What would social interaction be like *without* rules and roles?

2.  Think of a group to which you belong. In what ways is your membership in this group a *means*? In what ways is your membership in this group an *end*?

3.  If poor ideas and practices in organizations generally are punished to ensure organizational survival, how does an organization *encourage* constructive "foolishness" by its employees? How does the organization know when an employee is acting foolishly

for the good of the organization, rather than just acting foolishly?

4.  What are the stages of group development outlined in this chapter? How do each of these stages contribute to the effective functioning of the group?

5.  Are group influences on judgment and group influences on behavior equally likely to occur at each of the different stages of group development?

6.  As a student of group dynamics, what group

processes discussed in this chapter would you suspect to be contributing causes to the mass suicide at Jonestown? To the massacre at My Lai?

7. What can be done during team-development activities to prevent group interaction

from bringing out the "dark side" of human nature?

8. How do complexity, conflict, and uncertainty as defining characteristics of organizational behavior contribute to group influences on individuals?

IF YOU WANT TO KNOW MORE

Two excellent summaries of the influence of groups on individual thought and action are contained in the books *The Social Animal,* by Elliot Aronson (New York: Freeman & Co., 1984), and *The Individual in a Social World,* by Stanley Milgram (Reading, Mass.: Addison-Wesley, 1977). Aronson's book is accompanied by a collection of readings (entitled *Reading about the Social Animal*) that provides a good selection of papers on the behavior of individuals in groups. Milgram's book in particular focuses on how groups bring out the "dark side" of human nature. The release of the "dark side" of human nature also is considered in some detail in Phil Zimbardo's piece, "The Human Choice: Individuation, Reason, and Order versus Deindividuation, Impulse, and Chaos," in *Nebraska Symposium on Motivation,* eds. W. Arnold and D. Levine (Lincoln: University of Nebraska Press, 1969), 237–307.

Solomon Asch describes conformity and the effects of groups on individuals' thoughts in his classic article, "Effects of Group Pressure on the Modification and Distortion of Judgment," in *Groups, Leadership, and Men: Research in Human Relations,* ed. H. Guetzkow (New York: Russell & Russell, 1963).

Robert Zajonc wrote the seminal article "Social Facilitation" for *Science* (1965, 149, 269–274). The most re-

cent thorough review of the topic is provided by G. S. Sanders in "Driven by Distraction: An Integrative Review of Social Facilitation Theory and Research" (*Journal of Experimental Social Psychology* 17 [1981]: 227–251). A good starting point for understanding social-inhibition effects is a book by Bibb Latané and John Darley entitled, *The Unresponsive Bystander: Why Doesn't He Help?* (New York: Appleton-Century-Crofts, 1970).

Paul Goodman reviews the specific applications of social-comparison theory to understanding behavior in organizations in his article, "Social Comparison Processes in Organizations," in B. Staw and G. Salancik (eds.), *New Directions in Organizational Behavior* (Malabar, Fla.: Krieger, 1982), 97–132.

Researcher Connie Gersick recently has proposed a new model of group-development processes that highlights the role of time deadlines. This new model is described in Gersick's article, "Time and Transition in Work Teams: Towards a New Model of Group Development" (*Academy of Management Journal* 31 [1988]: 9–41).

A good general overview of the psychology of group processes is provided in an article of the same name by Alvin Zander in *Annual Review of Psychology* 30, eds. M. Rosensweig and L. Porter (1979): 417–452.

ON YOUR
OWN

Think of a group of which you are a member. This can be a formal group, such as a softball team or a work group. Or it can be an informal group, such as a study or discussion group you use to prepare for exams. Complete the following questionnaires to assess (A) your group's *need* for team development, and (B) your group's *readiness* for team development.

**A. Need for Team Development**   To what extent is there evidence of the following problems in your work unit?

| | Low Evidence | | Some Evidence | | High Evidence |
|---|---|---|---|---|---|
| 1. Loss of production or work-unit output | 1 | 2 | 3 | 4 | 5 |
| 2. Grievances or complaints within the work unit | 1 | 2 | 3 | 4 | 5 |
| 3. Conflicts or hostility between unit members | 1 | 2 | 3 | 4 | 5 |
| 4. Confusion about assignments or unclear relationships between people | 1 | 2 | 3 | 4 | 5 |
| 5. Lack of clear goals or low commitment to goals | 1 | 2 | 3 | 4 | 5 |
| 6. Apathy or general lack of interest or involvement of unit members | 1 | 2 | 3 | 4 | 5 |
| 7. Lack of innovation, risk taking, imagination, or initiative | 1 | 2 | 3 | 4 | 5 |
| 8. Ineffective staff meetings | 1 | 2 | 3 | 4 | 5 |
| 9. Problems in working with the boss | 1 | 2 | 3 | 4 | 5 |
| 10. Poor communications: people afraid to speak up, people not listening to each other or not talking together | 1 | 2 | 3 | 4 | 5 |
| 11. Lack of trust between boss and members or between members | 1 | 2 | 3 | 4 | 5 |
| 12. Decisions made that people do not understand or agree with | 1 | 2 | 3 | 4 | 5 |
| 13. Feeling that good work is not recognized or rewarded | 1 | 2 | 3 | 4 | 5 |
| 14. No encouragement to work together in better team effort | 1 | 2 | 3 | 4 | 5 |

Source: William Dyer, *Team Building* © 1977, Addison-Wesley Publishing Co., Inc., Reading, Massachusetts. Pages 36–39. Reprinted with permission of the publisher.

*Scoring*   Add the scores for the fourteen items in questionnaire A. If your score is between 14 and 28, there is little evidence your unit needs team building. If your score is between 29 and 42, there is some evidence but no immediate pressure, unless two or three items are very high. If your score is between 43 and 56, you should seriously think about planning the team-building program. If your score is over 56, then team building should be top priority for your work unit.

## B. Readiness for Team Development

| | Disagree | | | | Agree |
|---|---|---|---|---|---|
| 1. You are comfortable sharing organizational leadership and decision making with subordinates and prefer to work in a participative atmosphere. | 1 | 2 | 3 | 4 | 5 |
| 2. You see a high degree of interdependence as necessary among functions and workers in order to achieve your goals. | 1 | 2 | 3 | 4 | 5 |
| 3. The external environment is highly variable or changing rapidly and you need the best thinking of all your staff to plan for these conditions. | 1 | 2 | 3 | 4 | 5 |
| 4. You feel you need the input of your staff to plan major changes or develop new operating policies and procedures. | 1 | 2 | 3 | 4 | 5 |
| 5. You feel that broad consultation among your people as a group about goals, decisions, and problems is necessary on a continuing basis. | 1 | 2 | 3 | 4 | 5 |
| 6. Members of your management team are (or can become) compatible with each other and are able to create a collaborative rather than a competitive environment. | 1 | 2 | 3 | 4 | 5 |
| 7. Members of your team are located close enough to meet together as needed. | 1 | 2 | 3 | 4 | 5 |
| 8. You feel you need to rely on the ability and willingness of subordinates to resolve critical operating problems directly and in the best interest of the company or organization. | 1 | 2 | 3 | 4 | 5 |

| | | | | | |
|---|---|---|---|---|---|
| 9. Formal communication channels are not sufficient for the timely exchange of essential information, views, and decisions among your team members. | 1 | 2 | 3 | 4 | 5 |
| 10. Organization adaptation requires the use of such devices as project management, task forces, or ad hoc problem-solving groups to augment conventional organization structure. | 1 | 2 | 3 | 4 | 5 |
| 11. You feel it is important to bring out and deal with critical, albeit sensitive, issues that exist in your team. | 1 | 2 | 3 | 4 | 5 |
| 12. You are prepared to look at your own role and performance with your team. | 1 | 2 | 3 | 4 | 5 |
| 13. You feel there are operating or interpersonal problems that have remained unsolved too long and need input from all group members. | 1 | 2 | 3 | 4 | 5 |
| 14. You need an opportunity to meet with your people to set goals and develop commitment to these goals. | 1 | 2 | 3 | 4 | 5 |

*Scoring*   Add the scores for the fourteen items in questionnaire B. If your total score is between 50 and 70, you are probably ready to go ahead with the team-building program. If your score is between 35 and 49, you should probably talk the situation over with your team and others to see what would need to be done to get ready for team building. If your score is between 14 and 34, you are probably not prepared to start team building.

CLOSING CASE
FOR CHAPTER 7

# THE MANAGER'S MEMO

FROM: H. Barbieri, Vice President, Consumer Electronics Division

TO:    B. Jones, Production Manager

RE:    Quality First Program

I think it's time to look at a new approach to our Quality First program. We've had the suggestion box out for a year, and so far we've received only two suggestions for quality improvements, of which only one made any sense.

　　Let's try a group approach. We can divide the employees into teams that can meet to come up with ideas for improving the quality of our products and production process.

　　I'd like you to prepare a plan for these groups. How should they operate? How often should they meet? Should we divide the groups into engineers, production workers, maintenance personnel, and so on, or should we put a variety of workers into each group? What problems can we anticipate with the group format, and how can we try to resolve them?

　　These questions are meant as a starting point. If you have other ideas or concerns, please include them in your plan.

CASE DISCUSSION
QUESTIONS

Assume you are the production manager, and respond to the vice president's memorandum with a memo outlining the plan requested. Be sure to respond to the specific questions. Use as many of the concepts in the chapter as you can to develop a complete plan that minimizes the pitfalls of group dynamics.

# Power and Influence

## THE POWER BEHIND THE FBI

The J. Edgar Hoover FBI headquarters, its windows set deeply back behind cast stone frames, seems to squint suspiciously down Pennsylvania Avenue toward the Capitol and at the Justice Department building across the street. The interior plan of the complex is obscured by heavy barriers of stone and metal. Between protective pillars and behind steep walls only deep shadows can be seen, concealing activities whose nature outsiders can only imagine. The massive FBI headquarters is a concrete monument to the man who ran the Federal Bureau of Investigation for 48 years.

As chief of federal law enforcement and guardian of domestic security, Hoover moved within the innermost rings of the most powerful circles of government and bore critical responsibilities during the greatest political crises and national emergencies of the century. The Bureau he led—powerful, efficient, completely subordinate to his will—was a resource presidents and the public came to depend on for decisive, effective performance under the most sensitive and difficult circumstances.

In his time, the man and his Bureau were cloaked in a selective secrecy and protected by power so formidable that few dared to pry. Hoover's secrets—the files on Communists and spies, the hundreds of millions of fingerprints, the dossiers on the great and the famous—were whispered to have silenced his critics and destroyed his enemies. To those who saw it as a threat to political freedom, Hoover's secret power was a frightening specter that haunted the nation.

Paradoxically, that secrecy and power, so terrifying to some, were what made Hoover a hero to many more, perhaps even most, Americans. Hoover's imposing presence gave much of the country a sense of stability and safety as he gathered to himself the strands of permanence that connected Americans to their past: religion, patriotism, a belief in progress and a rational moral order. To attack him was to attack Americanism itself.

Part of Hoover's power arose because only the FBI policed the FBI. Hoover decided which criminals ended up on the FBI's "most wanted" list. Hoover could make sure that only those the FBI would soon catch made their way to the top of the list. Further, since only the FBI published national crime statistics, Hoover himself kept score of his agency's accomplishments. Naturally, these figures always justified larger appropriations when Congress reviewed the FBI budget. One rumor had Hoover keeping "office-confidential" files on all of Washington's political heavy-weights. While the existence of these files was confirmed only shortly before Hoover's death, the mere possibility of their existence was enough to dampen any

enthusiasm in Congress to challenge or investigate the FBI.

Of all Hoover's secrets, the most tightly guarded were his own. Head of what was arguably the most powerful agency in the nation, his influence extending thoughout government and society, he managed to block every effort by outsiders to take an independent look at what he was doing and how he was doing it, what he knew and how he knew it. A half century of tightly restricted access made him a figure of mystery and of nervous apprehension; legends grew up around him, and his reputation was haunted by rumors and superstition. Presidents, congressmen, attorneys general, and the public knew only what Hoover wanted them to know about the Bureau and himself.

Source: R. G. Powers, *Secrecy and Power* (New York: Macmillan, 1987), pp. 2–3 and N. J. Welch and D. W. Marston, *Inside Hoover's FBI: The Top Field Chief Reports* (Garden City, N. Y.: Doubleday, 1984), pp. 25–27.

## INTRODUCTION

Power is a cornerstone of organizational behavior. As noted in Chapter 1, **political conflict** is a defining characteristic of organizational behavior. Political conflicts occur when different members of an organization pursue conflicting *personal* (rather than organizational) agendas. The distribution of power in an organization settles political conflicts. Politics doesn't mean doing what's best for the organization—politics means doing what is favored by the person (or persons) with the most power.

Political scientist Robert Dahl has defined power in the following way: "A has power over B to the extent that he can get B to do something B would not otherwise do."[1] There are two parts to this definition. First, power is something between or among people. No one simply has power; an individual (or group) has power *over* another particular individual or group. That means that *power is part of the relationships among*

[1] R. Dahl, "The Concept of Power," *Behavioral Science* (July 1957): 202–203.

*people* and therefore exists only as a characteristic of a social system (such as a group or organization). Outside of the social system in which power exists, power relationships may dissolve or even be reversed. J. Edgar Hoover was a powerful presence in Washington, D. C. Political hopefuls could not afford to cross him. But it is doubtful that his word would have carried as much weight in Moscow.

In addition to locating power in the relationships among people, Dahl's definition also emphasizes that power refers to the capacity of one individual to change the attitudes or actions of another individual. Power causes two forms of change: influence and control. These two forms of change parallel the two effects of groups on individuals discussed in Chapter 7. Groups influence individuals *indirectly* by altering individual thoughts (through social evidence and social anchoring) or *directly* by altering individual behaviors (through social inhibition and social facilitation). Similarly, power refers to one individual *influencing* the thoughts of another or *controlling* that other individual's behaviors. In fact, social influence is one example of the power that group members have over each other.

POWER AS SOCIAL EXCHANGE

How do these attempts at influence and control work? One simple explanation is the **theory of social exchange.** According to this theory:

> Social behavior is an exchange of goods, material goods but also non-material ones, such as symbols of approval or prestige. Persons that give much to others try to get much from them, and persons that get much from others are under pressure to give much to them. This process of influence tends to work out at an equilibrium to a balance of the exchanges.[2]

According to the theory of social exchange, power occurs because of resource dependencies. A **resource dependence** occurs when one individual needs or desperately wants something (the resource) that another individual possesses. The person who wants or needs the resource is dependent upon the person who has it. In the terms of social exchange, power or influence occurs when individuals who need or desire the resource take possession of it *in exchange for* changes in their personal thoughts (influence) or actions (control).

Politics is one obvious demonstration of power, but power also can be exercised in more subtle ways through implicit resource exchanges. The "Focus on: Power as Social Exchange" describes how Dale Carnegie courses teach sales personnel how to influence and control potential customers by offering them something in addition to the product, something that is valuable to the customer and that the sales force has in

[2]G. C. Homans, "Social Behavior as Exchange," *American Journal of Sociology* 63 (1958): 597–606.

FOCUS ON:

Power as Social
Exchange

**Sales Power through Self-Esteem**
In his renowned book, *How to Win Friends and Influence People*, Dale Carnegie revealed his "big secret" for dealing with people. The big secret was that there is one human need that is "almost as deep, almost as imperious, as the desire for food or sleep and which is seldom gratified"— namely, the need to feel important. The psychologist William James even described this need as "the craving to be appreciated." Carnegie believed that we satisfy this need in other people by giving them attention and esteem. Perhaps of more importance, Carnegie also believed that anyone who masters the ability to satisfy this need in others can "hold people in the palm of his hand." In defense of this contention, Carnegie's book offers the experiences and insights of several famous millionaires, including John D. Rockefeller:

> Sincere appreciation was one of the secrets of Rockefeller's success in handling men. For example, when one of his partners, Edward T. Bedford . . . lost the firm a million dollars by a bad buy in South America, John D. might have criticized; but he knew Bedford had done his best—and the

incident was closed. So Rockefeller found something to praise; he congratulated Bedford because he had been able to save 60 percent of the money he had invested. "That's splendid," said Rockefeller. "We don't always do as well as that upstairs."

In his book Carnegie also notes that steel millionaire Andrew Carnegie paid his right-hand man Charles Schwab more than $1 million per year because Schwab knew how to handle people. And what was Schwab's secret of success? He claimed, "I have yet to find the man, however great or exalted his station, who did not do better work and put forth greater effort under a spirit of approval than he would ever do under a spirit of criticism."

All of these comments share a common thread: The expression of appreciation and positive regard for someone is a powerful tool for influencing that person. According to Dale Carnegie, people are starved for compliments and respect. Personal esteem therefore is a valuable coin of the realm in social exchange. Interestingly, it is also an inexpensive coin to spend.

Source: Dale Carnegie, *How to Win Friends and Influence People* (New York: Simon Schuster, 1936).

unlimited quantities—compliments. In effect, the sales force exchanges compliments for successful sales.

Because power is a form of resource exchange does not mean that these exchanges are fair, or that what the parties exchange is equal. When power is exercised, both sides receive something in the transaction. However, as noted by Aristotle:

> . . . the benefits that one party receives and is entitled to claim from the other are not the same on either side . . . the better of the two parties, for

instance, or the more useful or otherwise superior as the case may be, should receive more affection than he bestows; since when the affect rendered is proportional to desert, this produces equality . . .[3]

In effect, the social exchanges of power transactions are governed by supply and demand; the benefit each party receives in the exchange will reflect the relative power of the two parties. More powerful individuals can give less and expect to get back more.

SLACK

If resource dependence and social exchange explain why and when power works, then slack explains why and when it doesn't. In the book *Equality*, political philosopher R. H. Tawney notes that to destroy power, "nothing more is required than to be indifferent to its threats and to prefer other goods to those which it promises."[4] Slack (discussed in Chapter 6) refers to any overabundance of a resource that decreases an individual's or group's dependence for it on any other individual or group. Slack provides an individual the ability to be indifferent to threats and promises. If power represents the capacity of one individual to influence or control a second individual, slack represents the capacity of that second individual to resist.

Slack comes in two forms: **stockpiles** and **alternative sources.** Stockpiles are quantities of a resource set aside for future use; alternative sources are other ways to fulfill a resource dependency, thereby reducing an individual's dependence on any one source. Nest eggs (money put into savings for a "rainy day") are stockpiles that represent a form of slack. If your boss makes an unreasonable request, you could refuse the request and be fired. Or you could go along with the request, regardless of how distasteful, in order to preserve your job. If you are dependent upon your paycheck to pay your rent and buy groceries, you may have to swallow your pride and go along with the boss's power play. On the other hand, if you have a nest egg you have a little slack. You know that the rent will get paid and you will eat (at least for a while) even if you wake up unemployed tomorrow morning. The nest egg reduces your resource dependency on the boss and thereby allows you to resist any attempt to influence or control you.

The other form of slack—alternative sources—also could allow you to refuse your boss's unreasonable request or quit your job without concern. In this situation, an alternative source would be an alternative source of employment. Another job would be another source of income; knowing another source of income is readily available reduces your dependency on your current boss for income. The "Focus on: Slack" describes the nature of resource dependencies and slack within professional sports.

[3]Aristotle, *The Nicomachean Ethic* (Boston: D. Reidel Publishing, 1975).
[4]R. H. Tawney, *Equality* (New York: Capricorn Books, 1961).

Focus on:
Slack

**Slacking Off in the NFL**   In September 1987, the NFL Players Association (NFLPA) went on strike. At issue were such items as unrestricted freedom for players to change teams ("free agency") and a larger cut of the $217 million TV pie for the players. Who had the power to win this dispute? An analysis of the slack available to each side is revealing.

Slack for the players would be strike "war chests"—money put away against the possibility of the strike. Unfortunately, the NFLPA chose to strike only two regular-season games into the 1987 season. Many NFL regulars are paid by the game and had earned only a very small portion of their annual salaries. These players found themselves cash poor virtually as soon as the strike began. Player slack also could arise in alternative employment opportunities. The existence of the USFL in the early 1980s, for example, had forced NFL owners to pay superstar salaries to journeymen players to prevent defections to the fledgling competitive league. Unfortunately for the players, by 1987 the USFL had folded its tent. The Canadian Football League never really offered a viable employment alternative.

On the owners' side of the ledger, slack would be a supply of players ready and willing to cross NFLPA picket lines for even the remotest chance at NFL stardom. The strike clearly showed that a supply of these "scab" players *is* available. As the strike's replacement games began, Chicago Bears fans found a bartender calling signals; both former prison guards and former prison inmates surfaced on other team rosters. The strike also showed why these players were only replacement players and not NFL regulars.

The proof was in fan reaction. The slack the NFL owners really were hoping for was fan loyalty—fans turning out to watch NFL games both live and on TV, even though the players were not NFL regulars. As soon as the novelty of the replacement teams wore off (about three-quarters into the first day's games), so did the interest of the fans and TV sponsors. The first Monday night game of the strike turned out to be the second-least-watched Monday night game in history.

In the end it became obvious that the real slack in the strike belonged to the fans. The NFL is, after all, entertainment, and therefore an unnecessary luxury. Perhaps pro football fans can otherwise fulfill their needs by overindulging in watching college football on Saturdays or by rediscovering the bracing benefits of crisp fall weekend walks. If so, the NFL players and owners must march to the beat of the same drummer—fan interest. After all, the customer is always right.

Source: T. Callahan, "Striking while the Owners Are Cool," *Time*, October 19, 1987, 73.

Interestingly, discussions about slack highlight the fact that power can be undermined by its use. If the resource that is the source of power is scarce and changes hands in the exchange (bribery money for example), the person receiving the money now may have newfound slack. A crooked politician's power to buy votes runs out when the supply of money runs out. Further, if early bribes have been big enough, the bribed no longer will be so desperate for money. Some sources of power are powerful only if *not* used. An individual who threatens to reveal sordid details about another's life (as Hoover may have done by keeping his "office-confidential" files) has power over that individual only so long as the details are not revealed.

Power also can be undermined by its use if the use reveals new sources of slack or new resource dependencies. If your boss makes an unreasonable request and you have read this book and put a little money into a nest egg, perhaps you would quit. The boss now has to fill the vacant position, and that may be difficult. In reality the boss may have been more dependent on you than he or she wished to admit, especially if you were particularly talented or specially trained.

A resource dependency in itself does not represent power if the resource dependencies are equal for both parties. The boss may have plenty of applicants to fill your position, while you have only one job. It is the inequality of the resource dependency in a social relationship— you need the boss much more than the boss needs you—that gives the boss power over you. Unfortunately, many times it is easier for us to see how we depend on others than to see how they depend on us. We may have slack and not know it. Once we find out how easy it is to find a new job (if it is easy), no boss will ever again be able to control or influence us with that resource. After the boss has unsuccessfully looked for your replacement for a while, the boss might even try to lure you back to your old job with a higher salary. And that would reveal the real power in that relationship!

Perception thus plays a key role in the exercise of power. You must perceive that you are dependent on another individual for that individual to have power over you. If you don't perceive a resource dependency (for money, a job, even affection or friendship) in your relationship with someone, there is no reason for you to go along with that individual's demands.

## POWER AND PERSONALITY

Individuals differ tremendously in their willingness or eagerness to search out and use their sources of power. As one prominent researcher in this area has concluded, "Analyses of intra-organizational power will be deficient and possibly misleading unless the intentions of the individual powerholder within the organizational context are taken into account."[5]

Harvard psychologist David McClelland has studied power for many years and has examined how individuals differ in their **need for power.** McClelland characterizes the need for power as the desire to have an

[5]V. E. Shein, "Individual Power and Political Behavior in Organizations: An Inadequately Explored Reality," *Academy of Management Review* 2 (1977): 64–72.

impact on others. According to McClelland's research, a high need for power is revealed in individuals who: are competitive and aggressive; who desire the outward trappings of power such as prestige possessions; prefer action situations; and join a number of groups. McClelland studied managers at AT&T and found that managers high in need for power when they joined the company were most successful 16 years later if they were low in need for affiliation and high in self-control.

McClelland's findings led him to conclude that two distinct forms of exchange characterize the use of power. The positive form is one in which the exchange is voluntary and both parties feel good about what they received. The negative form of power occurs when the influenced individual changes behaviors only reluctantly and does not make similar changes in thoughts. McClelland notes that this negative form of power:

> does not often lead to effective social leadership for the reason that such a person tends to treat other people as pawns. People who feel they are pawns tend to be passive and useless to the leader who gets his satisfaction from dominating them. Slaves are the most inefficient form of labor ever devised by man. If a leader wants to have far-reaching influence, he must make his followers feel powerful and able to accomplish things on their own.[6]

McClelland's two forms of power (positive and negative) correspond to two forms of exchange. Negative power occurs when subordinates feel forced to engage in a behavior—for example, because the price for not doing so is prohibitive. The exchange is involuntary and is perceived by the subordinates as inequitable; it produces changed behavior but not changed beliefs. Positive power occurs when managers use their power to convince subordinates of the wisdom of their position. The exchange is voluntary and is perceived as equitable; it produces changed behavior *and* beliefs.

McClelland's work highlighted the fact that power seekers are not necessarily bad people. Individuals high in need for power apparently can become quite effective managers when this need is developed and used appropriately. McClelland found those who need power were most ineffective when they channeled this need toward personal rather than organizational goals.

## SOURCES OF POWER

What kinds of resources do individuals have to exchange? What gives them power? Figure 8–1 presents six sources of power. Five of these, reward power, coercion power, expert power, legitimate power, and referent power, come from a classic article by French and Raven on the social bases of power.[7] The sixth source, task interdependence, was

[6]D. E. McClelland, *Power: The Inner Experience* (New York: Irvington, 1975).

[7]J. R. P. French and B. Raven, "The Bases of Social Power," in *Studies in Social Power,* ed. D. Cartwright (Ann Arbor, Mich.: Institute for Social Research, 1959): 150–167.

**FIGURE 8–1**                     Sources of Power

Individual power in organizations can come from a variety of sources. Structural sources of power refer to power that the organization gives an individual, such as the legitimate authority to give orders to others in the organization. Personal sources of power come from characteristics of individuals, such as charisma or expertise in a field.

**Structural Sources** (Work Relationships)

| | |
|---|---|
| Reward power | → The capacity to dispense rewards |
| Coercion power | → The capacity to dispense punishments |
| Task interdependence | → Power that accrues naturally to a particular role in an organization |
| Legitimate power | → Authority; the right to give orders |

**Personal Sources** (Personality Traits)

| | |
|---|---|
| Expertise | → Possession of valuable information or status |
| Referent power | → Power stemming from the desire of others to imitate an individual |

identified later by sociologist Michael Crozier in his studies of European factories. Of these six sources, reward and coercion are the two basic sources of power. Reward and coercion power arise in the control of rewards and punishments, respectively. The other four forms of power—expert, legitimate, referent, and task interdependence—refer only to different organizational forms of reward and punishment.

REWARD POWER

**Reward power** occurs when one individual possesses resources that another individual desires and has the ability to *reward* the second person in exchange for desired behavior.

Reward power is based on the "law of effect" discussed in Chapter 4. In the earlier discussions about motivation, the law of effect was illustrated through the phrase, "People engage in those behaviors that are most likely to be rewarded." If a particular behavior is followed by a reward, the individual will be more likely to engage in that behavior again. A supervisor can encourage subordinates to engage in appropriate work behaviors by making desired rewards contingent upon those behaviors. By making desired rewards contingent on subordinates' appropriate work behaviors, the supervisor exercises power over the subordinates.

Reward power is quite common in organizations. Supervisors often can offer subordinates pay raises, promotions, bonuses, favorable work assignments, or even extra training. Reward power doesn't come from just material rewards, though. Supervisors can reward subordinates with praise or recognition. For instance, the owner of a small machine shop in Oakland, California, has a "super employee" ceremony periodically.[8] In

[8]From the PBS video, "In Search of Excellence."

these ceremonies, unusually innovative or productive employees are presented cash awards documenting their achievements. The amounts of cash are small; far more important is the praise from the boss and recognition by the group for a job well done.

Reward power is a two-way street. If a supervisor rewards a subordinate for a job well done, the subordinate in turn may work harder, which rewards the supervisor for rewarding the subordinate! This reward cycle makes the subordinate's appropriate work behavior more likely to be repeated and the supervisor more likely to reward subordinate behavior in the future as well.

**Undermining Intrinsic Motivation**    There is danger in using reward power to elicit appropriate work behaviors. It revolves around the distinction between extrinsic and intrinsic rewards. **Extrinsic rewards are** rewards (for example, money or praise) provided *in exchange for* appropriate behaviors. An intrinsic reward, on the other hand, occurs naturally as a result of the behavior.

Extrinsic rewards can undermine a worker's intrinsic interest in work. If a worker does a particularly good job and receives a bonus from the boss, the bonus is an extrinsic reward—something provided by the boss in exchange for the appropriate behavior. In contrast, learning from a task is intrinsically rewarding, as are feelings of satisfaction and accomplishment from a job well done. Some work tasks are interesting, challenging, and engrossing. Involvement in tasks of this sort may be rewarding to a worker independent of (or in addition to) any extrinsic rewards provided by the organization. Many health-care professionals, for instance, find that the feeling of helping others is an important *intrinsic* reward in their work.

Are intrinsic and extrinsic rewards equally effective from the viewpoint of the organization? Definitely not. The attention of individuals who are working for extrinsic rewards is likely to be focused on those extrinsic rewards. The attention of individuals who are intrinsically interested in their work is likely to be focused on the work itself. This additional attention being paid to the work should lead to better execution of the task and a greater likelihood of discovering innovative ways to perform the work. Intrinsic interest in a job also means that the worker will need less supervision. If the worker is just working for extrinsic rewards, there is less reason to work when the boss isn't watching. If a task is intrinsically rewarding, it will be fun to work on even if no one is supervising the worker.

Of course, a worker cannot find out that a work task is intrinsically rewarding until the worker engages in the task. To get the worker that far may take some reward power—the promise of an extrinsic reward in exchange for the appropriate behavior. Once the worker is engaging in the behavior, however, the persistent use of reward power may prove harmful. If the rewards are kept up, the worker may continue to focus on the rewards rather than on the intrinsically rewarding aspects of the task.

In effect, the rewards might *undermine* any intrinsic motivation to do the task.

The secret of using reward power is that supervisors must know their subordinates well enough to know which tasks are most likely to be intrinsically motivating. If the supervisor uses a little reward power to get the subordinate started on an intrinsically rewarding task—and perhaps a little supervision to make sure the subordinate's first experiences with the task are intrinsically rewarding—intrinsic motivation should take over as the driving force behind the subordinate's behavior. Supervisors also need to make sure that subordinates' *inappropriate* behaviors are not maintained by other intrinsic or extrinsic rewards. Inappropriate behaviors perhaps may be encouraged socially as part of the "game" against management. Providing workers with intrinsically interesting work can get them working on a different "game"—the game of being productive. The most important form of reward power, then, is arranging work environments so that appropriate behaviors are intrinsically rewarding for workers, and inappropriate behaviors are neither intrinsically nor extrinsically rewarding.

## COERCION POWER

**Coercion** is the threat of punishment for *not* engaging in appropriate behaviors. Coercion can be based upon material forms of punishment, such as fines or the docking of pay. Coercion also can refer to less material forms of punishment, such as rejection. For instance, in the Asch study described in Chapter 7, an individual may feel coerced into going along with the group if he or she fears rejection or ridicule for voicing a lone dissenting opinion. Typically, in organizations, possible termination of employment or suspension is a threat used to coerce reluctant employees. Naturally, threats work best when there is no fear of retribution. As discussed in the "INTERNATIONAL FOCUS ON: Coercion," this is why a small group of terrorists can bring even a great nation to its knees.

As noted in McClelland's comments about the negative face of power and our general discussion in Chapter 4 about the use of punishment in organizations, coercion is effective in only a limited way. A supervisor who uses coercion to elicit appropriate behaviors by subordinates may succeed, but similar changes in their beliefs are unlikely. An employee who works only to avoid termination is not likely to be an enthusiastic contributor in the workplace. In fact, a coerced employee may even react like a cornered animal, by fighting back. If, as suggested by McClelland, coercion suggests an unfair or involuntary exchange of resources, the coerced worker is likely to seek ways to even up the exchange. Goofing off while the boss isn't looking, taking liberties with office supplies, even sabotaging work are all ways in which subordinates try to give back to the supervisor exactly what the supervisor gave them—trouble. Coercion may be an effective form of power in organizational settings, but only in a very short-sighted sense.

Coercion is power that comes from threats. Threats do not require the possession of valuable resources, only their *control.* Terrorists may possess little but can coerce a lot when they threaten to take away valued resources, such as lives. The best defense against coercion is indifference to threats.

INTERNATIONAL
FOCUS ON:
Coercion

**Fanaticism, Indifference, and Power** Janis Joplin captured the paradox of coercion in the phrase "freedom's just another word for nothing left to lose" from her song "Bobby McGee." And in this paradox lies the key to understanding how apparently powerless individuals can coerce great nations.

Coercion works when people have something important to lose. A supervisor can bully—coerce—subordinates because those subordinates don't want to lose their jobs. In effect the supervisor is saying, "Do it my way or lose your job!" An important assumption here is that the supervisor *controls* the subordinates' access to valued resources such as employment, work assignments, raises and promotions, or even praise.

In our world of haves and have-nots, we often assume that those individuals who possess the resources have all the power. But does possession of valued resources equal control of them? Those who possess valued resources can offer access to them as inducements for action. But Janis Joplin's song suggests that the haves also may be particularly vulnerable to coercion precisely because they have the resources and therefore have the most to lose. And just because the haves *possess* the valued resources doesn't mean that they *control* them.

Fanatics are the ultimate example of powerful have-nots. Fanatics apparently are willing to give up everything—including their lives—to get their way. Americans got a strong taste of fanaticism from the Japanese kamikaze pilots of World War II. In the early 1980s, fanatics in the Middle East—such as those who carried out several suicide truck-bomb attacks on U. S. facilities in Beirut—professed that giving their lives for the cause was the path to paradise. How can you coerce people who don't care if they die? Fanaticism is indifference to punishment, even death. Indifference destroys any sense of social exchange in a power relationship. In the terms of Janis Joplin's song, you cannot coerce someone who has nothing left to lose.

Brinksmanship is a form of coercion that entails *feigning* indifference. Brinksmanship means going to the brink to see who really values resources that they claim not to value. In a labor negotiation, the management team must feign indifference to a strike and the union must feign indifference to lost income during a strike. Both sides want to appear immune to coercion. When hijackers seize a plane, it is important for the negotiating authorities to appear indifferent to the terrorists' threats. The negotiators must say, "We won't do anything for the hijackers because we don't think they'll kill the hostages." This takes the negotiation to the brink: Are the authorities unwilling to give in to save the hostages, and are the hijackers really willing to die for their demands? If the negotiating authorities appear indifferent to the terrorists' threats, then the hijackers control no valued resources and have no coercive power.

A traditional view of management is that you control workers by keeping them "hungry" and therefore dependent upon management for valued resources, such as their jobs. Janis Joplin's paradox of coercion suggests instead that the best way to keep workers in line is to give them everything they want—good wages, good benefits, and good jobs—so that they will always have something left to lose if they are not good employees.

Sources: H. Anderson, "The Agony of Pan Am Flight 73," *Newsweek*, September 15, 1986, pp. 20–26; and M. Whitaker, "Beirut: Who's to Blame?" *Newsweek*, October 8, 1984, pp. 32–34.

## EXPERT POWER

Experts are highly experienced or highly trained in a field. **Expert power** refers to our general willingness to defer to experts and be swayed by their opinions. There are really two components of expert power: information and status.

Expert power derives from information when an individual possesses special information, knowledge, or an ability that another individual needs. As we noted in Chapter 1, uncertainty and complexity are defining characteristics of organizations. There is never enough information available for all important decisions to be cut-and-dried. A stockbroker, for instance, may have a dizzying array of financial-analysis information. The information that the stockbroker chooses to share with clients, and the manner in which that information is presented, will have a tremendous impact on the decisions they make.

In organizations, power from special information or a special ability is not always reflected on the organizational chart. Certainly the top executives in the organization possess certain knowledge that gives them the power to influence the beliefs and actions of those below them. However, executives often complain that they really don't know what's going on below them in the organization. They feel out of touch with the actual work being done and the daily problems faced by the rank-and-file workers. That information is available elsewhere in the organization. Perhaps it is known by middle managers, or first-line supervisors. These managers and supervisors then possess information that gives them power over the top executives in the organization—the ability to sway the top executives' beliefs and actions.

Apparently powerless members of organizations often have tremendous potential to influence the opinions and actions of others. Take, for example, the job of administrative assistant to the general manager for the organization pictured in Figure 8–2(a). The division heads no doubt are more senior, more experienced, higher in status, and higher paid than the administrative assistant. The organization chart shows a direct connection between the general manager and the division heads. However, on a daily basis the administrative assistant probably acts as the representative of the busy general manager.

The administrative assistant may have the general manager's ear— even be the general manager's confidante or confessor. Similarly, in day-to-day dealings the division heads may be willing to share with the administrative assistant impressions, concerns, and fears that would never reach the ears of the general manager. The operating procedures of the organization—the use of the administrative assistant as a go-between to the division heads—places the administrative assistant in a central position for information gathering. The administrative assistant is the "pipeline" for information between the division heads and the general manager. If power derives from information, this organization's chart may be captured more accurately by Figure 8–2(b). While the administrative assistant's job may appear powerless in the job description, in reality it has lots of potential for influence through the control of information.

Information certainly represented an important source of power for J. Edgar Hoover. During Hoover's reign as director, the FBI's reach in gathering information was virtually unchecked. As a result, Hoover's dossiers and files contained information that allegedly gave Hoover power over much higher-ranking Washington officials—including U. S. presidents.

As noted in Chapter 7, another form of expert power comes from the status of experts as sources of special information or ability. The title "expert" refers to individuals who have impressive credentials, such as a

**FIGURE 8–2**                    Expert Power

Organizational charts capture the formal (legitimate) power structure of an organization: who takes orders and who gives them. However, expertise can give even formally powerless subordinates power over their bosses. The administrative assistant in (a) holds the formally powerless job of gofer for the general manager. However, as the information liaison between the general manager and the department heads, the administrative assistant in (b) may gain substantial power because of access to important information.

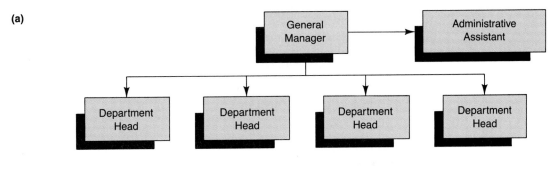

(a)

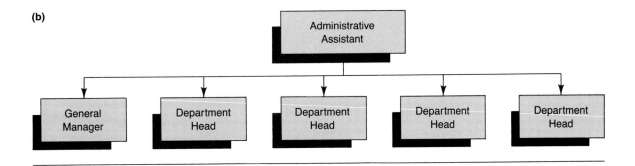

(b)

Ph.D., a medical degree, a law degree, or an equivalent amount of experience or ability. These credentials *imply* the possession of knowledge or ability, which should make the opinions of these experts particularly trustworthy or informative. Expert status thus elicits deference and respect. The result is that expert opinions have a tremendous influence on beliefs and behaviors even when they are *not* based on sound information or deduction. In fact, the *appearance* of expertise (and the status it conveys) can be more influential than actual knowledge. The opinions of a mature and distinguished, silver-haired professor may be given much more weight than those of a young assistant professor, even though the assistant professor may be more knowledgeable about the latest developments in the field.

Expert status can prove particularly powerful because of "halo" effects, discussed in Chapter 3. Halo effects occur when we incorrectly generalize from beliefs about one thing to beliefs about another—for example, when we believe that someone who is very good-looking is also very smart. Halo effects in expert power occur when we assume that an expert in one area will also have expert opinions in other areas. A wise and experienced doctor may be a great medical advisor, but may give terrible financial advice. Nevertheless, status as an expert in the field of medicine may make us more likely to give credence to the doctor's opinions on financial management. We may be inappropriately influenced by generalizing the trustworthiness of the doctor's opinions on medical matters to an area in which he or she is no more an expert than anyone else.

## LEGITIMATE POWER

One of the most pervasive forms of power in organizations is **legitimate power**—the *right* to give orders. What does it mean to have the right to give orders? It means that a social system (such as an organization or a society) has given an individual the authority to exercise control over the behaviors of others for their own good and for the good of the social system. One's role in a social system is the source of legitimate power.

Organization charts like the one shown in Figure 8–2(a) detail the formal authority relationships in a typical work organization. The chart explains who is a boss and who is a subordinate. The bosses have the *right* to give orders—to control the behaviors of their subordinates.

Why does legitimate power work? Why would a subordinate obey the orders of the boss? There are two reasons. First, authority (or legitimate power) is often simply an implicit form of reward, coercion, or expert power. If your boss tells you to make a sales call, you could sit down and decide for yourself if the ordered action is a good idea. However, if you decide against going out on the sales call, you could risk the eventual loss of a valued reward that the boss controls, or you could face immediate punishment—such as termination for insubordination (failure to follow orders). Or it may be that the boss is the boss because the boss is smarter or more experienced than you, and not following the boss's orders will result in the loss of an important sale. If you truly believe that the sales call is unwarranted but decide to go anyway, you may be reacting to the implict control the boss exercises over rewards, punishments, and important information.

There are also relatively subtle reasons for being obedient under the watchful eye of the boss, and these have to do with the survival of social systems. People join social systems such as organizations because they offer advantages over going it alone. Failure to obey orders is a challenge not only to the particular order given, but also to the social system that allows the order to be given. If the system has advantages, then challenging the system risks losing the advantages of having a system at all.

Work organizations have authority relationships (typically captured in the organization chart) that give individuals the right to give orders to others. Individuals who refuse to obey an order may be setting an example. Would those same individuals want their *own* subordinates to refuse orders as well? Wouldn't they expect their subordinates to obey when they take over the boss's job? Challenging the legitimate power given to individuals by the system not only challenges (and potentially undermines) the right of your boss to give you orders, it also challenges (and potentially undermines) your right to give orders to your subordinates. While it may be overstating the case, the logical consequences of disobedience are anarchy, the eventual destruction of the system, and the loss of any advantages the system provides. If an organization is to avoid the trap of having all bosses and no subordinates, a little obedience clearly is a good thing.

Unquestioned obedience is just as clearly not a good thing. As noted in Chapter 7, unquestioned subordination of individual judgment to norms or rules is bad for an organization. Unquestioned obedience of authority figures also can be detrimental to an organization's best interests. Decision makers can be wrong, just as rules and norms can be wrong. The dangers of unquestioned obedience to authority—and the strengths of legitimate power—were dramatically demonstrated in a series of studies by Stanley Milgram.

Milgram was particularly interested in why, during wartime conditions such as those in Germany during World War II, individuals often commit atrocities against others that they excuse as simply "following orders." Milgram devised an experimental procedure that allowed him to ask the question: Under what conditions are people willing to obey an instruction to intentionally hurt another person?

The participants in Milgram's experiment were volunteer adult males of various ages and occupations in New Haven, Connecticut. They arrived at Milgram's laboratory and learned that the experiment would examine the effects of punishment on learning. The study would involve two participants working together: a teacher and a learner. The participants drew lots to see who would be the learner and who would be the teacher. In fact, one of the participants was one of Milgram's assistants. The drawing was arranged so that Milgram's assistant always drew the role of learner.

After the drawing for roles, the experimental assistant took the learner into an adjacent room and connected the learner to an electric shock apparatus. The real participant was informed that his job would be to administer a word-pair memory task for the learner to learn. After each incorrect response, the teacher was to punish the learner by administering an electric shock. The teacher was given a sample 45-volt

The Milgram studies stand as a testament to the power of formal authority. The subjects in Milgram's study could have walked out at any time. Yet they continued to shock the innocent fellow subject (shown here being connected to the shock apparatus) simply because they were told to do so.

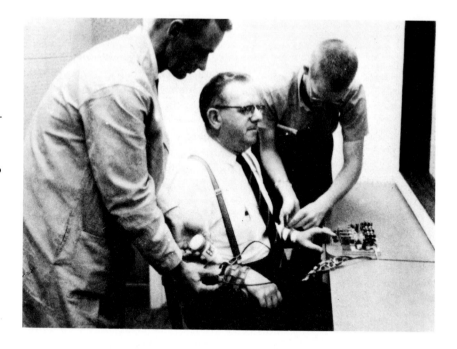

shock. At this point the teacher was seated at a simulated shock generator, with an array of switches and labels corresponding to shocks ranging from 15 volts ("slight shock") to 450 volts ("danger: severe shock"). The teacher was told to give the learner one shock for each incorrect response, and to increase the voltage of the shocks for each succeeding incorrect answer. (In fact, no electric shocks were administered at all.)

The learner's responses had been carefully orchestrated and they were the same for each new teacher. The learner gave many incorrect responses, so the teacher had to administer many shocks. And with the shocks came the apparent painful suffering of the learner:

> Starting with 75 volts, the learner begins to grunt and moan. At 150 volts he demands to be let out of the experiment. At 180 volts he cries out that he can no longer stand the pain. At 300 volts he refuses to provide any more answers to the memory test, insisting that he is no longer a participant in the experiment and must be freed.[9]

The experiment continued until the teacher refused to give the learner another shock.

Before making available the results of his study, Milgram asked a panel of 40 psychiatrists to predict the behavior of his real subjects. How far would the subjects go in the experiment? At what voltage level would

[9]D. Katz and R. L. Kahn, *The Social Psychology of Organizations* (New York: Wiley, 1966).

**FIGURE 8–3**      Actual and Predicted Obedience in Administering
(Fictitious) Shocks

Many of us probably un-
derestimate the extent to
which we are intimidated
by the trappings of legitimate authority. As part of
the Milgram studies, 40
psychiatrists were asked
to predict how far sub-
jects would go in shock-
ing another subject just
because an experimenter
ordered them to do so. As
shown in this graph, even
these experts on human
behavior grossly underes-
timated the amount of
compliance that was ob-
tained in the study.

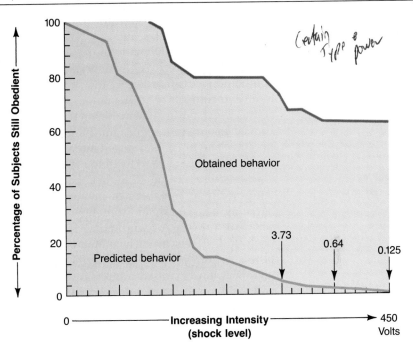

Source: Stanley Milgram, *The Individual in a Social World* (Reading, Mass.: Addison-Wesley,
1977), 119.

the subjects refuse to continue administering shocks to the helpless
learner? The psychiatrists suspected that most subjects would refuse to
continue the experiment as soon as the learner made his first plea to be
released (at 150 volts). The psychiatrists also predicted that only 1 of the
1,000 participants in Milgram's study would continue to be obedient all
the way up to the highest level of shock (450 volts).

A comparison of the psychiatrists' predictions and the actual behavior
of Milgram's' subjects is shown in Figure 8–3. In fact, 62 percent of
Milgram's subjects (620 of the 1,000 subjects) remained obedient and
administered shocks all the way to the end of the range on the generator
to a protesting and (eventually) ominously silent learner.

The **Milgram study** stands as a testament to the strength (and the
danger!) of legitimate power. In the study, the participants were
volunteers and could have quit at any time. No participant was
threatened or explicitly coerced into shocking the learner. In fact, many
subjects did register complaints during the experimental procedure.
Many were obviously tense and anxious during the experiment and

demonstrated concern about and sympathy for the learner. These complaints and concerns were met by a simple comment from the experimenter that "the experiment requires that you continue." And that command was enough for 62 percent of the subjects to continue to the end of the shock scale.

What sense can be made of the subjects' behaviors? Legitimate power is a strong force. We are socialized to believe that if someone in command gives an order, we may have the right to complain but we have a duty to comply.

It is worth noting in conclusion that the orders of the experiment were backed by a temporary organization, and one in which the subjects could not have had much of a vested interest. Most people hearing of this study for the first time ask, "Why didn't the real subjects just get up and leave?" The answer may be that they had voluntarily agreed to participate temporarily as members of an organization (the experiment), and in agreeing to participate somehow felt bound to obey the authority structure of the organization. If legitimate power can have such profound effects in such a flimsy organizational setting, imagine the power of authority in real, permanent work organizations where the members have a vested interest in both the survival of the organization and their continued membership in it. Even if a lot of obedience is a good thing in organizations, a little *dis*obedience is not only good but necessary. If someone is giving the wrong orders, survival of the organization could just as easily depend on workers disobeying those orders as on their obeying them.

The abuse of legitimate power provides one definition of unethical behavior. Organizations give individuals legitimate power to accomplish organizational goals. An employee who uses legitimate power to further personal objectives that are irrelevant to the organization has breached ethical standards. For instance, a supervisor could convince a subordinate to go out on a date in exchange for better work assignments (rewards) or just to remain employed (coercion). This abuse of legitimate power to accomplish personal goals is unethical.

## TASK INTERDEPENDENCE

Sociologist Michel Crozier has identified a source of power not included in French and Raven's classic list. This source of power accrues to a particular job (or group of jobs) in an organization because of **task interdependence.** Task interdependence occurs when two or more employees must depend on each other to complete assigned tasks.

The power dynamics between executives and their assistants illustrate power from task interdependence. The executive has legitimate power over the assistant. The organization gives the executive the right (within the limits of the assistant's job description) to give orders to the assistant. The executive's dependence on the assistant in the flow of work, however, gives the assistant some power over the executive. Once the executive has given an order, the executive actually becomes dependent upon the assistant to complete the task correctly and on time. Certainly the executive has the power to replace the assistant if the task is done poorly or late. Unfortunately for the executive, firing the assistant for failing is not equivalent to getting the task done well and on time! Therefore, the executive and assistant have an interdependent work relationship. The assistant depends on the executive for task assignments, resources, and a job, while the executive depends on the assistant for efficient and effective fulfillment of assignments. The organization gives the executive legitimate power over the assistant; the arrangements for getting work done give the assistant task interdependence power over the executive. Legitimate power comes with the job description; task interdependence power comes with the territory.

Crozier studied manufacturing organizations in France and discovered an example of power from task interdependence in a French tobacco factory. The maintenance engineers in the factory occupied only modest positions of authority in the formal organizational hierarchy. Nevertheless, they seemed to have tremendous power in the plant. For instance, they were able to dictate their own work schedules and dress codes, and they seemed always to have management's sympathetic ear. Crozier found that a key source of uncertainty in the plant concerned breakdowns of the manufacturing machinery. Over the years the machinery had been modified and customized to fit the facility's needs, so that now it only vaguely resembled the original manufacturer's specifications. Due to these modifications, the maintenance personnel were the only members of the organization capable of coping with breakdowns, so everyone else in the plant was highly dependent upon their goodwill. Thus, their position in the work arrangements gave them great power.[10]

Crozier's discoveries later were the basis for a formal theory about power from task interdependence. According to the theory, an individual accrues power from task interdependence because of the function that individual performs for the organization. Power accrues to those organizational functions that possess the most potential for disrupting the productivity of others in the organization. Functions can differ in their ability to disrupt the work of other employees along five dimensions: centrality, criticality, flexibility, visibility, and relevance.

**Centrality**   Centrality is primarily a matter of the reach of a particular individual or group. The secretary of the CEO of a large conglomerate may have no more formal status or authority than the secretary of a division vice-president. However, the CEO's secretary has much more power because her actions (such as postponing the mailing of a memorandum with which she disagrees) can disrupt the productivity of

[10]M. Crozier, *The Bureaucratic Phenomenon* (Chicago: University of Chicago Press, 1964).

virtually everyone else in the organization. The power of the division vice-president's secretary, on the other hand, is most likely limited to matters within the division.

**Criticality**   Individuals (or groups) in an organization are critical if there are no available substitutes for the function or role they perform. In Crozier's tobacco factory, the maintenance personnel were critical because only they were intimately familiar with the modifications to the machinery and knew how to fix it in the event of a breakdown. Even outsiders brought in to help would be helpless. In contrast, the role of typist often is not very critical in an organization. If there is a pool of typists, any one typist may be interchangeable with any other. Further, the entire pool may be interchangeable with temporary replacements.

In general, criticality has to do with redundancy. If a manager can easily locate substitutes to fulfill a subordinate's or group's function in the organization, the individual or group is not critical to the mission of the organization.

**Relevance**   An individual's role or function in an organization may be central, but only to minor goals of the organization. The relevance of a position concerns the centrality of the organization's goals to which it is critical. In Crozier's tobacco factory, customized restrooms also may have required a specialized maintenance crew, but that crew would not have had the power of the manufacturing maintenance crew because the restrooms are not as central to the mission of the organization (processing tobacco) as the tobacco machinery. By way of contrast, centrality has to do with the ability of a person to disrupt progress on tasks; relevance has to do with the importance of the disrupted tasks to the mission of the organization.

**Visibility**   The centrality, criticality, and relevance of an individual's role or function all must be perceived as such if they are to translate into power or influence. If no one else in the organization is aware of a job's centrality, criticality, or relevance, the position may be accorded little or no power. This suggests that individuals must cultivate others' appreciation of their power. In the case of Crozier's tobacco factory maintenance engineers, an occasional failure to keep things running smoothly would remind the rest of the work force of the maintenance engineers' centrality, criticality, and relevance. In contrast, individuals who always anticipate and smoothly discharge their duties may perform important and even critical functions invisibly. Invisibility of this sort may encourage other workers (or supervisors) to take them (and the power of their positions in the flow of work) for granted.

Individuals also can increase their visibility as a way of cultivating power. If a jobholder has a centrally located office or participates in lots of voluntary office functions, that individual will be more visible. This visibility will heighten the salience of the job's centrality, criticality, and relevance—if the job has any, that is.

**Flexibility**   A job has flexibility if the jobholder has opportunities to make choices, innovate, and take the initiative. A vague or incomplete job description gives a job incumbent lots of flexibility—flexibility that an industrious employee can parlay into power. A job that has no flexibility can be easily routinized, and the jobholder therefore easily replaced. Also, if a job is routine, the jobholder has the opportunity to do only what is dictated by the job description and not anything personally desired. There are no opportunities, for instance, to develop power by assuming command of a critical organizational function. A job with little flexibility can have only limited power.

In sum, these five characteristics of roles and functions determine whether an individual's position in the flow of work in the organization will be powerful or not. Centrality, criticality, and relevance have to do with the ability of one individual's actions to disrupt the work of another's. Visibility is a matter of whether actual centrality, criticality, and relevance are perceived as such by other organization members. Finally, a role has flexibility if it provides opportunities to exercise power (by making choices) that accrues from centrality, criticality, and relevance.

REFERENT POWER

Perhaps the most mysterious form of power is **referent power.** Jill has referent power over Jack when Jack willingly imitates or obeys Jill because Jack identifies with or admires her. Identifying with an individual means seeing in that individual traits that you would like to have. For example, many young people dress like the rock star or sports heroes they aspire to be like. The young people communicate their aspirations by imitating their heroes in fashion and behavior.

Much of the strength of referent power is believed to derive from **charisma.** Charisma is a personal style that captures the attentions, hearts, and imaginations of people. Charisma arises when an individual seems to possess the characteristics that define the model person for many admirers. This means that an individual's charisma will be quite specific to a particular reference group. An individual will have charisma not because of personal characteristics, but because of a *fit* between those characteristics and those desired or admired by others.[11] For instance, T. E. Lawrence (better known as the legendary "Lawrence of Arabia") possessed certain characteristics that made him an admired leader of the Arabs during World War I. By contrast, his personal style was unappealing in his home country of England, where his political aspirations failed upon his return.

[11]J. MacGinnis, *Heroes* (New York: Viking Press, 1976).

Chicago Bulls fans adore Michael Jordan and identify with his accomplishments. This makes the fans highly susceptible to the persuasion of referent power, as in product endorsements. In the business world, the results of a junior executive's emulation of and identification with the boss may be more subtle but just as powerful.

The personal style of Winston Churchill, on the other hand, became charismatic only when England faced certain defeat during World War II. When the crisis was resolved and the needs of the population changed, Churchill and his government quickly lost favor.[12] People's willingness to identify with another individual—and therefore to be influenced by that person—is highly situationally dependent. If the situation changes, people's needs change, and so do their definitions of a model person. As the definitions of the model person change, so do the people who are perceived as charismatic.

In comparison to other sources to power, referent power is most like expert power. Both are based almost exclusively on *personal* characteristics of the individual. A person is an expert because of background credentials or experience; a person has charisma because that person's personality traits match what the people think they need. In both cases, power derives from the individual. Reward, coercion, task interdependence, and legitimate power, on the other hand, are primarily *structural* sources of potential influence. The ability to dispense rewards and punishments, or the authority to act as if one could, arise from work relationships rather than personal traits.

# USING POWER: STRATEGIES AND TACTICS

With many sources of power available, power is actually well distributed in organizations rather than just concentrated at the top. Any member of an organization has access to some sources of power. What may be less clear is how lower-level participants in organizations can make effective

[12]J. E. Mack, *A Prince of Our Disorder: The Life of T. E. Lawrence* (Boston: Little, Brown, 1976). Cited in D. R. Hampton, C. E. Summer, and R. A. Webber, Organizational Behavior and the Practice of Management (Glenview, Ill.: Scott, Foresman, 1987).

**FIGURE 8–4** Some Upward-Influence Tactics

Even apparently powerless members of organizations have some sources of power at their disposal. An organizational newcomer can develop expertise in an important arena as a way of capturing control over a valued organizational resource. Alternatively, individuals in an organization can band together and mobilize their collective power through coalitions.

**Individual Sources of Power**

| | |
|---|---|
| Effort | Time and persistence |
| Ingratiation | Giving up something of little value in the hope of invoking valuable reciprocity |
| Control of valued resources | Developing valued expertise in order to increase others' dependence |

**Group Sources of Power**

| | |
|---|---|
| Compromise coalitions | Building alliances by compromising personal goals to satisfy others' goals |
| Logrolling | Building alliances by ceding influence on one issue to gain influence on another |

*(handwritten margin note: Where do get their power)*

use of the power they have. The next section of this chapter reviews several ways lower-level participants in organizations can individually mobilize the powers they do have, then focuses on one very important group source of lower-level power: the coalition. These power tactics are summarized in Figure 8–4.

TACTICS OF UPWARD INFLUENCE

If you are a newly hired executive assistant in a large industrial corporation, how can you get things rolling your way? There are two answers: (1) identify which valuable resources (information, rewards, punishments) already are at your disposal, or (2) go out and capture some resources that are available for you to control.

The most important and abundant resource available to lower-level participants for upward influence is effort. The higher individuals are in an organization, the busier they are and the less time they have to deal with problems below them in the hierarchy. This is an advantage for any lower-level organization member. If an issue seems important to you and you continue to bring it up, eventually it will become less expensive for those above you to let you have your way than to take the time necessary to dissuade you or even meet with you. Effort provides power because effort can become a form of coercion. Persistent effort carries the implicit threat of continuing to be a nuisance until things are changed. As noted in the "Focus on: Effort as Power," persistent effort also can translate into expert power.

Lower-level participants in an organization also have available the power of **ingratiation**.[13] Ingratiation occurs when an individual does

[13]E. E. Jones, *Ingratiation* (New York: Appleton-Century-Crofts, 1964).

FOCUS ON:
Effort as Power

**The Power of Just Showing Up**
The power of persistence highlights the relative scarcity of attention as a resource. An example is provided by the case of the San Francisco School Board in the early 1970s. The decision making of this board was dominated by middle-class, white, nonworking women. Traditionally, this particular group had been quite powerless and disenfranchised. How did it come to have such power, particularly in view of the presence of several apparently powerful special-interest groups?

These women became powerful because they had the time to go to meetings and carry out the business of the School Board. In short, they took over the board because they put in the effort to do so. In comparison, several active representatives of significant minority groups failed to play any role in the board's decision making because their participation in *other* board meetings was more pressing. This generated a self-perpetuating cycle. Though all participants on the board began on equal footing, the greater time and effort spent by the white, middle-class women on board activities eventually earned them a certain amount of expert power, which made other board members more reluctant to challenge their initiatives.

The American Association of Retired Persons (AARP) provides another example of the power of effort. AARP is a well-oiled money and propaganda machine of more than 29 million members that is growing by thousands of members a day. Much of AARP's income (from its bimonthly magazine, *Modern Maturity,* and commissions from the insurance packages it promotes) is turned directly into political clout through public-relations efforts ($5.6 million in 1986) and lobbying efforts ($8.8 million in 1986). In the courts, AARP submits "friend of the court" opinions in cases with implications for its membership.

However, AARP's real power is in its size. Local AARP chapters can muster up to 400,000 members to testify before state legislatures or to sign petitions. Head counts of that magnitude are enough to capture any politician's attention. The amount of time AARP members and staff spent on the phone turning out voters to back their positions may have produced even more clout in the 1988 presidential election than AARP's $8 million advertising budget.

Sources: Richard Phalon, "Empire Builders," *Forbes,* February 22, 1988, pp. 36–37; Lee Smith, "The World According to AARP," *Fortune,* February 29, 1988, pp. 96–98; S. S. Weiner, "Participation, Deadlines, and Choice," in *Ambiguity and Choice in Organizations,* eds. J. G. March and J. P. Olsen (Bergen, Norway: Universitetsforlaget, 1979).

nice things for someone in the hope of creating a sense of obligation in that individual to return the favor. Subordinates can ingratiate themselves with the boss by supporting the boss's ideas in group meetings, going out of their way to do little things for the boss, or even simply playing up to the boss with compliments or gifts.

Ingratiation is a powerful influence tactic because social exchange transactions are governed by the **norm of reciprocity.** The norm of reciprocity states that if someone does something nice for you, you are *obligated* by social convention to return the favor, even if you didn't want it in the first place. Cicero once noted that, "There is no duty more indispensable than returning a kindness . . . all men distrust one forgetful of a benefit."[14] Reciprocation is quite different from compensation—direct payment for services rendered. In fact, any attempt to repay a kindness quickly and directly in order to avoid obligation "is unseemly and conveys distrust."[15] The norm of reciprocity not only entails repayment of a previous kindness, it often suggests an *ongoing exchange relationship* in which favors are traded. If I scratch your back, I expect that at some point you will scratch mine, *and* that exchanges of this sort are part of our ongoing relationship.

The norm of reciprocity probably arose in early societies as a way to stabilize social interaction. As we have noted several times in this book, the pooling of individual efforts through groups and organizations makes life better for everyone. However, without a norm of reciprocity the pooling of individual effort would be a risky enterprise. If I loan my efforts to the group hunt, how do I know that I will receive some of the spoils of the hunt in exchange? Without the assurance provided by the accepted social convention of fair exchange of favors, no one would be willing to pool individual effort into a group effort in the first place. The norm of reciprocity is a cornerstone of social-exchange interactions. We all must believe that in the long run we will get back what we put in.

Ingratiation represents something of a perversion of the reciprocity norm. The norm of reciprocity allows low-power individuals to give others in the organization things they may not want or need and expect something in return. Ingratiation creates an obligation of repayment that can produce desired outcomes almost as surely as coercion.

Lower-level participants also have power available through flexibility. There is always some room to maneuver between doing what was asked and doing what was desired. A letter can take longer to type than expected. Rules can be broken for one person, but not another. In general, subordinates possess tremendous potential to "gum up the works" (a form of coercion arising in task interdependence) while still faithfully discharging the letter of their duties. Even the threat that this might occur should be enough to keep the boss reasonably in line.

In addition to gaining power by controlling resources already at their disposal, lower-level members of organizations also can gain power by finding a valuable resource to control. Access to this resource then can be traded for other desires, such as better task assignments. For instance, if a new and very complex software package has just been delivered to your department, you could take the time to learn all about it before anyone

[14]A. Gouldner, "The Norm of Reciprocity," *American Sociological Review* 25 (1960): 161–178.

[15]P. Blau, *Exchange and Power in Social Life* (New York: Wiley, 1964).

else gets a chance. You will have captured control of a critical resource: expertise about how to use the new software. The first time someone needs something done with this new software, only you will have the expertise to help out. And in *exchange,* who knows what you might be able to acquire? Further, once you have learned how to use it, it will be easier for others to give you what you want to run the software for them than to learn how to use it themselves.

Notice that this tactic does not require that you need the resource. If you are interested in changing the vacation-leave policy at your company, taking control of the new software gives other members of the organization a reason to listen to your concerns. It is not important for you to care about the software, only for *others* to care about the software. If you have something they want, you can exchange it for anything else you might find valuable. Knowing more about the new software than anyone else makes you a scarce but valued commodity. Exclusive information about the new software gives you reward and coercion power with which the organization might never have entrusted you. Once you have what everyone else wants, even if you don't want it yourself you can exchange it for whatever you *do* want.

Informal resources provide an important variation on identifying a critical resource in the flow of organizational work. The office "clown" or "cheerleader," for instance, fulfills an important role for office morale. If this role is perceived as critical to the healthy functioning of the office, higher-ups may be willing to forgive other shortcomings, such as mediocre performance on assigned tasks.

In the end, all the sources of power for lower-level organization participants so far discussed share an assumption that the subordinates are not easily replaced. After all, a boss who has lots of fawning subordinates will not be willing to exchange much for flattery, and a boss with an abundance of secretarial help is unlikely to be persuaded to do much by one recalcitrant clerical employee—except maybe to fire him or her. It should not be surprising, then, that the most important source of power for lower-level organization participants is not one source of power at all, but the union of many through the formation of coalitions.

## COALITIONS

Nowhere is the political nature of organizations more obviously on display than it is in the formation of coalitions. A **coalition** is a collection of individuals who have banded together to combine their individual sources of power. As noted by Thomas Hobbes in Chapter 7, no individual has the power to stand alone against the rest of the organization. The secret to power in organizations is alliances with others. When you join a coalition, your individual power is increased by the power of the others in the group. If you have one vote in an election, you cannot elect anyone on your own. But if you can gather together a large group of voters (each with one vote), that group of voters can decide who gets elected. Similarly, one disgruntled employee exercising the power to disrupt work by walking off the job may have little or no effect; several thousand employees walking out simultaneously can move mountains.

Coalitions represent a form of power *sharing*, and there are costs to joining a coalition. If you are a middle manager in a large corporation, undoubtedly you have some sources of power at your disposal, but who is going to listen to your one lone voice? You don't have enough power to affect a major change in corporate policy by yourself. Perhaps you could find some other managers who want the same change. Then it would be more than just your one voice—then your voice would have the strength of numbers behind it.

One of the problems with this strategy, of course, is that it may be difficult to find other managers who want *exactly* what you want. If only a few managers were interested in your agenda, what other options would you have for increasing your power base?

You could form a **compromise coalition.** In Chapter 6 we defined a compromise decision as one in which two or more parties each give a little to reach an agreement. The parties don't get exactly what they wanted, but they get something better than they would have gotten had they not compromised. In a compromise coalition, all of the members of the coalition are interested in the same issues, but they all don't get exactly what they want. The members of the coalition *compromise* on what each wants to make sure that the coalition gets anything at all.

If the issue is maternity leave, perhaps you think that six weeks of maternity leave at half pay would be appropriate. Someone else thinks that three weeks at full pay would be best. Both of you agree that *anything* is better than the company's current policy of two weeks at half pay. So the two of you compromise on four weeks at three-quarters pay. It is not really what either of you wanted, but you both prefer it to the company's alternative. And by finding a way to agree, you now can *both* put your sources of power behind the one compromise suggestion.

Coalitions don't always form because of shared interests, however. Many coalitions form only because their members share one *need*—the need for more power. If you searched out all the managers interested in your version of maternity leave, toned down your demands to get a few others interested, but still found yourself short of the power you needed, what else could you do? The answer is "logroll."

**Logrolling** is a form of coalition in which participants lend each other power so that each can pursue interests *not* shared by other coalition members. If you were the only manager in the company interested in changing the maternity-leave policy, to get others to join your coalition you would have to give them something. And what do you have to give? Your limited sources of power, of course.

Imagine you found an employee (we'll call him Sam) who couldn't care less about maternity leave but cared dearly about getting the company to sponsor a softball league. If you yourself had no strong opinions about softball leagues, the two of you could logroll a coalition. You would support Sam's initiatives on company softball leagues in exchange for Sam's support of your proposed changes to the company's maternity-leave policy. Both proposals would have the strength of two people behind them even though only one employee was interested in each proposal. Logrolls are coalitions that produce strange organizational bedfellows.

Notice that there are two important differences between compromise coalitions and logrolls. In a logroll, you can preserve the integrity of your original interests—you may not have to compromise your suggested changes to the company's maternity-leave policy. On the other hand, in a logroll you may find yourself supporting some pretty strange initiatives to pay back the support you received. The cost of joining a compromise coalition is the compromise of your initiative; the cost of joining a logroll coalition is your obligation to support issues in the future in which you have no interest. Both forms of coalitions have costs, although the costs differ.

Given the costs of joining a coalition, it should not be surprising that some researchers claim that coalitions never will be larger than necessary to make things happen. If it takes 51 votes to pass a resolution in the U.S. Senate, most winning coalitions should have exactly 51 members. Certainly this makes sense. There are costs (compromises or obligations) to adding members to a coalition. Once the coalition has amassed enough power to accomplish its goals, what reason could there be for enduring the costs of adding new members?

Unfortunately, research results do not support this view. Instead, winning coalitions often have many more members than needed to pass a resolution or affect change. There are three reasons why winning coalitions are usually larger than necessary: insurance, implementation, and goodwill.

**Insurance**   The exercise of power in an organization is an uncertain enterprise. In the U.S. Senate, it is clear how many votes are needed to pass a resolution. There are 100 senators, so a majority of 51 votes will do. In most organizations, however, the exercise of power is not a matter of majority vote. The manager who wants to get the maternity-leave policy changed needs to put pressure on the "higher-ups," but how *much* pressure? Are two supportive division heads enough to affect major changes? Are six division heads too many? Often it is difficult to determine. What is not so difficult to determine is that the costs of amassing too little power (and not getting anything accomplished for

Unions are the classic form of coalition. An individual worker would gain little ground with management by threatening to walk out on strike. However, a similar threat made by an entire work force allied together through a union carries tremendous clout.

your trouble) are much worse than the costs of amassing too much (and compromising or obligating yourself a little more than necessary).

Furthermore, power does have a funny way of changing sides. Ideas that seemed good in closed discussions may not sound good anymore to some coalition members when it comes time to take a public stance. Thus, a more-than-winning coalition has a little slack (more amassed power than necessary) to guard against eleventh-hour desertions.

**Implementation**   We can think of the use of power as being a two-step process: getting a proposal accepted and implementing the accepted proposal. Even after the winning coalition has won—that is, gotten its proposal accepted—that coalition still must implement the proposal. The biggest problem with putting together a minimally winning coalition to get a proposal accepted is that it leaves a maximally losing minority in the organization for the implementation stage. As sociologist Lloyd Bucher has noted, "Most of the opposition to an idea is worked through . . . or else the proposal dies."[16] If those organization members not on the winning coalition are dissatisfied with the winning proposal, they can (and will) use their own sources of power to prevent its successful implementation. Thus, a minimally winning coalition may win the battle but lose the war.

An obvious way to avoid trouble during implementation is to continue generating support for a proposal by adding members to the coalition even *after* it is big enough to win. Continuing to compromise and logroll with additional organization members builds consensus support in the organization, and thereby heads off opposition that might occur later

[16]R. Bucher, "Social Process and Power in Medical School," in *Power in Organizations*, ed. M. N. Zald (Nashville, Tenn.: Vanderbilt University Press, 1970): 3–48.

during implementation of the winning proposal. This prevents the battle won at proposal acceptance from being fought all over again during proposal implementation.

**Goodwill**   Just as it is important to remember that getting a proposal accepted is only half the battle, it is also important to remember that in an organization there is always another deal. Whatever a coalition wins today, it can lose tomorrow. Again, the problem with a minimally winning coalition is that it leaves a maximally losing minority. If there is something to be gained by being on the winning side—part of the "spoils," or perhaps just the sense of being part of the winning team—allowing unnecessary members in the winning coalition can generate some very useful goodwill:

> In any ongoing institution, the ability to get important things done is dependent upon maintaining a reservoir of goodwill. The person who fights every issue as though it were vital exhausts his resources including, most especially, the patience and goodwill of those on whom he has to depend to get things done. Therefore, it should be considered neither surprising nor immoral that, when an issue is of low importance the sensible individual may use it to build goodwill for the future, or pay off past obligations, by going along with some individual for whom the issue is of high importance.[17]

This suggests that even after a coalition has the minimally needed power to win, it may want to court additional members to secure their goodwill for *future* deals. In effect, being on the winning team is a resource that the minimally winning coalition can offer other organization members in exchange for future support. The comments above also suggest that logrolling often builds up a reservoir of goodwill. If you are willing to support someone else's concerns that seem trivial to you, in exchange you can expect future support on issues important to you.

## CONSEQUENCES OF THE USE OF POWER

Two major problems surface when we consider the consequences of using power in organizations. The first has to do with how the use of power affects perceptions of power holders. The second is the addictiveness of power.

## PERCEPTIONS OF POWER USERS

Social scientist D. J. Moberg has noted that it is critical that the objects of power plays not attribute the behaviors of powerholders to self-serving motives.[18] Ingratiation, for instance, is particularly ineffective in evoking

[17]*The Study of Policy Formation*, eds. R. Bauer and K. Gergen (New York: Free Press, 1968).

[18]D. J. Moberg, "Organizational Politics: Perspectives from Attribution Theory" Paper presented at the annual meetings of the American Institute of Decision Sciences, Chicago, 1977.

feelings of obligation when it is an obvious attempt to do so. Similarly, the relationship between the powerful and the powerless often depends more on the way power is used than on its outcomes.

Toni Falbo explored this problem by asking 141 students each to write an essay entitled, "How I Get My Way."[19] The essays were scored for the use of 16 general power tactics, shown in Figure 8–5. Each student was rated by other students on six dimensions: consideration, friendliness, quality of self-expression, honesty, desirability as a participant (in another discussion group), and liking. Falbo determined statistically how the use of each power tactic influenced others' perceptions of the user.

Some of the results of Falbo's study are shown in Figure 8–6 on page 358. Falbo found that her power tactics could be described by two major dimensions: direct/indirect and rational/nonrational tactics. The direct/indirect dimension is concerned with whether the influence attempt is oriented toward changing the individual (direct) or getting the individual to *choose* to change (indirect); the rational-nonrational dimension is concerned with whether the influence attempt entails providing good reasons for the change (rational) or not (nonrational). In general, Falbo found that power users who used rational and indirect tactics such as bargaining and persuasion were perceived much more favorably.

A major limitation of Falbo's work is that it measured only *perceptions* of power users. It is entirely possible that direct and nonrational power tactics may be tremendously effective in the short run. However, if such tactics cause negative perceptions of the powerholder, in the long run they can spell only disaster. Thus, McClelland's negative side of power eventually may have negative consequences for the power user as well.

ADDICTIVENESS OF POWER

The second major problem with the use of power concerns its addictiveness. This problem is described quite well in the observations of two anthropologists in the primitive Indian village of Karimpur:

> If you were to take one of the most harmless men in the village and put him in the watchman's place, he would be a rascal within six months . . ..
> The sense of power and sudden popularity which a man experiences on finding himself an agent of power is in itself a danger.[20]

This transformation occurs in a series of steps. First, the availability of power leads to its use. Second, the use of power then fuels a perception of control over others, often eclipsing any realization of the *shared* resource dependence of all social exchanges. Third, this perception of control in turn leads power users to view themselves as more worthy and others as less worthy of taking control. Finally, this leads power users to

[19]T. Falbo, "Multidimensional Scaling of Power Strategies," *Journal of Personality and Social Psychology* 35 (1977): 537–547.

[20]W. Wiser and C. Wiser, *Behind Mind Walls* (Berkeley: University of California Press, 1967).

**FIGURE 8–5**           Sixteen Strategies for Exercising Power

In an attempt to understand how power users are perceived, Toni Falbo had students write essays about "How I Get My Way." Each of the essays was examined to see which of these 16 power strategies were used, and each student was rated by other students on six dimensions.

| Strategy | Definition | Example |
|---|---|---|
| Assertion | Forcefully asserting one's position | I voice my wishes loudly. |
| Bargaining | Explicit statement about reciprocating favors and making other two-way exchanges | I tell her that I'll do something for her if she'll do something for me. |
| Compromise | Both agent and target give up part of their desired goals in order to obtain some of them | More often than not we come to some sort of compromise, if there is a disagreement. |
| Deceit | Attempts to fool the target into agreeing by the use of flattery or lies | I get my way by doing an amount of fast talking and sometimes by some white lies. |
| Emotion-agent | Agent alters own facial expression | I put on a sweet face. I try to look sincere. |
| Emotion-target | Agent attempts to alter emotions of target | I try to put him in a good mood. |
| Evasion | Doing what one wants by avoiding the person who would disapprove | I got to read novels at work as long as the boss never saw me doing it. |
| Expertise | Claiming to have superior knowledge or skill | I tell them I have a lot of experience with such matters. |
| Fait accompli | Openly doing what one wants without avoiding the target | I do what I want anyway. |
| Hinting | Not openly stating what one wants; indirect attempts at influencing others | I drop hints. I subtly bring up a point. |
| Persistence | Continuing in one's influence attempts or repeating one's point | I reiterate my point. I keep going despite all obstacles. |
| Persuasion | Simple statements about using persuasion, convincing, or coaxing | I get my way by convincing others that my way is best. |
| Reason | Any statement about using reason or rational argument to influence others | I argue logically. I tell all the reasons why my plan is best. |
| Simple Statement | Without supporting evidence or threats, matter-of-factly stating one's desires | I simply tell him what I want. |
| Thought manipulation | Making the target think that the agent's way is the target's own idea | I usually try to get my way by making the other person feel that it is his idea. |
| Threat | Stating that negative consequences will occur if the agent's plan is not accepted | I'll tell him I will never speak to him again if he doesn't do what I want. |

Source: Toni Falbo, "Multidimensional Scaling of Power Strategies," *Journal of Personality and Social Psychology* 8 (1977): pp. 537–547.

**FIGURE 8–6**          Relationship between Power Strategies and Peer Ratings

The results of Falbo's study provide a glimpse of how different power tactics are perceived. Falbo analyzed 16 power strategies along two dimensions: (1) the directness of the influence attempt and (2) the extent to which the influence attempt involved rational reasoning as opposed to threats or emotional appeals. In general, Falbo found that indirect, rational strategies such as bargaining were perceived most favorably.

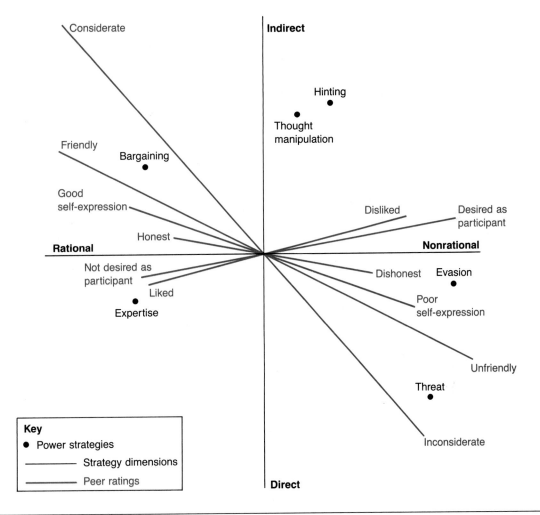

Source: Toni Falbo, "Multidimensional Scaling of Power Strategies," *Journal of Personality and Social Psychology* 8 (1977): pp. 537–547.

believe that their use of power is justified and appropriate, and that others are incapable of self-control or governance.[21]

In effect, a power user comes to see the use of power as appropriate and even necessary because others are weak and unworthy, even when the source of the power is in the resource-dependence relationship. Often this distorted belief that others are unworthy encourages the power user to use more direct and nonrational power tactics, such as coercion. These tactics invoke angry reactions from others, and the demise of the power user often follows. Thus, when the addictiveness of power causes the powerholder to lose sight of the symmetry of resource dependencies, the emergence of the dark side of the power user leads to the loss of power as well.

## SUMMARY

Power is a cornerstone of organizational behavior. Power is a form of social exchange in which the resource dependencies of two individuals allow one to change, influence, or control the beliefs or actions of the other. In a power play, both sides receive something. The more powerful person simply receives more for less. Slack refers to the overabundance of a resource, which insulates an individual from power plays by another.

Power arises from the control of a variety of resources. Reward and coercion power are the basic resources. Expert, legitimate, referent, and task-interdependence power all refer to different organizational forms of control over rewards and punishments.

Even the lowliest member of an organization has access to some forms of power. Tactics of upward influence include effort, ingratiation, and the development of expertise critical to the organization.

The most important power tactic for upward influence, however, is coalition formation. Coalitions such as unions represent the gathering and sharing of power in organizations so that relatively powerless individuals can achieve more than they could through their individual power alone.

Certain power tactics—particularly direct and nonrational influence attempts—are poorly received in organizations. Their use may destroy relationships and eventually undermine the power of the powerholder. Unfortunately, their use also is fostered by perceptual changes that accompany the acquisition of power. Powerholders often lose sight of the symmetry of resource dependencies in power exchanges. When this happens, they may be more likely to revert to more direct and nonrational power tactics. Thus, the inappropriate use of power may be self-limiting.

---

[21]D. Kipnis, *The Powerholders* (Chicago: University of Chicago Press, 1976).

# KEY TERMS

**Alternative sources**  Other ways to fulfill a resource dependency, thereby reducing an individual's dependence on any one source; a form of slack.

**Charisma**  Persuasiveness derived from personal characteristics desired or admired by a reference group.

**Coalition**  Collection of individuals who band together to combine their individual sources of power.

**Coercion**  Threat of punishment for not engaging in appropriate behaviors.

**Compromise coalition**  Coalition in which all members are interested in the same issues but each is flexible enough about specifics to make sure that the coalition gets its way.

**Expert power**  Individual power based on the possession of special information, knowledge, or ability.

**Extrinsic rewards**  Rewards like money or praise provided in exchange for appropriate behaviors.

**Ingratiation**  Doing nice things for someone in the hope of creating a sense of obligation in the individual to return the favor.

**Legitimate power**  Individual power based on individuals' authority to control the behavior of others for their own good and for the good of a social system.

**Logrolling**  Form of coalition in which participants lend each other power so that each can pursue interests not shared by other coalition members.

**Milgram study**  Stanley Milgram's classic experiments at Yale University in the early 1960s that examined the extent to which volunteer participants would obey, even if the demands of authority violated their moral responsibilities.

**Need for power**  Desire to control or to have an impact on others; David McClelland's research revealed that it is high in individuals who are competitive and aggressive, who desire the outward trappings of power such as prestige possessions, who prefer action situations, and who join a number of groups.

**Political conflict**  Occurs when different members of an organization pursue conflicting *personal* (rather than organizational) agendas.

**Referent power**  Individual power based on a high level of identification with, admiration of, or respect for the powerholder.

**Resource dependence**  Individual's need for resources, which exposes the individual to influence.

**Reward power**  Individual power based on the control of resources valued by another; the opposite of coercive power.

**Stockpile**  Resource set aside for future use, such as money put into savings for a "rainy day"; a form of slack.

**Task interdependence**  Power accruing to a particular job or group of jobs in an organization when two or more employees must depend on each other to complete assigned tasks.

**Theory of social exchange**
Theory suggesting that social behavior is an exchange of material and nonmaterial goods (such as approval and prestige), and that in relationships people continually monitor the rewards and costs to work out balanced exchanges.

DISCUSSION
QUESTIONS

1.  What sources of power were available to J. Edgar Hoover? Could these sources of power have made him even more powerful than a U.S. president?

2.  Imagine that the students and the instructor in a university course are unhappy with the way the course is going. What sources of power are available to university students to change things in the classroom? What sources of power are available to the instructor? Are the students or the instructor more powerful in this setting?

3.  What does it mean to say that *all* exercises of power are examples of exchanges? When a supervisor gives an order to a subordinate in an organizational setting, what is being exchanged?

4.  In what ways can the exercise of power undermine its future use?

5.  Why are coalitions such an important way for lower-level participants in organizations to mobilize the power they have?

6.  What is meant by the phrase, "those who govern do so at the consent of those governed"? What source of power does this describe?

7.  Economics suggests that coalitions should always be just big enough to win. Why in practice are winning coalitions almost always bigger than the minimum necessary to win?

8.  What sources of power depend on the existence of an organization? What sources of power are personal? What does it mean to say that reward power and coercion are the two *basic* forms of power?

IF YOU
WANT TO
KNOW
MORE

Stanford University Professor Jeff Pfeffer provides a good general discussion of power in his book, *Power in Organizations* (Marshfield, Mass.: Pitman, 1981). Included is a particularly good chapter on the use of coalitions to mobilize power. A good book of readings on power and influence is *Organizational Influence Processes,* by Robert Allen and Lyman Porter (Glenview, Ill.: Scott, Foresman, 1983).

An excellent discussion of ways in which lower-level members of organizations can gain power is provided in an article by David Mechanic entitled, "Sources of Power of Lower Participants in Complex Organizations" (*Administrative Sciences Quarterly* 7, 1962). A. O. Hirschmann, in his book *Exit, Voice, and Loyalty* (Cambridge, Mass.: Harvard University Press, 1972) also discusses the sources of power available at all levels of organizations and the consequences of their use.

Stanley Milgram's studies on obedience to authority are described in detail in his book, *Obedience to Authority* (New York: Harper & Row, 1974).

Two classic articles on different types of power are: J. R. P. French and B. H. Raven's piece, "Bases of Social Power," in *Studies in Social Power,* edited by Dorwin Cartwright (Ann Arbor: University of Michigan, 1959); and H. C. Kelman's article, "Processes of Opinion Change" (*Public Opinion Quarterly* 25, 1961, 57–78).

The notion of power as a social-exchange process is explained in detail in Peter Blau's book, *Exchange and Power in Social Life* (New York: Wiley, 1964).

ON YOUR
OWN

### Social Power Inventory

*Introduction*   The questionnaire in this exercise is designed to measure your predisposition to be responsive to certain forms of social power. In responding to these questions, you will learn something about the types of power that you are most responsive to, or least responsive to, depending on who is exercising the power.

### Procedure

*Step 1: 5 Minutes*   Identify three *different* people who have influence over you. One must be a teacher, a second may be a roommate or spouse, a third may be a boss. Others might include friends, business associates, parents, or people that you negotiate with regularly. Specify the three people you have identified:

Source: Questionnaire developed by David W. Jamieson and Kenneth W. Thomas, in R. J. Lewicki and J. A. Litterer, *Negotiation: Readings, Exercises, and Cases* (Homewood, Ill.: Richard D. Irwin, 1985), 490–493.

- Person 1:
- Person 2:
- Person 3:

*Step 2: 20 Minutes*   For *each* of the three people work completely through the following questionnaire with that person in mind. For each of the 30 questions, pick A or B depending on which one of the two best describes the way that they affect you. Make sure to *pick one* even if neither is a very good answer.

*Step 3: 30 Minutes*   Your instructor will hand out a scoring key. Follow the key in order to score your questionnaire.

**Person 1  Person 2  Person 3**

———  ———  ———   1. A. I sometimes do what that person says in order to get something I want.
B. I sometimes have to go along to avoid trouble.

———  ———  ———   2. A. That person always convinces me with his/her reasoning.
B. I sometimes do things for that person because I admire him/her.

———  ———  ———   3. A. That person might do good things for me in return.
B. I don't know as much about it as that person does.

———  ———  ———   4. A. That person's suggestions always make sense.
B. I could receive things I want from that person.

———  ———  ———   5. A. I want that person to like me.
B. I often feel that it is legitimate for that person to influence my behavior.

———  ———  ———   6. A. I take his/her word for things.
B. I sometimes try to avoid trouble by doing what is asked.

———  ———  ———   7. A. That person has the right to tell me what to do.
B. That person is able to harm me in some way.

———  ———  ———   8. A. That person knows better.
B. I will receive something I want.

———  ———  ———   9. A. That person's friendship is important to me.
B. That person seems fairly intelligent.

———  ———  ———   10. A. The reasoning of the request usually agrees with my way of thinking.
B. That person is in a position to legitimately ask things of me.

———  ———  ———   11. A. I will receive something I want.
B. I sometimes go along with that person to make him/her happy.

| | | | |
|---|---|---|---|
| \_\_\_\_\_ | \_\_\_\_\_ | \_\_\_\_\_ | 12. A. That person's knowledge usually makes him/her right.<br>B. I feel that person has the right to ask things of me. |
| \_\_\_\_\_ | \_\_\_\_\_ | \_\_\_\_\_ | 13. A. I want that person to like me.<br>B. I sometimes have to go along to avoid trouble. |
| \_\_\_\_\_ | \_\_\_\_\_ | \_\_\_\_\_ | 14. A. I would sometimes like to get things from that person.<br>B. Sometimes I feel that person might do something unpleasant to those who do not do what is suggested. |
| \_\_\_\_\_ | \_\_\_\_\_ | \_\_\_\_\_ | 15. A. That person's suggestions always make sense.<br>B. I do what is asked to keep that person from taking actions which could be unpleasant for me. |
| \_\_\_\_\_ | \_\_\_\_\_ | \_\_\_\_\_ | 16. A. That person should be listened to.<br>B. That person's friendship is important to me. |
| \_\_\_\_\_ | \_\_\_\_\_ | \_\_\_\_\_ | 17. A. That person can do things which I would not like.<br>B. That person always knows what he/she is doing. |
| \_\_\_\_\_ | \_\_\_\_\_ | \_\_\_\_\_ | 18. A. I sometimes have to go along in order to get things I need.<br>B. I often feel that it is legitimate for that person to influence my behavior. |
| \_\_\_\_\_ | \_\_\_\_\_ | \_\_\_\_\_ | 19. A. The request is sometimes appropriate, considering that person's position.<br>B. At times, that person's suggestions make sense. |
| \_\_\_\_\_ | \_\_\_\_\_ | \_\_\_\_\_ | 20. A. I sometimes do so because I feel that person is my friend.<br>B. That person's expertise makes him/her more likely to be right. |
| \_\_\_\_\_ | \_\_\_\_\_ | \_\_\_\_\_ | 21. A. That person has the right to tell me what to do.<br>B. That person could do something unpleasant to me. |
| \_\_\_\_\_ | \_\_\_\_\_ | \_\_\_\_\_ | 22. A. That person is able to do things which benefit me.<br>B. That person always convinces me with his/her reasoning. |
| \_\_\_\_\_ | \_\_\_\_\_ | \_\_\_\_\_ | 23. A. That other person's position permits him/her to require things of me.<br>B. That person's knowledge usually makes him/her right. |
| \_\_\_\_\_ | \_\_\_\_\_ | \_\_\_\_\_ | 24. A. I trust that person's judgment.<br>B. I agree with what that person says. |
| \_\_\_\_\_ | \_\_\_\_\_ | \_\_\_\_\_ | 25. A. Sometimes I feel that person might do something which is unpleasant to those who do not do what is suggested.<br>B. I always do what is asked because that person's ideas are compelling. |

_____ _____ _____ 26. A. That person might help me get what I
                            want.
                       B. It would not be proper sometimes for
                            me to do otherwise.

_____ _____ _____ 27. A. That person can make things
                            uncomfortable for me if I don't
                            comply.
                       B. I do what is asked to make that person
                            happy.

_____ _____ _____ 28. A. I would like to be his/her friend.
                       B. That person can help me.

_____ _____ _____ 29. A. That person always gives me good
                            reasons for doing it.
                       B. I sometimes do what is asked to gain
                            that person's friendship.

_____ _____ _____ 30. A. What that person says seems to be
                            appropriate.
                       B. That person has had a lot of
                            experience and usually knows best.

## Discussion Questions

1. What was your score for each of the different forms of power?

### Scoring Key

|          | Expert | Legitimate | Coercive | Reward | Referent | Informational |
|----------|--------|------------|----------|--------|----------|---------------|
| **Person 1** |        |            |          |        |          |               |
| **Person 2** |        |            |          |        |          |               |
| **Person 3** |        |            |          |        |          |               |

2. Find others in the class who rated the same *type* of person (teacher, parent, roommate, and so on). How do your scores compare to theirs in terms of the types that are most and least influential? Why do you suppose that this is so?

3. How do the *situations* that these people are in—for example, their objectives and your objectives, the differences in your ages, the kind of resources they control and you want, etc.—affect the kind of power they are likely to use, and the kind of power that has impact on you? Explain.

4. If you were the powerful party in these situations, would you try to use different forms of power from those now being used? Explain.

5. As a power user yourself, which forms of power are you most comfortable using? Least comfortable? In which situations?

CLOSING CASE
FOR CHAPTER 8

THE MANAGER'S MEMO

FROM: E. Grainger, Vice President

TO:    F. Blackstone, President

RE:    Potentially Damaging Resignation

Pat McDonnell has just given me his resignation, effective in two weeks. Because Pat was responsible for designing the high-powered telescope we sell to the Pentagon, his departure will be a great loss for the company.

I am particularly concerned because the Defense Department has just asked us to submit a bid to produce a miniaturized version of our telescope. In the future, the miniaturized version will be the only version purchased by the military. I believe that two other companies also are bidding on this contract.

As you know, the Defense Department represents over 90 percent of our business. I am afraid that, without Pat, we will be unable to come up with an acceptable design and will therefore lose our major customer.

Pat has hinted that for a substantial raise plus a stock interest in the company, he might be willing to reconsider. To me, this sounds vaguely like blackmail. I find his tactics unpleasantly coercive. Perhaps it's time we ceased being a one-product, one-customer company. What do you advise?

CASE DISCUSSION
QUESTIONS

Assume you are the president, and write a response to the vice president's memorandum. What power does Pat McDonnell have relative to the company? What power does the company have relative to the Pentagon? Use your answers to these questions and your knowledge about power to guide you in considering the alternatives available to the company.

# Group Decision Making

**The Nature of Group Decision Making**
Why Use Groups?
Types of Group Decisions
The Participation Controversy

**Problems with Group Decision Making**
Greater Complexity
Groupthink
Choice Shift Effects

**Solutions in Group Decision Making**
When to Use Group Decision Making
How to Use Group Decision Making
*Focus on Nominal Group Technique: ARA Services*
*Focus on Quality Circles: Honeywell and General Dynamics*
Why Group Decision Making Works
*International Focus on Group Decision Making: Making Decisions in Japanese Companies*

## LAUNCHING THE EAGLE

Adopting a remote, managerial point of view, you could say that Eagle was a project where a local system of management worked as it should: competition for resources creating within a team inside a company an entrepreneurial spirit, which was channeled in the right direction by constraints sent down from the top. But it seems more accurate to say that a group of engineers got excited about building a computer. Whether it arose by corporate bungling or by design, the opportunity had to be grasped. In this sense, the initiative belonged entirely to Tom West and the members of his team at Data General. What's more, they did the work, both with uncommon spirit and for reasons that in a frankly commercial setting, seemed remarkably pure.

. . . a large percentage of engineers in America are not content with their jobs. Among the reasons cited are the nature of the jobs themselves and the restricted ways in which they are managed. Among the terms used to describe their malaise are declining technical challenge, misutilization, limited freedom of action, and tight control of working patterns. No one who made it through the Eagle project could in fairness have raised these objections. The work was divided, but it was not cut to ribbons. Everyone got responsibility for some important part of the machine, many got to choose their piece, and each portion required more than routine labor. The team's members were manipulated, to be sure, and the unspoken rules of the group were Darwinian, but many of those who made it through declared they had been given as much freedom as they could have wished for . . .

Now it was done. The Eclipse Group and the many others who had worked on the machine—including, especially, Software and Diagnostics—had created 4,096 lines of microcode, which fit into a volume about eight inches thick; diagnostic programs amounting to thousands of lines of code; over 200,000 lines of system software;

367

several hundred pages of flow-
charts; about 240 pages of sche-
matics; hundreds and hundreds of
engineering changes from the de-
bugging; twenty hours of videotape to describe the new machine;
and now a couple of functioning
computers in blue-and-white cases,
plus orders for many more on the
way. Already you could see that
the engineers who had participated fully would be looking back
on this experience a long time
hence. It would be something un-
forgettable in their working lives.
All this, at last, was no canard.

Source: Tracy Kidder, *The Soul of the New Machine* (Boston: Little, Brown, 1981).

## THE NATURE OF GROUP DECISION MAKING

Tom West and Data General were clearly the beneficiaries of the positive effect of individuals coming together as a group to solve problems and make decisions. Groups such as the one at Data General are productive above and beyond the ability of their individual members. What is it about groups that can give rise to such an extraordinary level of performance?

### WHY USE GROUPS?

Groups have some obvious advantages over individuals when it comes to making decisions. One is that groups are composed of a number of individuals with differing perspectives who can contribute ideas and suggestions. Unlike a lone individual, groups have the potential for **resource pooling.** There is obviously more information in the group than there is in any of its members. Even if one member knows much more than anyone else, the unique information of less-skilled individuals can fill in the knowledge gaps of other group members. For example, a worker on an assembly line could tell management how other workers are likely to respond to a new fringe-benefit package.

Group members can stimulate and encourage each other. This mutual influence process is called **synergy.** Individuals working alone on a problem may persist in viewing the problem in a particular way. This mindset may be wrong and, thus, the individual will fail to solve the problem. Individuals in a group have the same tendency, but the number of different approaches may knock group members out of their solution ruts. The information contributed by a member of my group may catalyze my thinking or alter its direction, indirectly aiding my contributions to the group's solution.

Because of the number of different skills found in groups, individual members have the luxury of working on problems or parts of a problem. Groups offer the opportunity for specialization of labor, which is unavailable to individual decision makers.

The benefits of group decision making are not limited solely to the solution-generation stage. Many solutions depend upon the commit-

Organizational planning provides an ideal setting for participative decision making. When line managers are encouraged to provide planning inputs, this increases the likelihood that the organization's long-range planning will realistically reflect operational limitations. It also provides line managers a large measure of satisfaction and respect.

ment of those involved for their successful implementation. Because more people are involved in group decision making, implementation is easier because a larger number of people feel responsible for making the solution work. It is even possible that a low-quality solution that has good group commitment can be more effective than a high-quality solution that lacks such commitment.[1]

Not only are group decisions more accepted than individual decisions, they are likely to be better understood. Decisions made by an individual must be carried out by others. Thus, individual decisions have an additional step—that of relaying the decision to the implementing parties. Failure to convey the solution effectively (poor communication) can reduce its attractiveness and create greater problems than the one the solution was designed to solve. For example, after attending a seminar on motivating employees, a company CEO may decide to replace the current seniority-based compensation system with a merit-based system. Regardless of the wisdom of this decision, employees may believe that the company is just trying to make them work harder for less money—that the company really does not care about them, only about its bottom line. Further, because it is difficult to implement almost any solution, the solution that is imposed from above does not have the added benefit of "ownership." The only person to whom this particular decision belongs is the CEO of the company. If the decision had resulted from a group interaction, the sense of ownership would be much more widespread. The result of the CEO's decision may be lowered morale and reduced productivity, even though the CEO intended to give the workers more direct rewards for productivity.

If the CEO had included others in the decision-making process, the likelihood of this type of failure would have been reduced. The

[1]N. R. F. Maier, "Assets and Liabilities in Group Problem Solving: The Need for an Integrative Function," *Psychological Review* 74 (1967): 239–249.

individuals who would be implementing the system would understand not only why the particular compensation package was chosen, but also why other potential solutions were not chosen. The general assumption that the behavior of the CEO is arbitrary or adversarial would have less impact, because those involved in the decision would know how this particular choice was reached.

## TYPES OF GROUP DECISIONS

**When Are Many Heads Better Than One?**   Given the advantages of group decision making suggested above and the number of skilled individuals in a typical organization, perhaps all decisions should be group decisions. Yet many organizational decisions are made by one or two key individuals. Why is there such a wide gap between the benefits of group decision making and its use? Let's examine exactly which types of decisions can benefit from the unique contributions of groups.

Group decision making is usually superior to individual decision making in tasks requiring judgments about uncertain events. These types of decisions are primarily concerned with quality outcomes and usually have the following characteristics:

1. The potential benefits are substantial, the costs of error are high, and it is difficult to reverse or salvage a poor decision after action has begun.
2. Information is incomplete or uncertain.
3. Many feasible alternatives exist.
4. Identifying the optimal alternative is difficult.
5. Feedback about results from the chosen alternative will not be available until long after it has been implemented.[2]

When solving a problem involves generating many or unique ideas, recalling information accurately, and evaluating ambiguous or uncertain situations, then groups will likely outperform individuals. If group members can perform their jobs relatively independently of each other, individual decision making is probably more appropriate. If, however, group members are interdependent and must cooperate with each other, then effective performance will hinge on their ability to coordinate their decisions.[3]

While groups have been shown to produce judgmental decisions of generally higher quality than individuals,[4] the need for high-quality decisions is not sufficient in and of itself to require group involvement.

[2]D. E. Zand, "Collateral Organizations: A New Change Strategy," *Journal of Applied Behavioral Science* 10 (1974): 63–89.

[3]M. Sashkin, "Changing toward Participative Management Approaches: A Model and Methods," *Academy of Management Review* 1 (1976): 75–86.

[4]J. K. Murnighan, "Group Decision Making: What Strategy Should You Use?" *Management Review* (Spring 1981): 55–62.

A ~~second~~ factor to be considered is the need for acceptance of the decision for its successful implementation. As mentioned in the previous section, ~~a major benefit of group decision making is the greater acceptance by organizational members of the decision~~.

THE
PARTICIPATION
CONTROVERSY

Another way of deciding whether to use groups or individuals to solve problems is to ask the more general question of whether or not to let employees participate in decision making. ~~The decision to involve others in the decision-making process depends on a number of factors, such as the abilities of the group members, their willingness to search for and share information, and the nature of the decision to be made~~. In fact, if we ignore these factors, research indicates that in terms of productivity, there is no benefit to participative decision making. That is, participation has no effect on productivity in more than 50 percent of the studies. However, participation does have a positive impact on satisfaction, regardless of the existence of these factors, in more than 60 percent of the studies.[5]

It should be noted that ~~participation can be voluntary or involuntary, direct and indirect, and can vary in degree, content, and scope~~. For example, participation can be forced through laws, governmental regulation, or decree. Once a union is certified, then both management and labor must participate in contract negotiations. Before creating policies, many governmental regulations require citizen input. Thus, because of the nature of our political system, we must at times participate in its decision making, regardless of our unique desires or preferences.

Participation also may be direct or indirect. As members of a quality circle, individuals have the opportunity to make their views known directly. Alternatively, when each of us votes to elect representatives (who, in turn, participate directly in decision making), we are indirectly participating in the decision-making process.

Finally, ~~participation may be formal or informal~~. If an employee is elected to represent other workers on a work-safety committee, the employee's participation in the decision-making process is formal. However, if the supervisor asks the employee's opinion on a particular work-safety issue, that participation is informal—based not upon the employee's position, but rather upon his or her personal relationship with the supervisor.

The complexity of participation may, in part, account for its poor impact on performance in studies. Current research has suggested that participation is very likely *not* to work in some situations. For example, a survey of senior business executives showed that over three-fourths believed that (1) they knew what had to be done and (2) they had the

[5]E. A. Locke and D. M. Schweiger, "Participation in Decision Making: One More Look," in *Research in Organizational Behavior, vol. 1*, ed. B. M. Staw, 265–339.

right to make organizational decisions. In such situations, when management sees little benefit in employee participation in decision making, it is unlikely that requiring participation will work.[6]

Employee characteristics also influence the usefulness of participation. If employees have no knowledge of or interest in a decision, their input will probably do little to improve its outcome. Expecting employees to participate in decisions about which they have little knowledge or concern can also increase their sense of frustration. In fact, it seems that too much participation can lead to lower performance, stress, and dissatisfaction.[7]

## PROBLEMS WITH GROUP DECISION MAKING

Participative decision making has great potential for improving the decision outcomes of organizations, but it also has a number of inherent pitfalls. One obvious pitfall is that groups take considerably more time to reach a decision than do individuals. The additional time is required because group decision making involves increased information-processing demands and requires decision rules and more complex interpersonal processes.[8]

## GREATER COMPLEXITY

**Information-Processing Demands**   While any decision involves complex processes, the complexity is multiplied when more parties are involved. More decision makers may mean greater opportunities for creative solutions, but they also generate greater cognitive demands on each member of the group.

**Decision Rules**   Individuals in groups must decide on rules concerning how dissenting opinions will be incorporated in a group decision. Decision rules such as requiring consensus, majority rule, and so on, influence the decision-making process.

Groups can make decisions in a number of ways.[9] Groups can make decisions by a lack of response. Alternatives for which no one voices a preference are dropped from consideration. The one idea for which there is support is the one accepted. A second way in which group decisions can be reached is by authority rule. The leader of the group makes a decision based upon the group's discussion. Note that here, the

---

[6]R. Krishnan, "Democratic Participation in Decision Making by Employees in American Corporations," *Academy of Management Journal* 17 (1974): 339–347.

[7]G. Hespe and T. Wall, "The Demand for Participation among Employees," *Human Relations* 29 (1976): 411–429.

[8]M. H. Bazerman, E. A. Mannix, and L. L. Thompson, "Groups as Mixed Motive Negotiations," in *Advances in Group Processes: Theory and Research, vol. 5,* eds. E. J. Lawler and B. Markovsky (Greenwich, Conn.: JAI Press, 1988).

[9]L. L. Thompson, E. A. Mannix, and M. H. Bazerman (in press) "Group Negotiation: Effects of Decision Rule, Agenda, and Aspiration," *Journal of Personality and Social Psychology.*

group plays only an advisory role to the decision maker. A third way in which group decisions are made is by the minority. A small subset of the group's membership may be able to convince other group members to accept an alternative it favors. This is also known as "railroading" a particular decision. A common way groups reach decisions is through majority rule. The primary mechanism for majority rule is the vote. The problem here is that there are clear winners and losers. The losers may feel left out and without a say in the direction of the group. Their lack of commitment to a group's decision may lead to difficulties in its implementation. The last two mechanisms by which groups can make decisions are consensus or unanimity. While similar in outcome—all group members accept the final decision—consensus acknowledges that there may be some dissension among members of the group. By contrast, unanimity occurs when all group members agree on the course of action to be taken.

Each of these decision-making rules has its benefits and its costs. If a group member knows that to get a particular solution to a problem, all the group member needs do is convince the majority, that member's strategy is likely to be very different than if all members of the group must be convinced (unanimity).[10]

**Complex Interpersonal Processes**   The greater the number of individuals involved in the decision process, the wider the range of skills, abilities, and knowledge available to produce an effective solution. However, the larger the group membership, the greater the potential number of interpersonal relationships. Subgroups and coalitions are more likely to form, and the potential for conflict is greater.

Earlier we indicated that decisions requiring judgments about uncertainty or requiring widespread acceptance are prime candidates for group decision making: the additional complexity involved in getting a group to make the decision is worth the gain in the final decision. However, groups are often required to make a variety of decisions, whether or not the final result merits the group's attention. Consider, for example, the following decision whether or not to go to Abilene.

> The July afternoon in Coleman, Texas, was particularly hot—104 degrees, as measured by the Walgreen's Rexall Ex-Lax temperature gauge. In addition, the wind was blowing fine-grained West Texas topsoil through the house. But the afternoon was still tolerable—even potentially enjoyable. There was a fan going on the back porch; there was cold lemonade; and finally there was entertainment. Dominoes. Perfect for the conditions. The game required little more physical exertion than an occasional mumbled comment, "shuffle 'em," and an unhurried movement of the arm to place the spots in the appropriate perspective on the table. All in all, it had the makings of an agreeable Sunday afternoon in Coleman—that is,

[10]Ibid.

until my father-in-law suddenly said, "Let's get in the car and go to Abilene and have dinner in the cafeteria."

I thought: What, go to Abilene? Fifty-three miles? In a dust storm and heat? In an unairconditioned 1958 Buick?

But my wife chimed in with "Sounds like a great idea. I'd like to go. How about you, Jerry?" Since my own preferences were obviously out of step with the rest I replied, "Sounds good to me," and added, "I just hope your mother wants to go."

"Of course I want to go," said my mother-in-law. "I haven't been to Abilene in a long time."

So into the car and off to Abilene we went. My predictions were fulfilled. The heat was brutal. We were coated with a fine layer of dust that was cemented with perspiration by the time we arrived. The food at the cafeteria provided first-rate testimonial material for antacid commercials.

Some four hours and 106 miles later, we returned to Coleman, hot and exhausted. We sat in front of the fan for a long time in silence. Then, both to be sociable and to break the silence, I said,

"It was a great trip, wasn't it?"

No one spoke.

Finally, my mother-in-law said, with some irritation, "Well, to tell the truth, I really didn't enjoy it much and would rather have stayed here. I just went along because the three of you were so enthusiastic about going. I wouldn't have gone if you all hadn't pressured me into it."

I couldn't believe it. "What do you mean, 'you all'?" I said. "Don't put me in the 'you all' group. I was delighted to be doing what we were doing. I only went to satisfy the rest of you. You're the culprits."

My wife looked shocked. "Don't call me a culprit. You and Daddy and Momma were the ones who wanted to go. I just went along to be sociable and to keep you happy. I would have had to be crazy to go out in heat like that."

Her father entered the conversation abruptly. "Hell!" he said.

He proceeded to expand on what was already absolutely clear. "Listen, I never wanted to go to Abilene. I just thought you might be bored. You visit so seldom I wanted to be sure you enjoyed it. I would have preferred to play another game of dominoes and eat the leftovers in the icebox."

After the outburst of recrimination, we all sat back in silence. Here we were, four reasonably sensible people who, of our own volition, had just taken a 106-mile trip across a godforsaken desert in a furnacelike temperature through a cloudlike dust storm to eat unpalatable food at a hole-in-the-wall cafeteria in Abilene, when none of us had really wanted to go. In fact, to be more accurate, we'd done just the opposite of what we wanted to do. The whole situation simply did not make sense.[11]

Dilemmas such as the one experienced by this family are typical of problems that can derail even the best of work groups. While the foregone resources of taking the trip to Abilene may be minimal, the same factors can work to offset the benefits of groups in making

[11]Jerry Harvey, "Managing Agreements in Organizations: The Abilene Paradox," *Organizational Dynamics* (Summer 1974):63–80. Reprinted by permission of publisher. American Management Association, New York. All rights reserved.

decisions. Two forms of problems associated with group decision making have been identified—groupthink and choice shift effects. Both of these problems result from how groups function. They will be discussed next.

GROUPTHINK

The trip to Abilene is an example of groupthink. First described by Irving Janis, **groupthink** occurs in highly cohesive groups because their members have a tendency to lose their willingness and ability to evaluate one another's ideas critically.[12] Because of this, there is an overemphasis on agreement and consensus and an unwillingness to critically evaluate alternative courses of action. Consider the following organizational example of a trip to Abilene:[13]

> The Ozyx Corporation is a relatively small industrial company whose managers have embarked on a trip to Abilene. The president of Ozyx has hired a consultant to help discover the reasons for the poor profit picture of the company in general and the low morale and productivity of the R&D division in particular. During the process of investigation, the consultant becomes interested in a research project in which the company has invested a sizable portion of its R&D budget.
>
> When the consultant asked about the project in the privacy of their respective offices, the president, vice-president for research, and research manager each describe it as an idea that looks great on paper but will ultimately fail because of the unavailability of the technology required to make it work. Each of them acknowledges that continued support of the project will create cash flow problems that will jeopardize the very existence of the organization.
>
> Furthermore, each has not told the others about these reservations. When asked why, the president says he cannot reveal his true feelings because abandoning the project, which has been widely publicized, would make the company look bad in the press. In addition, it would probably cause the vice-president's ulcer to kick up or cause her to quit "because she has staked her professional reputation on the project's success."
>
> Similarly, the vice-president for research says she cannot let the president or the research manager know her reservations because the president is so committed to it that "I would probably get fired for insubordination if I questioned the project."
>
> Finally, the research manager says he cannot let the president or the vice-president know of his doubts about the project because of their extreme commitment to the project's success. All indicate that, in meetings with one another, they try to maintain an optimistic facade so that the others will not worry unduly about the project. The research director, in particular, admits to writing ambiguous progress reports so the president and the vice-president can "interpret them to suit themselves." In fact, he

[12]Irving Janis, *Victims of Groupthink: A Psychological Study of Foreign Policy Decisions and Fiascos* (Boston: Houghton-Mifflin, 1972).

[13]Harvey, "Making Agreements in Organizations."

The Kennedy administration's ill-advised backing of the Bay of Pigs invasion of Cuba revealed their vulnerability to groupthink. To their credit, their handling of the Cuban Missile Crisis reflected a more mature, unbiased group decision-making process.

says he tends to slant them to the positive side, "given how committed the brass are."

The scent of the Abilene trail wafts from a paneled conference room, where the project budget is being considered for the following fiscal year. In the meeting itself, praises are heaped on the questionable project, and a unanimous decision is made to continue it for yet another year. Symbolically, the organization has boarded a bus to Abilene.

The group described above is having difficulty managing its disagreements. It is in cases such as these that greater conflict and disagreement among the members likely would result in a far superior solution. The benefits of confronting differences of opinion are missing. Instead, the organization has made a unanimous decision that *no one* privately supports.

Examples of groupthink are found throughout our history. The lack of preparedness of the U.S. Naval Forces for the Japanese attack on Pearl Harbor, President Kennedy's handling of the Bay of Pigs, and many of the roads paved for our entry into and continued involvement in the Vietnam War are a few very salient examples. From studying these and other examples of groupthink, Irving Janis has identified a number of symptoms that should signal a potential "groupthink situation" to decision makers. Fortunately, Janis provides managers and other decision makers with some guidelines for avoiding groupthink. His lists of symptoms and guidelines appear in Figure 9–1. As suggested in Chapter 7, cohesiveness is often viewed as a critical group trait. It is an extreme emphasis on cohesiveness (and consensus) that produces groupthink. However, note that not all cohesive groups are equally

**FIGURE 9–1**  Groupthink

Groupthink occurs when the members of a highly cohesive group lose their willingness to evaluate each other's inputs critically. The symptoms of groupthink listed here can be avoided by following several procedural guidelines for appropriate group discussion and choices.

**Symptoms of Groupthink**

- **Illusions of invulnerability:** Members of the group overemphasize the strength of the group and feel that they are beyond criticism or attack. This symptom leads the group to approve risky actions about which individual members might have serious concerns.

- **Illusions of unanimity:** Group members accept consensus prematurely, without testing whether or not all members *really* agree. Silence is often taken for agreement.

- **Illusions of group morality:** Members of the group feel that it is "right" and above reproach by outside members. Thus, members feel no need to debate ethical issues.

- **Stereotyping of the "enemy" as weak, evil, or stupid:** Members do not realistically examine their competitors and oversimplify their motives. The stated aims of outside groups or anticipated reactions of outsiders are not considered.

- **Self-censorship by members:** Members refuse to communicate concerns to others because of fear of disturbing the consensus.

- **Mind-guarding:** Some members take responsibility to ensure that negative feedback does not reach influential group members.

- **Direct pressure:** In the unlikely event that a note of caution or concern is interjected, other members quickly respond with pressure to bring the deviant back into line.

**Guidelines for Avoiding Groupthink**

- Assign the role of critical evaluator to each group member; encourage the sharing of objections.

- Avoid, as the leader, clear statements about your preferred alternative.

- Create subgroups or subcommittees, each working on the same problem.

- Require that members of the group make use of the information available to them through their subordinates, peers, and networks.

- Invite outside experts to observe and evaluate group process and outcome.

- Assign a member to play the devil's advocate role at each meeting.

- Focus on alternative scenarios for the motivation and intentions of competitors.

- Once consensus is reached, reexamine the next (but unchosen) alternative, comparing it to the chosen course of action.

Source: Irving L. Janis, *Groupthink,* 2d ed. (Boston: Houghton-Mifflin, 1982).

vulnerable to groupthink. ~~When the group is cohesive because it functions well, groupthink is less likely to occur. When cohesiveness is based upon the group's attractive social milieu, then groupthink poses a bigger threat.~~[14]

CHOICE SHIFT
EFFECTS

Consider the following situation: You are one of six members of the R&D advisory committee for a large computer manufacturing firm for which you work. During your monthly meeting, your task is to determine which projects are to be funded. One of the decisions that faces your group in tomorrow's meeting is whether or not to fund a $2.2 million request for the development of a 128K memory chip. The product is so far ahead of today's chips that if the company is able to manufacture this chip successfully, there will be a minimum 50 percent return on your investment in the first two years of production. Other projects are also competing for these scarce resource dollars; their expected rate of return runs between 10 percent and 20 percent. What minimum probability for success would you consider necessary to invest the R&D money into the chip-manufacturing project?

Given the advantages of group decision making, should this decision be made by a group or by an individual? That is, which will require a lower probability of success for the computer chip manufacturing project? In such cases, research suggests that ~~groups will behave in a more risky manner than the average individual member of the group.~~[15] Thus, if your individual position is that the probability for success must exceed 25 percent before you are willing to fund this project, it is likely that the group will settle on a lower probability. This is known as the **risky shift.** In fact, both the group as a whole and each individual will be more willing to accept greater levels of risk after the group discussion than prior to it.

Yet groups do not always make risky shifts. In fact, there is documentation of just the opposite occurring—a **cautious shift.** A cautious shift ~~occurs when group members make less risky decisions than the average of the individual members' decisions.~~

While many researchers have proposed mechanisms first to explain risky shift and then later to explain the cautious shift (both are now termed choice shifts), they have focused on two primary explanations: ~~information exchange and social comparison.~~ They ~~suggest that individ-~~uals shift to more extreme positions following group discussion because members holding the dominant view (either risky or cautious) exchange

[14]J. Longley and D. G. Pruitt, "Groupthink: A Critique of Janis's Theory," in *Review of Personality and Social Psychology,* ed. L. Wheeler (Beverly Hills, Calif.: Sage Publishing Company, 1980).

[15]J. A. Stoner, "A Comparison of Individual and Group Decisions Involving Risk," unpublished master's thesis (M.I.T., Sloan School of Industrial Management, 1961); and H. Lamm and D. G. Myers, "Group-Induced Polarization of Attitudes and Behavior" in *Advances in Experimental Social Psychology,* vol. 11, ed. L. Berkowitz (New York: Academic Press, 1978).

information during these discussions and are exposed to views they had not previously considered. Further, individuals may also shift their perspectives to be more "in synch" with the group's attitudes. If the group favors risk, then the individual may see the advantages of being perceived as being even more risk seeking than the group, thus gaining idiosyncrasy credits.[16]

However, this notion of choice shift does little to aid managers in predicting whether the group in which they are involved will tend towards a cautious or a risky shift. Recent research, however, has suggested a different explanation for this choice-shift phenomenon that incorporates the decision biases discussed in Chapter 5.[17] It seems that whether groups shift towards risk or towards caution depends upon the type of decision being made. For example, a risky shift occurs in the decision described in Figure 9-2 of a choice between keeping one's current job and taking a new, potentially more lucrative position (a choice between potential gains). The decisions that commonly produce a cautious shift involve evaluating a choice among potential losses. A common example is a decision involving protecting the endangered life of an expectant mother.[18] Dichotomizing the choices in this way makes the framing of the issue (described in detail in Chapter 5) very salient. That is, it may be that groups move away from the risk level of individuals, but group decisions may not be affected by the framing bias. When individuals consider risky decisions involving potential gains, they are risk averse rather than risk neutral. Groups may appear to be shifting toward risk in these situations when, in reality, they are simply behaving in a risk-neutral manner.

The same logic can apply to the cautious shift. When individuals are confronted with decisions involving potential losses, they are risk seeking rather than risk neutral. Groups may appear to be less risky when, in fact, they are simply behaving in a risk-neutral manner. While these findings are tentative, they certainly are compatible with the belief that group decision making is often superior to individual decision making. The whole area of whether or not group decision making can reduce the vulnerability of decision makers to cognitive bias is just beginning to receive attention.[19]

[16]E. Burnstein, "Persuasion as Argument Processing," in *Group Decision Processes*, eds. M. Brandstatter, J. Davis, and G. Stocker-Kreschgauer (London: Academic Press, 1983).

[17]M. A. Neale, M. H. Bazerman, G. B. Northcraft, and C. A. Alperson, "Choice Shift's Effects in Group Decisions: A Decision Bias Perspective," *International Journal of Small Group Research* 2 (1986):33–42.

[18]Stoner, "A Comparison of Individual and Group Decisions Involving Risk."

[19]M. A. Neale, et al., "Choice Shift's Effects in Group Decisions."

Were choice-shift effects to blame for the Carter administration's ill-fated decision in 1980 to attempt to rescue the hostages in Iran? Carter and his advisors may have felt they were facing only continued frustration if they did nothing and a chance to "get even" if they gambled, leading them to take an unjustifiably large risk.

---

**FIGURE 9–2**      Sample Decision Involving Potential Gains

---

*Framing* refers to the way a choice is worded or presented; for instance, protecting gains (as with this choice) versus avoiding losses. The presentation of a choice influences a decision maker's willingness to take risks. Many choices can be presented or worded either way.

Mr. A., an electrical engineer who is married and has one child, has been working for a large electronics corporation since graduating from college five years ago. He is assured a lifetime job with modest, although adequate, salary, and liberal pension benefits upon retirement. On the other hand, it is very unlikely that his salary will increase much before he retires. While attending a convention, Mr. A. is offered a job with a small, newly founded company with a highly uncertain future. The new job would pay more to start and would offer the possibility of a share in ownership if the company survived the competition of the larger firms.

Imagine that you are advising Mr. A. Listed below are several probabilities or odds of the new company's proving financially sound. Please check the *lowest* probability that you would consider acceptable to make it worthwhile for Mr. A. to take the new job.

_____ The chances are 1 in 10 that the new company will prove financially sound.

_____ The chances are 3 in 10 that the new company will prove financially sound.

_____ The chances are 5 in 10 that the new company will prove financially sound.

_____ The chances are 7 in 10 that the new company will prove financially sound.

_____ The chances are 9 in 10 that the new company will prove financially sound.

_____ Place a check here if you think Mr. A. should *not* take the new job no matter what the probabilities.

---

SOLUTIONS IN
GROUP DECISION
MAKING

When a manager is faced with making a decision, he or she may (1) unilaterally make the decision based solely on the information at hand, (2) unilaterally make the decision but solicit input on the problem from others, or (3) involve others in both providing input and making the actual decision. Because the goal of a manager is making a good decision—one that is timely, acceptable, implementable, and high in quality—it is critical that the manager be able to use these three levels of participative decision making when they are most appropriate and most likely to produce a good decision.

WHEN TO USE
GROUP DECISION
MAKING

**Levels of Participation in Decision Making** Victor Vroom and Phillip Yetton have developed guidelines for helping managers choose the most appropriate decision-making methods for a variety of situations routinely encountered in daily activities. Initially, they divide the three levels of participative decision making (authoritative, AI or AII; consultative, CI or CII; and group decision making, G) into five levels:

- *AI.* In this the most authoritarian decision-making level, the manager solves the problem or makes the decision based upon information available at that time.
- *AII.* The manager obtains the necessary information from subordinates or peers and then makes the decision. The manager may or may not tell those subordinates or peers the nature of the problem. Further, they do not have the option of suggesting or evaluating alternatives.
- *CI.* The manager conveys the problem to relevant peers or subordinates, soliciting their ideas and suggestions without bringing them together as a group. While the other group members have input, the manager makes the decision, which may or may not reflect the others' influence.
- *CII.* The manager conveys the problem to subordinates or peers, soliciting their ideas and suggestions as a group. While the group members may collectively make suggestions and provide input, the manager still makes the decision, which may or may not reflect the input of the group.
- *G.* The manager conveys the problem to subordinates and peers as a group and the group, through consensus, determines the final solution.

From the manager's perspective, then, the first aspect of making a decision is deciding who will be in the cast of characters that determines the solution. Consider the following problem:

> You are the head of the staff unit reporting to the vice-president of finance. He has asked you to provide a report on the firm's current portfolio to include recommendations for changes in the selection criteria currently employed. Doubts have been raised about the efficiency of the existing system given current market conditions, and there is considerable dissatisfaction with the prevailing rates of return.

You plan to write a report, but at the moment, you are quite perplexed about the approach you should take. Your own specialty is the bond market, and it is quite clear to you that a detailed knowledge of the equity market—which you lack—would greatly enhance the value of the report. Fortunately, four members of your staff are specialists in different segments of the equity market. Together they possess a vast amount of knowledge about the intricacies of investment. However, they seldom agree on the best way to achieve anything when it comes to the stock market. Although they are obviously conscientious as well as knowledge-able, they have major differences when it comes to investment philosophy and strategy.

You have six weeks before the report is due. You have already begun to familiarize yourself with the firm's current portfolio and have been provided by management with a specific set of constraints that any portfolio must satisfy. Your immediate problem is to come up with some alternatives to the firm's present practices and select the most promising for detailed analysis in your report. Given this problem, would you make your decision using AI, AII, CI, CII, or G?[20]

**Problem Characteristics**   Vroom and Yetton suggest that the correct level of participation in decision making depends upon various characteristics of the problem at hand.[21] They have identified seven characteristics that can be used to diagnose the problem and determine what level of decision making should be used. The seven characteristics and their associated questions are described in Figure 9–3. These characteristics are arranged in the form of questions on a decision tree. The end of each path identifies the optimal level of participation in decision making recommended. The full decision tree is illustrated in Figure 9–4 on page 384. While each path ends with a specific level of decision participation, Vroom and Yetton suggest that when there is enough time, the manager may choose an option in the feasible set that lends itself to greater subordinate participation. That is, when the decision suggests an autocratic solution is appropriate, the manager might also use a more participative style—C or G; when a consultative solution is appropriate, the manager might also use a G decision.

Now let's consider the problem facing you the manager. Examining the problem from the perspective of the Vroom and Yetton decision tree in Figure 9–4, the first question concerns a quality requirement. Is one solution likely to be significantly better than others? In the case of the stock portfolio, the answer is yes. The second question concerns whether you have sufficient information to make the decision on your own. Clearly, you do not. Since the problem of stock portfolio selection criteria is not a structured one, the last question you will have to answer is

[20]V. H. Vroom and P. Yetton, *Leadership and Decision Making* (Pittsburgh: University of Pittsburgh Press, 1973).

[21]Ibid.

**FIGURE 9–3**

## Problem Characteristics and Diagnostic Questions in the Vroom and Yetton Model

| | |
|---|---|
| A. The importance of the quality of the decision | Is there a quality requirement such that one solution is likely to be more rational than another? |
| B. The extent to which the leader possesses sufficient information or expertise to make a high-quality decision alone | Do I have sufficient information to make a high-quality decision? |
| C. The extent to which the problem is structured | Is the problem structured? Do I know what information is required and where it is located? |
| D. The extent to which acceptance or commitment on the part of the subordinates is critical to the effective implementation of the decision | Is acceptance of the decision by subordinates critical to effective implementation? Can I do it without their support? |
| E. The probability that my autocratic decision will receive acceptance by subordinates | If I were to make the decision by myself, is it reasonably certain that it will be accepted by my subordinates? |
| F. The extent to which the subordinates are motivated to attain the organizational goals as represented in the objectives explicit in the statement of the problem | Do subordinates share the organizational goals to be obtained in solving this problem? Or do they have personal considerations that might dominate? |
| G. The extent to which subordinates are likely to be in conflict over preferred solutions | Is conflict among subordinates likely in preferred solutions? |

Source: V. H. Vroom, "A New Look at Managerial Decision Making," *Organizational Dynamics* (Spring 1973): pp. 69–70. Reprinted by permission of publisher. American Management Association, New York. All rights reserved.

whether acceptance by subordinates is critical to implementation. Since the decision will be implemented by your superiors, acceptance of the solution by subordinates is irrelevant. This particular path ends after the fourth question and indicates that you should use the CII level of participation. Thus, you should involve the subordinates as a group in offering ideas and suggestions, but make the final decision as to the preferred stock portfolio selection criteria yourself.

This model has been supported by research. Vroom and Yetton found that managers who had been trained to use these problem characteristics to diagnose the optimal level of participation in decision making were better able to classify decision problems and choose appropriate participation levels than managers without such training.[22] There is also

[22]V. H. Vroom, "A New Look in Managerial Decision Making," *Organizational Dynamics* (Spring 1973):66–80.

## FIGURE 9–4　Decision Tree for Determining Appropriate Decision Strategy

A.　Does the problem possess a quality requirement?
B.　Do I have sufficient information to make a high-quality decision?
C.　Is the problem structured?
D.　Is acceptance of the decision by subordinates important for effective implementation?
E.　If I were to make the decision by myself, am I reasonably certain that it would be accepted by my subordinates?
F.　Do subordinates share the organizational goals to be attained in solving this problem?
G.　Is conflict among subordinates likely in preferred solutions?

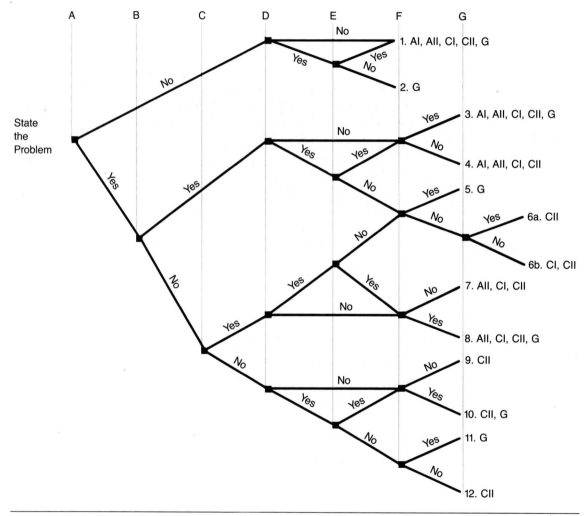

Source: V. H. Vroom and P. Yetton, *Leadership and Decision Making* (Pittsburgh: University of Pittsburgh Press, 1973).

evidence that increased managerial skill in determining the correct level of participation increases the effectiveness of managerial decision making.[23]

**HOW TO USE GROUP DECISION MAKING**

Once the number of individuals to be involved in making the decision has been determined, the next step is to determine how the group is to reach a decision. In selecting a particular group decision-making process, the intent is to minimize the liabilities of groups and maximize their benefits. Five different techniques will be described below—brainstorming, nominal group technique, the Delphi technique,[24] quality circles, and computer-assisted decision support systems.

**Brainstorming.**  An advertising executive developed **brainstorming** over 30 years ago as a means of enhancing creativity by encouraging the free discussion and exchange of ideas. Brainstormers are encouraged to produce as many and as creative a set of ideas or alternatives as possible and simultaneously prohibited from being critical of the ideas generated. When practiced correctly, brainstorming separates the evaluative stage from the idea-generation stage of decision making. The basic structure of a brainstorming session is determined by four rules:[25]

1. *No criticism!* Adverse judgments about your own or others' ideas are to be withheld.
2. *"Freewheeling" is invited.* No idea is too wild or crazy. The more creative or unusual the idea, the better.
3. *Quantity is desired.* Generate as many ideas as possible. The greater the number of ideas, the greater the likelihood that one will work.
4. *"Piggybacking" is encouraged.* Participants should build upon the ideas and suggestions of others. Combining and extending other ideas is a critical aspect of successful brainstorming.

The primary intent of brainstorming is to reduce the participants' fears of criticism and provide multiple sources of stimulation for creative problem solving. In general, brainstorming can work to improve the quantity and quality of ideas or alternatives generated. However, for brainstorming to work, it is critical that evaluation and criticism be suppressed until all ideas are "on the table."[26]

[23]See V. H. Vroom and A. G. Jago, "On the Validity of the Vroom-Yetton Model," *Journal of Applied Psychology* 63 (1978):151–162; and R. H. Field, "A Test of the Vroom-Yetton Normative Model of Leadership," *Journal of Applied Psychology* 67 (1982):523–532.

[24]See A. F. Osborn, *Applied Imagination* (New York: Scribner's, 1957) and A. L. Delbecq, A. L. Van de Ven, and D. H. Gustafson, *Group Techniques for Program Planning: A Guide to Nominal Groups and Delphi Techniques* (Glenview, Ill.: Scott, Foresman, 1975).

[25]Osborn, *Applied Imagination.*

[26]S. J. Parnes, R. B. Noller, and A. M. Biondi, *A Guide to Creative Action* (New York: Scribner's, 1977).

**Nominal Group Technique**   While brainstorming focuses on generating new and creative ideas, the **nominal group technique (NGT)** focuses on generating alternatives and selecting among them. Conducted within the context of a group meeting, NGT has the following structure:

1. Individuals silently and independently write down their ideas and alternative solutions to a stated problem.
2. All members take turns presenting their ideas, and these ideas are recorded on a chart or chalkboard.
3. The ideas are discussed only in terms of clarification. Evaluative comments are not allowed.
4. A written voting procedure is followed, which results in a ranking of the alternatives.

The exact voting procedure is determined in advance, and the winning alternative becomes the selected alternative. NGT is a very useful process when there is considerable inhibition, hostility, or a dominant individual. An example of the use of NGT is described in the "Focus on: Nominal Group Techniques."

**The Delphi Technique**   For situations in which group members cannot meet face to face, the RAND Corporation developed a group decision-making technique that offers many of the benefits of face-to-face interaction—the **Delphi technique.** Like the NGT, the Delphi technique minimizes the effects of different levels of status and influence on group decision making, but it does not require that the group members convene in the same physical space. Instead of reporting and recording alternatives as in the NGT, participants in the Delphi technique answer a series of questionnaires. A Delphi group might function as follows:

1. The first questionnaire distributed to members identifies the problem and asks for alternative solutions to it.
2. The Delphi coordinator summarizes the solutions, and the summary is returned to participants in the form of a second questionnaire specifically designed to identify areas requiring further clarification and consideration.
3. The results of the second questionnaire are presented to the participants, who rate the various alternatives presented.
4. The members' ratings are tabulated, and a summary of the data and resulting decision is returned to the participants.

NGT and the Delphi technique are very similar. The primary differences lie in the physical presence or absence of the group. The Delphi technique allows group members to remain anonymous (very helpful for particularly sensitive issues), but requires considerably more time.

Group members who interact often spend much time developing interpersonal relationships, discussing tangential issues, and maintaining

Focus on:

Nominal Group
Technique

**ARA Services**  ARA Services used a nominal group technique to identify and resolve a number of the problems encountered during its reorganization from a product-based organizational structure to a geographical-based structure. In particular, the NGT was used to focus on the human problems associated with the change in structure. They had initially tried to break up the affected managers into teams to discuss their concerns. Realizing that this technique was not producing the desired outcomes, the company then tried the NGT. Using this technique they were able to generate alternatives for solving specific problems that had been identified within the groups. Many of the solutions were put into effect, and through the use of NGT the reorganization was completed in one year rather than the proposed two years. In addition, there was no reduction in sales volume, but there was a reduction in managerial turnover.

Along with identifying problems with and developing solutions for the organizational restructuring, NGT was also used at ARA to identify new leaders in the restructured organization. The persons who were selected to lead the new divisions were trained in NGT before meeting the new members of their teams. During the initial meeting with their new subordinates, the new division heads used their skills in NGT to develop group goals, provide direction for achieving these goals, and consider each person's contribution to the group's performance. This became the primary means of establishing new management teams.

Source: Andre L. Delbecq, Andrew H. Van de Ven, and David H. Gustafson, *Group Techniques for Program Planning: A Guide to Nominal Group and Delphi Processes* (Glenview, Ill.: Scott, Foresman, 1975) pp. xii–xiv.

pressure for conformity. They also may be unduly influenced by the status, persuasiveness, or seniority of various group members.[27] Thus, when a manager is confronted with a problem in which the generation of creative alternatives is critical and criticism must be held to a minimum, the NGT or Delphi technique may be most appropriate.

The manager, however, should not ignore the potential pitfalls of these methods. In using these two methods of group decision making, managers run three risks. First, because of a lack of discussion and clarification, group members may lack understanding about the problem or the final solution. Second, it is difficult to adopt a truly creative solution through these techniques because the ideas of the minority are usually not clarified. Third, because of the lack of face-to-face interaction, the group members may have developed little commitment to the solution.[28]

[27]G. P. Huber, *Managerial Decision Making* (Glenview, Ill.: Scott, Foresman, 1980).

[28]Delbecq, Van de Ven, and Gustafson, *Group Techniques for Program Planning.*

Participative decision making in the form of Corrective Action Teams increases operating profits at Amoco Chemical Company by as much as $100 million annually. The two Amoco workers shown here—James D. Walker (left) and Ben Pafford (right)—designed a loom modification that strengthened fabric edges, thereby improving the product and reducing waste.

**Quality Circles**   Probably the newest innovation in group decision making, **quality circles (QCs)** have recently received considerable attention among U.S. manufacturers. Their interest in this technique stems from its having been described by the Japanese as critical to their recent manufacturing success. Ironically, Edward Deming, an American, first brought the notion of "statistical quality control," a management tool, to the Japanese in the early post–World War II years. The Japanese combined these ideas with the assumption that the person who performs a job is the one who best knows how to identify and correct its problems. As a result, the Japanese with Deming's help developed the "quality circle." A quality circle is a group of persons (approximately ten) who meet periodically to discuss and develop solutions to problems related to quality, productivity, or product cost.[29]

A QC is a voluntary group whose members come from the same work group. They receive special training in information gathering and problem analysis. Their task is to use the resources of the group members to identify and analyze problems and choose among decision alternatives. Proposed solutions to problems are presented to management, along with a cost-benefit analysis.

The intent of QCs is to direct the positive attributes of group decision making (such as group resources and synergy) towards solving key organizational problems. This problem-solving technique is quite visible

[29]J. B. Keys and T. R. Miller, "The Japanese Management Jungle," *Academy of Management Review* 9 (1984):342–353.

in U.S. companies. In fact, a recent survey reported that 44 percent of all companies with 500 or more employees and over 90 percent of the Fortune 500 companies have these programs.[30] However, as with other group decision-making techniques, QCs are effective only in the right situations. A number of characteristics seem to be necessary to ensure their effective performance:

1. The groups should receive managerial support.
2. Management should be patient and tolerant of QC failures. One duty of the QC leader is to keep management informed of progress on the group's projects.
3. Participation in the QCs should be voluntary, but management should encourage participation.
4. QC leaders should be chosen with a particular set of skills in mind. While the role of the QC leader often falls to supervisory personnel, whoever fills that role should be able to work with individuals at all levels of the organization, be aware of the political environment in the organization, and be creative and flexible in solving problems.
5. QCs should be used only when they are most likely to be helpful, such as when there are clear problems, when employees are enthusiastic about the process, and when management is committed to product improvement.
6. Participants must be well trained in group dynamics and problem-solving methods—the basic technology of QCs.[31]

The "FOCUS ON: Quality Circles" illustrates how quality circles benefited two companies in a variety of ways.

When QCs work, they can have a major impact on organizational productivity. Creation of quality circles in the purchasing department of Westinghouse Electronics Corporation's Defense and Electronic Systems Center outside Baltimore resulted in a savings of over $600,000 by improving the way in which vendors sent supplies to the Center. The worker-management QC at Bethlehem Steel's Los Angeles plant reduced operating costs by $225,000 over two months by creating ways to use mill downtime for production activities.[32] Chapter 12 provides more detail on quality circles and their impact on organizational performance.

Groups do have a great deal to offer management in producing good decisions. However, it is important to remember that there are both advantages and disadvantages to group decision making. The four methods discussed here are based upon the notion that the effectiveness

[30]E. E. Lawler III and S. A. Mohrman, "Quality Circles after the Fad," *Harvard Business Review* (January-February 1985):65–71.

[31]See both C. N. Greene and T. A. Matherly, "Quality Circles: A Need for Caution and Evaluation of Alternatives," *Readings in Personnel and Human Resource Management,* 3d ed., eds. R. Schuler, S. Youngblood, and V. Huber (St. Paul, Minn.: West, 1987):509–517; and R. Wood, F. Hull, and K. Azumi, "Evaluating Quality Circles: The American Application," *California Management Review* 26 (1983):37–53.

[32]D. Hage, "Goal Is Improving the Workplace," *Minneapolis Star,* November 19, 1981, 1C.

## FOCUS ON:
Quality Circles

**Honeywell and General Dynamics**
Quality circles can have a positive impact on organizational performance in a variety of arenas. Consider, for example, the benefits of quality circles at Honeywell and General Dynamics.

In a nonunion electronics assembly shop at Honeywell, ten quality circles with approximately 120 members reduced costs of their high-technology, high-reliability, low-volume production by 46 percent over two years. In another Honeywell facility—a hybrid microelectronics laboratory—involved in high-volume, technologically complex work, eleven quality circles with 94 members implemented solutions to problems which resulted in $86,000 of documented savings, a

36 percent reduction in assembly costs per unit of production, and a significant increase in cooperation, management response, feedback, effectiveness, and satisfaction (as measured by an in-house survey).

In the six months prior to joining a QC, 13.7 percent of the General Dynamics employees eventually involved in a QC submitted suggestions. In the six months after joining a QC, 74.5 percent submitted suggestions. Submission of suggestions by non-QC members dropped from 8.8 percent to 6.7 percent. Over the same period of time, the turnover rate for QC members was 8 percent, while the turnover for all other employees was 25 percent.

Source: P. C. Thompson, *Quality Circles* (New York: AMACOM, 1982), pp. 12–13.

of group decision making is equal to the potential effectiveness of the combined inputs of the members minus the losses in effectiveness that follow from the group processes plus the gains in effectiveness from group processes.[33] In other words:

$$\text{Actual Effectiveness} = \text{Potential Effectiveness} - \text{Process Losses} + \text{Process Gains}.$$

*Process gains* include many of the benefits of group decision making outlined early in this chapter, such as synergy, resource pooling, and task specialization. *Process losses* are the costs of group decision making, such as groupthink, undue social influence, or time.

## WHY GROUP DECISION MAKING WORKS[34]

Since the Hawthorne studies described in Chapter 2, managers and organizational scholars have known about the profound influence that groups can have on individual productivity. American managers have even witnessed our own group-oriented technologies being exported to

[33]J. R. Hackman and C. G. Morris, "Group Tasks, Group Interaction Process, and Group Performance Effectiveness," *Advances in Experimental Social Psychology* vol. 7, ed. L. Berkowitz (New York: Academic Press, 1975).

[34]Much of this discussion is based upon Harold Leavitt's 1975 article "Suppose We Took Groups Seriously . . .," which appeared in E. L. Cass and F. G. Zimmer, eds., *Man and Work in Society*, Van Nostrand Reinhold.

Japan with amazing results. Participative management is a very close relative of work-group activities. Although the nature of group decision making is not novel or unique to American managers, if you examine exactly how decisions are made in organizations and how they are structured, you will likely find individuals—not groups—are primary. Why is it that group decision making has been so consistently eschewed in favor of individual decision making?

A primary reason for this bias towards individual decision making lies in the rationality notion, which assumes that the individual is the elemental unit of organization. This traditional view of organizations is consistent with the assumptions underlying much of American culture. That is, individuals are taught the value and importance of individual achievement. From the individual's perspective, organizations merely represent arenas in which to compete for individual accomplishment, recognition, and satisfaction.

Organizations, however, need to control, or at least direct, this individual achievement along the lines of common organizational objectives. This individual achievement-orientation, coupled with the organization's attempt to mold and direct activity, leads to constant tension between the organization and the individual. Groups first make their appearance in response to this tension, through the development of worker coalitions to resist the control and influence of the organization.

With the discovery that groups could positively influence individual performance, groups took on an entirely new light. They were used by management to (1) relieve or reduce the tension between the individual and the organization, (2) coordinate individual activities, and (3) discipline and control nonconforming group members. However, organizations were not designed around groups. Rather, groups were tacked on to existing organizational structures—structures that were based on the individual. Thus, the very structure of the groups and the processes that would heighten productivity became a two-edged sword. Groups were too slow and too democratic. They created in-groups that were hard for outsiders to penetrate, and they diffused responsibility for decision making. Although management could never completely remove groups as a source of influence on organizational members, their importance in the structure of the organization has remained ancillary. It is as if "someone had insisted that automobiles be designed to fit the existing terrain rather than build roads to adapt to the automobile".[35]

What might be the advantages of an organization designed around groups? First, the amount of control required would be reduced. Rather than having to supervise every individual directly, the group would supervise its members. Second, individuals have many fewer units with whom they must interact. Rather than interacting with each individual on the traditional organizational chart, the group member would

[35]Ibid., p. 3.

interact with many fewer organizational units or groups, although each unit would be larger. Finally, the increased cohesiveness, motivation, commitment, and higher-quality decisions that flow from group interactions would become a routine benefit for an organization so structured.

What must happen for organizations to take advantage of the potential productivity and decision benefits of groups? Must organizations be restructured to incorporate groups, and if so, what might they resemble? Such organizations would have to select, train, pay, evaluate, and promote groups rather than individuals. Jobs would have to be designed for groups, and an entire group would be at risk for termination or relocation if it did not meet performance expectations.

While these ideas initially go against our embedded ideas about how organizations should function, consider, for a moment, whether managing groups might not be easier than managing individuals. For example, it would probably be easier for upper-level management to evaluate the performance of a work group than to evaluate the contribution of an individual member. Paying groups rather than individuals would increase the collaboration and cooperation among group members.[36] Allocation of rewards to individual members could be delegated to the group. Thus, the likelihood of yoking productivity contributions to rewards may be greater, since group members would have considerable opportunity to observe each other and would be much closer than a supervisor to the activities involved in producing the good or service.

Selecting a group rather than an individual may pose some unique problems. However, an organization could certainly hire individuals not only for their skills and abilities but also for their ability to work together. A step in this direction has been undertaken by the J. L. Kellogg Graduate School of Management at Northwestern University. Unlike most top business schools, Kellogg requires that all applicants—over 3,800 in 1986—be interviewed as part of the admission procedure. The interview is held to ensure that the 400-plus students admitted to the master's in management program "fit" together—a critical component of an education that relies heavily on classroom experiences structured around the concept of small-group decision making.[37] A slightly different perspective on group selection is illustrated by the hiring practices of the Macintosh group at Apple Computer. The Macintosh group interviewed all candidates for inclusion in the group. To become a member of the Macintosh group, an applicant had to garner group approval. The use of groups as decision-making entities is commonplace in other cultures. The importance of groups in the decision making of Japanese companies is illustrated in the "INTERNATIONAL FOCUS ON: Group Decision Making."

[36]M. Deutsch, "Equity, Equality, and Need: What Determines Which Will Be Used as the Basis of Distributive Justice?" *Journal of Social Issues* 31 (1975):137–149.

[37]"Business Schools: Money Majors," *U.S. News and World Report*, November 2, 1987, 81–83.

INTERNATIONAL
FOCUS ON:
Group Decision
Making

**Making Decisions in Japanese Companies** An increasing number of Americans are employed by Japanese firms, primarily firms that have plants or factories here or need to have a major presence in the United States. These employees have a unique opportunity to observe in detail the decision-making styles of Japanese managers. Geoffrey Tudor, an employee of Japan Air Lines, reports that the Japanese manager who made a decision unilaterally would quickly be removed from his or her position (in a way that would "save face"). Thomas Cappiello, a public relations officer for Nissho Iwai, a Japanese trading company, believes that the Japanese definition of a good leader is not one who makes decisions; but one who discovers the decisions subordinates have made.

If Japanese managers want to make sure a certain alternative is selected, they must plant the idea of this particular solution with some subordinates. The subordinates will then analyze the suggested solution, among others, and determine how best to solve the problem. According to John Macklin, an executive at Fujitsu, a manager whose preferred solution is accepted will then compliment the subordinates on their good idea and decision.

Source: "Outsiders in Japanese Companies," *Fortune*, July 12, 1982, pp. 114–128.

Promoting, transferring, relocating, or terminating an entire group seems considerably more problematic. As one moves up the hierarchy in most organizations, the importance of individual action looms larger, particularly as it relates to leadership. Without individual leaders, the task of directing, coordinating, and controlling the organization may be ignored or poorly orchestrated. Interestingly, however, in a few organizations, such as Hartmarx Corp., a management group, troika, or triumvirate controls the direction of the organization.[38] Further, as we will discuss in Chapter 10, work groups may serve as a substitute for leadership.

Transferring groups seems expensive until one considers the benefits of such transfers. Transferring groups of people and their families may make such a change more bearable. Support groups and networks would remain unbroken, and the need to develop new working relationships would be minimized.

While the hiring of groups is not yet a reality, a number of organizations are now involved in the first steps along such a path. O'Melveny & Myers, one of the nation's largest law firms, has hired several married couples. Martin Marietta, the aerospace and defense contractor, actually has a hire-a-couple policy. Personnel administrator Joseph Weiner notes "eight out of ten times, the recruited person is married to someone with skills we can use."[39] (Interestingly enough, the

[38]S. Weiner, "A New Cut for the Gray Flannel," *Forbes*, December 28, 1987, 61–62.
[39]A. Toufexis, "Dual Careers, Doleful Dilemmas," *Time*, November 16, 1987, 90.

hiring of couples would require a two-person decision-making process on the part of the applicants. In the case of the group, the decision to accept the offer would entail a group decision-making process!)

Terminating the group is probably the most difficult problem to confront. Wholesale dismissal of work groups may unnecessarily limit the flexibility of management. Of course, the poor performance of a group does not always reflect the poor performance of all individual members. It might well be that a poorly performing group should be dissolved and its members reassigned to other groups.

Some of these notions concerning group-based organizations seem unwieldy at first glance. However, such group-oriented activities are occurring in a variety of modern organizations. The issue seems to be to what extent such changes will be institutionalized in future organizations. More detailed comments on the future of organizations and organizational behavior are presented in Chapter 18.

## SUMMARY

Using groups to make decisions is not a new idea. For years, group decision making has been known to foster increased communication, commitment, development, and ownership of the problem and solution among group members. Groups are often able to outperform individuals in making decisions, particularly when the quality and acceptability of the decision are important.

Unfortunately, group decision making is not without its difficulties. Using groups as the basis for a decision increases the complexity of the decision process. The more individuals involved in coming up with a solution, the more information each individual member must process, the more complex the rules governing decision acceptance, and the more complex the interpersonal processes. As a result, groups require considerably more time and resources to make a decision than do individuals. Groups may also be influenced by factors or processes that do not affect individuals, such as group-

think or choice shift. Groupthink occurs primarily among highly cohesive groups and results in a decision process that emphasizes conformity and suppresses criticism. Choice-shift effects indicate that groups may be either more or less risky than their average individual members.

Deciding when to take advantage of the benefits of group decision making and when to rely on an individual decision-making process is an important component in solving organizational problems. Vroom and Yetton have developed guidelines for determining whether a group or an individual is the most appropriate decision maker. If the decision requires acceptance by subordinates, if one alternative is qualitatively better than another, and if the group possesses information necessary for the selection of an alternative, then group decision making is likely to be the preferred option.

After deciding who should make the decision, one must decide how the decision is to be made. Four methods of group decision making were described in this chapter—brainstorming, the nominal group technique, the Delphi technique, and quality circles. All are designed to enhance the benefits and reduce the costs of group decision making. For example, brainstorming, the nominal group technique, and the Delphi technique separate the creative, idea-generation process from the critical, idea-evaluative phase of decision making.

Quality circles probably represent the most widely accepted form of group decision making in current organizational practice. These groups of approximately ten individuals, whose task is to improve product quality, now exist in almost half of American corporations with 500 or more employees.

Given the acceptance and effectiveness of many quality-circle programs, the lack of more group decision-making activities in organizations is puzzling. Groups, it seems, have not been taken seriously in organizations in the United States. Rather, groups and their decision-making processes are often viewed as temporary or Band-Aid measures to reduce the tension between worker and organization, to coordinate individual activities, and to control or discipline group members. They have not been the basis for new organizational structures and, as such, have been doomed to play a tangential role in organizational life.

While converting our individual-oriented organizations to group-oriented structures may take some creative problem solving, a number of organizations are beginning to head in that direction. Groups have been shown to be effective in both manufacturing and service organizations. Group decision making, however, is not without its costs. The decision facing today's manager, then, is how to improve the decision process. Part of the eventual solution will likely be the involvement of groups and group decision making.

## KEY TERMS

**Brainstorming** Group creativity technique facilitating free discussion and exchange of ideas by withholding criticism of ideas, encouraging unusual ideas, generating as many ideas as possible, and piggybacking ideas.

**Cautious shift** Tendency of a group as a whole and each member to be less willing to accept risk after a group discussion than prior to it.

**Delphi technique** Group decision-making technique that minimizes interaction among members; members complete mailed questionnaires and a coordinator summarizes results.

**Groupthink** Tendency in highly cohesive groups for members to seek consensus so strongly that they lose the willingness and ability to evaluate one another's ideas critically.

**Nominal group technique (NGT)** Group decision-making technique that focuses on generating alternatives and selecting among them by asking group members to independently write down ideas, present them in turn, clarify them for the group, and rank them by voting privately.

**Quality circle (QC)**   Voluntary group of approximately ten people from the same work group who meet periodically to discuss and develop solutions to problems related to quality, productivity, or product cost.

**Resource pooling**   An advantage groups have over individuals by combining the perspectives, ideas, suggestions, and information of all members.

**Risky shift**   Tendency of a group as a whole and each member to be more willing to accept greater levels of risk after a group discussion than prior to it.

**Synergy**   Mutual influence process of stimulation and encouragement among members of a group.

DISCUSSION
QUESTIONS

1.  Consider the decision-making process in a group project you are involved in. What are some benefits you as an individual experienced that directly related to the group and its decision-making process? What are some liabilities you as an individual incurred?

2.  Quality circles have been extraordinarily successful in Japanese organizations. What factors might contribute to the less successful performance of quality circles in the United States?

3.  When groups convene to make decisions, one of their first acts typically is to determine *how* a decision will be made. What type of decision rule is likely to encourage the greatest amount of information exchange? The most political behavior? Coalition formation among group members? High commitment to the decision? Why?

4.  Even when it is in the best interest of a manager to involve subordinates in making a decision, he or she often makes it autocratically. What are some reasons why managers choose an autocratic decision-making process over a group decision-making process, regardless of the quality of the outcome?

5.  What are the advantages and disadvantages of brainstorming?

6.  Why might a manager choose to collect group members' suggestions and preferences with a Delphi method, rather than using a nominal group technique?

7.  Groupthink is typically viewed as a group decision-making *error*. In what types of groups or situations might a manager encourage groupthink?

8.  What are some of the major advantages and disadvantages to managing by groups?

**IF YOU WANT TO KNOW MORE**

While the study of group decision making has a rather long history, it has received more practitioner and scholar interest in recent years. Part of this resurgent interest can be traced to two books that illustrated the importance and influence of groups in making decisions. First was Graham T. Allison's book, *Essence of Decision* (Boston: Little Brown, 1971). Second was Irving Janis's initial work, entitled *Victims of Groupthink: A Psychological Study of Foreign Policy Decisions and Fiascos* (Boston: Houghton-Mifflin, 1972), and his subsequent book *Groupthink* (Boston: Houghton-Mifflin, 1982).

In attempting to maximize the benefits derived from groups while simultaneously avoiding their liabilities, different group processes were described and tested. A. F. Osborn's *Applied Imagination* (New York: Scribner, 1957) and A. Delbecq, A. Van de Ven, and D. Gustafson's *Group Techniques for Program Planning: A Guide to Nominal Groups and Delphi Techniques* (Glenview, Ill.: Scott, Foresman, 1975) provided three different decision-making processes for groups. The current interest in participation and group decision making is most likely a result of the Japanese experience with quality circles. While a number of texts explain quality circles, three fairly readable examples are P. C. Thompson's *Quality Circles* (New York: AMACOM Publishing, 1982), R. Barra's *Putting Quality*

*Circles to Work: A Practical Strategy for Boosting Productivity and Profits* (New York: McGraw-Hill, 1983), and D. Hutchins's *Quality Circle Handbook* (New York: Pitman Publishing, 1985).

Many of the topics presented in this chapter on group decision making are addressed in greater detail in J. McGrath's *Groups: Interaction and Performance* (Englewood Cliffs, NJ: Prentice-Hall, 1984) as well as in two edited volumes: H. Brandstatter, J. Davis, and G. Stocker-Kreichgauer's *Group Decision Making* (New York: Academic Press, 1982) and R. Guzzo's *Improving Group Decision Making in Organizations* (New York: Academic Press, 1982). Another series of articles directed towards the beginning student of group decision making is in the book *Group Decision Making*, edited by W. Swap and his associates (Beverly Hills: Sage Publishing, 1984).

For a recent review of the participation research to which group decision making is an important contributor, see E. Locke and D. Schweiger's "Participation in Decision Making: One More Look" in B. Staw's *Research in Organizational Behavior* (Greenwich, Conn.: JAI Press, 1979). For a more practical perspective on when to use participative decision making, the interested reader may wish to examine V. Vroom and P. Yetton's *Leadership and Decision Making* (Pittsburgh: University of Pittsburgh Press, 1973).

**ON YOUR OWN**

In the discussion of when to use group decision making, we presented an example of a managerial problem and used the Vroom-Yetton model of decision making to determine who should be involved in the decision-making process. Below are two other problem scenarios. Should the manager in each case use an autocratic (I or II), consultative (I or II), or group decision-making process?

Source: V. H. Vroom and P. Yetton, *Leadership and Decision Making* (Pittsburgh: University of Pittsburgh Press, 1973).

SCENARIO ONE
You are on the division manager's staff and work on a wide variety of problems of both an administrative and technical nature. You have been given the assignment of developing a universal method to be used in each of five plants in a division for manually reading equipment registers, recording the readings, and transmitting the scorings to a centralized information system. All plants are located in a relatively small geographic region.

Until now there has been a high error rate in the readings and/or transmittal of the data. Some locations have considerably higher error rates than others, and the methods used to record and transmit the data vary between plants. It is probable, therefore, that part of the error variance is a function of specific local conditions rather than anything else, and this will complicate the establishment of any system common to all plants. You have the information on error rates but no information on local practices that generate these errors or on the local conditions that necessitate the different practices.

Everyone would benefit from an improvement in the quality of the data because they are used in a number of important decisions. Your contacts with the plants are through the quality-control supervisors, who are responsible for collecting the data. They are a conscientious group committed to doing their jobs well, but are highly sensitive to interference on the part of top management in their own operations. Any solution that does not receive the active support of the various plant supervisors is unlikely to reduce the error rate significantly.

SCENARIO TWO
You are supervising the work of twelve engineers. Their formal training and work experience are very similar, permitting you to use them interchangeably on projects. Yesterday, your manager informed you that a request had been received from an overseas affiliate for four engineers to go abroad on extended loan for a period of six to eight months. For a number of reasons, you agreed that this request should be met from your group.

All your engineers are capable of handling this assignment, and from the standpoint of present and future projects, there is no particular reason why any one should be retained over any other. The problem is somewhat complicated by the fact that the overseas assignment is in what is generally regarded in the company as an undesirable location.

CLOSING CASE
FOR CHAPTER 9

# THE MANAGER'S MEMO

FROM: P. Dorian, Administrator

TO:     J. Sternberg, M.D.

RE:     Ethics Task Force

I have been considering your request that the hospital convene an ethics
panel whenever we receive a request that some or all treatment be
withheld from a patient presumed to be dying. I can't help but be
concerned by the idea of tying up the time of a doctor, nurse, social
worker, chaplain, family members, and possibly others every time we
need to make such a decision. Obviously, this would be costly.
    When I started in the business, we took it for granted that doctors
made all the decisions about treatment—with the OK of the patient and
family members, of course. I'm afraid I don't understand the benefits of
the change you are proposing. What do we gain from all the time we
would have to invest?

CASE DISCUSSION
QUESTIONS

Assume you are Dr. Sternberg, and respond to the hospital administrator's memo. Support your position with what you have learned about
when and how group decision making can be beneficial. Who will benefit
most from the group process? Who will bear most of the costs and
disadvantages? If you wish, you can assume that you have changed your
mind about recommending the formation of a task force. If so, use
material from the chapter to support this new viewpoint.

CHAPTER

# 10

# Leadership

*Focus on the Burdens of Leadership: Personal Responsibility at Japan Air Lines*

## Formal and Informal Leadership

## Leadership as a Managerial Role

## Universal Approaches to Leadership
Trait Approaches
*Focus on Transformational Leaders: WANTED: Leaders Who Can Make a Difference*
Behavior Approaches
*Focus on Leader Behaviors: Women Executives: What Makes for Success?*

## Contingency Approaches to Leadership
Trait Approaches
*Focus on Leadership Contingencies: Leader Intelligence and Effectiveness*
Behavior Approaches

## Alternative Theories of Leadership
Vertical Dyad Linkage Model
Attribution Model of Leadership
Substitutes for Leadership
*International Focus on Substitutes for Leadership: Power Sharing among Leaders*

## MRS. FIELDS COOKIES: GOOD ENOUGH NEVER IS

Setting aside the fact that she is a mere 32 years old, it is safe—very safe—to say that Debbi Fields, founder, president, and chief executive officer of Mrs. Fields Cookies, Inc., is the antithesis of the stereotypical corporate executive. Consider that she (1) is not profit motivated; (2) is energetic and spontaneous; (3) operates her company on instinct; and (4) says becoming a Mrs. Fields employee is joining a team that has fun. Consider, too, that all this corporate unorthodoxy brought the Mrs. Fields holding companies sales of $150 million in 1988. Further, what is believed to be the country's fastest-growing specialty food company expects to have more than 600 U.S. stores by the end of 1989.

Fields, who once chased foul balls for the Oakland Athletics baseball team, performed with dolphins at Sea World, and worked as a retail clerk and Christmas elf in a department store, opened her first store, Debbi's Chocolate Chippery,

in Palo Alto, California, on August 18, 1977, using a $50,000 loan from her husband, Randy.

This daughter of an Oakland, California, welder for the U.S. Navy claims that you should do what makes you and the customers happy and not work only for money. "You become successful by contributing, not by worrying what you'll get in return. My desire is to provide an environment that is fun and makes people smile," she says.

"There are special ingredients in our people. With our employees, their jobs are really a matter of pride. When a customer tells them how delicious the cookies taste, our people can be proud because they baked them, not me."

In managing her first store, she established hourly sales goals, creating a competition among employees to see who could record the day's best sales record. "We still hire people based upon their warmth, friendliness, and the ability to have a good time, because, in reality, that's what we're selling when we sell our cookies," she says.

In addition to having a good time, she maintains a zeal for quality, which is highlighted by her motto: "Good enough never is." To this end, Fields makes unannounced visits to her stores to test the enthusiasm and sales techniques of her staff, the quality of her products, and "to see how the customer sees us." More than once, she has found cookies not to her satisfaction, dumped the inventory into the garbage can, and closed the store until it could meet her standards. Her personal atten- tion coupled with her management style keeps her corporate staff requirements sparse. One hundred thirty corporate employees manage the 5,500 store-based employees.

Fields fears neither the future nor the prospects of the so-called "cookie fad" fading. When confronted with such inquiries, she relies on her belief that her stores are not merely selling premium cookies. "They are selling a 'feel-good feeling,' and that's something that people will always want."

Source: M. Korologos, "Debbi Fields," *Sky*, July 1988, pp. 42–50.

## INTRODUCTION

In previous chapters, we examined group decision making and the phenomenon of power and influence. The focus of these chapters was on how group behavior influenced the individual or how an individual influenced another individual. In this chapter on leadership, however, we shall focus on how an individual can influence the behavior of groups.

Good leadership may be critical to organizational performance. The success of any venture is often largely attributed to its identified leader. The importance of Debbi Fields to the success of Mrs. Fields Cookies is obvious. She is clearly identified as a necessary component of the success of her company. At the same time, the responsibility for failure of a venture is often placed squarely on the shoulders of the leader as well. When the Chrysler Corporation performs poorly, the person held responsible is Lee Iacocca. As described in the "Focus on: The Burdens of Leadership," after the August 12, 1985, crash of the Japan Air Lines (JAL) flight that killed more than 500 people, JAL president Yasumoto Takagi resigned his post as evidence of his assuming personal responsibility for the failure of JAL to protect its passengers. (An American CEO is not likely to take personal responsibility as far as Takagi, but leaders are given the lion's share of responsibility for the failure or success of their companies.)

FOCUS ON:

The Burdens of
Leadership

**Personal Responsibility at Japan Air Lines**   With the crash on August 12, 1985, of a Japan Air Lines Boeing 747 and the loss of over 500 lives, JAL president Yasumoto Takagi resigned but remained on the company's roster through the end of that year. During that time, Takagi began a personal campaign to visit the relatives of each of the crash victims.

Taking his place at the helm of JAL is Susumu Yamaji, a former senior executive in the Ministry of Transport. Further, airline officials have begun negotiations with approximately 70 of the 400 families affected by the loss of the 505 passengers. Offers of compensation for losses varied from $142,857 to $428,571 in 6 of the 70 cases.

Source: "JAL Reorganization," *Aviation Week and Space Technology,* November 11, 1985, p. 28.

While all would agree that good leadership is important to the successful organization, agreeing on the definition of leadership is considerably more difficult. Leadership has been defined in terms of individual traits, behavior, influence over other people, interaction patterns, role relationships, and incumbency in administrative positions.[1] For our purposes, however, we will use Katz and Kahn's definition of leadership, which distinguishes it from other forms of influence by suggesting that leadership is the influential increment over and above an employee's mechanical compliance with routine directives of the organization.[2]

Leadership is a difficult phenomenon to grasp. Organizational scholars have traditionally had trouble pinning down exactly what leadership is. At best, we can say that it is a complex phenomenon that involves exercising influence in an organization and that involves the interplay of many different organizational actors and issues. Perhaps it is because leadership has been perceived as such an important component of a successful organization that researchers and practitioners over the years have continued to try to understand it. One factor contributing to the confusion is that there are many different kinds of leaders. The next section examines two major types of leaders: formal and informal.

[1]G. Yukl, *Leadership in Organizations* (Englewood Cliffs, N.J.: Prentice-Hall, 1981).
[2]D. Katz and R. L. Kahn, *The Social Psychology of Organizations* (New York: Wiley, 1978).

FORMAL  AND
INFORMAL
LEADERSHIP

Formal leadership differs from informal leadership in the organizational legitimacy of the individual in that role. For example, the person occupying the role of executive vice-president of sales has a formal leadership role in the sales division of an organization. However, because that individual is assigned a particular role does not guarantee that the person will be a leader or the only leader of the sales force. Informal leadership is exerted by persons who can influence group members because of factors beyond the formal leader's organizational assignment. The formal leader will often exert influence in one dimension of the task and informal leaders will emerge to fill in the leadership gaps.

Individuals can increase their likelihood of being perceived as informal leaders in several ways. Generally, group members are more likely to be perceived as informal leaders if they provide salient contributions to the attainment of the group's goals and adhere to important group norms.

Contributions to group performance can come in three forms: special expertise or skills, unusually high involvement in activities necessary for group performance, and active participation in group discussions. Specifically, informal leaders are likely to be those perceived to (1) aid the group's attainment of its goals because of direct knowledge or expertise or indirect influence of those with the necessary knowledge or expertise; (2) volunteer relatively more time in pursuing the group's task; or (3) be more visible in group discussions by contributing ideas and suggestions. It is interesting to note that while contributing high-quality suggestions results in greater perceptions of influence, frequency of participation—independent of quality—significantly increases the perceived influence of the individual by group members.[3]

LEADERSHIP  AS  A
MANAGERIAL  ROLE

There is sometimes confusion between the role of a *leader* and the role of a *manager*. The activities of these two roles can differ radically. It is not necessary that the manager of the group also be the group's formal or informal leader. The manager may be the leader or perform functions separate from the tasks traditionally described as leadership activities. For example, the manager may be involved in developing and securing the necessary budget for the group's activities. While this is clearly not a leadership function, it is critical to the effective functioning of the group.

In addition to ability to accomplish the organization's goals, true leadership has at least two other important characteristics: the situation and the follower. It is interesting to note that early definitions of leadership focused almost exclusively on the identified leader. Students of leadership concerned themselves with the traits and demographic

[3]R. M. Sorrentino and R. G. Boutillier, "The Effect of Quantity and Quality of Verbal Interaction on Rating of Leadership Ability," *Journal of Experimental Social Psychology* 11 (1975): 403–411.

characteristics that differentiated leaders from followers. As leadership theory evolved, so did its emphasis on the situation in which the leader exists. Situational characteristics include the organization, the broader culture, goals, characteristics of the task or project, and the educational, professional, or maturity level of the followers. The most recent development of leadership theory focuses on the reciprocal influence process between leaders and followers. This influence that leaders exert on followers and followers exert on their leaders goes beyond mere characteristics of the followers. It extends into the interdependent relationship between followers and leaders.

The primary reason for the continuing evolution of leadership theory has been to identify what separates good leaders from poor leaders. That is, what are the critical components of an *effective* leader? Social scientists and practitioners have approached this question from a number of directions and assumptions about the nature of effective leadership. To bring some order to the various theories and perspectives on leadership presented in this chapter, consider the framework presented in Figure 10–1.

Traditional theories of leadership may be categorized into two dimensions: traits and behaviors. The first dimension focuses on what aspect of the leader (trait) is emphasized. Leadership has been described in terms of both who the leader is (enduring personality traits) and how the leader behaves (observable behavior). The second dimension focuses on the type of influence the leader's behavior has. Some theories of

**FIGURE 10–1** Framework for Traditional Leadership Theories

Traditional theories of leadership can be categorized into two dimensions. The first dimension focuses on what aspect of the leader is emphasized in the theory: personality traits or behaviors. The second dimension focuses on the type of influence the leader exerts: universal or situation-contingent.

|  | **Leader** | |
| --- | --- | --- |
|  | **Trait** | **Behavior** |
| **Universal** | "Great person" approach<br>Transformational leaders | Socioemotional and task leaders<br>Managerial grid |
| **Situation-Contingent** | Fiedler's contingency model of leadership | Path-goal theory of leadership<br>Vroom-Yetton's model of decision making |

leadership assume that the traits or behaviors of a leader are consistent, without regard to situational or follower demands. These theories assume that the leader responds consistently or universally to many different situations. Alternatively, other theories assert that the leader may adjust the expression of unique personality traits or behaviors to fit the demands of the situation. From this perspective, then, the leader expresses situation-contingent behavior.

As shown in Figure 10–1, the intersection of these two dimensions yields four theoretical perspectives: the universal-trait approach, the universal-behavioral approach, the situation-contingent trait approach, and the situation-contingent behavioral approach. In this chapter, leadership effectiveness will be considered from each of these four theoretical perspectives.

## UNIVERSAL APPROACHES TO LEADERSHIP

One popular perspective on leadership is that leaders are leaders because of some enduring aspect of their personality or behavior. That is, regardless of the situation in which these individuals find themselves, their leadership abilities will emerge. The primary consideration here, however, is whether such leadership is a function of the individual or the way in which that individual behaves. In the following sections, we will examine (1) theories that leadership is dependent on the person and (2) theories that leadership is dependent on behavior.

## TRAIT APPROACHES

The universalist trait approach provided the earliest and also some of the most intuitively appealing of the leadership theories. This approach was also known as the "great man" approach to leadership (or the "great person" approach, to bring this term into modern usage). This theory is based upon the notion that certain individuals are destined to be leaders. It contends that individuals such as Martin Luther King, Jr., Winston Churchill, or Indira Gandhi would have been leaders regardless of the situations in which they found themselves. That is, leaders possess a constellation of personality characteristics that separates them from others—their followers.

The "great person" perspective on leadership makes the implicit assumption that such individuals are **transformational leaders** as opposed to **transactional leaders.** A transactional leader motivates followers by exchanging rewards for services. The transactional leader:

- Recognizes what subordinates want from their work and tries to see that they get it (if their performance warrants it).
- Exchanges rewards and promises of rewards for subordinates' effort.
- Is responsive to subordinates' immediate self-interests if they get the job done.[4]

[4]B. M. Bass, *Leadership and Performance beyond Expectations* (New York: Free Press, 1985).

Universalist trait or "great person" theories of leadership contend that certain individuals, such as Martin Luther King, Jr., or Indira Gandhi, possess traits that set them apart as leaders regardless of the situations in which they find themselves.

Transactional leadership focuses on situational determinants of leadership. In the terms of Chapter 8, transactional leaders rely on reward and coercive power. Situation-contingent theories will be discussed in greater detail later in this chapter. For now, let us note that this approach fails to explain individuals who emerge as leaders no matter where they find themselves. Such exceptional people have the unique ability to go beyond transacting with their subordinates and transform the situation and their followers.

Transformational leaders arouse intense feelings and generate turbulent one-to-one relationships with their followers. They are inspirational and concerned with ideas rather than process. They heighten expectations and engender excitement. They are likely to be dramatic and unpredictable.

Transformational leaders rely on such personal sources of power as referent power, discussed in Chapter 8. They motivate their followers to do more than the followers had originally intended by transforming the group's expectations. Such transformations can occur when the leader:

- Raises the level of follower awareness, consciousness, and commitment to designated outcomes as well as knowledge of how to achieve these outcomes.
- Gets followers to transcend their self-interests for the sake of the organization.
- Alters the followers' needs or expands their wants.

Thomas J. Watson transformed IBM; George Patton transformed the Third Army; Adolf Hitler transformed Germany. These types of leaders have an almost magical appeal for followers. They identify for their followers a way to achieve a superordinate goal. Through their appeal, they are able to change the organization, its environment, and the organizational participants. Self-confidence and self-esteem, low internal conflict, self-determination, and enthusiasm all contribute to the success of transformational leaders.[5] They have the ability to both conceive and articulate goals that lift people out of their petty preoccupations.[6] Such leaders can unite people to seek goals worthy of their best efforts. As Steven Jobs suggested while the CEO of Apple Computer, "the greatest people are self-managing . . . what they need is a common vision, and that's what leadership is is having a vision, being able to articulate it, and getting a consensus on a common vision." The value of such leadership is discussed in the "FOCUS ON: Transformational Leaders."

If we reconsider our earlier discussion of the differences between managers and leaders, it seems that transactional leaders are more like

---

[5]See, for example, B. M. Bass, *Leadership and Performance;* R. J. House, "A 1976 Theory of Charismatic Leadership," *Leadership: The Cutting Edge,* eds. J. G. Hunt and L. L. Larson (Carbondale, Ill.: Southern University Press, 1977); W. Keichell III, "Wanted: Corporate Leaders," *Fortune,* May 30, 1983, 135–140; M. Weber, *The Theory of Social and Economic Organization,* trans. and eds. T. Parsons and A. M. Henderson (New York: Oxford University Press, 1947).

[6]J. W. Gardner, *Excellence: Can We Be Equal and Excellent Too?* (New York: Harper, 1961).

Transformational leaders like Steven Jobs, founder of Apple Computers, lift their followers to new heights of awareness and accomplishment by articulating common goals and visions. Transformational leaders are likely to be successful in small, entrepreneurial organizations where enthusiasm and excitement are more valuable than rules, routines, and procedures.

managers, making sure tasks get done right, and transformational leaders are what we generally refer to as leaders. David Berlew describes this latter form of leadership as Stage 3, or **charismatic leadership,** and differentiates it from the two other stages (or types) of leadership.[7] Stage 1 leadership is termed **custodial;** custodial leaders are concerned more with improving working conditions, compensation, and fringe benefits. Stage 2 leadership is termed **managerial.** Managerial leaders focus on providing subordinates work that is less routine and more challenging, building cohesive work teams, and giving employees more say in decisions that affect them directly. These first two stages of leadership seem much more consistent with what we consider to be transactional leadership. In contrast, Stage 3 *(charismatic)* leaders concern themselves with developing a common vision of what could be, discovering or creating opportunities and strengthening organizational members' control of their own destinies.

Few leaders fall cleanly into this third category. The demands of maintaining the charismatic hold over followers are extreme. For example, leaders of complex organizations must represent and articulate goals for many different groups simultaneously. Only the exceptional leader of a large, complex organization can identify a vision truly common to such diversity. Transformational leaders are more likely to be found in small, entrepreneurial organizations, since they are more concerned with a vision than with maintaining the rules, routines, and

[7]D. E. Berlew, "Leadership and Organizational Excitement," *Organizational Psychology: A Book of Readings,* eds. D. A. Kolb, I. M. Rubin, and J. M. McIntyre (Englewood Cliffs, N.J.: Prentice-Hall, 1979).

FOCUS ON:
Transformational
Leaders

**WANTED: Leaders Who Can Make a Difference** Say farewell to the classic postwar American manager, the model of rational decision making who coolly piloted us through the prosperity of the fifties and the go-go of the sixties, only to begin stubbing his toe in the seventies. Vanguard corporations are deciding that this generally amiable character—he did get a bit autocratic at times—isn't up to the challenges of today. No, what's required now, the emerging wisdom indicates, are not mere managers, but *leaders*—people like Lee Iacocca of Chrysler, Jack Welch of General Electric, and John Reed of Citicorp. The new paragon is an executive who can envision a future for his or her organization and inspire colleagues to join in building that future. Perhaps the most notable departure from managerial practice: Leaders do not fear change, but instead embrace it and create it. They know that their most important job is probably to transform the way the company does business.

Corporate America has always maintained a nodding interest in the subject of leadership, but the exigencies of global competition, deregulation, and accelerating technological change have whipped that interest into an anxious search for new answers to old questions: Can leadership be taught? How do you spot

potential leaders? And what, precisely, sets leaders apart from everyday managers?

Much of the current thinking on leadership had its beginnings in a famous 1977 *Harvard Business Review* article entitled "Managers and Leaders: Are They Different?" Yes, concluded the article's author, Abraham Zaleznik, a Harvard Business School professor. Managers do the same things over and over again, but it takes a leader to innovate. While a good leader needs to be a manager, too, a manager is not necessarily a leader. The corporate chief must be able to change things, to make a substantive difference in the organization, in contrast to the merely "transactional" manager who keeps on cutting the same kinds of deals with employees, customers, and society at large.

Corporations do not take kindly to transformational leaders. "The natural state of an organization is conservative, to maintain the status quo," says Walter Ulmer, Jr., president of the Center for Creative Leadership. Which is why, of course, a leader is exactly what's required when only radical change will preserve the organization in the face of new realities. These individuals must possess a "divine discontent with the status quo."

Source: Jeremy Main, "Wanted: Leaders Who Can Make a Difference," *Fortune*, September 28, 1987, pp. 92–102.

procedures necessary for larger organizations to survive. Second, the charismatic leader must give meaning to the organization for followers. Figure 10–2 identifies different opportunities that transformational leaders can provide to organizational participants to help them find meaning in their jobs.

**FIGURE 10-2**                    Sources of Meaning in Organizations

A charismatic leader must provide for followers a sense of meaning in organizational activities. Meaning comes when employees can see their organizational activities in a new light—as a chance to change or contribute something important to society.

| Type of Opportunity | Related Need or Value |
| --- | --- |
| 1. A chance to be tested; to make it on one's own | Self-reliance<br>Self-actualization |
| 2. A social experiment; to combine work, family, and play in some new way | Community<br>Integration of life |
| 3. A chance to do something well; for example, to return to real craftsmanship, to be really creative | Excellence<br>Unique accomplish-<br>ment |
| 4. A chance to do something good; for example, to run an honest, no-rip-off business or a youth counseling center | Consideration<br>Service |
| 5. A chance to change the way things are; for example, from Republican to Democrat to Socialist, from war to peace, from unjust to just | Activism<br>Social responsibility<br>Citizenship |

In addition to identifying a common vision and giving meaning to the organization and its related activities, the charismatic leader also must empower followers—make them feel stronger, more confident, more in control of their destinies, and more competent. Berlew suggests that charismatic leaders engender this feeling of power among followers by having high expectations of them, rewarding good performance rather than punishing poor performance, encouraging collaboration among individuals, helping only when asked, and creating success experiences for followers.[8]

Given the attraction and effectiveness of such leaders, it is little wonder that behavioral scientists have searched for ways to identify them. However, the search for specific factors that clearly and consistently predict which individuals will be effective transformational leaders has not been overly successful. Thousands of studies have investigated the impact on leader effectiveness of demographic characteristics (such as height, weight, and age), social characteristics (such as educational level, socioeconomic background, grades, appearance, and popularity), and personality characteristics (such as dominance, introversion-extroversion, initiative, and cooperation). While the transformational perspective has considerable intuitive appeal (especially considering the success of such transformational leaders as John Kennedy, Lenin, and Hyman Rickover), research provides only minimal support for the ability to identify charismatic leaders.

[8]Ibid.

After an exhaustive review in 1948 of over 100 review and empirical studies, one researcher reported that leadership is not a matter of possessing some combination of traits.[9] It appeared to emerge instead from a working relationship among members of the group. Thus, an individual who may be a leader in one situation is not necessarily a leader in other situations. A more recent review by this same researcher paints a more positive picture of the importance of personality traits on leader potential.[10] While the appropriateness of specific leader characteristics varies with the situation, there appears to be a constellation of leadership traits that distinguishes leaders from followers, effective from ineffective leadership, and higher-status from lower-status leaders. These characteristics include a strong sense of social and personal responsibility for decisions and outcomes, a desire for task completion, originality in problem solving, initiative in social situations, willingness to tolerate frustration and delay, self-confidence and a strong sense of self, and a capacity to structure social situations to achieve specific goals.

If we assume that transactional leaders are managers, one example of a recent application of universal trait perspectives to modern management is the identification of individuals with leadership potential through assessment centers. Assessment centers are testing mechanisms for identifying potential managerial talent. First developed by the OSS in World War II to select spies, assessment centers are now used by many major corporations. Participants in an assessment center undergo a series of role-playing exercises, psychological tests, simulations, and management games that measure their managerial talent. Assessment centers use both trait and situational information, and the accuracy of their selections is quite impressive. For example, the results of AT&T's management progression study showed that of the 422 men originally tested, 78 percent of those who reached middle management were correctly identified by the assessment center.[11] In addition, the assessment center was able to identify 95 percent of those who did not reach middle-management positions within ten years of their evaluation. Additional studies reported in 1983 based on 1,200 male and female employees of AT&T supported the usefulness of combining both individual traits and situational responses in selecting managerial talent.

Traits alone demonstrated very weak predictive power. It seems that trait measures are not sufficiently sturdy to stand alone as predictors of leadership talent and success. It should also be noted that, while assessment center results have shown good predictive validity for

[9]R. M. Stodgill, "Personal Factors Associated with Leadership," *Journal of Psychology* 25 (1948): 35–71.

[10]R. M. Stodgill, *Handbook of Leadership* (New York: Free Press, 1974).

[11]D. W. Bray and D. L. Grant, "The Assessment Center in the Measurement of Potential for Business Management," *Psychological Monographs* 80, no. 17, Whole N. 625 (1966).

managerial jobs,[12] these assessment centers were not designed to identify transformational leaders. Because of the potential overlap between what makes a successful manager and a successful leader, however, these findings are certainly intriguing. It seems that although traits are poor predictors of leader effectiveness, they do a fair job of predicting leadership *perceptions*. That is, we all have some ideas about how leaders are, and these traits can predict who we will believe to be leaders.

## BEHAVIOR APPROACHES

Although research into the specific traits of leaders is still being conducted, leadership research in the late 1940s began to focus on *behaviors* of leaders rather than their personality and demographic characteristics. Thus, rather than attempt to use personal characteristics to separate leaders from followers, this stream of research attempted to determine exactly which leader behaviors resulted in follower satisfaction and high performance.

The focus on leader behaviors rather than leader traits has a number of advantages. First, examining behaviors rather than traits allows us to consider informal as well as formal leaders. If we focus only on leaders identified by personal traits, then leadership is limited to those individuals in stable positions of leadership. Identifying leaders by their behaviors is more likely to include both stable, formal leaders and more volatile, informal leaders. Second, if critical and effective leader behaviors can be identified, our ability to train leaders will be enhanced. The "FOCUS ON: Leader Behaviors" pursues this line of thinking. Finally, the behaviors of a leader and the reciprocal behaviors of the followers allow us to examine closely the exchange relationship between leaders and followers. Exchange theory (the basis for transactional leadership), described in Chapter 8, contends that all social interactions involve some form of trade-off of benefits or costs. For example, the leader may give the group direction, coordination, legitimacy, and access to valued resources. The followers, then, reciprocate these benefits with resources of their own such as compliance and deference.[13]

In addition to this ongoing exchange of benefits, leaders can build up reserves, or idiosyncrasy credits (discussed in Chapter 7), with group members. For example, when leaders contribute to the group's performance, they gain idiosyncrasy credits. However, when leaders detract from group performance, they can lose these credits.

The importance of idiosyncrasy credits to leadership can be seen in the difference in initial power and influence between those *elected* and

---

[12]A. Howard, "An Assessment of Assessment Centers," *Academy of Management Journal* 17 (1974): 115–134; R. J. Ritchie and J. L. Moss, "Assessment Center Correlates of Women's Advancement into Middle Management: A Seven Year Longitudinal Study," *Journal of Applied Psychology* 68 (1983): 227–231.

[13]E. P. Hollander, *Leadership Dynamics: A Practical Guide to Effective Relationships* (New York: Free Press/Macmillan, 1978).

## FOCUS ON:
## Leader Behaviors

**Women Executives: What Makes for Success?** While executive men and women score similarly on measures of personality, intelligence, and behaviors in problem-solving groups and are just as able to lead, influence, and motivate other group members, women are not making the same progress as men in achieving the executive rank. Among Fortune 500 companies, only 1.7 percent of the corporate officers are women. To try to understand how women's movement up the corporate ladder compares with men's, 76 women at or near the general-management level in Fortune 500 companies were compared with similar male managers. In addition, 22 "savvy insiders" (16 men and 6 women) in ten companies—people responsible for identifying and selecting executives for top positions—were interviewed. These interviews identified the factors contributing to success or derailment among executives.

In this study, the criteria for success included reaching one of the top ten to twenty positions in the corporation and living up to one's full potential in the eyes of the company. Derailment was achieving a very high level in the company but not going as high as the organization had expected. In attempting to distinguish those individuals who had succeeded from those who had derailed, the insiders identified roughly the same number of derailment factors for men and women (on the average, 4 for men and 3.5 for women), but they listed nearly twice as many success factors for women (19.4) as for men (5.7).

The women described as successful and as derailed were put through a number of tests as they progressed up the corporate ladder. They had to show toughness and independence and at the same time depend on others. It was essential that they contradict the stereotypes that their male bosses and coworkers had about women. They had to be seen as different, "better than women" as a group, but they couldn't go too far and forfeit all traces of femininity because that would make them too alien to their superiors and colleagues. In essence, their mission was to do what *wasn't* expected of them while doing enough of what was expected of them as women to gain acceptance. Based upon the results of this study, women must reconcile themselves to four such contradictory expectations to succeed in corporate life:

1. Take risks, but be consistently outstanding.
2. Be tough, but don't be macho.
3. Be ambitious, but don't expect equal treatment.
4. Take responsibility, but follow others' advice.

These demands (which do not exist in such contradictory forms for men) are in response to stereotypic views of women. These unrealistic expectations are a part of the environment in which women must work and live, even though mounting evidence suggests that, when careers are matched, women are remarkably similar to men in their characteristics, abilities, and motives. This qualitatively different environment, then, may be the crucial—and only meaningful—difference between male and female executives.

Source: A. M. Morrison, R. P. White, and E. Van Velsor, "Executive Women: Substance Plus Style," *Psychology Today*, August 1987, pp. 18–26.

those *appointed* to leadership roles. Research has found that elected leaders are more likely than appointed leaders to make decisions in opposition to group preferences.[14] Election to leadership represents group acceptance and provides the flexibility to make decisions in what the leader perceives to be the group's best interest. Appointment to a leadership position does not necessarily include a reserve of idiosyncrasy credit. Thus, such leaders are more likely to gain these credits by maintaining the status quo or proving (by behaving consistently with group preferences) that they have the best interests of the group at heart. Once sufficient credit or acceptance is gained, then the leader must begin to introduce some form of change into the group to improve performance or these idiosyncrasy credits will deteriorate. Because a leader is expected to introduce change or provide some mechanism for improving group performance, ignoring this expectation can seriously erode a leader's influence and acceptance by group members.

From the perspective of exchange theory, leader behavior has the potential to significantly influence both group performance and follower satisfaction. Researchers at the University of Michigan and The Ohio State University were early leaders in determining the critical aspects of leader behavior.

These two research centers conducted independent research programs, yet it is interesting to note that both described two distinct types of leader behavior: **production(task)-oriented leadership** (initiating structure) and **employee(socioemotional)-oriented leadership** (initiating consideration). Production or task-oriented leadership focuses almost exclusively on activities related specifically to the task. Employee-oriented or socioemotional leadership emphasizes the individual worker's needs in managing group performance.

**The Ohio State University and University of Michigan Studies**    The Ohio State studies sought to identify the basic types of behaviors that all effective leaders use. To identify these behaviors, almost 1,800 descriptions of leader behavior were collected. Through statistical analyses, the 1,800 descriptions were reduced to 150 descriptions of good leader behavior. When these items were transformed into questions, they became the Leader Behavior Description Questionnaire (LBDQ).

These behaviors fell into a variety of categories, the two most important of which were those of initiating structure (task leadership) and consideration (socioemotional leadership). Given that any individual may rank either high or low on initiating structure and high or low on consideration, there were four different types of leaders, described in Figure 10–3. The important research question, then, was this: Which of

[14]E. P. Hollander and J. W. Julian, "Studies in Leader Legitimacy, Influence, and Innovation," *Advances in Experimental Social Psychology*, vol. 5, ed. L. Berkowitz (New York: Academic Press, 1970): 33–69.

FIGURE 10-3

## Outcomes of The Ohio State University Leadership Studies' Behavior Model

Researchers at the University of Michigan and The Ohio State University were pioneers in the attempt to identify critical aspects of leader behavior. Their studies identified several primary dimensions of leader behavior, but they have been unable to identify consistently effective leader behaviors.

|  |  | **Manager's Initiating Structure** | |
|  |  | **High** | **Low** |
| **Manager's Initiating Consideration** | **High** | High Performance<br>Low Grievance Rate<br>Low Turnover | Low Performance<br>Low Grievance Rate<br>Low Turnover |
|  | **Low** | High Performance<br>High Grievance Rate<br>High Turnover | Low Performance<br>High Grievance Rate<br>High Turnover |

Source: J. R. Gordon, *Organizational Behavior,* 2d ed. (Boston: Allyn & Bacon, 1987).

these general categories of leader behavior routinely results in superior group performance?

After large investments of time and energy, the results of this line of research have been disappointing. A recent review of this literature shows that it has yielded very inconsistent and inconclusive results.[15] There does not seem to be any combination of initiating structure and consideration that *consistently* results in superior group performance.

The work conducted at the University of Michigan led to a four-factor theory of leadership.[16] The four factors are:

1. *Support:* Behaviors that enhance group member's feelings of personal worth and importance.
2. *Interaction facilitation:* Behaviors that encourage group members to develop close, mutually satisfying relationships.
3. *Goal emphasis:* Behaviors that stimulate enthusiasm for meeting group goals and achieving high performance.
4. *Work facilitation:* Behaviors that directly aid goal attainment by providing resources such as tools, materials, and technical knowledge.

[15]B. M. Bass, *Stodgill's Handbook of Leadership: A Survey of Theory and Research,* rev. ed. (New York: Free Press, 1981).

[16]D. G. Bowers and S. E. Seashore, "Predicting Organizational Effectiveness with a Four-Factor Theory of Leadership," *Administrative Science Quarterly,* 1966, 238–263.

It should be noted that the first two factors are associated with behaviors common to socioemotional leaders, while the latter two factors are associated with task-oriented leader behaviors. As with the Ohio State two-factor theory of leadership, the Michigan studies also yielded inconsistent results. In his review of this research, Yukl found no support for all four of these categories taken together or individually as predictors of leadership effectiveness.[17]

**The Managerial Grid**   Even though the research on universal leader behaviors has received mixed support at best, the notion of an ideal leadership style continues to be intuitively appealing. This idea has served as the foundation for many leadership training programs over the years. The most famous of these—called the managerial grid—is conducted by Robert Blake, Jane Mouton, and their associates. The **managerial grid,** described in Figure 10–4, reflects the two dimensions of leader behavior—concern for production (task-oriented leadership) and concern for people (socioemotional leadership). While Blake and Mouton identify five different types of leadership—country club, impoverished, authority, organizational man, and team management— they believe that high production *and* high concern for people (team management) is the only style that will result in superior performance. With a team-management style, the leader is able to elicit high-quality performances from a group of highly committed followers who share a common purpose. The team leader uses mutual trust and respect to accomplish both individual and organizational goals.[18]

Despite its appeal and the large number of dollars spent training managers to adopt the team-management leadership style identified by Blake and Mouton, again research has revealed little empirical support for any relationship between a style of leadership and such factors as productivity, absenteeism, and turnover.[19] Given the lack of support for this universalistic notion, we now turn to the next set of leadership theories, the contingency theories.

CONTINGENCY APPROACHES TO LEADERSHIP

The fruitless search for a universal or trait perspective of leadership has led leadership researchers to reformulate their questions. Rather than search for a Holy Grail of executive leader behaviors, researchers in the last three decades have turned their attention to the situations in which leaders find themselves. Determining which set of leader behaviors is most appropriate for which situation requires an understanding of situational differences, or *contingencies* (such as the nature of the task, subordinate attributes, and group characteristics).

[17]Yukl, *Leadership in Organizations.*

[18]J. R. Gordon, *Organizational Behavior* (Boston: Allyn & Bacon, 1987).

[19]A. K. Korman, " 'Consideration,' 'Initiating Structure,' and Organizational Criteria: A Review," *Personnel Psychology* 19 (1966): 349–361.

*Jungle*

**FIGURE 10-4**  The Managerial Grid

The managerial grid is a variation of the two-dimensional perspective of leader behavior. These two dimensions result in five distinct leadership styles.

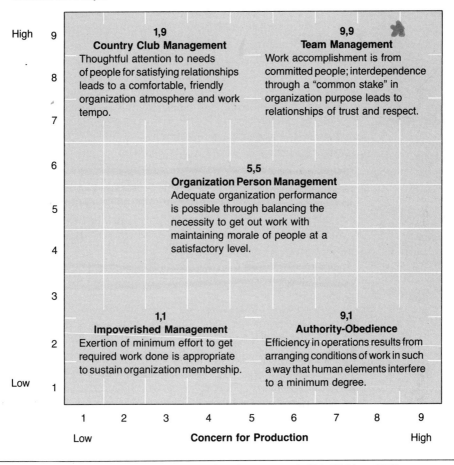

**Concern for People**

**High 9**

**1,9**
**Country Club Management**
Thoughtful attention to needs of people for satisfying relationships leads to a comfortable, friendly organization atmosphere and work tempo.

**9,9**
**Team Management**
Work accomplishment is from committed people; interdependence through a "common stake" in organization purpose leads to relationships of trust and respect.

**5,5**
**Organization Person Management**
Adequate organization performance is possible through balancing the necessity to get out work with maintaining morale of people at a satisfactory level.

**1,1**
**Impoverished Management**
Exertion of minimum effort to get required work done is appropriate to sustain organization membership.

**9,1**
**Authority-Obedience**
Efficiency in operations results from arranging conditions of work in such a way that human elements interfere to a minimum degree.

**Low 1**

1    2    3    4    5    6    7    8    9
Low            **Concern for Production**            High

Source: R. R. Blake and J. S. Mouton, *The New Managerial Grid* (Houston: Gulf Publishing, 1978).

**TRAIT APPROACHES**

**Contingency Model of Leadership**  The earliest theory specifically called a contingency theory was Fred Fiedler's **contingency model of leadership.** The basic assumption of his model was that the nature of the situation determined the effectiveness of the leader's behavior. To determine what style a leader possessed, he developed the **Least-Preferred Coworker (LPC) scale.**

Consistent with previous work on leader behavior, Fiedler's LPC scale measured two basic styles of leader behavior: (1) task-oriented and (2) relationship-oriented behavior. Research conducted by Fiedler and

Contingency theories of leadership emphasize the importance of fit between individual characteristics and situational demands. When companies grow beyond their small entrepreneurial beginnings, their need for leadership changes. John Sculley was brought in as the new CEO of Apple Computers in 1976 because his administrative skills matched the needs of the now large industrial concern.

Rice[20] suggests that low-LPC leaders emphasize completing tasks—even at the expense of interpersonal relationships—and gain self-esteem through task completion. In contrast, high-LPC leaders derive satisfaction and a sense of accomplishment from relationships with others. Fiedler argued that the importance of the LPC scale was in ferreting out an individual's ability to overlook negative traits in followers. Individuals unable to overlook such traits because of potential influence on future task accomplishment are more likely to be task oriented. Those who can maintain a strong relationship with an individual, regardless of negative traits, are more likely to be relationship-oriented individuals. The LPC scale, reproduced in Figure 10–5, produces scores between 18 and 144. Low-LPC leaders are usually described as those scoring below 58 points. High-LPC leaders score 64 or more points.

Once an individual's leadership style is ascertained, it is then important to diagnose the particular situation in which the leader works. Because Fiedler believed that leadership style was a trait—a stable personality characteristic—he suggested that organizations assign leaders based on a fit between their LPC and the situation. He felt that it was considerably easier (and more appropriate) for individuals to find situations that required their leadership style than to change their style to fit a situation.

Fiedler identified three situational characteristics that influenced whether a high-LPC or low-LPC leader would be more effective. These factors are:

1. *Leader-member relations:* The extent to which the group trusts and respects the leader and will follow the leader's directions.
2. *Task structure:* The degree to which a task is clearly specified and defined as opposed to unstructured and ambiguous.
3. *Position power:* The extent to which the leader has official power or the potential or actual ability to influence others in a desired direction because of the leader's position in the hierarchy.

Despite their bias that people are better off finding situations that require their leadership style, Fiedler and his colleagues have identified strategies for individuals to fine-tune situations to better fit with their leadership styles. These strategies are described in Figure 10–6.

Figure 10–7 illustrates the style of leadership most appropriate for a particular combination of situational characteristics. These recommendations are based on the amount of control a leader has. In high-control situations, where the group will expect *and* allow the leader to take charge, task-oriented leadership is more effective. Task-oriented leadership is also more effective in low-control situations. In a low-control situation, task-oriented leadership allows the leader to focus the activities

[20]F. E. Fiedler, *A Theory of Leadership Effectiveness* (New York: McGraw-Hill, 1967); R. W. Rice, "Construct Validity of the Least Preferred Co-Worker Scale," *Psychological Bulletin* 85 (1978): 106–118.

**FIGURE 10-5**     Least-Preferred Coworker (LPC) Scale

Fred Fiedler's contingency model of leadership contends that situational characteristics determine which leadership traits or skills are effective. Fiedler developed the LPC scale to measure an individual's leadership skills.

Think of all the people with whom you have ever worked, and then think of the person with whom you could work *least well*. This person may be someone with whom you work now or with whom you have worked in the past. This does not have to be the person you liked least well, but should be the person with whom you had the most difficulty getting a job done, the *one* individual with whom you could work *least well*.

Describe this person on the scale that follows by placing an *X* in the appropriate space.

Look at the words at both ends of the line before you mark your *X*. *There are no right or wrong answers.* Work rapidly; your first answer is likely to be the best. Do not omit any items, and mark each item only once.

Now describe the person with whom you can work least well.

*Scoring*

| | | | | | | | | | | |
|---|---|---|---|---|---|---|---|---|---|---|
| Pleasant | 8 | 7 | 6 | 5 | 4 | 3 | 2 | 1 | Unpleasant | ___ |
| Friendly | 8 | 7 | 6 | 5 | 4 | 3 | 2 | 1 | Unfriendly | ___ |
| Rejecting | 1 | 2 | 3 | 4 | 5 | 6 | 7 | 8 | Accepting | ___ |
| Tense | 1 | 2 | 3 | 4 | 5 | 6 | 7 | 8 | Relaxed | ___ |
| Distant | 1 | 2 | 3 | 4 | 5 | 6 | 7 | 8 | Close | ___ |
| Cold | 1 | 2 | 3 | 4 | 5 | 6 | 7 | 8 | Warm | ___ |
| Supportive | 8 | 7 | 6 | 5 | 4 | 3 | 2 | 1 | Hostile | ___ |
| Boring | 1 | 2 | 3 | 4 | 5 | 6 | 7 | 8 | Interesting | ___ |
| Quarrelsome | 1 | 2 | 3 | 4 | 5 | 6 | 7 | 8 | Harmonious | ___ |
| Gloomy | 1 | 2 | 3 | 4 | 5 | 6 | 7 | 8 | Cheerful | ___ |
| Open | 8 | 7 | 6 | 5 | 4 | 3 | 2 | 1 | Guarded | ___ |
| Backbiting | 1 | 2 | 3 | 4 | 5 | 6 | 7 | 8 | Loyal | ___ |
| Untrustworthy | 1 | 2 | 3 | 4 | 5 | 6 | 7 | 8 | Trustworthy | ___ |
| Considerate | 8 | 7 | 6 | 5 | 4 | 3 | 2 | 1 | Inconsiderate | ___ |
| Nasty | 1 | 2 | 3 | 4 | 5 | 6 | 7 | 8 | Nice | ___ |
| Agreeable | 8 | 7 | 6 | 5 | 4 | 3 | 2 | 1 | Disagreeable | ___ |
| Insincere | 1 | 2 | 3 | 4 | 5 | 6 | 7 | 8 | Sincere | ___ |
| Kind | 8 | 7 | 6 | 5 | 4 | 3 | 2 | 1 | Unkind | ___ |
| | | | | | | | | | Total | ___ |

Source: Fred E. Fiedler, Martin M. Chemers, and Linda Mahar, *Improving Leadership Effectiveness* (New York: Wiley, 1976), 7.

**FIGURE 10–6**   ✓   Leader Actions to Change Situations

Contingency theory implies that individuals are better off finding situations that require the leadership skills they possess. Nevertheless, there are some strategies that individuals can use to alter their situations to fit their leadership skills.

**Modifying Leader-Member Relations**

1. Spend more—or less—informal time with your subordinates (lunch, leisure activities, and so on).
2. Request particular people for work in your group.
3. Volunteer to direct difficult or troublesome subordinates.
4. Suggest or effect transfers of particular subordinates into or out of your unit.
5. Raise morale by obtaining positive outcomes for subordinates (special bonuses, time off, attractive assignments, and so on).

**Modifying Task Structure**

If you wish to work with less-structured tasks, you can:

1. Ask your boss, whenever possible, to give you the new or unusual problems and let you figure out how to solve them.
2. Bring the problems and tasks to your group members, and invite them to work with you on the planning and decision-making phases of the tasks.

If you wish to work with more highly structured tasks, you can:

1. Ask your superior to give you, whenever possible, the tasks that are more structured or to give you more detailed instructions.
2. Break the job down into smaller subtasks that can be more highly structured.

**Modifying Position Power**

To raise your position power, you can:

1. Show your subordinates who's boss by exercising fully the powers that the organization provides.
2. Make sure that information to your group gets channeled through you.

To lower your position power, you can:

1. Call on members of your group to participate in planning and decision-making functions.
2. Let your assistants exercise relatively more power.

Source: F. E. Fiedler, "How Do You Make Leaders More Effective?" *Organizational Dynamics* (Autumn 1972): 3–8.

of the group on the task rather than on the unfavorable nature of leader-follower interactions. Only in the moderate-control situation does Fiedler recommend a relationship-oriented leadership style. In such conditions, leaders must elicit the cooperation and commitment of their subordinates to accomplish the task.

Research has supported Fiedler's approach to leadership. However, there is controversy over the use of the LPC as a measurement of leadership style. The LPC does not directly measure leader behavior; instead, it measures an individual's *feelings* about a coworker. This concern, coupled with a lack of consistent scores among individuals who complete the scale on different occasions, has called into question the

**FIGURE 10–7**     Results from the Contingency Model Research

Task-oriented leadership fits best with both high-control and low-control situations. Only in moderate-control conditions does contingency theory recommend relationship-oriented leadership.

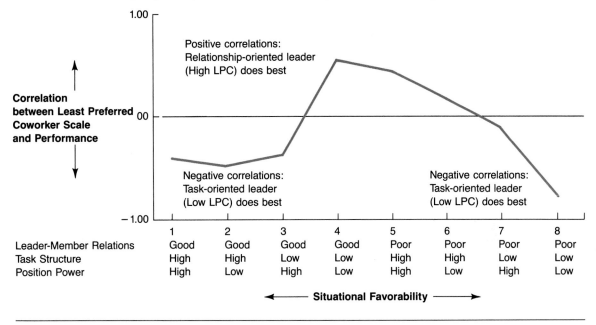

Source: F. Fiedler, *A Theory of Leadership Effectiveness* (New York: McGraw-Hill, 1967).

usefulness of the LPC questionnaire. However, Fiedler and his colleagues have provided us with a useful notion: *contingency* leadership. While clearly wedded to a contingency model of leadership and the importance of a situation-style fit, Fiedler acknowledged in a recent article (highlighted in the "FOCUS ON: Leadership Contingencies") that personality factors such as intelligence can enhance or inhibit a leader's effectiveness, even if the situation-style fit is correct.

**BEHAVIOR
APPROACHES**

✓ **Path-Goal Theory of Leadership**     In contrast to Fiedler's view that specific individuals should be chosen to be leaders based upon the match between their leadership style and the amount of situational control, this notion of contingency suggests that leaders *can and should* adapt their styles to various situational demands. Specifically, the task of a leader is to strengthen subordinates' expectancy links.[21] These expectancy links

[21]R. J. House and T. R. Mitchell, "A Path-Goal Theory of Leadership," *Journal of Contemporary Business* 3 (1974): 81–97.

FOCUS ON:

Leadership
Contingencies

**Leader Intelligence and Effectiveness** The importance of context in determining the better leadership style has been demonstrated by everyday experience as well as research. Leaders must be smart enough to communicate clearly and to monitor the task at hand, but a high level of intelligence doesn't always help.

In a recent set of studies involving high school students, Army mess personnel, Reserve Officers Training Corps cadets, and Army infantry squads, the tasks performed ranged from highly structured (running a mess hall) to unstructured (decoding messages). Group performance on these tasks was rated by various knowledgeable observers, and in one study was rated objectively by how many messages the group decoded in 30 minutes.

Leader intelligence contributed highly to performance only if the leader was directive and had a stress-free relationship with a supportive group. In all other conditions, either the leader's intelligence did not contribute to group performance or, much to the researchers' surprise, high intelligence was related to poor performance.

Why the most intelligent leaders did poorly in participatory situations can be understood in a number of ways. First, they are likely to throw a lot of ideas into the pot—too many to be integrated into a solution. The group members may be confused about which of the leader's many ideas to consider and whether to come up with their own ideas. Second, the members may expect bright leaders to provide guidance and feel betrayed or let down if the leaders let them flounder on their own. A third possibility is that the bright, nondirective leaders spend too much time listening and not enough time getting the job under way.

The data make intuitive sense: If you've got brains, tell the group what to do; if you are not so bright, let others do the talking. Leader intelligence, then, is not the only factor to influence effective job performance. There are many tasks that do not require intelligence and some in which highly intelligent individuals may perform worse than those with lower intelligence scores, but with more practical knowledge and experience. Being a mathematical genius will not be of much help if the job is to coach football or direct a musical comedy!

Source: Fred E. Fiedler, "When to Lead, When to Stand Back," *Psychology Today,* September 1987, pp. 26–27. Reprinted with permission from *Psychology Today* Magazine. Copyright © 1987 (PT Partners, L.P.).

come from expectancy theory (discussed in Chapter 4) and are the subordinates' perception of the ties between effort, performance, and desired outcomes. An effective leader will (1) encourage subordinates' desires for outcomes over which the leader has some control; (2) ensure that performance is rewarded as expected (that the link between performance and expected outcome is strong); (3) coach and direct subordinates along the path of successful performance; (4) help subordinates clarify expectations (set goals, specify organizational expectations, identify the route to successful job performance); (5) ensure that the necessary resources (skills, equipment, training) for successful task performance are available to subordinates; and (6) develop both the extrinsic and *intrinsic* motivational forces of subordinates. To the extent that the leader is able to accomplish these tasks, the path-goal model of leadership suggests that subordinates will:

1. *experience higher job satisfaction* as the path to job performance and subsequent rewards is more direct,
2. *accept the leader* as the leader aids in the attainment of valued rewards, and
3. *become motivated* (they will come to believe that they are performing the task required of them and that, in doing so, they will receive valued rewards).

*Choosing a Leadership Style*　The path-goal theory identifies four styles of leader behavior: directive, supportive, achievement-oriented, and participative. The first two styles are similar to the task-oriented and socioemotionally oriented leader behavior of other leadership theories. The third, achievement-oriented style, focuses on performance, goal setting, and other aspects consistent with McClelland's theories of motivating subordinates (discussed in Chapter 4). The fourth leadership style is participative. It focuses on behaviors that enlist the subordinates in the decision-making process of the organization. Examples of these specific leader behaviors are outlined in Figure 10–8.

In determining which leadership style to implement, the path-goal approach suggests that *both* subordinate and situational characteristics are important. Subordinate characteristics to be considered are their level of authoritarianism (rigidity), locus of control, and level of ability. The greater the subordinates' perception of their ability relative to task demands, the less willing they are to accept a directive style of leadership. The more authoritarian the subordinates, the more likely they are to accept a directive style of leadership. Individuals with an internal locus of control (who believe that rewards are contingent upon their behavior—that they control what happens to them) are more satisfied with a participative style of leadership than are those with an external locus of control (who believe that their behaviors have little to do with the rewards they receive—that fate controls their destinies).

The situational or environmental variables to consider include the nature of the task, the formal authority structure of the organization, and the norms of interpersonal relationships within the organization. The more unstructured or ambiguous the task, the more likely subordinates are to be satisfied with a directive style of leadership. The more structured the task, the more important a supportive leadership style is to subordinate performance and satisfaction.[22] Figure 10–9 illustrates the situations in which each of the leadership styles results in

[22]R. J. House and G. Dessler, "The Path-Goal Theory of Leadership: Some Post Hoc and A Priori Tests," *Contingency Approaches to Leadership,* eds. J. G. Hunt and L. L. Larson (Carbondale, Ill.: Southern Illinois University Press, 1974).

**FIGURE 10–8**     Leader Behavior Dimensions in House and Mitchell's Path-Goal Theory

In the path-goal theory, there are four styles of leader behavior. The path-goal theory suggests that both subordinate and situational characteristics are important determinants of the appropriate leadership style.

**Leader Directiveness**

Letting subordinates know what is expected.

Providing specific guidance as to what should be done and how.

Making leader's part in the group understood.

Scheduling work to be done.

Maintaining definite standards of performance.

**Leader Supportiveness**

Showing concern for status and well-being of subordinates.

Doing little things to make work more pleasant.

Treating members as equals.

Being friendly and approachable.

**Leader Achievement-Orientedness**

Setting challenging goals.

Expecting subordinates to perform at their highest level.

Showing a high degree of confidence in subordinates.

Constantly emphasizing excellence in performance.

**Leader Participativeness**

Consulting with subordinates.

Soliciting subordinate suggestions.

Taking subordinate suggestions seriously.

Source: R. J. House and T. R. Mitchell, "Path-Goal Theory of Leadership," *Journal of Contemporary Business* (Autumn 1974): 81–94.

positive outcomes. This figure illustrates, for example, that subordinates with a high need for achievement will respond satisfactorily only to a leader using an achievement-oriented leadership style.[23]

The path-goal theory of leadership provides some specific, testable predictions about leader effectiveness. Unfortunately, a review of the recent research on the path-goal theory of leadership has provided only marginal support for some of these predictions. For example, there is consistent evidence that subordinates will be more satisfied to perform in a structured situation when the leader effects a supportive style of leadership. With a directive style of leadership in a highly structured task

[23]J. C. Wofford and T. N. Srinivasan, "Experimental Tests of the Leader-Environment-Follower Interaction Theory of Leadership," *Organizational Behavior and Human Performance* 32 (1983): 35–54.

**FIGURE 10–9**

## Effective Leadership Styles under Certain Conditions: Predictions from the Path-Goal Theory of Leadership

According to path-goal theory, subordinate characteristics that determine appropriate leadership style include social and achievement needs; situational determinants include the nature of the task.

| Sample Situational Characteristics | Leadership Styles | | | |
|---|---|---|---|---|
| | Directive | Supportive | Achievement | Participative |
| **Task** | | | | |
| Structured | No | Yes | Yes | Yes |
| Unstructured | Yes | No | Yes | No |
| Clear goals | No | Yes | No | Yes |
| Ambiguous goals | Yes | No | Yes | No |
| **Subordinates** | | | | |
| Skilled in task | No | Yes | Yes | Yes |
| Unskilled in task | Yes | No | Yes | No |
| High achievement needs | No | No | Yes | No |
| High social needs | No | Yes | No | Yes |
| **Formal Authority** | | | | |
| Extensive | No | Yes | Yes | Yes |
| Limited | Yes | Yes | Yes | Yes |
| **Work Group** | | | | |
| Strong social network | Yes | No | Yes | Yes |
| Experienced in collaboration | No | No | No | Yes |
| **Organizational Culture** | | | | |
| Supports participation | No | No | No | Yes |
| Achievement-oriented | No | No | Yes | No |

Source: J. C. Wofford and T. N. Srinivasan, "Experimental Tests of the Leader-Environment-Follower Interaction Theory of Leadership," *Organizational Behavior and Human Performance* 32 (1983): 35–54.

situation, the findings are mixed. Sometimes subordinate satisfaction suffers; sometimes subordinate satisfaction is enhanced.[24]

The evolution of leadership theory from a trait or behavior approach to a contingency perspective is critical to our understanding of this complex phenomenon. Just as the need theorists in Chapter 4 provided us with the insight that people are different and their needs and motivations cannot neatly fit into simple economic models, the contingency theories of leadership have illuminated the association between appropriate leadership style and task characteristics.

[24]C. A. Schriecheim and A. Denisi, "Task Dimensions as Moderators of the Effects of Instrumental Leadership: A Two-Sample Replicated Test of Path Goal Leadership Theory," *Journal of Applied Psychology* (October 1981): 589–597.

# ALTERNATIVE THEORIES OF LEADERSHIP

Unfortunately, contingency theories of leadership have not answered all our questions about leadership. In fact, such models are primarily descriptive—that is, they describe which leadership style is best associated with which task or situation. Therefore, they leave gaps in our understanding of leadership. For example, what is the real impact of leader-subordinate interactions? Is it the leader who influences the subordinate, or does the subordinate's behavior subtly influence and shape the leader's behavior? What impact do leaders' perceptions of their subordinates have on their choice of leadership style? What characteristics of the task, the subordinates, or the situation make leaders more or less necessary? Finally, are there substitutes for leadership, such as work arrangements that make leadership less necessary?

Researchers recently have begun to fill in these gaps by examining leadership from different and relatively novel perspectives. For the most part, these new theories do not assume that leadership as an objective and consistent construct exists. Rather, they assume that leadership is a *social construction* of reality—a way that people talk about the relationships among employees in organizations. According to these new theories, leaders and leader behavior cannot exist independently from the task, situational, and subordinate components of the work environment. The final section of this chapter will address these more radical notions of leadership.

# VERTICAL DYAD LINKAGE MODEL

In the behavioral theories of leadership discussed earlier, the leader's behavior was assumed to be consistent across all subordinates. However, the **vertical dyad linkage (VDL) model,** which is based on exchange theory, focuses on the differential patterns of leader interaction within the work group. As an extension of exchange theory, it suggests that the leader does not interact with the group as a whole. Rather, the leader has individual relationships with each work-group member, and the nature of these dyadic (two-person) relationships determines the behaviors of subordinates.[25]

The relationships between individual work-group members have been categorized based on each member's association with an in-group or an out-group. Whether or not a person is a member of the in-group depends on that individual's association with the leader. Subordinates are members of the in-group if they share common interests with the leader and are part of the leader's communication and support network. Members of the out-group, then, have less in common with the leader and are less likely to support or associate with the leader.

In-group membership results in a better understanding between the subordinate and the leader. As supervisors become more knowledgeable

[25]G. Graen, F. Dansereau, and T. Minami, "Dysfunctional Leadership Styles," *Organizational Behavior and Human Performance* 7 (1972): 216–236.

The vertical dyad linkage model of leadership focuses on the importance of individual relationships between supervisors and subordinates. These relationships usually lead to the development of in-groups and out-groups in organizations, which can prove detrimental to both work-force morale and employee performance.

about the specific strengths and weaknesses of their in-group subordinates, they are likely to express more faith in their performance potential and judgment than in those of out-group members. The competitive advantage of in-group membership is that it is a self-fulfilling prophecy. While differences in the performance potential of in-group and out-group members may be low initially, over time these differences will be magnified. For example, if a task is sufficiently critical or complex, the supervisor is more likely to assign it to an individual in whom that supervisor has more trust. Particularly valued assignments will likely go to someone who deserves to be rewarded—a member of the in-group. Out-group members are likely to be assigned the remaining tasks—tasks that are repetitive, unimportant, and repugnant.[26]

Over time, then, the leader will come to see in-group members (whose abilities have been challenged and rewarded) as better able to handle the responsibilities of important hierarchical positions. The performance of out-group members, on the other hand, will have deteriorated, thus completing the cycle of the self-fulfilling prophecy. Not only will these employees be unchallenged by their assignments, but also both the employees' and their leader's perceptions of their capabilities will be seriously eroded. Job satisfaction will be low and turnover high.

Given human nature, the development of in-groups and out-groups is difficult to avoid in organizational settings. Such a split may not be damaging to work-group effectiveness if there are tasks that do not require a great deal of coordination among the groups. Tasks that can be accomplished through the skills of a few exceptional individuals also may not suffer from the existence of in-groups and out-groups. However, overreliance on a small portion of the work force to the exclusion of other members can seriously hamper a work group's overall performance. As suggested in Chapter 9, one of the clear advantages of group decision making lies in the added benefit accruing from the full use of the unique knowledge and skills of group members. Systematically excluding the contributions of some individuals clearly is undesirable. Leaders trying to avoid such a split should examine their patterns of work assignment and reinforcement carefully. In some cases, they might have to behave counter to their instincts by assigning challenging and critical tasks to those about whom they are unsure.

That the leader's perception of the subordinate influences leader behavior and, in turn, influences subordinate behavior should not be surprising. The mutual influence processes of exchange theory, equity theory, and negotiation have been described in other chapters. The notion that subordinate performance may be more influenced by leader perceptions and subsequent behavior than by innate ability and skill is also critical to the second alternative theory of leadership, the attribution model.

[26]L. Larwood, *Organizational Behavior and Management* (Boston: Kent, 1984).

ATTRIBUTION
MODEL OF
LEADERSHIP

Unlike other leadership models, the attribution model of leadership deals specifically with perceptions and subsequent behaviors of organizational actors. This model has two facets: (1) leader attributions for and reactions to poor performance by subordinates, and (2) observer attributions for and reactions to poor performance by the leader. Like the VDL model, it is based upon the notion that leaders and followers are involved in a mutual influence process.

**Leader Attributions**   In the daily performance of work, a leader obtains information about subordinates and their behaviors. Based upon this information, the leader makes a determination—an attribution—of the cause of each subordinate's behaviors and selects strategies to deal with any poor performers. The leader's attributions as much as the subordinate's behaviors determine how the leader responds to poor performers.

As detailed in Chapter 3, attributions are based upon three dimensions of behavior: distinctiveness (Did the behavior occur on this task but not on other tasks?), consensus (Is this level of performance common to other organizational actors?), and consistency (Is this level of performance common for this employee?). The answers to these three questions identify for the leader either an external (situational) or internal (personal) cause for the employee's poor performance.

This attribution is critical to leader-follower relations. A subordinate whose successes or failures are attributed to personal traits such as skill or natural ability will have very different interactions with the leader than a subordinate whose successes or failures are attributed to environmental factors, such as luck.[27] These attributions can influence many different facets of a leader's behavior. The perceived causes of a subordinate's poor performance have important implications for how a leader rewards or punishes a behavior. Typically, leaders attempt to change a subordinate's behavior only when an internal (personal) attribution is made. These types of changes are most clearly amenable to the influence of rewards and punishments. If the leader attributes a subordinate's performance to an external cause, then the leader likely will focus on changing the environment: what the leader perceives to be the *real* cause of the subordinate's poor performance.

A second aspect of leader behavior affected by a leader's attributions for subordinate performance is the level of supervision. If the leader believes that a subordinate's earlier successes were due to intense supervision, then the leader likely will continue the previous level of supervision. If the subordinate's performance is attributed to an internal

---

[27]F. Dansereau, G. Graen, and W. J. Haga, "A Vertical Dyad Linkage Approach to Leadership in Formal Organizations," *Organizational Behavior and Human Performance* 13 (1975): 46–78; T. R. Mitchell, S. G. Green, and R. E. Wood, "An Attribution Model of Leadership and the Poor Performing Subordinate: Development and Validation," *Research in Organization Behavior,* vol. 3, eds. L. L. Cummings and B. M. Staw (Greenwich, Conn.: JAI Press, 1981): 197–234.

**FIGURE 10–10**     An Attribution Model of Leader Behavior

As with the vertical dyad linkage model, the attribution model of leadership emphasizes the mutual influence of leaders and followers. The core of this model is attributions for and reactions to poor performance by either the leader or followers.

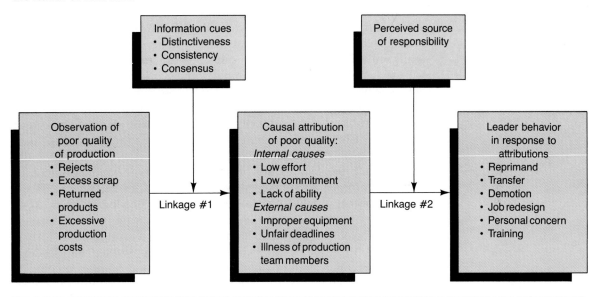

Source: T. R. Mitchell and R. E. Wood, "An Empirical Test of an Attributional Model of Leader's Responses to Poor Performance," in *Academy of Management Proceedings,* ed. R. C. Huseman, (Academy of Management, 1979), p. 94.

cause such as personal skill or effort, then supervision is likely to be less intense.

Finally, a leader's performance *expectations* of subordinates also will be influenced by attributions. If a subordinate's success is attributed to ability or skill, then the leader will be more likely to expect future performance to be consistently high than if success is attributed to an external cause such as luck.[28] Further, the stronger the internal attribution for success, the higher the leader's aspirations for future follower performance. The complete model of the attribution process from the leader's perspective is illustrated in Figure 10–10.

**Observer Attributions**     As mentioned earlier in this chapter, leaders often are given credit for organizational successes and blamed for

[28]B. Weiner and A. Kukla, "An Attributional Analysis of Achievement Motivation," *Journal of Personality and Social Psychology* 15 (1970): 1–20; B. Weiner, R. Nierenberg, and M. Goldstein, "Social Learning (Locus of Control) versus Attributional (Causal Stability) Interpretations of Expectancy of Success," *Journal of Personality* 44 (1976): 52–68.

organizational failures, regardless of their real causes. Leadership is a concern of organization observers (such as stockholders, employees, or anyone but the leader) who are attempting to understand and subsequently control their world. It is tempting to trace all organizational successes and failures back to individual leaders, rather than try to understand the complex web of individual, organizational, and environmental factors involved. People want to believe that individuals can significantly influence organizational performance. One study found that when observers were told that a work group had performed well, they concluded that the leader had been more consistent and provided more task structure than he or she did when the work group performed poorly.[29] Thus, the importance and reliance on leaders as the causal agent for organizational success or failure imbues them with considerable (and possibly undeserved) power.

The belief that leaders are responsible for organizational outcomes may be reinforced by such organizational actions as the investment of critical resources in selecting a leader or the firing of a leader whose work group's performance is inadequate. If there is an elaborate and detailed search and selection process to identify a new leader, followed by formal ceremonies to install that individual in the position, that leader's legitimacy is much greater than it is if chosen by the flip of a coin. In professional team sports, it is unlikely that an owner will fire the entire team when it performs poorly. Instead, the firing of the team's manager or coach as the obvious scapegoat symbolizes management's conviction that steps must be taken to enhance organizational performance.

From this perspective, successful leaders will be those who associate themselves with successes and dissociate themselves from failures—who figure out where the group is heading and arrive there first. When they know that a group or division is about to improve because of economic cycles, successful leaders will visibly and vividly associate themselves with that group and its performance. When failure of a group or division is imminent, then successful leaders will distance themselves from the actions of that group, perhaps going as far as transferring to another group or to a completely different organization.[30]

Both the attributional model of leadership and the vertical dyad linkage model assume that the perception of hierarchical leadership and its subsequent influence are important for organizational performance. A third and final perspective on leadership suggests that many individual, organizational, and task characteristics have the capacity to serve as **substitutes for leadership.**

[29]J. R. Larson, J. H. Lingle, and M. M. Scerbo, "The Impact of Performance Cues on Leader-Behavior Ratings: The Role of Selective Information Availability and Probabilistic Response Bias," *Organizational Behavior and Human Performance* 33 (1984): 323–349.

[30]J. Pfeffer, "The Ambiguity of Leadership," *Academy of Management Review* 2 (1977): 104–112.

## SUBSTITUTES FOR LEADERSHIP

Many of the theories introduced in this chapter make the implicit assumption that leadership makes a difference. While it is generally accepted that no one leadership trait is dominant enough to be effective in all situations, the focus in most modern theories of leadership is on determining in which situational contingencies a particular style of leadership will be more effective. Sometimes, however, hierarchical leadership does not have its intended influence. Even some of the more traditional leadership theories such as path-goal theory suggest that when both paths and goals are clear, attempts by the leader to clarify them will be redundant and will be seen by subordinates as imposing unnecessary, close control.[31] Such close control may enhance performance by reducing goldbricking, but it will reduce participant satisfaction as well. While leader behavior is redundant in such situations, a number of research studies now go further, arguing that, in many situations, leader behavior and hierarchical leadership are irrelevant.

Studies examining the impact of leader behaviors in organizations occasionally find that situational factors can neutralize or substitute for the formal leader's ability to influence work-group satisfaction or performance.[32] A **neutralizer** is a factor that paralyzes, destroys, or counteracts the effectiveness of leader behaviors, making it impossible for them to have an impact. A **substitute** makes leader behaviors not only impossible but also unnecessary. Thus, all substitutes are neutralizers, but all neutralizers are not necessarily substitutes for leadership. For example, a professional orientation (a commitment to a profession rather than to an organization) is more of a substitute for leadership than a neutralizer. Individuals who are seriously committed to their professions care more about horizontal than vertical relationships, give considerable credence to peer reviews and evaluations rather than to hierarchical evaluations, and tend to develop relationships external to the employing organization.[33] Alternatively, hierarchical leadership is neutralized when the work is very standardized, machine-paced, or serially interdependent. In these situations, the employee has little autonomy or ability to be influenced by leader behaviors. Examples of potential substitutes for or neutralizers of leadership are presented in Figure 10–11.

Leadership substitutes or neutralizers are often aspects of the task sought by employees and employers alike. For example, Figure 10–11 identifies task-provided performance feedback as a mechanism that can supplant leader usefulness. Since task-provided feedback is the most immediate, accurate, and intrinsically motivating source of performance

[31]House and Mitchell, "A Path-Goal Theory of Leadership."

[32]S. Kerr, "Substitutes for Leadership: Some Implications for Organizational Design," *Organizational Administrative Science* 8 (1977): 135–146.

[33]A. C. Filley, R. J. House, and S. Kerr, *Managerial Processes and Organizational Behavior* (Glenview, Ill.: Scott, Foresman, 1976).

**FIGURE 10–11**     Potential Substitutes for and Neutralizers of Hierarchical Leadership

Factors embedded in situations can neutralize or substitute for a leader's influence on group satisfaction and performance. Substitutes and neutralizers include characteristics of the worker, the worker's task, or the organization.

| Worker | Worker's Task | Organization |
|---|---|---|
| Ability | Repetitiveness and ambiguity | Formalization |
| Experience | Methodological invariance | Inflexibility |
| Training | Intrinsic satisfaction | Highly specific, active advisory and staff functions |
| Knowledge | Task-provided feedback concerning accomplishment | |
| Professional orientation | | Closely knit, cohesive work group |
| Need for independence | | Rewards outside leader's control |
| Indifference toward organizational rewards | | Spatial distance between leader and subordinate |

information, a leader's ability to influence employee performance through performance evaluation may pale in comparison.[34] Organizations should create mechanisms for including such factors as task-provided feedback or peer evaluation systems or goal setting in their daily activities. If the organization is to benefit from these substitutes, it is essential that such factors be incorporated in the routine of the firm. The extent to which organizations use substitutes for leadership varies around the world. For example, in the "INTERNATIONAL FOCUS ON: Substitutes for Leadership," it seems that leaders at different levels of the organization in different countries vary in their willingness to share power with their subordinates.

The concept of substitutes for and neutralizers of hierarchical leadership is an interesting one. It is unlikely that any organization will have so many such factors that leadership is rendered totally useless. On the other hand, it is equally unlikely that they will be so rare that followers will be forced to rely exclusively on leaders. Thus, in attempting to better understand the impact of leaders and leader behaviors, it is important that we consider when leadership is useful *as well as* when it is irrelevant or harmful to organizational performance.

[34]S. Kerr and J. Jermier, "Substitutes for Leadership: Their Meaning and Measurement," *Organizational Behavior and Human Performance* 22 (1978): 375–403.

# INTERNATIONAL FOCUS ON:
## Substitutes for Leadership

**Power Sharing among Leaders**

In recent research comparing the decision-making styles of upper- and lower-level managers in eight countries, consistent differences were found both between countries and within countries. In general, the research suggests that across all the countries, there was a general tendency for lower-level managers to share *less* power with their subordinates than did higher-level managers. Further, managers in countries such as the United Kingdom, Spain, and Israel report using many more central-ized decision-making processes than do managers in countries such as France and Sweden. Managers in the United States, Germany, and the Netherlands tend to cluster around the center of the distribution. Interestingly, the results of this study have clustered countries in groups that are not necessarily based on similar culture or background. So, while it seems that there may be differences in leadership style based on national differences, the concept of cultural differences has not been supported.

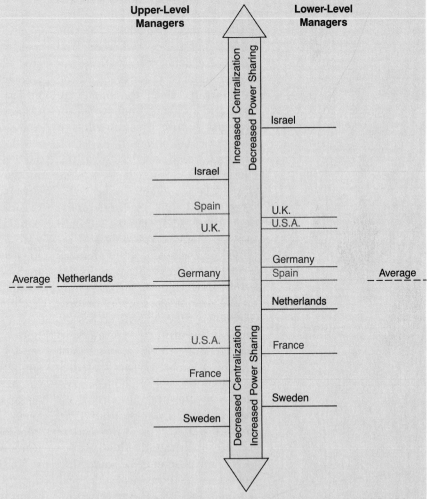

Source: F. A. Heller and B. Wilpert, *Competence and Power in Managerial Decision Making: A Study of Senior Levels of Organizations in Eight Countries* (New York: Wiley, 1981), 98–102.

SUMMARY

Leadership is a broad and difficult topic within organizational behavior. Researchers and practitioners alike have wrestled with this concept, trying to understand its specific components. Early in its history, leadership research focused on the personalities of those identified as leaders. The basic assumption of this research was that a set of unique personality and demographic characteristics differentiated leaders from followers. As this method proved less than useful, emphasis was placed on specific leader behaviors—whether the leader was concerned with the socioemotional or task aspects of the work group. Both the universal-trait and universal-behavior approaches ignore the influence of the particular situation in which the leader works. In contrast, the contingency approach to leadership—that leadership makes a difference and that its effectiveness depends on the specific situation—provides a more complex and interactional view of leader behavior. No longer is the efficacy of leader behaviors thought to be based only on the unique personality or predilections of the designated leader. Rather, the efficacy of leadership may be tied to the favorableness of the situation. However, Fiedler recommends that leaders be chosen to fit the situation in which they will be working rather than situations altered to fit the leadership style of the individual.

The intransigence of leadership style was at odds with the experience of many organizational actors, creating a theoretical and practical vacuum. What was needed was a theory of leadership that incorporated a responsibility for organizational leaders. In the path-goal theory of leadership, the leader's effectiveness is influenced by various situational components. The leader's task is to make the paths to performance and rewards for performance clearly visible to subordinates. While this perspective on leadership provided more flexibility for the leader in responding to organization demands, it (along with its predecessors) implicitly assumed that leadership was real; that it was a construct that could be identified and studied, separate from other organizational influences—particularly subordinates.

Alternative views of leadership such as the vertical dyad linkage model suggest that, while leadership is important, it is by no means one-dimensional. The same leader behavior can influence subordinates in a variety of ways, depending on their in-group or out-group membership. The primary assumption of the VDL model is that leadership is *interactive*.

An extension of this interactive notion is found in the attribution model of leadership. This model suggests that leadership exists because people (subordinates and leaders alike) have certain expectations about how individuals will behave. Therefore, what people think is more important than what is. If leaders develop attributions about the behavior of subordinates, they will behave consistently with those attributions, regardless of their veracity. Subordinates also make attributions about individuals in the role of leader. Those attributions influence the leader's ability to impact subordinate performance.

The final model of leadership presented here assumes leadership may be more or less useful, depending upon the existence of substitutes for or neutralizers of leadership. That is, the greater the presence of particular task, subordinate, and organizational characteristics (such as intrinsically satisfying work, ability and experience, and inflexibility, respectively) the less relevant or necessary the role of the leader.

Regardless of the particular perspective on leadership, of whether it exists as a unique psychological construct, or of the inability of leadership theories to predict leader effectiveness, the importance of leadership to organizational effectiveness is an intriguing and amorphous topic. It would be premature to suggest either that leadership is a topic that has outlived its usefulness or that all the answers have been found. Most likely, this is an area that will continue to motivate both researchers and practitioners to search for better answers.

## KEY TERMS

**Charismatic leadership**  Process used by transformational leaders to develop a common vision of what could be, discover or create opportunities, and strengthen organizational members' control of their own destinies.

**Contingency model of leadership**  Theory suggesting that leadership effectiveness is determined both by the characteristics of the leader and by the level of situational favorableness that exists.

**Custodial leadership**  Process used by transactional leaders to improve working conditions, compensation, and fringe benefits.

**Employee (socioemotional)-oriented leadership**  Process used by leaders that emphasizes the individual worker's needs in managing group performance; also called *initiating consideration.*

**Leadership**  Increment of influence over and above an employee's mechanical compliance with routine directives of the organization.

**Least-preferred coworker (LPC) scale**  Questionnaire that measures how respondents characterize their feelings about a person with whom they work least effectively. A high LPC score (favoring the least preferred coworker) suggests that the leader derives satisfaction and a sense of accomplishment from relationships with others; a low LPC score suggests that the leader emphasizes completing tasks, even at the expense of interpersonal relationships.

**Managerial grid**  Leadership training program conducted by Robert Blake and Jane Mouton that reflects two dimensions of leader behavior: concern for production (task-oriented leadership) and concern for people (socio-emotional leadership).

**Managerial leadership**   Process used by transactional leaders to provide subordinates work that is less routine and more challenging, build cohesive work teams, and give employees more say in decisions that affect them directly.

**Neutralizers of leadership**   Factors that paralyze, destroy, or counteract the effectiveness of leader behaviors, making it difficult for them to have an impact.

**Production (task)-oriented leadership**   Process used by leaders to direct activities related specifically to the task; also called initiating structure.

**Substitutes for leadership**   Individual, organizational, and task

characteristics that have the capacity to serve the same purposes as leader behaviors.

**Transactional leader**   Leader who motivates followers by exchanging rewards for services.

**Transformational leader**   Leader who arouses intense feeling and generates turbulent one- to-one relationships with followers and is inspirational and concerned with ideas rather than processes.

**Vertical dyad linkage model**   Model based on exchange theory that stresses the importance of individual relationships between leader and subordinates. Each relationship is termed a vertical dyad.

**DISCUSSION QUESTIONS**

1.  The current wisdom—based on leadership theories—is that effective leaders must be flexible in implementing specific leader behaviors. What, if any, are the potential problems with this perspective?

2.  Although they are very different, Fiedler's contingency theory of leadership and House and Mitchell's path-goal model of leadership are categorized as contingency models. What does the term *contingency* really mean in these instances?

3.  Based on your knowledge of leadership theory, how would you go about selecting an effective leader from a group

of managers? What is an "effective" leader?

4.  What is it that the LPC scale *really* measures? What background characteristics would distinguish a person with a high LPC and a low LPC score?

5.  While most organizational behavior theorists would support a contingency perspective as the premier model of leader behavior, articles such as the recent *Fortune* article highlighted in this chapter's "FOCUS ON: Transformational Leaders" indicate the increasing attraction of a trait approach to leadership. What is it about transformational

leaders that practitioners find so compelling? What are some of the problems with the "great person" notion?

6. Why should managers be sensitive to the existence of sub-

stitutes for leadership in their organizations? How might such substitutes enhance or detract from their leadership efforts?

**IF YOU WANT TO KNOW MORE**

Leadership is a topic for which there is no dearth of material or interest. For a more traditional perspective on leadership research and findings, Gary Yukl's *Leadership in Organizations* (Englewood Cliffs, N.J.: Prentice-Hall, 1981) is a useful starting point. *Stodgill's Handbook of Leadership,* authored after Stodgill's death by Bernard Bass (New York: Free Press, 1981) is a classic in the area of leadership. Stodgill was instrumental in moving the leadership field away from its preoccupation with the trait approach. For a more practitioner-oriented perspective, Edwin P. Hollander's *Leadership Dynamics: A Practical Guide to Effective Relationships* (New York: Free Press/Macmillan, 1978) is helpful.

Examining the latest perspectives on transformational leadership is the purpose of Noel Tichy and May Anne

Devanna's *The Transformational Leader* (New York: Wiley, 1986). Their book examines the unique kind of leader demanded by organizations and corporations in the 1980s.

From a different perspective, the interested reader may wish to consider Kathy Kram's *Mentoring at Work* (Glenview, Ill.: Scott, Foresman, 1985). This book is based upon Kram's research examining the mentoring process in the development of managerial and leadership talent. Finally, one might also wish to read Jim Wall's *Bosses* (Lexington, Mass.: Lexington Books, 1986). Modeled in part after Studs Terkel's *Working,* this book examines the leadership process, expectations, and behaviors of a variety of individuals, including transients, air controllers, and gangsters.

**ON YOUR OWN**

**T–P Leadership Questionnaire: An Assessment of Style**   Some leaders deal with general directions, leaving details to subordinates. Other leaders focus on specific details with the expectation that subordinates will carry out orders. Depending on the situation, both approaches may be effective. The important issue is the ability to identify relevant dimensions of the situation and behave accordingly. Through

Source: The T-P Leadership Questionnaire was adapted by J. B. Ritchie and P. Thompson in *Organization and People* (New York: West, 1984). Copyright 1969 by the American Educational Research Association. Adapted by permission of the publisher.

this questionnaire, you can identify your relative emphasis on two dimensions of leadership: task orientation and people orientation. These are not opposite approaches, and an individual can rate high or low on either or both.

*Directions:*   The following items describe aspects of leadership behavior. Respond to each item according to the way you would most likely act if you were the leader of a work group. Circle whether you would most likely behave in the described way: always (A), frequently (F), occasionally (O), seldom (S), or never (N).

A F O S N     1. I would most likely act as the spokesperson of the group.
A F O S N     2. I would encourage overtime work.
A F O S N     3. I would allow members complete freedom in their work.
A F O S N     4. I would encourage the use of uniform procedures.
A F O S N     5. I would permit members to use their own judgment in solving problems.
A F O S N     6. I would stress being ahead of competing groups.
A F O S N     7. I would speak as a representative of the group.
A F O S N     8. I would needle members for greater effort.
A F O S N     9. I would try out my ideas in the group.
A F O S N     10. I would let members do their work the way they think best.
A F O S N     11. I would be working hard for a promotion.
A F O S N     12. I would tolerate postponement and uncertainty.
A F O S N     13. I would speak for the group if there were visitors present.
A F O S N     14. I would keep the work moving at a rapid pace.
A F O S N     15. I would turn the members loose on a job and let them go to it.
A F O S N     16. I would settle conflicts when they occur in the group.
A F O S N     17. I would get swamped by details.
A F O S N     18. I would represent the group at outside meetings.
A F O S N     19. I would be reluctant to allow the members any freedom of action.
A F O S N     20. I would decide what should be done and how it should be done.
A F O S N     21. I would push for increased production.
A F O S N     22. I would let some members have authority which I could keep.
A F O S N     23. Things would usually turn out as I had predicted.
A F O S N     24. I would allow the group a high degree of initiative.
A F O S N     25. I would assign group members to particular tasks.
A F O S N     26. I would be willing to make changes.
A F O S N     27. I would ask the members to work harder.
A F O S N     28. I would trust the group members to exercise good judgment.
A F O S N     29. I would schedule the work to be done.

A F O S N       30. I would refuse to explain my actions.

A F O S N       31. I would persuade others that my ideas are to their advantage.

A F O S N       32. I would permit the group to set its own pace.

A F O S N       33. I would urge the group to beat its previous record.

A F O S N       34. I would act without consulting the group.

A F O S N       35. I would ask that group members follow standard rules and regulations.

T_____ P_____

The T–P Leadership Questionnaire is scored as follows:

a. Circle the item number for items 8, 12, 17, 18, 19, 30, 34, and 35.

b. Write the number 1 in front of a *circled item number* if you responded S (seldom) or N (never) to that item.

c. Also write a number 1 in front of *item numbers not circled* if you responded A (always) or F (frequently).

d. Circle the number 1's that you have written in front of the following items: 3, 5, 8, 10, 15, 18, 19, 22, 24, 26, 28, 30, 32, 34, and 35.

e. *Count the circled number 1's.* This is your score for concern for people. Record the score in the blank following the letter P at the end of the questionnaire.

f. *Count uncircled number 1's.* This is your score for concern for task. Record this number in the blank following the letter T.

CLOSING CASE
FOR CHAPTER 10

# THE MANAGER'S MEMO

FROM: I. Rand, President

TO:     T. Meyers, Vice President, Human Resources

RE:     Leadership Development Program

To support our plans to open ten new stores over the next five years, I think we need a program to develop future store managers. I would like your support in creating a leadership development program.

This program would have two phases: (1) identifying employees with leadership potential and (2) developing in them the skills that make a person a good leader.

Please submit to me your recommendations for how to carry out each phase of this program. If you would submit these recommendations in the form of a general outline of what the program should include, we can discuss the details in a meeting next week.

CASE DISCUSSION
QUESTIONS

Assume you are the vice president of the human resources division, and write a response to the president's memo. Use the material in the chapter as a resource for outlining a program you think will most likely succeed in meeting the president's objectives. Consider also the type of leadership most likely to be important in a store manager.

# Exercise for Part 3: The Desert Survival Situation

The situation described in this exercise is based on over 2,000 actual cases in which men and women lived or died depending upon the survival decisions they made. Your "life" or "death" will depend upon how well your group can share its present knowledge of a relatively unfamiliar problem so that the team can make decisions that will lead to your survival.

When instructed, read about the situation and do Step 1 without discussing it with the rest of the group.

## THE SITUATION

It is approximately 10:00 a.m. in mid-August, and you have just crash landed in the Sonora Desert in southwestern United States. The light twin-engine plane, containing the bodies of the pilot and the copilot, has completely burned. Only the air frame remains. None of the rest of you has been injured.

The pilot was unable to notify anyone of your position before the crash. However, he had indicated before impact that you were 70 miles south-southwest from a mining camp that is the nearest known habitation and that you were approximately 65 miles off the course that was filed in your VFR Flight Plan.

The immediate area is quite flat and except for occasional barrel and saguaro cacti appears to be rather barren. The last weather report indicated the temperature would reach 110° that day, which means that the temperature at ground level will be 130°. You are dressed in lightweight clothing: short-sleeved shirts, pants, socks, and street shoes. Everyone has a handkerchief. Collectively, your pockets contain $2.83 in change, $85.00 in bills, a pack of cigarettes, and a ballpoint pen.

## YOUR TASK

Before the plane caught fire your group was able to salvage the 15 items listed in the following table. Your task is to rank these items according to their importance to your survival, starting with "1," the most important, to "15," the least important.

You may assume the following:

1.  The number of survivors is the same as the number on your team.
2.  You are the actual people in the situation.
3.  The team has agreed to stick together.
4.  All items are in good condition.

**Step 1**  Each member of the team is to individually rank each item. Do not discuss the situation or problem until each member has finished the individual ranking.

Source: J. Clayton Lafferty, Patrick M. Eady, and Alonzo W. Pond, "The Desert Survival Situation: A Group Decision Making Experience for Examining and Increasing Individual and Team Effectiveness," 8th ed. Copyright © 1974 by Experiential Learning Methods, Inc., 14539 Harbor Island, Detroit, MI 48215, (313) 823-4400.

**Step 2**   After everyone has finished the individual ranking, rank order the 15 items as a team. Once discussion begins do not change your individual ranking. Your instructor will inform you how much time you have to complete this step.

| Items | Step 1: Your Individual Ranking | Step 2: The Team's Ranking | Step 3: Survival Expert's Ranking | Step 4: Difference between Step 1 and Step 3 | Step 5: Difference between Step 2 and Step 3 |
|---|---|---|---|---|---|
| Flashlight (4-battery size) | | | | | |
| Jackknife | | | | | |
| Sectional air map of the area | | | | | |
| Plastic raincoat (large size) | | | | | |
| Magnetic compass | | | | | |
| Compress kit with gauze | | | | | |
| .45 caliber pistol (loaded) | | | | | |
| Parachute (red and white) | | | | | |
| Bottle of salt tablets (1,000 tablets) | | | | | |
| 1 quart of water per person | | | | | |
| A book entitled *Edible Animals of the Desert* | | | | | |
| A pair of sunglasses per person | | | | | |
| 2 quarts of 180 proof vodka | | | | | |
| 1 top coat per person | | | | | |
| A cosmetic mirror | | | | | |
| **Totals** (the lower the score, the better) | | | | Your Score, Step 4 | Team Score, Step 5 |

|  | Team Number | | | | | |
|---|---|---|---|---|---|---|
| Please complete the following steps and insert the scores under your team's number. | 1 | 2 | 3 | 4 | 5 | 6 |

**Step 6: Average Individual Score**
Add up all the individual scores
(Step 4) on the team and divide by
the number on the team.

**Step 7: Team Score**

**Step 8: Gain Score**
The difference between the Team
Score and the Average Individual
Score. If the Team Score is lower
than Average Individual Score, then
gain "+". If Team Score is higher
than Average Individual Score, then
gain is "−".

**Step 9: Lowest Individual Score on the
Team**

**Step 10: Number of Individual Scores Lower
Than the Team Score.**

What makes a policeman go sour? I can tell you. I was a Denver policeman until not so long ago. Then I quit so I could hold my head up.

Don't get me wrong. I'm not trying to shift the burden of responsibility for the burglaries, break-ins, safe jobs, and that sort of thing. That is bad, very bad. But I will leave it to the big shots and the newspapers and the courts to say and do what needs to be said and done about that.

My concern is about the individual officer, the ordinary, hard-working, basically honest but awfully hard-pressed guy who is really suffering now.

Young fellows don't put on these blue uniforms to be crooks. There are a lot of reasons, but for most of the guys it adds up to the fact they thought it was an honorable, decent way of making a living.

Somewhere along the line a guy's disillusioned. Along the way the pressures mount up. Somewhere along the way he may decide to quit fighting them and make the conscious decision to try to "beat" society instead.

But long before he gets to that point, almost as soon as he dons the uniform, in fact, he is taking the first little steps down the road that does, for some, eventually lead to the penitentiary.

Let me back up a little. I want to talk about how you get to be a policeman, because this is where the trouble really starts.

Almost any able-bodied man can become a policeman in Denver. If he is within the age brackets, if he is a high school graduate, if he has no criminal record, he is a cinch.

There isn't much to getting through the screening, and some bad ones do get through. There are the usual examinations and questionnaires. Then there is the interview. A few command officers ask questions. There is a representative of civil service and a psychiatrist present.

They ask the predictable questions and just about everybody gives the predictable answers: "Why do you want to become a policeman?" "I've always wanted to be a policeman. I want to help people." Five or ten minutes and it is over.

Five or ten minutes to spot the sadist, the psychopath—or the guy with an eye for an easy buck. I guess they weed some out. Some others they get at the Police Academy. But some get through.

Along with those few bad ones, there are more good ones, and a lot of average, ordinary human beings who have this in common: They want to be policemen.

The job has (or had) some glamour for the young man who likes authority, who finds appeal in making a career of public service, who is extroverted or aggressive.

Before you knock those qualities, remember two things: first, they are the same qualities we admire in a business executive. Second, if it weren't for men with these qualities, you wouldn't have any police protection.

Source: Reprinted by permission of The Denver Post.

The Police Academy is point No. 2 in my bill of particulars. It is a fine thing in a way. You meet the cream of the Police Department. Your expectations soar. You know you are going to make the grade and be a good officer. But how well are you really prepared?

There are six weeks at the academy—four weeks in my time. Six hectic weeks in which to learn all about the criminal laws you have sworn to enforce, to assimilate the rules of evidence, methods of arbitration, use of firearms, mob and riot control, first aid (including, if you please, some basic obstetrics), public relations, and so on.

There is an intangible something else that is not on the formal agenda. You begin to learn that this is a fraternity into which you are not automatically accepted by your fellows. You have to earn your way in; you have to establish that you are "all right."

And even this early there is a slight sour note. You knew, of course, that you had to provide your own uniforms, your own hat, shoes, shirts, pistol, and bullets out of your $393 a month.

You knew the city would generously provide you with the cloth for two pairs of trousers and a uniform blouse.

What you didn't know was that you don't just choose a tailor shop for price and get the job done.

You are sent to a place by the Police Department to get the tailoring done. You pay the price even though the work may be ill-fitting. It seems a little odd to you that it is always the same establishment. But it is a small point, and you have other things on your mind.

So the rookie, full of pride and high spirits, his head full of partly learned information, is turned over to a more experienced man for breaking in. He is on "probation" for six months.

The rookie knows he is being watched by all the older hands around him. He is eager to be accepted. He accepts advice gratefully.

Then he gets little signs that he has been making a good impression. It may happen like this: The older man stops at a bar, comes out with some packages of cigarettes. He does this several times. He explains that this is part of the job, getting cigarettes free from proprietors to resell, and that as a part of the rookie's training it is his turn to "make the butts."

So he goes into a skid-row bar and stands uncomfortably at the end waiting for the bartender to acknowledge his presence and disdainfully toss him two packages of butts.

The feeling of pride slips away and a hint of shame takes hold. But he tells himself this is unusual, that he will say nothing that will upset his probation standing. In six months, after he gets his commission, he will be the upright officer he meant to be.

One thing leads to another for the rookies. After six months they have become conditioned to accept free meals, a few packages of cigarettes, turkeys at Thanksgiving, and liquor at Christmas from the respectable people in their district.

The rule book forbids all this. But it isn't enforced. It is winked at on all levels.

So the rookies say to themselves that this is OK, that this is a far cry from stealing, and they still can be good policemen. Besides, they are becoming accepted as "good guys" by their fellow officers.

This becomes more and more important as the young policeman begins to sense a hostility toward him in the community. This is fostered to a degree by some of the saltier old hands in the department. But the public plays its part.

Americans are funny. They have a resentment for authority. And the policeman is authority in person. The respectable person may soon forget that a policeman found his lost youngster in the park, but he remembers that a policeman gave him a traffic ticket.

The negative aspect of the job builds up. The majority of the people he comes in contact with during his working hours are thieves, con men, narcotics addicts, and out-and-out nuts.

Off the job his associations narrow. Part of the time when he isn't working, he is sleeping. His waking, off-duty hours do not make him much of a neighbor. And then he wants to spend as much time as he can with his family.

Sometimes, when he tries to mix with his neighbors, he senses a kind of strain. When he is introduced to someone, it is not likely to be, "This is John Jones, my friend," or "my neighbor"; it is more likely to be, "This is John Jones. He's a policeman." And the other fellow, he takes it up, too. He is likely to tell you that he has always supported pay increases for policemen, that he likes policemen as a whole, but that there are just a few guys in uniform he hates.

No wonder the officer begins to think of himself as a member of the smallest minority group in the community. The idea gradually sinks into him that the only people who understand him, that he can be close to, are his fellow officers.

It is in this kind of atmosphere that you can find the young policeman trying to make the grade in the fraternity. But that is not the whole story.

A policeman lives with tensions, and with fears.

Part of the tensions come from the incredible monotony. He is cooped up with another man, day after day, doing routine things over and over. The excitement that most people think of as the constant occupation of policemen is so infrequent as to come as a relief.

Part of the tensions come from the manifold fears. I don't mean that these men are cowards. This is no place for cowards. But they are human beings. And fears work on all human beings.

Paramount is the physical fear that he will get hurt to the point where he can't go on working, or the fear that he will be killed. The fear for his family.

There is the fear that he will make a wrong decision in a crucial moment, a life-and-death decision. A man has been in a fight. Should he call the paddy wagon or the ambulance? A man aims a pistol at him. Should he try to talk to him, or shoot him?

But the biggest fear he has is that he will show fear to some of his fellow officers. This is the reason he will rush heedlessly in on a cornered burglar or armed maniac if a couple of officers are present—something he wouldn't do if he were alone. He is tormented by his fears and he doesn't dare show them. He knows he has to present a cool, calm front to the public.

As a group, policemen have a very high rate of ulcers, heart attacks, suicides, and divorces. These things torment him, too. Divorce is a big problem to policemen. A man can't be a policeman for eight hours and then just turn it off and go home and be a loving father and husband—particularly if he has just had somebody die in the back of his police car.

So once again, the pressure is on him to belong, to be accepted and welcomed into the only group that knows what is going on inside him.

If the influences aren't right, he can be hooked.

So he is at the stage where he wants to be one of the guys. And then this kind of thing may happen: One night his car is sent to check on a "Code 16"—a silent burglar alarm.

The officer and his partner go in to investigate. The burglar is gone. They call the proprietor. He comes down to look things over. And maybe he says, "Boys, this is covered by insurance, so why don't you take a jacket for your wife, or a pair of shoes?" And maybe he does, maybe just because his partner does, and he says to himself, "What the hell; who has been hurt?"

Or maybe the proprietor didn't come down. But after they get back in the car his partner pulls out four $10 bills and hands him two. "Burglar got careless," says the partner.

The young officer who isn't involved soon learns that this kind of thing goes on. He even may find himself checking on a burglary call, say to a drugstore, and see some officer there eyeing him peculiarly.

Maybe at this point the young officer feels the pressure to belong so strongly that he reaches over and picks up something, cigars perhaps. Then he is "in," and the others can do what they wish.

Mind you, not all officers will do this. Somewhere along the line all of them have to make a decision, and it is at that point where the stuff they are made of shows through. But the past experience of the handouts, the official indifference to them, and the pressures and tensions of the job don't make the decision any easier.

And neither he nor the department has had any advance warning, such as might come from thorough psychiatric screening, as to what his decision will be.

Some men may go this far and no further. They might rationalize that they have not done anything that isn't really accepted by smart people in society.

This is no doubt where the hard-core guy, the one who is a thief already, steps in. A policeman is a trained observer, and he is smart in back-alley psychology. This is especially true of the hard-core guy, and he has been watching the young fellows come along.

When he and his cronies in a burglary ring spot a guy who may have what it takes to be one of them, they may approach him and try him out as a lookout. From then on it is just short steps to the actual participation in and planning of crimes.

Bear in mind that by this stage we have left all but a few policemen behind. But all of them figure in the story at one stage or another. And what has happened to a few could happen to others. I suppose that is the main point I am trying to make.

### Questions for Discussion

1. From what you have read and learned in Part Three, what are decision-making, leader, group, and political influences that contribute to the making of a bad cop?
2. What recommendations would you make to restructure the selection, training, and apprenticeship processes to reduce the likelihood of a police rookie "going bad"?

# PART

# 4

# Managing for Performance

# 11

# Organizational Entry and Socialization

### Entry: Organizational Perspective
Selection and Placement
*INTERNATIONAL FOCUS ON Selection: Making the Grade at Toyota-Kentucky*

### Entry: Individual Perspective
The Realistic Job Preview
*FOCUS ON Unrealistic Expectations: When a New Job Proves to Be Different Than Expected*
The Psychological Contract

### Organizational Commitment
Factors Influencing Commitment

### Organizational Culture
*FOCUS ON Corporate Culture: NCR's Corporate Culture Crosses International Boundaries*

### Organizational Socialization
*FOCUS ON Easing Organizational Entry: The Cray Style*
Mentors and Role Models
Orientation Training
Career Paths and Career Ladders

## PACKAGING EMPLOYEES

The impossible is about to happen. New York cabbies, infamous for their cavalier disregard for most rules of civilization, are about to improve their professional image—not by curbing their tongues or their madcap driving, but by sprucing up their wardrobes. The City Taxi and Limousine Commission recently approved a dress code for drivers. This unlikely development is but the latest example of "packaging" employees to boost professionalism and improve the look of a business, occupation, or city.

More than 23 million Americans wear some type of uniform, and the National Association of Uniform Manufacturers and Distributors projects annual sales of more than $2 billion by the end of the decade. In addition to such traditional users as nurses, police, and airline personnel, large companies such as Hertz and Coca-Cola have initiated extensive "ca-

reer apparel" programs. These companies rely on uniforms to project an image of consistent quality, good service, and uniqueness.

One function of service apparel is to communicate a company's selling points, whether they be cleanliness, professionalism, safety, or just plain good taste. Thus, like a chameleon, service apparel assumes the properties of the group it represents. It embodies the group's ideals and attributes, allowing its wearer to transmit the dominant values of the company or organization. Effective uniforms can go a long way towards establishing a desirable impression: the hygienic nurse, the brave soldier, the law-and-order-upholding police officer.

Most organizations recognize the vital role of indoctrination in helping new service workers learn the organization's rules, shed their idiosyncrasies, and become team players. It is no coincidence that the apparel of new recruits among such varied groups as soldiers, nuns, and physicians is immediately standardized upon induction. Admission to the group is indicated symbolically by permission to don its uniform. Looking like other members of the group helps new recruits to think in terms of "we" rather than "they."

As group members move up the organizational ladder, their self-concept changes; the group goals become more internalized and they rely increasingly on the group for rewards. One way of acknowledging and rewarding rising status is through changes in uniform. For example, when recruits of the New York City Police Department graduate from probationary status, they shift from a gray uniform to a blue one. Recruits often refer to this process as "moving up to the blues."

Uniforms can influence employee performance as well. Many organizations believe that uniforms contribute to productivity and morale and ensure that workers are loyal to the organization's goals. A uniform can help to minimize role confusion and lowered performance by defining employees' roles and reminding them of their primary allegiance. Uniforms also help control employees' behavior by making group members more easily identifiable—deviations from desired standards are less likely to occur if they are conspicuous.

The military, which has always used uniforms as a way of keeping people in line, recently provided a telling example of the wisdom of its prevailing policy. At one time, expectant U.S. servicewomen were permitted to wear civilian clothes once pregnancy was well advanced. But the military encountered problems as these women began to lose their identification with their soldier roles; their temporary return to civilian symbolism interfered with commitments to the organization. Maternity uniforms are now required for pregnant women in the U.S. Army, Air Force, and Navy. They are also issued by Eastern Airlines, U.S. Air, Hertz, Safeway, McDonald's, and the National Park Service.

Although many employees do not wear an official uniform, their attire is nonetheless restricted through unwritten or implicit dress codes. At IBM, long known as the "white shirt company," even high-level executives must conform to company expectations about proper appearance. These requirements are subtle, but the penalties for deviation may be severe. Tales of "eccentric" people whose careers were torpedoed by inappropriate dress are part of many corporate cultures.

Source: M. Solomon, "Standard Issue," *Psychology Today*, December 1987, pp. 30–31.

**INTRODUCTION**

While uniforms may make many service businesses stand out in the crowd and can help build patronage and customer loyalty, they also clearly help identify who is part of the company and who is not. The type of uniform individuals wear can also convey information about their place in the organizational hierarchy. As the opening vignette in Chapter 3 suggested, the blue suit/white shirt uniform necessary for a woman's initial acceptance into the world of business may evolve into a more personal statement as she moves up in the corporate hierarchy. Thus, becoming an organizational member requires more than being selected for a new position.

The purpose of this chapter is to examine some of the factors that influence an individual's association with and commitment to an organization. While many of these issues may be discussed in considerably more depth in other management courses, our intent is to give you a beginning point for thinking about how an individual becomes an organizational member. Starting with the selection process, we will examine critical issues in how organizations choose individuals and how individuals choose organizations. However, this is simply the first step in becoming a member of an organization.

Once an individual joins an organization, the next step is to link the organization and the individual—to commit the individual to the goals, expectations, and aspirations of the organization. After focusing on the situational characteristics that lead to commitment—such as the visibility of behaviors, the irreversibility of choices, and the responsibility for making those choices—we will examine how organizational commitment is transmitted from one member to another via the organization's culture.

Next, we will consider the process by which a newcomer learns how work is done in a particular organization. Organizations transmit their culture by socializing their employees. The ways in which they socialize their employees (such as by providing mentors, role models, and training) are the focus of the final section of this chapter.

**ENTRY: ORGANIZATIONAL PERSPECTIVE**

Getting the best individuals into the organization is critical to the organization's performance. If all applicants were able to perform the job equally well, then organizational selection would require little more than hiring the right number of "warm bodies." However, in the vast majority of instances, who is hired makes a big difference. In fact, research on worker productivity suggests that a high-ability worker will be two to three times as productive as a low-ability worker.[1] Thus, the

[1]N. H. Mackworth, "High Incentives versus Hot and Humid Atmospheres in a Physical Effort Task," *British Journal of Psychology* 38 (1947): 90–102; and F. L. Schmidt and J. E. Hunter, "Individual Differences in Productivity: An Empirical Test of Estimates Derived from Studies of Selection Procedure Utility," *Journal of Applied Psychology* 68 (1983): 407–414.

benefits of identifying and hiring the best-qualified candidate for a job can be considerable.

Finding the right employee is a question of fit—a fit between the person and the job as well as the person and the organization. The importance of such a fit stems from the organization's need for shared outlooks or a common purpose among its members and the individual's need to be comfortable within the working environment. A good fit between the organization and the employee may improve performance, since tasks will be completed more efficiently. This efficiency advantage occurs because individuals with similar views are better able to form teams and cooperate with each other.[2]

The lack of such a fit certainly contributes to high levels of turnover among new organizational members as well as first-year college students and transfers.[3] Further, a lack of fit between the person and the organization may also result in lost potential for innovation and cooperation.[4] Lack of fit can occur because the individual selected for the position is underqualified or overqualified. In the 1960s, there were many stories of cab drivers and waiters with PhDs in engineering or chemistry. Their job satisfaction and longevity in their positions were often quite limited. The 1990s equivalent of being underemployed may be fueled by the rising number of two-income couples. When one member of the couple accepts a new position or is transferred, the spouse may have to settle for a less-than-desirable position, depending upon the size, prospects, and economy of the new location.

One of the best ways an organization can enhance the fit between itself and its employees is through the process of selection.[5] The next section examines selection from the perspective of the organization.

## SELECTION AND PLACEMENT

How do people become members of particular organizations? Selection can be viewed as a matching process in which organizations seek out (recruit) specific individuals and individuals select among a variety of organizations. Thus, organizational entry can be examined from the perspective of both the organization and the individual.

---

[2]S. Keisler, *Interpersonal Processes in Groups and Organizations* (Arlington Heights, Ill.: AHM Publishing Corp., 1978).

[3]J. Wanous, *Organizational Entry* (Reading, Mass.: Addison-Wesley, 1980); and L. Pervin and D. Rubin, "Student Dissatisfaction with College and the College Dropout Rate: A Transactional Approach," *Journal of Social Psychology* 72 (1980): 285–295.

[4]C. A. O'Reilly and J. A. Chatman, "Organizational Commitment and Psychological Attachment: The Effects of Compliance, Identification, and Internalization on Prosocial Behavior," *Journal of Applied Psychology* 71 (1986): 492–499.

[5]J. A. Chatman, *Matching People and Organizations: Selection and Socialization in Public Accounting Firms.* Unpublished dissertation, University of California at Berkeley, 1988.

| FIGURE 11–1 | Major Steps in the Selection Process |
| --- | --- |

Selecting the right employee for a job entails three steps. Job analysis catalogs the tasks in a job and the skills required of job incumbents. Assessment procedures that test applicants for these skills must be developed. Finally, the assessment procedures are used to identify qualified applicants.

Job Analysis
(Identification of Tasks Performed, Skills and Abilities Required)
↓
Development and Validation of Assessment Devices to Measure Knowledge, Skills, and Abilities
↓
Use of Assessment Devices in Processing of Applicants

Source: R. D. Gatewood and H. S. Feild, *Human Resource Selection* (Hinsdale, Ill.: Dryden, 1987).

For an organization, **selection** is the process of collecting and evaluating information about an individual in order to extend an offer of employment.[6] Selection is typically perceived as occurring at the point when the employee accepts the organization's offer of employment. However, there is a growing realization that the usefulness of the selection decision in creating a person-job fit is known only over time. When the match between the individual's talents and needs and the organization's demands is good, then the organization can reduce the costs associated with rapid turnover, lower performance levels, and the friction between employee and organization that results from such a mismatch.[7] An example of the growing importance of the selection process is illustrated in the "INTERNATIONAL FOCUS ON: Selection."

Three steps are necessary for a good selection process. As illustrated in Figure 11–1, they include job analysis, selection of assessment devices, and the processing of applicants via screening, interviewing, and testing of the applicant pool. The selection process is most likely to succeed in identifying interested, qualified candidates and to be worth its costs when the process itself is valid, when there are more qualified applicants than positions to fill, and when a small percentage of applicants is successful.[8]

**Job Analysis** The logical starting point for an organization to ensure a good person-job fit is via a thorough understanding of the position to

[6]R. D. Gatewood and H. S. Feild, *Human Resource Selection* (Hinsdale, Ill.: Dryden Press, 1990), 5.

[7]J. P. Kotter, "The Psychological Contract," *California Management Review* 15 (1973): 91–99.

[8]W. Cascio, *Applied Psychology in Personnel Management* (Reston, Va.: Reston Publishing Co., 1978).

INTERNATIONAL
FOCUS ON:
Selection

**Making the Grade at Toyota-Kentucky** Nobody lands a job with Toyota Motor Corp. in Georgetown, Kentucky, by simply showing up at the plant gate. Just ask Michael Warren. The 31-year-old resident of nearby Lexington spent 25 hours proving himself to the Japanese automaker. He underwent paper-and-pencil tests, workplace simulations, and a probing interview. Going through all that "shows a commitment to working for Toyota," says Warren, who meanwhile held down a job with a jeans maker. He scored high in his Toyota tests and was hired as a manager in quality control. Toyota is grading report cards by the thousands as it starts to fill the 3,000 jobs at its new auto-assembly plant in this rural community just north of Lexington. A battery of tests is required for anyone who would so much as handle a fender or paint a hood. Not only literacy and technical knowledge are examined, but also more subjective things like "interpersonal skills."

The initial tests cover reading and math, manual dexterity, "job fitness," and, for skilled trades, technical knowledge. Then come the workplace simulations. Traditionally such simulations have been reserved in the United States for identifying white-collar workers suitable for management posts. In contrast, at Toyota, groups of applicants are assigned such problems as ranking features of a hypothetical auto according to how well the market would accept them. There are also mock production lines, where applicants assemble tubes or circuit boards. The idea is to identify applicants who can keep a fast pace, endure tedious repetition, and yet stay alert. Only one in twenty applicants makes it to the interview.

Toyota says it is hiring so carefully because it wants to find workers who will conform to the Japanese emphasis on teamwork, corporate loyalty, and versatility along the production line. Observing the Japanese, a regional United Auto Workers official notes the contrast with the way he was hired at an American-owned auto plant years ago. "You wrote down what work you had done before, and that was the end of it," he recalls. "If you knew somebody who worked in the plant and would put in a good word for you, that helped."

Source: Richard Koenig, "Exacting Employer: Toyota Takes Pains, and Time, Filling Jobs at Its Kentucky Plant," *Wall Street Journal*, December 1, 1987, p. 1.

be filled. **Job analysis** is the gathering of information about a job in an organization. The information collected should describe the tasks and activities, the results (products or services), and the equipment, materials, and working conditions that characterize the job.[9]

The primary purpose of a job analysis is to determine the critical job dimensions and worker characteristics needed in successful job incumbents. Relevant job dimensions are those aspects of the job essential for good performance. For example, promptness, low absenteeism, or participation in an advanced training program may be critical to an

[9]Gatewood and Feild, *Human Resource Selection.*

individual's success on the job. Worker characteristics include the specific knowledge, skills, and abilities that an individual must possess to qualify for the position. Thus, the job analysis conveys not only the important job characteristics, but also the critical worker qualifications.

In addition to specifying who should be recruited, the job analysis aids in the organization's performance appraisal, training, and compensation functions. To evaluate employees effectively, the performance appraisal system must reflect the job's important duties. Selection into training programs also must be related to the position's important dimensions. Only by knowing the skills the position requires can the organization train and promote employees effectively. A job analysis also evaluates the relative worth of a position to the organization. A good job analysis assures that each position is appropriately compensated relative to other positions within the organization.

**Identification of Assessment Devices**  Assessment devices can include application blanks, references, intelligence tests, special ability tests, personality tests, work simulation exercises, and the selection interview.[10] While not all of these components are used in every selection decision, the use of most is supported by empirical or anecdotal evidence.[11] The critical factor in deciding which selection devices should be used in a particular situation is their ability to differentiate among applicants and, given the litigious environment in which selection takes place, their defensibility in a court setting.[12] Because a particular job requires certain skills, abilities, and knowledge, the process used to screen applicants should be able to identify those who possess those particular traits and abilities.

**Identification and Processing of Applicants**  Once the organization understands both the position (through the job analysis) and how to measure the needed worker characteristics (through assessment devices), it is ready to identify and evaluate applicants. Applicants can be identified through a number of different mechanisms, including the classified sections of newspapers and journals, personal contacts and references, executive-search firms, employment agencies, college and university placement centers, and outplacement services.[13]

[10]Chatman, *Matching People and Organizations.*

[11]See, for example, Andrews, Schmitt, and Schneider, "Current Issues in Personnel Selection," in *Research in Personnel and Human Resource Management*, vol. 1, eds. K. Rowland and G. Ferris (Greenwich, Conn.: JAI Press, 1983), 85–126; J. Holland, *Making Vocational Choices: A Theory of Careers* (Englewood Cliffs, N.J.: Prentice-Hall, 1973).

[12]Chapter 14 includes an extended discussion of the legal (regulatory) environment and its impact on organizations.

[13]G. Kenny, D. Fisher, L. Katzenstein, and J. A. Sonnenfeld, "Note on Executive Search, Career Counseling, and Other Placement Services (Cambridge, Mass.: Harvard Business School Case 9–482–034, 1981).

Mazda wants to hire new employees who can work well with others—good team players. Part of Mazda's selection process includes a test of team-work skills, in which a group of applicants work together on a task, like this one of assembling flashlights.

Executive search firms, or "headhunters," are under contract to organizations to find candidates for specific jobs. Private employment agencies that charge fees for their services often advertise job openings (so that the actual company remains anonymous), screen applications, and conduct initial interviews. Governmental employment agencies often work with much lower-level employees, because their services are often a required aspect of unemployment benefits. In addition to supplying job applicants to organizations, they may assist employers in employee testing, job analysis and evaluation, and community wage surveys, among other activities. Outplacement firms are a recent phenomenon created in response to the "leaning" (trimming down) of large American organizations, through either downsizing or mergers and acquisitions. Typical outplacement activities include job counseling and job placement for employees who have been dismissed from firms. They are described in additional detail in Chapter 13.

Recent research suggests that the source of recruitment is an important factor in predicting the future performance of an employee. In general, it seems that candidates who apply directly to organizations or are recruited at professional meetings or conventions are more dependable, are absent less often, and report higher levels of job satisfaction and involvement than those recruited through newspaper ads or college placement offices.[14] One reason for this difference may be that individuals who apply directly to the organization or are recruited at professional meetings and conventions are likely to have more accurate

[14]J. A. Breaugh, "Relationships between Recruiting Sources and Employee Performance, Absenteeism, and Work Attitudes," *Academy of Management Journal* 24 (1981): 142–147.

**FIGURE 11–2**          Steps in Processing Applicants:
                                    The Organizational Perspective on Entry

From the organization's perspective, selection of new employees resembles a series of hurdles. When an applicant successfully passes all the qualification screens, the process culminates in a job offer from the organization.

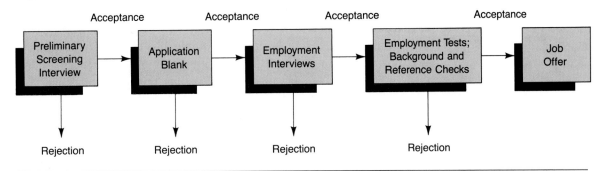

Source: R. D. Gatewood and H. S. Feild, *Human Resource Selection* (Hinsdale, Ill.: Dryden Press, 1987), p. 16.

information about the position than do individuals recruited through newspaper advertising or college placement offices. Thus, it seems that having accurate information about the position is significantly associated with success in that particular position.

Once the applicants have been identified, they may complete an application blank, participate in a preliminary screening interview and selection interview, take a variety of employment tests, and provide references to be checked. The culmination of this process occurs when a job offer is made to a candidate. Figure 11–2 graphically represents this process.

**ENTRY: INDIVIDUAL PERSPECTIVE**

While the organization is processing the applicants, the individual applicants are processing the organization. That is, applicants are simultaneously determining whether or not this is the type of organization they would like to join. Two mechanisms help an individual understand the organization so that such a decision can be made: the realistic job preview and the psychological contract.

**THE REALISTIC JOB PREVIEW**

In seeking a position, job candidates sometimes have unrealistically high expectations about the organization. For one thing, organizations trying to hire a recruit are likely to present their best sides. In addition, if the position is attractive, the applicant is likely to pay more attention to the positive aspects of the job and downplay the negative aspects. However, once the individual has begun the job, then the difference between what the now-incumbent thought the job was going to entail and what it actually entails becomes quite salient. So, early in the employee's tenure with the organization, job satisfaction may be low because of unmet expectations. The implications of these unrealistic expectations are described in the "Focus on: Unrealistic Expectations."

One way to avoid such unrealistic expectations is through the use of a **realistic job preview.**[15] A realistic job preview is a mechanism used by organizations to present both the desirable and undesirable aspects of

[15]Wanous, *Organizational Entry.*

---

## Focus on:
### Unrealistic Expectations

**When a New Job Proves to Be Different than Expected**  To Lynda McDermott, the job offer sounded ideal. So she left her position at an accounting firm and became executive vice-president of a fledgling management consulting company in New York, a job that her new boss said would allow her to play a major role in landing new business. Eleven months later, she quit. Her boss, she says, had immediately relegated her to administrative duties, a far cry from the role she had expected. As McDermott sees it, she was the victim of a job bait-and-switch. Promised the world as an applicant, she eventually realized as a new employee that the job was something quite different. Such realizations often lead to employee disgruntlement, stalled careers, and costly turnover.

New employee disillusionment has several sources. Some companies unduly hype a position to snare a particular person; sometimes the personnel department or manager is unfamiliar with the details of the job or managers cannot deliver on their promises. Alternatively, eager applicants can deceive themselves about a position by minimizing its shortcomings. Both applicants and employers may gloss over the job description, particularly if the applicant believes that such probing behavior will irritate the interviewer or if such information is not what the applicant wants to hear. The employer or recruiter may be at fault if the company is new or the job is difficult to fill.

Avoiding this pitfall is difficult. Consider the speechwriter who will soon leave his job after 15 months. He was promised that he wouldn't have to write speeches on nuts-and-bolts financial instruments for narrow audiences. In fact, that is all he writes. Now he finds himself in the ironic position of having agreed to select his successor. "I see three possibilities," he says. "I could tell the total truth about the job and thereby only have people accept who are not totally qualified. I could say it's a 'real challenging' job and so on, but that's not honest, and ultimately the needs of the corporation and the individual aren't served. Or I could leave the job unfilled." Thus far, he is telling the applicants the truth and the job remains unfilled.

Source: L. Reibstein, "Crushed Hopes: When a New Job Proves to Be Something Different," *Wall Street Journal,* June 10, 1987, Section 2.

the job and the organization—to provide the potential employee with more complete and accurate information about the position. Videotapes, work simulations, and interviews with current jobholders are just some of the ways in which a realistic job preview can be accomplished.

Providing a clear picture of the organization and the position is not without its risks. Individuals who are undecided may be persuaded to withdraw their names from consideration as their view of the organization becomes more realistic. However, those who do take the position are likely to be more committed and remain in the position longer.[16] As suggested earlier, candidates who have more complete and accurate information about a position are more likely to succeed in that position.[17] In addition, the organization's candidness in realistically portraying a position may increase the recruit's feeling of being fairly treated by the organization.[18]

Given the costly nature of the selection process (each employee selected is a potential half-million-dollar asset or a half-million-dollar liability to the organization[19]), weeding out the "undecideds" may have considerable long-term benefits for the organization. The experience of such organizations as Texas Instruments, Prudential Insurance Company, and West Point Military Academy suggests that candidates should receive a realistic job preview to assess their own fit with the organization.[20] This increases the likelihood of a good person-job match.

## THE PSYCHOLOGICAL CONTRACT

Individuals who decide to accept a position with an organization enter into a **psychological contract** with the employing organization. A psychological contract is a set of unwritten, reciprocal expectations between an employee and an organization.[21] It is the bedrock of the individual-organization link because employment is based upon an implicit exchange of beliefs and expectations about the actions of the individual vis-à-vis the organization and the organization vis-à-vis the individual. Psychological contracts usually involve expectations about working conditions, work requirements, the level of effort to be

[16]J. P. Wanous, "Organizational Entry: The Individual's Viewpoint," in *Perspectives on Behavior in Organizations,* eds. J. R. Hackman, E. E. Lawler, and L. W. Porter (New York: McGraw-Hill, 1977).

[17]Breaugh, "Relationships between Recruiting Sources and Employee Performance."

[18]R. J. Bies and J. Moag, "Interactional Justice: Communication Criteria of Fairness," in *Research on Negotiating in Organizations,* vol. 1, eds. R. J. Lewicki, M. H. Bazerman, and B. Sheppard (Greenwich, Conn.: JAI Press, 1986): 43–55.

[19]P. M. Podsakoff, M. L. Williams, and W. E. Scott, "Myths of Employee Selection Systems," in *Readings in Personnel and Human Resource Management,* eds. R. S. Schuler, S. A. Youngblood, and V. L. Huber (New York: West Publishing Co., 1987): 178–192.

[20]J. A. Breaugh, "Realistic Job Previews: A Critical Appraisal and Future Research Directions," *Academy of Management Review* 8 (1983): 612–619.

[21]E. A. Schein, *Organizational Psychology* (Englewood Cliffs, N.J.: Prentice-Hall, 1980).

expended on the job, and the amount and nature of authority the employer has over the employee in directing work.[22] They are different from other types of contracts in that they may contain thousands of items (although the employee and employer may be aware of only a few); both parties may have different expectations, since some may have been explicitly discussed and others, only inferred; and they change as individual and organization expectations change.[23]

The psychological contract is based upon the exchange of **contributions** and **inducements.** Individuals entering into a psychological contract contribute their productive capacity towards achieving the organization's purpose. Organizations provide inducements to employees in exchange for their contributions. That is, organizations compensate employees for their contributions. The psychological contract is generally viewed as committing both sides to the relationship, with employees contributing loyalty and the company, steady employment.[24] Figure 11–3 illustrates the contribution-inducement link that is the basis of the psychological contract.

Balanced psychological contracts are necessary for a continuing, harmonious relationship between the employee and the organization. Since psychological contracts are entered into as individuals join the organization, whether or not the individuals' expectations about the contract are met is crucial to their ongoing relationship with the organization. For example, if an individual accepts a position with the expectation of full autonomy in structuring the workday only to find out that the supervisor views planning employees' workdays as his or her prerogative, then the employee is likely to suffer considerable job-related dissatisfaction, based primarily on the perception that the psychological contract has been violated. An employee who had no such expectations prior to starting the job would not experience this level of dissatisfaction. The violation of the psychological contract can signal to the participants that the parties no longer share (or never shared) a common set of values or goals. Once this happens, one can expect a breakdown of communication between the parties, a failure in mutual understanding, and increasing frustration (and emotional responses) in both parties.[25]

Realistic job previews, by implicitly adjusting a recruit's expectations about life as a member of the organization, can have an impact on the psychological contract and, hence, the employee's job satisfaction. In

[22]Ibid.

[23]See both Kotter, "The Psychological Contract," 91–99; and D. M. Rousseau, "Psychological and Implied Contracts in Organizations," working paper, Evanston, Ill.: Northwestern University, 1987).

[24]M. L. Marks, "The Disappearing Company Man," *Psychology Today* (September 1988): 34–39.

[25]Schein, *Organizational Psychology.*

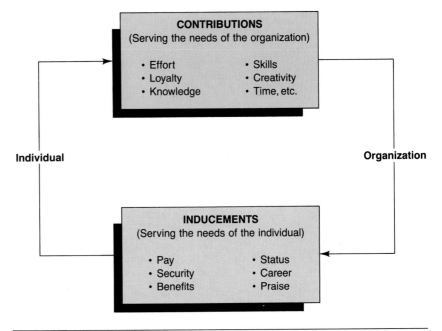

**FIGURE 11–3**

# The Psychological Contract:
# The Contribution-Inducement Exchange Process

An individual accepting a job enters into a psychological contract with the employer consisting of unwritten expectations on both sides. Balanced, equitable psychological contracts are necessary to harmonious relationships between employees and employers.

**Individual**

**Organization**

**CONTRIBUTIONS**
(Serving the needs of the organization)

- Effort
- Loyalty
- Knowledge
- Skills
- Creativity
- Time, etc.

**INDUCEMENTS**
(Serving the needs of the individual)

- Pay
- Security
- Benefits
- Status
- Career
- Praise

Source: J. R. Schermerhorn, J. G. Hunt, and R. N. Osborn, *Managing Organizational Behavior* (New York: Wiley & Sons, 1988), p. 38.

fact, the psychological contract may be the central determinant in whether a person is working effectively; generating commitment, loyalty, and enthusiasm for the organization and its goals; and obtaining satisfaction from work. The delicate balance of the psychological contract depends to a large measure on two conditions: (1) the degree to which employee expectations of what the organization will provide and what is owed in return match the organization's expectations of what it will give and get; and (2) agreement on what is actually to be exchanged. Examples include money in exchange for time at work; social-need satisfaction and security in exchange for work and loyalty; opportunities for self-enhancement and challenging work in exchange for high productivity, quality work, and creative effort in the service of organizational goals; or various combinations of these and other things.[26] Figure 11–4 illustrates the importance of the match between inducements and contributions for organizational productivity.

[26]Ibid.

**FIGURE 11–4**   The Importance of the Match between Contributions and Inducements in the Psychological Contract

A good match between what an organization gives its employees and the contributions it receives in exchange is critical to work-force morale. Realistic job previews may facilitate equitable psychological contracts by stimulating thoughts and discussion about employee and employer expectations.

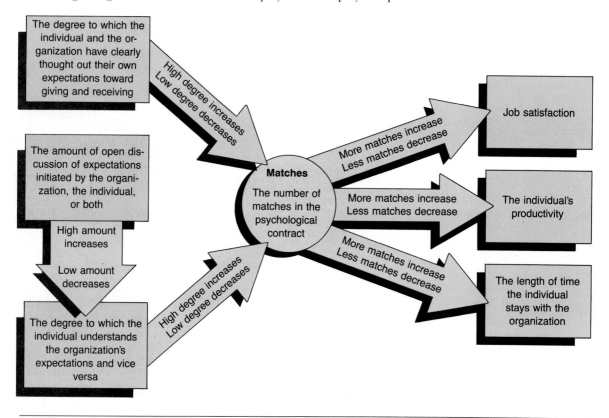

Once the organization has extended an offer to an applicant and that individual has decided to enter into a psychological contract by accepting the offer, then the applicant becomes an organizational member. However, the preparation needed to become a functioning part of the organization has just begun. The applicant must now become schooled in and committed to the organization's goals, objectives, and ways of conducting business.

Simply defined, **organizational commitment** is the relative strength of an individual's identification with and involvement in a particular organization.[27] It usually includes three factors: (1) a strong belief in the organization's goals and values; (2) a willingness to exert considerable effort on behalf of the organization; and (3) a strong desire to continue as an organizational member. Organizational commitment, then, is not simply loyalty to an organization. Rather, it is an ongoing process through which organizational actors express their concern for the organization and its continued success and well-being.

There are many reasons why an organization should want to increase the level of organizational commitment among its members. For example, research has found that the more committed the employee is to the organization, the greater the effort expended by the employee in performing tasks.[28] In addition, highly committed workers are likely to remain with the organization for longer periods of time—that is, there is a positive relationship between the level of organizational commitment and job tenure.[29] Finally, given the contribution of a highly productive, trained employee can make to organizational productivity, keeping such an employee should be a high priority for the organization. Because highly committed employees wish to remain associated with the organization and advance organizational goals, they are less likely to leave. Thus, high levels of organizational commitment are associated with low levels of employee turnover.[30]

FACTORS
INFLUENCING
COMMITMENT

Once individuals select membership in an organization, what is it about their early experiences that leads them to be more or less committed to the organization? To answer this question, we must first consider exactly what leads to the phenomenon of commitment. Gerald Salancik suggests that four major factors lead to commitment.[31] The visibility, explicitness, and irreversibility of our behaviors and personal volition for our behaviors are the factors that commit us to our acts.

[27]R. T. Mowday, L. W. Porter, and R. M. Steers, *Employee-Organization Linkages: The Psychology of Commitment, Absenteeism, and Turnover* (New York: Academic Press, 1982).

[28]R. M. Steers, "Antecedents and Outcomes of Organizational Commitments," *Administrative Science Quarterly* 22 (1977): 46–56.

[29]See, for example, R. T. Mowday, R. M. Steers, and L. W. Porter, "The Measurement of Organizational Commitment," *Journal of Vocational Behavior* 14 (1979): 224–247; Steers, "Antecedents and Outcomes of Organizational Commitments"; and J. L. Koch and R. M. Steers, "Job Attachment, Satisfaction, and Turnover among Public Employees," *Journal of Vocational Behavior* 12 (1978): 119–128.

[30]H. Angle and J. Perry, "An Empirical Assessment of Organizational Commitment and Organizational Effectiveness," *Administrative Science Quarterly* 26 (1981): 1–14; Mowday, Steers, and Porter, "The Measurement of Organizational Commitment"; and Steers, "Antecedents and Outcomes of Organizational Commitments."

[31]The following section draws heavily from G. R. Salancik, "Commitment Is Too Easy!," *Organizational Dynamics* (Summer 1977): 207–222.

**Visibility**     One major determinant of how committing a particular behavior may be is how observable that behavior is to others. Behaviors that are secret or unobserved do not have a committing force behind them because they cannot be linked to a specific individual. One of the most simple and straightforward ways to commit individuals to an organization is to make their association with the organization public information. If they are part of the organization, they (by association) support that organization and its goals. Many organizations are already taking advantage of this visibility notion to increase employee commitment. When a new employee joins an organization, the employee's photograph and a formal announcement are sent to the local newspapers, in-house publications, and other such outlets to inform others of the new arrival. As suggested in the opening vignette, the new employee may also be outfitted in the company's uniform—an obvious and visible sign of organizational membership.

Maintaining **visibility** is not a difficult task. For instance, it takes about the same time for inspectors to write a number after their task is completed as it does to write their names, or for the company to provide a nameplate on a door as to leave it blank. Very little additional effort is required to associate individuals with their work, their accomplishments, and their organization. The more visible individuals and their contributions, the more committed they are likely to be to the organization.

On some occasions, however, an organization does not want its members clearly associated with their acts. For example, there is a conscious attempt through the use of uniforms to reduce the visibility of individual soldiers, prison guards, and police officers so a particular individual is not associated with some of the more unpleasant tasks. Thus, the uniform in this case clearly identifies the individual as a soldier or police officer, but the individual within the uniform is not unique. In addition, organizations may decrease the visibility of individuals performing onerous tasks or tasks with a high likelihood of failure. This reduced visibility is likely to enhance the willingness of an individual to take on a task with negative overtones.

**Explicitness and Irreversibility**     Visibility alone is not sufficient to commit individuals to their actions. It must be combined with explicitness; the more explicit the behavior, the less deniable it is. Thus, **explicitness** is the extent to which the individual cannot deny that the behavior occurred. How explicit the behavior is depends on two factors: its observability and its unequivocality. When a behavior cannot be observed but only inferred, it is less explicit. For example, if I left a sensitive document on my desk and later heard one of my subordinates talking about the content of that document, I could not know that the subordinate had been in my office and read the document. At best, I might suspect that he or she had, but all I know for sure is that this sensitive information is now public. If I had seen that subordinate reading the document in my office, then I would know which subordinate released the information. Equivocality is the difficulty of pinning down the act or behavior. It can be seen in the way people qualify the statements they make (such as "It sometimes seems to me that . . ." versus "I think . . .").

**Irreversibility,** on the other hand, means that the behavior is permanent—it cannot easily be revoked or undone. The importance of irreversibility can be observed in the circumstances that committed Great Britain and France to building the Concorde.[32] The Minister of Aviation, James Avery, included a clause in the 1961 agreement with France that made both France's and Britain's decision to produce the Concorde virtually irreversible. The clause required that if either of the two partners withdrew from the collaboration, the entire development cost up to that point would be borne by the withdrawing party. Interestingly, the more rational it became to withdraw (because of escalating costs), the more committed the parties were to continuing. This type of commitment is typically referred to as behavioral commitment or escalation, which was described in detail in Chapter 5.

Organizations also are aware of the committing aspect of irreversible acts. Many organizations have developed benefit packages that are not transferable from one firm to another. The irreversible loss of these benefits, should an individual choose to leave the organization, commits the individual to continued employment. Training an employee in a skill that is specific to the organization or developing an employee's abilities to match the unique constellation of an organization's expectations also reduces the likelihood that the person will disengage from the organization.

Consider, for example, the cost a bookkeeper might incur in learning a particular accounting software package. Consider the much greater cost to this individual of relearning if this accounting package is unique to the organization. This is an example of knowledge that is very useful within a particular organization but may be completely irrelevant elsewhere. The time contributed to learning this system has a payoff in the current organization, but may be irreversibly lost if the bookkeeper were to transfer to any other organization.

Other factors influence a person's perceived attachment to the organization. Personal or family-related factors may foster an individual's commitment to an organization. Children in school, the cost of housing in other parts of the country, the circle of friends and acquaintances, and the spouse's job are all personal factors that may bind a person to an organization.

Of course, the commitment may be more to the status quo than to the organization. Imagine that an organization were to offer its employee a promotion that required relocation of the employee's family. The

[32]Ibid.

Irrevocable commitment to an organization can bias our perceptions of it. Some students joined ROTC in the late 1960s only to evade the draft. Many of them came to view the ROTC more favorably if they had signed contracts irrevocably committing them to the program.

personal factors that may have initially enhanced the employee's commitment to the organization may now be enhancing a similar commitment to a locality. The unique problems of dual-career couples are a salient example of the factors that tie individuals to an area.

An organization may attempt to compete with the personal factors that tie an individual to a locality by creating a network of relationships at work that become important. Developing work or project teams or fostering collaborations among specific coworkers are primary ways to connect workers to the organization. Further dependencies upon coworkers are fostered when employees are unable to develop relationships outside the organization because of frequent moves.

All of these are attempts to entangle the individual in organizational relationships. The greater the employee's entanglement with these relationships, the more costly termination would be to the employee. Employees' perceptions of the irreversibility of their positions in an organization develop naturally over time. The longer they are employed by an organization, the more their skills are tailored to the unique demands of that firm. What they know and how they think about a business become, in reality, what they know and how they think about the particular way their organization does business.

In fact, given the committing nature of organization-specific skills, it is probably against the best interests of the organization to encourage employees to develop general skills that would make them more attractive to other organizations. Developing generalized skills reduces the uniqueness of an individual's fit with a particular organization while simultaneously increasing that individual's attractiveness to others. The organization should clearly consider the potential costs and benefits of encouraging such skill development.

The irreversibility of behavior is important because it influences the psychological contract. Consider, for example, the plight of college-student cadets who had joined the Reserve Officers Training Corps (ROTC) in the late 1960s and early 1970s. Some were required to sign two-year contracts and others were not. During the Vietnam War, joining ROTC was viewed as a way to avoid the draft or to control the site and type of war experience one could expect. Because the war and thus the need for military personnel was limited, a lottery based on birth dates was designed to rank the order in which young men were subject to being drafted into the services. If you were assigned a low number through the lottery process, the odds were that you would soon receive a draft notice. If you were assigned a high number in the draft lottery, you were almost assured of not being drafted.

Barry Staw, a researcher with an interest in organizational commitment, examined the impact on ROTC cadets' behaviors of having a birth date with a very low probability of being drafted into the service.[33]

[33]B. M. Staw, cited in G. R. Salancik, "Commitment Is Too Easy," *Organizational Dynamics* (Summer 1977): 207–222.

Among those who had joined ROTC to avoid the draft, one would expect little reason to continue with the program. This was true, but only for those who had not signed a contract committing them to a specific period of service. While those without a contract began to be openly hostile towards ROTC, those with a contract became increasingly attached to the program. Thus, the irrevocable nature of the contract they had signed now influenced their commitment to the organization, regardless of the fact that the reason for their joining ROTC no longer existed.

These findings suggest that when the instrumental nature of our associations ceases to exist, we justify our continued association with emotional, rational, or socially desirable trappings. Once we have accepted a position, then the perceived attractiveness of that position and our commitment to that position and the organization increase. Of course, this commitment increase also occurs when we accept a marriage proposal, buy a home, or make any choice we perceive to be irrevocable (or revocable only at great cost).

**Volition**   We have been considering the importance of irreversibility in the commitment process, but there is still a piece of this puzzle missing. For example, if someone makes an irrevocable choice under duress or pressure, does that choice commit the person? Suppose your supervisor assigns you the task of firing several subordinates. How might you feel about the appropriateness of firing the employees if your supervisor applies a great deal of pressure on you to perform this task ("Either fire them or I will fire you!") or applies very little pressure ("Please terminate the following employees.")? It is likely that if you carry out your supervisor's instructions, you will feel more justified in terminating the employees when there is little pressure than you will when there is considerable pressure to comply. If there is very little pressure applied to get you to comply, then you are more likely to believe that the employees deserved to be fired. (After all, you did terminate the individuals; they must have deserved it.) However, if your supervisor applied considerable pressure to you and then you fired the employees, you are more likely to perceive that you had little choice in the matter. That is, you made the choice to act, but it was not of your own volition; you were forced to make that decision.

Volition, then, and its observable equivalent—personal responsibility—is the fourth mechanism that binds us to our actions. Without volition, behaviors are not committing. "Since I have no choice," one might reason, "I really cannot be held responsible for the consequences of my behavior." When trying to separate ourselves from our actions, we might protest that we do not like what we are doing, but the money was too good to refuse. Another way in which we try to distance ourselves from certain behaviors (usually those associated with unpleasant circumstances) is to insist that we have little personal responsibility for the behavior or the outcome. For example, in trying to explain why he did not turn in a paper by the deadline, a graduate student might report that his car had been stolen and the only copy of the paper was in the car at the time. Because he could not control the stealing of his car, he believes that his not meeting the deadline was not volitional.

If we reconsider the ROTC example, volition was certainly a factor. Because many ROTC cadets had avoided signing a contract, those who signed such a contract must have done it of their own volition. Those who signed contracts but had no other reasons for being in ROTC (the lottery indicated they had a low probability of being drafted) must be in ROTC because they enjoyed it. Thus, they became more committed because they were choosing to be cadets.

Enhancing employees' personal responsibility for their actions is critical to establishing and maintaining their commitment to the task and the organization. A number of organizational interventions acknowledge the importance of personal volition. For example, organizations are designing tasks in ways that increase an individual's personal responsibility for performing or scheduling them. In Chapter 12, the importance of volition in task design will be explored in more detail.

A second form of organizational intervention that emphasizes volition or personal responsibility is *participative decision making* (discussed in Chapter 9). If a work group is involved in making a decision or solving a problem, its members will be more committed to the implementation of that decision or solution than if they were simply informed of it. Their reasoning might be that if they chose to participate in the development of a solution, then they must be committed to it. This feeling of personal responsibility in turn increases employees' stake in the solution's successful implementation.

We have established that visibility, explicitness and irreversibility, and volition are important in the creation of commitment. Further, commitment to the organization and its goals is important because individuals adjust their attitudes and expectations in situations to which they are committed. While enhancing organizational commitment is an ongoing process, it is probably most critical early in an employee's association with an organization to assure continued attachment.

Mowday, Porter, and Steers suggest a number of factors that may lead to greater organizational commitment early in an employee's tenure with an employer.[34] Their complete model is pictured in Figure 11–5. According to this model, commitment depends on (1) personal factors such as the employee's initial level of commitment (deriving from initial job expectations, the psychological contract, and so on), (2) organizational factors such as an employee's initial work experiences and subsequent sense of responsibility, and (3) nonorganizational factors,

[34]Mowday, Porter, and Steers, *Employee-Organization Linkages: The Psychology of Commitment, Absenteeism, and Turnover.*

**FIGURE 11–5**

## Major Determinants of Organizational Commitment during Early Membership

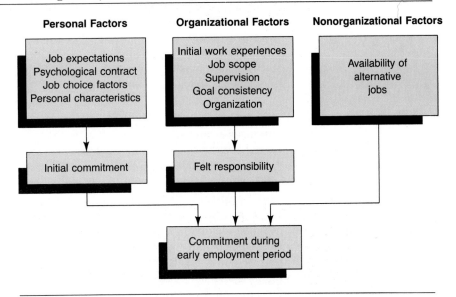

Source: R. T. Mowday, L. M. Porter, and R. M. Steers, *Employee-Organization Linkages: The Psychology of Commitment, Absenteeism, and Turnover* (New York: Academic Press, 1982), p. 56.

such as the availability of alternative jobs. Each of these three factors will be discussed in turn.

*Personal Factors* The primary personal factor is the amount of potential attachment an employee brings to work on the first day—the employee's propensity to develop a stable attachment to the organization. Individuals who are highly committed to an organization on their first day are likely to stay with the organization.[35] Individuals who are highly committed at entry are likely to be willing to take on additional responsibilities and contribute more to the organization. This early commitment process may become a self-reinforcing cycle. That is, if individuals, early in their tenure with an organization, put forth extra effort, then they may justify that extra effort by being more committed to the organization.

[35]W. Crampon, R. Mowday, F. Smith, and L. W. Porter, "Early Attitudes Predicting Future Behavior," paper presented at the 38th annual meeting of the Academy of Management, San Francisco, August 1978.

*Organization Factors*    Such organizational factors as job scope—the job's feedback, autonomy, challenge, and significance—increase behavioral involvement. The ability to participate actively in task-related decision making will also influence level of commitment. Consistency between work-group and organizational goals will increase commitment to those goals. Finally, organizational characteristics such as concern for employees' best interests or employee ownership are also positively associated with increased commitment to the organization.[36]

*Nonorganizational Factors*    The primary nonorganizational factor that enhances commitment is the availability of alternatives after the initial choice has been made. Research has found that Master's in Business Administration (MBA) students who did not take the job with the highest salary (insufficient external justification for the choice) reported significantly higher levels of job commitment six months later when no other job offers had been received than when alternative positions were available. Individuals who had accepted the position offering the highest salary (sufficient external justification for the choice) reported approximately equal levels of job commitment, regardless of whether subsequent alternative offers existed or not. Thus, it seems that the highest level of initial commitment occurs among those who (1) have insufficient external justification for their initial choice and (2) view the choice as relatively irrevocable; that is, believe they have had no subsequent opportunities to change their initial decision.[37]

Commitment to the organization and its goals is a major factor in predicting performance. Thus it is critical that organizations have mechanisms to enhance the development of organizational commitment among new employees. In fact, one way in which organizations with high levels of employee commitment differ from organizations with low levels of employee commitment is that the former are "strong culture" firms. For employees to be part of a strong culture, they must be educated as to the expectations and practices of the organization. The extent of their commitment to their jobs and the organization may well hinge on their ability to understand, accept, and become a part of the **organizational culture**—"the way we do things around here."[38]

# ORGANIZATIONAL CULTURE

Every organization has a culture. Sometimes that culture is very fragmented and difficult to perceive; other times, it is very strong, cohesive, and clear to insiders and outsiders alike. Whether weak or

[36]See, for example, R. M. Steers and S. R. Rhodes, "Major Influences on Employee Attendance: A Process Model," *Psychological Bulletin* 63 (1978): 391–407. Steers, "Antecedents and Outcomes," 46–56.

[37]C. A. O'Reilly and D. Caldwell, "Job Choice: The Impact of Intrinsic and Extrinsic Factors on Subsequent Satisfaction and Commitment," *Journal of Applied Psychology* 65 (1980): 559–565.

[38]J. S. Ott, *The Organizational Culture Perspective* (Chicago, Ill.: Dorsey Press, 1989).

strong, the culture of an organization has a profound influence on how work gets done in the organization. It can affect aspects of organizational life from who gets promoted and what decisions are made to how people dress, act, and play at work. As such, the culture *is* the organization; much more so than buildings, five-year plans, or bottom lines.[39] The importance of a culture to the organization and its members is illustrated in the "Focus on: Corporate Culture."

## Focus on:
### Corporate Culture

**NCR's Corporate Culture Crosses International Boundaries** It was August 1945, and S. C. Allyn, chairman of the board of National Cash Register Corporation (NCR), was one of the first allied civilians to enter Germany at the end of the war. He had gone to find out what had happened to an NCR factory, built just before the war, that had been promptly confiscated by the German military command and put to work on the war effort. He arrived via military plane and traveled through burned-out buildings, rubble, and utter desolation until he reached what was left of the factory. Picking his way through bricks, cement, and fallen timbers, Allyn came upon two NCR employees whom he hadn't seen for six years. Their clothes were torn and their faces grimy and blackened by smoke, but they were busy clearing out the rubble. As he came closer, one of the men looked up and said, "We knew you'd come!" Allyn joined them in their work, and together the three men began cleaning out the debris and rebuilding the factory. The company had even survived the ravages of war.

A few days later, as the clearing continued, Allyn and his coworkers were startled as an American tank rumbled up to the site. A grinning GI was at its helm. "Hi," he said. "I'm NCR, Omaha. Did you guys make your quota this month?" Allyn and the GI embraced each other. The war may have devastated everything around them, but NCR's hard-driving, sales-oriented culture was still intact.

Source: T. Deal/A. Kennedy, *Corporate Cultures*, © 1982, Addison-Wesley Publishing Co., Inc., Reading, Massachusetts, p. 3. Reprinted with permission of the publisher.

Strong organizational cultures generally have five elements: (1) a widely shared philosophy, (2) a view that people are a critical resource, (3) charismatic leaders and heroes, (4) rituals and ceremonies, and (5) clear expectations about the direction of the organization.[40] To the extent that an organization has a strong culture, the *guiding philosophy* of its leaders will be widely shared among its employees. Developing the management philosophy and direction of such companies is not a sideline of top management; it is the essence of the company. Individuals

[39]T. Deal and A. Kennedy, *Corporate Culture: The Rites and Rituals of Corporate Life* (Reading, Mass.: Addison-Wesley, 1982).
[40]Ibid.

in strong-culture organizations are viewed as critical organizational resources. Most of the rules of the organization center around its philosophy. Authority is often dispersed.

Charismatic leadership is common among strong-culture organizations.[41] Myths and stories of company heroes who provide tangible role models for employees are well integrated into such organizations' oral histories. They show the newcomer how to succeed in the company. Finally, many strong-culture firms have daily, systematic, and programmed routines and rituals that illustrate to employees the kind of behavior expected of them. Formal ceremonies provide vivid and potent examples of what the organization stands for.

Four major components assure the continuity of the strong-culture organization and convey its culture: selection, socialization, training, and mentoring. We have already addressed selection as a means of bringing into the organization the "right kind" of individuals—those who have values and beliefs consistent with the organization or who can be inculcated with the organization's values. Once the individual is an organizational member, then the actual process by which culture is conveyed and commitment is produced—organizational socialization—begins.

## ORGANIZATIONAL SOCIALIZATION

**Organizational socialization** is the process of conveying the organization's goals, norms, and preferred ways of doing things to the new employee. Socialization molds the new employee to fit the organization.

Through organizational socialization, the employee comes to appreciate the values, abilities, expected behaviors, and social knowledge essential for assuming an organizational role and participating as an organizational member.[42] In essence, organizational socialization conveys the organization's culture. How the new employee is socialized is often unique to particular organizations and strongly influenced by their cultures.

Richard Pascale, in a recent article, suggests that organizational socialization is necessary for organizational effectiveness.[43] He suggests a seven-step approach to successful organizational socialization:

1. *Selection.* Careful selection of entry-level candidates is paramount.
2. *Humility-inducing experiences.* Such experiences lead employees to question prior behaviors, beliefs, and values and may lower their

---

[41]Charismatic leadership is discussed in detail in Chapter 10.

[42]See both M. R. Louis, "Surprise and Sense Making: What Newcomers Experience in Entering Unfamiliar Organizational Settings," *Administrative Science Quarterly* 25 (1980): 226–251; and J. Van Maanen and E. H. Schein, "Toward a Theory of Organizational Socialization," in *Research in Organizational Behavior*, ed. B. M. Staw (Greenwich, Conn.: JAI Press, 1979).

[43]R. T. Pascale, "The Paradox of Corporate Culture: Reconciling Ourselves to Socialization," *California Management Review* 27 (1985): 26–27.

resistance to accepting the organization's norms and values. A common example is the hazing of underclass students or fraternity pledges.

3. *Training*. Mastery of one of the core disciplines of the business cements the orientation to the organization's way of doing things.

4. *Meticulous attention to systems for measuring operational results and rewarding individual performance*. Such systems should be comprehensive and consistent and should focus on those aspects of the business that are tied to competitive success and corporate values.

5. *Careful adherence to the firm's transcendent values*. This most critical step is the foundation of trust between the organization and the individual.

6. *Reinforcement of folklore*. Organizational folklore emphasizes a code of conduct about "how we do things around here."

7. *Consistent role models*. "Heroes" and mentors identify appropriate traits and behaviors necessary for organization members to be successful.

These seven steps suggest that how people are brought into the organization can have a major impact on their future relationship with the organization and subsequent productivity. Figure 11–6 illustrates some important ways organizations can facilitate a newcomer's entry process. They include developing a welcome package to ease an individual's transition from outsider to insider. In addition to the information in Figure 11–6, other factors in bringing a new person into the organization are particularly salient to the maintenance of organizational culture. For example, new employees at Cray Research receive a formal statement—the "Cray Style"—of the values, mission, and philosophy of the company. This document is reproduced in the "Focus on: Easing Organizational Entry."

Individuals involved with helping newcomers adjust to the organization should also consider the impact of mentors or role models, training programs, reward systems, and career paths—all of which reinforce the culture and expectations of the organization. While Chapter 13 will focus specifically on compensation and reward systems as mechanisms for maintaining performance, the following sections describe how these three other socialization mechanisms can be used to reinforce the organization's culture.

It should be kept in mind, however, that what makes an organization attractive to newcomers or job applicants may be contingent upon where they are in their career development. In fact, Dalton, Thompson, and Rice have identified four distinct phases in career development.[44] In the first stage, individuals work under the direction of others, similar to

[44]G. W. Dalton, P. H. Thompson, and R. Rice, "The Four Stages of Professional Careers," *Organizational Dynamics* (Summer 1977): 19–42.

**FIGURE 11–6**          A Newcomer's Welcome Package

Many employees do not receive a good first impression of their firms. They often must search for information about how to do their jobs—a task that is frequently burdensome and frustrating. To combat this information deficit, some organizations have established a welcome package.

The welcome package is a compilation of useful information that employees need to conduct their routine activities. At the very least such a package should include:

1. *Phone listings:* Because much of the modern employee's work requires telephone contact, having to search for such numbers is very time consuming. To offset this, the welcome package should contain a section of frequently called numbers of organizations, services, and people.

2. *Mailstop listings:* This section contains a complete listing of employee and organizational internal mail locations to expedite routing of critical documentation that the employee will receive and mail.

3. *Forms:* Because of the importance of standard forms to the smooth flow of information on a variety of topics, the package should also contain a listing of all important forms. This listing would provide the name, purpose, destination, and special characteristics of all such forms.

4. *Equipment and facilities listings:* All major equipment such as personal computers, word processors, modems, and copiers should be listed, along with their locations and functions. A separate listing of the locations of any facilities such as a library or recreational and dining facilities and their hours of operation should also be included.

5. *Schedules:* The package may also include a schedule of daily operations such as breaks, lunch hours, and holidays.

6. *Glossary:* An important section, this listing should include common acronyms of projects and organizations and frequently used esoteric terms. This enhances the newcomer's ability to "speak the language" of the firm.

7. *Organizational descriptions:* This section should identify the mission of the organization, the top managers, and other pertinent information.

8. *Project descriptions:* This section should include a compendium of the major projects with which the organization is involved to give an employee a wider view of its direction and functions.

9. *Procedures:* A very important component of the package, this section should include a listing of all policies and procedures of which the new employee must be aware.

Source: R. L. Kliem, "Welcoming New Employees the Right Way," *Administrative Management* (July 1987): pp. 14–15.

apprentices. In the second stage, they begin to make independent contributions. In the third stage, they serve as mentors for others in the first stage.

In the fourth stage, they provide direction for their organizations. In the remaining sections of this chapter, we will focus on factors influencing those in the first stage—the apprenticeship—of their careers.

FOCUS ON:

Easing
Organizational
Entry

**The Cray Style** At Cray Research, we take what we do very seriously, but don't take ourselves very seriously.

There is a sense of pride at Cray. Professionalism is important. People are treated like and act like professionals. But people are professional without being stuffy.

Cray people trust each other to do their jobs well and with the highest ethical standards. We take each other very seriously.

We have a strong sense of quality—quality in our products and services, of course; but also quality in our working environment, in the people we work with, in the tools that we use to do our work, and in the components we choose to make what we make.

Economy comes from high value, not from low cost. Aesthetics are part of quality. The effort to create quality extends to the communities in which we work and live as well.

The Cray approach is informal and nonbureaucratic. Verbal communication is key, not memos. "Call, don't write" is the watchword.

People are accessible at all levels.

People also have fun working at Cray Research. There is laughing in the halls, as well as serious discussion. More than anything else, the organization is personable and approachable, but still dedicated to getting the job done.

With informality, however, there is also a sense of confidence. Cray people feel like they are on the winning side. They feel successful, and they are. It is this sense of confidence that generates the attitude of "go ahead and try it, we'll make it work."

Cray people like taking responsibility for what they do and thinking for themselves. At the same time, they are proud to share a single mission—making the world's fastest computers.

Because the individual is key at Cray, there is a real diversity in the view of what Cray Research really is. In fact, Cray Research is many things to many people. The consistency comes in providing those diverse people with the opportunity to fulfill themselves and experience achievement.

The creativity, then, that emerges from the company comes from the many ideas of the individuals who are here. And that is the real strength of Cray Research.

Source: Courtesy Cray Research, Inc.

**MENTORS AND ROLE MODELS**

A mentor is a senior employee whose primary role is to instruct a younger, less experienced protégé.[45] **Mentoring** is another component of the socialization process and one which unites those in the first stage with those in the third stage of their careers. In addition, mentoring is a political activity. A mentor-protégé relationship is a form of vertical coalition. As we suggested in Chapter 8, the developing of political relationships and the forming of coalitions are common organizational activities. Taking advantage of the natural bond between mentor and protégé is one way to help develop a coalition. Whether we consider mentor-protégé relationships from a socialization or a political perspec-

[45]K. E. Kram, *Mentoring at Work: Developmental Relationships in Organizational Life* (Glenview, Ill.: Scott-Foresman, 1985).

A mentor-protégé relationship is a form of vertical coalition. Such relationships with successful, experienced managers are very important to newcomers throughout much of their tenure with an organization. In fact, younger managers are more satisfied and progress faster when they have this form of intergenerational cooperation than when they do not.

tive, such relationships with successful, experienced managers are very important to newcomers throughout much of their tenure with an organization. In fact, research suggests that younger managers are more satisfied and progress faster when they have this form of intergenerational cooperation than when they do not.[46]

The mentoring process is a socialization process. Four distinct phases have been identified: initiation, cultivation, separation, and redefinition.[47] The initiation stage usually lasts for about six months to a year, during which time the parties get to know each other. The second stage, cultivation, is the major stage of mentoring. During this stage, the mentor supports, directs, and counsels the protégé. It is this stage in which the "teacher-student" relationship is most evident. The third stage is the separation stage, in which the nature of the relationship changes significantly. In fact, virtually all mentor-protégé relationships end with some negative emotion, ranging from feelings of ambiguity to outright anger at being rejected. The separation phase is difficult for both parties, but if the mentoring relationship has been successful, they may be able to recognize and value both the old and new forms of the relationship. This reconceptualization of the mentor-protégé relationship is accomplished in the last, the redefinition, stage.

Mentoring relationships are not without their risks. If there is a mismatch between the mentor and protégé, their relationship can be anything but supportive. Some individuals may feel pressured into a mentoring role, regardless of their lack of enthusiasm for the assignment. Finally, it is not clear that mentoring is required for organizational success. Some organizational scholars suggest that a newcomer can obtain the information necessary to navigate the corporate system from a variety of people. A newcomer may take advantage of sponsors (strong supporters, but less powerful than mentors), guides (individuals conversant with the policies, procedures, and obstacles in the organization), and peers (equals who can act as sounding boards and information sources).[48]

A mentor-protégé relationship is often a formal or, at least, acknowledged interchange between an inexperienced and an experienced manager. However, the term *mentor* is often applied to relationships of much shorter duration. For example, a "designated mentor" is a person assigned to an organizational newcomer to aid the newcomer's transition from outsider to organizational member. Unlike in the mentoring

[46]G. R. Roche, "Much Ado about Mentors," *Harvard Business Review* (January-February 1979): 14–28.

[47]K. E. Kram, "Phases of the Mentor Relationship," *Academy of Management Journal* 26 (1983): 608–625.

[48]See, for example, J. G. Clawson, "Mentoring in Managerial Careers," in *Work, Family, and the Career,* ed. C. B. Derr (New York: Praeger, 1980) 144–165; and E. C. Shapiro, F. B. Haseltin, and M. P. Rowe, "Moving Up: Role Models, Mentors and the 'Patron' System," *Sloan Management Review* 19 (1978): 51–58.

Teams can provide an important source of role models for new employees. Well-managed teamwork programs, like the one at The Travelers Corporation, also quickly establish a sense of belonging in the new employees, a favorable initial work experience that can help develop early organizational commitment.

process we have described above, the designated mentor is a role assigned to a particular individual by the organization. In the same vein as the welcome package, the designated mentor is an information source—but one with a considerably more personal touch.

Sometimes an experienced manager can help in the socialization of a newcomer without even knowing it, by serving as a role model. A role model is a person whose behavior, attitude, image, or performance sets an example that we wish to imitate. Role models are common components of our learning how to respond in new or unfamiliar situations. Parents, teachers, public figures, and friends are common role models for conveying "the right way to do things" in different aspects of our lives. In unfamiliar social situations, we commonly defer to role models. When faced with a vast array of silverware at a formal dinner party, a common response is to wait and observe the behavior of others. Using their behavior as a role model, we may imitate or adopt what they do. Thus, whether as mentors, designated mentors, or role models, experienced organizational members play a vital role in the socialization of new employees. But their responsibilities lie primarily in the informational and political arenas. To teach new employees core aspects of the organization or commit them to a long-term relationship with the organization is the function of training programs and career paths, respectively.

ORIENTATION
TRAINING

While there are many kinds of training programs, training that focuses specifically on the newcomer is called **orientation training.**[49] Orientation training gets new employees "up to speed." Poor orientation training can be financially damaging to an organization because it will reduce the productivity of new employees for at least the first few weeks on the job and can heighten their anxiety, leading to greater dissatisfaction and turnover.[50]

Orientation training is typically conducted jointly by the training staff of an organization and the individual's supervisor. The division of labor among these two parties must be carefully delineated for this process to work. One common way in which the newcomer's orientation training is handled is illustrated in Figure 11–7. As you can see, the general company orientation is routinely handled by the training staff, while the specifics of departmental activities are handled by the line supervisor.

Since supervision is such a critical component of successful socialization, the quality of the interaction between supervisor and subordinate is of considerable concern. The supervisor should be schooled in the kind of information to be conveyed to the newcomer. For example, standards of performance, standard operating procedures, attendance policies, and other written and unwritten rules of conduct—even if included in a welcome package of information—should be conveyed by the supervisor. The better the supervisor is able to transmit this information to the employee, the quicker the employee will adapt to the organization.[51]

Because of the benefit on their future productivity of "stretching" employees early in their history with the organization, it is important that supervisors monitor their performance progress to ensure that they are challenged. Nothing is more likely to kill a new employee's enthusiasm for the job faster than sitting around "stacking paper clips." Thus, the orientation training of the employee as well as the supervisor's interaction will reinforce future productivity and job satisfaction.

CAREER PATHS
AND CAREER
LADDERS

Career paths are job-progression routes along which employees advance through the organization. While career paths are often designed for a particular employee, they may be drawn up by the organization as

[49]K. N. Wexley and G. P. Latham, *Developing and Training Human Resources in Organizations* (Glenview, Ill.: Scott-Foresman, 1981).

[50]E. R. Gomersall and M. S. Myer, "Breakthrough in On-the-Job Training," *Harvard Business Review* 44 (1966): 62–72.

[51]L. Chancey, "An Orientation System for New Employees. Seven-Phase Process at LTV Missiles and Space Division," *Training and Development Journal* 22 (1966): 52–56.

**FIGURE 11–7**            Typical Orientation Training Agenda and Responsibility

Orientation training typically is conducted by both training personnel and the new employee's supervisor. Responsibilities must be explicitly divided between these two parties for the process to work.

**Training Staff: General Company Orientation**

The following items are among those typically included in this first phase:
1. Overview of the organization— brief history, what the organization does (products/ services), where it does it (branches, etc.), how it does it (nature of operations), structure (organization chart), etc.
2. Policies and procedures—work schedules, vacations, holidays, grievances, identification badges, uniforms, leaves of absence (sickness, educational, military, maternity/paternity, personal), promotion, transfers, training, etc.
3. Compensation—pay scale, overtime, holiday pay, shift differentials, when and how paid, time clock, etc.
4. Benefits—insurance, retirement, tax sheltered annuities, credit union, employee discounts, suggestion system, recreational activities, etc.
5. Safety information—relevant policies and procedures, fire protection, first-aid facilities, safety committee, etc.
6. Union—name, affiliation, officials, joining procedure, contract, etc.
7. Physical facilities—plant/office layout, employee entrance, parking, cafeteria, etc.

**Line Supervisor: Specific Departmental Orientation**

The following items are typically covered in this phase:
1. Department functions— explanation of the objectives, activities, and structure of the department, along with a description of how the department's activities relate to those of other departments and the overall company.
2. Job duties—a detailed explanation of the duties of the new employee's job (give the employee a copy of the job description) and how the job relates to the activities of the department.
3. Policies and procedures—those that are unique to the department, such as breaks, rest periods, lunch hour, use of time sheets, safety, etc.
4. Department tour—a complete familiarization with the departmental facilities, including lockers, equipment, emergency exits, supply room, etc.
5. Introduction to departmental employees.

Source: R. W. Hollman, "Let's Not Forget about New Employee Orientation," *Personnel Journal*, May 1976. Reprinted with the permission of *Personnel Journal*, Costa Mesa, California; all rights reserved.

common highways for career advancement. Such routes usually consist of a combination of lateral, downward, and upward moves through the organizational hierarchy to gain needed experience. When career paths are formalized, they become career ladders. Thus, a **career ladder** is a specific series of jobs or experiences necessary to advance in the organization. For example, in most airline companies, a clear career ladder must be followed to achieve the command of an aircraft. An individual qualified to be a pilot must first serve as a navigator and then as a second officer before advancing to the rank of captain.

The existence of career paths and career ladders plays a role in socializing the new employee. While much of the benefit that employees will receive from these paths and ladders lies in the future, understanding how one advances in the organization provides critical information to (1) the individual deciding whether to join the company and (2) the newcomer searching for a mentor or role model. In addition to providing information, career paths also play a more symbolic role. They let employees know that the organization is interested in a long-term relationship with them—that it is committed to them not just for now, but for the future as well. In fact, one major reason for turnover in organizations is the lack of clear opportunities for career advancement.[52]

By now it should be clear that many factors help to socialize newcomers into an organization and its culture. The importance of a strong culture and appropriate socialization to organizational performance is gaining credibility among both practitioners and researchers in the field. Structuring the way in which newcomers are brought into an organization can enhance their level of organizational commitment and, thus, their long-term productivity.

## SUMMARY

This chapter focused on how individuals become organizational members. In recent years, considerable attention has been paid to the processes—such as selection and socialization—that ensure a good person-organization and person-job fit.

The selection process is the first contact with potential organizational members—the applicants. From the organization's perspective, a good selection process can identify the "right kind" of people for the organization. Such individuals may be those with specific skills, values, and expectations, or those who are amenable to the values and expectations of the organization. From the applicant's perspective, selection of an appropriate organization is aided by gathering the "right kind" of information. Knowing both the desirable and undesirable aspects of the job requires a realistic job preview. Clarifying the inducements and the contributions that the organization and the individual will exchange is the basis of the psychological contract between the individual and the employer.

After the individual accepts an offer of employment and becomes an organizational member, then the next task is to commit the individual to the goals and expectations of the organization. Such a commitment is in the organization's best interest, because committed employees are more likely to remain with the organization

[52]Wexley and Latham, *Developing and Training Human Resources in Organizations.*

and expend greater effort in the accomplishment of their tasks.

Organizational commitment is generated through the visibility of individuals as organizational members, through the explicitness and irreversibility of their choices and behaviors, and through the volition or personal responsibility they feel for their actions. Organizations can enhance the visibility, irreversibility, and volition of behaviors by selecting the appropriate individuals and structuring their tasks and work groups accordingly.

A primary way in which organizations with highly committed employees differ from those with less committed employees is their possession of a strong organizational culture. An organization's culture is composed of five elements: a widely shared philosophy, a view of people as critical resources, charismatic leaders and heroes, rituals and ceremonies, and clear expectations about the direction of the organization.

To convey the culture of an organization to newcomers requires organizational socialization—communication of the organization's goals, norms, and preferred ways of doing things. Specific mechanisms to accomplish this socialization include mentors and role models, welcoming packages, orientation training, and clearly defined career paths and career ladders. The importance of a strong culture and efficient socialization mechanisms in creating highly productive organizations cannot be ignored.

## KEY TERMS

**Career ladder** Specific series of jobs or experiences necessary to advance in an organization.

**Contributions** The productive capacity toward achieving an organization's purpose offered by an individual who is entering into a psychological contract.

**Explicitness** Extent to which individuals cannot deny that a behavior occurred, serving to commit individuals to their actions.

**Inducements** The compensations of steady employment and payment offered to an individual by an organization that is entering into a psychological contract.

**Irreversibility** Extent to which behavior cannot easily be revoked or undone, serving to commit individuals to their actions.

**Job analysis** Gathering of information about a job in an organization, including a description of tasks and activities, results (products or services), and the equipment, materials, and working conditions that characterize the job.

**Mentoring** Process of senior employees instructing younger, less experienced protégés.

**Organizational commitment** Relative strength of an individual's identification with and involvement in a particular organization.

**Organizational culture** Expectations and practices of the organization, including shared philosophy, attitude toward employees, leaders and heroes, rituals and ceremonies, and belief about the direction of the organization.

**Organizational socialization**
Process of conveying the organization's goals, norms, and preferred ways of doing things to new employees.

**Orientation training**   Process of introducing newcomers to organizational procedures that is conducted jointly by the training staff and the new employee's supervisor.

**Psychological contract**   Set of unwritten, reciprocal expectations between an employee and an organization.

**Realistic job preview**   Mechanism used by organizations to present both the desirable and undesirable aspects of the job and the organization, to provide the potential employee with more complete and accurate information about the position.

**Selection**   Process of collecting and evaluating information about an individual in order to extend an offer of employment.

**Visibility**   The observability of behaviors serving to commit individuals to organizations by making their association with them public knowledge.

**Volition**   Extent to which individuals believe they have a choice in their behaviors, serving to commit them to their actions.

DISCUSSION
QUESTIONS

1. The selection process in organizations has taken on increasing importance in the last decade. What factors are responsible for this change?

2. Realistic Job Previews (RJPs) are one way organizations can convey their expectations of employee performance to potential organizational members. In what ways do RJPs facilitate the development of an effective psychological contract?

3. One way in which organizations deal with newcomers is to try to humble them early in their tenure with the company. Why might organizations put their employees through such experiences, and why might the newcomers learn from them and find them useful?

4. In recent years fraternity hazing has become a larger problem on college campuses. In fact, such hazing activities have resulted in a number of highly publicized deaths. What is the purpose of hazing? If you were asked to solve this problem by the president of your university, how would you go about making sure that the practice of hazing would be eliminated?

5. Distinguish between organizational commitment and behavioral commitment.

6. Why are socialization activities so important in bringing employees of newly acquired firms up to speed in productivity?

7. Under what conditions might a firm want to maintain a "weak" culture?

8. Career paths and career ladders are often one way an organization can convey its commitment to its employees. One obvious example of a career path is the promotion and tenure process for faculty at colleges and universities. What are the advantages and disadvantages of such a system for the organization? For the individual?

IF YOU
WANT TO
KNOW
MORE

The new employee is the focus of much recent organizational behavior research. There are a number of interesting readings written from both the organization's perspective and the new employee's perspective. Organizational selection is the topic of Gatewood and Feild's book, *Human Resource Selection,* published in 1990 by Dryden Press. This book presents a detailed description of the selection process and is an excellent reference on this topic.

Realistic job previews are the specific focus of organizational entry, the general focus of a book by John Wanous entitled *Organizational Entry: Recruitment, Selection, and Socialization of Newcomers,* published by Addison-Wesley (Boston, 1980). Probably one of the more detailed descriptions of psychological contracts can be found in E. H. Schein's book, *Organizational Psychology* (Englewood Cliffs, N.J.: Prentice-Hall, 1980).

To get more information on the general process of commitment, a good article to read is Jerry Salancik's piece "Commitment Is Too Easy," published in *Organizational Dynamics* (Summer, 1977). Focusing specifically on organizational commitment is the book by R. T. Mowday, L. W. Porter, and R. M. Steers, *Employee-Organizational Linkages: The Psychology of Commitment, Absenteeism, and Turnover* (New York: Academic Press, 1982).

Organizational culture is the topic of T. Deal and A. Kennedy's book, *Corporate Culture: The Rites and Rituals of Corporate Life* (Boston: Addison-Wesley, 1982). Our understanding of organizational socialization is examined in a review written by E. A. Schein, "Toward a Theory of Organizational Socialization," which appears in volume 1 of *Research in Organizational Behavior* (Greenwich, Conn.: JAI Press, 1979). Those interested in additional reading on mentors and the mentoring process should examine K. E. Kram's book, *Mentoring at Work: Developmental Relationships in Organizational Life* (Glenview, Ill.: Scott-Foresman, 1985). For those interested in training, K. N. Wexley and G. P. Latham wrote a good overview entitled *Developing and Training Human Resources in Organizations* (1981). Finally, an excellent sourcebook for information about various aspects of career management is J. Sonnenfeld's *Managing Career Systems: Channeling the Flow of Executive Careers* (Homewood, Ill.: R. D. Irwin, 1984).

ON YOUR
OWN

**Alien Invasion**   Organizational cultures are so ubiquitous that we often overlook the information they can convey to an observer. The trick to deciphering a culture is learning to read the clues. What do the building style and layout say about the company? What symbols does it use in dealing with the public, and what do those symbols say about how the company wants to be seen? What can we interpret from the activities of employees? Are they energetic or apathetic? Are they friendly or hostile? What stories do they tell about the organization and its major executives? What are the norms of dress? How formal are relationships between people, particularly people of different status levels, such as supervisors and secretaries? It is surprising how much of a feel for an organization one can acquire simply by looking and listening carefully.

Consider an organization to which you belong, such as your family, university, volunteer agency, fraternity or sorority, or church. Now look at your chosen organization through the eyes (and antennae!) of an alien. You have just arrived on the first spaceship to Earth from your planet. Your supervisors have ordered you to learn how Earthlings behave without doing anything to make them aware that you are from another planet. It is vital to the future plans of your superiors that you do nothing to disturb the Earthlings. Unfortunately, your people communicate by electromagnetic waves and are incapable of speech, so you cannot talk to the natives. Even if you could, it is reported by the usually reliable Bureau of Interplanetary Intelligence that Earthlings may become cannibalistic if annoyed. A crash course in Earth languages taught by the bureau has enabled you to read and understand the language.

These instructions limit your ability to interact verbally with the organization you are observing. There are two reasons for this. First, your objective is to learn about what the organization does when it is simply going about its normal business and not responding to specific questions. Second, you are likely to be surprised at how much you can learn by simply observing if you put your mind to it. Many skilled managers employ this ability in sensing what is going on as they walk through their plant or office area. When you have completed your observation of the chosen organization, develop a short description of the culture of the organization, focusing on its ideologies, myths, values, and norms of behavior.

Source: Donald D. Bowen, "Alien Invasion: An Organizational Culture Assignment," in *Experiences in Management and Organizational Behavior,* 3d ed., R. J. Lewicki, D. D. Bowen, D. T. Hall, and F. S. Hall, eds. (New York: Wiley, 1988).

CLOSING CASE
FOR CHAPTER 11

# THE MANAGER'S MEMO

FROM: H. Roadruck, Vice President, Pickle Division

TO: T. Phinney, Production Supervisor

RE: High Turnover

It has seemed to me that turnover among the pickle production workers has been high. I obtained some figures from the Personnel Department, and the numbers show my assumption was right. Out of a 135-person work force, we have lost the following numbers during the last 12 months:

| | |
|---|---|
| Within 5 years of hiring | 6 |
| Within 1 year of hiring | 23 |
| Within 6 months of hiring | 31 |
| Within 1 month of hiring | 97 |

These figures show that we are constantly replacing our production work force. We cannot afford to keep this up. We also cannot afford to pay any more than we do now. Our wages are already above the industry average.

The numbers also tell me that a lot of the people you are hiring either are unqualified or quickly become disillusioned with their jobs. According to the Personnel Department, some of the departing workers have been saying that working here is a lot more boring than they were led to believe it would be. I even heard that one worker said he was on the job for a full week before he was allowed to touch the packaging machine. Another said he was getting embarrassed to tell his friends he makes pickles all day long.

Please provide some ideas on how you can rectify this situation.

CASE DISCUSSION
QUESTIONS

Assume you are the production supervisor, and respond to the vice president's memorandum. Review the concepts in the chapter, and apply the ones you think would be most effective in selecting and assimilating production workers. Be sure to support your recommendations.

# Job Design

## Notes from Underground

According to ex-Chief of Naval Operations Elmo (Bud) Zumwalt, the Navy assumes that "everyone below the rank of commander is immature." Do most managers feel this way about their subordinates? Do most organizations treat their employees this way? A General Motors executive discovered this poem circulating among the auto workers. He believes that "most organizations are governed by that assumption that the *average* worker is an incompetent ne'er-do-well, just itching to screw up." He also believes that this assumption has a monumentally negative impact on productivity.

Are these men and women
Workers of the world?
or is it an overgrown nursery
with children—goosing, slapping, boys
giggling, snotty girls?
What is it about that entrance way,
those gates to the plant? Is it the
guards, the showing of your badge—the smell?
is there some invisible eye
that pierces you through and
transforms your being? Some aura
or ether, that brain and spirit washes you
and commands, "For eight hours
you shall be different."
What is it that instantaneously makes
a child out of a man?
Moments before he was a father, a husband,
an owner of property,
a voter, a lover, an adult.
When he spoke at least some listened.
Salesmen courted his favor.
Insurance men appealed to his family responsibility
and by chance the church sought his help. . . .
But that was before he shuffled past the guard,
climbed the steps,
hung up his coat and
took his place along the line.

Source: T. Peters and R. H. Waterman, *In Search of Excellence* (New York: Random House, 1981), pp. 235–236.

## INTRODUCTION

Philosopher and historian David Hume once wrote, "the richest genius, like the most fertile soil, when uncultivated, shoots up into the rankest weeds: and instead of vines and olives for the pleasure and use of man, produces to its slothful owner the most abundant crop of poisons." Hume's quotation highlights the challenge facing an organization's management. Finding the right personnel and successfully getting them into the organization is only the first step in the long journey of developing a healthy and productive work force. This chapter addresses the second step in this managerial challenge. This second step is designing jobs and roles for workers in the organization that take full advantage of each individual's ability to contribute to the organization's efficiency and effectiveness. The chapter presents three perspectives on the design of jobs: (1) the tradition of work simplification, (2) job characteristics approaches to job design, and finally (3) work-group approaches to job design. The chapter concludes with several important qualifications to the success of all job design efforts.

## JOB DESIGN IN PERSPECTIVE

As noted in Chapter 2, the field of organizational behavior traces its roots to shortcomings of the traditional job design efforts of the early 1900s. Traditional job design—as exemplified by Frederick Taylor's "scientific management" and Henry Ford's revolutionary assembly line—focused almost exclusively on efficiency. All too often this focus on efficiency meant **work simplification.** Managers designed work tasks to be simple and therefore easily mastered and quickly accomplished. Each worker specialized at a small number of very simple tasks, such as screwing several nuts onto several bolts. The basic philosophy behind this approach to job design was that each worker could become expert at some very small number of tasks and learn to do them repeatedly with lightning speed and no mistakes. In the electronics industry, for example, simplified jobs may have a "cycle time"—the amount of time it takes an employee to complete the entire task—as short as 10 seconds.[1] That translates into more than 2,500 cycles per eight-hour workday.

## THE WORK-SIMPLIFICATION PARADOX

The philosophy behind a work-simplification strategy is very appealing, and by some estimates as many as 50 percent of all manufacturing jobs today still are designed on the premise that simpler is better.[2] However, work simplification takes into account only what is the most efficient way to design a work task *assuming that workers are indifferent* to what they are doing. The truth is that workers are not indifferent to the design of their work. The Hawthorne studies (discussed in Chapter 2) proved that what workers feel and need can be just as important to efficiency as specialization and simplification of tasks.

[1] E. E. Lawler III, *High-Involvement Management* (London: Jossey-Bass, 1986), 84.
[2] Ibid.

Whatever simplified, routinized jobs gain in potential efficiency they often more than lose in boredom and alienation. This woman feels like a part of the machine as she merely keeps the product flowing along the production line. There is virtually no variation or interest in her day.

In his book *High-Involvement Management,* management theorist Edward Lawler III summarizes the effects of work simplification on worker behaviors:

> . . . the work simplification approach is often associated with (1) low quality because individuals do not care about product quality, (2) low productivity because individuals are not motivated to be productive, and (3) high wages because individuals demand them for repetitive, boring, unsatisfying jobs. In addition, it often leads to high levels of turnover and absenteeism, and therefore overstaffing to replace absentees and people who quit. Further, despite the fact that jobs are relatively simple to learn, training costs may be high because of the high turnover rate. Finally, the social costs are high. Although largely undocumented, it is thought that the dissatisfying nature of simplified, repetitive work causes mental problems, alcohol and substance abuse, and a general alienation from society."[3]

The message here is that a job that is sensibly designed from the viewpoint of the task may not be sensibly designed from the viewpoint of the worker. This is the paradox of work simplification. A job that consists of continuous repetition of several simple tasks may be easy to do in principle. However, when a job is too easy, a worker's attention will wander; the worker will become bored and alienated. Quality and productivity both will suffer.

The literature on job design is filled with managers' horror stories of what happens when workers are assigned tasks that are too simple and repetitive. The comments of one manager of a large microelectronics manufacturer in Holland are revealing. The workers in his plant were required to wear gloves to protect the product from fingerprints and skin oil. When management wasn't looking, the workers would roll their gloves into a ball and play "soccer" in the work bays. Each work bay also was equipped with an air hose for blowing dust off the work surfaces. Somehow the workers figured out how to disconnect the nozzles and use the hoses to shoot rubber drawer-knobs at each other across the work bays. This kind of disfunctional playfulness on the assembly line represents alienation, lost productivity, and even potential hazards for the worker. Further, it usually means that the organization must spend money to provide more supervisors to keep employees in line. Some further examples of this problem are provided in the "Focus on: Worker Alienation."

In addition to lost productivity, the issue of lost employees is not trivial for organizations. Small amounts of worker turnover no doubt are healthy for organizations and represent natural renewal of the work force.[4] However, the departure of an organization's potentially valuable and productive but alienated human resources can be extremely costly.

---

[3]Ibid., 86.

[4]J. R. Hollenbeck and C. R. Williams, "Turnover Functionality versus Turnover Frequency: A Note on Work Attitudes and Organizational Effectiveness," *Journal of Applied Psychology* 71 (1986): 606–611.

FOCUS ON:

Worker Alienation

**A Case of the Blue-Collar Blues**

What was it like to work on a Detroit automobile assembly line in the 1970s? Henry Belcher, a 40-year-old welder at a Dodge plant, described it this way: "I am as much a machine as a punch press or a drill motor is." A local UAW president at Cadillac summed it up grimly: "Every single unskilled young man in that plant wants out of there. They can't face it. They hate to go in there." What is it that they hate? Consider the following description of Henry Belcher's job:

Promptly at 5 a.m., the assembly line begins sending cars past his work station, and from then on Belcher is part of the line, like the well-oiled gears and bearings. The noise is deafening; Belcher could not talk to the men at the next stations three feet away even if there were time. There never is. Partially assembled cars move past him at the rate of 62 an hour; in less than one minute he is expected to look over each auto, pound out a dent in a fender, or reweld an improperly joined seam. Cars that cannot be fixed that quickly are taken off the line. In the winter, drafts from ill-caulked windows chill Belcher's chest, while hot air blasts from rust-proofing ovens 30 feet away singe his back. After two hours of standing on the concrete floor his legs ache, but the whistle does not blow for lunch until 10 a.m.

. . . Says Belcher . . . "Everything is regulated. No time to stop and think about what you are doing; your life is geared to the assembly line."*

Belcher's experience was hardly unique. Workers would do anything to avoid feeling like part of the machinery—have water fights, paint fights, whatever. Drugs and heavy drinking were common, and so was product sabotage—an ignition key dropped in the gas tank, a lighted glove locked in the trunk, slit upholstery, severed ignition wires. And in the back of everyone's mind was the same slim hope that the line would break down. It was no surprise that when the United Auto Workers union voted to strike the Vega plant in Lordstown, Ohio, 85 percent of the work force turned out to vote and 97 percent supported the strike.

For many of the workers, old age was not unwelcome because retirement looked like the only escape. But Richard Janowski realized the autoworker's dream of leaving the line for good. He went to night school and qualified for a job teaching high school. In his last day on the line, he reflected on his experiences there: "I almost cry when I see kids coming into the shop today. Working in a factory is nothing to be ashamed of, but you look at men who are 35 and look 50 and you say, is that going to be me?"

*"The Grueling Life on the Line," *TIME*, September 28, 1970, p. 70.
Source: "The Luddites in Lordstown," *Harper's* magazine, June 1972, pp. 68–73; and "Blue-collar Blues on the Assembly Line," *FORTUNE*, July 1970.

Replacing an employee may cost an organization anywhere from 5 to 25 times an employee's monthly salary in interim lost productivity, search, socialization, and training costs.[5]

The bottom line is that workers have a reservoir of interest and energy. If this reservoir is not tapped by the job itself, it will be wasted or will surface in other forms—such as counterproductive playfulness on the assembly line. The challenge of job design is this: How can managers harness this reservoir of worker interest and energy and direct it toward the accomplishment of organizational objectives?

In this chapter, we will consider two approaches to redesigning jobs to tap this reservoir of worker interest and energy: redesign focused on characteristics of individual jobs, and work-group approaches to job redesign.

# JOB CHARACTERISTICS

Management attempts to harness worker interest and energy by changing the characteristics of individual jobs generally are of two sorts: job enlargement and job enrichment. **Job enlargement** redesign strategies change the range of a job—the number of tasks that a worker performs—to make the job more interesting and involving. **Job enrichment** redesign strategies instead make jobs more interesting and involving by allowing workers to fulfill higher-order needs—such as achievement and control—through work.

## JOB ENLARGEMENT

Job enlargement is based on the simple premise that a job will be more interesting and involving if the worker has a wide range of skills (rather than just one) to master and perform. Consider the range of tasks required to produce a shirt, as portrayed in Figure 12–1(a). A work-simplification strategy would assign each worker one of these three tasks. Each worker then could master one particular task, providing (in principle at least) the best potential for efficiency through specialization. This specialization approach, however, would run the risk of worker alienation. Job enlargement, on the other hand, decreases the probability of worker alienation or boredom by increasing the variety of skills each worker has to master. In its simplest form, managers increase skill variety in workers' jobs by giving workers more tasks. In Figure 12–1(b), for instance, each worker does *all three* tasks.

A slightly different way to increase the skill variety of a job is job rotation. As shown in Figure 12–1(c), **job rotation** increases skill variety by allowing workers to switch jobs occasionally. The first worker does Task #1 (stitching on collars) only for a while, and then moves on to Task #2 (ironing and folding) for a while, and finally on to Task #3

[5]P. H. Mirvis and E. E. Lawler III, "Accounting for the Quality of Work Life," *Journal of Occupational Behavior* 5 (1984): 197–212.

**FIGURE 12–1**     Comparison of Job Specialization, Job Rotation, and Job Enlargement Strategies

Simplifying the tasks assigned to a worker in principle should make a job easy to do, but in practice will make the job boring and alienating. Job rotation and job enlargement make jobs more interesting by increasing the variety of skills a worker uses.

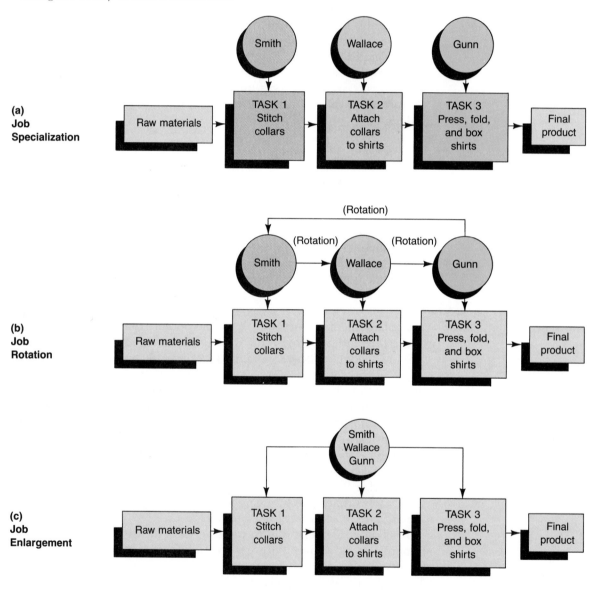

(boxing). Rotation breaks up the monotony of working a single repetitive task by changing a worker's task every once in a while. Rotation might occur every week, every day, or even every few hours. In one version of job rotation—the "work module" approach—management divides the workday into four two-hour modules and assigns workers different tasks during each module.[6]

Skill variety also can be increased through cross-training. **Cross-training** occurs when management encourages employees to learn their coworkers' jobs. Cross-training provides benefits for both the individual and the organization. For the individual, learning new skills increases variety on the job and breaks up the monotony of working on only a small number of tasks. In Shell's Sarnia plant, it takes workers as long as 9 or 10 years to master all the different tasks.[7] That gives every worker some new challenges to look forward to every day. For management, cross-training provides additional flexibility; if an employee calls in sick or leaves the organization, or if a particular task becomes a temporary bottleneck, work assignments can be shifted around to handle the temporary changes in task demands. At a Chrysler plant in New Castle, Indiana, cross-training was used effectively to reduce manufacturing costs by 30 percent, resulting in a savings of over $3 million.[8] Cross-training also allows management to train personnel for supervisory roles. An employee who has been cross-trained on all the jobs in a work group should make a better work-group supervisor than someone who has learned only one task in the work group. Cross-training is seen as such an overall benefit that some companies even use compensation schemes (known as "pay-for-knowledge" plans) that reward employees for each new skill acquired.

While job enlargement, rotation, and cross-training are certainly improvements over work simplification as ways to design jobs, they just as certainly have drawbacks. Perhaps most critically, increases in the range of jobs do not go far enough in tapping the interest and energies of most workers. A 1987 survey found that most workers want more than just enlarged jobs; they want a say in deciding how their work is organized.[9] Workers want a chance to fulfill their "higher-order" needs through work.

## JOB ENRICHMENT

The origins of job enrichment are found in Herzberg's two-factor theory of motivation (discussed in Chapter 4). Herzberg maintained that workers will be interested and involved in work when their jobs provide

[6]R. L. Kahn, "The Work Module: A Tonic for Lunchpail Lassitude," *Psychology Today*, February 1973, 35–39.

[7]Lawler, *High-Involvement Management*, 104.

[8]W. F. Cascio, *Managing Human Resources* (New York: McGraw-Hill, 1986), 130.

[9]"Managers Underrate Employee Values," *Administrative Management*, July 1987, 8.

**FIGURE 12–2**    Positive Task-Related Experiences

1. *Accountability.* Workers should be held responsible for their performance.
2. *Achievement.* Workers should feel that they are accomplishing something worthwhile.
3. *Control over resources.* If possible, workers should have control over their task.
4. *Feedback.* Workers should receive clear and direct information regarding their performance.
5. *Personal growth and development.* Workers should have the opportunity to learn new skills.
6. *Work pace.* Within constraints, workers should be able to set their own work pace.

Source: F. Herzberg, "The Wise Old Turk," *Harvard Business Review,* September/October 1974, pp. 70–80.

opportunities for "positive, task-related experiences" such as control and achievement.[10] A list of these positive, task-related experiences is shown in Figure 12–2. We will consider four ways to enrich jobs: providing task identity, task significance, decision-making responsibility, and feedback.

**Task Identity**    When the set of tasks a worker is assigned allows the worker to see a process through from start to finish, **task identity** occurs. Task identity provides the worker with a sense of completion and achievement. Management at Continental Illinois National Bank and Trust learned just how important task identity can be. Check processing at the bank used to be done on an "assembly line," where each clerical worker performed one function over and over. The work was boring and the workers were prone to make errors. That changed when the bank went to a "modular" arrangement that allowed workers to handle entire transactions from start to finish. With the modular arrangement, a single worker processed an incoming check, transferred funds in the account by computer, telephoned the customer if necessary, and mailed out a confirmation of the transaction. "I like it," noted one worker, "because you see the package from beginning to end." The bank liked it, too, because error rates went down.[11]

Naturally, task identity is dependent upon skill variety. A job must incorporate a fair number of skills in order to take a process through from start to finish. Job enlargement also may enrich a job if added tasks increase the task identity in a worker's job. The lesson of identity is simply that while in tasks, more is better, skill variety works best when the

[10]R. W. Griffin, *Task Design: An Integrative Approach* (Glenview, Ill.: Scott, Foresman, 1982), 31.

[11]"You See the Package from Beginning to End," *Business Week,* May 16, 1983, 103.

At the Federal Reserve Bank of Chicago, checks used to be processed assembly-line style—one task per worker. Now check processors handle multiple tasks through the use of high-speed sorters, thereby increasing skill variety and task identity. Productivity and satisfaction have both benefited.

variety of tasks assigned to an individual adds up to something—like a sense of completion.

**Task Significance** Managers also can enrich jobs by increasing **task significance.** A task is significant when a worker can see that good or poor performance makes a difference to someone. Task significance often is tied to contact with the consumer of a product or service. Any chance a worker has to experience a customer's appreciation for a job well done will enhance that worker's feeling that the task is significant.

Task significance is an important component of job design at Chantiers Beneteau, a custom sailboat manufacturer. When Xavier Fontanet, chief executive, took over the small company, he quickly learned that his work force had lost interest and was turning out seaworthy but undistinguished craft. To reverse this trend, Fontanet encouraged the company's customers to send along some personal information with their orders—photographs, personal background information, even descriptions of the adventures they were planning with their new boat. Suddenly, workers were not just building sailboats, they were building a racer for Ted Hall to parade around San Francisco Bay, and a summer sailing vacation for the Schmidt family in Hamburg. Their work had become significant, and within a year their workmanship had improved dramatically.[12]

Task significance also has to do with workers being able to imagine that their effort and workmanship make a difference in the overall quality of a product, and therefore in its value to someone. A worker on a traditional assembly line doing just one of twelve tasks in an assembly process probably has a hard time believing that quality of workman-

[12]R. H. Waterman, *The Renewal Factor* (New York: Bantam Books, 1987), 4.

ship—how well or poorly that worker does just one task on the line—makes much of a contribution to the overall quality of the final product. On the other hand, when a job is enlarged in variety, a worker can feel responsible for a significant portion of the overall product (for example, three of the twelve component tasks—fully 25 percent of the total product!). And if the enlargement includes task identity, it becomes easy for a worker to imagine that the quality of the overall product makes a significant difference to the final consumer.

**Decision-Making Responsibility**   Job enrichment often goes beyond job enlargement by allowing workers to take responsibility for decision making on the job. The lament of the poem that began this chapter is that management often lacks the trust necessary to delegate decisions to workers. Job enrichment becomes a big step in job design when it represents the first move by management to share control in the workplace and get workers to act less like slave labor and more like organizational resources. Managers can increase workers' decision-making responsibility either by allowing them to participate in management decision making (perhaps by soliciting worker opinions through problem-solving groups) or by allowing workers limited decision-making autonomy within the scope of their jobs.

Consider again our shirt assembly line. In the Figure 12–3 depiction of job enrichment, each worker not only has responsibility for all the component tasks (collar stitching, folding and ironing, and boxing), but also *controls* the arrangement of these tasks. Should all the collars be stitched on first, then all the folding and ironing done, and finally all the boxing? Perhaps the whole process could be run through in lots of five or ten shirts? Management has delegated these decisions to the worker. The worker controls the immediate work environment and has the option of changing the order of the tasks when the current arrangement gets boring.

The worker in Figure 12–3 also now has responsibility for quality-control decisions—checking the work and certifying it to be error free. In a traditionally designed job, quality assurance would be the job of another worker. After all, can workers be trusted to police their own work? In an enriched job, the responsibility for quality comes with the job. Management trusts the workers to check their own work.

Worker feelings of control and responsibility also are enhanced when managers consult workers about management decisions, such as how to design a new manufacturing line. Participation in organizational decision making allows workers to feel control over the direction of the organization and feel that management respects their opinions. For the organization, worker participation in decisions opens up a communication channel so that management can access an important source of knowledge and innovation—the workers. A 1986 article entitled "The Golden Nuggets on the Factory Floor" provides some striking examples

**FIGURE 12–3**    Comparison of Job Specialization and Job Enrichment

Job enrichment increases the decision-making responsibility of the worker. In this example, the workers' enriched jobs give them responsibility for quality and task arrangement.

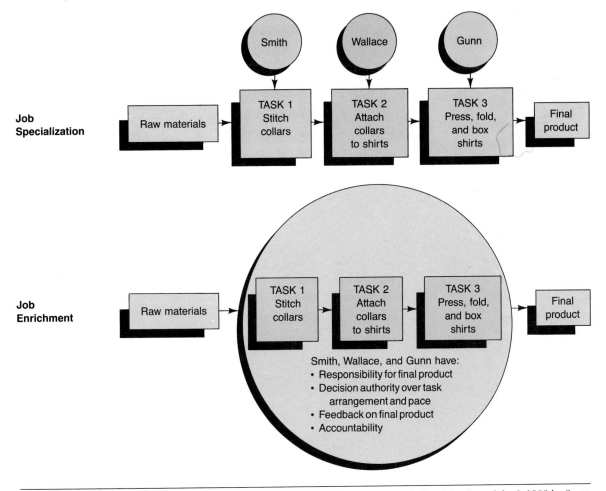

Source: *Managing Behavior in Organizations*, by Marc J. Wallace, Jr., and Andrew D. Szilagyi, Jr. Copyright © 1982 by Scott, Foresman and Company. Reprinted by permission.

of the thoughtfulness of factory workers. Consider the insightful comments of one cannery employee:

> We change over an awful lot from 8-oz. to 16-oz. cans. Why can't they drop the size but keep the same diameter for the base as in the 16-oz.? That would save half the amount of changeover time. It would save three to four hours once a week of six to eight expensive people. I am the mechanic, so I know. Now we have to change everything. If we made the change as

suggested, all you would have to do is lower all the machines. That's a half hour's work.[13]

Workers on the factory floor like this one are, after all, closest to the work and often have a perspective on the production process that is quite different from—and often clearer than—that of management.

In practice, enriching jobs by giving workers more decision-making control—either through limited autonomy within their jobs or participation in management decision making—is not only a big step for management. It can also be a big step for workers. Workers often are unfamiliar with taking responsibility on the job or making innovative suggestions. Time and even training may be required before workers can productively exercise the decision-making control management is willing to give them.[14]

**Context Enrichment**   Decision-making responsibility in a job also can be increased by enriching the *context* of work; for example, by giving workers decision-making control over the context of their work. One example of context enrichment is **flextime work scheduling.** In a flextime program, management delegates to each individual worker the responsibility for deciding when to come to work. Naturally this does not mean that flextime workers can just come in any time they please. That would create chaos, since no one in a work setting ever could depend on anyone else being there. In fact, flextime represents a good example of the *limited* autonomy management can provide workers in an enriched job. As shown in Figure 12–4, even in flextime scheduling management specifies certain times when *everyone* is expected to be at work. That means that workers who have important dependency relationships at work know that there is always a time when needed others will be around. Outside of the required work periods, however, workers can decide for themselves which hours they will be at work in order to fill out their eight hours per day. Schedules then are set up quarterly or yearly so other workers will know when they can count on someone being there, and so that management can be sure that the minimally required work force always is present during business hours.

In the flextime schedule in Figure 12–4(a), for example, all workers are required to be at work between 10 a.m. and 3 p.m., with everyone taking a standard noon to 1 p.m. lunch break. However, that only accounts for four hours of the eight-hour workday. For the other four hours, a worker could choose to come in at 6 a.m. to begin work and be done for the day at 3 p.m. Or a worker could choose to come in at 10 a.m. and stay until 7 p.m. A standard 8 a.m. to 5 p.m. job also is an option. The key is that management leaves the decision with the individual

---

[13]W. Imberman, "The Golden Nuggets on the Factory Floor," *Business Horizons,* July/August 1986, 64.

[14]R. M. Kanter, "The Dilemmas of Participation," in *The Changemasters* (New York: Simon & Schuster, 1983), 241–278.

**FIGURE 12–4**    Two Sample Flextime Schedules

Flextime scheduling en-
riches a job by giving
workers decision-making
responsibility over the
*context* in which they
work. With a flexible
working schedule, work-
ers decide when to work
and can arrange work
around nonwork commit-
ments or interests.

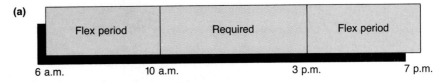

(a)

| Flex period | Required | Flex period |

6 a.m.          10 a.m.                3 p.m.          7 p.m.

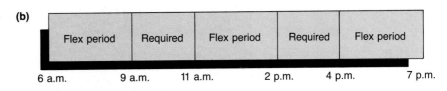

(b)

| Flex period | Required | Flex period | Required | Flex period |

6 a.m.      9 a.m.     11 a.m.        2 p.m.    4 p.m.      7 p.m.

worker. Figure 12–4(b) provides a second example of a flextime schedule where the required times are from 9 a.m. to 11 a.m. and 2 p.m. to 4 p.m., allowing for flexible scheduling around the lunch break as well.

Flextime scheduling works best when workers do not need to interact with other workers to do their work. For a typical assembly line, flextime work scheduling is not appropriate. In our shirt assembly line (Figure 12–1), if the worker who folds and irons the shirts comes in at 6 a.m. to begin work but the collar stitcher doesn't arrive until 9 a.m., that second worker on the line may have nothing to do for three hours! For secretaries in a typing pool, however, flextime may be perfect. Work left the night before (perhaps by someone working till 7 p.m.) will be waiting at 6 a.m. when the first typist arrives.

Flextime allows workers to schedule work around the rest of their lives. Single parents, for instance, may want to start work early in order to be home by 4 p.m. when the children return from school. Ambitious workers may want to schedule classes at the local university to supplement their skills and increase their chances for promotion. Flextime scheduling allows these workers to fit work hours around class offerings. In both cases, flextime scheduling allows workers the freedom to fit the rest of life around work.

Flextime scheduling programs enrich jobs by enriching their *context* rather than their contents. Flextime scheduling allows workers to exercise decision-making control in fitting their obligations at work around their obligations or needs outside the work setting. Another example of job enrichment through enrichment of the job context is provided by the McDonald's "Crew Olympics" competitions. These competitions, described in the "Focus on: Context Enrichment," enrich the context of the job by providing for fun and rewarding job challenges.

At Pace Foods, the context of work has been enriched by making quality control a "family affair." Here company president Kit Goldbury joins his employees for their daily picante sauce taste testing.

**Feedback**    Feedback occurs when management provides workers with information about their performance. Feedback plays an important psychological role by reducing uncertainty in workers. Practically, it makes sense for management to give workers control over decisions only if management also is willing to give them the information necessary to make good decisions. Timely feedback can help alert workers to the existence of problems and also help pinpoint their source. If different arrangements of work are more or less efficient or effective, this information needs to be made available to workers so that their decisions can be informed and intelligent. *Any* form of worker participation or autonomy will work only if the workers making the decisions have enough information to make high-quality decisions.

Several years ago, Professor David Garvin of Harvard University conducted a study comparing the defect rates of American and Japanese air-conditioner manufacturing plants. He found 63.5 defects per 100 air-conditioning units produced in the U.S. plants, compared to 0.9 defects per 100 units produced in Japan. Worse yet, the study took longer than Garvin had anticipated because the Americans hadn't even

FOCUS ON:

Context
Enrichment

**Turning Work into Play at McDonald's** All the excellent companies celebrate superior performance. But when it comes to tailoring hoopla to fit its own needs, McDonald's is the master.

In the coming year, about 17 million customers will visit the "golden arches" each day, consuming some 50 billion burgers in the process. In fact, it's safe to say that the vast majority of Americans have at least sampled a Big Mac. Dining at McDonald's is no gourmet experience. But in a world full of unpleasant surprises, what you do get at McDonald's is the comfort of knowing what to expect. The burgers are never burned or raw, the service is sunny, and the restaurants generally are spotless inside and out. McDonald's stays far ahead of its competition in the fast-food industry by maintaining its standards throughout a worldwide system. This is no easy trick since over 75 percent of McDonald's 8,000 restaurants are independently owned franchises, outside the reach of corporate control.

How are the standards so rigidly maintained? By making sure each worker understands McDonald's values and visions and has the requisite pride and purpose to pursue them. And how does McDonald's maintain pride and purpose? Job content does not seem to be the key here; the rules and standards for tasks at McDonald's are rigidly specified in the 700-page operations manual. Working at a McDonald's, from a job-content point of view, is the equivalent of working on a fast-food assembly line. But what McDonald's jobs lack in content they make up for in *context*.

Consider the McDonald's "Crew Olympics." McDonald's management spent six months and $500,000 on a competition *for its workers* prior to the 1984 Olympics in Los Angeles. The competition featured a McDonald's decathlon; counter workers at every McDonald's around the world had the opportunity to compete at each of the tasks McDonald's workers perform on the job every day. "Compete" meant doing a task as fast as possible while still adhering to the rules and standards laid out in the McDonald's operations manual, which includes every attitude and gesture to be used in dealing with McDonald's customers. In-store and local competitions led up to regional competitions. Eventually the finalists—the best McDonald's hamburger flippers in the world—all were flown to Los Angeles for a culminating competition and awards ceremony, not to mention a few visits to the real Olympic games.

This kind of hoopla may sound corny, but it works. To compete successfully, counter workers had to know the operations manual cold. So, by the way, did the judges—the independent owner-operators of individual McDonald's outlets that McDonald's headquarters had referee the local and regional competitions. McDonald's couldn't enrich the contents of assembly-line food preparation, so they enriched the context in which that job takes place. The result was that McDonald's made doing the job right a game—a giant competition that every McDonald's worker in the world could practice for every day at work.

Source: Adapted from the television special, "In Search of Excellence," PBS.

bothered to calculate defect rates before Garvin asked for them. The numbers had to be reconstructed in the American plants! In the Japanese plants, these numbers were posted publicly for all workers to see and consider.[15] The importance of timely performance feedback is illustrated by the experiences of Emery Air Freight, which are described in the "FOCUS ON: Feedback."

While feedback is critical to effective worker participation in decision making, participation also can prove important in the *collection* of feedback. Research suggests that feedback works best when workers participate in the collection and analysis of performance feedback data. Workers place greater trust in feedback they themselves have generated, and being entrusted to collect it seems to have positive effects on worker effort.[16] At Emery Air Freight, management asked dockworkers to collect the container utilization information that became the impetus for dramatic performance improvements. Similarly, by the late 1980s, some major electronics firms in the United States had begun to follow Japan's lead and train their manufacturing workers to collect statistical quality-control data—data that those workers then could use to improve the efficiency and effectiveness of their own jobs.

Feedback works best when it is diagnostic and timely. Feedback is diagnostic to the extent that it reveals problems with performance. A videotape of your public speaking style, for instance, may reveal aspects of your performance that you were not aware needed to be changed. Feedback is timely when it arrives as soon as possible after performance. Feedback about your performance three or four weeks after the fact may not tell you what you're doing wrong *now*—and will have allowed you to continue making mistakes for three or four more weeks!

**Quality Circles**   Quality circles already have been discussed briefly in this book in Chapter 9 as a form of group decision making. Quality circles are volunteer employee groups that meet to discuss work-related problems. They are an extremely popular form of job enrichment and worker decision-making participation in the United States. A New York Stock Exchange study in 1982 found that 65 percent of companies with over 25,000 employees were using quality circles. Most had only been using circles since 1980.[17] A second study conducted in 1984 found that more than 75 percent of companies surveyed were using circles.[18] In fact, in the mid-1980s, most Fortune 500 companies were using quality circles in one form or another.

While the format of quality circles (QCs) is a little different in every company, most QC programs share several defining characteristics. First,

[15]D. A. Garvin, "Quality on the Line," *Harvard Business Review* 61(5), (1983): 65–75.

[16]G. B. Northcraft and P. C. Earley, "Technology, Credibility, and Feedback Use," *Organizational Behavior and Human Decision Processes* 44 (1989): 83–96.

[17]Lawler, 44.

[18]H. Gorlin and L. Schein, *Innovations in Managing Human Resources* (New York: Conference Board, 1984).

FOCUS ON:

Feedback

**Putting Information Where It Matters Most** Employees at Emery Air Freight have found that a little information can go a long way in saving money. One example: Emery's costs for small shipments intended for the same destination are lower when shipped together in a large container than when shipped separately. Through the use of continuous feedback, Emery increased large container use by its workers from 45 percent to 95 percent of possible shipments, with the increase occurring in *one day* in most of its offices. The net savings: $650,000 annually.

How does continuous feedback work? Consider "callbacks" from the customer service department. The customer service department at Emery had a standard: When a customer calls in with a question, the customer should always get a "callback"—a response—within 90 minutes of the initial query. To keep track of this, each customer representative was given a daily sheet on which to keep track of calls received and "callbacks." It took no special skills or training for the customer reps to compare their times with the standard of 90 minutes. Similar tracking sheets—all easily filled out by the employees themselves—were provided in other departments as well.

And what is the value of continuous feedback in a setting like this? At first, feedback helps employees know if they are meeting the standard. Later, when the standard is being met on a regular basis, feedback becomes a form of reinforcement—corroboration that the employee has done a fair day's work by meeting the standard.

Judging from what has happened at Emery Air Freight, there can be no doubt that continuous feedback is a powerful tool. In the customer service department, standards were met only 30 percent to 40 percent of the time before employees began to collect their own continuous feedback. After the feedback system was instituted, standards were met 90 percent to 95 percent of the time. In one office, the percentage jumped from 30 percent of standard to 95 percent of standard in one day! And the effects lasted. Four years later, performance in Emery's customer service departments continued to average 90 percent to 95 percent of standard. Across all the departments where continuous feedback was instituted, Emery saved over $3 million in three years.

Edward J. Feeney, vice-president for system performance, was the man responsible for emphasizing the importance of feedback systems at Emery. "We found that when we provided daily feedback only one week out of four or one out of five, performance in the periods without feedback reverted to the previous level or was almost as bad," he says. Feeney also sees the accuracy of the performance standard as key. If standards are too low, the company loses performance and the employee loses potential job satisfaction. If the standards are too high, the employee will be frustrated and may even revert to a performance level *below* that before standards were used.

Interestingly, Emery has achieved the benefits of continuous reinforcement *without* accompanying monetary incentives. At Emery Air Freight, the recognition of a job well done—especially recognition through self-collected continuous feedback—seems to be enough.

Source: "At Emery Air Freight, Positive Reinforcement Boosts Performance," in *The Applied Psychology of Work Behavior*, ed. D. Organ (Plano, Tex.: Business Publications, Inc., 1987), 138–149.

membership is voluntary and only rarely do all employees volunteer initially. Over time, membership may change as some members become disenchanted and leave the circle while others become curious and join. QCs are made up of individuals who either work side by side—for example, as part of an assembly line—or have the same job in a plant. They meet for a specified period of time (such as an hour) on a very regular basis (such as once every two weeks). Typically there is no extra pay for participating in the QC (though meetings are held during paid work hours), and most QCs are not rewarded for making good suggestions.

Quality circles can be thought of as a form of job enrichment because they empower workers to make suggestions and some decisions. The agenda of QC meetings is limited to discussing ways to improve quality, reduce costs, or improve productivity in the QC members' immediate jobs. QCs are never given a broad mandate to come up with suggestions to change the overall organization. Further, QCs do not have budgets. They are urged to come up with suggestions that require changes in procedures rather than expenditures. Finally, management typically retains veto power over QC suggestions, especially if expenditures are required. In such cases, the QC will have to present its suggestion formally to management for approval.

Quality circles can be costly for organizations. Naturally, the organization must forego some productivity to allow members the time to participate in circle activities. Further, many QC volunteers are not well prepared to handle the group dynamics in problem-solving meetings. To give a QC a good chance to succeed, training in group problem solving is recommended, at a cost of about $200 per member.[19]

As a form of job enrichment, there are two reasons for having QCs: benefits to the organization and benefits to their members. For the organization, quality circles represent an attempt to take advantage of the greater problem-solving synergy of groups. An article in *Industry Week* touted the "tremendous" savings produced by QC suggestions. Loopco Industries claims to have reduced production costs by *70 percent* as a result of QC suggestions. The payback for expenditures to support QC activities and to implement their suggestions has been estimated to be as high as 8 to 1.[20]

For the members of quality circles, membership seems to have a positive impact on job satisfaction, which in turn can lead to reduced absenteeism and turnover.[21] QCs provide a forum in which employees can make suggestions and decisions concerning ways to improve efficiency and effectiveness. And many employees enjoy the social interaction and camaraderie of quality circle activities. Quality circles have their downsides, however, as evidenced by the following comments:

[19]Lawler, 48.

[20]P. Pascarella, "Quality Circles," *Industry Week* 213(7), (1982): 50–55.

[21]R. E. Cole and D. S. Takachi, "Forging International Links: Making Quality Circles Work in the U.S.," *National Productivity Review* 3(4), (1984): 407–429.

**FIGURE 12-5**       Limited Autonomy and Rising Expectations

1.  Expectation of making a difference
       New self-image as a contributor
       Feelings of power
       Feelings of accomplishment

2.  Expectation of being asked again
       Self-image as an organizational resource
       Expectation of supervisor's respect
       Expectation of timely feedback about suggestions
       Expectation of further expansion of role

3.  Expectations about compensation
       Equitable repayment for valuable suggestions
       Expanded compensation to fit the new expanded role
       Possible training for expanded role
       Possible promotion for valuable suggestions

---

> I recently visited a major company that was in the expansion phase of its circle activity. The plant I visited was the one whose early successes encouraged the corporation to increase circles corporate wide. A week after I was there, the company president was scheduled to visit in order to hear about their successes. They had a problem, however. Their groups had stopped meeting, so they were frantically looking for a member of an old group who could present their successes to the president. No one, it seems, was willing to tell the president that the groups were no longer meeting.[22]

Why would even *successful* quality circle programs eventually die? In fact, successful quality circle programs eventually die for the same reasons virtually any job enrichment approach to job design can prove self-destructive. In using job enrichment programs, management is trying to allow workers to experience the psychological benefits of exercising control in the workplace. At the same time, the organization reaps invaluable benefits in improved efficiency and effectiveness. Job enrichment programs are designed to accomplish these objectives *within* the well-defined limits of workers' job descriptions. (Remember that management generally restricts quality circle agendas to discussion of ways to improve the members' immediate job functions.) In effect, job enrichment may be a way for management to have its cake and eat it too—to allow the benefits of limited autonomy while retaining the control of an essentially autocratic organizational decision-making structure.

The problem is that allowing workers a taste of control through limited autonomy raises rank-and-file worker expectations in three critical ways, as shown in Figure 12-5. First, limited autonomy allows workers to see that their suggestions can make a difference in the workplace. Good suggestions save the organization money, and the workers come to see themselves as important organizational resources.

[22]Lawler, 54–55.

This sense of power and accomplishment is not easily forgotten, or surrendered, by workers. It can prove to be a particularly touchy matter if supervisors are threatened by the successes of their subordinates' suggestions.

Second, when limited autonomy works, the workers come to expect the organization to value their opinions. Once management solicits worker opinions, an expectation is created that opinions will be solicited in the future. Nothing kills a participation program faster than management's failure to respond to a QC suggestion in a timely fashion—except perhaps management's failure to solicit worker opinions about issues when workers expect to be consulted. Finally, limited autonomy raises expectations about compensation. An enriched job may be more interesting and more involving for the worker, but it also entails more responsibility and therefore deserves more pay.

In the long run, the successes of limited autonomy in job enrichment programs may become a journey rather than a destination. If management thwarts the expectations that job enrichment programs engender in the work force, enthusiasm for participation will wane. This may be why many attempts by American corporations to become more participative end up being only "gimmicks"—short-lived fads whose time in the organization comes and goes.[23] The other choice, of course, is for management to accept and build on workers' expectations for a larger role in their organization. The "INTERNATIONAL FOCUS ON: Job Enrichment" on page 510 provides one example of what can happen when management cultivates the benefits of worker participation and autonomy.

## THE JOB CHARACTERISTICS MODEL

Job enrichment is a big step for management. It signals a change in management's philosophy about the role of workers. Job enlargement strategies typically don't give workers credit for being much more than physical resources for the organization. Job enlargement is an attempt by management to increase the probability that workers will perform their role as physical resources well (by not becoming bored) and to decrease the probability that workers will quit or be absent (by making jobs less alienating). Job enrichment, on the other hand, represents the acceptance by management that workers are a dual resource of the organization—both a physical and mental resource.

Job enrichment programs have proven successful in two different ways. First, job enrichment often leads to improvements in product *quality*. Product defect rates may drop anywhere from 10 to 60 percent when a job enrichment program is instituted. In one review of 21 job enrichment programs, job enrichment improved product quality (as measured by error rates) by an average of 28 percent.[24] Why does job

[23]T. Peters and R. H. Waterman, *In Search of Excellence,* from the chapter "Productivity through People" (New York: Random House, 1981).

[24]R. E. Kopelman, "Job Redesign and Productivity: A Review of the Evidence," *National Productivity Review* 4(3), (1985): 237–255.

**FIGURE 12–6**  The Job Characteristics Model of Job Enrichment

The job characteristics model summarizes the relationships among features that can be designed into jobs (such as skill variety), the psychological effects of these features (such as meaningful work), and the outcomes for workers and organizations (such as productivity and satisfaction).

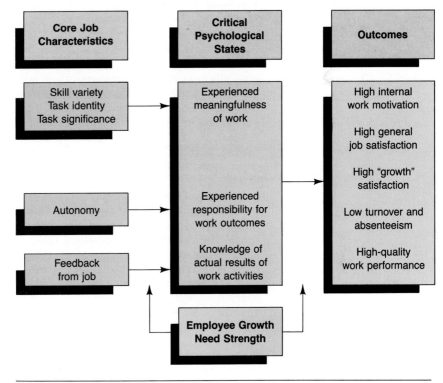

Source: J. R. Hackman and G. R. Oldham, *Work Redesign* (Reading, Mass.: Addison-Wesley, 1980), p. 77.

enrichment lead to quality improvement? First, job enrichment increases the responsibility workers feel for the product. Workers are much more motivated to turn out something they can be proud of. Second, job enrichment invests workers with a broader perspective on their work. In the shirt assembly example, when management entrusts a worker with responsibility for quality control, the worker may begin to think about what quality means in a shirt. This broader perspective may lead the worker to think of innovations that would never occur to a worker who was concentrating just on fulfilling the letter of the tasks. On the worker's side of the coin, job enrichment programs also improve job satisfaction. The review of job enrichment programs cited earlier found an average decrease of 14.5 percent in turnover and absenteeism when job enrichment was instituted. Apparently, workers enjoy the opportunity for achievement and control on the job.

The combined effects of both enlargement and enrichment job redesign strategies are captured in the **job characteristics model,** shown in Figure 12–6. The model proposes three "critical psychological states":

INTERNATIONAL
FOCUS ON:
Job Enrichment

**Participatory Management at a Paris Hotel**   Few of the wealthy tourists who visit the opulent George V, Plaza Athénée, or La Tremoille in Paris would ever suspect it, but this small chain of hotels is a showcase for the beneficial effects of industrial democracy. Even in a country where the law requires managers to involve their workers in organizational decision making, workers in these hotels are given a remarkable degree of responsibility.

The story of these hotels began in the 1920s, when they were owned by a wealthy banker. They were his hobby. He filled them with priceless antiques and artwork and cultivated a guest list that read like *Who's Who*. By the 1960s, though, the banker's health was declining—and with it the fortunes of his hotels. At the time of his death in 1967, staff morale and occupancy rates both were miserably low, so his widow sold the chain. This also turned out to be a time of social reform in France. Pressured by pro-

communist sentiment in the voter ranks, French President Charles de-Gaulle pushed a law through parliament requiring all French businesses with more than 50 employees to give workers a voice in running things and a share of the profits.

For French business on the whole, the impact of this new law was minor. Many firms simply found a way to involve workers without giving them any real say in things. At the Plaza Athénée Hotel, a different story unfolded. When the staff at Plaza Athénée heard that their hotel was being acquired by a British fast-food and motel chain, head porter Paul Bougenaux organized a strike. The strike had two goals: to preserve the hotel's historic traditions and to ensure that the new laws about worker participation in decision making were taken seriously.

The new owner did the workers one better. At the heart of each of the hotels in the chain was a "staff committee"—required by the worker par-

meaningfulness of work, responsibility for work outcomes, and knowledge of work activity results. According to the model, a redesigned job must foster these three psychological states in workers to achieve such desired outcomes as worker satisfaction and high-quality performance. The model suggests that these critical psychological states are likely to occur when managers redesign jobs to contain five of the characteristics favored by job enlargement and enrichment strategies: skill variety, task identity, task significance, autonomy, and feedback.

Plenty of anecdotes about job redesign programs support the job characteristics model, and it unquestionably has become the dominant model of job design theory.[25] Research on the effectiveness of actual job redesign programs based on the model has not been so positive, however. One survey of 30 redesign efforts found that successes of the model were as common as failures.[26] Even the researchers who

---

[25]M. G. Evans, M. N. Kiggundu, and R. J. House, "A Partial Test and Extension of the Job Characteristic Model of Motivation," *Organizational Behavior and Human Performance* 24 (1979): 354–381.

[26]Kopelman, "Job Redesign and Productivity," 239.

ticipation law—made up of elected representatives of each department in the hotel. In many French businesses these staff committees are steered away from any serious decisions. At the Plaza Athénée and its sister hotels, they became important sources of ideas, sounding boards for management, and problem-solving forums. Though hotel management personnel typically make the decisions, they explain them to the workers and even respond to the committees' opposing viewpoints. And to make sure the workers realized that the staff committee contributions would be taken seriously, head porter and strike leader Paul Bougenaux was made manager of the Plaza Athénée.

The results of the changes at Plaza Athénée were striking. Enhanced staff morale led to a 35 percent increase in efficiency and a 15 percent increase in occupancy, despite substantial hikes in room rates. For the new owners, after-tax profits have been as high as 50 percent annually. Of course, a centerpiece of the French participation movement is profit sharing, and in this hotel chain the employees' share is substantial—fully a third of the pre-tax profit. But even Paul Bougenaux admits that "money is not the main thing, you know—especially for the young people. For them it is to be happy. If they are happy to work, they are happy to share profit, of course. But it is not the center of their lives." According to Daniel Cochonneau, maître d' in the Plaza's dining room, what makes the workers happy is the great freedom of expression and decision they have in running the hotel. The managers at these hotels still have the power, but they don't have to use it.

Source: B. Nelson, "Participative Management at a Paris Hotel," *Business and Society Review* 41 (1982): 29–32.

developed the model, J. R. Hackman and G. R. Oldham, stated several years after introducing it, "While there is support in the research literature for the basic Job Characteristics Model, it would be inappropriate to conclude that the model provides a correct and complete picture of the motivational effects of job characteristics."[27] The amount of supportive research on the model does suggest, though, that it contains important insights about job design.

Hackman and Oldham's research on the model also revealed that the relationships among job characteristics, psychological states, and outcomes (such as job satisfaction and productivity) would be stronger for workers high in "growth need strength"—workers who want to grow and develop in their jobs.[28] This and other qualifications concerning the

[27]J. R. Hackman and G. R. Oldham, *Work Redesign* (Reading, Mass.: Addison-Wesley, 1980), 97.

[28]E. F. Stone, R. T. Mowday, and L. W. Porter, "Higher-Order Need Strengths as Moderators of the Job Scope–Job Satisfaction Relationship," *Journal of Applied Psychology* 62 (1977): 466–471.

power of job characteristics to enhance job design will be discussed in the final section of this chapter.

## WORK-GROUP PERSPECTIVES

What happens when management takes the successes of limited autonomy job enrichment programs seriously? Successes with job enrichment force on management the refreshing insight that rank-and-file workers are an important—if not critical—problem-solving ally of management. This conclusion can lead only to a different approach to the way organizations function. Two of these different approaches will be discussed next: semiautonomous work groups and sociotechnical systems.

## SEMIAUTONOMOUS WORK GROUPS

A **semiautonomous work group** is a team of workers assigned full responsibility for a series of tasks. Semiautonomous work groups represent a radical departure from quality circles. Even with quality circles, management retains responsibility for assigning particular tasks to each individual worker. When semiautonomous work groups are used, management assigns groups of tasks to groups of workers; the work group (rather than management) then has responsibility for deciding what tasks are performed by which workers. With quality circles, management retains responsibility for making day-to-day operational decisions; the quality circle acts in an advisory capacity. When semiautonomous work groups are used, management delegates responsibility for day-to-day operational decisions to the work group.

In effect, the semiautonomous work group acts as an independent contractor within the larger organization. Management provides task assignments for the work group, but how those tasks are accomplished is up to the work group itself. Often the work group elects its own leaders, develops its own work rules and culture, and makes its own task assignments to individual workers. As long as the work gets done, management may leave well enough alone. In fact, one of the *indirect* benefits of using semiautonomous work groups is that the demands on the organization for supervisory, support, and management personnel may be reduced substantially. For example, in one General Motors plant only 24 white-collar employees were needed to manage a blue-collar manufacturing work force of nearly 500 employees. An electronic service organization found that the need for first-line supervisors was cut in half when the organization moved to work teams. The Scott Paper Company found that supervisory personnel simply weren't needed during off-shifts in one of their plants once work teams had been implemented.[29] These reductions in white-collar manufacturing support personnel represent substantial savings in labor costs. These are savings

---

[29]Lawler, 112, 176.

in addition to those generated by improved worker performance. In one survey of companies using autonomous work groups, 14 of 15 companies reported increased worker productivity.[30]

Semiautonomous work groups first gained widespread notice when they were successfully implemented in one of England's coal mines. However, the best-known (and most-written-about) implementation of semiautonomous work groups in a traditional manufacturing setting occurred at the Topeka, Kansas, plant of General Foods. The Topeka plant is part of the Gaines Pet Food division of General Foods. General Foods management was concerned about the seriousness of productivity problems in other Gaines Pet Food plants when the final plans for the Topeka plant were being drawn up. Gaines Pet Food decided to try out semiautonomous work groups as a potential solution to these productivity problems.[31]

The procedures by which the Topeka work groups functioned became known as the Topeka System. The Topeka System addressed aspects of the plant's supervision structure, reward system, and social system.

**Supervision**   The work force of the plant was divided into three kinds of teams: processing teams, packaging teams, and an office team. Processing teams (about 8 employees per shift) managed receipt and storage of the raw materials (corn, soya, vitamins, and meat meal delivered to the plant in railroad cars) and mixed the ingredients in predetermined percentages to produce the Gaines dog-food mixture. Their objective was to produce at least 100 tons of dog food per shift so that the packaging teams would never run out of work. The packaging teams (17 employees per shift) coated the dog food, packaged it in bags or boxes, and had responsibility for warehousing the completed product. The office team handled both personnel and distribution paperwork.

These teams were entirely self-managed. It was up to each team to assign tasks to team members. The teams also were given responsibility for controlling quality, maintaining the facility, counseling employees who did not perform well, appointing team members to serve on plant safety and recreation committees, and even screening and selecting new team members. Plant management imposed few rules on the teams and tried to provide them with much of the economic, quantity, and quality information provided only to supervisors or management in most manufacturing settings.

**The Reward System**   Compensation at the Topeka plant was linked to *skill acquisition*. There were four pay levels: starting rate, single rate (for

[30]T. G. Cummings and E. S. Molloy, *Improving Productivity and the Quality of Work Life* (New York: Praeger Press, 1977).

[31]D. A. Whitsett and L. Yorks, "Looking Back at Topeka: General Foods and the Quality of Work Life Experiment," *California Management Review* 24(4), (Summer 1983): 93–109.

mastery of a single job), team rate (for mastery of all jobs performed by the team), and plant rate (for mastery of all jobs performed in the plant). Team members also could qualify for supplemental increases if they acquired special skills needed by the team.

Management designed this pay system to encourage team members to learn all jobs within the team, thereby giving the teams additional job assignment flexibility. No limits were placed on the number of workers in the plant who could achieve a given pay rate; it was hoped that this would encourage team members to teach each other. (This turns out to be an important benefit of using teams. Since a productive team member helps everyone else on the team, there is a clear incentive for team members to help each other acquire needed skills.) Further, in keeping with the overall team philosophy of the plant, decisions about compensation (for instance, deciding when a team member had mastered all the team's jobs) also remained with the team.

**The Social System**   To convey management's commitment to the semiautonomous work group philosophy, many of the status symbols that segregate managers and workers at most plants were eliminated at the Topeka facility. There were no assigned parking places for management in the parking lot, office decor was uniform throughout the plant, and all employees used the same entrance and the same lunchroom.[32] Offices were designed with glass walls facing the plant floor. Further, because the teams were self-managed, workers had a high level of freedom to circulate and socialize on the job.

One thing the Topeka System did *not* include was alteration of the plant's physical design or technology to accommodate the move to semiautonomous work groups. Technologically, Topeka was very much like any other modern processing/packaging facility.

How well did Topeka's radical experiment in job design work? Industrial engineers had estimated that 110 employees would be needed to run the plant; the work force stabilized at something less than 70 employees. After 18 months, the teams at the Topeka plant had lowered fixed overhead 33 percent, were reporting 92 percent fewer quality rejects, had achieved an absenteeism rate 9 percent below industry standards and lower turnover, and had one of the best safety records of any plant in General Foods. Annual savings were estimated to be about $600,000. Visitors to the plant also reported high satisfaction, involvement, and openness and mutual respect among the plant's employees.[33]

While the Topeka plant today remains innovative in many of the ways noted above, General Foods was unable to duplicate the successes of Topeka at any of its other plants. This may be because the Topeka plant

[32]Lawler, 173.

[33]R. E. Walton, "How to Counter Alienation in the Plant," *Harvard Business Review* 50(6), (1972): 70–81.

was a new plant, so prior values and practices ⟍
overcome or changed. Further, the successes of th
not without problems. The open social system
some workers, who reverted back to traditional
relations with other team members. The pay system
tension in the plant. Since pay was tied to task mastery and
judgments were the province of the teams, questions about
consistency of mastery standards arose. In sum, some problems arose at
Topeka precisely because the work force was not prepared to deal with
the uncertainty and autonomy that self-governance requires. Training
personnel to handle the new demands of more participation-oriented
jobs often turns out to be a major hurdle in introducing job redesign
innovations.

Problems also arose at the level of plant management. Less than six
years after the start of the Topeka experiment, virtually all of the key
management personnel in the plant had left General Foods. It appears
that the delicate alliance of management personnel at Topeka was a key
to its success. When Topeka's initial successes led General Foods to
promote the alliance's originator and corporate protector, Lyman
Ketchum, beyond direct responsibility for the plant, understanding and
support for the plant's philosophy waned. While the importance of the
problems experienced at Topeka will be discussed later in this chapter, in
retrospect the successes of the Topeka plant probably stand as a
testament to the *potential* of job redesign using semiautonomous work
groups.[34]

## SOCIOTECHNICAL SYSTEMS

Most job redesign efforts (like General Foods' Topeka plant) take the
existing production technology as the starting point around which
redesign efforts must revolve. Unfortunately, the existing production
technology often stands as a significant barrier to the success of job
redesign efforts. The **sociotechnical systems** approach to job redesign
takes a big step beyond autonomous work groups by making *technology* a
central concern in redesigning jobs to be more interesting, involving, and
motivating for workers.

Figure 12–7 summarizes the major components of sociotechnical
systems design principles: the social system, moderators, and the
technological system. The "social system" refers to all the human
elements (including needs and desires) that are part of the work context
and that can (as discussed in previous chapters) influence worker
productivity dramatically. The "technological system" refers to the nuts
and bolts of production—the type of production technology required,
the complexity of the assembly tasks, work interdependence issues, and

[34]A. D. Szilagyi and M. J. Wallace, *Organizational Behavior and Performance* (Glenview, Ill.: Scott, Foresman, 1987), 170–172.

RE 12–7         Sociotechnical Systems Model of Job Design

iotechnical systems theory deals with designing jobs to find a fit between the social system of an organi-
ation (including such social needs of workers as affiliation needs) and the technical requirements or limits
of an organization's production system.

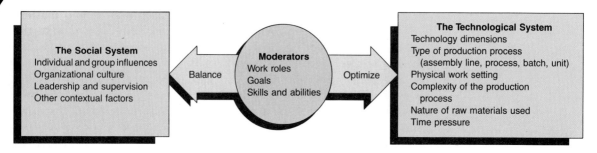

Source: T. Cummings, "Self-Regulating Work Groups: A Socio-Technical Synthesis," *Academy of Management Review* 3, 1978,
pp. 625–634; Don Hellriegel, John W. Slocum, and Richard W. Woodman, *Organizational Behavior* (St. Paul, Minn.: West,
1986), 382.

even the nature of the final product. Worker roles, goals, and worker
skills and abilities all act as moderators. The moderators help define an
optimal balance among what the workers want or need, what they are
capable of, what kinds of tasks need to be done, and how they can get
done. In effect, sociotechnical systems design asks and answers the
questions: How can we adapt our technological production demands to
meet the needs of our workers, and how can we adapt our workers to
meet our production system needs? How can we strike a balance between
what our workers want and what the manufacturing of our product
requires?

No one really knows how many major corporations in the United
States have experimented with sociotechnical systems redesign of their
production operations. In contrast to the widespread publicity afforded
the General Foods Topeka plant, most companies are reluctant to
publicize their sociotechnical job redesign efforts. Certainly many
Fortune 500 companies—including AT&T and General Motors—have
tried sociotechnical systems approaches at one time or another, and
reliable sources estimate that probably several hundred U.S. manufacturing facilities have been completely redesigned along the lines of
sociotechnical systems principles.[35] Procter and Gamble is a leading
advocate of sociotechnical systems redesign, having used these principles
to design or redesign 20 plants by the late 1980s.[36]

The origins of the sociotechnical systems design efforts of U.S.
corporations are found in the pioneering work redesign efforts in

[35]R. E. Walton, "From Control to Commitment in the Workplace," *Harvard Business Review*
63(2), (1985): 76–84.
[36]Lawler, 171.

Scandinavia in the late 1960s and early 1970s. At the time, the Swedish automotive industry used traditional assembly lines and was having serious problems. Annual turnover among assembly-line workers was more than 50 percent and absenteeism ran as high as 35 percent. Further, a national survey indicated that fewer than 5 percent of high school graduates in Sweden were willing to work on the factory floors.[37]

Both Saab and Volvo first decided to experiment with autonomous work groups to address these problems. At Saab, the assembly lines were reorganized into work groups. The groups in turn were assigned overall production goals (470 engines every two workweeks) and given responsibility for organizing their own work. Under traditional assembly-line production methods, the average assembly operation for each worker lasted only 2 minutes. The semiautonomous work groups instead could combine tasks and assemble half of each engine at once (about 10 minutes) or even follow an engine completely through the assembly process (about a half hour). Work pace and timing and length of breaks also were left up to the work groups, just as long as their production goals were met.

The results of Saab's efforts were mixed. Production flexibility increased, some costs decreased, turnover was cut in half, and product quality improved. On the negative side, production speed decreased and absenteeism remained essentially unchanged. Saab learned some important lessons from these efforts about the limits of job enlargement and enrichment. In one factory, a work group had been assigned the assembly of truck diesel engines. This turned out to be too much—1,500 parts and six hours—for a single group to handle easily, so that assembly was returned to a more traditional assembly line. Eventually management at Saab realized that the success of its enlargement and enrichment attempts was highly dependent upon the *technology* of the tasks involved. Highly complex tasks offered sufficient challenge that enlargement or enrichment was not only unnecessary but in some cases undesirable. This led to a typical sociotechnical systems conclusion: Job redesign efforts at Saab became dependent upon an analysis of the manufacturing *technology* required for assembly.

Volvo's initial attempts at job redesign were quite similar to those at Saab. Production teams were established among workers with common work assignments; the teams set up their own work schedules, divided up the work, and handled their own quality control. Job enlargement was tried, with workers changing jobs sometimes several times per day, or following the same automobile through a number of consecutive work stations on the assembly line. Unlike at Saab, however, initial mixed results convinced management at Volvo that something different was necessary.

---

[37]Ibid., 111; Szilagyi and Wallace, *Organizational Behavior and Performance*, 148.

**FIGURE 12–8**     Diagram of a Workshop at Volvo's Kalmar Assembly Plant

The Volvo Assembly Plant at Kalmar is considered a prototype of sociotechnical systems design. The innovative floor plan of the plant reflects management's concern that jobs be designed to meet both workers' needs and the requirements of the production process.

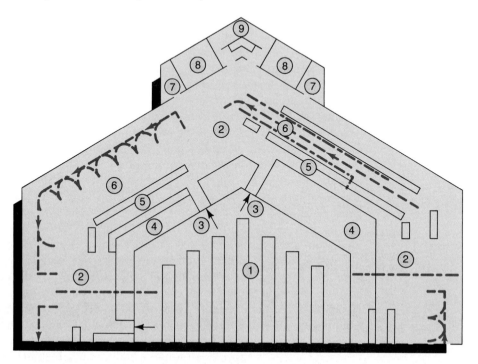

| | | |
|---|---|---|
| 1. Stores | 4. Preassembly | 7. Pause area |
| 2. Body buffers | 5. Materials | 8. Toilets, etc. |
| 3. Material intake by | 6. Bodies (on the left, stationary; | 9. Changing rooms |
| electric trucks | on the right, moving) | |

Source: William F. Dowling, "Job Redesign on the Assembly Line: Farewell to Blue-Collar Blues," *Organizational Dynamics*, Autumn 1973, p. 62. Copyright © 1973 American Management Association, New York. All rights reserved.

The something different turned out to be radical changes in the technical design of Volvo's Kalmar automobile assembly plant. At the Kalmar plant, traditional automotive assembly *line* technology was abandoned. In its place instead appeared an assembly technology that was suited perfectly to the use of semiautonomous work groups.

A schematic of Volvo's innovative Kalmar plant is provided in Figure 12–8. Several features of the Kalmar operation are worth noting. Primarily, the Kalmar plant does not look like a typical automotive assembly plant. There is no endless assembly line. Instead there are compartmentalized workshops with large windows. The workshops are designed to accommodate the use of separate semiautonomous work teams. Each work team has its own discrete space on the shop floor and can make its own decisions about timing and length of breaks. Computer screens beam production rates out to employees every hour, providing instant feedback. The automobiles being assembled are mounted on trolleys that track from workshop to workshop by following a computer tape affixed to the floor.

Kalmar represents the ultimate in sociotechnical systems design—the redesigning of a factory to accommodate and even enhance job enrichment efforts. Kalmar has its detractors, however. The plant cost $25 million to build, which is between 10 percent and 30 percent more than comparable traditional plants. The plant has limited capacity (only up to 60,000 autos per year, compared to as many as 400,000 per year at similar U.S. facilities), leading to questions about the generalizability of Volvo's successes to higher-volume operations. Finally, production costs at Kalmar are *higher* than at comparable plants, though management claims that productivity is high and absenteeism quite low compared to other facilities.[38]

The experiences of Saab, however, suggest that sociotechnical design principles need not necessitate such a radical redesign plan. At Saab, designing jobs with sociotechnical principles in mind meant tailoring enrichment programs to address the distinguishing characteristics of a production technology. The expanding role of technology in determining workplace behavior will be discussed further in Chapter 17.

## QUALIFICATIONS

The different approaches to job redesign reviewed in this chapter promise tremendous *potential* benefits. However, statistics (such as those presented in Figure 2–8 in Chapter 2) show only indifferent successes of employee involvement programs. These statistics stand as a sobering testament to the fact that choosing a good system for redesigning jobs is hardly enough to guarantee success. If job redesign efforts are not properly managed, they are likely to increase only job satisfaction and not productivity.

Many job redesign efforts *have* increased job satisfaction of workers, which is nothing to sneeze at, of course. Job satisfaction certainly plays a role in turnover, and current estimates place the costs of employee turnover at something between 5 and 25 times the monthly salary of the departing employee. Nevertheless, realization of the *full* benefits of job design—both work-force satisfaction *and* enhanced productivity—requires an understanding of its limits. Three limits will be addressed in the remainder of this chapter: social information processing, individual differences, and management support.

## SOCIAL INFORMATION PROCESSING

The job characteristics model and work-group approaches to job design discussed in this chapter both make an important assumption. They assume that workers perceive their jobs the way that managers intend

---

[38]Szilagyi and Wallace, *Organizational Behavior and Performance*, 450.

According to the social information processing view, a worker's reaction to a job often reflects the way surrounding coworkers appear to react to their jobs. The enthusiasm and satisfaction of these McDonald's employees are contagious, which underscores the importance of maintaining a positive and supportive work climate.

those jobs to be perceived. However, as we know from our discussions of perception in Chapter 3, this is an unrealistic assumption. Just because a manager decides to give a subordinate some autonomy on the job does not mean that the subordinate will perceive autonomy in the job. As we noted in Figure 3–6, subordinates' and supervisors' perceptions often differ dramatically.

The **social information processing** framework of job design emphasizes the importance of perception in understanding how workers react to their jobs.[39] According to the social information processing framework, how an employee perceives and reacts to a job will depend on cues provided socially by coworkers[40] and even the jobholder's supervisor.[41] For managers, the role of perception and social cues in worker reactions to jobs underscores the importance of positive attitudes, a positive atmosphere, and open channels of communication in a work group. Workers react to *perceptions* of their jobs rather than to their objective characteristics. A positive work-group climate, which encourages favor-

[39]G. Salancik and J. Pfeffer, "A Social Information Processing Approach to Job Attitudes and Task Design," *Administrative Science Quarterly* 23 (1977): 224–253.

[40]H. M. Weiss and J. B. Shaw, "Social Influences on Judgments about Tasks," *Organizational Behavior and Human Performance* 24 (1979): 126–140.

[41]R. W. Griffin, "Technological and Social Processes in Task Redesign: A Field Experiment," unpublished manuscript, Texas A&M University, 1981.

able perceptions of job characteristics, may be as important to work outcomes as a good job design.

INDIVIDUAL
DIFFERENCES

One of the important lessons of Chapter 4 was that no two employees are likely to be motivated by quite the same things. This becomes a critical issue in job design. Job design efforts that suit the needs of one employee may be hopelessly inappropriate for another employee.

The approaches to job design outlined in this chapter differ in what they require of the typical worker. Work simplification requires the least of the worker. Tasks are simple and repetitive. There is very little demand that the employee think on the job or take responsibility. A job enlargement approach assumes that employees at least want some variety in their work. Job enrichment programs and work-group redesign efforts assume quite a bit more. These approaches to job design assume that the rank-and-file worker is willing to take on the responsibility associated with making consequential decisions on the job, and that workers are interested in more than just being told what to do. This is not always true. In General Foods' highly successful Topeka plant, a small minority of workers resisted management's new philosophy. Researchers have found that there are always some workers who prefer highly repetitive, low-skill jobs, even when there are opportunities to bid for more interesting tasks.[42]

Even if workers are interested in going beyond just earning their paychecks, the particular job design scheme of a company may not match all employees' needs and interests. One researcher of radical job redesign efforts tells a story about a worker who said to him, "I don't care what those turkeys think, I just want to be left alone to do my job." The "turkeys" he was referring to were his coworkers! For this worker at least, programs such as quality circles would seem ill-advised.[43]

Differences among workers must be handled in a couple of ways. First, participation in job redesign efforts that increase worker autonomy should be *voluntary*.[44] If a worker is uninterested in playing a larger role in the workplace, forcing that worker to do so really violates the spirit of limited autonomy job redesign. Mandatory participation in limited autonomy job redesign is not more freedom for the worker but less—just another aspect of work where the worker has no choice. Further, it seems unlikely that a reluctant participant (for example, in a quality circle) will be a positive contributor.

If management wants to make enriched jobs a permanent part of its management approach, managers should assess employee interest

[42]M. Fein, "Job Enrichment: A Reevaluation," *Sloan Management Review,* Winter 1974, 69–88.

[43]Lawler, 182.

[44]Kanter, "The Dilemmas of Participation."

# FIGURE 12–9        Growth Need Strength (Measure B)

Because motivations differ across workers, job redesign that is correct for one worker may be incorrect for another. Questionnaires can help managers design jobs to fit their workers' abilities and needs.

**Instructions:** If you would prefer the job in the left-hand column (Column A), indicate how much you prefer it by putting a check mark in a blank to the left of the "neutral" point. If you prefer the job in the right-hand column (Column B), check one of the blanks to the right of "neutral." Check the "neutral" blank only if you find the two jobs equally attractive or unattractive. Try to use the "neutral" blank rarely.

**Column A**                                                                                              **Column B**

1. A job which offers little or no challenge.

   Strongly          Neutral          Strongly
   prefer A                           prefer B

   A job which requires you to be completely isolated from coworkers.

2. A job where the pay is very good.

   Strongly          Neutral          Strongly
   prefer A                           prefer B

   A job where there is considerable opportunity to be creative and innovative.

3. A job where you are often required to make important decisions.

   Strongly          Neutral          Strongly
   prefer A                           prefer B

   A job with many pleasant people to work with.

4. A job with little security in a somewhat unstable organization.

   Strongly          Neutral          Strongly
   prefer A                           prefer B

   A job in which you have little or no opportunity to participate in decisions which affect your work.

5. A job in which greater responsibility is given to those who do the best work.

   Strongly          Neutral          Strongly
   prefer A                           prefer B

   A job in which greater responsibility is given to loyal employees who have the most seniority.

6. A job with a supervisor who sometimes is highly critical.

   Strongly          Neutral          Strongly
   prefer A                           prefer B

   A job which does not require you to use much of your talent.

7. A very routine job.

   Strongly          Neutral          Strongly
   prefer A                           prefer B

   A job where your coworkers are not very friendly.

8. A job with a supervisor who respects you and treats you fairly.

   Strongly          Neutral          Strongly
   prefer A                           prefer B

   A job which provides constant opportunities for you to learn new and interesting things.

9. A job where you have a real chance to develop yourself personally.

   Strongly          Neutral          Strongly
   prefer A                           prefer B

   A job with excellent vacations and fringe benefits.

10. A job where there is a real chance you could be laid off.

    Strongly          Neutral          Strongly
    prefer A                           prefer B

    A job with very little chance to do challenging work.

11. A job with little freedom and independence to do your work in the way you think best.

    Strongly          Neutral          Strongly
    prefer A                           prefer B

    A job where the working conditions are poor.

12. A job with very satisfying teamwork.

    Strongly          Neutral          Strongly
    prefer A                           prefer B

    A job which allows you to use your skills and abilities to the fullest extent.

Source: J. R. Hackman and G. R. Oldham, "The Job Diagnostic Survey: An Instrument for the Diagnosis of Jobs and the Evaluation of Job Redesign Projects" (Tech Report #4, Department of Administrative Sciences, Yale University, May 1974).

through their selection process. The questionnaire in Figure 12–9 is a measure of **growth need strength:** the interest of the worker in growing and developing on the job. Hackman and Oldham identified growth need strength as an important determinant of the power of job characteristics in job redesign efforts. Responses to a questionnaire like the one in Figure 12–9 could be used to identify job applicants who would be more receptive to job enrichment, or to identify job incumbents who are prime candidates for enrichment of their jobs. The big three automakers—Honda, Toyota, and Nissan—already use this philosophy in selecting employees for their American plants.[45] Several other personal characteristics that similarly influence the effectiveness of job redesign efforts also have been identified.[46]

Finally, it is important to realize that interest is not the only barrier that might prevent an employee from being receptive to job redesign efforts. As noted in earlier discussions about worker autonomy and participation, many workers are shocked to hear that their input would be valued by management. For these people, expectations developed in the past that management-worker relationships are adversarial could be hard to shed. Often additional training is necessary before these workers can feel comfortable in their new roles as mental as well as physical resources for the organization.

These concerns about the appropriateness of job redesign for some employees should not, however, be used as an excuse to *not* initiate any form of substantial job redesign effort. Consider again the survey results mentioned early on in this chapter: Most managers seriously underestimate the desires of their employees to make positive contributions to the organization and play larger roles in organizational decision making. Ignoring this untapped resource can be costly.

MANAGEMENT SUPPORT

Many if not most job redesign efforts are aimed at the rank-and-file workers of an organization. Yet one key to the success of a job redesign effort may not be the rank-and-file workers at all but the layers of supervisors and management above them. Three major concerns about supervisors and management must be addressed if a job redesign effort is to succeed: their responsiveness, their feelings of being threatened, and how they handle success.

[45]R. Koenig, "Toyota Takes Pains, and Time, Filling Jobs at Its Kentucky Plant," *Wall Street Journal,* December 1, 1987, 1+.

[46]Griffin, *Task Design: An Integrative Approach,* 43–45.

**Responsiveness**    A critical issue in ceding limited autonomy to workers in a job redesign effort is that management *must appear sincere*. Sincerity often is a function of responsiveness—how quickly and completely management responds to worker suggestions. Consider the following tale about the demise of a quality circle:

> . . . In one change effort, a quality circle focused on the purchase of new trucks for the organization. After months of study an extensive set of specifications were developed. They promised to save the organization hundreds of thousands of dollars by buying trucks that were both easier to maintain and more effective. There was great resistance from the purchasing agent and the industrial engineer to changing the specifications, even though top management approved the idea. It literally took months to get them to change the specifications. By the time the specifications were changed and the actual trucks were purchased, the group had long since disbanded in discouragement, convinced that management was simply engaged in a sham exercise to keep them quiet.[47]

The sad part of this particular tale is that management really was taking the suggestions of the employee group seriously. However, their lack of feedback to the group unintentionally sent a different message, namely, that no one in management really cared about the suggestions that the group came up with. Since feedback is an important job characteristic (it figures prominently in our job enrichment schemes!), timely feedback should also be incorporated in management's treatment of workers' involvement.

Even if an employee-generated suggestion is not a good one—for example, if there are practical, budgetary, or political reasons for not implementing it—a thorough response from management can accomplish two important goals. First, even negative feedback sends the message that management is listening. If employees have the sense that management is just toying with them, they can "dry up" as a source of ideas pretty quickly. Second, if management takes the time to discuss with workers the reasons for rejecting an idea, management is providing invaluable input to workers so that future suggestions have a better probability of being adopted. An obvious key to a successful limited autonomy program is making sure the workers have enough information to be able to make good decisions. Only then will they be able to fulfill their roles as mental resources for the organization.

[47]Lawler, 55.

**Feelings of Being Threatened** If the lowest-level workers in an organization are given more control through limited autonomy job redesign programs, who is losing that control? For most supervisors, the obvious answer seems to be: supervisors.

At Topeka, the autonomous work group redesign effort achieved a personnel reduction of 33 percent. It was no secret that the savings in personnel came from the fact that semiautonomous work groups don't have supervisors. As noted earlier, a General Motors plant using autonomous work groups uses only 24 white-collar employees for a production work force of almost 500 workers. If limited autonomy job redesign is going to be pursued to its natural conclusions, supervisors may have reason to feel threatened. Obviously, this fear on the part of the supervisors must be dealt with if they are to support rather than obstruct the implementation of job redesign.

Even if elimination of supervisory personnel is not a legitimate concern, an increased role for rank-and-file workers still could seem like a loss to supervisory personnel. After all, the need for control and the desire to make a contribution are felt by workers at *all* levels of an organization. An attempt to enlarge or enrich the scope of jobs at the lowest level of an organization probably needs to be followed up at other levels of the organization as well. If management enlarges or enriches the scope of rank-and file jobs, supervisors are unlikely to feel that their authority has been usurped if the scope of their own jobs is similarly enlarged or enriched. In short, job redesign efforts should not be used as Band-Aids for productivity, quality, or morale problems. Behind every approach to job design lurks an overall philosophy about the role of workers at all levels of the organization. The most successful job redesign programs will be ones where the philosophy is implemented consistently across all levels of the organization, from rank-and-file workers to supervisors to middle managers and on up.

**How Management Handles Success** Interestingly, a final major stumbling block to the success of job redesign programs is what to do when they succeed. Many times this turns out to be a problem management is ill-equipped to deal with.

One big problem created by successful job redesign is the spiral of rising employee expectations detailed in Figure 12–5. All successful job redesign efforts develop in employees more self-respect, more self-confidence, and a stronger image of themselves as potentially valuable contributors to the organization's goals and objectives. This suggests that successful job redesign must be a journey, not a destination. Management must be prepared to meet the rising expectations of workers to contribute.

At one southwestern manufacturer, this particular challenge is being met. Intel, a large computer chip manufacturer, decided several years ago to institute a quality circle form of employee involvement. Management was, however, aware that employee successes in the program would give rise to new demands for further opportunities to contribute. To deal with this new demand, Intel coupled its job redesign efforts with a career counseling program. The counseling program served two extremely useful functions. First, if a rank-and-file worker acquired a new sense of self-worth and wanted to pursue it further, the counseling program could identify possibilities (both within and without Intel's own sphere) for career advancement that would meet the employee's newfound needs and expectations. Second, the counseling program could help the employee understand the additional training that might be needed to bring those career opportunities within reach. At Intel, management was not only prepared to deal with employees' rising expectations but also willing and able to help employees deal with their rising expectations themselves.

Successful job redesign programs can also lead to thorny compensation issues. As workers' jobs are enlarged or enriched, their beliefs in their ability to contribute is not the only thing that grows. Workers' belief that their work has become more valuable to the organization also can grow. If management is not prepared to adjust compensation schemes to reflect the enlarged contributions of the work force, again the well of worker ideas and energy may soon run dry. The "Focus on: Participation and Compensation" describes how one CEO decided to deal with this particular dilemma by extending autonomy to the realm of compensation and allowing workers to set their own wages. Some more traditional approaches to dealing with compensation issues—such as the profit sharing used at the Plaza Athénée hotel in Paris—will be discussed in the next chapter.

## Summary

American industry has come to an important crossroads in job design. The average educational level of the American worker is on the rise. In 1964, only 45 percent of the American work force possessed a high school diploma; by 1984, 60 percent of the work force had high school diplomas. For workers in the newest cohort of the work force—those between the ages of 25 and 29 in 1984—the percentage was closer to 86 percent.[48] Furthermore, this better-educated work force has an "entitlement" mentality. Workers now feel that they have a *right* to good wages, interesting work, and a say in management decision making.[49] In short, management in the 1990s must face up to the challenge of providing work for an American

[48]Ibid., 15.

[49]J. O'Toole, *Making America Work* (New York: Continuum, 1981).

**Arthur Friedman's Outrage** One thing for sure, Arthur Friedman will never become the chairman of the board at General Motors. It is mainly because Art Friedman has some pretty strange ideas about how one runs a business.

Five years ago, he had his most outrageous brainstorm. His idea was to allow employees to set their own wages, make their own hours, and take their vacations whenever they felt like it, and it worked.

Friedman first unleashed his proposal at one of the regular staff meetings. Decide what you are worth, he said, and tell the bookkeeper to put it in your envelope next week. No questions asked. Work any time, any day, any hours you want. Having a bad day? Go home. Hate working Saturdays? No problem. Aunt Ethel from Chicago has dropped in unexpectedly? Well, take a few days off, show her the town. Want to go to Reno for a week? Need a rest? Go, go, no need to ask. If you need some money for the slot machines, take it out of petty cash. Just come back when you feel ready to work again.

His speech was received in complete silence. No one cheered, no one laughed, no one said a word.

"It was about a month before anyone asked for a raise," recalls Stan Robinson, 55, the payroll clerk. "And when they did, they asked Art first. But he refused to listen and told them to just tell me what they wanted. I kept going back to him to make sure it was all right, but he wouldn't even talk about it. I finally figured out he was serious."

Instead of the all-out raid on the company coffers that some business-

people might expect, the 15 employees of the Friedman-Jacobs Co. displayed astonishing restraint and maturity. As a result they have developed a strong sense of responsibility and an acute sensitivity to the problems that face the American worker in general that would have been impossible under the traditional system.

George Tegner, 59, an employee for 14 years, has like all his coworkers achieved new insight into the mechanics of the free-enterprise system. "You have to use common sense; no one wins if you end up closing the business down. If you want more money, you have to produce more. it can't work any other way. Anyway, wages aren't everything. Doing what you want is more important."

In the past five years, there has been no turnover of employees. Friedman estimates that last year his 15 workers took no more than a total of three sick days. It is rare that anyone is late for work and, even then, there is usually a good reason. Work is done on time and employee pilferage is nonexistent.

"We used to hear a lot of grumbling," says Robinson. "Now, everybody smiles."

Skeptics by now are chuckling to themselves, convinced that if Friedman is not losing money, he is just breaking even. The fact is that net profit has not dropped a cent in the last five years; it has increased. Although volume is considerably less and overhead has increased at what some would consider an unhealthy rate, greater productivity and efficiency have more than made up for it.

Source: Martin Koughman, "Arthur Friedman's Outrage," *The Washington Post,* February 23, 1975. © The Washington Post. Used with permission.

work force that has more to offer than ever before and fully expects to have opportunities to offer it.

Traditional approaches to job design focused almost exclusively on work simplification in order to take advantage of efficiency through specialization. Unfortunately, these approaches ignore the message of the Hawthorne studies—that what people think about their work environment makes a difference in how hard and well they work. If the work is uninteresting, the workers are uninterested. Management pays the price.

More enlightened approaches to job design have attempted to take the needs of workers into account by providing more interesting and involving work. Job enlargement and job enrichment are two individual approaches to job design in which management focuses on changing the characteristics of jobs to fit the needs of workers. Job enlargement makes jobs more involving by increasing the range of skills that a job requires. Job enlargement does not, however, satisfy workers' needs to

feel control and accomplishment on the job. Job enrichment goes beyond job enlargement by allowing workers to fulfill higher-order needs (such as the need for control) in doing their work.

The successes of enlargement and enrichment job design programs may lead management to mold job design efforts around entirely different approaches to the management of organizations. Autonomous work groups take limited autonomy to its limits by delegating virtually all operational decisions to worker groups. Sociotechnical systems design molds job design efforts to match the needs and limitations of both human workers and technological advances. Both of these approaches have had noteworthy successes.

In the end, the success of management's job design efforts does not depend just on having a good approach to job design. Job design efforts will work only if workers and managers see jobs similarly, if the jobs match the needs of the work force, and if management supports the changes.

KEY TERMS

**Cross-training**   Encouraging workers to learn their coworkers' jobs; provides challenges for workers and flexibility for management.

**Flextime work scheduling** Method of context enrichment in which management gives workers limited discretion in arranging their work hours.

**Growth need strength**   Interest of a worker in growing and developing on the job.

**Job characteristics model**   Theory of job enrichment in which the presence of five job characteristics (skill variety, task identity, task significance, autonomy, and feedback) leads to critical psychological states (meaningfulness of work, responsibility for work outcomes, and knowledge of work activity results) that in turn result in positive work-related outcomes such as productivity and worker satisfaction.

**Job enlargement** Redesign of work tasks that increases the number of tasks in a job to make it more interesting and involving.

**Job enrichment** Redesign of work tasks that makes a job more interesting and involving by allowing workers to fulfill higher-order needs such as achievement and control.

**Job rotation** Method of increasing workers' skill variety by allowing them to switch jobs occasionally.

**Semiautonomous work group** Team of workers given full responsibility for a series of tasks (including arrangement and assignment of the work).

**Social information processing** Framework of job design that emphasizes the importance of perception and social cues from coworkers and supervisors in understanding how workers react to their jobs.

**Sociotechnical systems** Approach to job redesign that moves beyond semiautonomous work groups by making technology a central concern in making jobs more interesting, involving, and motivating for workers.

**Task identity** The sense of completion and achievement that occurs when the set of assigned tasks allows the worker to see a process through from start to finish.

**Task significance** Worker's sense that a good or poor performance on the job makes a difference to someone.

**Work simplification** Design of work tasks to be simple and easily mastered so each worker can become expert at some very small number of tasks and learn to do them repeatedly with lightning speed and no mistakes.

DISCUSSION QUESTIONS

1. Think of your role as a university student as a job. How could you redesign that job to enhance your performance? To increase your job satisfaction?

2. An acronym used in many organizations—KISS—is supposed to be the key to successful management. KISS stands for "Keep it simple, stupid." Would KISS be a good rule of thumb for designing jobs?

3. How do enrichment approaches to job design differ from enlargement approaches? Are there any dangers for management in moving from job enlargement to job enrichment?

4. What are some of the qualifications or barriers to the success of any job redesign effort? What steps do these qualifications suggest that management should take to ensure the success of a job design program?

5.  When would enriching the *context* of a job be a more effective or appropriate approach to job redesign than enriching the *content* of the job?

6.  When might a *group* approach to job design be more appropriate than an *individual* approach?

7.  Why should feedback be an important part of any individual job enrichment program?

8.  Who is likely to benefit when a company decides to use quality circles? Why do quality circle programs fail?

**IF YOU WANT TO KNOW MORE**

An excellent description of the horrors of traditional job design in coal mines is available in "Some Social and Psychological Consequences of the Long Wall Method of Coal Getting" (E. L. Trist and K. W. Bamforth, *Human Relations* 4, 1951, 3–38). The depressing realities of life on an automobile assembly line are described in detail in "Luddites in Lordstown" (*Harper's* magazine, June 1972, 68–73) and in "Blue-Collar Blues on the Assembly Line" (J. Gooding, *Fortune*, June 1970, 69–71).

A review and consideration of job enrichment is provided in "Is Job Enrichment Just a Fad?" (J. R. Hackman, *Harvard Business Review* 53(5), 1975, 129–139). A useful discussion of the use of quality circles is provided in "Quality Circles: Panacea or Pandora's Box?" (G. W. Meyer and R. G. Stott, *Organizational Dynamics* 13, Spring 1985, 34–50). R. M. Kanter discusses the dilemmas of managing participative systems in her book *The Changemasters* (New York: Simon & Schuster, 1983).

An excellent summary of the Topeka experiment at General Foods is provided by D. A. Whitsett and L. Yorks in "Looking Back at Topeka: General Foods and the Quality-of-Work-Life Experiment" (*California Management Review* 25, 1983, 93–109). A summary of the job reform efforts in Scandinavia is provided in a book by Volvo's president, Pehr G. Gyllenhammar, *People at Work* (Reading, Mass.: Addison-Wesley, 1977).

The best available overall discussion of job design issues is provided in E. E. Lawler III's book, *High Involvement Management* (London: Jossey-Bass, 1986). A good book of edited readings is *The Innovative Organization*, R. Zager and M. P. Rosow, editors (Elmsford, N.Y.: Pergamon Press, 1982).

Several good discussions of the resistance of supervisory personnel to job redesign efforts are available: "Stonewalling Plant Democracy" (*Business Week,* March 28, 1977, 78–82); R. E. Walton, "The Diffusion of New Work Structures: Explaining Why Success Didn't Take" (*Organizational Dynamics* 59, 1975, 616–622); and J. A. Klein, "Why Supervisors Resist Employee Involvement," *Harvard Business Review* 65 (5), 1984, 87. Some discussion of union resistance to job redesign efforts is included in "Detroit vs. the UAW: At Odds over Teamwork" (*Business Week,* August 24, 1987, 54–55); E. Kushell and E. Johnson, "Mobilizing Supervisors to Support Employee Involvement Programs," *SAM Advanced Management Journal* 51 (3), Summer 1986, 36–38; and R. E. Walton, "From Control to Commitment in the Workplace," *Harvard Business Review* 63 (2), 1985, 76–84.

ON YOUR
OWN

**Job Characteristics Instrument**   Think about a job you have held recently, perhaps last summer. With this job in mind, answer the following questions. The scoring instructions follow the questions. In what design areas was your job deficient? How do you think these deficiencies could be corrected?

The following questions are concerned with the characteristics of your job. Each of the questions should be evaluated according to the following responses:

| Very Little 1 | Little 2 | A Moderate Amount 3 | Much 4 | A Great Deal 5 |
|---|---|---|---|---|

Two separate responses are required. In column 1, please mark your response according to how you evaluate the *actual* characteristic of your job. In column 2, please mark your response according to how you would like, or *desire*, that characteristic to be.

| Question | Column 1 | Column 2 |
|---|---|---|
| 1. To what extent does your job provide the opportunity to do a number of different duties each day? | _____ | _____ |
| 2. How much are you left on your own to do your work? | _____ | _____ |
| 3. To what extent can you tell how well you are doing on your job without being told by others? | _____ | _____ |
| 4. To what extent do you feel like your job is just a small cog in a big machine? | _____ | _____ |
| 5. To what extent do you start a job that is finished by another employee? | _____ | _____ |
| 6. Does your job require a great deal of skill to perform it effectively? | _____ | _____ |
| 7. How much of your job depends upon your ability to work with others? | _____ | _____ |
| 8. To what extent does your job limit your opportunity to get to know other employees? | _____ | _____ |
| 9. How much variety of tasks is there in your job? | _____ | _____ |
| 10. To what extent are you able to act independently of supervisors in doing your work? | _____ | _____ |
| 11. Does seeing the results of your work give you a good idea how well you are performing? | _____ | _____ |
| 12. How significant is your work to the overall organization? | _____ | _____ |
| 13. To what extent do you see projects or jobs through to completion? | _____ | _____ |

Source: From *Organizational Behavior and Performance*, 4/e by Andrew D. Szilagyi, Jr. and Marc J. Wallace, Jr. Copyright © 1987, 1983 by Scott, Foresman and Company. Reprinted by permission.

14. To what extent is your job challenging?     \_\_\_\_\_  \_\_\_\_\_
15. To what extent do you work pretty much by your-
self?     \_\_\_\_\_  \_\_\_\_\_
16. How much opportunity is there in your job to
develop professional friendships?     \_\_\_\_\_  \_\_\_\_\_
17. To what extent does your job require you to do
the same thing over and over again each day?     \_\_\_\_\_  \_\_\_\_\_
18. To what extent do you have the freedom to decide
how to do your work?     \_\_\_\_\_  \_\_\_\_\_
19. To what extent does doing the job itself provide
you with feedback about how well you are
performing?     \_\_\_\_\_  \_\_\_\_\_
20. To what extent do you feel like you are
contributing something significant to your
organization?     \_\_\_\_\_  \_\_\_\_\_
21. To what extent do you complete work that has
been started by another employee?     \_\_\_\_\_  \_\_\_\_\_
22. To what extent is your job so simple that virtually
anyone could handle it with little or no training?     \_\_\_\_\_  \_\_\_\_\_
23. To what extent is dealing with other people a part
of your job?     \_\_\_\_\_  \_\_\_\_\_
24. To what extent can you talk informally with other
employees while at work?     \_\_\_\_\_  \_\_\_\_\_

**Scoring Instructions**   For each of the eight job characteristics (A through H), compute a total score by summing the responses to the appropriate questions. Note that some questions are *reversed* (e.g., #17), and that the response to these should be subtracted from 6 to get a response value. Transfer the scores to the *final* scores, where column 1 is *actual* scores, column 2 is *desired* scores, and column 3 is *comparative* scores to be provided by your instructor.

| Variable | Column 1 Actual | | | Column 2 Desired | | | Final Scores 1 | 2 | 3 |
|---|---|---|---|---|---|---|---|---|---|
| | *Question* | | *Response* | *Question* | | *Response* | | | |
| | (#1) | = | + \_\_\_ | (#1) | = | + \_\_\_ | | | |
| A | (#9) | = | + \_\_\_ | (#9) | = | + \_\_\_ | | | |
| | (6−#17) | = | + \_\_\_ | (6−#17) | = | + \_\_\_ | | | |
| | (Total ÷ 3) | = $A_1$ = | + \_\_\_ | (Total ÷ 3) | = $A_2$ = | + \_\_\_ | ( ) $A_1$ | ( ) $A_2$ | ( ) $A_3$ |
| | (#2) | = | + \_\_\_ | (#2) | = | + \_\_\_ | | | |
| B | (#10) | = | + \_\_\_ | (#10) | = | + \_\_\_ | | | |
| | (#18) | = | + \_\_\_ | (#18) | = | + \_\_\_ | | | |
| | (Total ÷ 3) | = $B_1$ = | + \_\_\_ | (Total ÷ 3) | = $B_2$ = | + \_\_\_ | ( ) $B_1$ | ( ) $B_2$ | ( ) $B_3$ |

| Vari-able | Column 1 Actual | | | Column 2 Desired | | | Final Scores 1 | 2 | 3 |
|---|---|---|---|---|---|---|---|---|---|
| C | (#3) | = | + _____ | (#3) | = | + _____ | | | |
|  | (#11) | = | + _____ | (#11) | = | + _____ | | | |
|  | (#19) | = | + _____ | (#19) | = | + _____ | | | |
|  | (Total ÷ 3) = $C_1$ = | | + _____ | (Total ÷ 3) = $C_2$ = | | + _____ | ( ) $C_1$ | ( ) $C_2$ | ( ) $C_3$ |
| D | (6−#4) | = | + _____ | (6−#4) | = | + _____ | | | |
|  | (#12) | = | + _____ | (#12) | = | + _____ | | | |
|  | (#20) | = | + _____ | (#20) | = | + _____ | | | |
|  | (Total ÷ 3) = $D_1$ = | | + _____ | (Total ÷ 3) = $D_2$ = | | + _____ | ( ) $D_1$ | ( ) $D_2$ | ( ) $D_3$ |
| E | (6−#5) | = | + _____ | (6−#5) | = | + _____ | | | |
|  | (#13) | = | + _____ | (#13) | = | + _____ | | | |
|  | (6−#21) | = | + _____ | (6−#21) | = | + _____ | | | |
|  | (Total ÷ 3) = $E_1$ = | | + _____ | (Total ÷ 3) = $E_2$ = | | + _____ | ( ) $E_1$ | ( ) $E_2$ | ( ) $E_3$ |
| F | (#6) | = | + _____ | (#6) | = | + _____ | | | |
|  | (#14) | = | + _____ | (#14) | = | + _____ | | | |
|  | (6−#22) | = | + _____ | (6−#22) | = | + _____ | | | |
|  | (Total ÷ 3) = $F_1$ = | | + _____ | (Total ÷ 3) = $F_2$ = | | + _____ | ( ) $F_1$ | ( ) $F_2$ | ( ) $F_3$ |
| G | (#7) | = | + _____ | (#7) | = | + _____ | | | |
|  | (6−#15) | = | + _____ | (6−#15) | = | + _____ | | | |
|  | (#23) | = | + _____ | (#23) | = | + _____ | | | |
|  | (Total ÷ 3) = $G_1$ = | | + _____ | (Total ÷ 3) = $G_2$ = | | + _____ | ( ) $G_1$ | ( ) $G_2$ | ( ) $G_3$ |
| H | (6−#8) | = | + _____ | (6−#8) | = | + _____ | | | |
|  | (#16) | = | + _____ | (#16) | = | + _____ | | | |
|  | (#24) | = | + _____ | (#24) | = | + _____ | | | |
|  | (Total ÷ 3) = $H_1$ = | | + _____ | (Total ÷ 3) = $H_2$ = | | + _____ | ( ) $H_1$ | ( ) $H_2$ | ( ) $H_3$ |

CLOSING CASE
FOR CHAPTER 12

# THE MANAGER'S MEMO

FROM: W. Johnson, Office Manager

TO:     M. Callahan, Clerical Support Supervisor

RE:     Performance of Clerical Staff

With regard to your concern that error rates and absenteeism are rising among the clerical support staff in our law firm, perhaps the problem lies in part with the design of their jobs. It may be that redesigning the work load could increase motivation and satisfaction.

In reviewing the procedures you sent me, I see that their tasks are quite specialized. One worker enters data into standard forms, another types documents, another makes corrections to previously entered work, and so on.

I also note that typically the clericals have no direct contact with the attorneys in the firm, presumably to insulate them from conflicts with the attorneys. You should know, however, that because the attorneys don't know which individuals are doing their work, they tend to criticize all the members of your department as a whole.

My suggestion is that you consider ways to expand and enrich the work of the clerical staff. If you will outline some general ideas, we can then meet to discuss them and how they fit in with the overall needs of the firm.

CASE DISCUSSION
QUESTIONS

Assume you are the clerical staff supervisor, and respond to the office manager's memorandum. Select the ideas from the chapter that you think will be most effective, and compile them into an overall redesign of the clerical staff's jobs. Be as specific as you can.

# Maintaining Performance

**Compensation Systems**
Wages, Salaries, and Nonrecurring Financial Rewards
*FOCUS ON Pay for Performance: Back to Piecework*
*INTERNATIONAL FOCUS ON Incentive Systems: Changing Reward Systems in China*
*FOCUS ON Employee Stock Ownership Plans: Employees as Owners*
Employee Benefits
Noneconomic Rewards

**Goal Setting**

**Performance Appraisal Systems**
Conflicts and Problems
Improving Performance Appraisal Systems

**Managing for Improved Performance**
The Poor Performer
*FOCUS ON Flextime: Turning Absence into Presence*
Downsizing the Organization: Handling the Survivors

## Pay for Performance: Quota System Raises Questions of Ethics

Is it, as defense lawyers argue, an unethical quota system that violates the concept of criminal justice? Or is it, as some prosecuting attorneys contend, a legitimate management technique for measuring their performance? Either way, the productivity formula used by the Pima County (Arizona) Attorney's Office is a novel way of evaluating its trial lawyers.

The formula awards points to the deputy county attorneys based on the number of cases they take to trial, compared with the number of cases that result in plea agreements. Points are also given according to the verdicts in the trials, and they can be taken away if the attorney has an excessive number of cases dismissed. These totals are then added to points awarded for more subjective criteria, such as "utilization of skills" and "general performance." Finally, the sum is compared to the established goals for each deputy county attorney to determine if that attorney will receive an annual pay raise or a promotion.

The county attorney developed this formula in an attempt to create an environment where people are paid for the actual performance they deliver. "Every organization that cares about its employees and its mission sets goals and measures employee productivity. That's all this is. It is a sound management technique," said Stephen D. Neeley, county attorney.

However, defense lawyers have a very different view of this performance appraisal system. From their perspective, the formula is unethical because criminal attorneys are barred from having a financial stake in the outcome of their cases. "It's a sort of quota system, which might work for traffic cops, but doesn't work in the criminal justice system," said one defense lawyer. "It's stupid. It might work OK in January, but at the end of the year, if you haven't met those performance measurements, you may take a lot of cases to trial that should have been settled out of court," he continued.

"What's troubling is your pocket-book may mandate one thing in a case when justice mandates another."

Other defense attorneys see this system as ripe for abuse. For example, in an open-and-shut case where the defendant is clearly guilty, the case might be most quickly and economically resolved with a plea agreement—unless the prosecutor saw it as a chance to earn some easy points and insisted on a trial. Similarly, a deputy county attorney might be less inclined to dismiss a weak case if it meant that points would be subtracted from the attorney's total.

According to Neeley, the "public is entitled to have its representatives. . .challenged by rigorous standards and producing at the highest level." For that reason, he sees nothing wrong with the com-

ponent of the formula that awards more points for a guilty verdict than for an acquittal or a mistrial. "Does the public pay me to get not-guilty verdicts?" he asked. "One of the things we do around here is convict criminals, so it stands to reason that a person should be commended for doing that."

One current deputy attorney indicated that the formula is not "based on the number of scalps you bring in at the end of the year—there certainly is concern that we try cases, but that's not the be-all and end-all." Another reported, "It's not perfect. Every burglar doesn't deserve to go to prison. Some of us have our complaints about it. Some of us don't care. Some of us do our jobs the best we can within the confines of the system."

Source: C. Warren, "Prosecutors' 'Quota System' Raises Questions of Ethics," *Arizona Daily Star,* January 24, 1988, p. 1.

## INTRODUCTION

The controversy highlighted in the opening vignette focuses on exactly what performance we, as managers, want to reward. The developer of this particular incentive system sees it as having very different goals and effects than do those outside the system who must interact with the deputy county attorneys.

This controversy—identifying appropriate behaviors and developing incentive structures to maintain them—is central to the topic of this chapter: maintaining individual performance. Managers often would prefer that employees behave a certain way, yet the organization's incentive structures may not reward the behaviors managers want. Throughout this chapter, we will be examining various mechanisms managers may use to promote and maintain effective organizational performance. One of the most obvious ways to maintain employee performance is through the use of compensation systems. However, designing and implementing effective compensation programs requires that employers tell employees what is expected of them and give them feedback about their performance. Thus, setting performance goals and conducting performance appraisals are critical to the success of any compensation system.

Even with all of these factors in place, managers still face the problems of improving the performance of poor performers. In addition, such organizational changes as downsizing will have an impact on the performance and morale of the survivors. Figuring out the causes of and solutions to poor performance and planning for the disruption in performance after organizational downsizing are the final components of this chapter.

## COMPENSATION SYSTEMS

Compensation systems are the primary mechanism by which organizations endeavor to influence employees' behavior. In fact, most compensation systems are developed with two broad goals in mind: (1) to produce the desired behaviors from employees, and (2) to accomplish the first goal within the limitations faced by the organization. The first goal includes motivating employees to join the organization, to remain with it, and to perform well for it. The second goal focuses on the constraints or limitations faced by most organizations, including their ability to pay, legal constraints such as minimum wage regulations, labor unions, and external labor markets (compensation levels for the internal labor pool are greatly influenced by the "market rate" for similar jobs in the external labor market).

**Compensation systems** include more than just the dollars employers pay to employees for their work. They include an employee's wage or salary, benefits, nonrecurring financial rewards (such as special commissions, prizes, or profit sharing), and noneconomic rewards for working (such as a sense of accomplishment or power from one's job and the opportunity to socialize with colleagues and peers).[1] Its compensation system is a major way an organization conveys to its employees what it wants done and how they should behave.

In designing their compensation systems, many organizations unfortunately find that what they want and what they get from their employees are very different. In fact, many compensation systems reward behaviors that employers are trying to *discourage* and do not reinforce the behavior they want. Consider the following examples.[2]

In business organizations where rewards are dispensed for unit performance or for individual goals achieved without regard for overall effectiveness, performance counter to the hopes of management is common. The organization is often in a position where it *hopes* for employee effort in the areas of team building, creativity, and interper-

---

[1]F. S. Hills, *Compensation Decision Making* (Hinsdale, Ill.: Dryden Press, 1987).

[2]This example was taken from S. Kerr, "On the Folly of Rewarding A while Hoping for B," *Academy of Management Journal* 18 (1975): 769–783.

sonal relations, but it formally *rewards* none of these activities. In cases where promotions and raises are tied to goal achievement, the system itself contains a paradox in that it "asks employees to set challenging, risky goals, only to face smaller paychecks and possible damaged careers if these goals are not accomplished."[3]

Organizations hope that managers will pay attention to long-run costs and opportunities and will institute programs that will focus on the future. However, many reward systems often pay off for short-run sales and earnings only. Thus, it is personally advantageous for such managers to sacrifice long-term profit and growth for short-term advantages; such a view, unfortunately, is not likely to be in the best interest of the organization.

These two general examples suggest that compensation systems are often put into place without a careful consideration of their impact on employee behavior. In developing a new compensation system or revising an existing system, managers should examine exactly what set of employee behaviors is desired. Second, if there is an existing compensation system, managers should identify exactly what set of employee behaviors *is being rewarded.* Given the way most compensation systems work, it would not be unusual for managers to find that their organization is not rewarding desired or expected behaviors. Setting up a compensation system consistent with the performance expectations of management reduces the likelihood that managers will have to depend upon the telepathic ability of employees to divine their intents. Relying on the good nature or responsibility of workers puts a greater burden on the organization's selection mechanism to find such people than if the organization relies on the compensation system to reward the appropriate type and level of employee performance.

In addition to rewarding the wrong behaviors, a number of other factors are common obstacles to the development and implementation of effective compensation systems. Probably the most crucial is the difficulty of knowing what behavior is desired *and* being able to measure that behavior reliably.[4]

There are several reasons why this task is so difficult. First, the changing nature of work performed by employees (for example, the big shift from manufacturing positions to service positions or the increasing number of managerial or professional jobs) means that work is becoming less quantifiable. It is certainly easier to count the number of widgets produced by an individual than to determine the quality of service provided by a mental-health counselor.

Second, work is becoming more complex and multidimensional. Technological advances and machine-paced performance may reduce

[3]Ibid.

[4]P. M. Podsakoff, C. N. Greene, and J. M. McFillen, "Obstacles to the Effective Use of Reward Systems," in *Readings in Personnel and Human Resource Management*, 3d ed., eds R. Schuler, S. Youngblood, and V. Huber (New York: West Publishing, 1987), 270–285.

**FIGURE 13–1**                The Importance of Incentives

Managers often have difficulty identifying rewards valued by their employees. Some rewards, such as continued employment, appeal to almost all employees.

Source: Reprinted with special permission of King Features Syndicate, Inc.

the variability in actual job performance, so that differences in evaluation are based upon subjective employee characteristics rather than objective performance.

Third, managers who are required to make distinctions among employees often neither are trained in how to assess performance nor have the desire to evaluate—and defend their assessment of—their employees. Finally, managers have difficulty identifying rewards valued by their employees. As the cartoon in Figure 13–1 suggests, there may be some commonalities among employees. More likely, however, some employees may find certain rewards very reinforcing while others may find those same rewards completely irrelevant.

The preceding discussion highlights only some of the difficulties a manager faces in trying to develop or implement a compensation system. Up until this point, we have been examining the compensation system as a whole. The next sections focus on the specific components of the compensation system—wages and salaries, employee benefits, nonrecurring financial rewards, and noneconomic rewards (see Figure 13–2). As you read the next four sections, consider the impact of each of these factors on motivating employees to perform in concert with management's desires and expectations.

**WAGES, SALARIES, AND NONRECURRING FINANCIAL REWARDS**

Most people define compensation systems as how much individuals are paid for the work they perform. Monetary rewards are the most salient of the forms of compensation under the control of organizations. The general notion is that monetary rewards are the primary mechanism for motivating high performance among employees. As we suggested in

**FIGURE 13-2**          Components of the Compensation System

The company's total com-
pensation package
includes a variety of economic rewards and also
nonmonetary rewards
such as autonomy, recog-
nition, and a sense of
achievement.

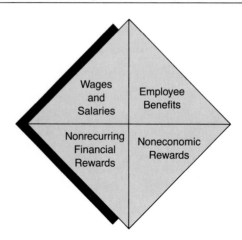

Chapter 4, a number of assumptions based upon expectancy theory must
be met for monetary rewards to be effective in influencing performance
levels. In the following list, we have described in parentheses which
component of expectancy theory relates to each assumption:

1. *Employees must be capable of performing at high levels.* Unless the work
   force has the capability to perform the task, there is no possibility
   that high-quality task performance can result (E→P).
2. *Employees must believe they can perform at high levels.* Even if
   individuals have the ability to perform the task, they are unlikely
   to try unless they believe they can accomplish it. (E→P).
3. *Employees must believe that higher performance will result in more money.*
   Employees must perceive a relationship between performance and
   monetary rewards. That is, they must realize that the level of
   reward varies systematically with the level of performance (P→O).
4. *Employees must value money.* While not all employees value money
   equally, for money to be motivating, they must value money
   sufficiently (Valence).
5. *Money must be valued relative to other rewards.* Money must be valued
   over other incentives, such as peer acceptance. If peer acceptance
   is valued more highly than money, then the possibility of
   antagonizing peers because of high performance will restrict the
   level of performance (Valence).
6. *Jobs must allow for performance variation.* The job must be designed
   so that individuals may perform at different levels. If the job is
   machine-paced, then levels of performance (because they are
   based upon the machine) are not subject to worker control. In this
   case, the notion of high performance is irrelevant (P→O).

**FIGURE 13-3**                     Types of Incentive Systems

The company has a variety of options for structuring its compensation system. These options include ways to reward individual performance or the performance of the group as a whole. The choice of an option depends in part on the individual's control over the desired outcome and the degree of cooperation required among group members.

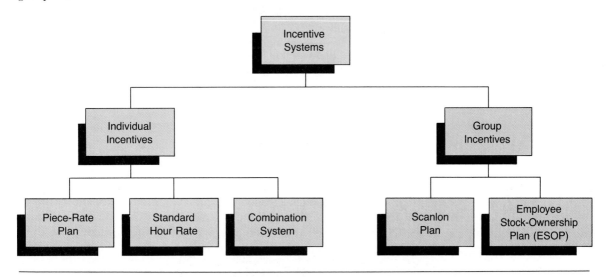

7. *Performance must be measurable.* Employees must be convinced that the level of their performance can be reliably measured. If, for example, an employee exerts considerable effort during one evaluation period and little effort in a subsequent period and there is no difference in the level of reward, then the "incentive" system has less of an influence on the individual's performance (P→O).

8. *The plan must be compatible with the nature of the work (individual versus group).* Unless the organization can assess who does the work, an incentive plan probably will not work because the organization will not be able to attribute contributions of the individual or the group (P→O).

If these assumptions are met, then it is likely that an incentive system will foster high performance. How the incentive system will be structured, however, is still in question. Consider the types of incentive systems (shown in Figure 13-3) from which one can choose. If one is rewarding individual performance, then employees can be paid on a piece-rate plan or on a standard hour rate. In the **piece-rate plan,** the employee is paid a given rate for each unit produced. Piece-rate incentive plans are based upon objective performance and are oriented

FOCUS ON:

Pay for
Performance

**Back to Piecework: Many Companies Base Workers' Raises on Their Productivity** Denise Wise, a San Francisco office worker who processes payroll accounts in BankAmerica Corp.'s business service division, has earned $4,000 in incentive bonuses this year under a pay-for-performance plan designed to reward the productive and punish the deadwood among the bank giant's 86,000 employees. She is understandably happy with pay for performance. "If you work effectively, there's something in it for you," Wise says. "That [incentive] wasn't always there before."

But 3 of her 24 colleagues in her office weren't pleased at all. Although the office achieved 100 percent of its incentive-plan goals in the first quarter of this year, the three, including a man who had worked there for more than 20 years, didn't get any bonus at all because their individual performance lagged behind the group's. That longtime employee eventually left the company, Wise says.

Pay for performance can be ruthless, but it is nonetheless one of the hottest management and labor trends around, according to compensation consulting firms. Under such plans, middle- or lower-level workers are supposed to be judged as their high-powered executive bosses often are, receiving higher raises, bonuses, or prizes for excelling on a variety of specific and often computer-measured indices. Employees who don't measure up receive little or no pay raise, or are even fired.

Many of the managers who must implement pay for performance and the employees who work under it are skeptical, even critical. According to management consultants, most workers dislike being judged, and most managers who work closely with their employees dislike sitting in judgment.

Workers and their unions say that performance on many jobs can't be measured objectively, that pay for performance may be an excuse for favoritism and for firing people. Some

towards future productivity. Thus employees' earnings are based upon what they are able to produce. Such an incentive system differs from merit-based pay, or pay-for-performance, in that merit systems reward past performance and usually are based upon a subjective evaluation of performance. Depending upon the nature of the task, such performance-based systems have always been an option in developing a compensation system. However, most organizations shy away from a purely merit-based or piece-rate system. An example of the benefits and problems of a piece-rate system can be found in the "FOCUS ON: Pay for Performance."

**Standard hour rates** differ from piece rates in that they are determined not by what the employee actually produces but by the amount of time (determined by industrial engineering standards) that it *should* take to produce each unit. Then the employee is paid a standard rate, regardless of the length of time it took to produce the unit.

companies agree that the system can destroy rather than lift morale, and even those employees who prosper under it complain bitterly if other groups of fellow workers—such as unionized blue-collar workers—are kept on the old system of automatic cost-of-living adjustments.

The difficulty of implementing pay for performance can be seen even at BankAmerica. Some division managers aren't convinced that the system works for everybody, and others don't want to rank their employees. William Carstens, a vice-president of business services, doesn't think all jobs can be measured objectively. And some workers, he says, might become so nervous working under a quota system that it hurts their work. "You don't want them so worried about being able to pay their rent they can't do their job," Carstens says. Another BankAmerica executive, who manages a group of branches, says he hasn't confronted any employees over poor ranking, nor has he fired anyone. "It's my biggest weakness," he says. "I find [such confrontation] very unpleasant."

Bashker Biswas, the former compensation manager at Memorex Corp., concludes that merit-based systems often just increase fixed costs because managers tend to conclude that everybody is in the top categories, and thus raise all salaries. "If you say your employees are poor performers, you have indicted yourself," he says. "It shows that you're not doing a good job of training and coaching your people." Biswas, now an instructor at Golden Gate University in San Francisco, adds, "It's tough not to give a raise to somebody you know has a family to feed. I was a typical manager. I always rated my people average or above."

Source: Carrie Dolan, "Back to Piecework: Many Companies Now Base Workers' Raises on Their Productivity," *The Wall Street Journal,* November 15, 1985, p. 4.

Combinations of these two forms exist as well. For example, salespeople who are paid a salary plus commission have parts of a piece-rate and a standard-hour incentive structure. Such employees are guaranteed both a minimum wage (standard-hour plan) and also rewards based directly on the sales they produce.

Rewarding individual performance, regardless of the system, is based on equitable distribution of rewards. This is a common assumption about how rewards should be distributed, but unquestioning acceptance of the equity norm of reward distribution does not exist among all workers. As illustrated in the "INTERNATIONAL FOCUS ON: Incentive Systems," Chinese workers are much more comfortable with equal distribution of rewards.

While such combinations reward individual performance, some tasks require group performance. Therefore, incentive structures should have sufficient flexibility to reward groups when appropriate. Group-level incentive plans operate under the same set of assumptions as individual

INTERNATIONAL
FOCUS ON:
Incentive Systems

**Changing Reward Systems in China** In the first quarter of 1978, one of the first companies to reinstate a bonus incentive system in China was the Capital Iron and Steel Company. This attempt to deviate from the path dictated by the "Iron Ricebowl" policy was met with considerable discomfort and debate among the various levels of the organization. The "Iron Ricebowl" describes the absolute egalitarian system under which China's work force operated during the Cultural Revolution. Under the old system, each worker was guaranteed a job, and in most cases that guarantee had little to do with the worker's performance. Under the new system, a series of bonuses based on superior performance would be allocated to the workers. With this bonus system, the factory was organized into 10 units. Each unit was evaluated on completeness and superiority. Completeness meant that all technical and economic indicators such as quantity, quality, and variety of products were evaluated. All workers who did not meet their quotas would forfeit part of their bonus. Under the criterion of superiority, the work unit that met its respective quotas and outperformed others in the same industry (nationwide) would receive a bonus.

However, this program met with considerable ideological differences. Some managers were concerned about the low wages of many workers and believed that their chances of receiving monetary bonuses should be greater than the probability of their forfeiting the bonuses. Some workers, because of the desire to abolish the evaluative criteria, recommended that the superior achievement bonuses be tied to individual quotas. Other workers demanded that the production quotas be lowered, and that although people could get more by exceeding the quotas, they should not forfeit their bonuses when they did not meet their quotas.

After two years of adjusting and implementing this bonus system, the Capital Iron and Steel Company has discovered a unique way to introduce such changes in incentive systems to their workers. They integrate ideological and political indoctrination with a rigorous system of personal responsibilities and clearly defined codes of rewards and penalties. To the extent that they did not successfully integrate ideological and political systems into explanations, but rather tried to separate them from the daily functioning of the new incentive system, they were unable to gain the cooperation of the workers.

Whereas American workers do not have to be convinced of the "appropriateness" of equity-based incentive systems, such incentive systems and the assumptions they include are indeed foreign to other cultures such as the Chinese. The Capital Iron and Steel Company is one of a new breed of Chinese organizations that are attempting to re-educate the Chinese worker on the multiple goals of an organization—goals that clearly include efficiency and productivity.

Source: M. A. Von Glinow and M. B. Teagarden, "The Transfer of Human Resource Management Technology in Sino–U.S. Cooperative Ventures," *Human Resource Management* 27 (1988): 201–229; and "The Capital Iron and Steel Company, The Reward System in China," *International Studies of Man and Organization* 12 (1982): 77–89.

Why are these people smiling? Because they work for high-tech manufacturer W. L. Gore, makers of Gore-Tex. Gore has no employees, only associates. Like more than 5,000 other firms in the United States, W. L. Gore associates are more than just employees because they all own stock in their company. Employee-owned companies generally outperform their competitors.

incentive plans. However, they are more effective in situations where productivity is a function of group rather than individual contributions. For example, if a project's success depends upon the contributions of an entire department, then it is important that all of the contributors be rewarded for their combined performance. Rewarding only certain individuals in a department is likely to lead to increased competitiveness among group members rather than the cooperation required for a successful outcome.

There are a variety of group-based incentive plans. These plans can focus on either rewarding groups for successful cost reduction or rewarding groups for gains in productivity. The most well-known example of a cost-reduction group-level incentive plan is the Scanlon plan.[5] Under such a plan, all employees share the benefits of efficiency increases among the work force.

Another, more recent development in group-based incentive plans allows the employees to share in the profits of the firm. Under **Employee Stock Ownership Plans (ESOPs),** companies make tax-deductible contributions of stock or cash to a trust fund to buy stock. The stock is then allocated to employees based upon their seniority. When they retire or leave the company, they receive their stock and can either sell it on the market or sell it back to the company.[6] The financial benefit of stock

[5]W. F. Whyte, "The Scanlon Plan," in *Compensation and Reward Perspectives,* ed. T. Maloney (Homewood, Ill.: R. D. Irwin, 1979).

[6]C. Rosen, K. J. Klein, and K. M. Young, "When Employees Share the Profits," *Psychology Today,* January 1986, 30–36.

ownership both to employee attitudes and employee performance is considerable. An ESOP can provide each employee with a considerable nest egg and may also serve as a visible symbol that the company views the employee as a critical and important resource. Further, managers in ESOP firms often see such employee participation and ownership as central to the organization's culture and mission. Such ownership may increase employee influence in decisions affecting the organization, enthusiasm, and commitment to the organization.

An important question, however, is what impact such employee-ownership programs have on firm performance. The "FOCUS ON: Employee Stock Ownership Plans" illustrates the performance effect often associated with ESOPs.

## FOCUS ON:
### Employee Stock Ownership Plans

**Employees as Owners**   People Express Airlines called its employees "managers." Quad/Graphics, among the most successful print companies in the United States, refers to its workers as "partners." W. L. Gore Associates, a 4,000-employee high-tech manufacturer, insists it has no employees, only "associates."

These companies are not unique. More than 8,000 firms in the United States now share some ownership with more than 10 million employees. In at least 1,000 companies, employees own the majority of the stock. Employee ownership can be found in every industry, every size of firm, and every part of the country.

Studies by the National Center for Employee Ownership, the Survey Research Center at the University of Michigan, and others indicate that employee ownership is strongly associated with corporate performance. Employee-owned firms have been shown to be 150 percent as profitable and to have twice the productivity growth rate of conventional companies. Firms that are mostly employee owned generate three times more new jobs than do their competitors, while high-tech companies that share ownership widely grow two to four times as fast as those that do not. Publicly held companies that are at least ten percent employee owned outperform from 62 percent to 75 percent of their competitors, depending on the measures of performance being used.

While these studies cannot prove a causal relationship between employee ownership and success (perhaps successful firms are simply more likely to set up ESOPs), they are suggestive—especially to managers of other companies looking for a way to compete more effectively. And they fit in well with currently popular management thinking. In his book, *The Year Ahead,* John Nasbitt argues that ownership will be a key emerging business trend "because it works," while management psychologist Tom Peters, in *A Passion for Excellence,* cites a "sense of ownership" as a striking characteristic among employees at successful firms.

Source: C. Rosen, K. J. Klein, and K. M. Young, "When Employees Share the Profits," *Psychology Today,* January 1986, p. 33.

**FIGURE 13–4**                A Menu of Employee Benefits

Employee benefits are all the indirect economic rewards that employees receive. These benefits can represent as much as 40 percent of a company's total compensation costs, but are rarely valued that highly by employees.

### Optional Benefits

| | |
|---|---|
| Pension plans | Dental insurance |
| Vacation time | Life and accident insurance |
| Holiday pay | Long-term disability insurance |
| Sick leave | Automobile insurance |
| Jury-duty pay | Liability insurance |
| Maternity/Paternity leave | Moving expenses |
| Funeral leave | Severance pay |
| Military-duty pay | Subsidized employee meals |
| Health insurance | Discount on goods or services |

### Legally Required Benefits

| | |
|---|---|
| Social security | Unemployment compensation |
| Workers' compensation | |

EMPLOYEE
BENEFITS

Employee benefits are all the indirect economic rewards that employees receive.[7] A lengthy list of potential employee benefits is illustrated in Figure 13–4. While the purpose of a compensation system is to influence an individual's willingness to behave in accordance with the organization's wishes, employee benefits are not likely to influence this process directly. Since the majority of employee benefits are given to all employees, regardless of level of performance, they are not likely to motivate performance. However, they probably do influence individuals in deciding to stay with an organization. This is particularly true of benefits that increase in value with employee seniority. Examples of such benefits are pension plans, vacation time, and sabbatical leaves.

In most organizations, a standard set of benefits is offered to each employee. Recently, some organizations have begun to offer customized benefits packages. In this "cafeteria" approach to benefits, the employee is given a core set of benefits that does not vary across employees, but is also offered the opportunity to select among other benefits. Usually, the employees are given a certain amount of "benefit dollars" to spend and can allocate those dollars across different benefits. For example, a member of a dual-income family with no children may forego additional health-care coverage. An employee with children may choose greater insurance benefits and a prepaid child-care option.

---

[7]See "Benefits Boosts: Most Firms Expand Health Coverage to Keep Pace with Inflation," *The Wall Street Journal,* February 23, 1982, p. 1; and Hills, *Compensation Decision Making.*

Allowing employees to customize their benefit plans has two major advantages. First, it increases the value of the benefits package to the individual employee while maintaining a set cost per employee. Second, it increases employee awareness of the actual value of the benefits the company is providing. Without such a system, employees often seriously underestimate the value of the benefits the company provides. For example, one group of employees reported that they thought the company made an average monthly contribution of $21.69 per employee for their health-care benefits, when in fact the company contributed $64.07.[8]

## NONECONOMIC REWARDS

Managers often focus solely on the economic rewards of employment, ignoring noneconomic rewards as a means of influencing individual performance. These nonpecuniary or noneconomic rewards do not directly affect the employee's wages and benefits. However, many rewards that flow from employment influence employee performance.

To assume the only important rewards are economic is naive. An individual who dislikes the duties of a job may leave it. Other workers may decide to stay in an organization because of the power they have, because they believe their jobs are significant and important, because they like their colleagues, or because they like the geographic area in which their positions are located.

Noneconomic rewards can take many forms. They can include intrinsic job rewards, extrinsic job rewards, and non-job-based rewards. Intrinsic job rewards are those reinforcers which relate directly to performing the task. They include such job-related factors as autonomy, power and control, and a sense of task completion and achievement. An example of a noneconomic, intrinsic job reward is the use of flextime. Extrinsic job rewards are those rewards external to or separate from the job itself, such as supervisory recognition and social interaction. Finally, non-job-based rewards are those which accrue to employees because they are employed by a particular organization, independent of their unique positions within the organization. Two such rewards are organizational status (status based upon association with the particular organization) and a favorable geographical location.

The rewards we have discussed all contribute to an organization's compensation system. However, as we know from previous chapters, compensation systems are not foolproof in rewarding good performance. In some cases, compensation can systematically discriminate among employees. In the next section we discuss comparable worth as a basis for determining the compensation of a specific class of employees.

[8]M. G. Wilson, G. B. Northcraft, and M. A. Neale, "The Perceived Value of Fringe Benefits," *Personnel Psychology* 38 (1985): 309–320.

The basis of comparable worth discrimination lies in the differential valuing of occupations because of the dominant gender of the jobholders. In Wisconsin, nurses argued that their positions were worth more than those of sanitation workers in terms of skill, ability, and effort. In most cases courts allow different wage rates for different jobs if based on market demands.

**Comparable Worth**   Among all the forms of compensation, monetary incentives are the most easily divisible and the easiest to allocate. As such, they are most likely to be the basis for discriminating among employees. Discrimination is an ominous term. However, in allocating rewards, organizations must discriminate between good and poor performers. This type of discrimination is vastly different from discrimination based on factors unrelated to job performance.

In fact, we can describe four different types of discrimination: legal and fair, legal and unfair, illegal and fair, and illegal and unfair. An example of legal and fair discrimination is to give the largest pay increases to younger workers if they outperform older workers. Discriminating by giving a friend a higher pay raise than another employee about whom you are indifferent is unfair but not illegal. An example of illegal but fair discrimination is requiring women to contribute more to employee pension plans. It is fair discrimination because women as a group live longer than men and are likely to receive more benefits from a retirement plan. However, recent court rulings have made it illegal to require higher pension contributions from women.[9] Illegal and unfair discrimination is granting a pay raise to a white employee whose performance is only average while not granting one to a black employee with above-average performance.

Currently, when the topic of discrimination is considered, the focus often turns to the comparable worth controversy. **Comparable worth** is based on two factors. The first is that the Equal Pay Act requires equal pay for jobs that are substantially equal in terms of skill, ability, and effort. Second, even though the Equal Pay Act has been around for over

[9]Manhart v. City of Los Angeles, Department of Water and Power, 552 F. 2d 581, 13 FEP 1625 (9th Cir. 1976); Norris v. Arizona, Governing Comm., 486 F. Supp. 645, 22 FEP 1059 (D. Ariz. 1980).

**FIGURE 13–5**          A Plan for Narrowing the Gap between Wage Rates

The most practical way to achieve equal pay for comparable worth is to gradually raise the wage rates of predominately female jobs to bring them in line with comparable jobs staffed predominately by males. The examples in this figure are part of such a plan designed for workers employed by the City of Colorado Springs.

Source: Peggy Simpson, "If the Wage System Doesn't Work, Fix It," *Working Woman*, October 1985, 118.

20 years, there is still a significant difference between the average pay of men and women. Women earn, on average, only 60 percent of what men earn. A substantial portion of this difference can be accounted for by occupational gender segregation. In a recent study, two researchers found that to alleviate occupational gender segregation in California, 96.3 percent of the men (or women) would have to change jobs.[10] The low pay associated with "female" occupations is not just a function of history. Occasionally, a largely segregated occupation (such as bank teller or public-school teacher) has begun to accept members of a different gender, and the pay has changed accordingly: increased if the new

[10]W. Bielby and J. Baron, "Men and Women at Work: Sex Segregation and Statistical Discrimination," *American Journal of Sociology* 91 (4), 1986.

jobholders were male and decreased if they were female.[11] Figure 13–5 shows a plan for narrowing the gap between wage rates.

The basis of comparable worth discrimination lies in the differential valuing of occupations based on the dominant gender of the jobholders. In Denver, for example, nurses argued that their jobs required more skill and ability than other jobs for which the employer paid more—tree trimmers and sign painters. In a similar case in Wisconsin, nurses argued that their positions were worth more than those of sanitation workers. In most cases the courts are accepting a market defense—that is, wage rates are based on market wage surveys for these occupations. Thus, to pay different rates for different jobs based on market demands currently is not considered discrimination.[12]

The issue of comparable worth discrimination is still being battled in the courts. Its potential impact on organizations could be incredible. Consider the case of the state of Washington. The state had conducted numerous job evaluations over several years and found that predominately female jobs were paid less than comparable jobs held predominately by males. The state had known this condition existed but failed to implement any changes in its compensation system. If states conduct job evaluations on comparable jobs and find systematic differences, the cost to rectify the inequities all at once would be staggering. It is unlikely that any organization would reduce the wage rate of the higher-paid jobs, such as maintenance engineers or tree trimmers, yet raising the wages of nurses, clerical assistants, and teachers could easily bankrupt a public system. The more likely alternative, if comparable worth discrimination is not recognized by the court, would be an incremental process of bringing the wage rates of predominately female jobs in line with those of comparable male jobs. In addition to assuring that employees are not the subject of discrimination, many other factors must be present to assure good performance. The next section focuses on one of those factors, the setting of performance goals.

## GOAL SETTING

Another important factor in the employee performance equation is the setting of performance goals. **Goals** specify a direction for action and a specific quantity of work to be accomplished.[13] Considerable research supports the notion that employees who are assigned difficult and specific goals perform at higher levels than those assigned easy goals. Further, those with specific, challenging goals outperform individuals told to "do your best."

[11]J. Pfeffer and J. Ross, "Gender-Based Wage Differences: The Effects of Organizational Contexts," in *Work and Occupations* (in press); and M. Strober, "The MBA: Same Passport to Success for Women and Men?" in *Women in the Workplace*, ed. P. Wallace (Boston: Auburn House, 1982), 25–55.

[12]Hills, *Compensation Decision Making.*

[13]E.A. Locke and G. P. Latham, *Goal Setting: A Motivational Technique That Works!* (Englewood Cliffs, N.J.: Prentice-Hall, 1984).

Goals specify a direction for action and a specific quantity of work to be accomplished. Athletes who set themselves difficult and specific goals perform at higher levels than those with easy goals. The running times of competitors displayed prominently can influence how committed the runner is to achieving the goal and provide feedback about her own performance.

It is not enough to simply set challenging, specific goals. For these goals to work, the employee must be *committed* to achieving them. **Goal commitment** implies the extension of effort, over time, toward the accomplishment of a goal and an unwillingness to give up or lower the goal.[14] However, goal commitment is inversely related to goal difficulty. That is, the more difficult the goal, the less commitment to it.[15] Increasing the difficulty of a goal while maintaining the necessary amount of goal commitment is an important task for the manager. Committing individuals to goals is, in many ways, similar to committing individuals to the organization (for a detailed discussion, refer to Chapter 11). In addition to volition, visibility, and explicitness and irreversibility, other factors influencing just how committed an individual is to a goal include ability and self-esteem, the complexity of the task, past successes, how involving the job is, and how supportive the supervisor is.[16] Figure 13–6 shows the steps involved in setting performance goals.

Commitment to challenging, specific performance goals provides many benefits to the employee *in addition to* raising productivity. If employees are to perform at high levels, it is critical that they understand exactly what is expected of them. Goals are a primary way in which management can convey performance expectations to employees. In addition, goals can relieve boredom.[17] Specifying a goal that is difficult but attainable adds a measure of challenge to a task, regardless of the job's innate interest level.

Finally, goal attainment provides feedback to employees about their performance. If goals provide a clue to management's expectations about employee performance, then meeting the goals set by management gives employees information about the level of their performance. Thus, goals provide a bench mark for employees to judge their performance. They also increase their pride and confidence in their ability to accomplish the assigned task.

In setting performance goals for employees, a manager should follow the following six steps:[18]

1.  *Specify the general objective or task to be accomplished.* What is it you want the employee to do? One way employees' attention can be

[14]M. A. Campion and R. G. Lord, "A Control Systems Conceptualization of Goal Setting and Changing Process," *Organizational Behavior and Human Performance* 30 (1982): 265–287.

[15]E. A. Locke, "Relation of Goal Level to Performance with a Short Work Period and Multiple Goal Levels," *Journal of Applied Psychology* 67 (1982): 512–514.

[16]J. R. Hollenbeck, and H. J. Klein, "Goal Commitment and the Goal Setting Process: Problems, Prospects, and Proposals for Future Research," *Journal of Applied Psychology* 72 (1987): 212–220.

[17]E. A. Locke and J. F. Bryan, "Performance Goals as Determinants of Level of Performance and Boredom," *Journal of Applied Psychology* 51 (1978): 120–130.

[18]Locke and Latham, *Goal Setting.*

**FIGURE 13–6**          Steps in Setting Performance Goals

Setting effective perfor-
mance goals not only
raises productivity, but
also clarifies for employees what is expected of
them. The six-step pro-
cess shown here helps the
manager ensure that the
goals will be effective.

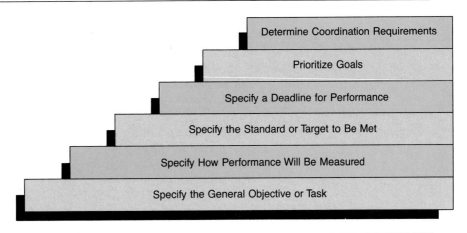

Determine Coordination Requirements

Prioritize Goals

Specify a Deadline for Performance

Specify the Standard or Target to Be Met

Specify How Performance Will Be Measured

Specify the General Objective or Task

focused on what they are to do is through job descriptions. As
described in Chapter 11, a job description usually conveys a great
deal of information to the employee, including what tasks need to
be performed, what outcome is expected, and what deadlines are
important.

2. *Specify how the performance in question will be measured.* Performance
on some tasks is more easily measured than on others. For
example, the performance of a salesperson is often evaluated on
the dollar value of generated sales; the performance of a secretary
may be measured by the number of assignments completed daily.
Other types of performance, such as the performance of the
prosecuting attorneys described in the opening vignette, are more
difficult to assess. For example, if the attorneys' supervisor only
counts the number of cases that are tried, then there obviously
will be a clear incentive to bring more cases to trial. Or, as one of
the opponents stated, if points are awarded based upon guilty
verdicts, the prosecutors may choose to try cases that may have
been handled better by a plea-bargaining agreement. Clearly,
managers should carefully consider exactly what they want and
develop goals to match their desires.

3. *Specify the standard or target to be met.* In addition to identifying
what will be evaluated, a manager should also specify exactly what
level of performance is expected. This is the challenging portion
of the goal.

4. *Specify a deadline for performance.* Generally, as the level of
responsibility of a task increases, so does the time allowed for
performance. For example, semiskilled or blue-collar workers may

be given daily or weekly goals. Upper-level managers may be evaluated yearly or even in three- or five-year cycles.

5. *Prioritize goals.* Employees are likely to have many goals to accomplish, especially as the complexity of their positions increases. Thus, setting goal priorities directs effort in proportion to the importance of the goals. Not knowing the priority of tasks can be dangerous. Consider the following example. An executive was hired by a national association to edit a series of publications. In an emergency, she was asked to take charge of a national convention, and she spent a great deal of time planning the convention at the expense of her editorial work. After the convention, she was fired for not doing the editorial work for which she was hired! She had incorrectly prioritized her goals. If her employer had prioritized her goals, her dismissal may have been avoided.[19]

6. *Determine coordination requirements.* Consider the amount of coordination and cooperation with other individuals needed to accomplish the set goals. Depending upon the amount of interdependence necessary to accomplish the task, the manager should be aware of and account for the increased conflict that is likely to occur.[20]

Goal setting has been shown to be a very effective mechanism for improving performance. However, there are a number of potential pitfalls that should be avoided if goal setting is to be effective. Setting extremely difficult goals may produce greater levels of effort, but it also increases the level of risk managers and employees are willing to take. While risk taking is a component of managing in uncertain environments, excessive risk taking (as we suggested in Chapter 5) clearly can be counterproductive. If goals are too difficult, they may produce unnecessary levels of stress for employees and may reduce their acceptance of and commitment to meeting them. While challenging goals that demand high levels of performance may be inherently stressful for employees, it is important to avoid levels of stress that hamper performance. Further, if goals are too difficult, employees' goal commitment may be lowered, which likely will offset the typical benefits of setting challenging goals.

Other potential pitfalls of goal setting include perceiving goals as *ceilings* on performance. Goals are usually intended to identify the minimum acceptable level of performance, not the maximum. Further, since goals direct employee effort, areas of performance for which goals are not set may be ignored. Along this line, goals set for short time

[19]Ibid., p. 34.

[20]G. B. Northcraft and P. C. Earley, "Goals Setting, Conflict and Task Interdependence," in *Conflict Management: An Interdisciplinary Approach*, ed. M. A. Rahim (New York: Praeger Publications, 1989).

**FIGURE 13-7**    Goal-Setting Pitfalls and Potential Solutions

Goal setting can be a very effective mechanism for improving performance in an organization, but only if managed well. There are a number of pitfalls that must be avoided for goal setting to be effective.

| Pitfall | Potential Solution |
| --- | --- |
| Excessive risk taking | Specify acceptable risk levels for the employee and the organization |
| Increased stress | Adjust goal difficulty, increase staff as needed, and ensure that employees have the skills necessary to accomplish their goals |
| View of goals as ceilings rather than floors | Reward those who exceed their goals |
| Ignoring of nongoal areas | Make sure that goals are comprehensive—developed for all important areas of performance |
| Encouragement of short-range thinking | Increase the time span of goals |
| Dishonesty and cheating | Set an example of honesty in actions, give frequent feedback, and be open to negative information to avoid a climate of high pressure and low support |

Source: E. A. Locke and G. P. Latham, *Goal Setting: A Motivational Technique That Really Works!* (Englewood Cliffs, N.J.: Prentice-Hall, 1984), 171–172.

periods may encourage short-term performance. An employee is likely to focus on whatever timeline is contained within the goal. Finally, in a high-pressure, unsupportive atmosphere, demanding and difficult goals can lead employees to take shortcuts, cheat, or misrepresent their actual levels of performance to meet performance demands. Figure 13–7 illustrates some ways in which each of these pitfalls can be avoided.

While setting specific goals can increase performance, it is important that employees have feedback about how they are doing. When employees are told how their behaviors measure up to an expected standard of performance, they can then modify their behavior if necessary to reach their set goals. Thus, feedback is necessary if goal setting is to work. While feedback that is timely and self-generated is probably the most useful in modifying work behavior, it is also important that employees receive formal feedback about their performance on a routine basis in the form of a performance appraisal.[21] The next section focuses on the importance of performance appraisals in maintaining employee performance.

[21]G. B. Northcraft, and P. C. Earley, "Technology, Credibility, and Feedback Use," *Organizational Behavior and Human Decision Processes* (in press).

Performance appraisals are an important organizational tool. They provide valuable opportunities for performance-enhancing discussions between supervisors and subordinates as well as diagnosing weaknesses in an organization's selection, socialization, and training programs.

## PERFORMANCE APPRAISAL SYSTEMS

Performance appraisals serve many purposes in organizations. They provide feedback to the employee and serve as the basis for decisions concerning promotion, salary and wage increases, demotion, transfer, training, and layoffs. The general strengths and weaknesses of the employee population can be evaluated and directions for training identified. Performance evaluations can also aid the individual in determining personal strengths and weaknesses. Finally, information garnered from a performance appraisal system can aid in the maintenance or modification of the current organizational selection process.

## CONFLICTS AND PROBLEMS

Using performance appraisals for so many diverse purposes can cause problems. If all the reasons for performance appraisal use are categorized, three major functions emerge: (1) to provide feedback, (2) to distribute rewards, and (3) to counsel employees. If we examine these three functions more closely, it is easy to see how they can conflict with one another.

Consider the obvious conflict employees must experience in trying to respond to both the counseling and the reward-distribution functions of performance appraisals. A supervisor trying to understand the obstacles that keep employees from performing their jobs will want to focus on the employees' perceptions of problems, weaknesses, and failures. However, if employees view the performance appraisal as an opportunity to make their case for a substantial promotion or salary increase, then the last thing they will want to do is to focus on the problems, weaknesses, and failures they have experienced in their positions. What they want to do is to present their performance in the best possible light. Thus, they are likely to gloss over difficulties and potential problems and present only their successes. It may be that expecting employees to be honest about their shortcomings while simultaneously evaluating them for a salary increase or promotion is asking too much. To answer the questions honestly would probably mean going against what employees see as their best interests.

Conflict engendered by performance appraisals is also responsible for vanishing performance appraisals. This conflict develops not only from the conflicting functions of a performance appraisal system, but also from the difficulty of the lack of incentives for conducting high-quality performance appraisals. The major difficulty with performance appraisals is the inability of supervisors to convey negative feedback in a constructive manner. Supervisors—especially those who must convey negative performance information—are often vague and indirect in conveying this information to their employees. As a result, supervisors may believe that an evaluation has been conducted while employees may be unaware that they have been evaluated.

The second reason for vanishing performance appraisals is the lack of organizational incentives for supervisors to spend the time and effort necessary to conduct good performance-appraisal interviews. In fact, this is probably a good example of the "folly of rewarding A while hoping for B."[22] Most organizations probably hope that their supervisors will spend the necessary time to diagnose the reasons behind poor performance and, together with the employee, implement solutions to address these problems. Yet the reward structures of most organizations actually *reward* supervisors for conducting superficial performance appraisals (they take less time away from "productive" activities) or ignoring them altogether.

Even supervisors who understand the importance of performance appraisals often find themselves in a no-win situation. For example, a supervisor's appraisal of an employee's performance may be very different from the employee's self-appraisal. In fact, because of disparate perceptions, it is difficult even for a supervisor with good interpersonal skills to conduct a positive performance interview. Employees often display considerable levels of discomfort when confronted with a performance evaluation, *regardless of their level of past performance*. Part of this discomfort can be explained by their anxiety about evaluation. However, some of the discomfort is probably based on a perceived lack of control over the outcome: the final evaluation. Recent research suggests that employees generally believe performance appraisals to be arbitrary and capricious, independent of their level of performance.[23]

[22]Kerr, "On the Folly of Rewarding A while Hoping for B."

[23]R. Folger and J. Greenberg, "Procedural Justice: An Interpretive Analysis of Personnel Systems," in *Research in Personnel and Human Resource Management*, vol. III, eds. K. Rowland and G. Ferris (Greenwich, Conn.: JAI Press, 1985), pp. 141–183.

That is, both poorly performing and highly performing employees view performance appraisals as unrelated to their levels of performance.

The reasons for this almost universal dissatisfaction with the process of performance appraisal are numerous. They include dissatisfaction with what is being rated, the performance-appraisal instruments, who conducts the actual ratings, and how often the ratings are conducted. The next section considers each of these concerns.

## IMPROVING PERFORMANCE APPRAISAL SYSTEMS

Creating an effective performance appraisal system is a difficult undertaking. Although 90 percent of organizations report having performance appraisal systems in place, approximately the same percentage report dissatisfaction with their current systems. Even in the military services, which traditionally invest considerable resources in developing accurate and effective performance appraisal systems, a newly implemented performance appraisal system has an expected life of only a few years. The search for an accurate, reliable, and well-received performance appraisal system may be never-ending, but managers could certainly improve the quality of their performance appraisal systems by focusing on the following issues, which are the root of much participant dissatisfaction with the evaluation process.

**Measure Behavior, Not Traits**   One of the most popular formats for evaluating employees is a **trait-rating scale.**[24] The trait approach typically asks the rater to evaluate the ratee on such factors as dependability, cooperation, leadership, obedience, and loyalty. While we often evaluate our acquaintances on such dimensions, there are serious problems associated with rating employees by traits. If performance appraisals exist to measure past *performance,* then evaluating employees' various personality traits is inconsistent with that purpose. Personality traits are measures of neither performance nor behavior. In fact, considerable research into the relationship between personality and behavior reports little relationship between the two.[25] Even if the correlation between personality and behavior were much higher, traits only *predict* behavior, they do not *measure* it. For example, there is a positive relationship between success in an organization and an individual's height.[26] However, a manager would be hard-pressed to justify using an employee's height as a measure of performance. While an individual's height may indeed predict performance, it does not *measure* performance!

[24]H. J. Bernardin and R.W. Beatty, *Performance Appraisal: Assessing Human Behavior at Work* (Boston: Kent Publishing, 1984).

[25]R. I. Henderson, *Performance Appraisal* (Reston, Va.: Reston Publishing, 1984).

[26]B. M. Bass, *Stodgill's Handbook of Leadership: A Survey of Theory and Research,* rev. ed. (New York: Free Press, 1981).

Further, evaluations based upon employee traits or personality characteristics are usually generic in nature, not based upon specific, identifiable (and thus modifiable) behaviors. For example, if you receive a performance evaluation that indicates that you are viewed by the supervisor as being low in leadership, how will you modify your behavior to reduce that deficiency? How would you, specifically, alter your level of "leadership"? On the other hand, if you are told that you "tell new people how to do the job, show them when it is done wrong, but don't explain why or check whether they understand what they are doing and the reason for the method,"[27] then you are likely to be able to alter your behavior to improve performance.

The difficulty of adjusting one's personality traits to meet organizational expectations is not lost on employees. Performance appraisal systems that primarily evaluate traits rather than observable behavior are typically viewed with suspicion by employees. For employees to be more accepting of performance appraisals, organizations must focus on measuring observable behavior. Along this line, then, the performance-appraisal instrument must measure such behaviors.

**The Proper Performance-Appraisal Instrument**   As we described previously, the most commonly used performance-rating form is the graphic rating scale, an instrument that purports to measure employee traits. On the other end of the performance-appraisal continuum are instruments that measure behaviors. The most common form of "behavioral" instrument is the **behaviorally anchored rating scale (BARS).** In developing a BARS, an organization must first analyze the particular job to determine what types of behavior reflect varying degrees of performance. That is, how does an "outstanding" employee behave? An "average" employee? An "unsatisfactory" employee? Actual descriptions of behaviors are then used to define, or *anchor*, the ratings on the scale. For example, in rating an employee's perseverance, a BARS might offer options from "keeps working on difficult tasks until job is completed" to "likely to stop work at the first sign of difficulty."[28]

While a BARS is often perceived by employees as a major improvement over trait scales, few organizations have implemented this particular form of appraisal instrument and the research on its superiority is sparse. The development of such scales requires lengthy job analyses and a considerable amount of the organization's resources—particularly money and time. In addition, BARS are designed for a specific job in a specific organization. Thus, one BARS cannot be developed and applied to all positions in an organization. Since they are unique to a position and they require such a large amount of resources to produce, BARS are

---

[27]Henderson, *Performance Appraisal,* p. 189.

[28]Berkeley Rice, "Performance Review: The Job Nobody Likes," *Psychology Today,* September 1985, 30–36.

usually developed only for job categories in which there are many incumbents, such as bank tellers, nurses, grocery clerks, bookkeepers, and secretaries. It is rare that a BARS will be developed for professionals or executives—the cost is just too great. Finally, some research suggests that ratings based upon memory may capture more accurately the essence of an individual's performance than ratings (such as a BARS) conducted immediately after viewing a sample of the employee's performance.[29] Probably the most common reason *for* using a BARS is that it seems to fare much better under judicial scrutiny; that is, it is legally more defensible. In a number of court cases, trait rating scales have been found not to be legally defensible.

While trait scales and BARS represent two ends of the continuum, there are other types of performance-appraisal instruments. They are briefly described and their position along this continuum illustrated in Figure 13–8.

**Who Should Rate Employees?**   The easy answer to this question is that the supervisor should rate employees. In fact, in the vast majority of organizations, supervisors are the ones who evaluate a subordinate's performance. Unfortunately, the easy answer is not always the correct answer. Deciding who should evaluate an employee's behavior should depend upon certain criteria. The ideal rater should be (1) aware of the objectives of the employee's position, (2) able to determine if the observed behavior is satisfactory, (3) able to observe the employee frequently, and (4) able to ascertain whether the employee is effective. Rather than assuming that the supervisor is most qualified to evaluate a subordinate's performance, let's first examine the cast of organizational—and nonorganizational—actors who might serve as raters.

*Supervisors*   Supervisors are often viewed as the only people in the organization who are familiar with the responsibilities and duties of each job within their purview. In addition to knowing the jobs, supervisors should also have a grasp of the various strengths and weaknesses of those individuals they supervise. Further, they are the obvious conduit between the employee and the organization. As the organization's agents, they often are able to influence the allocation of organizational rewards and punishments.

The problems with supervisory appraisals occur when the supervisor does not have adequate opportunity to observe the employee's performance. For example, a supervisor is unlikely to be able to rate a traveling salesperson's performance other than by comparing rates of completed sales. How such a salesperson actually performs the job can only be

[29]K. R. Murphy and W. K. Balzer, "Systematic Distortions in Memory-Based Behavior Ratings and Performance Evaluations: Consequences for Rating Accuracy," *Journal of Applied Psychology* 71 (1986): 39–44.

**FIGURE 13–8**      Types of Performance Appraisal Instruments

Graphic rating scales are the most commonly used performance-rating instruments. On the other end of the range of available techniques for measuring performance are behavior-based instruments such as the behaviorally anchored rating scale (BARS).

MEASUREMENT OF TRAITS   ⟶   MEASUREMENT OF BEHAVIORS

| **Trait Scale** | **Ranking** | **Paired Comparison** | **Forced Distribution** | **Weighted Checklists** | **Behaviorally Anchored Rating Scales (BARS)** |
|---|---|---|---|---|---|
| Evaluates the employee on such factors as commitment, creativity, loyalty, initiative, and so forth. It requires judgment of ratee performance along an unbroken continuum (from excellent to unacceptable) or by discrete categories (superior, satisfactory, unsatisfactory). | The simplest of all comparative techniques, it involves ranking all employees from the best to the worst on the particular dimension being considered. | Every person is rated against every other person; the final ranking depends on how many times a particular employee is ranked better than comparison employees. | The number of individuals who can be assigned certain performance categories is limited. For example, only 10 percent of employees may be rated very good; 20 percent good, and so on. | Group of statements that describe types and levels of behavior. Each statement has a weight attached to it. Not only is the actual rating considered in this form of performance appraisal instrument, but also the value of that behavior or level of behavior to the performance of the job or task. | This instrument is a set of rating scales. There is one scale for each important aspect of job performance. Each scale is composed of brief descriptions or critical incidents of effective and ineffective job performance. |

inferred from sales levels. Further, employee evaluations are often based upon supervisors' beliefs about how they *think* the work should be done rather than how well it is actually being done.[30]

*Employees* Self-appraisals are becoming an increasingly popular addition to performance reviews. This form of evaluation is consistent with the trend toward increasing employee participation in organizational decision making. In addition, having employees evaluate themselves reduces their level of defensiveness when confronting problem areas or weaknesses. Employees rate an evaluation based on self-appraisal as more satisfying, and they are less defensive. Such evaluations can provide the supervisor with new information about how the employee perceives the job and its associated problems. They can also help to

[30]R. S. Barrett, "Influence of Supervisor's Requirements on Ratings," *Personnel Psychology* 19 (1966): 375–387.

clarify differences between the performance expectations of a supervisor and subordinate. Self-appraisals have been shown to have greater validity when self-raters expect their ratings to be compared to an identified standard, raters have previous experience with self-evaluation, and the evaluation instructions stress the comparison with others.[31]

The disadvantages of self-appraisals focus primarily on the inexperienced employee. Employees who have had little experience in being evaluated by supervisors often express greater satisfaction with more traditional, supervisory evaluations. Employees who do not have clearly established performance standards or goals by which to measure their performance are likely to use a different yardstick than the supervisor. In addition, few employees believe their performance to be average. Since the very definition of the term *average* indicates that it describes the majority of individuals, the likelihood of consistency among supervisor ratings and self-ratings is low.[32]

*Peers*    Probably the best evidence of the usefulness of peer appraisals is the reliability and validity of these reviews. In fact, they routinely have higher predictive validity than do supervisory ratings. The differences in validity between peer and supervisory ratings can be accounted for by the opportunity each group has to observe the ratee. Peers often interact with the ratee in many different arenas; thus, they have a large sample of behavior by which to evaluate performance.

The problem with having peers as raters is that they often resist evaluating their coworkers, viewing it as a threat to their relationships with others. In fact, if performance reviews are tied to salary raises or promotions, peer reviews suffer. Rather than evaluate performance accurately, peers may choose to evaluate coworkers strategically—to evaluate others in a way that maximizes their own evaluations.[33]

*Subordinates*    Subordinates have the unique ability to appraise the leadership and management potential of the rated superior. Superiors can receive useful feedback from this type of appraisal. Accepting such feedback can enhance future cooperation among organizational actors.

However, the greatest disadvantage in using subordinates to rate superiors is their (understandable) concern about the impact of their evaluations on their relationship with the supervisor. Subordinates may be hesitant to rate their supervisors accurately for fear of reprisal. Subordinates also may have different ideas of the important perfor-

[31]Paul A. Mabe III and Stephen G. West, "Validity of Self-Evaluation of Ability: A Review and Meta-Analysis," *Journal of Applied Psychology* 67 (1982): 280–296.

[32]G. C. Thornton, "Psychometric Properties of Self-Appraisals of Job Performance," *Personnel Psychology* 33, (1980): 263–272.

[33]S. J. Carroll and C. E. Schneier, *Performance Appraisal and Review Systems* (Glenview, Ill.: Scott, Foresman, 1982).

mance criteria for their bosses, and may choose to rate their superior on dimensions unrelated to job success.[34]

*Outside Individuals*   Outside raters are individuals outside the organizational unit, such as members of the human resources management department, external consultants, or clients of the firm. The benefit of having these individuals rate performance is that they rarely have a vested interest in the final outcome. That is, their own promotions, raises, or evaluations are not dependent on or influenced by their evaluation of the ratee. Outside appraisers can also provide information from a completely different perspective. For example, clients or customers may see a very different side of a salesperson than that observed by either the supervisor or coworkers.

The major problem with outside reviews is that they reduce the meaningfulness of the discussions among supervisors and their subordinates. Further, employees may find fault with a supervisor who "abdicates" responsibility to review their performance. Finally, the greatest advantage of outsider evaluations—the outsider's perspective— is also their greatest weakness. Because outsiders typically have little opportunity to observe the employee in a variety of settings, their evaluations may be based upon too small a sample of behavior.

While there are clearly both advantages and disadvantages to every type of rater, some generalizations about raters can be made. First, it is important that there be multiple raters, if possible. Having multiple raters increases the probability of obtaining a comprehensive picture of an employee's performance. Second, whoever is chosen to evaluate an employee should have considerable opportunity to observe the employee directly. Finally, the type of rater used should be consistent with the type of evaluation desired. If a manager is being evaluated for promotion to upper management, then subordinate evaluations of performance may be critical. If the supervisor has little opportunity to observe the individual directly, then perhaps peers, clients, or customers may provide the best performance information. All in all, choosing the type and number of raters can have a significant impact on the quality of the performance appraisal process.

**The Timing of Performance Appraisals**   Most organizations conduct formal performance appraisals annually. As a result, supervisors are expected to remember and evaluate behaviors that have occurred over the last 365 days. In such cases, the most recent behaviors—especially if they differ significantly from the person's usual behavior—will have the greatest impact on an evaluation. It is difficult enough for us to remember what transpired 30 days ago, much less to accurately recall what occurred one year ago.

[34]Ibid.

There are two types of solutions to this problem. A rater could schedule multiple appraisal interviews—say, four—during the year and have each review cover only the period of time since the last review. One review each year could result in a summary evaluation to be used for salary and promotion decisions. The second solution involves the use of memory aids to help the rater remember a larger sampling of employee behavior. Formally, the rater might keep a **critical incidence file** on each employee. A critical incidence file contains examples of the employee's behaviors—instances that exemplify outstanding, good, and poor behaviors. Informally, the rater might record brief observations of employees in a "little black book."[35] Ratees might also keep such a diary, noting both good and poor examples of their performance.

The suggestions above represent ways in which any performance appraisal system can be adjusted to improve its acceptance by employees. However, improving the structure of a performance appraisal system is only part of the answer to maintaining performance. In fact, it may be that many of the problems associated with formal performance appraisal systems have less to do with their structure than with motivation—how willing managers are to commit the necessary time to producing high-quality evaluations of their employees.[36] Figure 13–9 contains some advice for managers who are motivated to improve the quality of their performance appraisal systems.

## MANAGING FOR IMPROVED PERFORMANCE

Until now, this chapter has discussed general techniques for maintaining employee performance. In this section, we will focus on identifying the poor performer and developing specific prescriptions for addressing the causes of poor performance. While designing specific incentive systems, setting performance goals, and developing an effective performance appraisal system will improve the performance of both good and poor performers, managing the poor performer demands more of the supervisor's resources and analytical skills.

## THE POOR PERFORMER

All supervisors hope that all of their employees will perform their respective jobs adequately. When this happens, the job of the supervisor is much easier, and the difficult interpersonal problems associated with negative evaluations and upset employees can be avoided. Unfortunately, this is not always the case. Most managers must face, from time to time, the specter of the poorly performing employee. In addition to identifying such an individual, the supervisor must diagnose the causes of the employee's poor performance *and* develop strategies for improving it.

[35]Henderson, *Performance Appraisal.*
[36]Rice, "Performance Review: The Job Nobody Likes."

**FIGURE 13–9**      Performance-Appraisal Reviews: Advice for Managers

Many of the problems encountered with performance appraisal systems may be less the fault of the system than of the motivation and skills of the managers using them. Listed here are some recommendations for managers who wish to improve their appraising of employees.

- Know precisely what you want to achieve (and what company policy says you should achieve) with your performance reviews, such as determining raises, evaluation, criticism, training, or morale-building.

- Don't wait until the review itself to let your staff know what you expect. Let them know early on exactly what the job requires, what specific goals, standards, and deadlines you expect them to meet and how you plan to evaluate and reward their performance.

- Keep a record of subordinates' performance so that you can cite specific examples to back up any criticisms or comments.

- Listen. Numerous surveys of employee attitudes reveal the feeling that "management doesn't care what we think." The review is your chance to get valuable feedback from your own subordinates about their jobs or company policy.

- Ask fact-finding questions to get employees to recall instances in which they performed well or poorly. See if they have a realistic estimate of their abilities.

- Go over your written evaluation with each employee. Find out if they feel your ratings are fair. They don't have to agree with you completely, but strong disagreements will lessen their motivation to improve.

- Focus steadily on each individual's performance. Show that you care about that person's career. Otherwise it looks like you're just going through the motions, and employees will get the message that the review, and perhaps their performance, doesn't really matter.

- When critiquing an employee's performance, do some stroking: Reinforce the good habits with praise.

- Be specific and constructive in your criticism. Don't just tell employees they're not "aggressive enough." Point out how they can improve, with specific examples.

- Critique the behavior, not the employee. Keep the discussion on a professional level.

- Be fair, but don't be afraid to give honest criticism when necessary. Most employees don't want a meaningless pat on the back. They want to know where they stand and how they can improve.

- Don't play the role of therapist. If personal problems are affecting an employee's performance, be supportive, but be careful about getting involved. Suggest outside professional help if necessary.

- Explain how the employee's performance in meeting goals contributes to department or corporate objectives. In this way, the review can help build morale and loyalty.

- Don't wait till the next performance review to follow up. Use informal progress reports or mini-reviews to help spot problems before they become serious.

- Use the occasion to get an informal review of your own performance. Encourage your staff to tell you about any of your habits that make their work difficult or to suggest changes you could make that would help them do their jobs better.

Source: Berkeley Rice, "Performance Review: The Job Nobody Likes," *Psychology Today*, November 1985, p. 35.

**Diagnosing the Poor Performer**   Knowing that a person is performing poorly is vastly different from knowing *why* a person is performing poorly. Poor performance can be highlighted by performance-appraisal ratings, behavior (missed deadlines, tardiness, absenteeism, poor work habits, or insubordination), or other such violations of performance expectations. Once poor performance has been observed, then the manager must determine its cause in order to find the appropriate remedy.

The most common way managers assign blame for poor performance is based on the attribution process. Recall that, in Chapter 3, we identified three principles people use to attribute the causes of behavior to internal or external causes: distinctiveness, consistency, and consensus. Internal causes are associated with the individual performer—that person's skills, abilities, effort, and personality. External causes are associated with the environment—task difficulty, resource availability, interpersonal demands, and information availability.[37] For example, if an employee is consistently absent from work, the employer needs to determine whether the absences are due to factors the employee can or cannot control. The "Focus on: Flextime" describes a solution to employee absenteeism arising from family demands.

In addition to the three principles for determining whether poor performance can be attributed to the individual or the environment, the fundamental attribution error will also influence the determination of blame. Supervisors are likely to believe that poor performance is caused by internal (or personal) failings of the subordinate. Alternatively, subordinates are likely to attribute their failure to external (or environmental) factors out of their control. Thus, because of their different perspectives, supervisors and employees rarely agree on the cause of poor performance.

Because of these differing perceptions, employees who are confronted with their poor performance are likely to respond in one or more of the following ways:[38]

- *Deny it.* Often, the initial reaction is denial. The facts concerning the poor performance are disputed or reinterpreted in a more favorable light, or employees may say they were working towards goals other than the unmet goals of the supervisor. This is a natural response to criticism and, if successful, relieves employees of the responsibility for correcting or improving their performance.
- *Justify it.* If poor performance cannot be denied, then the next step is to justify or rationalize it. Employees may diminish the

[37]G. P. Latham, L. L. Cummings, and T. R. Mitchell, "Behavioral Strategies to Improve Productivity," *Organizational Dynamics* (Winter 1981): 5–23.
[38]Ibid.

FOCUS ON:

Flextime

**Turning Absence into Presence**
Flextime, a catchall term for various ways of giving employees a say in scheduling their work hours, was initially developed in Germany in 1967 to cut down on rush-hour congestion. It soon became apparent, however, that the concept offered other potential benefits, including increased employee satisfaction and less job turnover. Research in the United States suggested that the ability to match working hours to employee needs also helped reduce absenteeism.

Flextime seems to be particularly helpful to married women and mothers, whose family responsibilities traditionally result in high absenteeism. It can also reduce absenteeism in single-parent and dual-career families. Recent research suggests that while women in these two situations had higher absenteeism rates than men when both worked fixed schedules, the rates were about the same when flextime schedules were used. This suggests that flextime makes it easier for caretakers to meet the needs of their families without taking time off. This flexibility may also help dual-career families cope with family demands.

Flextime schedules differ across organizations. Typical components of such schedules include core hours during which all employees must work; a "flexband," or range of times around these starting hours from which employees may select starting times, stopping times, and lunchtimes; and finally, a specified period of time during which employees must adhere to the chosen schedule.

Simply selecting a work schedule may also have positive effects. Choosing a schedule to adhere to over an extended period of time can generate high levels of commitment and may emphasize to employees that the organization is concerned about both attendance and the interests of employees.

Source: Gary Johns, "The Great Escape," *Psychology Today*, October 1987, p. 32.

significance of their poor performance by comparing their record to those of carefully selected others—others who are performing at similar or lower levels.

■ *Allocate it.* If strategic comparisons are impossible or unbelievable, then employees may attempt to allocate the responsibility for poor performance to an external agent such as the government, a competitor, the unusual difficulty of the task, bad luck, or other uncontrollable events. Similar in many respects to denial, allocating poor performance to external causes suggests that employees themselves are not responsible. Thus, they should not be blamed or held accountable.

These coping strategies are most likely to be used when any of the following three conditions exists:

1. When performance expectations and standards are ambiguous.
2. When public admission of poor performance is punished.

3. When commitments to performance goals are avoided to maintain organizational flexibility and responsiveness to change.

In determining how to handle poor performance, managers must not only be able to identify it, they must also be able to specify what good performance is and explain how the employee can attain it. In concert with the employee, the manager must develop strategies for better performance.

**Strategies to Improve Performance**   Many of the strategies needed to transform poor performers into good performers have been described in previous sections of this chapter: appropriately designed incentive systems, goal-setting activities, and effective performance appraisal systems. While these mechanisms are useful to all employees, they are uniquely important to the poorly performing employee.

In dealing with poor performance, managers should concentrate on the following four steps.[39] (See Figure 13–10.) First, managers should convey to employees the crucial aspects of performing their assigned tasks. In defining effective performance, managers may elucidate what behaviors are expected. Such behaviors are easily identified if the performance appraisal system uses a behaviorally anchored rating scale. Another way in which examples of good and poor performance can be distinguished for employees is through the use of the critical incidence or the diary that managers have been keeping on each employee.

Second, it is important for managers to be able to discern good performance when they observe it. Rarely are managers trained in how to observe, record, and evaluate behavior objectively. Instead, their evaluations may be tainted by various misperceptions such as the fundamental attribution error, stereotyping, halo effects, the similar-to-me bias, and contrast effects. While the first three biases have been described in Chapter 3, the latter two are particularly salient in evaluating performance. The **similar-to-me bias** reflects the tendency of evaluators to rate more positively those individuals whose background and experience are similar to their own. The contrast effect, a perceptual bias introduced in Chapter 3, makes managers tend to measure an employee's performance against the performance levels of other employees rather than against performance standards. Thus, an individual who is performing adequately in a poorly performing department is likely to be rated more highly than an equal performer in a high-performing department.

Third, specific, challenging performance goals need to be set and monitored and feedback routinely made available to the employee. Finally, there should be a direct and obvious relationship between attaining goals and receiving organizationally controlled rewards. To

[39]Ibid.

**FIGURE 13–10**    Steps for Improving Poor Performance

These steps for transforming poor performers into good performers are linked to the company's basic strategies for maintaining performance: incentive systems, goal setting, and performance appraisal.

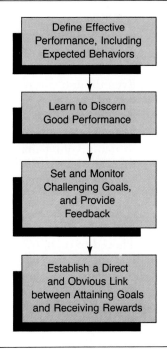

Define Effective
Performance, Including
Expected Behaviors

↓

Learn to Discern
Good Performance

↓

Set and Monitor
Challenging Goals,
and Provide
Feedback

↓

Establish a Direct
and Obvious Link
between Attaining Goals
and Receiving Rewards

reinforce the importance of goals and their acceptance by employees, it is important that some measurable response occur when goals are met. Thus, the incentive system of the organization must be consistent with the goals and objectives of that organization.

These are not easy tasks to accomplish in most organizations. Given the cost of replacing poorly performing employees or, even worse, the cost to the organization of lost productivity[40] if the employee remains, these factors are well worth considering and implementing in organizations.

**DOWNSIZING THE ORGANIZATION: HANDLING THE SURVIVORS**

A common response of troubled companies in the United States has been to reduce their work force. Because of the rapidly changing geography of organizations, one of the newer trends in American business is for successful companies to reduce the number of managerial and professional jobs, creating a survivor mentality among those who remain. Downsizing is only one of the stresses that employees must face;

---

[40]As we suggested in Chapter 11, each employee is a potential half-million-dollar investment or liability for the organization.

the recent merger and acquisition frenzy has also resulted in another group of "survivors."

Whether the organizational downsizing occurs because of an attempt to save a troubled organization or to make a profitable organization more competitive or in response to a merger, a major concern about the "new" organization is its ability to maintain the productivity of its survivors. Even though survivors are, in some sense, the winners of organizational downsizing, they often experience a sense of loss of control. It is demoralizing for survivors to discover that they are working for managers who have been demoted three grades. At Exxon, for example, so many young managers have been demoted that there is a layer of them in their early forties: a group that aspiring "up-and-comers" will never be able to penetrate. Those who get demoted may not take a salary cut, but they don't expect any salary increases for a long, long time.[41]

What can management do to maintain productivity of survivors? As survivors, they are likely to have two overriding concerns: "Why was I allowed to remain?" and "Will I be the next to go?" While management may never be able to answer the first question satisfactorily for the survivors, it can respond to the job-security issue. Of the four factors often identified as concerns by survivors, job security and related items such as pay and benefit issues and performance feedback ("How well am I doing?") are often uppermost in their minds.[42]

The best way for management to respond to the survivors' security needs is to manage the downsizing effectively. Recent research has suggested ways in which managers can reduce the loyalty loss, maintain morale, and reduce the flow of voluntary terminations. Managers need to do four things when managing the downsizing process:

1. *Remain committed to one's employees and serve as a companion.* Effective managers will attempt to protect their employees, serve as sounding boards, and create stability in the work unit.
2. *Be honest.* Managers should maintain an honest relationship with their employees, providing them with accurate information and giving them as much detail about future events as possible. Then the survivors are more likely to accept their statements about job security.
3. *Show understanding for employee concerns.* The "Why me?" question often plaguing survivors can be somewhat addressed in frank discussions with a manager. If done successfully, the manager-employee relationship will be strengthened and the

---

[41]B. Nassbaur et al., "The End of Corporate Culture," *Business Week*, August 4, 1986, 42–49.

[42]D. M. Schweiger, J. M. Ivancevich, and F. R. Power, "Executive Actions for Managing Human Resources Before and After Acquisition," *Academy of Management EXECUTIVE* 1 (1987): 127–138.

employee may emerge with an increased understanding of the process as well as an increased sense of self-worth.

4. *Handle terminations and outplacement with dignity.* How people are let go has a major impact on those who remain. It signals to the survivors how they might be handled in the future. Providing outplacement services, job leads, and workshops on interviewing skills conveys to both groups that the company does not consider those let go as worthless.

If handled appropriately, organizational downsizing can be a boon to certain survivors. Some employees may find themselves receiving new responsibilities and discovering new opportunities. Developing a lean organization may increase the entrepreneurial spirit of the survivors, opening new vistas for the company.

## SUMMARY

This chapter examined how managers and other organizational decision makers can maintain employee performance. The first component of this process is the organization's incentive system. Composed of both economic and noneconomic elements, the incentive system is the most visible way in which an organization can influence employee behavior. Wages, salaries, and nonrecurring economic benefits can influence an employee's behavior if the employee is capable of high performance, believes it is beneficial, sees the relationship between high performance and monetary rewards, values economic rewards, and is involved in tasks where performance can be measured. The incentive structure also must be consistent with the nature of the work performed (individual- or group-based). Examples of individual-based incentive structures are piece-rate or standard-hour systems. Group-based incentive structures include the Scanlon plan and employee stock-ownership plans.

Employee benefits are the indirect economic rewards that employees receive. One of the more recent innovations in the benefits area has been the development of cafeteria benefit plans. In such plans, the employees are allowed to customize their benefits package within a prescribed dollar amount per employee. Noneconomic benefits include the inherent interest of the job, the quality of the work life, the status associated with belonging to an organization, and the amount of power and autonomy associated with a position.

Unfortunately, having a well-developed incentive system is not sufficient to ensure high levels of employee performance. In addition, employees need performance goals. Goals specify the direction for action and the quantity of work to be accomplished. For goals to be effective, they must (1) specify the task to be accomplished, (2) indicate how performance will be measured, (3) specify the level of performance to be achieved, (4) specify a deadline for performance, (5) be accepted by the employee, and (6) set priorities for performance and coordination.

For an employee to reach a goal, feedback about performance is crucial. Providing employees with feedback is one of the purposes of a performance appraisal system. These systems have three major functions: providing feedback, distributing rewards, and counseling employees. Unfortunately, these three functions are often in conflict with each other. If managers use the same performance-appraisal interview to accomplish all three objectives, employees are likely to experience conflict in their responses. Should they present their accomplishments in the best possible light, or should they identify various problems and weaknesses encountered over the past year? In addition, the anxiety created by the evaluation may be so great that employees are unable to comprehend or even *hear* the information being provided.

To improve the organization's performance appraisal system, evaluations should be (1) based on observable behavior, (2) conducted by raters who have the opportunity to observe the ratee, (3) conducted several times a year, and (4) con-

ducted with instruments that measure behavior, not traits.

Even if all these components are in place, the manager is still likely to face two major performance-related problems: dealing with the poor performer and dealing with the survivors of organizational downsizing. With the poor performer, the manager must first determine the cause of the employee's poor performance. Whether to attribute the cause of poor performance to personal (internal) or situational (external) factors depends upon the distinctiveness, consensus, and consistency of the employee's behavior.

When an organization undergoes downsizing, there is considerable risk to the productivity of those who survive. To keep the motivation and morale of the survivors high, the organization needs to be proactive in managing this process. It must remain committed to its employees, serve as a sounding board, and convey information about future events. Finally, an organization must handle the termination and outplacement of other employees with dignity. This is particularly reassuring to employees who are expecting to be the next to leave.

KEY TERMS

**Behaviorally anchored rating scale (BARS)**   Employee evaluation format in which the organization analyzes a particular job to determine what types of behavior reflect varying degrees of performance, using actual descriptions of behavior to define the ratings.

**Comparable worth discrimination**   Discrimination in which men are paid more than women for jobs that are substantially equal in terms of skill, ability, and effort required.

**Compensation system**   A major way an organization conveys to its employees what it wants done and how they should behave, consisting of wages or salaries, benefits, nonrecurring financial rewards, and noneconomic rewards.

**Critical incidence file** A memory aid containing examples of an employee's behavior to help managers prepare for performance appraisals.

**Employee Stock Ownership Plan (ESOP)** Group-based incentive plan in which an organization contributes to a trust fund to buy stock, which is allocated to employees based on seniority.

**Goal** A specific direction for action and a specific quantity of work to be accomplished.

**Goal commitment** Extension of effort, over time, toward the accomplishment of a goal and an unwillingness to give up or lower the goal.

**Piece-rate plan** Incentive plan in which employees are paid a given rate for each unit produced.

**Similar-to-me bias** Rating bias in which raters tend to rate more positively those individuals whose background and experience are similar to their own.

**Standard hour rate** Payment rate per hour based on the amount of time, determined by industrial engineering standards, that it should take to produce each unit.

**Trait-rating scale** Employee evaluation format that asks the rater to evaluate the ratee on such factors as dependability, cooperation, leadership, obedience, and loyalty.

DISCUSSION QUESTIONS

1. Which of the major systems for maintaining performance is likely to be most effective among professional employees? Among blue-collar employees? Among white-collar employees? Why?

2. What factors, besides overt and intentional discrimination, might lead to the large difference in wages between the average male and female worker?

3. In early 1989, controversy arose over what was called the "mommy track" in organizations. What are the advantages and disadvantages to working women for organizations to have two career tracks, one for women with children and one for women without children?

4. How might a cafeteria benefits plan ensure that employers do not discriminate *in favor* of employees with families?

5. Even employees who are rated highly believe that performance appraisals are arbitrary and capricious. How might the typical organization respond to this charge? How might the review process be altered to increase its fairness?

6. In evaluating an employee's poor performance, what is likely to be the manager's first impression about the cause of the poor performance? What factors might lead the manager to adjust this evaluation?

7. How might a manager go about structuring an employ-

ee's workday to improve his or her performance?

8. What are the potential costs and benefits of downsizing an organization? Why is such an action becoming increasingly popular in U.S. businesses? What are the long-term implications of such a strategy?

**IF YOU WANT TO KNOW MORE**

Maintaining employee performance is probably one of the most written-about topics in organizational behavior. Despite the sheer magnitude of the writings, a number of books and articles stand out. In the area of compensation systems, the interested reader might consider Frederick Hill's *Compensation Decision Making,* published in 1987 by Dryden Press. Marc Wallace and Charles Fay have also written an interesting (and shorter) book on compensation systems, *Compensation Theory and Practice,* which was published in 1983 by Kent Publishing Company. Finally, David Balkin and Luis Gomez-Mejia have written a book that addresses many of the issues surrounding organizational compensation systems. Entitled *New Perspectives on Compensation,* it was published by Prentice-Hall in 1987. Readers interested in the financial consequences of poor performance might refer to Wayne Cascio's 1982 book, *Costing Human Resources: The Financial Impact of Behavior in Organizations,* published by Kent Publishing Company.

Performance appraisal is the subject of a large number of books. For a concise view of the current state of the art, the reader is directed towards the following two books: John Bernardin and Richard Beatty's 1984 *Performance Appraisal: Assessing Human Behavior at*

*Work,* published by Kent and Stephen Carroll; and Craig Schneier's *Performance Appraisal and Review Systems,* published in 1982 by Scott, Foresman. For a more detailed review of performance appraisal systems, see Frank Landy and James Farr's *The Measurement of Work Performance,* published in 1983 by Academic Press.

While reams have been published on goal setting, one of the more readable manuscripts is Edwin Locke and Gary Latham's *Goal Setting: A Motivational Technique That Works,* a 1984 book published by Prentice-Hall. An interesting review of the research on goal setting up through 1980 can be found in E. A. Locke et al.'s "Goal Setting and Task Performance," in *Psychological Bulletin* 90 (1981): 125–152. The most recent review of the effects of goal setting can be found in A. J. Mento, R. P. Steel, and R. J. Karren's "A Meta-Analytic Study of the Effects of Goal Setting on Task Performance," in *Organizational Behavior and Human Decision Processes* 39 (1987): 52–83.

Finally, to understand more about how to handle the poorly performing employee, the interested reader should consult a review article by T. R. Mitchell, S. G. Green, and R. E. Wood, entitled "An Attributional Model of Leadership and the Poor Performing

Employee." It may be found in *Research in Organizational Behavior,* vol. 3, eds. B. Staw and L. Cummings (Greenwich, Conn.: JAI Press, 1981): 197– 234, as well as in pp. 5–23 of the 1981 *Organizational Dynamics* publication entitled "Behavioral Strategies for Enhancing Productivity."

ON YOUR
OWN

**Developing a Performance Appraisal System for Faculty**    Think about your instructor for this course. How would you go about setting up a performance appraisal system to evaluate faculty at your university or college? First, consider what you as a student think are the important dimensions of an instructor's behavior. Next, consider what other faculty (your instructor's peers) might identify as important dimensions of behavior. What about the dean of the business school or the president of the university or college? List the major dimensions of behavior that are important to each:

| Students | Other Faculty | Dean | President |
|----------|---------------|------|-----------|
| _____ | _____ | _____ | _____ |
| _____ | _____ | _____ | _____ |
| _____ | _____ | _____ | _____ |
| _____ | _____ | _____ | _____ |
| _____ | _____ | _____ | _____ |
| _____ | _____ | _____ | _____ |
| _____ | _____ | _____ | _____ |
| _____ | _____ | _____ | _____ |

How are each of these dimensions valued by these four different constituencies? What would be good behavioral indicators of each? How would you choose which dimensions to use in the evaluation of your instructor?

CLOSING CASE
FOR CHAPTER 13

### THE MANAGER'S MEMO

FROM: P. Wilcox, President

TO:     O. Hansen, Vice President, Human Resources Management

RE:     Dissatisfied Former Employees

As you know, within the last six months, three of our most capable divisional vice presidents have left the company to take positions with our major competitor. Clearly, pay was not the problem, as they received a level of salary plus bonuses that was until then unprecedented in the industry.

From recent conversations with them and some of the remaining executive team, all I have been able to learn is that there is some dissatisfaction with our performance appraisal system. One of the departing executives made some comment about there being no incentive to be innovative.

I really don't understand these remarks. We spent a great deal of time trying to develop a performance rating scale that is fair and rewards results, not personality. I cannot think of a better system than our method of assigning points for each product that exceeds expected performance, deducting points for failed ideas, and paying a generous bonus based on accumulated points. The system admittedly penalizes executives for failures, but that encourages them to think carefully before launching into risky ventures. Furthermore, one of the departing executives never had a failing idea. Clearly, the performance-rating system was very good to them.

I would appreciate your letting me know what you learned from your exit interviews with these former executives. If the performance appraisal system really is the reason they left, how can we modify it to avoid losing our key people in the future?

CASE DISCUSSION
QUESTIONS

Assume you are the vice president of the human resources management division, and respond to the president's memo. Assume that the executives who left were in fact dissatisfied with the performance appraisal system. From the information given in the president's memo, what types of compensation was the company providing generously, and what types were lacking? How can the company modify its performance appraisal system to provide the missing rewards?

EXERCISE FOR
PART 4:
The Hovey and
Beard Company

The Hovey and Beard Company manufactured a variety of wooden toys including animals, pull toys, and the like. The toys were manufactured by a transformation process that began in the wood room. There, toys were cut, sanded, and partially assembled. Then the toys were dipped into shellac and sent to the painting room.

In years past, the painting had been done by hand, with each employee working with a given toy until its painting was completed. The toys were predominately two colors, although a few required more than two colors. Now, and in response to increased demand for the toys, the painting operation was changed so that the painters sat in a line by an endless chain of hooks. These hooks moved continuously in front of the painters and passed into a long horizontal oven. Each painter sat in a booth designed to carry away fumes and to backstop excess paint. The painters would take a toy from a nearby tray, position it in a jig inside the painting cubicle, spray on the color according to a pattern, and then hang the toy on a passing hook. The rate at which the hooks moved was calculated by the engineers so that each painter, when fully trained, could hang a painted toy on each hook before it passed beyond reach.

The painters were paid on a group bonus plan. Since the operation was new to them, they received a learning bonus that decreased by regular amounts each month. The learning bonus was scheduled to vanish in six months, by which time it was expected that they would be on their own—that is, able to meet the production standard and to earn a group bonus when they exceeded it.

**Questions**

1.   Assume that the training period for the new job set-up has just begun. What change do you predict in the level of output of the painters? Why?
2.   What other predictions regarding the behavior of these painters do you make based upon the situation described so far?

Source: Abridged and adapted from Chapter 10, "Group Dynamics and Intergroup Relations," by George Strauss and Alex Bavelas (under the title "The Hovey and Beard Case"), in *Money and Motivation*, ed. William F. Whyte (New York: Harper & Row, 1955). As appeared in John R. Schermerhorn, Jr., James G. Hunt, and Richard N. Osborn, *Managing Organizational Behavior* (New York: Wiley, 1982), pp. 64–66.

CASE FOR
PART 4:
Perfect Pizzeria

Perfect Pizzeria in Southville, in deep southern Illinois, is the second-largest franchise of the chain in the United States. The headquarters is located in Phoenix, Arizona. Although the business is prospering, it has employee and managerial problems.

Each operation has one manager, an assistant manager, and from two to five night managers. The managers of each pizzeria work under an area supervisor. There are no systematic criteria for being a manager or becoming a manager trainee. The franchise has no formalized training period for the manager. No college education is required. The managers for whom the case observer worked during a four-year period were relatively young (ages 24 to 27) and only one had completed college. They came from the ranks of night managers or assistant managers, or both. The night managers were chosen for their ability to perform the duties of the regular employees. The assistant managers worked a two-hour shift during the luncheon period five days a week to gain knowledge about bookkeeping and management. Those becoming managers remained at that level unless they expressed interest in investing in the business.

The employees were mostly college students, with a few high-school students performing the less challenging jobs. Since Perfect Pizzeria was located in an area with few job opportunities, it had a relatively easy task of filling its employee quotas. All the employees, with the exception of the manager, were employed part time. Consequently, they worked for less than the minimum wage.

The Perfect Pizzeria system is devised so that food and beverage costs and profits are set up according to a percentage. If the percentage of food unsold or damaged in any way is very low, the manager gets a bonus. If the percentage is high, the manager does not receive a bonus; rather, he or she receives only his or her normal salary.

There are many ways in which the percentage can fluctuate. Since the manager cannot be in the store 24 hours a day, some employees make up for their paychecks by helping themselves to the food. When a friend comes in to order a pizza, extra ingredients are put on the friend's pizza. Occasional nibbles by 18 to 20 employees throughout the day at the meal table also raise the percentage figure. An occasional bucket of sauce may be spilled or a pizza accidentally burned. Sometimes the wrong size of pizza may be made.

Source: Adapted from a case assignment prepared by Lee Neely for Professor James G. Hunt, Southern Illinois University at Carbondale. The case appears in John E. Dittrich and Robert A. Zawacki (eds.), *People and Organizations: Cases in Management and Organizational Behavior*, pp. 164–167. © Business Publications, Inc., 1985. All rights reserved. Used by permission.

In the event of an employee mistake or a burned pizza by the oven man, the expense is supposed to come from the individual. Because of peer pressure, the night manager seldom writes up a bill for the erring employee. Instead, the establishment takes the loss and the error goes unnoticed until the end of the month when the inventory is taken. That's when the manager finds out that the percentage is high and that there will be no bonus.

In the present instance, the manager took retaliatory measures. Previously, each employee was entitled to a free pizza, salad, and all the soft drinks he or she could drink for every 6 hours of work. The manager raised this figure from 6 to 12 hours of work. However, the employees had received these 6-hour benefits for a long time. Therefore, they simply took advantage of the situation whenever the manager or the assistant was not in the building. Though the night manager theoretically had complete control of the operation in the evenings, he did not command the respect that the manager or assistant manager did. This was because he received the same pay as the regular employees; he could not reprimand other employees; and he was basically the same age or sometimes even younger than the other employees.

Thus, apathy grew within the pizzeria. There seemed to be a further separation between the manager and his workers, who started out as a closely knit group. The manager made no attempt to alleviate the problem, because he felt it would iron itself out. Either the employees that were dissatisfied would quit or they would be content to put up with the new regulations. As it turned out, there was a rash of employee dismissals. The manager had no problem in filling the vacancies with new workers, but the loss of key personnel was costly to the business.

With the large turnover, the manager found he had to spend more time in the building, supervising and sometimes taking the place of inexperienced workers. This was in direct violation of the franchise regulation, which stated that a manager would act as a supervisor and at no time take part in the actual food preparation. Employees were not placed under strict supervision with the manager working alongside them. The operation no longer worked smoothly because of differences between the remaining experienced workers and the manager concerning the way in which a particular function should be performed.

Within a two-month period, the manager was again free to go back to his office and leave his subordinates in charge of the entire operation. During this two-month period, the percentage had returned to the previous low level and the manager received a bonus each month. The manager felt that his problems had been resolved and that conditions would remain the same, since the new personnel had been properly trained.

It didn't take long for the new employees to become influenced by the other employees. Immediately after the manager had returned to his supervisory role, the percentage began to rise. This time the manager took a bolder step. He cut out any benefits that the employees had—no free pizzas, salads, or drinks. With the job market at an even lower ebb than usual, most employees were forced to stay. The appointment of a new area supervisor made it impossible for the manager to "work behind the counter," since the supervisor was centrally located in Southville.

The manager tried still another approach to alleviate the rising percentage problem and maintain his bonus. He placed a notice on the bulletin board, stating that if the percentage remained at a high level, a lie-detector test would be given to all employees. All those found guilty of taking or purposefully wasting food or drinks would be immediately terminated. This did not have the desired effect on the employees, because they knew if they were all subjected to the test, all would be found guilty and the manager would have to dismiss all of them. This would leave him in a worse situation than ever.

Even before the following month's percentage was calculated, the manager knew it would be high. He had evidently received information from one of the night managers about the employees' feelings toward the notice. What he did not expect was that the percentage would reach an all-time high. That is the state of affairs at the present time.

### Questions for Discussion

1. How would you characterize the compensation plan for managers and student workers at Perfect Pizzeria? Would you want to work there?
2. What kinds of group dynamics are at work at Perfect Pizzeria during the case?
3. What do you think of the manager's attempts to solve the problems at Perfect Pizzeria? What would you suggest he do instead?

# The Larger Context
# of Organizational Behavior

CHAPTER

# The Environment

**The Myth of the Closed System**
Open Systems Theory
Resource Dependence
Knowledge of the Environment

**The Form of Environmental Forces**
Uncertainty
Instability
Complexity
Beneficence

**The Content of Environmental Forces**
Other Organizations
*Focus on Shareholder Activism: Stockholders with a Mission*
*International Focus on Other Organizations: Stateside Samurais*
The Regulatory Environment
*Focus on the Regulatory Environment: The Blind Scales of Regulatory Justice*
The Social Environment
Technology

**Managing Environmental Dependence**
Anticipation
Negotiation
*International Focus on Lobbying: Influence Peddling, European Style*
Control

**The Boundary-Spanning Role**

## Of Poison Pills, White Knights, And Pac-Men

Imagine that you are part of the top management team at a billion-dollar Fortune 500 corporation in America. One day, you hear that another large conglomerate is buying up your stock—quickly, and in large quantities. Your company has become a takeover target.

Is this a common scenario in American business? You bet it is. In the early 1980s, the number of major acquisitions in the United States grew at a rate roughly twice that of a decade earlier, reaching 2,000 per year by 1988. In the first two months of 1988 alone, more than $50 billion worth of deals were put together.

Why all the interest in takeovers? The answer is simply *resources*. The winners of a stock market takeover battle gain control of the acquired corporation's resources. And that can mean anything. Some acquisitions diversify holdings, so that a conglomerate doesn't have all its corporate eggs in one basket. Diversification is hardly the only reason for acquiring, however. If a company is

underproducing, the acquiring firm can bring in new management and with some hard work and a little luck turn a big loser into a big winner. If a company is undervalued, the acquiring firm can come in and sell off assets to turn a fast profit. In fact, one study of corporate acquisitions found that 75 percent of acquiring firms sold off their newly acquired assets within the first year.

For the top management team of a major corporation, these possibilities must be frightening. Takeovers invariably spell major changes—either in top management personnel or policies—and no one can feel safe. No wonder, then, that few top management teams go down without a fight. What are some of their battle plans?

**Poison Pills** If a company wants you for your assets, one way to become unattractive in a hurry is to lose them, or even use them. Selling off its particularly profitable divisions can make a potential takeover target considerably less attractive—especially if the cash then is used to fight the takeover by buying back stock. Alternatively, a potential takeover target can lose a lot of attractiveness in a hurry when it acquires another company itself. Or guarantees its top management team fatally large severance bonuses in the event of a takeover. These actions can quickly poison a takeover attempt—and relations with stockholders!

**White Knights**   Can't stand the idea of someone taking over your company without your consent? Maybe you can sell yourself *willingly* to someone else first. A "white knight" is a friendly acquirer— one who already has assured top management of a good deal (continued employment, for example, or a "golden parachute") after the acquisition. That way, top management gets to maintain an illusion of control.

**Pac-Man**   Perhaps the most daring defense to a takeover is a good offense—attempting to acquire the firm that is attempting to acquire you. In Bendix Corporation's wild attempt to acquire Martin Marietta, the hunted decided to fight back by becoming the hunter. When the smoke cleared, Bendix had acquired 67 percent of Martin Marietta, while Martin Marietta had acquired 50 percent of Bendix. It might have been a standoff except that Allied Industries then entered the fray—and bought out Bendix.

Who wins when a takeover succeeds? Invariably it's the stockholders of the acquired firm that come out on top. After all, a takeover target is most attractive when it's either underproducing or undervalued. Takeover battles can quickly remedy one—or even both—of these problems.

Source: M. C. Jensen, "Takeovers: Folklore and Science," *Harvard Business Review,* 62 (6), 1984, pp. 109–120; and J. H. Dobrzynski, "A New Strain of Merger Mania," *Business Week,* March 21, 1988, pp. 122–126.

## INTRODUCTION

Up to this point, this book has focused on the challenge of understanding and managing resources *within* an organization. We have explored how individuals behave, how groups interact, and how managers can use knowledge of individual behavior and group interaction to manage an organization's work force effectively. But the picture is not yet complete. The management of resources within an organization becomes important only if managers have acquired resources from the environment to manage. Managing the acquisition—and retention—of those resources presents another challenge altogether.

The purpose of this chapter is to paint a picture of the environment in which today's organizations must function. This picture will have two parts: first, the form and content of environmental demands on behavior in and of organizations; and second, some strategies that organizations use to manage those demands. Chapter 15 then will discuss one particularly important source of influence in today's business environment: technology. Chapter 16 follows with an examination of the ways in which organizations are designed both to adapt to the demands of the environment and to manage internal conflicts. Chapter 17 details the problems organizations face and the strategies they use when the larger context of organizational behavior requires change. Finally, Chapter 18 will close Part 5 with some thoughts about what new challenges the environment is likely to present organizations in the future.

## THE MYTH OF THE CLOSED SYSTEM

Large work organizations often are talked about as if they were **closed systems:** completely self-contained machines that function apart from and are unaffected by what goes on around them. Nothing could be further from the truth. Consider the convents and abbeys of the Middle Ages—the ultimate attempts to design completely self-contained social systems:

> Needs were kept to a minimum; foods were grown within; and many required utensils, tools, and clothing were made by the abbey's available labor. An attempt was made, consciously, to isolate the organizations as much as possible from the secular world outside. But, abbeys were peopled by people, usually of one sex, and humans are mortal. This meant that new members had to be recruited from the outside, which required the organization to maintain relations with sources of recruits. . . . Moreover, these religious organizations had land, and to maintain their land, it was necessary to ensure a position of social legitimacy and political acceptance so that other groups would not attempt to seize the land for themselves.[1]

The message here is that it is virtually impossible for any organization to be truly isolated or insulated from environmental influence or interaction. The abbeys and convents of the Middle Ages intended to be *totally* apart from the less-than-pure influence of society at large. Yet even these organizations were *required* for survival to interact with their environment.

Closer to home, many students probably think that the university classroom has the look of a closed system. The professor's management of classroom activities appears to be totally independent of the larger university system. In many universities the *right* of the professor to be independent in managing classroom activities appears to be protected under the doctrine of academic freedom—a doctrine that says that since the professor is an expert, no one has the right to tell the professor what to do in the classroom.

[1]J. Pfeffer and G. Salancik, *The External Control of Organizations* (New York: Harper & Row, 1978), 2–3.

**FIGURE 14–1**        Example of an Open System

The college classroom may seem to students to be a closed system where the instructor completely controls what goes on. In reality, classroom activities are open to influence from a host of environmental forces including social trends, accrediting agencies, curriculum committees, and even the kinds of jobs that are in demand.

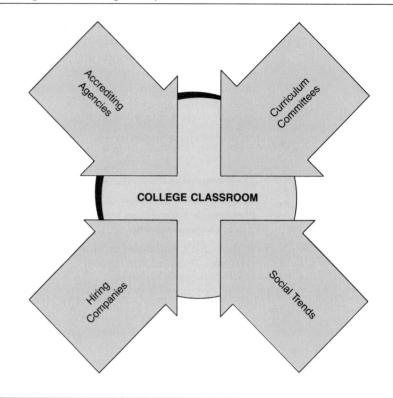

A professor's academic freedom in the classroom is an illusion, however. As depicted in Figure 14–1, the university classroom is hardly closed off from the influence of the external environment. Behaviors in the university classroom are influenced dramatically by what goes on in the larger university environment. If an instructor is good, word gets around, the number of students interested in taking the course goes up, and the instructor has a larger class to manage. Fluctuations in the number of students desiring to take the course also depend on factors over which the instructor has little or no control, such as the number of students that the university admits for study and whether the course is required or elective. Social trends may make some areas of study more popular than others. In the late 1980s, for example, international management and negotiation became hot topics for MBA courses.

What goes on in the classroom also will be influenced by the *quality* of the students (Are they highly intelligent? Are they well prepared for class?) and the *expectations* they bring to the course from other courses they have taken at the university. What happens in the classroom will further be influenced by developments in the field that need to be added to the curriculum. When the U.S. tax laws were dramatically changed in 1986, the contents of tax-accounting courses had to be changed as well. Similarly, developments in teaching materials—such as the availability of better texts, videos, or computer programs—also will change what happens in the classroom. Finally, what happens in the classroom often is *regulated* by college, university, or departmental curriculum committees, accrediting agencies (such as the American Association of Colleges and Schools of Business), and even licensing boards (such as the graduate college committees that decide who will be awarded Ph.D.s and therefore have the proper credentials for university instruction). Even the "customers" of the university—the companies that employ its graduates—indirectly influence what goes on in the classroom. If companies are interested in hiring business students with some understanding of international business issues, then international business issues are likely to turn up in business course curriculums.

The importance of environmental considerations in understanding behavior of and in organizations is illustrated in two concepts: open systems theory and resource dependence. Their importance to the relationship between organizations and their environments in turn depends upon a third concept: perception.

## OPEN SYSTEMS THEORY

Both the abbeys and convents of the Middle Ages and the university classrooms of the twentieth century demonstrate that organizations are open systems. An **open system** is an organization whose activities are inescapably influenced by its environment. Open systems share several defining characteristics, as shown in Figure 14–2.[2]

First, all open systems take inputs from the environment. For abbeys, convents, and university classrooms, the most salient input is people. For a manufacturing firm, the input might be raw materials such as iron ore, leather, or grain. However, for most organizations, inputs also include a production technology, the building that houses the organization, and even past learning.

Second, all open systems transform the inputs received. The key here is that the organization does something to the inputs that *adds value beyond any intrinsic value of the inputs themselves.* For instance, leather might be made into shoes, steel might be made into automobiles, paper into books, or a professor's time into learning by students. If nothing else, some organizations (such as distributors) simply *organize and store* inputs so that another organization can use them. Typically, the transformation process is *cyclical,* meaning that most organizations don't just take *any* inputs and transform them in *any* way. Organizations

[2]D. Katz and R. L. Kahn, *The Social Psychology of Organizations* (New York: Wiley & Sons, 1978), 23–30.

**FIGURE 14–2**          Defining Characteristics of Open Systems

The environment provides inputs such as raw materials and labor. The organization transforms these inputs to add value to them. Clients or customers in the environment then consume the outputs of this transformation process. The process is cyclical; in return for consuming the organization's outputs, the environment provides new inputs for the organization to restart the transformation cycle.

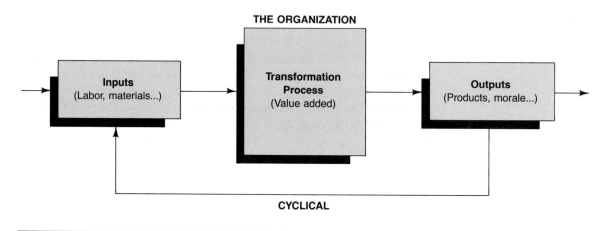

maintain some consistency over time; they repeat a transformation cycle over and over. The organization accepts roughly the same inputs and uses roughly the same transformation processes over and over again.

Third, the transformation process creates an *output*. An organization's outputs are its goals: shoes, automobiles, worker satisfaction, profit, perhaps a living wage for the organization's work force. The last two examples are particularly telling, since most organizations have as a goal continued survival over time. In fact, some organization theorists suggest that survival is *the* goal of organizations—that all organizations, from the first cave clans to today's General Motors, exist primarily to transform the environment into survival.[3] Any other outputs produced by an organization (such as automobiles or shoes) are simply indirect means of ensuring survival.

Finally, the idea that organizations exist as a means for survival has an important implication for the open systems model of organizations. The outputs of an organization must do more to enhance the organization's survival than to discourage it; in other words, the net value of the transformation process must be positive. If the net value of the transformation process is more destructive than creative (for instance, if

[3]Pfeffer and Salancik, *The External Control of Organizations*, 2–3.

byproducts of the transformation process such as pollutants or worker dissatisfaction are greater than the value of what is created), the organization eventually will lose the ability to take inputs from the environment and transform them.

**RESOURCE DEPENDENCE**

The open systems model of organizations exposes the susceptibility of organizations to environmental influence, and the origin of this influence is resource dependence. In Figure 14–2, the organization is only the black box, the transformation process. The organization is not a self-contained perpetual-motion machine. To do anything, it is dependent upon the environment for resources—inputs such as raw materials, labor, and energy. The organization is dependent upon the environment for a transformation technology. Great money-making inventions often are precisely transformation processes: new ways to turn raw materials and labor into something worth considerably more than the value of the inputs. However, rarely if ever does an organization develop a transformation process completely from scratch. Prior transformation systems, or their parts or components, and even education are resources available in the organization's environment that play a role in the development of innovative transformation technologies, and on which the organization therefore is dependent.

Finally, the organization is dependent upon the environment to accept or consume its outputs as value added. As we noted earlier, a key characteristic of open systems is that there must be a positive flow of "value added" for an organization to survive. In a traditional agricultural society, for instance, the farmers must make sure that they do not simply take and take and take from their farmland until it can give no more. Their transformation process must give something back to the land so that the land can continue to give. A modern work organization is dependent upon consumers' willingness to pay more for its outputs than the total cost of transforming those inputs. If not, over time the organization clearly loses its ability to continue taking inputs from the environment. The organization fails to survive.

The resource dependence described here between organizations and their environments is an example of a power relationship, discussed in Chapter 8. The environment has power over organizations because organizations depend upon the environment for resources. Organizations in turn may gain power over their environment by making the environment depend upon the organization's particular transformation skills for its survival.

**KNOWLEDGE OF THE ENVIRONMENT**

Open systems theory and resource dependence cast the organization in a fluid relationship with its environment. Organizations are not closed, self-contained entities. Organizations depend upon the environment for inputs to transform, for energy, labor, and ideas to carry out the transformation, and for consumers who desire their outputs.

A key issue here, however, is that the resource dependence between organizations and their environments is not deterministic. Many changes in an organization's environment are not directly and automatically reflected in commensurate changes in the organization. For example, if Congress passes a law about worker safety, one might suspect that an organization would change its behavior to conform to the law. However, managers in the organization might just ignore the law if they feel it will not be enforced. Or they might not even be aware of the change in the law—until one of their employees sues them for a violation!

This example highlights the fact that organizations and their environments usually are loosely coupled. What happens in the environment may or may not be reflected by immediate changes in the organization. **Loose coupling** has both advantages and disadvantages. To carry on an orderly transformation process, organizations must be somewhat insensitive to changes in the environment. An organization that reacts to *everything* that happens in its environment would spend more time reacting to the environment than it would transforming inputs into outputs. On the other hand, an organization that reacts too slowly (or not at all) to important changes in the environment can get left behind in the race to survive.

Perception is an important determinant of just how changes in the environment translate into reactions in the organization. In Chapter 3, we learned that people's perception of what goes on in their environment is determined by three processes: attention, construction, and interpretation. How individuals react to something that happens around them will depend on (1) whether they realize that it has occurred, (2) what they decide has occurred, and (3) what importance they attach to what has occurred.

These same perceptual processes of attention, construction, and interpretation are critical to the way organizations perceive and react to their environments as well. If the government passes a new law, an organization should change its behavior to conform to the law. However, whether an organization does in fact conform to a new law depends on (1) whether the organization is aware that the new law has been passed, (2) whether the organization's lawyers think the law applies to their organization, and finally (3) whether the organization thinks the government is serious about enforcing the law. In effect, unless the organization perceives a resource dependence (and therefore the need to change), changes in the environment are unlikely to cause changes in the organization.

The important point here is that while resource dependencies with the environment will determine the fate of an organization, it is the organization's *perceptions* of these resource dependencies that determine what actions it takes in response. Unfortunately, deciding which

Traditionally, organizational shareholders kept their hands off of the day-to-day management of major U.S. corporations, perhaps feeling it was not their place to interfere. In the early 1980s, that perception changed. Shareholders have begun to intervene in organizational decision making—for example, by taking legal action against corporate management teams that appear to be mismanaging shareholder equity.

environmental cues to attend to and how to interpret them are highly subjective processes. In fact, which environmental cues are attended to and processed by the organization's decision makers will depend upon such factors as what is readily available (is there a government report?) or highly salient (was there just an article in the *Wall Street Journal*?), not to mention personal agendas or biases of the environmental cue interpreters.

Examples of the role of perception of the environment in organizations' actions abound. One interpretation of "the day of infamy" (the December 7, 1941, decimation of the U.S. Pacific fleet in Pearl Harbor) was that decision makers in Washington, D.C., felt that Japan had neither the capability nor the gall to attack the United States in Hawaii. Obviously, this turned out to be a disastrously incorrect perception.

Closer to home, in the 1960s corporate boards and CEOs generally ignored stockholders because they viewed them as an impotent distraction. One CEO summarized the sentiment of the times with this comment about the annual stockholders' meeting: "I don't give a damn about the annual meeting. I'd like to see the thing abolished. The object of our meeting is to end as fast as possible without making a fool of the chairman."[4] In concert with this view, corporations rarely if ever responded to stockholder initiatives. No doubt this view of the stockholders' powerlessness was linked to the stockholders' own similar perception. By the mid-1980s, all that had changed, however. As stockholders have begun to realize the power they hold by virtue of the resources they control, they have forced that perception on corporate boards. The

[4]J. L. Hysom and W. J. Bolce, *Business and Its Environment* (St. Paul, Minn.: West, 1983), 167.

corporate boards in turn have responded by altering their behaviors to keep stockholders content and minimize dissident-sponsored revolutions.

## THE FORM OF ENVIRONMENTAL FORCES

The open systems and resource dependence orientations highlight the importance of its environment to an organization. In this section we will begin to paint a picture of the environment that faces work organizations. This picture includes four dimensions that determine environmental resource dependencies: uncertainty, instability, complexity, and beneficence. The following section then examines the particular sources of environmental resource dependencies.

## UNCERTAINTY

In Chapter 1, uncertainty was described as a defining characteristic of life in organizations. Uncertainty refers to a lack of information, an inability to know what exactly is going to happen or when. Much of the uncertainty that plagues organizational planning and action comes from the environment. Environmental uncertainty has three components.[5] First is the *lack of clear information* about the state of critical variables in the environment. If you were an automobile manufacturer, it would be critical for you to know the future price of gasoline so that you would know whether fuel mileage was going to be an important consideration for American consumers. If you were a university, it would be critical for you to know how social trends would change the popularity of certain subject areas in the foreseeable future. If you were a computer producer, it would be critical for you to know what new inventions were going to appear in the marketplace in the next few years. All of these pieces of information are critical to decision making, yet none of them can be known, only guessed at or estimated.

A second source of environmental uncertainty is in the *cause-and-effect relationships* between organizational actions and environmental responses. If banking customers want greater convenience, will putting in automated teller machines respond to that need? Even if organizational actions are followed by the resolution of identified problems, it can be difficult to know if the actions *caused* the problems to be solved. If a bank puts in automated teller machines and customer satisfaction increases, what does that mean? Did the new automated teller machines increase customer satisfaction, or did it increase for other reasons? These causal relationships often cannot be known ahead of time, and sometimes not even afterwards.

Finally, uncertainty also arises because of the *length of feedback cycles* in the response of the environment to organizational planning and action. It may take years for an organization to understand the effectiveness of

---

[5]P. R. Lawrence and J. W. Lorsch, *Organization and Environment* (Homewood, Ill.: Richard Irwin, 1964).

its work-force recruiting strategy. By the time it finds out whether a particular approach works or not, one or even two more recruiting seasons may have passed, thereby determining the fate of the organization's short-term performance.

In general, uncertainty means that some amount of what an organization does will be wrong because top management is always guessing. An uncertain environment is one in which "betting the ranch" on one decision is unwise. Organizations functioning in uncertain environments must distribute the risk inherent in uncertain plans and decisions (for example, by redundancy or diversification) in the hope of winning on the average.

INSTABILITY

**Instability** reflects the rate of change in an organization's environment. The rate of change in the environment determines the necessity for regular evaluation of environmental cues and reaction by the organization. In the electronics industry, for example, product life cycles are extremely short because the advance of technological innovation and invention is so rapid. This means that customers' needs and desires are changing constantly, and an organization in this environment must be willing and able to adapt to these rapidly changing needs to survive. In a rapidly changing environment, an organization must remain flexible and adaptive—it must be prepared to change quickly in response to changes in the environment.

COMPLEXITY

Complexity refers to the number of environmental cues that are critical to an organization's functioning and therefore must be monitored. A complex environment is one in which there is a lot going on that is important to the functioning of the organization. The U.S. Congress, for example, exists in a very complex environment. Many different interest groups and cause-and-effect relationships must be considered in every decision that is made. If Congress wants to fund a highway project in Georgia, how will environmental protectionists react? How will the residents of other states who wanted highway projects react? How will other interest groups who wanted the money for other projects react? All these concerns must be weighed when Congress makes its decision. Presumably the managers of the corner ice cream store face a less complex environment, though it may not seem so to them!

There are two costs to operating in a complex environment. First, more inputs require more information collection and evaluation if planning and decision making are to be of high quality. (Alternatively, a decision maker in a highly complex environment simply can choose to ignore some of the inputs, as long as the decision maker is willing to accept outcomes that are on the average lower in quality.) Second, environmental complexity generally means that plans and decisions are more constrained by resource dependencies. For example, if each environmental factor that a manager considers eliminates one possible course of action, the end result may be a very small range of alternatives. This could render decision making easy—after all, how difficult is it to choose if there is *only one* feasible alternative? But it could also make organizational decisions harder, for instance when the only feasible alternative from the viewpoint of environmental resource dependencies turns out not to be a practical solution to the problem.

**BENEFICENCE**

The final dimension of environmental resource dependencies is beneficence. **Beneficence** refers to the generosity, leniency, and helpfulness of the environment when it comes to resources. To grasp the importance of this concept, consider for a moment the fictional tale of two organizations, both located in a small southwestern town. One of the organizations is the city's only junior high school; the other the city's only pool hall. When both organizations run into financial difficulties, what is the environment's reaction? In this tale, the answer is that city tax dollars ride to the financial rescue of the junior high school while the pool hall is allowed to sink slowly into the sunset. While this might not be the outcome in every small southwestern city, the fact is that some organizations are likely to be helped by their environment in times of trouble, and some are likely to be attacked. (In this tale, for instance, the financial difficulties of the pool hall no doubt stemmed in part from the picketers outside its door threatening to take pictures of patrons—a clear example of a hostile environment.)

Why would an environment be beneficent (helpful) to some organizations and not others? There are two possibilities. First, the stated *goals or values* of an organization may be consistent with those of important resource holders in the environment. The town leadership, for instance, may feel it is important to have a junior high school in town to attract new residents with children. The presence of the junior high school thus is important for symbolic reasons and therefore is supported by its environment. Significantly, support provided to an organization because of its symbolic value may be enough to ensure the organization's survival but *not* its quality—in this case, the quality of education provided. (Some of the town leaders might be interested in retaining the pool hall as well, but unwilling to take a public stand to that effect.)

Environments also may be helpful to an organization if the transformation process it performs is *unique and highly desirable*. In 1987, the U.S. government guaranteed Maxime Faget, a struggling space-technology entrepreneur, $700 million in leases for his privately funded space station. These guarantees were, at the time, incentive enough for the entrepreneur to continue development of his project. Why did the federal government offer this support? The government's $30 billion funding of its own development efforts in this arena had begun to meet

The beneficence of a business environment can vary tremendously. In a highly competitive business environment, clients may be unforgiving and one serious mistake may put a company out of business. On the other hand, if your company is the sole supplier of a valued service, the environment may cater to your every need. Maxime Faget, as the only private party interested in building an industrial space platform, has found his environment very beneficent—to the tune of a $700 million federal subsidy for his project.

with strong public opposition and could not be continued. Nevertheless, many in power felt that somewhere, somehow, U.S. development efforts needed to continue. Otherwise, the United States would be conceding the development of space to Soviet bloc countries. Supporting a private effort seemed to be a low-cost compromise, and Faget's private effort was the only show in town. The environment came to his rescue because his organization provided a transformation process—low-cost, private-sector space station technology development—that was seen in some circles as both essential and unique.[6] Unlike symbolic support, the amount of environmental support an organization receives because of the transformational service it provides will depend on the effectiveness of the service.

## THE CONTENT OF ENVIRONMENTAL FORCES

The dimensions we have been discussing—uncertainty, instability, complexity, and beneficence—provide us with an understanding of how the forces in an organization's environment vary. But what are these forces? Where do they come from? As shown in Figure 14–3, the next

---

[6]E. Clark and T. Smart, "A Space Station That's Losing Its Boosters," *Business Week*, March 7, 1988, 116–118.

**FIGURE 14–3**               Sources of External Dependence

---

**Other Organizations**

Suppliers: organizations that provide inputs, including capital, raw materials, and labor.

Consumers: organizations that purchase the organization's outputs.

Competitors: other organizations that produce the same outputs.

**The Regulatory Environment**

Laws and court rulings that legislate the behavior of organizations, what the outputs look like, and how the transformation process creates those outputs.

**The Social Environment**

Social adjustment: societal trends to which the organization must adjust.

Social responsibility: the need to make sure corporate actions measure up to society's moral and ethical standards.

**Technology**

Changes in all the different ways available for an organization to transform its inputs into outputs.

---

section of this chapter examines four important sources of external dependence for organizations: other organizations, the regulatory environment, the social environment, and technology.

OTHER
ORGANIZATIONS

Perhaps the most prominent features of any organization's environment are other organizations. Our definition of organizations as open systems provides a framework for understanding what kinds of other organizations are in an organization's environment. An open system takes inputs from the environment, transforms them into outputs, and then provides the outputs to the environment. This three-stage definition of an open system suggests three types of other organizations, corresponding to the three stages of input, output, and transformation: suppliers, consumers, and competitors.

**Suppliers**  Suppliers provide an open system its inputs, such as raw materials. A cotton-garment manufacturer needs to have a source of cotton—perhaps a cotton growers' association or a cotton-cloth weaving company. It is important to realize, however, that an organization's inputs include far more than just its raw materials. Labor and capital also are critical inputs to any organization. Labor (the organization's work force) provides the energy to transform the organization's inputs into outputs. In a typical manufacturing organization, capital is needed to purchase the inputs from the supplier prior to transforming them. The garment manufacturer must buy raw cotton from the cotton growers or buy cotton cloth from cotton weavers. In a typical service organization, on the other hand, raw materials are not purchased at all. Instead, raw materials come from the eventual consumer of the outputs, the customer. A carpet-cleaning organization, for example, doesn't *buy* dirty carpets to clean. The service consumer provides the input (the dirty carpets) to the service organization. The service organization then uses labor and a transformation process (in this case, a carpet-cleaning machine) to transform the dirty carpets into clean ones. Manufacturing and service organizations thus differ in their relationships with the environment as a source of inputs.

Manufacturing and service organizations do not differ, however, in their need for capital, labor, and technology. Virtually all organizations need capital to get started. Capital (money) is needed to purchase the transformation technology and to hire the labor. Usually capital also is needed to make contact with consumers through marketing efforts. Sometimes the need for capital is not large. A computer-software-development organization, for example, may start out with one or two programmers working in their garages in their spare time. They may need only enough money at first so that they don't have to work evenings at other jobs to pay the rent and buy groceries. However, even an organization this small still needs paper and pencils to write computer codes and floppy disks to get its output to potential consumers.

As an organization gets larger, its need for capital grows as well. A large organization needs a building, furniture, telephones, typewriters, and so on, not to mention enough money to pay salaries until money starts coming in from consumers. Large organizations that need lots of capital will have to get it from the environment. Banks often provide business loans to organizations to get them started, or to help them develop beyond the scope of their immediate cash resources.

An organization also can get capital from the environment by selling itself, for example, by selling shares in the company or publicly issuing stock. When an organization sells shares or issues stock, it is selling its potential to make money through the value added by its transformation process. The person or company who buys the stock, the shareholder, provides the organization capital in exchange for ownership of a piece of the company. Thus, if a garment manufacturer owns sewing machines, theoretically a shareholder owns part of each of the company's sewing machines. Of course, the garment manufacturer's shareholders are not interested in sewing machines, but in the possibility of receiving more capital later if the organization is successful.

Shareholders are not necessarily inactive observers of an organization's performance. Shareholders and organizations are mutually dependent; organizations are dependent upon their shareholder for financial support, and shareholders depend on the organization to take good care of their capital. As long as an organization provides its shareholders a good return on their investment (through stock dividend payouts or stock-price appreciation), shareholders are likely to leave well enough alone.

But what happens when things are not going well? As part owners of an organization's assets, shareholders have the right to put in their two cents' worth about how the company should be run. If shareholders think an organization's top management is doing poorly, they can pressure the board of directors—often through election of board officers—to institute major changes. Shareholder activism can be reflected in corporate policy as well. Executive compensation in organizations with powerful and active shareholders tends to be much more performance based.[7] Responsiveness to shareholders can be a mixed blessing, however. If shareholder interests run in the direction of short-term financial gain, top management may find itself selling out the future in order to look good in the present.[8]

Top management defenses against hostile takeovers have been known to galvanize shareholders into action. If a takeover effort promises to inflate stock prices but results in major changes in management personnel, the management team has an incentive to fight the takeover to preserve its jobs—even though the takeover might be in the best interests of the shareholders. In 1985, the management team at the St. Regis paper company tried to thwart an attempted takeover by buying out the raider's interest in the company at $52 per share when the stock was trading at only $42.25. An angered shareholder group brought suit against the management team for improper use of shareholder equity.[9]

Shareholders also may act to alter company policies for reasons other than personal financial gain. As described in the "FOCUS ON: Shareholder Activism," many companies in the 1980s found themselves the targets of shareholder revolts not because of poor financial performance but because of their unwillingness to cease dealing with South Africa. Shareholders were not disappointed in their firms' financial performance. They were disappointed in their firms' *morality*.

Labor also provides an important interface between organizations and their suppliers. In most cases, acquiring and maintaining labor means dealing with individuals rather than organizations. Individuals respond to job ads and negotiate deals with organizations to compensate them for their efforts. In some cases, however, the individuality of the labor-management process disappears. Organizations in need of short-term assistance may turn to temporary-help organizations that maintain stables of potential employees. They also may turn to "headhunter" firms—companies that specialize in locating labor with the specific

---

[7]L. R. Gomez-Majia, H. Tosi, and T. Hinkin, "Managerial Control, Performance, and Executive Compensation," *Academy of Management Journal* 30 (1987): 51–70.

[8]C. W. L. Hill, M. A. Hitt, and R. E. Hoskisson, "Declining U.S. Competitiveness: Reflections on a Crisis," *Academy of Management Executive* 2 (1988): 51–60.

[9]R. Greene, "Greenmail: The Backlash," *Forbes*, December 2, 1985, 86–90.

FOCUS ON:
Shareholder
Activism

**Stockholders with a Mission** In 1972, a coalition of five Protestant churches banded together to try and stop apartheid practices in South Africa. What ammunition could five churches possibly have to wage a battle against the national policies of a foreign country? They had realized the importance of American commercial investments to the South African economy. The South African economy was dependent upon U.S. corporate involvement. The U.S. corporations, in turn, were, as always, dependent upon the goodwill and understanding of their shareholders. The churches assaulted this second source of resource dependence.

The churches put together a resolution to be voted on by the stockholders of several major U.S. corporations, including General Motors, Gulf Oil, Mobil, Goodyear, and IBM. The resolution simply demanded that these corporations discontinue their operations in apartheid South Africa. The churches further bolstered their position by seeking the support of other institutional investors such as banks, insurance companies, and even universities. By the early 1980s, pressure was being applied to 300 major U.S. corporations doing business in South Africa.

There was a simplistic elegance to the assault of the five churches, and they have won some important victories over the years. The threat behind stockholder revolts of this sort is that top management will be harassed or even removed if it fails to comply. As it turns out, though, the real key is that U.S. corporations doing business in South Africa are there because it is profitable. The resource dependence between South Africa and these corporations therefore is *mutual,* and this mutual dependence in turn has led many corporations with investments there not to abandon their operations in South Africa but—better still—*to work to change apartheid.*

Perhaps the best example is the work of the Polaroid Corporation. Polaroid has forced both its South African business partners and their suppliers to "improve dramatically the salaries and other benefits of their nonwhite employees." Polaroid also required its South African business partners "to initiate a well-defined program to train nonwhite employees for important jobs within their companies" as a condition of continuing to do business. Finally, Polaroid has even set up a nonprofit trust fund to provide educational funds for South African blacks.

Other major U.S. corporations also have heeded the call of their activist stockholders by initiating humanitarian programs in their South African affiliates. Goodyear has realigned wages in its South African operations to reflect job value rather than worker race. Mobil Oil has worked hard to train and promote nonwhites in its South African connections. And Colgate-Palmolive even funded a black township school in the local community of one of its South African facilities.

These actions by U.S. corporations in South Africa have not brought an end to apartheid, but they do seem to be a step in the right direction. Further, they reflect the ability of stockholder activists not only to assert their opinions but to make a difference. Can five churches possibly hope to change the behaviors of several major U.S. corporations and a foreign government? Through resource dependence, apparently so.

Source: J. L. Hysom and W. J. Bolce, *Business and Its Environment* (St. Paul, Minn.: West, 1983), pp. 166, 382–383.

talents an organization needs. In effect, these actions are attempts by an organization to delegate aspects of managing this interaction with the environment.

By far the most prominent example of labor organizations are unions. Unions are groups of workers that have banded together to give themselves more bargaining power with their employers. An organization and its labor are mutually dependent. There is no company if there is no work force, and there are no jobs for the work force if there is no company. However, for any individual worker this mutual resource dependence is unlikely to be balanced. With rare exceptions, most individual workers probably need their jobs more than the company needs them. It tends to be easier for a company to find a new worker than for a worker to find a new company.

Unions represent an attempt to balance this mutual resource dependence. When workers band together and speak with one voice, that of the union, they create the very real threat of having to replace an entire work force (for instance, because of a strike or walkout). Unions representing a work force can gain concessions that no individual worker would have the power to gain.

Unions initially arose because labor was being exploited by organizations. Management often took advantage of the imbalanced resource dependence between large organizations and individual workers. So workers banded together to form unions and get a better deal. Over many years, though, government legislation has restricted the power of organizations over their work force. Further, the competitive environment of modern business has forced organizations to appreciate their dependence upon the goodwill of their work force. While in the past fair treatment of workers had to be won in hard-fought negotiations between unions and management, today many organizations recognize the shortsightedness of adversarial relations with their workers. Organizations willingly provide their workers fair treatment in the hope that they will return the favor by being loyal, hard-working, and productive contributors. Not surprisingly, these dual trends of more legislation guaranteeing workers' rights and greater appreciation by organizations of their dependence upon their work force have decreased the power of unions in modern American business.

**Consumers**  Like suppliers, consumers are a feature of the environment linked in a resource-dependence relationship with the organization. And like suppliers, consumers may be either groups or organizations. As we have noted earlier in the chapter, organizations are highly dependent upon their consumers for resources. Shareholders provide only seed capital for an organization—money to get the input-transformation-output process under way. After that, consumers must compensate the organization for any value added to inputs by the organization's transformation process. This compensation paid to the

Recently, unions have tried to expand their control over organizational resource dependencies through secondary boycotts. In a secondary boycott, employees of an organization try to enlist the support of their own organization's customers or suppliers as a way of putting additional pressure on management to make changes. In the secondary boycott pictured here, workers at the *Chicago Tribune* encourage consumers to stop buying the newspaper.

organization for value added to the inputs is the profit. Some of the profit is returned to shareholders in the form of dividends, to ensure their continued future support. Some of the profit becomes working capital for the organization and is used to secure future inputs.

The resource-dependence balance between consumers and organizations often favors the consumer. Because organizations depend upon consumers to reimburse them for value added to the inputs, organization often are willing to tailor their outputs to meet consumer demands. On the other hand, resource dependence can be balanced in favor of the organization when its transformation process is unique or in short supply.

**Competitors**   In addition to suppliers and consumers, organizations also must deal with the existence of competitor organizations in their environment. Competitors stimulate an organization in two major ways: through financial pressure and modeling.

Financial pressure occurs when a competitor can transform the same inputs better, faster, or at lower cost. These characteristics typically make a competitor's outputs more attractive to consumers, therefore undercutting an organization's continued access to working capital. If consumers can get what they want better, faster, or at a lower price elsewhere they will, and an organization's survival will be threatened. Financial pressure will force the organization to look for ways to innovate and streamline in order to survive.

Not surprisingly, competitors themselves usually present the best model of how to respond to competitive pressures in the environment. For example, if consumers discovered that a sports equipment company

Competitors' successes can influence the way an organization chooses to do business. The success of Japanese management teams in American factories, such as the Nissan plant in Smyrna, Tennessee, pictured here, has forced many home-grown management teams to reevaluate their approach.

was producing a new tennis racket that was much easier to play with, financial pressure would be brought to bear on competitors as consumers flocked to purchase the new racket. A suitable competitor response would be to copy and start producing the new racket. But this may not be possible, or at least not easy. Patents may prevent direct copying.

Even in these cases, the behaviors of organizations in the environment may model solutions for a company feeling competitive financial pressure. If it became known that the new tennis racket design was dreamed up in an employee quality circle, some competitors no doubt would institute quality circles for product development the next day. Even if a competitor's outputs or transformation process cannot be copied directly, the behavioral process that led to its competitive edge—such as quality circles or incentive programs—can be copied to help get an organization back into the competitive picture. Many of the most innovative approaches to employee involvement in U.S. corporations today have come from America's "offshore" competitors. The success of these competitors in American markets has put financial pressure on American producers to become better, faster, and cheaper. In many cases the solutions American firms have adopted to become more competitive come from the model successes of their offshore competitors. An example is provided in the "INTERNATIONAL FOCUS ON: Other Organizations," which describes the invasion of Japanese management techniques in American manufacturing settings.

## THE REGULATORY ENVIRONMENT

In addition to other organizations, a significant feature of any organization's environment is regulation. **Regulation** refers to any way in which the actions of an organization are restricted. Laws are a primary source

INTERNATIONAL
FOCUS ON:
Other
Organizations

**Stateside Samurais** On a U.S. assembly line in Atlanta, American women assemble transistor panels according to a prescribed set of steps. At a Tokyo plant owned by the same company, 35 Japanese workers use the same procedures to manufacture the same panels. The only difference between the two manufacturing lines is productivity. The Japanese factory workers complete 15 percent more panels than the Americans.

This example is not an isolated one. In one comparison of two companies that assemble the same products in both the United States and Japan, the Japanese company demonstrated higher productivity in *both* locations *and* 25 percent to 50 percent lower turnover and absenteeism. A Japanese bank in California has grown twice as fast as its competitors. Americans working for the bank claim that the Japanese managers instill an unusual (at least for Americans) amount of esprit de corps and aggressive involvement in work. Employees of the bank are extensively cross-trained. This gives the bank more flexibility to staff teller windows during peak periods without hiring extra tellers. The employees' jobs are enriched, job security is enhanced, and group cohesiveness of the work force encourages low absenteeism.

These practices are the hallmarks of the Japanese management boom that swept through American management circles during the late 1970s. The components of Japanese management practices include: (1) emphasizing the flow of information from the bottom up, (2) encouraging management to delegate and to promote decision making from below rather than issue edicts, (3) stressing consensus as a goal in decision making, and (4) treating subordinates as whole persons rather than just as so many production units. The Japanese also have pioneered many operational techniques, such as "just-in-time" inventories and zero-defect manufacturing. However, their overall view of employees as respected first-line resources in organizational problem solving has probably had the biggest impact on American management thinking.

Of course, not all Japanese management techniques translate so easily into the American culture. "Hell Camp" is a Japanese technique for training salespeople and managers to be more aggressive. The curriculum includes memorization of rules, constant oral presentations and testing, and even strenuous physical activities. "Hell Camp" is particularly important for breaking down the traditional Japanese reserve, and toughens up its graduates for the no-holds-barred competitiveness of the Japanese marketplace. When introduced in California in 1988, however, "Hell Camp" was greeted with only limited enthusiasm. Nevertheless, it is probably worth a look. After all, if it is working for the competition, there must be something in it worth copying.

Source: R. T. Johnson and W. G. Ouchi, "Made in America (under Japanese Management)," *Harvard Business Review*, September/October 1974, pp. 61–69; and "Hell Week," *The Wall Street Journal*, March 2, 1987, p. 1.

of regulation. Consumers often think about regulation in terms of laws that prohibit organizations from producing certain outputs or from producing them in certain ways. Drug companies, for instance, are prohibited from marketing untested substances, toy companies are prohibited from marketing dangerous toys, and virtually all manufacturing organizations face regulations about such byproducts of the transformation process as carcinogens or toxic pollutants. Regulations also exist to maintain competitiveness in certain industries. For instance, the U.S. government has imposed quotas and heavy duties on some offshore imports to encourage the survival of stateside competitors.

However, regulation goes far beyond legislating the outputs that organizations can provide. Regulations also restrict the kinds of behaviors that organizations can engage in while transforming inputs into outputs. Laws protect the rights of workers by dictating which behaviors will be allowed in organizations and which will not. Some of these laws even include the appointment of a regulatory body that performs a watchdog function to ensure that organizations comply. Two examples of legal doctrines that regulate behavior in organizations are Equal Employment Opportunity and mandatory employee benefits.

The doctrine of Equal Employment Opportunity (EEO) traces its modern roots to the Civil Rights Act of 1964. One section of the Civil Rights Act (Title VII) specifically prohibits discrimination on the basis of race, color, religion, sex, or national origin in all areas of employment including selection, compensation, and promotion. The idea of this legislation was to give all individuals an equal opportunity to qualify for any job. Title VII of the Civil Rights Act of 1964 is probably the single piece of legislation most responsible for the origin of employee rights in American business. Courts have interpreted Title VII to mean that selection and promotion decisions must be based solely on consideration of job-related skills. In 1972, the Equal Employment Opportunity Commission (EEOC) was established to enforce Title VII by identifying and punishing violators. In 1978, the EEOC issued the Uniform Guidelines on Employee Selection Procedures. These guidelines outline the characteristics of appropriate employee selection strategies and specify at length how an organization can judge whether its personnel decision methods are in compliance with the guidelines. The guidelines are not laws and are not legally binding. However, they are used as a reference in court decisions and therefore have the force of law.[10]

A particularly good example of how EEO legislation regulates behavior in organizations are the Guidelines on Sexual Harassment. These guidelines specify that:

> Unwelcome sexual advances, requests for sexual favors, and other
> verbal or physical conduct of a sexual nature constitute sexual harassment

---

[10]R. D. Gatewood and H. S. Field, *Human Resource Selection* (Hinsdale, Ill.: Dryden Press, 1987).

when (1) submission to such conduct is made either explicitly or implicitly a term or condition of an individual's employment, (2) submission to or rejection of such conduct by an individual is used as the basis of employment decisions affecting such individual, or (3) such conduct has the purpose or effect of unreasonably interfering with an individual's work performance or creating an intimidating, hostile, or offensive working environment.[11]

These guidelines have done more than just regulate the sexual behaviors of employees in organizations. They also have led top management in organizations to establish both training programs to help supervisors identify and manage sexual harassment among subordinates and communication channels to help victims of sexual harassment to come forward without fear of retribution.

Unlike EEO legislation, the legislation concerning required employee benefits has more to do with behavior *of* than *in* organizations. The Fair Labor Standards Act (FLSA) and the Employee Retirement Income Security Act (ERISA) are two examples of the many laws that regulate organizations' behaviors with respect to their employees. The FLSA first established the minimum wage in 1938 at $.25 per hour for nonsupervisory labor, and mandated that overtime would be paid (at the rate of 1.5 times regular wages) for any work in excess of 48 hours per week. ERISA is a federal law that governs the operation of pension funds by organizations. Its primary objective is to ensure that employees eligible for pension benefits will receive those benefits at retirement. ERISA regulates how pension funds are maintained and managed, and thereby prevents abuses and exploitation by employers.

For the most part, government regulation provides an important service. Regulatory agencies police the fairness of behavior in and of organizations. Regulations ensure that organizations deal fairly with their employees and with their environments, including consumers and their immediate neighbors. In most cases, regulations impose on organizations standards of behavior that are socially beneficial in the long run. In the short term, however, regulation is a form of environmental constraint that must be managed. As described in the "Focus on: The Regulatory Environment," improperly managed regulation can prove catastrophic or even fatal to an organization.

## THE SOCIAL ENVIRONMENT

Another component of the environment arises because all organizations are part of a larger society. Social trends that occur in that larger society influence behavior of and in organizations in many ways. We will consider two examples: social adjustment and corporate responsibility.

**Social Adjustment**  Social trends that are unrelated to an organization's actions but to which the organization must adjust require **social**

---

[11]J. Ledvinka, *Federal Regulation of Personnel and Human Resource Management* (Boston: Kent, 1982), 66–67.

FOCUS ON:

The Regulatory
Environment

**The Blind Scales of Regulatory Justice** In November 1972, the Food and Drug Administration (FDA) notified The Marlin Toy Company that two of its most important toy products were unsafe. In the previous two years, the two toys in question, Birdie Ball and Flutter Ball, had accounted for 40 percent of Marlin's sales. The FDA's notification came as a great surprise to Marlin. There had not been one complaint to the company of any harm from the toys since their introduction ten years earlier, and the toys in the meantime had passed three safety tests—by an insurance company, by a department store, and by Marlin itself. Nevertheless, Marlin agreed to recall and redesign the toys.

One month later, the FDA notified Marlin that it was now satisfied with the safety of the toys and promised to remove the two toys from its next listing of banned products. This was little consolation to Marlin. Already it had lost considerable money both in the recall and in lost sales for Christmas 1972.

In 1973, Marlin's top management decided to make up for the loss by increasing advertising and production of the two toys for the upcoming Christmas season. In September 1973, however, the newly formed Consumer Product Safety Commission (CPSC) published a special holiday list of dangerous toys. *By clerical error,* this list included the two Marlin toys that had been redesigned to meet FDA standards only a few months before. By the time the error was discovered and acknowledged, it was too late. Stores all over the country had canceled Marlin toy orders for the 1973 Christmas season.

By January 1974, the Marlin Toy Company faced bankruptcy. Marlin had lost $1.7 million in sales and a great deal of goodwill. Management thought about taking legal action against the CPSC, but was told by a New York law firm that the CPSC

**adjustment.** For example, between 1960 and 1980 the proportion of one-earner households in the American economy declined from 49.6 percent to 22.4 percent, the percentage of married women in the American work force rose from 32 percent to 51 percent, and the number of working mothers rose beyond the number of nonworking mothers.[12] All of these statistics convey a strong sense of change in the fabric of American society: specifically, the entry of working mothers into the American work force.

There are other major changes occurring in the characteristics of the American work force. The age profile also is changing. The average American worker is getting older as a consequence both of the 43 million "baby boomers" born immediately following World War II and legislation repealing mandatory retirement. And, as mentioned earlier, the education profile of the American work force is changing. In 1964, only 45 percent of the American work force had graduated from high school.

[12]J. Cocks, "How Long till Equality?" *Time*, July 12, 1982, 20–29.

could not be sued for neglectful mis-representation of a product. Marlin eventually appealed to the U.S. Congress (with the support of CPSC) for a private bill for financial relief. Unfortunately, it takes two years for a private relief bill to pass Congress. When the bill finally was approved, the Marlin Toy Company was awarded only $40,000—not even enough to cover its legal costs—which it received several years later. By that time, the Marlin Toy Company had sold its toy molds and manufacturing equipment to other toy companies and closed its doors.

Are the results of government regulation always so negative? Hardly. Take the case of Richard J. Hogard, who was awarded more than a million dollars in 1980 in a judgment against Johns-Manville and Raybestos-Manhattan. Hogard had

the misfortune to contract asbestosis—a form of poisoning from exposure to asbestos fibers—after working in a Long Beach shipyard. For its role in exposing both its own workers and its customers to asbestos poisoning, Johns-Manville in the mid-1980s was forced to file for bankruptcy. At the time Johns-Manville faced up to 3,200 lawsuits and possible liabilities of as much as $25 billion. The courts have ruled that manufacturers like Johns-Manville are legally liable if they fail to warn their customers and employees of potential hazards the manufacturers could or even *should* have known about. The threat of potentially crippling lawsuits and sympathetic courts is another form of regulation, and one which in this case has led many employers to voluntarily rid their facilities of potentially harmful asbestos.

Source: Harrison W. Fox, Jr., and Martin Schnitzer, *Doing Business in Washington* (New York: Macmillan, 1981), pp. 158–160; as appeared in John L. Hysom and William J. Bolce, *Business and Its Environment* (St. Paul, Minn.: West, 1982, pp. 341–342 and 425–426.

By 1984, fully 59.7 percent were high school graduates, and 86 percent of the younger segment of the work force (25 to 29 years of age) had high school diplomas.[13]

At first blush, these sweeping social changes may not seem to have immediate implications for a corporation's top management. However, it is precisely these sorts of changes that create forces of *direct* interest to work organizations, such as the currently heightened interest of American workers in temporary employment, as discussed in Chapter 1. No one can predict the future directions in which society will move. Whatever they are, as social trends unfold, organizations must adjust to and evolve with them—or be left behind.

**Corporate Responsibility**   Standards for corporate responsibility are one aspect of the evolving social scene that modern business corporations must face. **Corporate responsibility** has to do with actions taken (or

[13]E. E. Lawler III, *High-Involvement Work Strategies* (San Francisco: Jossey-Bass, 1986), 16.

avoided) by an organization and how they measure up to society's moral and ethical standards. By way of example, consider the actions of Warren Beatty as the top executive of a major conglomerate in the movie, "Heaven Can Wait." Beatty finds his corporation under seige by citizen groups for a variety of transgressions, including the accidental killing of porpoises in its tuna-canning process (a very real problem for tuna fishermen). The problem for Beatty is that harvesting the tuna without killing the porpoises would be more expensive. But in his plea for the corporation to change its thinking, Beatty's character captures the crux of corporate responsibility. Killing the porpoises may be legal, he notes, but it isn't right. Implicit in his argument is a concern that any short-run savings the conglomerate realizes may lead only to long-term costs when the consuming public turns its back on the corporation.

This kind of corporate responsibility goes beyond fulfilling the letter of the law. Corporate responsibility includes such issues as good citizenship and social sensitivity. Good citizenship refers to returning something to the community which is an organization's home. For example, E. B. Industries and Fisher Price Toys contribute substantially to the emergency fire and ambulance services in their immediate communities by releasing volunteer employees from work on a regular basis.[14] Such actions cannot directly enhance a corporation's profit picture, but they will contribute to the development and well-being of a community, which in turn enhance a corporation's probability of survival.

Social sensitivity occurs when a corporation selects an alternative that will minimize negative impact on the surrounding social environment. Legislation requires organizations to give their workers 60 days' notice before closing a plant, but it does not require them to help workers find new jobs. Organizations that provide their displaced workers outplacement assistance during tough times will likely find the community more supportive when they later resume operations. In some cases social sensitivity may not cost the company anything. When a company is deciding between two prime locations for a new plant, choosing the one that minimizes damage to wildlife habitats may cost the company no more but make a big difference to the community. In the end, though, corporate responsibility is a bottom-line issue. Organizations are dependent upon their environments for resources. Adhering to the environment's dictates of acceptable corporate behavior—whether through good citizenship or social sensitivity—is one way for an organization to make sure its nest remains feathered.

## TECHNOLOGY

A final content of organizations' environments is technology. **Technology** includes all the different ways available to an organization to

---

[14]Hysom and Bolce, *Business and Its Environment*, 4.

transform inputs into outputs. Because of the recent rapid advance of technological development, an entire chapter (Chapter 16) will be devoted to an in-depth examination of this powerful environmental force.

MANAGING ENVIRONMENTAL DEPENDENCE

In the previous two sections of this chapter, we have described the form and the contents of the environment that today's modern business organizations must face. The challenge for today's organizations is managing the resource dependence that this environment presents. In this section we will consider three strategies that organizations use for managing environmental resource dependence: anticipation, negotiation, and control. As shown in Figure 14–4, these three approaches to dealing with the environment differ in the extent to which the organization's efforts are internally or externally focused. **Anticipation** focuses on making internal changes in the organization to *respond* to the demands of the environment, while **control** entails molding the environment to fit the organization's needs. Negotiation falls somewhere in between. Many organizations use a mixture of these strategies.

| FIGURE 14–4 | Strategies for Managing Environmental Dependence |
| --- | --- |

Organizations can try to manage resource dependencies in the environment by anticipating the actions of the environment or by negotiating or controlling the environment's demands. Which strategy a firm chooses to pursue may depend on how susceptible to influence it perceives its environment to be.

**Anticipation**

Scanning: collecting information about the environment and its possible actions.

Forecasting: predicting future actions of the environment, often using statistical models.

**Negotiation**

Lobbying: having agents plead the organization's case with regulatory bodies.

Interlocking directorates: having influential suppliers and consumers on the board of directors to provide policy input.

Public relations activities: attempting to build up the image of the organization in the environment.

**Control**

Contracts: obtaining legally enforceable promises from consumers or suppliers.

Buffers: stockpiling resources.

Vertical integration: acquiring or merging with a supplier to guarantee resource availability.

Horizontal integration: entering a different market to diversify risk.

Joint ventures: sharing resources on a project with another organization to share risk.

ANTICIPATION

Anticipation occurs when an organization collects information about what its environment is doing (or is about to do). The organization then can predict and respond appropriately to the environment's demands. Two component processes of anticipation are scanning and forecasting.

**Scanning**   Collecting information from the environment is known as **environmental scanning.** Environmental scanning may involve the creation of new data; for example, through surveys. Scanning also can be accomplished by tapping into existing data sources, such as government labor statistics. As we noted in the last section, government labor statistics suggest that the American work force on the average is becoming older and better educated. An organization that has collected this information may be able to use it to redesign future jobs to be more stimulating and involving for its work force.

**Forecasting**   An organization's use of information collected from the environment to predict future environmental demands is called **forecasting.** Last year's unemployment figures may provide only limited information about the labor supply in the immediately foreseeable future. However, a company that has collected unemployment figures for the last 20 years, as well as background information concerning the possible factors that drive unemployment statistics, is in a good position to *predict trends* in unemployment for the upcoming years. Forecasting uses statistical models to predict what the environment has in store for an organization in the future.

One example of environmental anticipation by an organization is the social audit.[15] The **social audit** is a mechanism that organizations use to see where they stand with respect to corporate responsibility demands placed on them by their social environments. Social audits have three goals. First, social audits identify and analyze important issues in a firm's social environment. These might include: (1) issues that affect the firm, such as changes in community demographics, which could require alterations in a company's recruitment policies; (2) issues that the firm affects, such as plant closures that could have widespread effects on a community's economy. Second, social audits catalogue the scope of socially responsive programs or actions that an organization is undertaking. Finally, social audits assess the effectiveness of a firm's social actions and programs in addressing identified social issues.

Social audits can serve two important functions for an organization. First and foremost, social audits help an organization realize any shortcomings it might have in addressing its social responsibilities. The social audit is the first step an organization takes to prevent or correct any problems it might have in managing its corporate responsibility demands. In addition, however, social audits provide an important

[15]Ibid., 47–51.

documentation function. An organization that had conducted a social audit will have documented its level of social responsiveness. Assuming it paints a pretty picture, this documentation can be made available to representatives of the social environment as proof of a firm's willingness to fulfill its social obligations. And a firm that conducts periodic social audits—and uses the information appropriately—can be sure the picture painted will be one of a socially responsive and responsible organization.

The potential ability of organizations to anticipate the actions and demands of their environments through mechanisms such as social audits has been enhanced greatly by the advent of computers. Computers allow organizations to store systematically and access instantly a great deal of information about the environment. Furthermore, many data bases have been computerized to provide organizations ready access to a wide variety of information that they could never collect themselves. Finally, computers provide organizations with virtually unlimited computational ability for generating forecasts with the information that is collected.

## NEGOTIATION

When practiced by itself, anticipation assumes that the resource dependencies of the environment are a given—something that the organization must face up to and react to. As a strategy for managing environmental demands, negotiation takes a different view—that the environment, in particular the *beneficence* of the environment, is susceptible to influence. An organization can bargain with its environment and negotiate the demands that it places on the organization.

**Lobbying**   Lobbying is one way that organizations bargain with their environments. **Lobbying** occurs when the representative of an organization tries to convince a source of resource dependence in the environment (such as another firm or the government) of the correctness of the organization's world view. An organization of grain farmers, having a vested interest in the passage of a bill guaranteeing price supports for their products, might lobby Congress. This lobbying effort would include personal visits by grain farmers' representatives. The representatives would present the grain farmers' position, provide information supportive of their views, and generally advocate their viewpoint in the hopes of gaining support. As noted in the "INTERNATIONAL FOCUS ON: Lobbying," attempts to persuade Congress of the correctness of constituents' viewpoints are not always just a matter of providing information. Threatened withdrawal of monetary or even voting support also may sway someone's way of thinking.

**Interlocking Directorates**   A slightly more elegant device that firms use to subtly negotiate their environmental resource dependencies is **inter-**

## INTERNATIONAL FOCUS ON:
### Lobbying

**Influence Peddling, European Style**

On the second floor of the European Parliament in Strasbourg, alongside the ceiling-high windows, stretches a long row of couches known as "lounge lizard row." This is the home of the European Parliament (EP) lobbyists, and on any given day the influence peddlers—animal protectionists and industry advocates alike—gather there by the dozens. They monitor the debates and resolutions on the Parliament floor, pass on reports (presumably favoring their clients) to key Members of Parliament, and keep tabs on issues moving through the EP's decision-making machinery. In short, their jobs appear to be similar to those of many American lobbyists in Washington, D.C.

Lobbying of this sort is relatively new to the European Parliament, however. In the early 1980s, the European Community's decision-making body in Brussels—the Council—represented a loose trade consortium of Western European countries. Since a single dissenting vote by any member country was enough to kill a resolution, interest groups defended their positions by bringing pressure to bear at home. Direct intervention by industrial lobbyists in Brussels was rare, and probably unnecessary.

This all changed in 1987, when the stifling "unanimous approval" requirement for European Community (EC) resolutions was abolished and the power to review and revise proposals before Council votes was given to the European Parliament in Strasbourg. As the notion of a "borderless market" (where goods would circulate freely among member countries) came closer to reality, interest groups swung their influence attempts away from national lawmaking to EC legis-lation. The previously "toothless" European Parliament, now endowed with the power to shape EC trade law, suddenly became a lobbying hotbed.

The EC's Commission also has become the focus of many Western European lobbying efforts. The Commission is charged with preparing first drafts of proposals before they are reviewed by the Parliament, making it a prime target for "first strike" lobbying. Noted one leading European industrial lobbyist, "Somewhere out there in the EC landscape is a low-level Commission functionary who has the chore of pulling together a first draft. The better lobbyists find him, and make their organizations available." One prize lobbying target in the Commission is Directorate General 16. Directorate General 16 controls the billion-dollar European Regional Development Fund, which underwrites industry modernization, infrastructure projects, and worker retraining in economically depressed regions of the European Community. In a year, as many as 700 regional, state, and local agencies might lobby Directorate General 16 for funding.

Even as lobbying has exploded in the European Community, there remain important differences between European lobbyists and their American counterparts. Free trips, extravagant meals, and expensive gifts for spouses of important functionaries are still considered out of bounds, and in some languages the translation for "lobbying" has a decidedly negative connotation. But influence peddling is a new art form in the EC, and it is rapidly gaining in respectability. Notes Walter Grunsteidl, director of international affairs at Philips, "Now it's improving. At least you can use the word 'lobbying'."

Source: Brooks Tigner, "Influence Peddling, European Style," *International Management*, June 1988, pp. 32–40.

**locking directorates.** A corporation can appoint to its board of directors representatives from a variety of organizations on which it is dependent. A major medical-supplies manufacturer, for instance, will have hospital and banking representation on its board of directors to cover the consumption and financing ends of its enterprise. These representatives typically possess either decision-making power or influence in their own organizations. In addition to any strategic insights or information they might have to offer, these representatives from the environment give the firm an opportunity to promote its views and gain their commitment. This commitment then becomes an invaluable asset when board members return to their own organizations to make decisions that affect the fate of the firm.

**Public Relations** Another way organizations negotiate the resource dependencies they face in the environment is through **public relations** activities. **Image advertising** is one form of environmental negotiation. Image advertising is advertising that attempts to influence the public's overall perception of an organization. Is the organization patriotic? Is the organization community-minded? Does it give you a good feeling? An organization also can influence its overall image in the environment by providing community services, such as McDonald's support of the Ronald McDonald Houses for critically ill children.

Why is it important for an organization to maintain a positive image in the environment? A good impression of an organization will influence the environment's beneficence. Consumers will be more willing to try the organization's products. Further, because of the constructive nature of perception, an organization's good public image will even influence consumers' perception of the quality of its outputs. Regulators, for example, will see a corporation's actions in a more favorable light if they have an overall favorable impression of the corporation. Just because an organization's community-service activities are unselfish does not mean that they also have to be unprofitable.

Each Ronald McDonald House is a unique facility, created by local citizens to meet their community's needs. The McDonald's Corporation helps the houses manage their environmental dependence by providing start-up funding for new houses and by lending its positive image and visibility to help increase public awareness and interest in the houses.

CONTROL

Negotiation as an environment-management strategy assumes that the environment can be influenced—that resource demands placed on an organization can be negotiated. An even more proactive approach to resource demands is to control them. A variety of strategies for controlling environmental resource dependencies are available to organizations, including contracts, buffers, vertical and horizontal integration, and even joint ventures.

**Contracts** A contract is one of the simple ways for an organization to control resource dependencies in its environment. A **contract** is a legally binding document that guarantees an organization delivery of and terms for a particular resource. A department store and a clothing manufacturer might have a contract specifying the delivery dates and terms for a line of sportswear. What does having the contract accomplish for either organization? The department store, through the contract, guarantees itself a supply of sportswear for the upcoming season. The clothing manufacturer, through the contract, guarantees itself a distributor for its clothes. In practice, a contract that simply guaranteed delivery of the clothes at a set price might not be enough for either party. The manufacturer might want the contract to include additional guarantees about how heavily the department store will advertise its clothes, and the department store might want some input into the design of the sportswear.

The point of having contracts is to reduce uncertainty about the availability of resources. Both the department store and the clothing manufacturer can rest a little easier knowing they have signed a contract. Naturally, contracts are no real guarantee. The clothing manufacturer might not come through with the clothes, and the department store might renege on its promise to market them. But a contract provides each organization legal recourse if that happens. The department store can sue the clothing manufacturer for lost revenues if the clothing manufacturer fails to deliver according to the terms of the contract. Suing the clothing manufacturer is not the same as getting the clothes delivered as promised, but in either case the contract provides the department store some protection against the whims of the environment.

**Buffers** Buffers provide an organization another way to insulate itself from the unpredictability of its environment. If an organization is concerned that its resource supplies might dry up, it can create a buffer against resource scarcity by stockpiling resources when they are available against the day when they will not be. A concerned department store might buy a warehouse and fill it full of clothes. In the event that a clothing supplier failed to deliver on time, the department store would have a buffer—a safety margin—of clothes in its warehouse to see it through the crisis.

Clothes, unfortunately, are a good example of a product that cannot be stockpiled easily. Because styles change rapidly, clothes that a department store stockpiles against the possibility of future shortages may be out of style when the department store attempts to use them. Grocery stores face a similar problem with fresh fruits and vegetables— they cannot be stockpiled against the possibility of future scarcity because they would not stay fresh. When resources cannot be stockpiled, **resource redundancy** can be used instead as a form of environmental buffering.

Resource redundancy is accomplished by maintaining relationships with multiple resource suppliers. A department store that has relationships (perhaps even contracts) with multiple clothing suppliers knows that one supplier's failure to deliver on its promises will not be fatal. The other suppliers will be able to step in and deliver on their promises, and may even be able to fill in the gaps left by the undependable supplier. Any clothing manufacturer, on the other hand, probably isn't depending on just the one department store either. Having multiple consumer outlets in line means that if one distributor fails to move its merchandise, the successes of other outlets will prevent any crisis.

**Vertical Integration**   Vertical integration is a much more aggressive way for an organization to control resources in its environment than either contracts or resource buffers. Contracts and buffers allow an organization some measure of control over important resources, but those resources still remain at arm's length in the environment. **Vertical integration** involves the *absorption* of important resources so that an organization's control of them becomes absolute.

Consider again our department store and clothing manufacturer. One way for the department store to increase the clothing manufacturer's dependability is to *buy* it. The department store then can control completely not only availability of the clothing but also styles, sizes, and so on. On the other side of the coin, a clothing manufacturer that is nervous about the dependability of the department stores that are retailing its goods can vertically integrate by acquiring a chain of factory-outlet stores that it completely controls. For the grocery store, vertical integration might include the acquisition of a dairy farm to ensure availability and terms for a variety of dairy products.

As shown in Figure 14–5, the term vertical integration means *integrating* different functions in the vertical chain of production under the umbrella of one organization. For clothing, the entire vertical chain might include cotton growers, cotton-cloth weavers, clothing manufacturers, and finally retail distributors. Each of the links in this vertical chain represents a source of resource dependencies. By integrating functions, these resource dependencies can be more closely controlled. Vertical integration is no final solution, however. The department store that acquires a clothing manufacturer eliminates one source of resource dependence, but in turn may learn just how undependable cotton-cloth weavers are as suppliers to the newly acquired business.

**Horizontal Integration**   Horizontal integration is a completely different approach to controlling resource dependence. An organization horizontally integrates by getting involved in multiple, often unrelated vertical chains of production, such as those shown in Figure 14–6. The point of vertical integration is to control resource dependencies; the point of **horizontal integration** is to control the *effects* of resource dependencies. A horizontally integrated organization is one that is in many different businesses. That way, the organization can balance the failures of any one of its businesses with the successes of its others.

**FIGURE 14–5**      Example of Vertical Integration

Panel (a) shows four component operations in getting clothing to market. Each of these component operations could be accomplished by a separate firm. In Panel (b), Firm C has vertically integrated by merging with or acquiring Firm B. Having acquired a cloth weaver, the clothing manufacturer no longer has to worry about the supply of cloth.

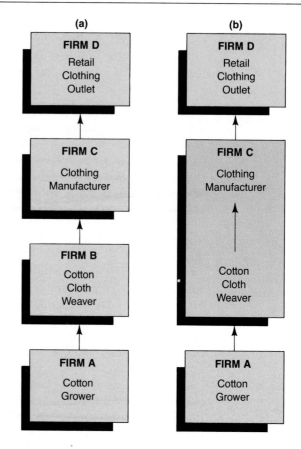

Horizontal integration allows an organization to distribute its resource-dependence risks across a variety of activities.

Department stores themselves actually provide an interesting example of horizontal integration. If a store sold only children's clothes, its success as a business would be highly dependent upon the success of the children's clothing industry as a whole. But what if that store also sold hardware, books, toys, and kitchen supplies? A bad year in children's clothes could be balanced by a particularly good year in kitchen goods. In fact, the term *department store* refers to the fact that department stores have many departments—many little businesses—all contained under the umbrella of one organization.

Horizontal integration works best when an organization gets into businesses with completely different sources of environmental resource dependence. Imagine, for instance, a corporation that was involved in

**FIGURE 14–6**   Example of Horizontal Integration

In this example, Firm C has horizontally integrated by acquiring a new business in a completely different market, bicycles. If the factors that determine when consumers buy clothing and bicycles are different, this kind of horizontal integration decreases the impact of a problem in either market. Horizontal integration works best when expertise can be pooled across the integrated units. In this case, for example, both units are manufacturing concerns.

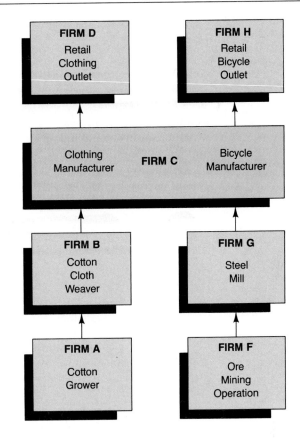

two businesses: photographic film and silver jewelry. The factors that determine who buys film and who buys jewelry probably are quite different, so that fluctuations in sales in one market would not likely be related to fluctuations in the other. However, both of these industries are highly dependent upon the supply of silver, which is used in the production of photographic film. A scarcity of silver could take both businesses down at the same time. Photographic film and dairy products, on the other hand, are unlikely to share either supplier or consumer resource dependencies, and therefore might make for effective horizontal integration.

The valuable asset that an organization may lose with horizontal or vertical integration is expertise. A top management team that is very adept at managing a department store might flounder if asked to manage a clothing manufacturer (vertical integration) or a dairy farm (horizontal integration) as well. Horizontal and vertical integration offer the possibility of controlling the stability and uncertainty presented by resource dependencies, but only at the expense of increasing environmental complexity.

**Joint Ventures**   An interesting variation on horizontal integration is the **joint venture.**[16] Joint ventures occur when two or more unrelated organizations pool their resources to collaborate on joint projects. Some well-publicized examples of joint ventures include the Alaska pipeline, which brought several major U.S. corporations together on a massive oil and gas exploration project; a factory in California producing automobiles made jointly by General Motors and Toyota; and McKids clothing, a joint effort by McDonald's and Sears to manufacture and market children's wear.

Why would two organizations—sometimes even competitors—be willing to work together on a project? There are a variety of answers, but they all come down to resource dependence. In the case of the Alaska pipeline, the project was too large and too risky for any one of the companies to underwrite alone. Interestingly, its potential also might have been too great for any of those firms to ignore. Thus, participation of any firm in the project prevented its competitors from gaining an advantage through participation, and also availed the firm of the possible benefits of the project without taking the risks all alone.

The case of the General Motors and Toyota joint venture was slightly different. Both companies were more than capable financially of going it alone, but both also knew that a joint venture could produce huge benefits. Toyota needed to improve its access to American car buyers; having its cars made by American workers in a General Motors plant in the United States was just the ticket. General Motors, on the other hand, knew that its U.S. manufacturing processes could not compete with the effectiveness and efficiency of the Japanese. Joining forces with the competition offered General Motors an opportunity to improve its product, its image, and its expertise in manufacturing automobiles. In effect, both companies had an important resource that the other desperately wanted. A joint venture gave each side control of that valued resource. The reasoning behind the Sears-McDonald's joint venture is similar. Sears has expertise in children's clothing, while McDonald's has the image and visibility that can sell clothes.

In the final analysis, the reasoning behind all joint ventures comes down to managing resource dependence. Joint ventures reduce uncertainty by sharing risk, and they also increase the ability of firms to manage environmental complexity by sharing their expertise.

[16]J. B. Levine and J. A. Byrne, "Corporate Odd Couples," *Business Week*, July 21, 1986, 100–105.

## THE BOUNDARY-SPANNING ROLE

As a closing comment on the importance of interactions between an organization and its environment, it should be remembered that organizations do not interact with their environments, nor do organizations interact with each other. The interfaces between an organization and its environment are **boundary spanners,** individuals who span the boundary between an organization and the forces in its environment.[17]

The boundary-spanning role is both important and difficult. It is important because of the importance of resource dependence. Boundary-spanning individuals who handle their role poorly put their organization at risk to lose access to important resources in the environment. The role is difficult because the boundary spanner often lives in two worlds. Take, for example, the job of liaison for a joint venture between two corporations. To be successful, such liaisons must learn the rules of both corporate cultures and be able to move freely back and forth between the two. And if successful, the boundary spanners' loyalty may come to be suspected by their own camp because of their exposure to the other side. Further, because boundary spanners must do much of their work in organizations to which they do not belong, they have little legitimate power to fall back on to accomplish their goals. Boundary spanners therefore must be well-schooled in the use of other forms of power to be effective. Corporate liaisons cannot order people around; they must rely on less direct tactics, such as ingratiation, to accomplish their mission.

While these problems provide only a glimpse at the challenge of boundary spanning, they do suggest that individuals cast in this role may need different skills than other organizational actors. The selection of such individuals may need to place greater emphasis on flexibility if the boundary spanner is to manage successfully regular transitions between environment and home organization. The boundary spanner will also need to be trained to manage interactions differently when outside the organization—for example, by using other sources of power. For an organization, resource dependence makes the correct selection and preparation of individuals for boundary-spanning roles at least as important as for any roles internal to the organization.

## SUMMARY

The goal of this chapter has been to paint a picture of the environment in which today's organizations must function. Organizations cannot exist independent of their environment. Organizations are open systems that depend upon the environment for resources and are influenced by their interactions with it. Organizations depend upon the environment for inputs to transform and for customers or

---

[17]D. W. Organ, "Linking Pins between Organizations and Environments," *Business Horizons*, December 1971, 73–80.

clients to consume their outputs.

The environmental forces that influence business organizations have both form and content. Environmental forces vary in their uncertainty, stability, complexity, and beneficence. These environmental forces include other organizations, governmental regulations, social trends, and the current state of technological development.

Successful management of environmental dependence is key to an organization's survival. Three broad strategies for managing environmental forces include anticipation, negotiation, and control. Anticipation requires scanning the environment in order to forecast—and therefore be prepared to respond appropriately to—environmental action. Negotiation is the process of influencing resource dependencies an organization faces in its environment. Organizations can successfully influence environmental resource dependencies through lobbying, the formation of interlocking directorates, and even public relations activities. Finally, organizations can control resource dependencies in their environments through contracting, buffering, vertical and horizontal integration, and even joint ventures.

While any one individual may pale in the face of the enormity and complexity of environmental forces, it is nevertheless individuals that actually manage the boundaries between organizations and their environments. Because of the uniqueness and importance of boundary-spanning roles, organizations need special procedures for selecting and training boundary spanners to ensure successful management of environmental resource dependencies.

## KEY TERMS

**Anticipation**    Making internal changes in the organization to respond to the environment's demands.

**Beneficence**    Generosity, leniency, and helpfulness of the environment concerning needed resources.

**Boundary spanners**    Individuals such as liaisons who represent an organization in interactions with the forces in its environment.

**Closed system**    Completely self-contained organization that functions apart from and is unaffected by what goes on around it.

**Contract**    Control strategy of managing environmental demands using a legally binding document that guarantees an organization delivery of and terms for a particular resource.

**Control**    Molding the environment to fit the organization's needs.

**Corporate responsibility**    Need for an organization to take or avoid actions in order to measure up to society's moral and ethical standards.

**Environmental scanning**    Process of anticipation in which the organization collects information from the environment.

**Forecasting**   Process of environmental anticipation in which the organization uses mathematical models to predict future environmental demands.

**Horizontal integration**   Involvement of an organization in several different activities (e.g., product lines) in order to distribute its resource-dependence risks across a variety of activities.

**Image advertising**   Attempts to influence the environment's overall perception of an organization.

**Instability**   Rate of change in an organization's environment.

**Interlocking directorates**   Negotiation strategy for managing environmental demands in which a corporation appoints to its board of directors representatives from a variety of organizations on which it is dependent.

**Joint venture**   Two or more unrelated organizations that pool their resources to collaborate on projects.

**Lobbying**   Negotiation strategy for managing environmental demands in which a representative of an organization convinces a source of resource dependence in the environment of the correctness of the organization's perspective.

**Loose coupling**   Relationship of an organization and its environment in which what happens in the environment may or may not be reflected by immediate changes in the organization.

**Open system**   Organization whose activities are inescapably influenced by its environment.

**Public relations**   Negotiation strategy for managing environmental demands in which an organization actively controls its interactions with the environment using activities such as image advertising.

**Regulation**   Legal restriction of behaviors in or by organizations.

**Resource redundancy**   Preventing the lack of a particular resource by maintaining relationships with several suppliers.

**Social adjustment**   Changes the organization must make in response to environmental changes that are unrelated to its actions.

**Social audit**   Mechanism organizations use to see where they stand with respect to corporate-responsibility demands by identifying important issues in the social environment, cataloging the actions the organization is presently taking, and assessing their effectiveness.

**Technology**   The knowledge, tools, and techniques available to an organization to transform inputs into outputs.

**Union**   Group of workers who have banded together to give themselves more bargaining power with their employer.

**Vertical integration**   Acquisition of one organization by another with the goal of controlling resource dependencies that are important in its production process.

DISCUSSION
QUESTIONS

1. What does it mean to say that organizations are open systems? What are the defining characteristics of open systems?

2. In what ways are organizations dependent upon their environments? Explain what might be meant by the phrase, "Organizations are a way of turning the environment into survival."

3. In what dimensions of external dependence do the environments of service and manufacturing organizations differ? Does this have implications for how these two types of organizations might manage their environmental interactions differently?

4. Consider the following prayer: "Grant me the strength to change the things I can change, the patience to endure the things I cannot, and the wisdom to know the difference." Would this make a good corporate policy for managing resource dependencies? Why or why not?

5. What does it mean to say that an organization and its environment are "loosely coupled"? Is loose coupling an advantage or disadvantage?

6. Why is the boundary-spanning role particularly important? Particularly difficult? How could an organization prepare one of its employees for this role?

7. What strategies does an organization have for managing its dependence on the environment?

8. How might mergers, takeovers, and acquisitions be seen as a form of managing environmental dependence?

IF YOU
WANT TO
KNOW
MORE

For anyone interested in learning more about the interaction between organizations and their environments, three classic readings provide the foundation for our current understanding of these topics: Jeff Pfeffer and Gerry Salancik, *The External Control of Organizations* (New York: Harper & Row, 1978); P. R. Lawrence and J. W. Lorsch, *Organization and Environment* (Homewood, Ill.: Richard Irwin, 1964); and F. E. Emery and E. L. Trist, "The Causal Texture of Organizational Environments" (*Human Relations* 18, 1968, pp. 20–26).

The success of Korean and Japanese companies intensified interest in international management issues during the 1980s. An entire issue of the *Academy of Management Executive* (February 1988) was devoted to managing in the global marketplace, including an article by Richard Steers and Edwin Miller, "Management in the 1990s: The International Challenge." Several articles have looked specifically at the importation of Japanese management techniques into American industry, including James S. Bowan's two-article series entitled, "The Rising Sun in

America" (*Personnel Administrator,* September 1986, pp. 63–67+ and October 1986, pp. 81–91); the *Business Week* cover article "The Americanization of Honda" (S. Toy, April 25, 1988, pp. 90–96); and L. S. Dillon, "Adopting Japanese Management: Some Cultural Stumbling Blocks" (*Personnel* 32, July 1983, pp. 77–81).

Two interesting books on the issue of organizational stakeholders and their influence on organizations are *Stakeholders of the Organization Mind,* by Ian Mitroff (San Francisco: Jossey-Bass, 1983); and *Strategic Management—A Stakeholder Approach,* by E. Freeman (Boston: Pitman Publishing, 1984).

"State of the Unions," by Keith Atkinson (*Personnel Administrator,* Sep-

tember 1986, pp. 54–59) provides a look at the current state of unions in Europe and the United States. "U.S. Unions and Foreign Employers: A Clash of Cultures," by Martin and Susan Tolchin (*Management Review,* March 1988, pp. 47–53) discusses the problems foreign employers have experienced in dealing with American unions.

One of the early articles to consider the importance of the boundary-spanning role in organizations was "System Boundaries," by R. L. Kahn, D. Wolfe, R. Quinn, J. D. Snoek, and R. Rosenthal (*Organizational Stress,* New York: Wiley, 1964, pp. 99–124).

ON YOUR
OWN

Below is a table that provides a framework for analyzing the environmental forces that influence the behaviors of an organization. The table asks you to list different sources of environmental influence and to identify strategies for dealing with them. Using your school's football team as an example of an open system, fill in the boxes to complete an audit of the environmental forces influencing the behavior of the team. In the first column, list one or two examples of each source of environment dependence listed on the left. Then fill in examples for each of the strategies available to a football team to manage the influence of these environmental dependencies successfully.

|  | Source | Management Strategies | | |
|---|---|---|---|---|
|  |  | Anticipation | Negotiation | Control |
| **Other Organizations** |  |  |  |  |
| **Regulatory Environment** |  |  |  |  |
| **Social Environment** |  |  |  |  |
| **Technology** |  |  |  |  |

Are any of these boxes harder to fill in than others? Does this suggest anything about what types of strategies might be better for managing different types of environmental forces?

CLOSING CASE
FOR CHAPTER 14

## THE MANAGER'S MEMO

FROM: G. Irving, President

TO:    P. Rambowski, Vice President

RE:    Preparing for Hard Times

These days the antigun fanatics seem to be shooting their mouths off
more and more, and I'm getting concerned about the future of Top
Gun Shops. If the trend keeps up, our chain of gun and ammunition
stores could be under siege, maybe from the government, maybe from
community activists. And if the market gets any trickier, you can bet
that the competition will be stepping up the pressure.

The successful hunter keeps his eyes open at all times. So how can
we do the same in our business? We need a plan for keeping an eye
on what's going on, for anticipating changes, for taking action where
we can.

I'd like your suggestions. Where should we be watching? How should
we watch? And what can we do to head off problems?

CASE DISCUSSION
QUESTIONS

Assume you are the vice president, and respond to the president's
memorandum. Consider as many aspects of the environment as you can
apply to this situation. Besides identifying sources of environmental
dependence, describe ways in which the company might be able to
manage its environmental dependence.

CHAPTER

# Technology

**Technology and Organizational Behavior**
Technological Type
Technological Change

**Technology and Automation**
The Intelligence Issue
Limitations
*Focus on Limitations of Automation: The Human Side of Robotics*
The People Angle
*Focus on Automation: Factories with a Future*
Fighting Worker Obsolescence
*Focus on Fighting Worker Obsolescence: High-Tech Retraining*

**Technology and Information**
Information Availability
*Focus on Information Availability: Staying Home Is Paying Off*
Information Use
*International Focus on Technology and Information: Japan's Love for High Tech Stops at the Office*
Surprising Consequences?

**Smoothing the Transition**
Assessing Job Changes
Generating Ownership

## AT WESTINGHOUSE, "E-MAIL" MAKES THE WORLD GO ROUND

It was a typical summer weekend for Westinghouse Electric Corp. President Paul E. Lego. In between golf games and jogging near his home outside of Pittsburgh, Lego got in five hours on his IBM home computer. He sent a flurry of electronic-mail memos to managers located as far off as Japan and Australia. He read electronic progress reports from company representatives negotiating a new contract with Westinghouse's unions. He immediately responded via "E-mail" with bargaining suggestions and fired off another memo to a lieutenant, asking him to send data to Lego's office computer by Monday morning.

At 6 a.m. on Monday, during his 30-minute drive downtown, Lego called chief executive John C. Marous on his cellular phone to map out the day's strategy. Marous was motoring in from Fox Chapel, a town 10 miles northeast of the city. Arriving at his office, Lego checked his computer for messages and found the information he had requested the day before. Another workweek had begun.

Welcome to the brave new world of Westinghouse, where personal computers and telecommunications have dramatically changed the life-styles of Lego and thousands of employees. Electronic mail and voice-message systems have ended the annoyance of telephone tag. Teleconferencing has drastically reduced travel to meetings. The bottom line, Lego says, is that these tools have contributed up to one-third of the company's stunning 6 percent annual increases in white-collar productivity since the early 1980s. That's important since Westinghouse's salaried ranks have soared to 73 percent of its work force today, compared to 46 percent two decades ago. In terms of white-collar productivity, "Westinghouse is probably the best in the world," says Iwao Koshimae, deputy director of a think tank is Osaka. Japanese companies are studying Westinghouse's methods for use at home.

The centerpiece of Westinghouse's office system is E-mail, which was begun in 1980. Some

6,000 PCs connect 10,700 of the company's managers and employees as well as 1,000 customers. The system links operations around the United States with offices in 37 foreign countries. Lego may spend 15 hours of his 80-hour workweek using E-mail from his home and office. "It makes it possible both at home and at work for me to have continuous access to important information," he says.

It also makes life easier. A decade ago, if Lego wanted to contact a manager in Tokyo, he'd dictate a letter to his secretary, who would take it over to the telex center, where it would be retyped. It often took eight hours for the message to reach Tokyo. Or he might call at 5 p.m., forcing a Tokyo manager out of bed at 6 a.m. Now Lego can send a message before heading home and have an answer in his computer the next morning. Because E-mail costs 90 percent less than overseas calls and letters and 75 percent less than telex, the savings add up quickly.

Lately, Lego even has become a portable executive. At a recent meeting in Hawaii, Lego and Marous brought laptop computers. "Both of us stayed in constant contact with Pittsburgh and the rest of the world," says Lego.

The new technology isn't entirely wonder and light. Executive Vice-President William A. Coates concedes that the reams of electronic memos can mean too many weekend hours spent in front of the PC. Still, there's no going back. "People are amazed at how quickly we can move information around," says Coates. "It gives us a competitive advantage."

Source: G. L. Miles, "At Westinghouse, 'E-Mail' Makes the World Go 'Round," *Business Week*, October 10, 1988, p. 110.

## INTRODUCTION

What is technology? Broadly defined, technology is what people use to get things done. In the terms of Chapter 15, technology is whatever workers use to transform organizational inputs into outputs. Technology can refer to something as abstract as a recipe or formula, or something as concrete as a new piece of stainless-steel machinery. The opening vignette for this chapter described just one of the space-age information technologies currently available to modern organizations: electronic mail.

For many managers, technologies like electronic mail also represent "the edge." Technology is supposed to help us do things easier, better, and faster. The adventures of space cowboy Buck Rogers and the exploits of high-tech spy James Bond have left lasting impressions on the American public. Anyone with access to glasses that see perfectly at night, a new ray gun, or a car seat that ejects unwanted passengers at just the right moment has "the edge"—the ability to surprise the competition with an advantage that cannot be overcome.

The tragedy of the USS *Vincennes,* which mistakenly shot down a commercial airliner with 290 civilians aboard, offered an important lesson. Technological advancement is useful only if it helps workers do their jobs better. An information technology—such as the ultrasophisticated radar on U.S. warships—must fit the abilities of workers. Too much information for the human mind to digest can be just as useless as too little.

Not surprisingly, then, Americans have fallen in love with technology. The speed of technological development in America has been staggering. In 1960, no human had traveled in space and computers were just extremely large and boxy adding machines. By 1969 a man had walked on the moon, and by 1985 computer technology was going into its third or fourth generation of development. And through it all, Americans have gobbled up whatever new technologies have come along—even those they didn't understand—perhaps as much to avoid giving the edge to the competition as to get it themselves.

But is the advance of technology a mixed blessing? Are we using technology to take us where we want to go, or are we just going where technology takes us? The U.S. Navy got a quick lesson in this issue in July 1988 when the USS Vincennes shot down an Iranian commercial airliner in the Persian Gulf, killing 290 civilians. An inquiry revealed that the warship's state-of-the-art technology had performed flawlessly. The problem was that, in doing so, the ship's technology may have provided its decision makers with more information than they could digest and integrate into an appropriate decision in the heat of battle.[1] As the Navy learned, technology is not "the edge" after all. Technology represents only potential. Correct management of new technology is the real competitive edge.

This chapter explores the nature of the technological challenge: how to manage technological development for competitive advantage. The chapter begins with a review of two theories of technological determin-

---

[1] D. Griffiths, "When Man Can't Keep Up with the Machines of War," *Business Week,* September 12, 1988, 36.

ism. The first theory examines the effects of different classes of technology on behaviors in and of organizations; the second theory looks at how organizations adapt to rapid technological changes in their industry. Next, we explore the effects on organizational behavior of two major developments: automation and information technologies. Finally, the chapter closes with some thoughts about ways that managers can meet the challenge of using technology effectively.

## TECHNOLOGY AND ORGANIZATIONAL BEHAVIOR

In Chapter 14, technology was cast as one of the environmental forces that influence behavior of and in organizations. The effects of technology on organizations are described in theories of technological determinism. **Technological determinism** means that the way a firm is organized—how it makes decisions or how much training its line workers receive, for example—depends on the technology the firm uses to transform its inputs into outputs. Researchers have identified two different sources of technological determinism: technological type and technological change.

## TECHNOLOGICAL TYPE

English social scientist Joan Woodward first identified **technological type** as a determinant of behavior in organizations. Woodward studied 100 manufacturing firms in the South Essex region of England. One-third of the organizations she studied were branches of larger companies, and the majority of these organizations had fewer than 500 employees. Woodward's studies identified three primary types of production technology: (A) unit or small-batch, (B) large-batch, and (C) mass production or process manufacturing.[2] Woodward proposed a theory of technological determinism that has two components.

**Output Customization**   As shown in Figure 15–1, the first component of Woodward's technological determinism involves the amount of customization required of an organization's outputs by its consumers. Greater demand for **output customization** requires flexibility in the organization's transformation technology. Woodward's three primary types of technology differ in the extent to which an organization's outputs are influenced by customer needs. Output Type A in Figure 15–1 is customized to meet the needs of each consumer or small numbers of consumers (a haircut or dental work, for example). Each output is unique and must be produced individually or in small batches. For Output Type B, segments of the consumer market desire identical outputs (such as automobiles or clothing) from the organization, so outputs can be produced in larger batches. Finally, at the opposite

[2]J. Woodward, *Industrial Organizations: Behavior and Control* (London: Oxford University Press, 1970).

**FIGURE 15–1**          Technological Determinism

Woodward's technological determinism deals with the amount of customization required of an organization's outputs. When outputs must be customized to meet individual consumer needs (Output Type A), transformation technology and organizational processes must be flexible. When outputs do not require customization to meet consumer needs (Output Types B and C), transformation technology and organizational processes can be quite inflexible. Intelligent machines may be one way to defeat the trade-off between customization and production volume by making manufacturing systems both highly efficient and highly flexible.

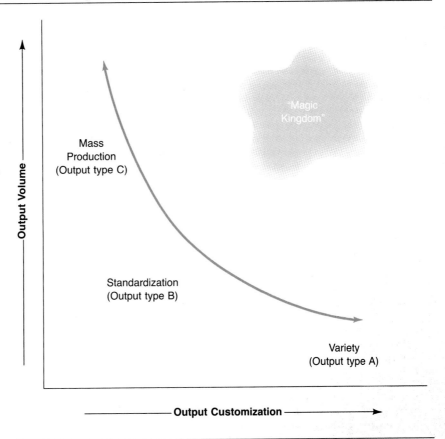

Source: N. Valery, "Factory of the Future," in *Organizations Close-Up: A Book of Readings,*
eds. J. Gibson, J. Ivancevich, and J. Donnelly, Jr. (Plano, Tex.: Business Publications Inc.,
1988), 274–301.

extreme from customized or individually tailored outputs, Output Type C consists of products that can be produced in mass quantities because needs or desires for the product do not differ from consumer to consumer. Process manufacturing occurs when a good (such as beer, dog food, or medicine) is produced in mass quantities and then packaged into units of varying sizes. Mass production occurs when goods (such as pencils or books) that do not need to be altered to fit individuals are produced in mass quantities.

Woodward's technological types illustrate the amount of potential consumer interference that an organization must put up with while it transforms inputs into outputs. If an organization produces a Type A output—one customized to the needs of each individual consumer—it needs a production technology that is extremely flexible. Every unit produced may need to be different from all others ever produced before it. The organization's ability to adapt the production technology swiftly and at low cost is critical to performance. On the other hand, if an organization produces a Type C output—one that requires no consumer customizing—it can plan long production runs. The organization can use a production technology that is inflexible—difficult and costly to change. The organization will not need to change the technology often and can write off the costs of changing the technology over many, many units of output.

**Uncertainty**   The second component of Woodward's technological determinism is *uncertainty*. A manufacturer may have the ability to deliver a product or service but be uncertain about the specifics, such as size or fit, until they are specified by the prospective consumer. Greater uncertainty exists when an organization must customize its outputs (Output Type A) to suit each and every consumer; little or no uncertainty exists when organizational outputs require no customization (Output Types B and C) for external consumption. As we have seen, uncertainty in the transformation function requires a flexible and responsive transformation technology. Woodward's technological determinism contends that uncertainty about customer demand will be mirrored in organizational processes. If consumer demands necessitate a flexible and responsive transformation technology, the processes of organizational interaction also must be flexible and responsive. If consumer requirements allow an inflexible and unresponsive transformation technology, then the processes of organizational interaction also can be rigid and autocratic.

Organizational decision making provides an example of the connection between technological flexibility and the flexibility of an organization's interaction processes. If an organization produces a Type A output, its decision-making style must match the demands inherent in managing a flexible transformation technology. In a hospital, for example, it would seem odd if the delivery of medical assistance involved centralized decision making—that is, if each physician had to check with a supervisor and each supervisor had to check with a manager and so on before the physician could provide a diagnosis or prescribe a cure. The demands for medical service require a flexible transformation technology since physicians must tailor the treatment they provide to each patient's individual needs. The advantages of this flexibility are diminished considerably if the line worker (in this example, the physician) is neither trained nor empowered to use it. If the transformation technology needs to be flexible, then organizational processes (such as decision making) have to match that flexibility.

On the other hand, soft drinks are not tailored to each consumer's needs. Rather, hundreds of thousands of identical gallons of the liquid are produced by a very rigid and fixed production technology. Decisions about altering the transformation technology are made infrequently, involve large costs since the transformation technology is relatively fixed, and therefore are centralized. Top management makes the decisions and passes them down through a prescribed hierarchy of reporting relationships.

These effects of technology on organizational decision-making practices similarly influence training. If an organization decentralizes its decision making to cope with the uncertainty inherent in transforming inputs into acceptable Type A outputs, its line workers will need substantial training to handle their decision-making responsibilities. On the other hand, an organization with centralized decision making leaves its line workers little opportunity for exercising discretion and can afford to hire low-skill individuals to staff its transformation technology.

Woodward's technological determinism does not really suggest that technology determines an organization's processes. What it does suggest is that technology *mediates* the effects of consumer demands on organizational processes. A flexible transformation technology will require skilled operators who can take advantage of this flexibility by exercising decentralized decision making. If a flexible transformation technology is needed, operators likely will be skilled and decision making likely will be decentralized.

Woodward's technological determinism ignores the ability of an organization to negotiate or even control output customization demands from its environment. The fast-food industry provides some striking examples. McDonald's became a major U.S. corporation by convincing consumers that customization of hamburgers isn't worth the price consumers have to pay to get them that way. This suggests that, at least for some organizational outputs, consumer demands for customization are negotiable.

On the other hand, a chief competitor of McDonald's, Burger King, has built a national reputation around its slogan, "Have it your way!" The implication of this ad campaign is that consumers can have customized outputs at standardized output prices. How is this possible? One way is to buffer the production technology from consumer influence, thereby achieving the benefits of customization. Customization then is "added on" later. In the case of Burger King, this means hamburgers are mass-produced and then customized with the requested items just before the consumer takes delivery.

Perhaps even more ingenious is the *delegation* of the customization process to the consumers themselves. By providing a sideboard containing all available toppings for a hamburger, a burger stand can allow the consumer to personally customize a mass-produced hamburger. The consumer receives a customized output at a mass production price by personally taking charge of customization. In effect, the burger stand has controlled the effects of consumer demand on organizational processes by delegating customization to the consumer. This is not the way a fancy restaurant would serve a hamburger. On the other hand, fancy restaurants don't charge McDonald's or Burger King prices. Organizational flexibility has its costs.

## TECHNOLOGICAL CHANGE

A second form of technological determinism arises in the rate of change of transformation technologies in an industry. In some industries, technological developments are quite rapid. In the early 1980s, the life cycle for typical manufactured goods—the time from fad to out-of-fashion—was three to six years. By 1987, the life cycle of consumer electronics in Tokyo was down to about three *months*.[3] This amount of product turnover in the consumer marketplace puts demands on organizations that are quite similar to the demands for output customization. The uncertainty is not what any particular consumer will demand in the output, it is what *all* consumers will demand.

In a market where even products that are not customized have a very short life cycle, an organization cannot afford to be inflexible and unresponsive. Just as an organization copes with the uncertainty of individual consumer demands by adopting a flexible transformation technology, it must cope with uncertainty in its market consumer demands by becoming flexible. Unstable product interest in the market requires a flexible and responsive transformation technology. And as we have already seen in the discussion of Woodward's technological determinism, a flexible transformation technology in turn requires similarly flexible organizational processes, such as decentralized decision making and skilled labor.

Technology is only one factor that influences the design of organizational processes. Chapter 16 will take a closer look at the important dimensions of organizational processes and structures and the factors—including technology—that influence their design. The remainder of this chapter will focus on current developments in technology and their potential influence on behaviors in organizations. The two major developments we will examine are automation and information technologies.

## TECHNOLOGY AND AUTOMATION

The 1980s provided American manufacturing moguls something of a reality shock. While the manufacturing productivity of American workers (their per capita contribution to gross national product) remained the highest anywhere in the world, other countries were catching up—and quickly. Between 1970 and 1985, American productivity increased less than 50 percent. The productivity of French and German workers during the same period increased by more than 75 percent, and the productivity of Japanese workers more than doubled.[4]

---

[3]N. Valery, "Factory of the Future," in *Organizations Close-up: A Book of Readings,* eds. J. Gibson, J. Ivancevich, and J. Donnelly, Jr. (Plano, Tex.: Business Publications, 1988), 274–301.

[4]E. E. Lawler III, *High-Involvement Management* (San Francisco: Jossey-Bass, 1986).

**FIGURE 15–2**   Labor Costs as a Percentage of U.S. Labor Costs

High labor costs in the United States make it difficult for American companies to compete in the global marketplace. Appropriate use of technology is critical if American companies are to get the most productivity for their labor costs.

| | |
|---|---|
| West Germany | 130% |
| Japan | 95 |
| France | 93 |
| Italy | 93 |
| Australia | 79 |
| Taiwan | 19 |
| Korea | 18 |
| Hong Kong | 16 |
| Mexico | 12 |
| Brazil | 11 |

Source: U.S. Department of Labor, Bureau of Labor Statistics, "International Comparisons of Hourly Compensation Costs for Production Workers in Manufacturing, 1988," March 1988, p. 5.

The slower growth of American productivity during the 1970s and 1980s is critical because of the cost of American labor. American labor is among the highest-priced labor in the world. As shown in Figure 15–2, the cost of labor in other industrialized countries—including some who regularly compete with American manufacturers in the international marketplace—is often only a fraction of U.S. labor costs. In Mexico and Brazil, for example, labor costs are as little as 11 percent of those in the United States. To put these figures in perspective, realize that in U.S. manufacturing companies, labor can account for as much as 30 percent of total costs; in service organizations in the United States, labor costs may be as much as 80 percent of total costs.[5]

Given the high costs of labor in the United States and their significance to company budgets, it is easy to understand why U.S. managers must get the most bang for their labor buck to survive in the international marketplace. This need to improve the cost effectiveness of U.S. workers has led managers to experiment with job design and performance enhancement programs such as those described in Chapters 12 and 13. On the other hand, management at many American companies has begun to imagine what corporate life would be like *without* labor costs. Corporate life without labor costs can mean only one thing: corporate life without labor, and that in turn means **automation.**

Defined simply, automation is the replacement of people with machines. In the service sector, the advent of ATMs (automated teller

[5]R. S. Schuler, *Personnel and Human Resource Management* (St. Paul, Minn.: West, 1987), 19.

machines) represented an important step in the automation of banking. Before ATMs, bank tellers handled a variety of tasks that included many simple (and quite "mindless") transactions such as account withdrawals, deposits, and fund transfers. When ATMs arrived on the banking scene, many banks encouraged their customers to use them for simple tasks and to call on the tellers only when human discretion was required, for example, to cash a check or set up a new account. ATMs also provide flexibility that live labor cannot, such as the opportunity to do banking outside of regular banking hours. ATMs allow customers to do their banking 24 hours per day seven days per week—a work schedule no live teller would ever put up with.

In this chapter, we will consider two levels of automation: mechanization and computer-integrated manufacturing. In **mechanization,** a machine is programmed to execute the component actions of a work task, but faster, more precisely, and more consistently than any human could ever hope to. Current attempts to mechanize work are extensions of what began with the steam-powered looms of the original Industrial Revolution. Today computer chips bring new levels of mechanical sophistication within reach.

Robots are the most visible part of the movement to replace people with machines. A **robot** is a machine that is guided by automatic controls to perform complex functions like a human being. At the General Dynamics plant in Fort Worth, a robot is used to drill 550 holes into the tail fins of an F–16 jet fighter. The task used to take three workers an entire eight-hour day to do; the robot does it in three hours.[6] The Japanese are world leaders in using robots in manufacturing, and have been more successful than their Western counterparts at integrating robots into a variety of industrial sectors. In the United States, automakers account for fully 50 percent of robot usage; only 10 percent of Japan's robots are used in automobile manufacturing.[7]

**THE INTELLIGENCE ISSUE**

While building robots is a billion-dollar industry, robots account for only 2 percent of expenditures on automation in manufacturing. Beyond robots and one step further down the road to unmanned factories— factories that operate around the clock with few or no workers—is the realm of **computer-integrated manufacturing (CIM).** As shown in the following passage, CIM represents a world far beyond mere mechanization:

> Imagine, if you will, an engineer sitting at a computer terminal punching in data for the design of a new product and sketching freely with a light pen on the screen before him. Happy with the design, he presses a

[6]G. Bock, "Limping along in Robot Land," *Time,* July 13, 1987, 46–47.
[7]Ibid.

button and the details are passed electronically to another computer running software that checks to see whether the design's stresses and strains are within prescribed limits. The information then zips along to a third computer which generates instructions that command the tools in the workshop to machine, assemble, and store the engineer's product ready for distribution—all done automatically, without hassle, delay, or hefty manhandling, and all before the morning's coffee break.[8]

What sets CIM apart from mere mechanization is the use of information by machines. CIM combines task mechanization with computerized information processing about the task. In the example above, the machines are doing more than just producing a custom part. The machines also are deciding what the part needs to look like and even telling other machines how to make it.

The value of CIM lies in its flexibility. "Unintelligent" mechanization—unthinking robots, for example—can be extremely valuable if an organization's product never changes. But what if customization is the way to the consumer's heart? The intelligent mechanization of CIM systems offers a path into the "magic kingdom" of volume with variety (shown earlier in Figure 15–1). CIM gets machines not only to produce efficiently, but also to defeat the limiting trade-off between customization and economies of scale by changing what they produce efficiently.

## LIMITATIONS

Despite the obvious promise for improved productivity offered by automation, manufacturers' experiences with both mechanization and CIM have been disappointing. General Motors, a pioneer in the introduction of new automotive manufacturing technologies, was fully convinced that automation was the wave of the future. GM invested $500 million in a new factory in Detroit that featured 260 fixed production robots to do painting, welding, and assembly work and 50 additional mobile robots to fetch parts. Unfortunately, quality in GM's factory of the future didn't measure up. In fact, quality turned out to be much higher at GM's sister plant in Fremont, California—a plant run by Toyota managers using *yesterday's* manufacturing technology. GM's Buick plant in Flint, Michigan, also received $400 million worth of automation upgrading, but its management found the benefits to be illusory, leading GM to cancel $88 million worth of orders for new robots and retreat to the drawing board.[9] Other manufacturers have had similarly discouraging experiences. As noted in the "Focus on: Limitations of Automation," the experiences of many companies have revealed robots to be downright human. Not surprisingly, the fallout of these disappointments has been a falloff in the pace of automation, as

[8]Valery, "Factory of the Future," 274.
[9]Ibid., 290.

Focus on:

Limitations of Automation

**The Human Side of Robotics**
Robots are being used in increasing numbers in offices and factories throughout the world. In general, robots can be thought of as machines that can sense, think, and act in repeatable cycles. Little is known about how robots affect either individual workers or the structure, functioning, and effectiveness of organizations.

To begin to understand how workers react to the introduction of a robot, data were collected at a manufacturing plant that was installing its first robot. The company had used a fairly comprehensive set of strategies to introduce the robot into the plant, including an open house to demonstrate the operation of the robot, talks by the plant manager, discussions with first-line supervisors, and notices posted in the cafeteria. The robot was introduced in a department that handled the milling and grinding of bar stock. The department had 40 employees who worked in three shifts. Placed at the beginning of the work flow in the department, the robot loaded and unloaded two milling machines. Production workers in the department were interviewed during two separate visits to the plant made about two and a half months before and after the introduction of the robot.

The workers in general seemed to feel that robots would increase productivity by decreasing fatigue and eliminating boring jobs. Interestingly,

the workers' responses suggest that they do not believe that robots will substantially increase product quality or become the overwhelming threat to job security that might be expected.

Workers' comments during the interviews also indicate that introduction of the robot altered the nature of work in the division. Many workers felt that the use of the robot made their job more demanding:

> The job now requires more skills . . .. You have to learn how to program the robot and run it . . .. With more skills, of course, comes more responsibility . . .. The job is more sophisticated.

While these comments appear to describe an enriched job, for some workers these changes led to more pressure and stress. The increased mental demands of working with the robot also changed social interaction patterns on the shop floor:

> I haven't been able to talk as much. . . . I'm too involved with the robot. . . . You really have to concentrate.

Some workers even seemed worried about working with the robot simply because it was "an expensive piece of equipment." On the other hand, workers also reported positive feelings created by the recognition received from and personal pride in successfully operating the robot.

Source: L. Argote, P. S. Goodman, and D. Schkade, "The Human Side of Robotics: How Workers React to a Robot," *Sloan Management Review* (Spring 1983): 31–42.

disappointed manufacturers like GM have cut back to rethink their positions.

Why has automation failed so far to live up to its early promise? There are several reasons. First, the potential benefits of automation probably have been oversold. When General Electric designed state-of-the-art CIM systems into its dishwasher factory in St. Louis, the new systems helped raise productivity by more than 30 percent, cut warranty calls in half, and boost GE's share of the U.S. dishwasher market from 31 percent to 43 percent. The new plant also cost $600 million, however, and many among GE's top management now are questioning whether even the dramatic benefits achieved were worth the price.[10]

A second problem is that the new generation of mechanized and "intelligent" systems cannot always be run by a company's traditional work force. As noted by one expert, managers in state-of-the-art plants can find themselves needing "experts in computer science, communications, and data-base technology. The number of people in factories with this expertise is probably zero."[11] Thus, while automation has led to large work-force *reductions*, an unanticipated side effect has been the need for some work-force *additions*— programmers and technicians who understand the new technologies. As the director of personnel relations at National Semiconductor Corporation put it, "We will be upgrading jobs through automation. I think we will be changing all our collars to white over the next few years."[12] In fact, by some estimates the advent of serious factory automation means that the proportion of white-collar jobs in U.S. manufacturing will rise from 50 percent of the work force in the mid-1980s to 90 percent by the early 1990s.[13]

If automation leads to drastic changes in the nature of work (from doing the tasks to maintaining machines that do the tasks) and in the nature of the work force (from blue collar to white collar), training will be a key to its successful implementation. The Chrysler Corporation managed to avoid the kind of automation debacle suffered by GM by giving its work force 900,000 hours of training before opening up its intelligent factory. The happy result was a relatively smooth transition to a futuristic factory that produces two new car models per year rather than just one every four years.[14]

The experiences of IBM also suggest that some of the problems with automation have come from a failure to fully appreciate the difference between mechanization and intelligent mechanization. IBM reportedly sunk $350 million into a state-of-the-art typewriter plant in Kentucky.

[10]Ibid.

[11]Bock, "Limping along in Robot Land."

[12]"America Rushes to High Tech for Growth," *Business Week,* March 28, 1983, 84–90.

[13]W. E. Cascio, *Managing Human Resources* (New York: McGraw-Hill, 1986), 19.

[14]Valery, "Factory of the Future," 291.

Automation reduced the work force of the plant from 6,000 to 2,000 while doubling the number of typewriters produced annually. Further, the new typewriters are much more reliable, needing service only once every four years instead of annually, and cost $1,000 less than their predecessors. The plant's automation expert claims that the plant is so flexible that it could handle *several hundred* different product lines. The problem is that IBM never intended to use the plant for several hundred different product lines, and the plant's critics are now saying that the facility is overautomated.[15] Automation, especially intelligent automation, is very costly and makes sense only if the additional capacity can be used. A mechanized system will be worth the price only if volume is high. The additional flexibility of a CIM system will pay off only if flexibility is needed to accommodate either individual customer needs or quick changes in product lines. American industry's fascination with and belief in technology has led to the misguided belief that automated is always better. Management's problem here is not automation itself, but knowing *when* to use it.

## THE PEOPLE ANGLE

As the U.S. Navy learned from the USS *Vincennes* incident, knowing *how* to use automation is equally important. The final consideration of making automation work concerns the fit between people and machines. The first industrial Revolution laid the foundation for a terrible misunderstanding: that the goal of automation is to *replace* people. As Japanese industrialist Haruo Shimada puts it, "Only people give wisdom to the machines."[16] Automation works best when people and machines are considered *complementary* rather than *competing* inputs.

If people and machines are to work together, what shall be the role of the people? Technology presents a danger for job design: alienation. Consider what happened when a museum put in a closed-circuit TV system monitored by one security guard to replace a staff of guards patrolling the grounds. The obvious advantage was a reduction in work-force size. But the *task* became totally different. Instead of walking and watching, the guard now sat and observed a bank of TV monitors. The task—monitoring instead of patrolling—became more passive and the guard more detached. What was the outcome? A federal agency did an 18-month test and found that, of several thousand experimental covert intrusions, only *5 percent* were detected.[17] The technology seems better, but the results certainly were not.

The nature of this paradox is portrayed in Figure 15–3. As automation is introduced, the immediate short-term effect often is

[15]Ibid., 298.

[16]R. Neff, "Getting Man and Machine to Live Happily Ever After," *Business Week,* April 20, 1987, 61–63.

[17]Cascio, *Managing Human Resources,* 104.

**FIGURE 15–3** Job Oversimplification through Automation

Automation can be a problem if it oversimplifies the work that remains for the work force. If mechanization of routine tasks leaves workers merely monitoring the machines, alienation may result. This alienation can lead to poor quality and low productivity, which in turn could encourage management to increase automation.

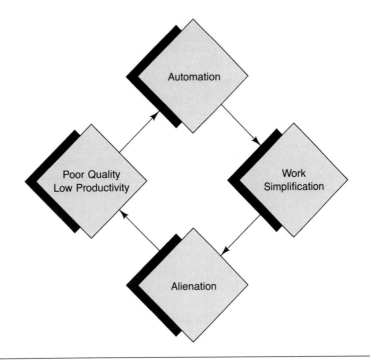

simplification of the task for the worker. In a factory, automation may change the job of a low-level worker from assembling a product to monitoring the machines that do the assembly. The task is much more passive and much less involving. The worker is more likely to become bored and alienated, and (as in the museum example) the quality of the worker's performance likely will reflect it. In the worst of all possible circumstances, the resulting decreases in efficiency may even encourage management to automate further, thereby further decreasing the worker's active role and further increasing boredom and alienation.

Does automation inevitably lead to work simplification? Not necessarily. The introduction of ATMs in banks in fact had the *opposite* effect. Automation took the most routine tasks (deposits and withdrawals) away from the tellers and left them with the more complicated tasks. Unfortunately, automation in service industries (such as banking) usually means less customer contact for employees, which can reduce task significance for workers.

Automation must be preceded by an understanding of the effects it will have on the jobs that remain. Automated is not always better if it means reduced employee involvement in tasks. Enlightened automation is done with an eye to the effects of automation on job design. When automation oversimplifies tasks, management must compensate, perhaps by increasing job scope.

In fact, this turns out to be a recipe for successful automation: increase the scope of automated low-level jobs by increasing worker participation in decision making. Increased participation compensates for the decreased job involvement brought on by automation. At Westinghouse, about 65 percent of the 830 employees in the automated Grand Rapids furniture plant are involved in an elaborate system of committees and task forces that discuss anything from business strategy to the redesign of work areas for product innovation. Using computer-aided design and computer-aided manufacturing (CAD/CAM), the plant can switch rapidly from one special order to another, combining standard parts in unlimited permutations. From 1983 to 1986, productivity in sales dollars per employee rose 74 percent.[18]

The importance of worker involvement in automation planning is explained best by the past masters of successful automation, Hewlett-Packard. HP's William Bowler found that "there were a lot of informal procedures which were not supposed to be there. There's a lot of 'fixing' done by people on the line which never gets shown on any organizational chart." Fixing means human discretion—the judgment that something is subtly wrong and needs to be altered. As long as this uniquely human function cannot be programmed into machines, the machines cannot compete with people.

For HP there are several messages here. HP now preaches that a very fine understanding of a task must precede its automation. Management needs to find out how work in its organization is really done—not just how it is supposed to be done—before trying to automate it. HP also preaches a slow transition into automation. It doesn't attempt wholesale automation of entire lines, but instead begins with "islands of automation" within a line. As bugs gradually are worked out within the islands, the islands can be expanded.[19]

The larger message of HP's approach to automation is that the correct view of automation is *assistance* rather than *replacement* of human workers. The experiences of Shenandoah Life Insurance reinforce this belief. Shenandoah thought it could dramatically reduce policy processing time by automating its processing and claims operations in Roanoke, Virginia. After installing a $2 million "automated" system, Shenandoah found that it still took 27 working days and 32 clerks to process a typical policy conversion request. Once Shenandoah realized its new automated system could never *replace* its employees, it formed semiautonomous work teams to decide how to best put the technology to use. Having people work *with* the technology dropped application-handling times to *two days*. In six years, Shenandoah was processing 50 percent more

[18]Neff, "Getting Man and Machine to Live Happily Ever After."
[19]Valery, "Factory of the Future."

applications despite having trimmed its work force by 10 percent.[20] As noted in the "Focus on: Automation," such diverse enterprises as computer makers and bicycle manufacturers have made automation work by linking it with participative management.

FIGHTING WORKER OBSOLESCENCE

The current party line is that the newest generation of machines is intended to complement rather than replace workers. Nevertheless, workers remain concerned that the increases in productivity achieved through mechanization will result in fewer jobs. In particular, job incumbents are concerned that increasing automation may decrease the skill level of their jobs or render their current skills obsolete, necessitating replacement of the skills (or the workers!). A related fear is that automation simply will do away with jobs.

Certainly workers have legitimate cause for concern. In high-technology manufacturing, output per worker is expected to rise by almost 50 percent between 1981 and 1993, which is nearly double the projected increases for traditional manufacturing and service industries. The dollar output of high-tech companies during this period will virtually double, but the work force will increase by only about 30 percent.[21] Thus, even in expanding industries, automation does not seem to promise equal expansion of job opportunities.

The most likely casualties of increasing automation are jobs in small- and medium-size companies. In the lumber industry, for example, automation has taken over in the last decade and is driving out small operators. In the modern sawmill, the mill hands rarely touch wood. An operator at Lakeland Mills, Ltd., sits at a console in a glass-walled booth, flipping switches to position logs; video monitors display the mill's operations. Computers use electronic scanners to measure each log and decide how to cut it up into the largest amount of usable lumber. The computer chooses from among 100,000 cutting patterns. Notes the operator, "I have to do a little physical labor, but not very often. I have to pick up a log if it falls off the conveyor." At the operator's side, a radio plays music all day to relieve the boredom.[22]

These new computer-driven sawmills are pictures of precision and efficiency. For better or worse, they require very few workers and through the wonders of computer programming waste far less wood than manually operated systems. In some of the most modern mills, work-force reductions can run as high as 80 percent. Consequently, many small lumber mills were forced to close their doors in the 1980s.

[20]J. Hoerr and M. A. Pollock, "Management Discovers the Human Side of Automation," *Business Week,* September 29, 1986, 70–75.

[21]"America Rushes to High Tech for Growth," 86.

[22]A. Bayless, "Technology Reshapes North America's Lumber Plants," *The Wall Street Journal,* October 16, 1986, 6.

FOCUS ON:
Automation

**Factories with a Future**   A decade ago, futurists envisioned robots operating factories, with only a few white-coated technicians on hand to tend to any problems. Unisys Corporation's factory of the future isn't quite like that. It does have computerized robots. But instead of white-coated technicians, it has workers like Joan Dudley. Dudley feeds electronic parts to a robot that inserts electronic chips into circuit boards, and then she checks the robot's work. From Dudley at the start of the manufacturing process to Richard Clader, who packs the finished machines into corrugated cartons, the 299 production workers at Unisys aren't much different from hourly workers at many of America's traditional manufacturing plants. But automation of materials handling and other steps has helped raise their productivity.

The totally mechanized factory, once seen as the only answer to low-wage foreign competition, continues to recede into the next century. Instead of the futuristic models once envisioned, factories of the 1990s will be more efficient versions of the 1970s models—partnerships of man and machine. Workers like Dudley will remain essential to a plant's operation for a long time to come.

Plant automation has turned out to be much more complex and costly than was forecast a decade ago. Instead, manufacturers from Caterpillar—a maker of heavy equipment—to Huffy—a bicycle maker—are successfully combining new production methods, imaginative management, a more cooperative work climate, and some of the latest computer-controlled equipment in their existing plants. The cost is far below that of new automated plants, if indeed the technology exists for total automation.

Caterpillar claims its upgrading program helped trim costs 20 percent between 1982 and 1988. The company adopted the slogan, "Plant with a Future" to underline its belief that older plants can be made competitive for years to come. The savings result mainly from lower materials and labor costs, fewer defective parts, and better inventory controls.

At Huffy's 32-year-old Celina, Ohio, bicycle factory, 1,700 employees turn out more than 15,000 bicycles a day. In 1982, 2,200 employees were required to make 10,000 bicycles daily. Visits to Huffy's sprawling factory in western Ohio and to the Unisys plant in New Jersey illustrate the principal elements in upgrading programs. At both plants, fresh attention is being paid to making blemish-free products and to ensuring a smooth and rapid flow of parts through the plant. Employees get involved in the decisions, making them more willing to continue to change. Officials talk constantly of new goals, in contrast to the old factory maxim, "If it ain't broke, don't fix it."

As a result, Huffy says, the Celina plant has become the most productive bike factory in the world, requiring only seven-tenths of an hour of work to make a bike. That is a quarter to a third of the time needed in the Orient, says Barry J. Ryan, Huffy's VP for finance. "Rust Belt manufacturing plants can compete," he says.

Managers at both plants are becoming adept at mixing people and electronically controlled machines. At Huffy an electrostatic painting system applies the basic coat of paint to the bike frames. But experienced workers with hand-held spray guns apply touch-up paint to areas that didn't get a thick enough coat. Robots don't have the judgment to do that.

Source: R. E. Winter, "Upgrading of Factories Replaces the Concept of Total Automation," *The Wall Street Journal*, November 30, 1987, p. 1.

Automation provides tremendous opportunities to improve jobs by mechanizing the most tedious and repetitive aspects of work. However, managers must examine carefully the jobs that remain. If automation reduces a job to watching the technology do the work, the work force will become more alienated.

From 1977 to 1984, the amount of lumber produced in the United States remained constant. At the same time, however, the size of the work force in U.S. lumber mills fell 25 percent and the number of mills decreased 18 percent. The fact is that some of the smaller mills cannot afford the up-front price tag of modernization—often $15 million or more. Further, some of the smaller mills are small precisely because they are located in small or low-volume forests that cannot provide enough work for a large, automated mill to break even on its investment. The smaller mills nevertheless must match prices with the larger mills in the lumber market. The production efficiency of larger, automated operations makes it impossible for the smaller mills to compete.

The possibility that technological advances will result in substantial work-force reductions has not been lost on labor organizers. Unions have adopted two defenses: protectionist and forward-looking strategies. Protectionist actions include labor contract clauses that protect employment in spite of technological innovation and prohibit management from lowering wages when the skill levels of job functions are decreased. On the forward-looking side, the International Association of Machinists at Boeing requires the company to hold briefings at least annually concerning potential technological innovations on the horizon; and the Graphic Arts International Union has gotten its employers to contribute a fixed amount per month per worker to a fund for retraining technologically displaced workers.[23]

Interestingly, the worker-displacement dilemma posed by technological advances may have technological solutions as well. As noted in the

[23]J. S. Solomon, "Union Responses to Technological Change: Protecting the Past or Looking to the Future?" *Labor Studies Journal* (Fall 1987): 51–65.

"Focus on: Fighting Worker Obsolescence," technological advances have altered more than just the way work is done. Technology is also changing *training methods* for jobs of the future. New methods for training and retraining displaced workers provide considerably more flexibility than before. Computerized courses allow students to work at their own pace. These courses also change the nature of the learning process to make it more like fun and less like work.

---

Focus on:

Fighting Worker Obsolescence

**High-Tech Retraining**   William Norris, the founder and chairman of Control Data Corporation, has long marched to a band that no one else in business could hear. With the computer industry watching in awe, the gruff septuagenarian poured $900 million and 11 years into a computer-based teaching system called Plato. Only by harnessing computers, Norris contended, could companies and schools cope with the quickening pace of technological change, upgrading workers' skill levels and educating youth for tomorrow's jobs. "There's just no other way you can train and retrain" on the massive scale necessary, Norris asserts. "Plato has to be the key."

A Plato terminal acts as a private tutor, asking questions and scoring responses, offering hints and advice, and helping users to learn at their own pace. Its screen has a pressure-sensitive, see-through covering so that when a drawing of equipment is displayed, a user can "operate" the machine by touching its control switches.

General Motors has been Plato's biggest industrial customer. It has used the system as one tool in training 2,000 employees in subjects ranging from basic electronics and hydraulics to programmable controllers and robotics. In April of 1983, GM installed a $2 million computer to extend Plato's availability from 7 to all 30 of its North American divisions.

GM says its employees learn with Plato terminals about 30 percent faster than they do in ordinary classrooms—an important time savings because workers get paid for time spent learning new skills. "People react favorably to it, much as they would to a Pac-Man game," says Gale King, training director for one of GM's divisions.

Du Pont Company spent $300,000 for 40 Plato terminals at two centers where 2,000 hospital employees have learned to use Du Pont's medical equipment. Du Pont's manager of learning resources figures Plato is saving $1 million per year, compared with traditional training.

Plato also has been harnessed to address the more general problem of retraining the unemployed. For example, laid-off steelworkers have been retrained in a state-funded program at the Pittsburgh Control Data Institute. The institute is one of 26 Plato-equipped retraining centers in major U.S. cities.

Norris thinks the future is bright for Plato. He contends that sometime in the 1990s, public schools will turn to computer tutors and Plato will become the biggest and most profitable division of Control Data Corporation. Says Norris, "We're looking at an infinite market."

Source: "Computerized Training May Finally Be about to Take Off," *Business Week*, March 28, 1983, p. 88.

**Telecourse systems** through which students access programs on television or by computer link from their own homes provide more options for workers who want or need more training against the possibility of layoffs or changes in the nature of their work. With telecourses, working parents can spend the evening hours at home with their children and still dial into a class for part of the evening. Long-distance or electronic learning—nicknames that have been attached to telecourse programs—also provides training opportunities for individuals and even groups who do not live close to training facilities.[24] With telecourses, a telephone or television may be enough to begin building the foundation for a new career.

Interestingly, one major benefit of these new teaching technologies may be that they are less threatening to workers who probably already are defensive about retraining later in life. Teachers who have worked with long-distance learners claim that traditional college or junior-college classrooms can be intimidating to someone going through a mid-life job displacement crisis. Telecoursing offers those individuals the opportunity to return to the learning well and make mistakes without any fear of public embarrassment or ridicule.

The question that remains unanswered is where the money for this kind of retraining comes from. Telecoursing requires a modem and personal computer (if the work is transmitted over computer lines) or a television and VCR (if the lessons are coming in by television), not to mention the cost of enrolling for credit in the classes. Where does this money come from? Current federal efforts in this area come from the Job Training Partnership Act of 1982, which serves about 200,000 workers. Through the early 1990s, about twice that many workers are expected to need retraining. Whether industry's sense of social responsibility will lead it to shoulder the burden of retraining technologically displaced workers remains to be seen.[25]

Companies who remember that maintaining good relationships with the local labor supply is part of managing the business environment can take several steps to minimize the negative impact of technology-driven changes in the work force. Anticipation and planning are critical. If a work-force reduction looms on the business horizon, an organization can take advantage of natural attrition to ease into the change. A hiring freeze will ensure that no new permanent employees are hired only to be released when reductions or changes occur. Temporary employees can be used to help weather the transition, by filling in permanent staff positions that become vacant. Alternative employment schedules—such as shorter workweeks or greater use of part-time positions—also can ease the burden of major technology-driven work-force reductions.

[24]L. R. Smeltzer and J. A. Davy, "Teleconferencing: Reach Out to Train Someone," *Personnel Administrator,* June 1987, 211.

[25]M. Ivey, "Long-Distance Learning Gets an 'A' at Last," *Business Week,* May 9, 1988, 108–110.

Temporary employees also can be used to handle changes in the nature of work brought on by technological advancement. When the current work force lacks the skills needed for a new technology, management may perceive retraining as too disruptive of productivity. This can lead employers to lay off the current work force and hire new employees with appropriate skills rather than tackle retraining. On the other hand, temporary labor can be used to keep the company ball rolling while the current work force is retrained to handle the new technology. Not only can some of the uncertainty of hiring an entire new work force be avoided, but the increased commitment and loyalty of current workers may more than make up for any expense incurred.

As a final thought on this issue, technological changes in the nature of work also may mean altering the career paths within an organization. As jobs change, career mobility will change as well. Organizations that help their employees put these changes in proper perspective will find the transition easier.[26]

## TECHNOLOGY AND INFORMATION

According to Warren McFarlan, a department head at the Harvard Business School, "We don't change our curriculum very often." Yet 1987 was a year that warranted a major change: Information-management classes were added to the list of required courses for earning a Harvard MBA. In explaining the logic behind this move, McFarlan commented that "the general managers of the next 30 years will be unable to do their jobs without a firm grasp of information management."[27]

Harvard's move to educate its business graduates about information management reflects the growing realization in business circles that technology is quickly changing the demands for managing information. On the one hand are claims such as those made in the book, *The Information Edge,* that correctly managed information technology can return a profit as high as 1,000 percent on investment.[28] On the other hand are concerns that incorrectly managed information systems increase job stress and pressures, leading productive workers to the brink of nervous breakdowns.[29]

The fact is that technological developments have changed the availability of information in organizations dramatically. In the next section of the chapter, we will examine the effects of technology on information availability, the effects of technology on information use, and finally some surprising consequences of the information-technology boom.

[26]K. Ropp, "Technology and Employment," *Personnel Administrator,* February 1987, 81–84.

[27]R. Farmanfarmaian, "Why Managers Are Asking: Is the Computer Stealing *My* Job?" *Working Woman,* November 1987, 70–76.

[28]N. D. Meyer and M. E. Boone, *The Information Edge* (New York: McGraw-Hill, 1986).

[29]Hoerr and Pollock, "Management Discovers the Human Side of Automation," 73.

As mechanization does away with menial tasks, familiarity with intelligent machines will become a basic requirement for work. Dean Witter is helping the next generation of workers get acquainted with computers at an early age through its support of Playing to Win, Inc., a nonprofit organization.

## INFORMATION AVAILABILITY

One of the primary benefits of new developments in information technology is the increased availability of information. Availability means both retrievability and transmission of information. Many companies have now turned to electronic record-keeping systems. A state-of-the-art electronic record-keeping system consists of an integrated computer system that includes a digital scanner, optical character recognizer, laser printers, and optical disk storage for the filing and retrieving of documents.[30] Original documents can include microfilm, sketches, bills, invoices, photographs—in fact, almost everything. An electronic camera scans the original to form an image, and the image is stored electronically for later retrieval.

While electronic filing systems offer obvious advantages by eliminating the need for manual storage of information, the real value of such systems is their *retrieval* capabilities. Using "key word" access systems, a worker can retrieve information stored in the system instantly. Such speed can be critical if the information is needed immediately—say, as a part of the sales pitch to a valued customer or as evidence to back up an important point in a meeting. Portable computers make instant information access portable as well. Critical information can be loaded into computer memory and literally carried to the point of sale or into meetings.

In one in-house study conducted by Hewlett-Packard in 1986, 135 sales representatives were given laptop computers to help handle the information storage and retrieval demands of their sales jobs. After six months, HP found that time spent in staff meetings had been cut by 46 percent and time spent traveling between customers and the office by 13 percent. The result: time spent with customers increased 27 percent and sales went up 10 percent.[31]

---

[30]W. A. Kleinschrod, "The Management Message in Electronic Messaging Media," *Administrative Management*, October 1987, 13.

[31]C. L. Harris, "Office Automation: Making It Pay Off," *Business Week*, October 12, 1987, 137.

FOCUS ON:

Information
Availability

**Staying Home Is Paying Off**  In all kinds of settings across the United States, from country homes to suburban high-rise apartments, more and more people need only take a few steps from their breakfast tables to their desks to start a day's work. Of course, working at home for pay has been around for as long as homemakers have taken in knitting, doctors have put up shingles outside their houses, and writers have set up typewriters in their dens. But the advent of personal computers and other advanced technology has vastly expanded the range of occupations that can be successfully pursued in studies or basements.

About 90 percent of home professionals are entrepreneurs who have started their own businesses or work for larger companies on a contract basis. The fastest-growing category, however, is that of the so-called telecommuter—a homebound but salaried worker on a corporate payroll. The rise of telecommuting has been predicted by futurists ever since home

computers appeared a decade ago, but the phenomenon is only now beginning to catch on. Since 1982, the number of corporate employees working at home has ballooned from 20,000 to 600,000.

The proliferation of home offices would not have been possible without the electronic revolution. Using computers linked by telephone lines, home professionals can rapidly exchange information with bosses or clients. Whatever appears on the computer screen, from reports and statistics to maps and charts, can be transferred to paper through the use of compact printers. Copies of documents can be electronically transmitted over telephone lines by facsimile machines. Says Jeff Gardner, who operates an advertising agency out of his split-level home, "I can't imagine how I could run this business from home without technology. It has liberated us from the constraints of the office."

People who work at home report several advantages. Bonnie Figgatt

Unfortunately, the experiences of the USS *Vincennes* remind us that information availability can prove to be a sword that cuts both ways. The phrase *"paralysis of analysis"* describes what happens when information systems make too much information readily available. Available information demands to be taken into account, even if it is irrelevant, too detailed, too general, obsolete, or poorly organized, and thereby not only useful but potentially detrimental to decisive decision making.[32] Information systems cannot simply be passive collectors of data. They must *manage* information, including its presentation, updating, and organization.

New technological developments have also dramatically reduced the time required to *transmit* information from one place to another. Facsimile (fax) machines allow documents to cross the country not in days (as regular mail would require) or overnight (as the best delivery

[32]"Computer No Help in Executive Suite," *The Denver Post*, November 15, 1981, 3D.

estimates that she saves at least $2,000 a year by not having to drive to work, go out to lunch as often, buy as many dressy clothes, or run up her dry cleaning bills. Other pleasures are more personal than financial. "It's a lovely thing to be sitting there, with no makeup on, coffee cup in one hand, closing a deal on the phone," says Beverly Neuer Feldman, a Los Angeles writer.

Working at home, however, is hardly problem free. People often miss the intellectual stimulation and socializing that occur in office settings. Many report that they have trouble sticking to the business at hand, especially when no one is around to see them cheat by taking a nap or turning on the TV set. Some telecommuters fear they will be passed over for promotions because they never see their bosses. Managers who can no longer look over

employees' shoulders worry about losing control over their work.

At many companies, however, telecommuting seems to please both labor and management. Mountain Bell claims that its telecommuters are 35 percent to 40 percent more productive than in-office counterparts. Says William Benham, chairman of the company's telecommuting division: "Employees who work at home develop independent work habits. They learn to set goals." He predicts that by 1995 one-third of the 69,000-member work force at Mountain Bell's parent company, US West, will be telecommuting.

As that trend spreads to other companies, traditional workplaces are not going to disappear. But more and more professionals will have a choice: the camaraderie of gathering around the office coffee machine or the freedom of working at home.

Source: Janice Castro, "Staying Home Is Paying Off," *Time*, October 26, 1987, pp. 112–113.

services would provide) but literally in seconds; cellular car phones provide individuals continuous communication contact with their place of work, even while traveling from one customer to another; and electronic mail systems allow users to flash their messages worldwide in a matter of seconds, to as many people as need access. All three of these innovations get information where it needs to be when it needs to be there, even instantly. The technologically derived 1,000 percent profit figure mentioned earlier in this chapter resulted when a geographically distributed problem-solving task force used an electronic mail system to speed communications among its members. The instant communication capabilities of electronic mail allowed the task force to beat its project completion deadline and get the product to market two months early, resulting in a net savings of more than $100,000.[33] The value of timely

[33]Harris, "Office Automation," 137.

New technological developments are rapidly changing the definition of an office. Marketing director Bernie Beleskey has his "office" on wheels, complete with phone, facsimile (fax machine), and personal computer. But are such arrangements changing the nature of social relationships at work?

information transmission is so high that the use of electronic mail systems is expected to double annually between now and the year 2000.[34]

One unexpected result of the advancement of information technology is a change in the definition of the term *office*. As discussed in the "Focus on: Information Availability," home computers—doubling as information storage and retrieval systems *and* electronic mail receipt and transmission stations—have created new opportunities for many employees to complete their duties just about anywhere outside the office. What remains to be seen is whether the growth of "**telecommuting**" will dramatically alter work by reducing face-to-face communication among organizational members.

Even without telecommuting, new information systems already have altered the social interaction patterns of workers within organizations. At banks, technologically advanced information systems allow clericals to complete entire operations at individual work stations. The new work stations give workers fewer reasons to interact with coworkers, resulting in fragmentation of *social* relationships at work. Given the importance of the social context of work to worker satisfaction, this potential disruption of the social community leaves many workers feeling at odds with the new technology.[35] As discussed in the "International Focus on: Technology and Information," it is interesting to note that the usually innovative Japanese have resisted some of the most recent technological office innovations.

[34]E. Mortensen, "Adapting Electronic Mail to Management's Needs," *Administrative Management*, August 1987, 26.

[35]S. Zuboff, "New Worlds of Computer-Mediated Work," *Harvard Business Review* 60 (September/October 1982): 142–152.

INTERNATIONAL
FOCUS ON:
Technology and
Information

**Japan's Love for High Tech Stops at the Office** It's rather puzzling. Japan's cities are some of the most congested and expensive in the world. Commuters in Tokyo are shoehorned into rush-hour trains, sometimes six days a week. Inner-city apartments can run $6,000 a month. The miracle products of the electronic age, many of them made in Japan, could be used to help offset these problems. But by and large, they aren't.

Take cellular phones: Japanese manufacturers have been selling them to Americans for years. But until recently, government regulation meant high prices and low volumes at home. Only 56,000 car phones were installed in Japan in 1987 compared to 1.1 million in the United States. Japan hasn't shown much gusto, either, for its laptop computers, which dominate the world market. Then there are desktop personal computers. The workhorse of American telecommuters, they're hard to find in Tokyo—even in large offices. Overall, personal computers are used in only 20 percent of Japan's offices. Even high-technology companies average 11 workers for each machine versus 4 in typical U.S. offices.

Why? Unlike in America, where IBM and Apple Computers have set strong personal-computer standards, the Japanese PC market is splintered among numerous, incompatible machines. That, some argue, has limited the availability of useful software and the ability to share data over networks.

Japanese writing also is a factor. It includes 2,000 commonly used Chinese characters and two phonetic scripts. As a result, there's never been an easily used Japanese typewriter— and few people take quickly to computer keyboards. Lately, Japanese word processors have caught on, but mainly among young people, not managers.

On the other hand, keyboarditis has made facsimile machines popular in Japan. "Americans like to sign their letters by hand. Japanese feel that way toward all personal communication," says Toru Maekawa, deputy director in the Ministry of International Trade & Industry. "If you get something printed, you assume the same thing has been sent to lots of other people." In technically advanced offices, there's one fax for every 22 workers.

Still, the national culture seems antithetical to telecommuting. "Japanese don't trust electronic information," says Takao Ogiya, planning section chief of the government's Small & Medium Enterprise Agency. A suburban merchant, he says, would much rather go to Tokyo to acquire business information than tap into a remote computer from his shop. "Business is built on interaction," Ogiya says. "Businessmen want to read each other's expressions." Moreover, he adds, Japanese prefer to make decisions in groups. "If one man decides, he's liable to get stuck with all the blame."

The government is trying to encourage more widespread use of new technology. One effort, called *zuno ritchi*, or "brain location," seeks to entice information industries to outlying communities. But success appears far off. "Electronic data is all in the past tense," says Yotaro Suzuki, vice-president of the Japanese Institute of Office Automation. People get the most valuable information, he says, face to face.

Source: N. Gross, "Tokyo's Love Affair with High Tech Stops at the Office," *Business Week*, October 10, 1988, p. 112.

Of course, not all technological innovations serve only management's needs. The computerization of human-resource information systems is making available to both managers *and* workers a host of information about career paths and opportunities both within and without organizations.[36]

## INFORMATION USE

Marshall McLuhan is probably best remembered for his contention that "the medium is the message"—an assertion that an era's medium of communication has a larger influence on the thinking of its generation than any of the messages sent via that medium.[37] Our generation might well ask, "How have electronic information systems changed the way we think about and use information?"

One development that has changed the way people think about and use information are expert systems. **Expert systems** are an outgrowth of the field of artificial intelligence: the attempt to construct machines that "think" like humans. An expert system is a computer program that mimics the thought processes of an expert decision maker or problem solver. At Midwest Metal Products, a small midwestern manufacturer, president William Wendt developed an expert system on his personal computer that has saved the company about $100,000 a year in salaries. Special fabrication shops such as Midwest Metal Products live or die by their price estimates. If the estimate is too high, they lose the order to a competitor; too low, and the work doesn't turn a profit; too slow, and the customer loses interest. Without the expert system, a careful estimate might take 15 to 20 minutes. With the system, estimation time is closer to 15 to 20 *seconds*. Wendt figures the system has allowed him to reduce his estimation staff from 10 or 12 to 6, and it has given him the edge in his industry.[38]

The foundation of an expert system is the decision-making or problem-solving expertise of a real expert or (better still) group of experts. To write an expert-system program, the creator must get an expert or group of experts to divulge their expertise. A programmer then captures this knowledge in computer language. Experts often find it difficult to articulate their expertise, but the process of describing and quantifying their knowledge puts it out in the open where it can be examined, explored, and even improved upon. Programming that expertise into a computer makes it accessible even to nonexperts. Anyone who can work a computer at Midwest Metal Products can make an expert estimate. Further, expert systems render comprehensive, expert judgments more quickly and consistently than any human expert

---

[36]M. Kustoff, "Assembling a Micro-based HRIS: A Beginner's Guide," *Personnel Administrator*, December 1985, 29–38.

[37]Kleinschrod, "The Management Message."

[38]Harris, "Office Automation," 142.

could ever hope to. Expert systems even can be programmed to be self-correcting or self-generating. By making judgments, compiling feedback on those judgments, and adjusting the weighting of inputs to the decision-making or problem-solving process accordingly, expert systems can teach themselves faster and more completely than their human rivals.

The greatest benefits of expert systems unfortunately turn out to be their biggest problems. Expert systems are intended to render the decisions that an expert would have rendered. They allow nonexperts to trust the answer the system generates. Unfortunately, all expert systems necessarily mirror some of the decision-making frailties of their creators. Worse yet, expert systems suffer from implementation problems such as input information that is outdated, invalid, or even just entered incorrectly. The result can be "expert" judgments that are catastrophically amateurish. And the poor quality of these judgments may go unrecognized. In one study of computer-generated judgments, researchers found that our trust in technology-generated computations is so high that answers off by as much as 50 percent routinely were not questioned.[39] While this may be unusual, it does suggest that a little suspicion of technology is probably healthy. Again this reveals the importance of viewing information systems as *complements* to rather than substitutes for human judgment.

SURPRISING
CONSEQUENCES?

One of the interesting benefits of the new information systems is their ability to collect and compile information on an ongoing basis. For example, a computer can tabulate the length and destinations of all phone calls made by a sales force. The organization in turn can use this information to analyze and possibly redirect the sales force's efforts. One of the important unintended consequences for organizations of having this monitoring capability is that some employees now feel that the new information systems are another way for management to watch over them. And they resent it.

Most employers rank job performance improvement as the top reason for putting in something like a telephone monitoring system. At American Express, an elaborate monitoring system produces daily reports for supervisors that summarize the frequency and length of calls as well as how quickly incoming calls are answered.[40] The ability to identify employee abuses has proven to be an attractive incidental benefit of such computer monitoring systems. For phone systems alone, the cost of abuses to a big employer can run as high as $1 million annually. To discourage misuse of resources, companies use computer monitoring to

[39]L. Timnick, "Electronic Bullies," *Psychology Today,* February 1982, 10–15.

[40]J. Rothfeder, "Memo to Workers: Don't Phone Home," *Business Week,* January 25, 1988, 88–90.

generate and publish usage reports that publicly identify heavy users. Public exposure often is sufficient to stop abuse. Unfortunately, computerized performance monitoring also generates negative feelings in employees. Computer performance monitoring systems have been blamed for increases in formal grievances against management, increased union organizing, high work-force absenteeism and turnover, and reports of low morale.[41]

In the final analysis, performance monitoring and the availability of instant feedback for employees are important benefits provided by new-age information systems. Technological advances decrease the psychological involvement of workers in their work, for example by making work more abstract. Some bank-statement processing no longer involves statements at all but only images on a computer screen; some manufacturing jobs no longer involve assembling products but only operating a computer console while the computer-controlled robots perform the assembly. In these cases, performance feedback can play a critical role in keeping workers psychologically involved in their work. How can this be accomplished without risking some of the negative aspects of oversurveillance? Allowing employees *direct* access to the information should minimize the impression that it might be used to punish or prod them. In turn, this should decrease negative feelings about computer monitoring and allow its potential benefits for performance to be realized.

## SMOOTHING THE TRANSITION

There is no question that advancing technology holds considerable promise for increasing worker productivity. Technology can even improve the quality of work life for workers by eliminating routine or mindless tasks, freeing them for more interesting work. There is also no question, unfortunately, that managing the introduction of technological changes is a delicate and difficult enterprise. The advantages of new technology can evaporate in the face of a poor implementation plan. In the final section of this chapter, we will examine several technological innovations in an attempt to discern what practices contribute to the successful implementation of new technology.

## ASSESSING JOB CHANGES

Consider the experiences of a bakery that implemented two major technological changes. The first was automation of the dough-making process. Previously, the job of mixing dough was overseen by master bakers. Each master baker supervised a team of workers that brought in flour and mixed ingredients in large, open-vat spindle mixers. The master bakers could see and hear the mix and were responsible for

---

[41]Office of Technology Assessment, *The Electronic Supervisor: New Technology, New Tensions*, OTA–CIT–33 (Washington, D.C.: U.S. Government Printing Office, 1987).

making small adjustments to the ingredients to ensure acceptable quality. When mixing became automated and computer-controlled, the job of the master baker changed dramatically. All ingredients were premeasured. The master baker had responsibility for starting the machine, adding certain premeasured ingredients when ordered to by the computer, and emptying the finished dough onto the hopper that would take it to the oven. The title of the job was changed to "mixer operator" to reflect changes in the nature of the work.

Not surprisingly, this technological change was not greeted with great enthusiasm by the master bakers cum mixer operators, as reflected in the observations of their managers:

> I can see they've really switched off. I've seen it happen to new people coming in as well. It destroys the human contact.
>
> The job has got much more boring and routine. It's changed the atmosphere of the work entirely. They used to have much more to do, but [the technological change] has done away with much of the manhandling. There's no outlet on the job now and people are desperate to get away from the job.
>
> If automatic control goes too far, operators may lose interest in the work. When the plant is running smoothly, operators start talking and stop checking. Operators may lose concentration on the job. . . .
>
> One problem with the whole mixer setup seems to be that the new generation of operators don't appreciate as fully as before the consequences of what they do. It's all so automatic they have difficulty visualizing the effects of, say, half a minute extra mixing time on later stages of production.[42]

The second major change implemented in the bakery was in the ovensman job. The ovensmen had responsibility for baking biscuits of the correct bulk and weight. Every mix of dough could have different properties, and the ovensmen had to adjust the baking process accordingly. At the end of the baking line, packets of biscuits traveled past a "checkweigher." The checkweigher made random checks on packet weights every half hour.

When the computer-controlled checkweigher was installed, instant feedback about the weight of the biscuit packets became available to the ovensmen. The feedback from the electronic checkweigher signaled that something was wrong but could not isolate the source of the problem or explain how to fix it. The ovensmen still had to take into account properties of the dough to decide on corrective action. Their reaction to this change was quite positive:

> The pressures on the operators have been reduced. The [computer] acts as a double check on the ovensman; it's an assistant, a second opinion.

---

[42]D. A. Buchanan and D. Boddy, "Advanced Technology and the Quality of Working Life: The Effects of Computerized Controls on Biscuit-making Operators," in *Readings in Industrial and Organizational Psychology*, ed. F. Landy (Homewood, Ill.: Dorsey Press, 1986), 374.

Computers can be set up to track performance and offer individuals virtually instantaneous feedback about their work progress. Acceptance of this kind of close monitoring may depend on whether employees perceive it as a way to help them improve performance or just another way to help the boss keep an eye on them.

More people can now see what is happening, are aware of the state of production and level of performance . . .. If things start to go wrong, we can regain the situation faster. Before, when packets were way over or under weight, everything had to be trayed off, which wasted time.

In both of these cases of technological change, new technology substantially altered the nature of work. In the case of the master bakers, the change was clearly detrimental. The new computer-controlled mixing system assumed many of the skilled portions of the master baker's job function, such as measuring and adjusting ingredients to ensure the proper dough consistency. The work also became more abstract and less involving because the new mixing vats were closed; the mixing system operators (previously master bakers) could no longer see how their dough was progressing during the mixing phase. Further, because the technological change completely removed any decision-making and supervisory responsibilities previously exercised by the master bakers, the mixing-operator position quickly became a dead-end job. No new knowledge or skills were developed through the task, so mixing operators had no chance for further advancement in the bakery. Finally, the change in job titles simply reinforced the decrease in status attached to the new job description.

For the ovensmen, technology had a different impact. In a job where feedback previously had been too slow to be useful, the computerized checkweighing system now provided instant performance feedback. The decision making previously performed by ovensmen remained, only now their decisions could be based on much more current information. Further, the instant information provided by the system allowed the ovensmen immediate feedback on the quality of their decisions, thereby improving their understanding of the impact of their adjustments to the ovens. The computerized checkweighing system helped them do their jobs better.[43]

The contrast between these two cases is striking. Technology diminished the master-baker job by taking over its most motivating and involving function—personal responsibility for ensuring correct dough consistency. Technology complemented the ovensman job by enhancing its most motivating and involving aspects—adjusting the oven to produce the correct bulk and weight of biscuits. The experiences of the bakery suggest that the introduction of technological innovations always should be preceded by an analysis of the current design of jobs *from the viewpoint of the workers.*

An analysis would have revealed that the two major aspects of the master-baker job were responsibility for ensuring the appropriate consistency of the dough mixture and supervisory responsibility over other workers. Both were completely undermined by the new technol-

[43]Ibid., 375.

ogy. The detrimental aspects of this change could have been avoided if management had established work teams of dough mixers and given them control over the entire mixing operation. This would have allowed the master bakers to retain a sense of responsibility in their jobs. Alternatively, the dough mixers could have been given more individual responsibility for the dough recipe or given expanded job functions. All of these suggestions derive from the need to maintain the quality of the job itself.

**GENERATING OWNERSHIP**

Sometimes a company can more easily realize the benefits of technological changes when workers are brought on board early in the implementation process. Consider the following case:

> Sophisticated computer technology allows the central office of a large company to begin monitoring electronic telecommunications switching equipment in remote locations. This may eventually allow for fewer and less-skilled employees at local sites. But the local technicians resist the central monitoring centers. They fear forced relocation, job loss, the inability to keep up with their skills, and loss of control over their work while they nevertheless remain accountable for the local operation. When a central monitoring center is implemented by management fiat, it fails. Technicians resist working in the center and taking orders from it. . . .
>
> [The] conflict between the center and local technicians led the general manager to shut down the center for one year to explore alternatives. After much consideration, he asked the local technicians to volunteer to be covered by the center. Local technicians could choose the shifts the center would cover. Because they now retained some control over their switches, the local technicians accepted this compromise. The monitoring center was reopened and put into successful operation.[44]

In contrast to the changes made at the bakery, the technological innovation in this case did not necessarily have to diminish the most desirable aspect of the local technicians' jobs—their autonomy. By involving the local technicians in the implementation phase of the change, the general manager was able to enlist their assistance in finding the best way to realize the full benefits of the new technology, and without undermining the positive aspects of their jobs. Through this kind of employee involvement, management helps the target work force better understand and prepare for a new technology by enlisting its assistance in planning implementation.

At the Harvard Business School, they call the newest generation of information-system cognoscenti **gold-collar managers:** MBAs who combine business know-how with technical expertise.[45] For these "gold-

[44]M. London and J. P. MacDuffie, "Technological Innovations: Case Examples and Guidelines," *Personnel*, November 1987, 26.
[45]Farmanfarmaian, "Why Managers Are Asking: Is the Computer Stealing *My* Job?"

collar" workers to be worth their hefty paychecks, their technical expertise must go beyond knowledge about information systems. As the experiences of other companies have proved, "gold-collar" expertise must include an understanding of how to get people and machines to fit together rather than fight each other in the workplace. Only then will America's newest generation of corporate leaders be able to meet the challenge of managing new technologies for maximum organizational benefit.

## SUMMARY

Broadly defined, technology is anything the workers of an organization use to transform the organization's inputs into outputs. Technology also represents "the edge" —the way for management to increase the productivity of its work force and increase profits, or at least maintain competitiveness. In reality, technology is no edge at all. The competitive edge comes when managers achieve a harmonious integration of their human and technological resources.

Technological determinism refers to the influence technology has on behaviors of and in organizations. The extent to which an organization must tailor its outputs to the needs of particular customers will determine what type of production technology it must use. The technology in turn affects the behaviors and design of the organization. The rate of technological change within an industry also will influence an organization's actions. Technology is an important source of environmental uncertainty that organizations must manage.

Two major sources of technological innovation are automation and information technology. Automation occurs when a task performed by a human worker is mechanized to be performed by a machine. Intelligent automation occurs when the design of automated technology includes the ability to adapt or make decisions. For better or worse, experiments with automation suggest that it works best when designed to complement the skills of rather than replace human workers. Implementation of automated production technologies must entail some awareness of the potential of worker alienation if automation oversimplifies their work. Employers also must plan for the effects of automation on their work force, whether they include worker displacement, replacement, or retraining.

Information technology is rapidly changing the availability and use of information in organizations. Both retrievability and transmission of information have been drastically changed by new information technologies, making it possible to find almost any piece of information and send it anywhere instantly. Some of these technological changes are even altering the definition of the term *office* by making it possible for employees to be in constant contact with coworkers regardless of their location. Expert systems also are changing the efficiency and effectiveness of human decision-making powers. Further, new information technologies are allowing management to continuously monitor worker performance. When managed appropriately, this new ability can put more useful feedback in the hands of workers when they need it most. If managed poorly, this monitoring capability can negatively affect work-force morale.

The term "gold collar" refers to a new generation of workers who have both business skills and technology expertise. Because of the rapid advance of technological developments, such expertise needs to include more than just an understanding of how to use particular new technologies. It also must include an awareness of how to correctly integrate the benefits of that new technology with the organization's human resources. "Gold-collar" managers must understand the effects of new technologies on the nature of work for their work force, and must work hard to encourage a sense of ownership of new technologies among their workers. For the current generation of managers, an understanding of technology is a plus; for the next generation of managers, it will be a necessity.

KEY TERMS

**Automation** Using machines to replace or assist workers.

**Computer-integrated manufacturing (CIM)** Manufacturing technologies that combine task mechanization with computerized information processing about the task.

**Expert systems** Computer programs that mimic the thought processes of an expert decision maker or problem solver.

**Gold-collar managers** Managers who combine business know-how with technical expertise in how to get people and machines to work together (rather than fight each other) in the workplace.

**Mechanization** Programming a machine to execute the component actions of a work task faster, more precisely, and more consistently than any human.

**Output customization** Extent to which an organization's products or services are influenced by customer needs.

**Paralysis of analysis** When timely and decisive decision making fails to occur because too much irrelevant, detailed, obsolete, or poorly organized information is readily available.

**Robot** Machine guided by automatic controls to perform various complex functions like a human being.

**Technological determinism** Perspective that the way a firm is organized (how it makes decisions or how much training its line workers receive, for example) depends on the technology the firm uses to transform its inputs into outputs.

**Technological type** Joan Woodward's classifications of ways an organization can transform inputs into outputs, which determine behavior in the organization: (A) unit or small-batch production, (B) large-batch production, and (C) mass production or process manufacturing.

**Telecommuting**   Employees completing their duties outside the office using home computers that double as information storage and retrieval systems and electronic mail receipt and transmission stations.

**Telecourse systems**   Training workers using television programs or computer links in the workers' homes.

**DISCUSSION QUESTIONS**

1. There is an old saying that "a little knowledge is a dangerous thing." With the advent of new information technologies, the reverse problem may be true. How might a lot of information be a dangerous thing, too?

2. What are some of the ways that the arrival of a new technology can threaten the jobs of current employees? What can a manager do to minimize the negative impact on work-force morale of a new technology?

3. What is the role of expert systems in organizational decision making? Does the use of expert systems guarantee that managers will make better decisions?

4. Describe the two forms of technological determinism discussed in this chapter. How do both of these reflect the powerful influence of uncertainty on behavior of and in organizations?

5. What does it mean to be a "gold-collar" worker? What specific skills will the "gold-collar" managers of the future need to have?

6. Why is work-force involvement critical to the successful implementation of a new technology?

7. As new information technologies allow the dissolution of the traditional office, how is the nature of work likely to change? Are these changes likely to alter organizational outcomes, such as the quality of organizational decision making?

8. Are advances and developments in information technology (such as high-speed computers and fax machines) making the concept of bounded rationality obsolete?

IF YOU
WANT TO
KNOW
MORE

An entire issue of *Organizational Dynamics* (Autumn 1985) was devoted to the issue of advancing technology and its effects on organizational behavior. The special issue includes three particularly insightful pieces. An article by Shoshana Zuboff entitled "Automate/ Informate: The Two Faces of Intelligent Technology" explores the differences between using technology for automation and information functions. An article by Karl Weick entitled "Cosmos vs. Chaos: Sense and Nonsense in Electronic Contexts" discusses how electronic media may alter the meaning of information. Finally, Peter Keen's article, "Computers and Managerial Choice," discusses the role of new technologies in helping managers make better decisions.

An article by Donald Gerwin, "Relationships between Structure and Technology" (in the 1981 Oxford University Press *Handbook of Organizational Design,* edited by P. Nystrom and W. H. Starbuck), discusses some of the issues raised in the beginning of the chapter concerning technology's influence on the design of organizations.

One important issue raised by advancing technology and not discussed in this chapter is information privacy in an age of electronic record-keeping.

This issue is addressed in an article entitled "Don't Tread on My Data: Protecting Individual Privacy in the Information Age," by Philip Elmer-DeWitt, in the July 6, 1987, issue of *Time*.

The issue of worker displacement by technological innovation is discussed in "Worker Obsolescence: The Human Resource Dilemma of the '80s," by Jeffrey Bracker and John Pearson, in the December 1986 issue of *Personnel Administrator.* Smoothing the introduction of new technology under these circumstances is discussed by Lisa Mainiero and Robert DeMichiell in their article, "Minimizing Employee Resistance to Technological Change," in the July 1986 issue of *Personnel.* Technology implementation issues also are discussed in "The Electronic Office: How to Make It User Friendly," by Wilbert O. Galitz and David J. Cirillo, in the April 1983 *Management Review.*

Finally, the ways in which information technologies may alter interactions between workers are explored in "Social Psychological Aspects of Computer-Mediated Communication," by Sara Kiesler, Jane Siegel, and Tim McGuire, in the October 1984 issue of *American Psychologist.*

ON YOUR
OWN

**Attitudes toward Computer Usage**   Are you ready to move into the age of information technology? Your responses to the following questions will provide you an indication of your own receptiveness to the introduction of new technologies in organizations. Answer the following questions using this scale:

**Strongly 1** . . . . . . . . **2** . . . . . . . . **3** . . . . . . . . **4** . . . . . . . . **5 Strongly**
    **Agree**                                                                **Disagree**

_____ 1. I would prefer to type a paper on a word processor rather than on a typewriter.

_____ 2. Whenever I use something that is computerized, I am afraid I will break it.

_____ 3. I like to keep up with technological advances.

_____ 4. I know that I will not understand how to use computers.

_____ 5. Using a computer is too time consuming.

_____ 6. I feel that having a computer at work would help me with my job.

_____ 7. I prefer not to learn how to use a computer.

_____ 8. I would like to own, or I do own, a computer.

_____ 9. I like to play video games.

_____ 10. I feel that the use of computers in schools will help children learn mathematics.

_____ 11. I prefer to use an automatic teller for most of my banking.

_____ 12. If I had children, I would not buy them computerized toys.

_____ 13. I have had bad experiences with computers.

_____ 14. I would prefer to order items in a store through a computer rather than wait for a store clerk.

_____ 15. I feel that the use of computers in schools will negatively affect children's reading and writing abilities.

_____ 16. I do not like using computers because I cannot see how work is being done.

_____ 17. I would prefer to go to a store that uses computerized price-scanners rather than go where the clerks enter each price into a cash register.

_____ 18. I do not feel I have control over what I do when I use a computer.

_____ 19. I think that computers and other technological advances have helped to improve our lives.

_____ 20. I do not like to program computerized items such as VCRs and microwave ovens.

Your instructor will supply you with directions for scoring your responses.

Source: P. M. Popovich, K. R. Hyde, T. Zakrajsek, and C. Blumer, "The Development of the Attitudes Toward Computer Usage Scale," *Educational & Psychological Measurement,* 1987, vol. 47, pp. 261–269.

CLOSING CASE
FOR CHAPTER 15

# THE MANAGER'S MEMO

FROM: P. Briggs, Purchasing Manager

TO:    T. Han, Sales Manager

RE:    Car Phones

I have just received literature on a product that you might be interested in: deluxe car phones. According to the manufacturer, this product could greatly increase the productivity of the sales department.

If you install a car phone in each salesperson's car, you can be in virtually continuous contact with the sales force. Whenever you want to talk to one of the sales reps, you simply call. Furthermore, each salesperson can use a portable computer to transmit orders and reports through the car phone to the office. With this communication power, the sales reps will seldom have to come into the office and can spend more time on the road making sales calls.

This means we can also lower overhead costs. Because the salespeople will be on the road most of the time, they will not each need an office. Instead, we can consolidate their offices into one bullpen, and use the extra space for other activities.

A special benefit of this particular car phone is that it has a long-range beeper. The beeper sends back a signal, so you can use an electronic map to track where each salesperson goes. This information will enable you to review and improve the efficiency of their call patterns.

Would you like to pursue this idea? Please let me know what you think about it.

CASE DISCUSSION
QUESTIONS

Assume you are the sales manager, and write a response to the purchasing manager's memorandum. Do you think the purchasing manager has thought out the impact of this technological innovation carefully? How is this innovation likely to alter the nature of work for the sales force? How are the salespeople likely to react? What can the sales manager do to improve the likelihood that the new phone will enhance the productivity of the sales force?

CHAPTER

# 16

# Organizational Structure and Design

## Structuring Ceramics, Inc.

Grace Raku made pottery in her basement. That involved a number of distinct tasks—wedging clay, forming pots, tooling them when they were semidry, preparing and applying the glazes, and firing the pots in the kiln. The coordination of all these tasks presented no problem; she did them all herself.

The problem was that orders exceeded Raku's production capacity. So she hired Janice Bisque, who was eager to learn pottery making. But this meant that Raku had to divide up the work. Since the craft shops wanted pottery made by Raku, she decided that Bisque would wedge the clay and prepare the glazes, and she would do the rest herself. This decision required coordination of the work —a small problem with only two people in the pottery studio. They simply communicated informally.

The arrangement worked well —so well that, before long, Raku was again swamped with orders. More assistants were needed. But this time, foreseeing the day when they would be forming pots them-selves, Raku decided to hire them right out of the local pottery school. While it had taken some time to train Bisque, the three new assistants knew exactly what to do at the outset and blended right in; even with five people, coordination presented no problem.

When two more assistants were added to the group, however, co-ordination problems did arise. One day Bisque tripped over a pail of glaze and broke five pots; another day, Raku opened the kiln to find that the hanging planters had all been glazed fuchsia by mistake. At this point, she realized that seven people in a small pottery studio could not coordinate all their work through the simple mechanism of informal communication. Making matters worse was the fact that Raku, now calling herself president of Ceramics, Inc., was forced to spend more and more time with customers; indeed, during those days she was more apt to be found in a Marimekko dress than a pair of jeans. So she named Bisque studio manager and entrusted her

669

with supervising and coordinating the work of the five producers of the pottery.

The firm continued to grow. Major changes again took place when a work-study analyst was hired. He recommended that each person perform only one task for one of the product lines (pots, ashtrays, hanging planters, and ceramic animals): the first wedge, the second form, the third tool, and so on. Thus, production took the form of four assembly lines. Each person followed a set of standard instructions worked out in advance to ensure the coordination of everybody's work. Of course, Ceramics, Inc., no longer sold to craft shops; Raku would only accept orders by the gross, most of which came from chains of discount stores.

Raku's ambition was limitless, and when the chance came to diversify, she did—first into ceramic tiles, then bathroom fixtures, and finally clay bricks. The firm was subsequently partitioned into three divisions: Consumer Products, Building Products, and Industrial Products. From her office on the 55th story of the Pottery Tower, she coordinated the activities of the divisions by reviewing their performance each quarter of the year and taking personal action when their profit and growth figures dipped below those budgeted. It was while sitting at her desk one day going over these budgets that Raku gazed out at the surrounding skyscrapers and decided to rename her company "Ceramico."

Source: H. Mintzberg, *Structure in Fives: Designing Effective Organizations* (Englewood Cliffs, N.J.: Prentice-Hall), pp. 1–2.

---

## INTRODUCTION

As suggested by the story of Ceramico, the structure of an organization is the formal means by which it coordinates the activities of its work force to accomplish its goals and objectives. At Ceramico, Raku needed to adjust the structure of her organization periodically to remain competitive and efficient in the ceramics industry. Specifically, Raku restructured her organization several times to improve the coordination of the work and her workers.

Virtually all organized human activity requires two forms of organizational structure: the division of labor into various component tasks to be performed, and the coordination of these tasks to produce the organization's outputs. As noted in Chapter 1, organizations typically form because some goal or mission entails a variety of component tasks, more than any one individual could hope to accomplish alone. In an organization, different members of the work force are assigned component tasks of the organization's mission, known as their roles.[1] At

[1] James D. Thompson, *Organizations in Action* (New York: McGraw-Hill, 1967).

Ceramico, for instance, Raku deals with the public side of the business, while Bisque manages the pottery studio. The different roles and behaviors of the organization's work force then must be coordinated. This is where structure emerges.[2] **Organizational structure** is the skeleton of an organization that captures the relationships among different roles in the organization. **Organization design,** on the other hand, is the process of *creating* structure: grouping roles and activities to coordinate the interdependencies among organizational actors effectively.[3]

A common way to represent the organization's structure to employees (and outsiders as well) is through an organizational chart, such as the one shown in Figure 16–1. An organizational chart is a representation of the formal lines of authority in an organization. Each box on the chart represents a position. Boxes are connected to each other with vertical solid lines (indicating a direct reporting relationship). Horizontal solid lines represent communication (but not authority) relationships. Broken lines represent informal or infrequent relationships.

In this chapter, we will describe the most common organizational structures and examine the ways they influence the relationships and interactions among members of an organization. Then we will identify the factors that influence the effectiveness of a particular organizational structure and examine what happens to organizational performance when there is a fit between the organizational structure and the various factors that influence it. We conclude the chapter by examining some symptoms of inappropriate organizational structures.

## ELEMENTS OF ORGANIZATIONAL STRUCTURE

An organization's structure reflects the way the organization divides up and coordinates work. An appropriate structure (the division and coordination of tasks) is essential to the efficient attainment of an organization's goals. In this section, we will consider four design features that organizations use to divide up and coordinate work: job specialization, departmentalization, centralization, and span of control.

## JOB SPECIALIZATION

The overall task of any organization can be divided into various component tasks. At Ceramico, the overall task is selling pottery. The component tasks include production and sales; production itself requires wedging the clay, throwing the pots, and glazing the pots. The major benefit of **job specialization**—assigning each member of the work force a limited number of component tasks—is that employees can become very skilled and productive at a limited number of assigned tasks. Further, when workers' roles are limited in scope, the skills for a

[2]Jeffrey Pfeffer, *Organizational Design* (Arlington Heights, Ill.: AHM Publishing, 1978).
[3]Jay Galbraith, *Designing Complex Organizations* (Reading, Mass.: Addison-Wesley, 1973).

672

**FIGURE 16–1**    A Hospital: An Organization Structured by Knowledge and Skills

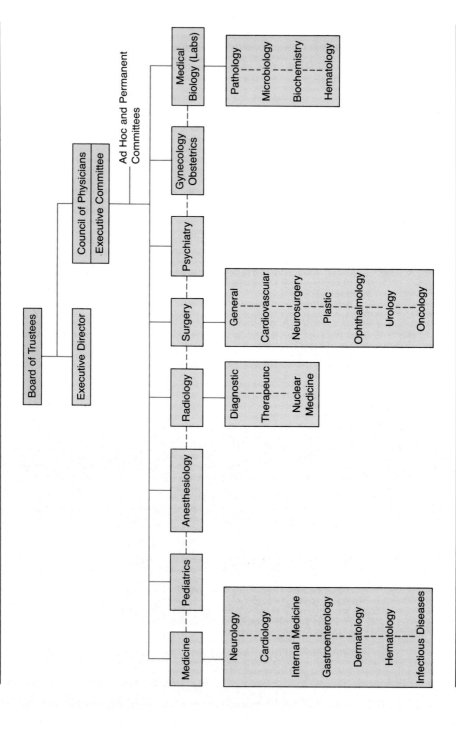

Source: H. Mintzberg, *The Structuring of Organizations* (Englewood Cliffs, N.J.: Prentice-Hall, 1979).

particular role are easily taught to another employee, such as a newcomer.

Jobs can be specialized along two dimensions: the number of tasks assigned to a role (horizontal specialization) and the amount of responsibility for organizing tasks assigned to a role (vertical specialization). Jobs are specialized horizontally to increase productivity and to match employees with tasks. Horizontal specialization increases productivity by using repetition and standardization and by making the task easier to perform. When five different people were assigned five distinct jobs by the work-study consultant at Ceramics, Inc., the company was able to take advantage of increased task specialization. As noted in Chapter 12, however, the increases in productivity achieved by horizontal specialization may be short-lived if they lead to worker boredom or alienation.

While horizontal specialization limits the number of component tasks assigned to a particular role, vertical specialization separates those who perform tasks from those who administer or organize them. Vertical specialization is useful because it takes different skills or perspectives to organize tasks than to perform them.[4] Often jobs that are horizontally specialized also must be vertically specialized. With horizontal specialization, the job incumbent sees only a small piece of the task. This may make it difficult for job incumbents to relate or integrate their work into the larger picture that includes the work of others. Raku recognized this when she assigned Bisque the job of studio manager. Bisque's new job was vertically enlarged; her previous job had been horizontally and vertically specialized.

## DEPARTMENTAL-IZATION

**Departmentalization,** the grouping of organizational roles by determining which jobs fit together, is another feature used to structure organizations. Related tasks can be assigned to the same subunit (a department, for instance) because of similarities in the required knowledge and skills members bring to the job. For example, universities divide faculty into colleges, schools, and departments; the members of each group become more similar as we move down the list.

In addition to similarity of skills and knowledge, departmentalization can be based on similar levels of skills and abilities. For example, traditional hospitals and health maintenance organizations (HMOs) have somewhat different structures. The skills required in each setting are similar, but the goals of the two types of organizations are different (curing illness in hospitals versus preventing illness in HMOs). The HMO is focused on efficiently handling patients. The task of seeing patients at an HMO is more specialized, and each member of the medi-

---

[4]H. Mintzberg, *The Structuring of Organizations* (Englewood Cliffs, N.J.: Prentice-Hall, 1979).

cal team has a task to complete. Physicians see patients in both hospitals and HMOs, but in an HMO the patient typically is first screened by another health-care professional, such as a nurse's assistant. The time the physician spends with a patient is limited, to make the most efficient use of the physician's time. In contrast, the hospital is more focused on effectiveness. Consequently, hospitals are structured by skills. There is a cardiology unit, a trauma unit, and so on. The physicians in each unit spend more time with each patient and the goal is to cure the illness. Hospitals place less emphasis on efficiency, which is reflected in their organizational structures.

An organization's component tasks also can be grouped by the functions of the component tasks. In functional departmentalization, typical organizational functions include production, marketing, finance, personnel, and accounting. The major advantage of functional depart- mentalization is that experts in an area are concentrated and can share their expertise to accomplish their tasks. A disadvantage of this method of organizational design is the creation of barriers between departments. These barriers limit communication, decrease the salience of organiza- tional goals, and create unnecessary competition for resources among groups.

An organization's component tasks can also be departmentalized by the types of outputs or products they produce. In a diversified organization, all the jobs required to produce and sell a product or group of related products are under the direction of one individual. The firm grows by increasing the number and types of products it produces. In fact, as firms grow, it becomes increasingly more difficult to coordinate the functional areas. A common response to organizational success in the form of growth is to reorganize from functional to diversified (product) departmentalization.

An organization's tasks can also be organized by the type of client they serve (for example, retail versus wholesale) or by geographic region. Banks, for example, have different departments for consumer loans, business loans, mortgage loans, and the like. If an organization is geographically dispersed, then it may be necessary to divide groups based on their geographic relationship. It is very difficult to manage an organization over large distances, and diverse social and cultural expectations add to the problems. Examples of product, function, client, and geographic departmentalization are illustrated in Figure 16–2.

The advantage of these forms of departmentalization is that they allow quick responses to changes in the product, in the client base, or in a geographic region. These structures also encourage departmental loyalty by focusing employees' attention on the attainment of a common goal (such as the success of a particular product line, satisfying the customer, or serving a geographic region). The disadvantage of these forms of structure is redundancy. An organization with a product, client, or geographic orientation must assign people in all functional areas

**FIGURE 16–2**   Four Types of Departmental Structure

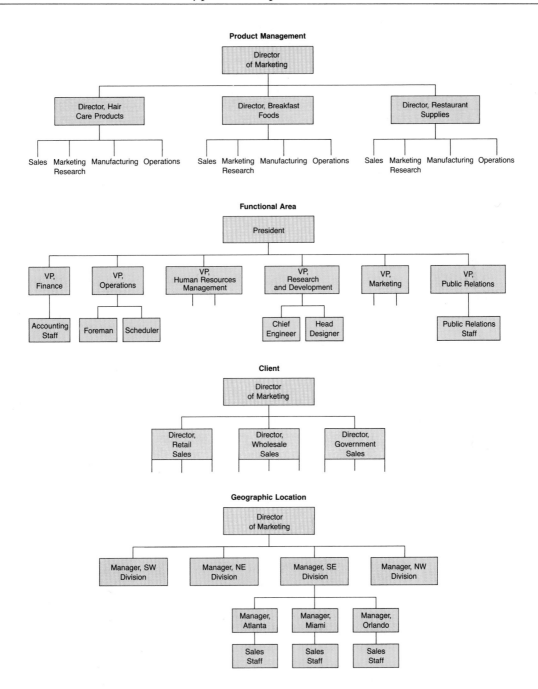

Source: J. R. Gordon, *A Diagnostic Approach to Organizational Behavior* (Boston: Allyn & Bacon, 1987).

(such as sales and personnel) to each product, customer, or geographic area. In addition, the attention of these functional area specialists will not be focused on their area of expertise, so they may be less likely to keep pace with changes in their profession.

## CENTRALIZATION

In 1985, CEO John Young centralized Hewlett-Packard's loose federation of entrepreneurships to improve co-ordination among product groups. The reorganization cost HP a few employees who preferred the older, more entrepreneurial culture, but it has improved HP's responsiveness in the computer marketplace.

**Centralization** of organizational structure is based on the dual needs of division and coordination of labor. An organization is centralized to the extent that its decision-making power rests with one or a few individuals. In a highly centralized organization, all decisions are made by one person and implemented through formal authority channels. While centralization typically improves the coordination of an organization's activities, it does have problems. Centralized decision makers often do not have all the information necessary to make good decisions, or cannot make decisions and send them back down the organization's formal authority channels quickly enough to be effective. In the past 30 years, the trend among companies in the United States has been to decentralize. Decision-making authority is being pushed lower and lower in American organizations so that decisions can be made quickly and at the point where the most diagnostic information is available.

In spite of this trend, decentralization is not right for all companies. The "Focus on: Centralization" provides one example of a highly successful centralization effort at Hewlett-Packard. However, a number of factors might lead an organization to decentralize:

1. The more change an organization faces and the more quickly decisions must be made, the more likely that decentralization will prove beneficial. Decentralization allows a work group (for instance, a product division) to respond quickly to changes, rather than having to request instructions through the organization's formal authority channels.

2. As organizations increase in size, centralized decision makers get further and further from the information they need to make high-quality decisions, and it takes longer and longer for information and their decisions to travel up and down the organization's formal channels of authority. Thus, growth inevitably leads to decentralization of decision making.

3. Risk often tends to centralize decision making. Where the consequences of making poor decisions are great, top management will be unlikely to give up control.

4. Finally, centralization may be a function of the quality of an organization's channels of communication. If an organization's channels of communication are highly efficient, centralized decision makers may be able to gather information and return decisions quickly enough to remain effective.[5]

[5]E. Dale, *Organization* (New York: American Management Association, 1967).

FOCUS ON:
Centralization

**Hewlett-Packard—The End or the Beginning?** Ever since William Hewlett and David Packard started the company in Packard's garage back in 1939, Hewlett-Packard (HP) has been a company run by engineers for engineers. Organizationally it has been a loosely knit federation of highly autonomous production divisions, with each responsible for its own marketing.

HP has long been recognized as a great place to work. Long before Japanese management practices became the rage, HP pioneered practices like flextime, no layoffs, and open-door management. Also largely absent was the them-versus-us division between workers and management. There was a lively sense of everyone being in the same boat, even though different people pull different oars. In August of 1985, for example, faced with slowing sales as the computer slump persisted, the CEO informed the division that all HP workers would be expected to take off two days a month, without pay, to avoid having to lay off personnel. What happened? Although production ceased in most divisions, a number of nonproduction employees showed up on payless Fridays, working for free. It seems that the company cared about its workers and the workers cared about the company.

But the computer world was changing. Big corporate customers stopped buying equipment piecemeal and insisted that whatever they bought fit coherently into a systematic whole. No longer were computer companies selling to other engineers.

While the old HP organization encouraged a healthy entrepreneurial spirit that saved HP from hardening of the bureaucratic arteries, it began to create problems. Coordination among groups (specifically, the computer and instrument groups) became problematic. The old system of organizing contributed to a pattern of product delays. HP fumbled in the important market for engineering workstations when the software to make the HP–9000 useful to customers didn't arrive on time.

For all its problems, HP was doing well. In 1985, it earned 20.6 percent on its equity. So, rather than waiting until the coordination issue became a real problem, CEO John Young decided to restructure HP by pulling HP's loose federation of entrepreneurships into an integrated company capable of designing and selling the integrated systems and networks the big corporate customers demanded. The old structure was replaced with a market-oriented structure, which meant bringing the fiercely independent instrument and computer sides of the company together and redefining how much autonomy to allow HP's 50+ divisions. The reorganization had its casualties. The centralization move cost Young several valuable HP players who left to work for other, more entrepreneurial firms.

In the years since the restructuring, much has happened. HP shipped the first of its Spectrum computers using the new RISC (Reduced Instruction Set Computing) technology in 1986. These computers complete office tasks in 30 percent less time than existing machines and cost less than half as much. In addition, the company has revamped nearly its entire line of computers and is paying more attention to industry-standard software and hardware. Says Young, "We have the best product portfolio in my 29 years at HP."

*(Continued)*

SPAN OF CONTROL

A fourth element of organizational structure is the span of control. **Span of control** is the number of people reporting to a manager. The size of an organization's work groups is determined by its managerial span of control. Span of control is directly related both to the closeness of supervision and the "depth" of the organization. With fewer subordinates, a manager can supervise more closely. Such a narrow span of control is important in an organization or work unit with a task in which close interpersonal control of subordinates is desired. If the task requires machine-paced, well-learned, or easily monitored behaviors, there is less need for a narrow span of control.[6] In fact, to assess the appropriate span of control, a manager must consider both the routineness of the task and the time required to monitor and coordinate subordinates' activities.[7]

Span of control is also directly related to the number of levels in (or "depth" of) an organization. Typically, the greater the span of control in an organization, the fewer the number of hierarchical levels. An organization with few hierarchical levels appears "flat" in its organizational chart. An organization with many hierarchical levels (and typically a narrow span of control) appears "tall" in its organizational chart. Figure 16–3 illustrates both a flat and a tall organizational structure.

Are tall or flat organizations more effective? In terms of overall performance of organizations with the same tasks, it seems that flat organizations have a slight edge over tall organizations. In a study of Sears, Roebuck and Company, those Sears stores with flat structures had

[6]P. M. Blau and W. R. Scott, *Formal Organizations* (San Francisco: Chandler, 1962).

[7]K. D. Mackenzie, *Organization Structures* (Arlington Heights, Ill.: AHM Publishing, 1978).

**FIGURE 16–3**     Tall and Flat Organizations Compared

Span of control is a major determinant of the number of administrative levels in an organization: the more subordinates managed by each supervisor, the flatter the organization's administrative structure.

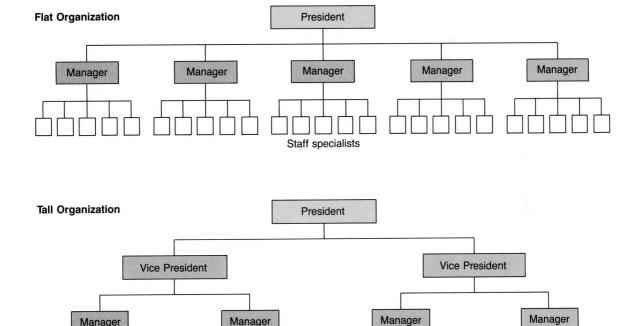

relatively better sales, profitability, and employee job satisfaction than stores with taller structures.[8] While the performance of flat organizations may exceed that of tall organizations in companies with a constellation of tasks such as Sears, a review of the research in this area suggests that there is no one best number of subordinates for a manager's span of control or best number of hierarchical levels.[9] Rather, the optimal span

[8]J. C. Worthy, "Organizational Structure and Employee Morale," *American Sociological Review* 15 (1950): 169–179.

[9]D. R. Dalton et al., "Organizational Structure and Performance: A Critical Review," *Academy of Management Review* 5 (1980): 49–64.

of control depends on the degree of job specialization, the members' need for autonomy and direct access to the supervisor, and the similarity of jobs in the unit.[10]

Related to span of control is **administrative intensity,** the proportion of administrators and managers in an organization's total work force. In recent years, administrative intensity has become a proxy for productivity. Since managers and administrators do not directly produce an organization's outputs, the more administrators or managers an organization has, the higher the number of employees required to transform the raw materials into the organization's output. The differences in administrative intensity between Japanese and American companies is touted as one of the reasons for Japan's lower production costs.

## COMMON ORGANIZATIONAL STRUCTURES

These four elements of organizational structure—job specialization, departmentalization, centralization, and span of control—all provide ways for organizations to coordinate their employees to create outputs. Using these features to divide up and coordinate the component tasks of an organization's mission, three primary forms of organizational structure emerge: the simple structure, the bureaucracy, and the organic structure.[11] Figure 16–4 provides an overview of these three types of structure and the types of task coordination and control used in each.

## SIMPLE STRUCTURE

**Simple structure** most often occurs in young or small organizations. Coordination is largely a function of direct supervision, and the top manager has significant control. In fact, it is common for all employees to report directly to the top manager. Employees have very little discretionary decision-making power, although there is rarely a formal policies and procedures statement. The best illustration of this type of firm is the entrepreneurial firm. Such a firm is aggressive and often innovative, although it is usually careful to remain in the market niche best understood by the founding entrepreneur. Inside the firm, all revolves around the entrepreneur. Its goals are the entrepreneur's goals; its strategy, the entrepreneur's visions. Entrepreneurial firms are often founded by individuals who resist the type of control imposed by bureaucratic organizations and who view more formal structure as constraints on their flexibility.[12]

## BUREAUCRACY

In a survey of electronics firms in Scotland, two organizational researchers, Tom Burns and G.M. Stalker, classified all the firms they studied into

---

[10]Mintzberg, *The Structuring of Organizations.*

[11]Ibid.

[12]Ibid.

**FIGURE 16–4**     Overview of Organizational Structures

The amount of control needed to coordinate interdependence among employees yields one of three types of organizational structure: simple, bureaucracy, or organic.

**Coordinating and Control Mechanism**

| | |
|---|---|
| **Simple Structure** | Direct supervision |
| **Bureaucracy** | Standardization of work process or skills |
| **Organic Structure** | Mutual adjustment |

Source: Henry Mintzberg, *The Structuring of Organizations* (Englewood Cliffs, N.J.: Prentice-Hall, 1979).

Wal-Mart has avoided the pitfalls of growth and bureaucracy through a formal policy of "management by walking around." Corporate management, led by 14 regional vice-presidents, visits stores and support facilities every week to gather new ideas. They reassemble at their Bentonville, Arkansas, headquarters on Friday mornings to exchange information and formulate plans for the weeks ahead.

two categories: mechanistic and organic.[13] Mechanistic organizations embody Max Weber's bureaucratic organizational form, described in Chapter 2. The major goal of bureaucratic organizations is predictability. In a bureaucracy, tasks are carefully planned in advance and the quantity and quality of performance is closely monitored. In addition, roles tend to be narrow in scope with extremely well-defined responsibilities. A detailed formal authority hierarchy exists to control and coordinate task performance. Rewards are allocated on the basis of following instructions, and compensation and selection are tied to ability to perform within narrow job functions.

Bureaucracies may be either machine or professional, depending on whether the organization's transformation technology is machines or people. A **machine bureaucracy** has highly specialized and routine tasks, formalized procedures for the transformation process, a proliferation of rules, regulations, and communication channels, a functional departmentalization structure, a large span of control, and an elaborate administrative and technical structure. The technical support staff's primary role is to develop formalized work policies and procedures for other units in the organization. Even though there is considerable formalization of policies and procedures, machine bureaucracies are often criticized for their alienated work forces and lack of innovation. Their large size makes them more suited to efficiency than to creativity. Examples of these organizations include the U.S. Postal Service, steel companies, and automobile manufacturing firms.

Professional bureaucracies differ from machine bureaucracies in that the production technology of a professional bureaucracy is composed of professionals who also control most of the organizational power. However, rather than standardizing policies and procedures as a machine bureaucracy would, the professional bureaucracy seeks to standardize skills. A professional bureaucracy's major mechanism for

[13]T. Burns and G. M. Stalker, *The Management of Innovation* (London: Tavistock, 1961).

coordination is training and indoctrination designed to internalize a set of performance and professional standards. These types of organizations often provide services rather than products. Examples of professional bureaucracies are hospitals, universities, social work agencies, and public accounting firms.

## ORGANIC STRUCTURES

The organic organizational structures identified by Burns and Stalker were more flexible; they could adapt more easily to new demands placed on them. In fact, the defining feature of an **organic structure** is being able to respond efficiently and effectively to new demands. In organic organizations:

1. Knowledge and ability rather than job descriptions or position titles determine who will participate in solving a particular problem. People are valued for their abilities rather than their organizational status.
2. Organizational status and expertise are not assumed to be related. Decision making is decentralized, and the responsibility for decisions is pushed as low as possible in the organization, to take advantage of the "hands-on" expertise of even the lowest-level members of the organization.
3. Communication flows freely in a lateral direction. The use of project teams and task forces is common (as are liaisons between departments or work groups) in order to encourage information sharing across diverse areas of expertise.[14]

The most complex and formal form of organic structure is the matrix. Unlike other organizational structures, in which employees usually report to only one supervisor, the matrix structure has a dual reporting structure. That is, the head of the functional area *and* the project or matrix manager have authority over members of the staff.

A matrix organizational structure has helped Tenneco Inc.'s Newport News, Virginia, shipyard tackle big projects like the construction of the attack submarine *Newport News*, pictured here. The matrix structure facilitates coordination of efforts along both functional and project lines.

The matrix structure is particularly useful when an organization wishes to focus its attention on the development of a particular product. Texas Instruments is a typical example of a matrix organization. The use of the matrix structure to build different types of computers for different markets allows specialization of skills and attention to both the product and its market to develop.[15] Of course, high-technology organizations are not the only ones for which matrix structures are effective. The "INTERNATIONAL FOCUS ON: Matrix Organizations," describes the reorganization of a German multinational corporation. As one would expect, matrix organizations are difficult to manage. Because each employee has

[14]C. R. Gullett, "Mechanistic versus Organic Organizations: What Does the Future Hold?" *Personnel Administrator* 20 (1975): 17–19.

[15]R. Duncan, "What Is the Right Organizational Structure? Decision Tree Analysis Provides the Answer," *Organizational Dynamics* (Winter 1979): 59–80.

INTERNATIONAL
FOCUS ON:

Matrix
Organizations

**Reorganization for Growth and Flexibility** With a total of 175,000 employees, Bayer Aktiengesellschaft of Leverkusen, West Germany, is one of the largest chemical and health-care products companies in the world. Since its founding in 1863, the company has diversified considerably in both geographic and product activities. On January 1, 1984, Bayer announced that it would restructure the organization to respond to tripled sales and the increasingly important role of its foreign activities, subsidiaries, and foreign companies. Specifically, the changes included adjusting the organizational structure to:

1. Shift management emphasis from the parent company to Bayer World by integrating Bayer's foreign activities and those of the subsidiaries more closely into the organization.
2. Regroup and restructure the various business areas and clearly define their responsibilities.
3. Delegate certain duties and decisions to lower levels of management so that the Board of Management could concentrate on the development of corporate strategy and policy.

Bayer implemented these changes by creating a quasi-matrix structure from the organization's initial functional and departmentalized structure. The matrix structure was formed by grouping all business activities of Bayer World into six Business Sectors, each of which consisted of several Business Groups, such as organic chemicals, dyestuffs, rubber, fibers, etc. The central and staff functions were combined into a corporate staff division, which serves the company worldwide. The remaining service functions, such as human resources, administrative services, and plant administration were regrouped into service divisions. In addition, each member of the Board of Management was given responsibility for a geographic region rather than a functional area as in the previous structure.

In analyzing the impact of the restructured organization one year after its implementation, the Chairman of the Board of Management, Hermann J. Strenger, reported the following effects:

1. The Board of Management was able to devote more of its time to developing corporate policy.
2. The sector heads established their roles as connecting link pins between Business Groups and the Board of Management.
3. By regrouping the 9 departments into 19 Business Groups, the company became more flexible and responsive to environmental changes.
4. Each national organization was strengthened at its respective location, and interaction with Bayer World improved.
5. The plant administration and service divisions were streamlined.

Because of the cooperation and commitment of Bayer's employees, the implementation of a matrix structure enabled Bayer World to be more responsive to global influences and environmental shocks.

Source: H. Vossverg, "Bayer Reorganizes in Response to Growth," *Long Range Planning* 18 (1985): 13–20.

**FIGURE 16–5**    Weaknesses and Strengths of Matrix Organizations

In a matrix organization, staff members report to *both* functional and product (or project) managers. A matrix organizational structure presents both advantages and disadvantages.

**Weaknesses**

It is costly to maintain the personnel pool to staff the matrix.

Participants experience dual authority of the matrix manager and functional area manager.

There is little interchange with functional groups outside the matrix, so that duplication of effort—"reinvention of the wheel"—may occur.

Participants in the matrix need to have good interpersonal skills in order for this structure to work.

**Strengths**

Personnel are able to focus full time on the project of the particular matrix.

The matrix manager is coordinator of functions for a single project.

The matrix structure reduces information requirements, as the focus is on a single product and/or market.

The matrix structure focuses specialized skills on the product and/or market.

Source: R. Duncan, "What Is the Right Organizational Structure? Decision Tree Analysis Provides the Answer," *Organizational Dynamics* (Winter 1979): pp. 59–80.

two supervisors, the potential for conflict is great. Only when the information and geographical and technological demands are so great that they require the full-time attention of a subgroup of the organization should a matrix structure be considered. The strengths and weaknesses of a matrix organization are listed in Figure 16–5.

**FACTORS INFLUENCING ORGANIZATIONAL STRUCTURE CHOICE**

Examples of each of these common organizational forms—simple, machine and professional bureaucracies, and organic structures—can be observed among successful *and* unsuccessful organizations. What determines whether a particular structural form will prove successful for an organization? The open systems view of organizations described in Chapter 14 emphasizes the fact that an organization must manage its dependence on the environment. The strategies an organization uses to manage its environment are reflected in the structure of the organization. As noted in Chapter 15, the design of the organization's structure also is influenced by the technology necessary to produce the organization's outputs. Other factors besides technology and environment have an impact on the appropriateness of organizational structure. For example, the size and age of the organization play an important role in the interdependencies within an organization and, as such, in the optimal organizational structure. In the following sections, we will examine each of these factors in detail.

INTERNAL
ORGANIZATIONAL
ENVIRONMENTS

The organization's internal or task environment has a major impact on the kind of interdependencies it must coordinate. The internal or task environment is whatever managers define as relevant to organizational decision making. It can be subdivided into three components: the organization's personnel, its functional and staff units, and its organizational levels. Figure 16–6 provides a master list of internal environmental factors. It is unlikely that any one organization would have to address all of these components in evaluating its internal environment. The list serves as a guide for managers by highlighting the environmental elements they should consider when deciding the type and intensity of coordination demanded by the organizational task. Examples of the internal environment at the personnel level include the selection and socialization process of employees, their level of job-relevant and interpersonal skills, and their commitment to the organization's goals and objectives. Other examples of the internal environment at the functional- and staff-unit level include the amount of conflict and interdependence between line and staff employees. Organizational-level characteristics focus primarily on the mechanisms the organization uses to direct its employee's efforts to achieve its goals.

**FIGURE 16–6**

## Characteristics of an Organization's Internal Environment

An organization's internal (or task) environment also provides interdependencies that the organization must coordinate. The internal environment of an organization includes personnel, functional and staff unit, and organizational level components.

**Organizational Personnel Component**

Educational and technological background and skills

Previous technological and managerial skills

Individual members' commitment to attaining system's goals

Interpersonal behavior styles

Availability of manpower for use in the system

**Organizational Functional and Staff Units Component**

Technological characteristics of organizational units

Interdependence of units in carrying out their objectives

Intraunit conflict among functional and staff units

**Organizational Level Component**

Organizational goals and objectives

Process of integrating individuals and groups into contributing maximally to attain organizational goals

Nature of organization's product or service

Source: R. Duncan, "What Is the Right Organizational Structure? Decision Tree Analysis Provides the Answer," *Organizational Dynamics* (Winter 1979): pp. 59–80.

**FIGURE 16–7**              Classification of Organizational Environments

The stability and complexity of the external environment also influences an organization's structure. Environmental stability leads to bureaucracy; environmental complexity leads to decentralization.

|            | **Stable**                                                          | **Dynamic**                                        |
|------------|---------------------------------------------------------------------|----------------------------------------------------|
| **Complex** | Decentralized Bureaucratic (standardization of skills)             | Decentralized Organic (mutual adjustment)          |
| **Simple**  | Centralized Bureaucratic (standardization of work processes)       | Centralized Organic (direct supervision)           |

Source: C. Perrow, *Organizational Analysis: A Sociological Review* (New York: Wadsworth, 1970).

**EXTERNAL ORGANIZATIONAL ENVIRONMENTS**

Once the internal environment has been specified, the external environment must be classified next. Typically, external environments have been categorized into four groups along two dimensions: the simple-complex dimension and the stable-dynamic dimension. The simple-complex dimension focuses on the number of different environments in which the organization or its units must function. A simple environment might be one faced by a lower-level manufacturing group that is dependent only on its suppliers for raw materials and on the market for sales. A complex environment is one faced by a strategic planning unit. For a successful product to be produced, the planning unit must gather inputs from many different departments in the organization; similarly, its output (the strategic plan) is consumed by many different organizational subunits. Because the planning unit must consider many different factors in the different environments it faces, it has a complex environment.

The stable-dynamic dimension is concerned with the amount of change in environmental factors that the organization must face. A stable environment is one in which there is little uncertainty. In the past, banks operated in a stable environment. However, since the deregulation of the banking industry, banks have had to face a dynamic environment. That is, banks today must confront a rapidly changing environment to be successful. Figure 16–7 illustrates the classification of organizational environments based on these two dimensions.

**TECHNOLOGY**

Chapter 15 was devoted exclusively to technology, but it is important here to reconsider the impact of technology on organizational or unit structure. As defined in Chapter 15, technology is the transformation process, the mechanism by which an organization accomplishes its

The production technology available to an organization dramatically influences span of control. Complex technologies (like the one used at the Genetic Systems division of Bristol-Myers) require more attention, so supervisory span of control must be smaller.

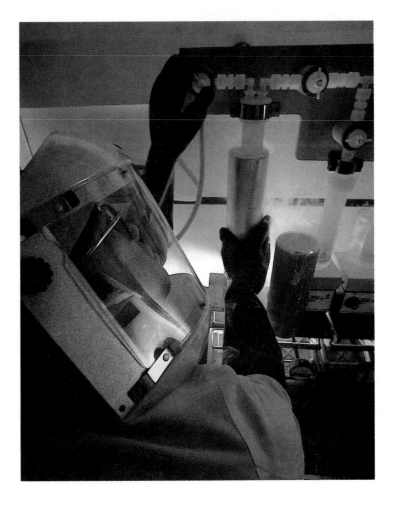

tasks.[16] An important issue in technology is the demand for output customization by an organization's clients or customers. Related to this is the rapidity with which products must be altered. When there is a high demand for output customization or product change, stable organizational structures (for instance, a machine bureaucracy) will be ill-suited for coordinating and controlling the production process. To respond efficiently and effectively to output customization and change demands, an adaptive structure (for instance, organic) will be most effective. Alternatively, if outputs are standardized, customer exceptions are few, and product life-cycles are long, more bureaucratic or mechanistic structures will suffice. In fact, it seems that organizations with relatively fixed transformation technologies ("routine" technologies) are more concerned with efficient performance, and those facing high demands

[16]Pfeffer, *Organizational Design*.

for output customization or change ("nonroutine" technologies) are more concerned with effective problem solving.[17]

In addition to the mechanistic-organic dimension, we can also examine other structural issues. Employees in organizations with routine technologies require less education and training because their work is standardized. In organizations with nonroutine technologies, employees are more likely to be professionals with considerable training and on-the-job experience.

Span of control also differs with type of technology. The more complex the technology, the more that problems requiring a supervisor's involvement are likely to occur. This increased level of involvement requires a smaller span of control because of the amount of subordinate-supervisor interaction. However, in nonroutine technologies that rely on professional employees, the span of control can be larger: professionals have expert knowledge and personal performance expectations that reduce the need for close supervision. The resulting span of control with professional employees in organizations with nonroutine technologies is smaller than with comparable groups in organizations with routine technologies.[18] Thus, as one would expect, the largest span of control occurs within organizations with routine technologies.

Centralization of decision making is another characteristic of organizations with routine technologies. Coordination and control are also under the purview of a centralized management structure. When the organization's task is analyzable, communication is frequent and tends to be in the form of memos, reports, and rules and procedures.[19] When tasks are less analyzable (more nonroutine), information is usually transmitted through interpersonal communication such as face-to-face or telephone conversations and group meetings. In organizations with nonroutine technologies, decision-making authority is pushed far down the organization, as are coordination and control activities.

Finally, organizations with routine technologies typically have very clear, standardized performance expectations; their efficiency and output-quantity goals are identifiable and measurable. In firms with nonroutine technologies, the goals are not nearly so obvious. Rather than aiming for efficiency and quantity, such firms are more concerned with the reliability and quality of their products.

From this discussion on technology, we can make some predictions about which organizational structures work best with which forms of technology. For example, machine bureaucracies provide a good fit *only*

[17]R. G. Hunt, "Technology and Organization," *Academy of Management Journal* 13 (1970): 235–252.

[18]P. M. Blau and R. A. Schoenherr, *The Structure of Organizations* (New York: Basic Books, 1971).

[19]R. L. Daft and R. H. Lengel, "Information Richness: A New Approach to Managerial Behavior and Organizational Design," in *Research in Organizational Behavior*, vol. 6, eds. B. Staw and L. Cummings (Greenwich, Conn.: JAI Press, 1984).

for organizations with routine technologies. Organic structures are appropriate for other types of technologies, although the fit is probably best with nonroutine technologies.

AGE AND SIZE

In the previous sections, we have largely examined factors external to the organization: the environment and technology. Now we will examine the influence of organizational demographic characteristics on structure. In the following discussion, we will assume that the technology and the environment remain constant. This will allow us to observe the impact of age and size on organizational structure.[20]

**Age**  In general, it seems that the older an organization, the more formal its structure. As organizations age, they are likely to repeat the cycle of tasks they accomplish. Thus, as the task is better understood and the likely complications are more predictable, rules and procedures for performing the task are more likely to be promulgated.

Not only does the age of an organization seem to be related to its level of formalization, but when that particular industry was founded seems to have a big impact on its structure, too. In fact, one researcher found that the age of an industry was inversely related to its use of professionals in staff positions and of job specialization.[21] He also found that industries founded in each of four periods were vastly different. For example, organizations founded in the "prefactory" period (such as farms, construction firms, and retail stores) relied more on unpaid family members and self-employed owners than organizations founded in any other period. In the second period—during the rise of factories—industries such as apparel, textiles, and banking used virtually no unpaid family members. They relied instead on many paid clerks, indicating the birth of the bureaucracy. Much control during this period, however, remained with the self-employed owners.

The next period, "bureaucratization of industry," marks a time when professional managers took control of railroads and related industries. The final period, the "modern age," includes the founding of the automobile, chemical, and utility industries. These industries introduced the use of professional employees and the development of staff support units. Since 1965, when this particular study was reported, it is likely that a fifth period of industry foundings has occurred. With the development of the aerospace and electronics industries as well as consulting firms, we may well have witnessed a fifth organizational form.[22]

---

[20]The following discussion is based in large part on the 1979 edition of Mintzberg's *The Structuring of Organizations*.

[21]A. L. Stinchcombe, "Social Structure and Organizations," in *Handbook of Organizations*, ed. J. G. March (Chicago: Rand McNally, 1965).

[22]Mintzberg, *The Structuring of Organizations*.

**Size**  The size of an organization may be measured in a variety of ways, such as the amount of its sales, the size of its capital investment, the size of its budget, or its number of employees. For the purposes of our discussion here, we will use the number of employees as our measure of organizational size.

Research into the relationship between organization size and structure is convincing. It seems that the larger the organization, the more specialized are its tasks, the larger is its administrative component, and the more differentiated are its organizational units.[23]

As organizations grow, they must add new workers. These workers can be assigned to existing departments or units or put into newly created units. As organizations grow in size, they also seem to increase the average span of control for their managers. In fact, it seems that as organizations grow, they increase the size of each unit *and* increase the average span of control at all levels.[24]

Just as older organizations become more structured, larger organizations are more formalized than smaller organizations. The larger the organization, the more the task can be broken down (the more people there are to do parts of the task), and the more predictable the task becomes. The more predictable the task, the more it can be controlled and coordinated through rules, policies, and procedures.

In general, the following organizational characteristics are associated with increased organizational size:

1.  Increased number of management levels
2.  Greater number of jobs and departments
3.  Increased specialization of skills and functions
4.  Greater formalization
5.  Great decentralization
6.  Smaller percentage of top administrators
7.  Larger percentage of technical, professional, clerical, and maintenance support staff
8.  Greater levels of written communication and documentation.[25]

Having a large, well-run organization makes it possible for relatively few managers to manage large numbers of people and resources. From this ability comes the orientation towards efficiency. However, sometimes the organization becomes too large to be managed efficiently. This was the case with Sears, Roebuck and Company in 1980. The "Focus on: Size and Effectiveness" examines what happened to Sears and what the company has done to effect a change.

---

[23]See, for example, P. N. Khandwalla, *The Design of Organizations* (New York: Harcourt Brace Jovanovich, 1977); P. M. Blau, C. M. Falbe, W. McKinley, and D. K. Tracey, "Technology and Organization in Manufacturing," *Administrative Science Quarterly* 21 (1976): 20–40; and D. S. Pugh, D. J. Hickson, C. R. Hinings, and C. Turner, "Dimensions of Organizational Structure," *Administrative Quarterly* 13 (1968): 65–105.

[24]Blau and Schoenherr, *The Structure of Organizations.*

[25]R. L. Daft, *Organizational Theory and Design* (St. Paul, Minn.: West, 1983).

FOCUS ON:

Size and
Effectiveness

**How Sears Became a High-Cost Operator** In 1973, when Sears, Roebuck and Company moved its headquarters, it seemed fitting that it was placed in the world's tallest building. Sears had always been associated with superlatives: biggest, best, and sharpest. The envy of its competitors, the huge retailer was second to none in its ability to ferret out innovative products and to get suppliers to provide them at the lowest cost. Its mail-order catalog was the largest of its kind, and its 860 stores, many located in the first suburban shopping centers, represented the epitome of convenience. Its staff was huge—more than 400,000 employees—and where other retailers made do with just two buyers for a single line of merchandise, Sears could seek out sources with as many as ten.

But no one is envying the giant today. It has become the highest-cost mass merchandiser in the business, with general and administrative expenses siphoning off 29 percent of its sales dollars, compared with J. C. Penney at 23 percent and K mart at 19 percent. One competitor estimates that Sears needs a 50 percent markup to make a profit on items that others need mark up only 35 percent. The seriousness of the problems at the country's largest retailer became painfully clear in March of 1988, when an early Easter boosted spring apparel sales around the country. Though sales of retailers such as K mart increased nearly 10 percent, Sears's reportedly dropped 7 to 8 percent.

The point hasn't been lost on Sears executives. In the last two years, the retailer has modernized its antiquated distribution system and signed agreements with McDonald's Corp. and Walt Disney Co. for children's apparel. Sears has also set up a specialty stores operation and announced a three-year restructuring that could trim as many as 4,000 jobs from its huge headquarters staff. In an interview, Sears Chairman Edward A. Brennan said that the "primary focus" of the restructuring, which analysts say is critical to the success of its other moves, is to streamline the organization, not to cut costs.

However, this is not the first time Sears has responded to the obvious success of its competitors. In the past, Sears has used an apparent trial-and-error approach to managing its way out of trouble—an approach that has given aid and comfort to its competitors. Consider the following tried-and-failed solutions Sears has used:

- An attempt to lure more affluent customers into its solid blue-collar base by stocking expensive, high-fashion merchandise (completely ignoring its image as the merchandiser of America's heartland).
- An attempt to woo the specialty stores' customers by stocking products in depth. Customers still saw no reason to buy sporting equipment at Sears rather than at Herman's and grew even more confused about what to buy at Sears at all (thus Sears wound up with a lot of very expensive inventory).
- An attempt to woo K mart customers ( the other end of the line) by embarking on a very successful price war. Sales shot up 16 percent, but the price cuts had destroyed profits.

At the root of most of these ill-conceived decisions lies an increasingly ponderous management structure. Sears, until 1981, had an almost

*(Continued)*

*Focus on (Continued)*

schizophrenic approach to management. It gave its field people virtual autonomy on promotional pricing, store size, and product selection. Yet it continually enlarged corporate management staff in futile attempts to coordinate its diverse activities into a coherent whole. While this practice was relatively harmless in periods of unbridled growth, it created an almost knee-jerk reaction to solving problems: adding still more managers.

Sears's management structures on top of management structures have grown into a hindrance to timely decisions and good execution as well as an enormous cost burden, one observer suggests. The first round of staff cuts occurred in 1980. A massive early retirement program was accepted by 1,600 managers older than 55. Sears also consolidated its 9 merchandising groups into 7 and dropped 6 of its 41 buying departments and 5 of its 46 field administrative units. The southwestern territory, which employed more than 300 people, was shut down altogether. By the middle of 1980, merchandising staff decreases saved the company $125 million annually.

Of all Sears's recent moves, Wall Street was most impressed with the restructuring, noting that only a leaner Sears would be able to execute new strategies fast enough to be competitive. But the jury is still out on whether Sears and its top management will be able to get the proper blend of cost cutting, aggressive image rebuilding, and organizational centralization and decentralization to pull it off. A consultant for a competitor sums it up: Sears forgot its primary purpose is to please the customer by stocking the right goods and sticking by its principle of satisfaction guaranteed. Those things will be hard to regain.

Source: "How Sears Became a High-Cost Operator," *Business Week,* February 16, 1981; and Janet Key, "Sears Struggling to Stay Atop the Nation's Retailing Heap," *Chicago Tribune,* April 18, 1988, Section 4, p. 1.

## ORGANIZATIONAL LIFE CYCLES

The story of Raku and her company, Ceramico, which began this chapter suggests a final influence on organizational structure. Organizations change over time, and as they do the forces that influence their structure change with them. In fact, organizations (like the people that compose them) go through predictable life cycles, and organizational structure is determined in part by the particular stage of development in which the organization finds itself.[26] During each stage in the **organizational life cycle,** the structure, leadership style, and administrative systems follow a predictable pattern of evolution. Recently, some researchers have suggested that organizations evolve through four different phases or cycles.[27] The four phases are the entrepreneurial

[26]J. R. Kimberly and R. H. Miles, *The Organizational Life Cycle* (San Francisco: Jossey-Bass, 1980).

[27]R. E. Quinn and K. Cameron, "Organizational Life Cycles and Some Shifting Criteria of Effectiveness: Some Preliminary Evidence," *Management Science* 29 (1983): 33–51.

stage, the collectivity stage, the formalization stage, and the elaboration stage. Each of these stages has its own unique problems or concerns.

ENTREPRENEURIAL
STAGE

When an organization comes into existence, the primary concerns of the founders are to create the product or service and to survive as an organization. There is little formal control in the **entrepreneurial stage;** what control there is comes from the commitment and supervision of the owner-entrepreneur. The working hours are long, and the entire focus of the organization is on the development and marketing of the product or service.

As the organization becomes successful, it grows. Growth, with its demands for more employees, requires the entrepreneur to address management issues. Because entrepreneurs would rather deal with the interesting and creative components of the business, such as creating and selling the product or service, they are not likely to be skilled or interested in management issues. A crisis of leadership often develops. Either the owner restricts the growth of the organization, or it will begin to falter. What is needed at this juncture is the introduction of a strong manager who can inject managerial control processes into the organization. If such a manager is available or the entrepreneur can provide the necessary structure and control, then the organization progresses into the second stage of its life cycle. The "FOCUS ON: The Entrepreneurial Stage" examines the problems of Donald D. Kingsborough, chief executive and founder of Worlds of Wonder, Inc.

COLLECTIVITY
STAGE

In the adolescence of an organization, it is typically most concerned with human resource issues such as cooperation, employee commitment, morale, cohesion, and personalized leadership. Employees feel a part of the organization in the **collectivity stage** and value its goals and objectives. During this stage of an organization's existence, we see the beginnings of such formal systems as structured departments, job assignments, and a hierarchy of authority.

The beginning of the formal structure also leads to the major problem at this stage: the simultaneous need for delegation and desire to maintain control. Solving the leadership crisis was the first step; now that very solution catalyzes a second problem. The strong management presence—so successful in the past—now restricts the activities of low-level managers. Because of the development of competent lower-level managers, management must learn to delegate authority and control down the hierarchy—to overcome its fear of losing control of the organization. To survive this crisis, the organization needs to develop formal mechanisms to manage organizational interdependence without direct intervention by top management.

FOCUS ON:

The
Entrepreneurial
Stage

**From Wall Street Charmer to Chapter 11** Donald Kingsborough lounges in an office so large and lavishly furnished that employees call it the "Oval Office." It's vintage Kingsborough. He is unrelentingly upbeat. Forget that WOW—the toy company's still-apt acronym—owes creditors $260 million and that it has missed $3.6 million in interest payments to bondholders. Forget that the company lost $189.9 million in its third quarter, which ended December 31, 1987. Kingsborough's equanimity just never seems to fade, even though he's still holding some 4 million shares of a stock that has plummeted from 29 to 1 in 18 months.

Kingsborough pins the blame mostly on the company's out-of-control growth, adding that 1987 was a bad year for all toymakers. Then he cites all those second-string executives he put in first-string jobs, some of whom he has since fired. But some former WOW executives and managers say Kingsborough himself was largely responsible for the problems. He had thumbs up or down on every decision made, one says.

Now, Kingsborough must persuade his creditors—including the banks whose credit is secured—to work with him. He has already persuaded the bankruptcy court to let WOW show up at the February New York toy fair with a slew of new products. But even Kingsborough realizes that he needs more than a handful of promising new toys to cure WOW's ills. Besides slashing employment to 130 and cutting costs by 70 percent, he has replaced his manufacturing manager and is looking for a new chief financial officer. And he's putting the finishing touches on a reorganization plan to be filed with the bankruptcy court by late March. Some believe the plan should include a new CEO. "Kingsborough should know he's not capable of managing a company from a financial standpoint," says a Hong Kong manufacturer and creditor.

Kingsborough claims he has no intention of stepping down, although he is willing to consider selling the company. To get WOW back on its feet, he must use all his talents to sell the toughest product of all—his ability to manage Worlds of Wonder, Inc.

Source: R. Brandt, S. Benway, and D. Jones Yang, "Worlds of Wonder: From Wall Street Charmer to Chapter 11," *Business Week,* March 21, 1988, pp. 77–78.

FORMALIZATION
STAGE

In the midlife of the organization, corresponding to the adult years of a person, the organization values stability, efficiency, rules and procedures, and other bureaucratic trends. New employees, particularly specialists, are hired. Communication among employees is less frequent and more formal. Effectiveness in such organizations is typically measured quantitatively through efficiency ratios and productivity measures. Although goal attainment and productivity are important concerns throughout the life of an organization, they are more salient as measures of organizational effectiveness during the **formalization stage.**

During this stage of the organization's life cycle, a crisis of increased bureaucratization occurs. The development of various mechanisms, rules, policies, and procedures to coordinate and control the increasingly large organization now begins to suffocate middle management. Because of this stranglehold, creativity is stifled by the demands of standard operating procedures. Conflict develops between line and staff employees, and the overall impression is that the organization is too large to be managed effectively solely through formal rules, regulations, policies, and procedures.

## ELABORATION STAGE

As the organization matures, it enters the final portion of the cycle. The **elaboration stage** redirects the organization's emphasis from bureaucracy to a renewed interest in cooperation and teamwork. Decentralization of the organization occurs to balance the conflicting demands for differentiation and integration. Rather than rules and standard operating procedures, social control and self-discipline limit the need for direct, hierarchical supervision. More than in other stages, the firm's reputation and stature are important. Innovation and creativity are once again valued. The managerial process is adjusted to augment rather than impede the flow of new ideas. Formal systems are simplified, and integrating mechanisms such as project teams or task forces are created to improve communication across the organization.

The major concern for an organization in the elaboration stage is to monitor its product cycles, paying attention to changes in the environment and technology in order to revitalize itself.[28] Top management is often replaced during this part of the organization's life; the intent is to bring new blood into the organization. Organizations that fail in this revitalization process may become stagnant or enter into a period of organizational decline. The "Focus on: Elaboration," is an example of the recent revitalization of Control Data Corporation.

## Symptoms of Design Deficiencies

What happens when the organizational structure does not fit neatly with the demands of the environment, organizational task, age, and size of the organization? In the final sections of this chapter, we will examine the potential problems that may arise in an organization when the "right" organizational structure is not in place: organizational conflict and organizational decline.

## Organizational Conflict

Much of what we learned about individual conflict in Chapter 6 also applies to conflict at the organizational level. Organizational conflict occurs because of poorly managed division and coordination of tasks

---

[28]D. A. Whetten, "Sources, Responses and Effects of Organizational Decline," in *The Organizational Life Cycle,* eds. J. Kimberly and R. Miles (San Francisco: Jossey-Bass, 1980).

**Control Data Is Moving Forward by Looking Back** Restoring Control Data Corporation's past glory in the computer industry is a tall order. From the early 1960s through the late 1970s, CDC was the foremost maker of scientific computers. Some of its earliest machines are still used in nuclear research and aerospace design. By 1979, it had 7 percent of the market for big mainframes, giving it the fourth-largest installed base.

But then its computer business declined. "They got away from being a scientific systems company; they lost their perspective," says Ray Argo, head of an association of CDC computer customers.

Thomas C. Roberts runs CDC's $1.4 billion Computer Systems Group. And he's out to win back the prestige and profits CDC once enjoyed as one of the world's premier makers of large computers. To do it, he's steering CDC back to its original strategy: building speedy, sophisticated computers for engineers and scientists.

When Roberts arrived at CDC's Minneapolis headquarters, he found its computer business mired in bureaucracy. It took 300 people in 30 departments to process a mainframe order, he says. And while customers clamored for faster, lower-priced machines to run the software they already had, CDC was pouring money into more software. "We didn't know where our machines were, what they were being used for, where the market was going, and where we fit into it," Roberts says.

Almost immediately, he laid off 20 percent of the work force, slashing $55 million in costs. Then he installed new management. Its strategy was to make CDC a one-stop shop for technical computing, a market that's expected to grow 30 percent per year into the early 1990s. In addition, CDC is hoping it can win new accounts with a widening variety of smaller systems. It has priced one Cyber mainframe as low as $60,000 and is selling $25,000 graphic workstations made by Silicon Graphics in Mountain View, Calif., in which CDC acquired a 20 percent stake for $70 million.

Roberts's initial moves showed results. After two years of losses (a total of $832 million), the Computer Systems Group had operating earnings of about $26 million in 1987. And that figure hit $47 million in 1988, when CDC earned about $142 million before taxes on revenues of $3.9 billion. But the turnaround is not complete. Ironically, CDC is now short of software for its big machines. Amassing a broadly competitive product line could require more capital than CDC can afford, given all of its recent changes. And CDC must convince customers that it is a solid contender.

Source: Patrick Houston, "Control Data Is Moving Forward by Looking Back," *Business Week*, April 18, 1988, pp. 71–72.

among interdependent organizational units. Conflicts can arise from problems in task clarity (the degree to which daily task requirements are known), task complexity (the number of elements to be considered when completing the task), the rapidity of technological change, feedback cycles (how quickly a manager can know the results of a decision), and the goals of the organization.[29] Thus, the more interdependence required to complete the task, the greater the potential for organizational conflict.

While interdependence alone may be sufficient to produce some organizational conflict, the way in which organizational members must interact can exacerbate its level. The appropriate organizational structures can moderate such conflict. If we examine the following prescriptions for managing organizational conflict, the common thread running through them is for managers to reduce the interdependencies among organizational units.

**Bureaucratic Authority**   This form of conflict management is based on the acceptance by organizational members of the right of top management to invoke rules, regulations, and procedures to structure how groups and individuals interact within the organization. Within such a system of conflict management, the response to conflict across and within groups is to pass the issues to be resolved to the next higher authority level.

**Limited Interaction**   When the bureaucratic structure gets overloaded with demands, an alternative way to manage conflict is to limit interaction among conflicting groups. Interaction between conflicting groups is often limited to controversial issues, which does not allow the participants to focus on a common goal. Instead, these two groups can be given a superordinate goal that requires them to coordinate their activities. This strategy works best when the rules and procedures necessary to complete the task or meet the goal are well known and well understood.

**Integrating Devices**   The previous strategies focus on managing conflict that is not a permanent experience because of the amount of environmental and technological uncertainty. What happens when the interdependence and uncertainty inherent in performing the organizational task is so great that conflict is unavoidable? In this case, perhaps the organization should implement more formal conflict management devices. These devices include liaisons, integrators, task forces, and project teams. The goal of such **integrating devices** is to enhance communication across groups and maintain an appropriate level of interaction.

Liaisons are boundary spanning individuals who facilitate coordination and communication between interdependent organizational units (for instance, production and sales departments). Liaisons typically are located in one department or organizational unit but have responsibili-

[29]J. M. Brett, "Managing Organizational Conflict," *Professional Psychology: Research and Practice* 15 (1984): 664–678.

ties for working with both units. When coordination of different organizational units becomes more complex, an organization may choose to establish an integrator role. The more different organizational units are in structure, goals, and orientation, the greater the opportunity for conflict. The role of the integrator is to manage (coordinate and moderate) relationships among diverse organizational units. Integrators need (1) a wide set of contacts within various organizational units, (2) some understanding of each unit's goals, orientations, and organization, (3) the ability to talk the language of each unit, (4) some trust of the members of the units, (5) some expertise that members of the units respect, and (6) skills in conflict management and resolution.[30]

While liaisons and integrators are individuals, coordination also may be enhanced by the use of task forces. The task force is a group of people brought together to accomplish a specific assignment. Typically, task forces are disbanded when their assignment is completed. Each member of the task force represents the interests of one organizational unit (a department, for instance) and communicates the task force's decisions or recommendations back to that constituency. Task forces are created by upper-level management to solve problems that require horizontal coordination, thereby taking pressure off the organization's formal structure to create solutions.

When long-term interdepartmental activities demand strong coordination efforts, a project team is likely to be formed. A project team is a permanent task force. It is often composed of mid-level organizational members or those at the executive level (often referred to as an administrative committee or an operations review committee). For example, when the Florida Power and Light Company built a nuclear power plant, the coordination achieved through the use of project teams was critical in reducing construction time in half, from an industry average of 12 years to just 6. The construction manager assigned critical personnel to 15 different project teams. One team orchestrated the completion of 25,000 tasks needed to finish the plant.[31]

Organizational conflict is only one problem that can arise when organizations are not structured to handle their unique sets of problems and opportunities. In addition to excessive conflict, an organization may experience a performance decline resulting from a poor fit between an organization, its demands, and its structure.

## ORGANIZATIONAL DECLINE

There are at least two meanings to the term **organizational decline.** The first describes a cutback in the size of an organization's work force, budget, resources, clients, and the like. The second definition refers to the view that mature organizations become stagnant, bureaucratic, and

[30]Duncan, "What Is the Right Organizational Structure?"

[31]Ron Winslow, "Utility Cuts Red Tape, Builds Nuclear Plant Almost on Schedule," *The Wall Street Journal,* February 22, 1984, 1, 18.

passive. These conditions may herald an organization's increasing inability to stay in touch with changing markets, technologies, and client preferences. Rather than lead to a reduction in revenues, the latter form of decline may simply reflect a reduction in the rate of growth.[32] In fact, some authors have made the argument that decline-as-cutbacks occurs in times of resource scarcity, and decline-as-stagnation occurs in times of resource abundance.[33]

Researchers in this area have identified four causes or sources of organizational decline: organizational atrophy, vulnerability, loss of legitimacy, and reduced environmental support.[34] **Organizational atrophy** occurs when an organization continues to use a particular response to a situation long after the situation has changed. In this form of perseverance, successful organizations may continue to behave in ways that were once successful and, as a result, be increasingly vulnerable to failure in the future.

Both slow- and fast-growing organizations are vulnerable to organizational atrophy. Fast-growing organizations are at risk when they fail to identify sagging performance as a problem, as opposed to not trying hard enough. Alternatively, slow-growing organizations are more responsive to changes in their vital signs, but they err in the amount of their response to a problem. Such organizations have so little slack that they may not be able to survive long enough to respond to the problem.

Vulnerability is the second source of organizational decline. At some point in the organization's life, it is more susceptible to decline. Most organizations experience a "liability of newness."[35] The difficulty that new organizations have clearing such barriers as the inefficiency of the inexperienced, the lack of a stable set of suppliers and customers, and their more frequent interpersonal conflict is reflected in their higher death rate, compared to that of older organizations.

Loss of legitimacy occurs when an organization focuses its energy on economic gains and ignores the cultivation of its political acceptance. This issue of legitimacy is probably more salient in public rather than private organizations. The test of legitimacy commonly revolves around the development of a powerful constituency that resists the efforts of other groups to dismantle the organization. Of the four sources of decline, it seems that organizations are most capable of combating this one.

The fourth source of decline is reduced environmental support. The environment in which the organization exists can no longer support the organization. Organizations faced with this situation can either find another niche, product, or service (a new environment) or downsize. The

---

[32]K. S. Cameron, R. I. Sutton, and D. A. Whetten, *Readings in Organizational Decline: Frameworks, Research and Prescriptions* (Cambridge, Mass.: Ballinger, 1988).

[33]Whetten, "Sources, Responses and Effects of Organizational Decline."

[34]Ibid.

[35]Stinchcombe, "Social Structure and Organizations."

first option suggests that the decline can be reversed if management makes appropriate strategic choices. The second option assumes that the set of circumstances in which the organization is mired is beyond the control of management. As such, management's only option is to scale down the operation.[36]

**MANAGING DECLINE**

After managers have figured out the source of the decline, the next step is to develop an organizational response to the problem. Much of what is known about how organizations respond to decline has been taken from the organizational change literature. While there are four general categories of responses to decline, they can be placed on the continuum illustrated in Figure 16–8. The two reactive responses are defending and responding. The two proactive responses are generating and preventing.

The organization using a defending response is usually a large, bureaucratic organization. A common example of this response occurs when adhering to the organization's rules and policies becomes more important than addressing the goals behind them. A second, reactive way in which organizations respond to decline is retrenchment. Retrenchment is commonly characterized by cutting back: layoffs based on seniority or performance or across-the-board cuts in funding and resources. The focus here is on solving the "problem." Unfortunately, management may respond to the decline by either attaching the wrong solution to the right problem (such as responding to a lack of innovation by cutting the research and development budget) or finding a solution to the wrong problem (laying off production workers when the problem is with research and development). In either case, attaching a solution to a problem will allay management's concerns, as it will believe it has done something to resolve the problem.

The next two responses to organizational decline, preventing and generating, differ from the reacting and defending responses in that they are proactive; that is, they take steps to remove hazards that may cause the organization to decline in the future. In the first, preventing, the organization attempts to increase its competitive advantage and remove potential threats. Such tactics include participating in mergers and acquisitions, changing public opinion and influencing consumer preferences, and shaping economic and social policy.[37] These actions by management are based on the notion that organizations must act to reduce uncertainty by circumventing the need to respond reactively to the environment.

---

[36]R. M. Cyert, "The Management of Universities of Constant or Decreasing Size," *Public Administration Review* 38 (1978): 344–349.

[37]See, for example, C. Perrow, *Complex Organizations: A Critical Essay* (Glenview, Ill.: Scott, Foresman, 1979); J. Pfeffer, "Merger as a Response to Organizational Interdependence," *Administrative Science Quarterly* 17 (1972): 382–394; and J. E. Post, *Corporate Behavior and Social Change* (Reston, Va.: Reston Press, 1978).

**FIGURE 16–8**            Management's Responses to Organizational Decline

There are four categories of organizational responses to decline. Defending and responding are reactive responses, and generating and preventing are proactive responses.

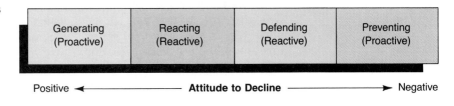

| Generating (Proactive) | Reacting (Reactive) | Defending (Reactive) | Preventing (Proactive) |

Positive ◄─────────── **Attitude to Decline** ───────────► Negative

Source: D. A. Whetten, "Sources, Responses and Effects of Organizational Decline,"in *The Organizational Life Cycle*, eds. J. Kimberly and R. Miles (San Francisco: Jossey-Bass, 1980).

The intent of the fourth response to organizational decline—generating—is to develop "self-designing" organizations. Such organizations are characterized by informal lines of communication, loose criteria for performance evaluation, slack resources, experimentation, tolerance for occasional failure, frequent movement of personnel within the organization, and a high regard for innovation.[38] Interestingly, such organizations would have a high reliance on the integrating structures of liaisons, task forces, project teams, and matrix structures. While this generating point of view has been promoted by organizational scholars, it remains to be seen if organizations can, in fact, achieve this self-designing status when facing a crisis in the form of decline.

The following effects of organizational decline can be felt throughout the organization:

1.  Increasing levels of stress among organizational actors as the importance of making good decisions and the penalties for bad decisions increase.
2.  Increasing levels of interpersonal conflict as the organization's resource base dwindles.
3.  Layoffs and cutbacks directed at the most vulnerable organizational members—the low-skilled, low-income, and minority employees—coupled with attrition among the most mobile and best qualified employees, resulting in a reduction in the variability of employees and the ability of the organization to respond creatively to the decline.
4.  Death of the organization, either through failure of management to adapt to changes in the environment, political vulnerability, decision demands, or through a transformation (such as a merger or acquisition).

[38]For example, see K. E. Weick, "Organizational Design: Organizations as Self-Designing Systems," *Organizational Dynamics* 6 (1977): 30–46; B. M. Staw, "The Experimenting Organization," *Organizational Dynamics* 6 (1977): 2–18; and B. L. Hedberg, P. C. Nystrom, and W. H. Starbuck, "Designing Organizations to Match Tomorrow," in *Perspective Models of Organizations*, eds. P. C. Nystrom and W. H. Starbuck, North-Holland/TIMS Studies in the Management Sciences, vol. 5 (Amsterdam: North-Holland, 1977).

## SUMMARY

The purpose of this chapter was to examine the components of an organization that determine its structure, the factors that determine which organizational structure should be put into place, and the problems organizations face when their structures do not meet the demands placed on them.

The four elements of organizational structure include job specialization (how the organizational task is divided into jobs), departmentalization (how jobs fit together), centralization (the degree to which decision making in an organization is handled by a small, central group of decision makers), and span of control (how many employees report to a manager). These elements of organizational structure differ depending on how an organization coordinates and controls its employees to create organizational outputs.

Typically, organizations are structured in one of three ways. A simple structure is most common in young or small organizations. In a simple structure, employees typically report to one person, usually an entrepreneur who views a more formal organizational structure as restrictive. When greater structure is required and tasks are specialized and routine, an organization may become bureaucratic, with an elaborate administrative structure.

When an organization must remain flexible, the appropriate organizational form is organic. Within this structure, an organization can respond quickly to changes in the market, technology, and product mix. Integrating mechanisms such as liaisons, integrator roles, task forces, project teams, and matrix structures are the markers of an organic structure.

An organization's structure will be influenced by demands from its internal and external environments, the technology required to produce its product or service, and its age and size. A machine bureaucracy is more appropriate for an older, larger organization with a routine technology and a predictable, stable environment. An organic structure is best suited for a smaller, younger organization with a turbulent, unpredictable environment and a nonroutine technology.

The structure of an organization is not stable; rather, organizations like people follow a well-ordered evolution of structure (a life cycle). This life cycle includes the entrepreneurial stage, the collectivity stage, the formalization stage, and the elaboration stage. At each stage of its life, an organization will face a major problem associated with its transformation into the next stage.

Finally, two major problems may occur if an organization has a poor fit between its structure and the demands placed on it, or if its structure cannot successfully handle the problems associated with its stage in the life cycle. Organizational conflict and organizational decline are both related to deficiencies in organizational design.

KEY TERMS

**Administrative intensity**  Proportion of administrators and managers in an organization's total work force.

**Centralization**  Resting decision-making power with one or a few individuals, based on the competing needs of coordination and division of labor.

**Collectivity stage**  Second phase of the organizational life cycle, in which management concentrates on human resource issues such as cooperation, employee commitment, and morale, and in which the beginnings of formal systems such as structured departments, job assignments, and a hierarchy of authority are seen.

**Departmentalization**  Grouping tasks into organizational units according to the knowledge and skills required or based on similar levels of skills and abilities.

**Elaboration stage**  Fourth and last phase of the organizational life cycle, in which management redirects the organization's emphasis from bureaucracy to a renewed interest in cooperation and teamwork, and in which decentralization often occurs and innovation and creativity are once again valued.

**Entrepreneurial stage**  First phase of the organizational life cycle in which the organization comes into existence and the founders concentrate on creating the product or service and surviving as an organization.

**Formalization stage**  Third phase of the organizational life cycle, in which management val-

ues stability, efficiency, rules and procedures, and other bureaucratic trends.

**Integrating device**  Strategy of conflict management aimed at enhancing communication across groups and maintaining appropriate levels of interaction.

**Job specialization**  Division of the overall mission of an organization into various smaller tasks.

**Machine bureaucracy**  Organizational structure using highly specialized and routine tasks, formalized procedures for the transformation process, a proliferation of rules and communication channels, a functional departmentalization structure, a large span of control, and an elaborate administrative and technical structure.

**Organic structure**  Flexible organizational structure that can respond efficiently and effectively to new demands placed on it.

**Organizational atrophy**  Organization's use of a particular response to a situation long after the situation has changed.

**Organizational decline**  (1) Cutback in the size of an organization's work force, budget, resources, clients, and so on. (2) Mature organization's inability to stay in touch with changing markets, technologies, and client preferences, leading to stagnation, bureaucracy, and passivity.

**Organizational life cycle**  Predictable pattern of evolution of organizations' structure, leadership style, and administrative systems.

**Organizational structure**  Skeleton of an organization based on the relationship among its positions or roles.

**Organization design**  Process of actively creating a structure composed of groups of activities, roles, or positions to coordinate the interdependencies among organizational actors effectively.

**Simple structure**  Organizational structure common in young or small organizations in which coordination is largely a function of direct supervision, the top manager or entrepreneur has significant control, employees have very little discretionary decision-making power, and there is little formal policy or procedure.

**Span of control**  Number of people reporting to a manager.

**DISCUSSION QUESTIONS**

1. How does organizational design differ from organizational structure?

2. If organizations face considerable task interdependence, uncertainty, and a dynamic environment, what structural mechanisms can they use to manage these factors more effectively?

3. In a matrix organization, how does the role of a functional manager differ from that of a project manager?

4. What two prime factors might cause an organization to decline? How would management respond to these two factors?

5. What are the costs and benefits of a machine bureaucracy? An organically structured organization?

6. What is the basis for the crisis of leadership in young, entrepreneurial firms?

7. What is the importance of creativity and innovation in older organizations?

8. Why must increased interaction among organizational units be managed to avoid excessive amounts of conflict?

**IF YOU WANT TO KNOW MORE**

To really understand the issues behind organizational structure, it is important to consider the original work on bureaucracy by Max Weber, *The Theory of Social and Economic Organizations,* translated by Henderson and Parsons and published by Free Press in 1947. In the same vein, one of the first examinations of the relationship of structure to factors unique to an organization is Alfred Chandler's 1966 book entitled *Strategy and Structure,* published by Anchor Press. He developed his perspective on this subject by interviewing managers at General Motors, DuPont, Standard Oil of New Jersey, and Sears, Roebuck and Company.

While Chandler's notion was that the organization's strategy drove the development of structure, other authors have proposed different contingency models. Jay Galbraith (*Designing Complex Organizations,* Addison-Wesley, 1973) and J. D. Thompson (*Organizations in Action,* McGraw-Hill, 1967) both propose such models. Interdependence of the task is what drives Thompson's model, while task uncertainty and the demand to process information drive Galbraith's. While much material has been written about the factors that influence organizational design, one of the better overviews of the contingency notion of organizational structure can be found in Robert Duncan's article, "What Is the Right Organizational Structure?" in the Winter 1979 issue of *Organizational Dynamics.*

A more detailed description of different organizational structures and the factors that influence their fit or lack of fit can be found in Henry Mintzberg's 1979 *The Structuring of Organizations,* published by Prentice-Hall. Focusing particularly on matrix organizations is a book entitled *Matrix,* written in 1977 by Stanley Davis and Paul Lawrence and published by Addison-Wesley.

Issues of organizational structure and conflict are addressed in R. David Brown's 1983 book, *Managing Conflict at Organizational Interfaces,* published by Addison-Wesley. The idea that organizational structure is a strategy for resolving or preventing conflict is the focus of an article, "Intergroup Relations in Organizations," by Jeanne Brett and Jorn Rogness that appeared in the 1986 volume of *Designing Effective Work Groups,* edited by Paul Goodman and associates and published by Jossey-Bass.

The area of this chapter probably receiving the most attention these days is organizational decline. An excellent overview of the research and prescriptions in this area can be found in a book edited by Kim Cameron, Robert Sutton, and David Whetten. Entitled *Readings in Organizational Decline,* it was published by Ballinger in 1988. The interest in organizational decline was probably sparked by earlier work elucidating organizational life cycles. In 1980, John Kimberly and Robert Miles authored *The Organizational Life Cycle,* which was published by Jossey-Bass.

ON YOUR
OWN

**Analysis of an Organization's Structure**    For this exercise, you should select an organization with which you are familiar. Such an organization may be your family, church, fraternity or sorority, your class, or a firm with which you have been associated through a summer job or part-time employment. Answer the following questions about that organization:

*Description*    Draw the firm's organizational chart, showing lines of authority, influence, and communication.

Source: J. R. Gordon, *A Diagnostic Approach to Organizational Behavior* (Boston: Allyn & Bacon, 1987).

*Diagnosis*   Describe and evaluate the organization's departmentalization, span of control, and job specialization.

Describe and evaluate the coordinating mechanisms.

Describe and evaluate the internal environment and the technology, age, and size of the organization.

Is the organizational structure appropriate, given the answers to the questions above?

*Prescription*   What changes could be made in the organization's structure to enhance its fit *and* its performance?

CLOSING CASE
FOR CHAPTER 16

# THE MANAGER'S MEMO

FROM: W. Hightower, Manager, Support Services

TO:    J. Weintraub, President

RE:    Conflicts and Confusion

Ever since we added the Tax Preparation Division with its staff of 12 people, I have been swamped with complaints from my people. They don't know how to stay in control of their work. This was never a problem when we just had the Consumer Lending business.

In the Copy Room, my people are bombarded with "priority" requests. First someone from the Consumer Lending Division comes in with a major job. Then someone from Tax Prep brings in a stack of tax returns that are supposed to be photocopied immediately. We call both division heads, and both say their job must be done first. We try to call you, but you're often away from the office or in a meeting.

In the Mail Room, it's the same thing. Someone from each division comes in with a mailing that must go out the same day. We can't do it all at once, and the division heads won't agree on what we should do first. The Mail Room is constantly full of people coming in to pick up their mail and look for deliveries. Also, we sometimes have to call the recipient when an overnight delivery comes in, just to find out where that person's office is. It was easier when we knew everybody.

I could go on and on. The Supply Room can't keep up with supplies, because people forget to sign out what they've taken from the shelves. The Word-Processing Pool gets caught in arguments about which division's jobs to do first. I try to call you when I have a problem, like you suggested, but to tell you the truth, if I reached you every time, we'd be on the phone all day long.

What can you do about this?

CASE DISCUSSION
QUESTIONS

Assume you are the president, and respond to the memo of the manager of support services. What appears to be the source of the problems? Should the company president be handling these day-to-day matters? How can changes in the company's structure and design improve the situation?

CHAPTER

# Managing Change

**The Dynamics of Change**
Forces for Change
Sources of Resistance to Change
*INTERNATIONAL FOCUS ON External Forces for Change:*
*The Great Soviet Computer Screw-Up*

**A Model for Change in Organizations**
Diagnosis
*FOCUS ON Support Systems: Giving Quality the Green Light*
Unfreezing
*FOCUS ON Selling the Diagnosis: AT&T Answers the Call*
Movement
Refreezing

**Organizational Development**
Behavioral Health
Survey-Guided Development
Quality-of-Work-Life Programs
*FOCUS ON Quality-of-Work-Life Programs: Learning from Tarrytown*

**Change in Corporate America**
Corporate Reorganizations
*FOCUS ON Corporate Change in America: Easing the Pain*

## STAYING FOREVER YOUNG?

The scenario is a familiar one. A small company—in this case, one started in a local gas station—becomes astonishingly successful. The success leads to growth and the growth forces the company to change. Soon, what made the company great when it was young and small threatens to disappear.

The company is Ben & Jerry's Homemade, Inc., Vermont's astonishingly successful super-premium ice cream maker. Two real guys, Ben Cohen and Jerry Greenfield, began the company in 1978 as a small ice cream parlor. A decade later it had become a financier's dream, doubling in size every year and surpassing $30 million in sales. But there is another story within this financial success story, for Ben & Jerry's has never been a normal company.

Throughout its growth, the culture of Ben & Jerry's has emphasized fun, charity, and goodwill, not only within the company but throughout its corporate reach. In 1985, The Ben & Jerry's Foundation was established. It receives 7.5 percent of the company's pretax income to spend on a broad mission of social responsibility. Projects have included the refurbishment and maintenance for one year of a New York City subway station and efforts to open an ice cream parlor in Moscow whose profits will be used to support East-West exchange programs. Internally, the company hires the handicapped, provides free therapy and counseling for employees, takes workers on company outings, and even brings in masseurs for workers during high-stress production periods. The monthly staff meetings are attended by *all* employees, the work climate is informal, and there has been a strong sense of family in the business since its inception. There is even a corporate "Joy" committee (with Jerry as its nominal head) to infuse more joy into the workday. More to the point, these characteristics of social responsibility and a feeling of family are not just add-ons at this company. They are at the core of Ben & Jerry's corporate mission. Financial success and growth are the added dimensions.

Yet it is the core characteristics of the Ben & Jerry's culture which now seem under attack. When the company was small, everyone knew everyone, everyone bought into the mission, and Ben & Jerry's really did feel like family. But rapid growth has brought with it a disturbing malaise. There are now departments and memorandums, and suits and ties and MBAs have begun to appear. Several times communication within the company has broken down. At one monthly meeting, the head of retail operations announced plans to open 50 new stores—plans that came as a complete shock to the disbelieving head of production. Employees also claim to have found out about the new Springfield, Vermont, plant through newspaper accounts. Noted Wendy Yoder, a supervisor and five-year Ben & Jerry's veteran, "It's hard to feel you're part of a big family if you don't know the brothers and sisters."

Chico Lager, Ben & Jerry's chief financial officer, feels that growth can't be stopped; and anyway, it's not growth that kills the culture in a company. "It's a convenient scapegoat. You can say we can't grow because we're not going to be the same company we used to be, and we're not going to be a family.

I don't agree with that. I say you can be every bit as much the company you used to be as you grow, *if*—underline the word *if*—you pay attention to those issues and deal with them."

Ben & Jerry's has fought back. The compromise struck by the board of directors was that growth would continue but with more effort devoted to development of the internal organization. A consultant was brought in to strengthen the management team, improve its communications, and help it hammer out a statement of corporate mission. Some insiders believe that the company needs to find a new balance, and that a bit more "corporate"-ness will help preserve some of the best of the old culture.

Even Jerry admits that they can't go home again. "The idea, I think, is to maintain the values of your culture, and yet bring it along with you. I mean, you don't want to stay stuck in the past. The gas station we started in was an amazing place, but it is there no longer. It's a parking lot. You can tell wonderful stories about the place —but tell the wonderful stories about what happened at the plant last month. I think our company will be changed. I think there's no doubt about that. It will be changed. We just have to make it a good change."

Source: "Forever Young," *Inc.*, July 1988, 50–62.

INTRODUCTION

Even when top management gets an organization off to a good start, there are no guarantees that the organization's initial successes will continue. In fact, there are no guarantees—as Ben & Jerry's of Vermont has learned—that management techniques that have worked in the past will continue to work in the future. There are no guarantees because organizations exist in uncertain business and social environments that are constantly changing. Therefore, organizations must be prepared to change constantly as well to respond effectively to the ever-changing demands around them. For companies like Ben & Jerry's, success in business is a journey—a continuing battle to adapt—not a destination. In a constantly changing environment, the management challenge is not only to *reach* a successful level of organizational performance but to *maintain* that successful level of performance over time by meeting the demands for change.

This chapter is about how management can meet the demands for change in organizations. It begins with a discussion of the forces that clash in organizations—forces for change and sources of resistance to change—then describes the characteristics of an organization that is ready for change. Next, a four-stage model of change in organizations is presented, followed by a discussion of organizational development as an alternative approach to managing the change process. The chapter concludes with a discussion of an important example of change in contemporary American business—corporate reorganizations.

THE DYNAMICS
OF CHANGE

Organizations, like people, are creatures of habit. **Habit** is the tendency of a person or an organization to do things the same way, over and over again. People take comfort in doing things in familiar ways. And as we discussed in Chapter 7, habits in the form of group rules or norms for behavior often represent accumulated organizational experience and learning. It should not be surprising, then, that change is resisted. In fact, it would be surprising if it weren't.

In physical terms, the equivalent of habit is inertia. **Inertia** is the tendency of an object to continue in the same direction with the same velocity or intensity unless influenced by some force of change. A billiard ball on a pool table, for instance, will continue in the same direction until it encounters something—another ball, a side rail, a human hand. According to the laws of physics, inertia must be altered when the object encounters a force of change. This is an important difference between people and physical objects: People can decide whether to alter their path when they encounter a force for change, and sometimes people make the wrong decision. At Ben & Jerry's, for instance, management resisted changes in the organization's structure and procedures to accommodate growth. Continued growth, and the corporate malaise it brought with it, eventually forced these changes to occur.

The challenge for top executives trying to keep an organization afloat in an uncertain, constantly changing environment is how to manage the delicate tension between two forces: forces for change and sources of resistance to change. When managed correctly, the outcome should not be only a financially profitable organization, but one that is healthy from an organizational behavior point of view.

## FORCES FOR CHANGE

In 1976, Atari Corporation introduced a new product—the VCS–2600. The VCS–2600 was the first programmable home video player, and its success was astonishing. The VCS–2600 became the best-selling home electronics product of all time, with over 10 million sold between 1979 and 1982. Atari's star rose with the VCS–2600, with total sales skyrocketing from $39 million to $2.7 billion. Atari controlled 75 percent of the market for video games and employed more than 7,000 workers.

Then, in 1983, things changed. Atari sales dropped 30 percent. The company lost more than half a million dollars. New management proved unable to stem the tide of Atari's collapse, and in 1984 the company was sold. By this time Atari's work force had dwindled to only 1,000 employees.[1]

Atari's rise and fall in the early 1980s stands as a testament to the power of the forces of change. In the late 1970s, consumers apparently couldn't get enough of whatever Atari was selling. By 1982, they had had enough. In the late 1970s, these consumers built Atari up into an economic powerhouse; in 1983 those same consumers tore that house down. Perhaps if Atari executives had better understood the forces of change surrounding them, they could have built on their early successes instead of swooning. Even Emery Air Freight, singled out in Chapter 12 for its innovative and effective use of employee-performance feedback in the late 1970s, fell on hard times in the 1980s and filed for bankruptcy in 1987. The message here is the power of the forces of change—forces that can make and break companies. If an organization ever hopes to be more than just a leaf blowing in the winds of capricious environmental forces, it must learn to recognize the forces of change and meet their demands.

In the early 1980s, futurologist John Naisbitt wrote *Megatrends,* a book about the future of American business and society. *Megatrends* turned out to be a best-seller, and throughout the 1980s it played a major role in shaping managers' views about the coming forces of change in America. Some of the primary forces of change—or "megatrends"— identified by Naisbitt are presented in Figure 17–1.

While some of these "megatrends" may have been extremely consequential in the 1980s, to students who plan to be practicing managers in

---

[1]R. I. Sutton, K. M. Eisenhardt, and J. V. Jucker, "Managing Organizational Decline: Lessons from Atari," *Organizational Dynamics* 14 (Spring 1986): 17–29.

**FIGURE 17–1**                    Some of Naisbitt's Megatrends

These "megatrends" are important sources of change that one organizational observer has identified. The important sources of change in our society will, however, change over time. Managers must understand where to look for sources of change and how to deal with them once they have been identified.

- From an industrial society to an information society (an economy based on the creation, processing, and distribution of information).
- From high technology that was imposing in its complexity to high technology with a more inviting and personal touch.
- From a predominantly national economy to a more interdependent world economy.
- From a short-term managerial orientation to a focus on long-range planning.
- From centralized organizational structures to greater decentralization.
- From an emphasis on organizational hierarchy to an emphasis on networking (greater sharing of ideas, information, and resources).
- From limited personal choices to a greater variety of acceptable lifestyles, careers, and other options.

Source: John Naisbitt, *Megatrends: Ten New Directions Transforming Our Lives* (New York: Warner Books, 1982).

the 1990s they are at best of historical interest. What is important are not just the currently "hot" forces for change, for those "hot" forces are constantly changing. Equally important is knowing *where* to look for the forces for change as they develop. For managers in organizations, there are two kinds of forces for change: internal forces and external forces.

**Internal Forces**   Internal forces for change are signals coming from *inside* an organization that change is necessary. Sometimes the signs are quite direct, such as inexplicably skyrocketing costs for operations. When employees go on strike, the clear message is that they are dissatisfied. The strike leads to negotiations that correct major problems concerning compensation arrangements or working conditions. Other times, the signals may be more subtle. High levels of absenteeism or turnover may indicate smoldering dissatisfaction among the work force. A certain amount of employee discontent is probably normal. The challenge for management is to realize when the numbers are getting out of hand so that more serious—even catastrophic—problems (such as a walkout, work slowdown, or wholesale work-force desertion) can be avoided further down the road.

Internal problems also can be reflected indirectly. Increasing numbers of employee grievances may indicate a high level of tension between supervisors and the rank-and-file work force. Internal squabbling that is out of proportion to the nature of the problem—for instance, two managers arguing for days in a department head's office about which direction a secretary's desk should face—is often symptomatic of deeper problems that need to be brought to the surface and addressed. Tasks that don't get done on time, messages not received or returned (like the expansion plans at Ben & Jerry's), workers who don't seem to understand their roles, meetings that go on and on and on without resolution—all of these are indirect indications that an organization's management habits are not working and need to be overhauled.

Internal forces for change often reflect an organization's failure to accomplish its mission. For all organizations, survival is the primary mission. Problems such as excessive turnover and dwindling market share threaten an organization's survival, and so it must respond. For many organizations, however, monetary survival is only one aspect of the corporate mission. At Ben & Jerry's, the effectiveness of the organization also is measured by fulfillment of its social responsibilities. Whatever the organization's goals, its success in managing the forces of change will be measured by its attainment of those goals—or their abandonment in the face of external pressures.

**External Forces**   The impact of the external environment on behavior of and in organizations was considered in detail in Chapter 14. At this time, it is worth reviewing several environmental forces that act as major catalysts for organizational change.

Social forces are a major force for change in organizations. For instance, in 1964 only 45 percent of the American work force had a full high school education. By 1984, U.S. Labor Department statistics indicated that almost 60 percent of the work force had high school diplomas, and in the young segment of the work force—those 25 to 29 years old—the percentage was closer to 85 percent.[2] What does this rise in general levels of education mean for American corporations? It may mean that workers will be better able to contribute ideas on the job. As noted in Chapter 12, surveys have shown that workers indeed *want* to play a greater role in organizational decision making. This suggests that managers need to rethink selection criteria and design jobs to meet the needs of a changing work force. (Some other aspects of the changing American work force will be discussed in Chapter 18.)

Political forces also have a tremendous impact on behavior of and in organizations. Certain political actions—for example, the Affirmative Action policies of the 1970s and the comparable worth debates of the 1980s—simply change the internal management habits of organizations. Comparable worth in particular probably led many organizations to reexamine their compensation schemes, giving rise to an entire generation of merit-based compensation plans. Other political winds, such as movements to encourage or discourage mergers and acquisitions or the

[2]E. E. Lawler, *High-Involvement Management* (San Francisco: Jossey-Bass, 1986), 16.

Legislation such as the "plant closing" bill sponsored by Senator Edward Kennedy's Labor and Human Resources Committee provides a major force for change in organizations. While the bill requires only that employers inform their work force of facility shutdowns in advance, this change in notification requirements no doubt will encourage employers to manage the transition process more responsibly.

antitrust rulings that broke up AT&T, more directly affect the climate in which an organization exists by regulating the behaviors of other companies in the environment.

The effects of legislation can be subtle as well. The deregulation of banks in the early 1980s altered the business of banking. Opportunities to develop new products or new markets became available, but many banks were not positioned to take advantage of them because banking traditionally had not been an opportunistic business.[3]

The rapid advance of technology also constitutes a major force for change external to organizations. The Industrial Revolution forever changed the face of manufacturing, and it has been followed by a variety of smaller revolts, including the birth of interchangeable parts and the modern assembly line. The advent of computerized typesetting and word processors similarly revolutionized newspaper production techniques, while automated teller machines changed bank access from "banker's hours" (typically 10 a.m. to 4 p.m., five days per week) to 24 hours every day of the week. The "INTERNATIONAL FOCUS ON: External Forces for Change" describes the Soviet Union's struggle with the computer, a major technological force for change. The increasing role of technology as a force for change in organizations was discussed in detail in Chapter 15.

Finally, market factors also provide an important impetus for change in organizations. A decreasing market share should tell any company that some changes need to be made. Predatory pricing by competitors

[3]R. B. Chase, G. B. Northcraft, and G. Wolf, "Designing High-Contact Service Systems: Application to Branches of a Savings and Loan," *Decision Sciences* 15 (1984): 542–556.

INTERNATIONAL
FOCUS ON:

External Forces for
Change

**The Great Soviet Computer Screw-Up** Though sometimes reluctantly, business executives in the Western world by and large have not only adapted to computers, they have become dependent on them. By 1984, undoubtedly all American manufacturing facilities employing 500 or more workers were using some form of mainframe computer to run plant operations.

The Soviet Union is another story, however. At the enterprise (or business) level, the Soviet Union has failed miserably to exploit the fantastic efficiencies made possible through computerization. By 1984, barely one-third of all large Soviet manufacturing facilities had mainframe computer capabilities. This is an economic disaster of sorts, and a major reason why the gap between Soviet and Western economies should continue to widen.

It also is a major embarrassment to the Soviet system. Computers were once hailed as the ultimate ally of socialist central planning. In fact, in 1971, the Soviet Communist party endorsed a 5-year plan that included a goal of establishing a vast computer network in the Soviet Union. The network was to link all enterprises and ministries in the economy, making timely central planning at last a reality. Three 5-year plans later, that network remains only a goal.

Many of the Soviet Union's problems in adapting to the age of computers are practical. Its equipment is outdated, usually two or three generations of development behind Western state-of-the-art technologies. Further, the technical support systems necessary to advanced computer applications—including service, training, and repair personnel—simply do not exist. Even installation can be a problem. There are stories about computers left in boxes in the snow at Soviet factories for as long as a year, apparently because no one knew how to set them up.

Some of these problems can be traced to the absence of an informal

may mean that a company has to slash its own prices, or that internal cost-savings programs must be implemented to maintain profit margins. New products on the market and changes in the tastes and preferences of consumers are market forces that also demand responses from companies. Market forces that influence the behaviors of an organization's *suppliers* need to be watched carefully as well.

SOURCES OF
RESISTANCE TO
CHANGE

Even with all these internal and external forces pushing organizations to change, some individuals and organizations resist the need to change. For these individuals and organizations, the signals to change never get translated into appropriate responses or actions. Sometimes resistance takes the form of ignoring the signals. Sometimes top management heeds the signals and plans appropriate actions, but those actions never happen—at least not the way they were planned. Several sources of resistance to change are habit, resource limitations, threats to power and influence, fear of the unknown, and defensive perception.

computer "hacker" youth culture in the Soviet Union. Because computers provide an excellent means for both collecting and disseminating information, they represent a first-class vehicle for mobilizing dissent. Consequently, access to computers has been jealously guarded by state institutions. In turn, this means there is no generation of youthful computer wizards in the Soviet Union to fuel their country's emergence into the computer era.

Even some of the benefits of computers may be standing in the way of their acceptance and implementation in the Soviet Union. The Soviet economy is run "by the numbers," with enterprise managers responsible for meeting quotas and projections. Computers pose a threat to these managers precisely because they represent that dream of total central monitoring

of local enterprise activity. Total central monitoring would deprive enterprise managers of the opportunity to juggle their production numbers for impression management purposes.

At a recent NATO briefing, one astute observer of Soviet computer developments noted that the Soviets are acutely aware of and distressed by their shortcomings. "They sit there and watch this competition between Japan and the West over development of a fifth generation of computers. They know they can't just sit out the contest. They know they have to at least look as though they're doing the same kinds of things, but that's not easy." Meanwhile, Soviet central planners can only think wistfully about what might have been. To date at least, progress through computers in the Soviet Union just doesn't compute.

Source: D. Seligman, "The Great Soviet Computer Screw-Up," *FORTUNE*, July 8, 1985, pp. 32–36.

**Habit** Inertia is the tendency for objects to keep doing the things they already are doing—their habits. Inertia is a primary cause of resistance to change. Even with the proliferation of word processors in the 1980s, many people continued to use typewriters. Did they not realize just how much more efficient a word processor would be? Unlikely. Did they not have access to training? Even more unlikely. Probably the typewriter had become a familiar and comfortable companion, and they didn't want to learn the whole new set of habits required to use a word processor.

In many cases, inertial resistance to change stems from an individual's realization that changing a habit will entail some short-term costs. Figure 17–2 shows three typical patterns of individual performance when a change occurs. Pattern A is what top management hopes for. In Pattern A, the change occurs at Time 0. There is no immediate decrease in performance level and, over time, performance gradually increases, reaching a stable new level. Patterns B and C are what usually happens instead. Pattern B represents a classic "Hawthorne effect." (The "Hawthorne effect" and the Hawthorne studies were discussed in

**FIGURE 17–2**     # Three Patterns of Change

Changes in organizations can affect organizational performance in different ways. Most organizations hope that changes (a) will immediately and permanently improve organizational functioning. In some cases changes (b) cause immediate improvements that unfortunately do not last. Most of the time, though, changes (c) result in short-run losses that are eventually recouped when the changes are fully institutionalized.

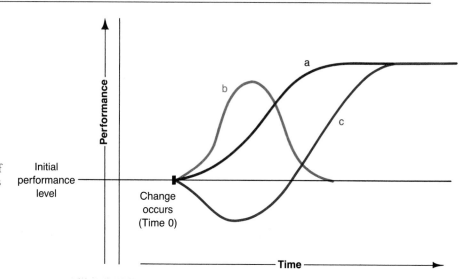

Source: James R. Gibson, John M. Ivancevich, and James H. Donnelly, Jr., *Organizations*, 6th ed. (Plano, Tex.: Business Publications Inc., 1988).

Chapter 2.) Top management hears of or reads about something that it thinks is a great idea—quality circles, for instance. The idea is implemented and work-force performance immediately improves. Unfortunately, the improvement in performance is not really because the idea is a good one, but rather because the idea is a *new* one and people are enthusiastic about trying something new. When the enthusiasm for the new idea disappears, so do the improvements in performance.

Pattern C provides a classic example of a short-term loss from a change that has long-term value. Imagine that you own a small chain of hardware stores and for years your staff has kept the inventory manually, using large paper-and-pencil inventory registers. You are convinced by a computer salesperson that putting your entire inventory system on a desktop computer will save you both time and money in the long run. Further, you can use the computer for other functions such as payroll. This computerized inventory system clearly is your ticket into the twentieth century. There is only one problem: No one on your staff knows how to use a computer.

In such cases, some short-term costs have to be absorbed to get to the long-term benefits. Everyone will have to be trained to use the new computerized inventory system. That may mean closing your store for a couple hours per week for a few weeks, which means lost sales. Or it may mean having your staff come in evenings or weekends, which means overtime pay. Perhaps you will need to add some temporary employees to run the new system while your regulars observe and learn the ropes. You may even need to let some workers go and hire some others with different qualifications. Further, during the training period people are bound to make mistakes, which undoubtedly will translate into lost sales and maybe even lost customers. Some of your staff may even get discouraged and quit. Finally, when you announce the upcoming change to the new computerized system, some of your staff may stop recording inventory in the registers, creating further chaos when the new system is installed.

Knowing ahead of time that many of these costs are unavoidable can create a substantial psychological barrier to change. Any lost revenues and lost goodwill likely to occur as a result of the changeover *should be* recouped eventually. But those short-term costs can be painful, while the old managerial habits are probably familiar, comfortable, and workable, even if not spectacularly efficient.

**Resource Limitations**    Sometimes obvious changes are avoided because the costs are prohibitive. If a manager faces probable initial losses (Pattern C change), those short-term losses may represent more than just a psychological roadblock. In our previous example, the owner of the hardware-store chain had no one else to answer to for that short-term loss. What if instead that short-term loss was going to show up as red ink on a CEO's annual report to the shareholders, or as a quarterly loss on a division manager's performance appraisal? Even if the long-term benefits look pretty good, the long term is only potential. The short-term bad news may cost the CEO or division manager any opportunity to find out what the long term looks like—especially if the company or division is making a profit *without* the benefit of any changes. In these cases, inertia may be traced to a manager's short-run need to survive.

**Threats to Power and Influence**    One of the effects of many changes in organizations is the rearrangement of power relationships. In particular, changes often undermine power arising from expertise. Consider again the example of the hardware-store chain. If one or two people in the chain have become influential because of their in-depth understanding of the traditional inventory system, the adoption of a new system about which they know nothing would be quite threatening. Their power in the organization would evaporate, and they would have to start all over on an equal footing with every other computer novice in the company. Worse yet, a brand-new employee who was knowledgeable about computers would suddenly become quite powerful, even though computer experience previously was irrelevant as a condition of employment.

**Fear of the Unknown**    The sources of resistance that we have discussed so far all arise from an understanding of the probable consequences of a change in managerial habits. Some consequences, of course, cannot be foreseen, and the uncertainty that is part and parcel of any organizational change presents another source of resistance.

New employment opportunities provide a classic example of resistance that arises from uncertainty about the actual consequences of a change. If you are offered a transfer to another part of your company, should you go? Salary and job assignments, even housing costs and climate, can be known prior to making the decision. But what about the friendliness of your new coworkers? What about the quality of the new schools for your children? What about the quality of your life-style in a different town? These are all big question marks. If your current situation is good or even just OK, is a transfer worth the risk of losing the nice parts of your life as it is now? In the terms of Figure 17–2, maybe those short-term losses will never be recouped.

For organizationwide changes, similar uncertainties arise. Will I still be able to perform well under the new management? Will I ever be able to work the new computer inventory system? Will I still be respected as a typist when all the others have a word processor on their desk? These fears breed resistance to any changes to the old, familiar, and comfortable.

**Defensive Perception**    Managers who understand their own susceptibility to these sources of resistance to change—habit, resource limitations, loss of power or influence, fear of the unknown—may well be able to correctly perceive the need for change and act on that need despite their reservations or trepidations. A larger fear is that these sources of resistance to change will *bias* a manager's ability to construct an accurate perception of the need for change.

In Chapter 3 we noted that perception is a constructive process, and one that can be biased. Managers who sense trouble on the horizon if a particular change occurs may be less likely to perceive the need for that change. The signals may be there; managers just may be unwilling to see them or interpret them for what they are. An old-timer who has mastered the hardware chain's traditional inventory registers may have a hard time understanding the need for computers. A supervisor who fears the consequences of any short-term productivity losses may fight tooth and nail against the introduction of new machinery, if for no other reason than to be absolved of any personal responsibility for the outcome.

Defensive perception is really a result of resistance to change—a reflection of an individual's or organization's wish to maintain the status quo. When managers engage in defensive perception, the opportunity to change is missed. Resistance also can surface *after* the wheels of change already have been put in motion. An organization's work force may voice its resistance to change by sabotaging implementation of management's new plans, perhaps in the hope of changing management's mind. The craftsmen who wrecked the textile mills in the early days of the Industrial Revolution were demonstrating their fears about the possible consequences of such a major change and hoping to reverse the trend. Whether such fears manifest themselves in defensive perception, sabotage, or even just fearful depression and paralysis, they will oppose any alteration in managerial habit, no matter how justified or necessary. The manager must be able to face this opposition and balance it against the need for change. Our attention turns next to how these changes occur.

## A MODEL FOR CHANGE IN ORGANIZATIONS

While there are many ways of conceptualizing the process of change in organizations, the model devised by psychologist Kurt Lewin is probably the best known and provides the simplest framework for understanding change processes. Lewin's model proposes three phases for change: unfreezing, movement, and refreezing.[4] Over the years, researchers have revised Lewin's model in a variety of ways and identified other phases of the change process.[5] In our discussion, we will consider one additional phase: diagnosis. The relationships among these four phases of change are depicted in Figure 17–3.

## DIAGNOSIS

Realizing that change is needed, or even having systems for meeting the demands of change, is not equivalent to knowing exactly what to change. The forces for change will signal the need to alter managerial habits; the next challenge for management is figuring out what actions to take in response to the signals. **Diagnosis** involves three separate tasks: identifying the problem, isolating its primary causes, and coming up with an appropriate and effective solution. Figure 17–4 shows one framework for thinking about where to find appropriate responses to the need for change. This framework includes six places to search for problems, their causes, and solutions when a change is needed: purposes, structure, relationships, rewards, support systems, and leadership.[6]

**Purposes**  Purpose is what an organization is supposed to be doing—its charge, or mission. In 1987, a small home-movie videotape distributor

---

[4]K. Lewin, *Field Theory in Social Science* (New York: Harper & Row, 1951).

[5]R. Lippitt, J. Watson, and B. Westley, *Dynamics of Planned Change* (New York: Harcourt Brace, 1958).

[6]M. R. Weisbord, *Organization Diagnosis: A Workbook of Theory and Practice* (Reading, Mass.: Addison-Wesley, 1978).

**FIGURE 17–3**    Four Phases of Change

There are four distinct phases to organizational change efforts. Diagnosis identifies what needs to be changed; unfreezing prepares the organization for change; in movement, the change actually occurs; and refreezing ensures that the change had its intended effects and no unintended ones.

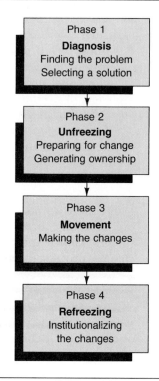

Phase 1
**Diagnosis**
Finding the problem
Selecting a solution

Phase 2
**Unfreezing**
Preparing for change
Generating ownership

Phase 3
**Movement**
Making the changes

Phase 4
**Refreezing**
Institutionalizing
the changes

called Vestron watched as the videotape-distribution market became saturated and its revenues plummeted. The response? Vestron's management decided that to remain financially healthy Vestron could no longer be just a videotape distributor. It had to become a *movie* company in a much larger sense of the word. So Vestron made a movie, "Dirty Dancing," that netted the company over $50 million.[7] Enlarging an organization's mission, for instance, through vertical or horizontal integration, is a common way to respond to the need for change.

Sometimes the shift in an organization's purpose will be more subtle. Following deregulation, many bank managers found it necessary to adjust their perceptions of the business of banking. After deregulation, banking remained a financial-services industry, but with a new proactive flavor for marketing and product development. In fact, marketing and product development always had been parts of the banking picture, but passive parts. Deregulation meant less a change in overall mission than a reordering of the mission's priorities.

[7]R. King, "Is There More Where *Dirty Dancing* Came From?" *Business Week,* February 15, 1988, 110.

## FIGURE 17–4    A Framework for Diagnosis

Weisbord's "six-box" organizational model provides a road map for identifying problem areas in an organization. Each of Weisbord's six boxes represents one aspect of the organization that may be inhibiting its effective response to environmental forces for change.

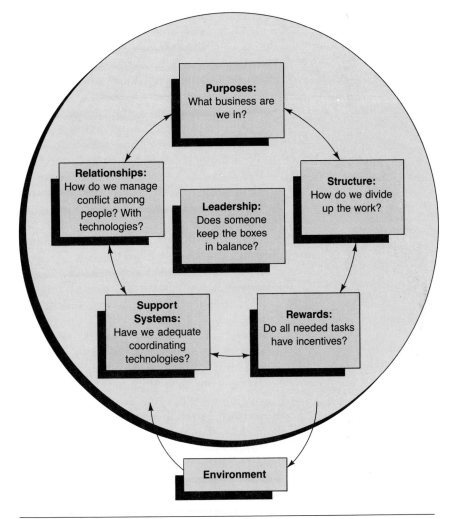

Source: M. R. Weisbord, "Organizational Diagnosis: Six Places to Look for Trouble With or Without a Theory," *Group and Organization Studies* 1 (1976): pp. 430–447; W. Warner Burke, *Organizational Development: A Normative View* (Reading, Mass.: Addison-Wesley, 1987).

**Structure**   Organizational structure (which was the focus of Chapter 16) consists of an organization's reporting relationships. These reporting relationships in turn reflect how work is divided up in the organization. Organizational structure usually is reflected in a company's organizational chart.

Centralization is an aspect of organizational structure often tinkered with in response to signals for change. In a decentralized conglomerate, each division will act as a virtually independent company with its own marketing and purchasing operations. In a centralized organization, the marketing and purchasing operations for separate product divisions might be handled by central marketing and purchasing units. Marketing and purchasing in a centralized organization might even be divisions themselves. Centralization affords opportunities to avoid duplication of effort and consequently to achieve substantial economies of scale—for example, by having only one person order all the clerical supplies for the whole company. Decentralization, on the other hand, can increase understanding and responsiveness. Purchasing and marketing units that are part of a product division are in a position to be more in touch with that particular division's unique needs and therefore can respond better and more quickly to the division's concerns.

**Relationships**    Relationships have to do with the ways in which people in an organization get along—the group dynamics. Are there obvious conflicts, and if so, what are their origins? Are communication channels in place to ensure that work groups or individuals who need to share information have a way to do so?

Relationships also may involve the roles that different workers are assigned. If someone is not doing the job, perhaps that person's role expectations are unclear. If two people are in conflict, perhaps their roles define their jobs so that conflict is inevitable. A supervisor who is rewarded for production quantity and a quality-control engineer who is rewarded for quality are bound to find their daily agendas in conflict. These kinds of relationship problems dictate a hard look at the roles of workers as one possibility for change.

**Rewards**    As we noted in Chapter 4, the law of effect suggests that the behaviors that get rewarded are the behaviors that occur. If an organization wants quality, it needs to reward quality; if it wants quantity, it needs to reward quantity. Too often compensation schemes are busy rewarding one set of behaviors (say, individual achievement) when another set of behaviors altogether (such as cooperative collaboration) is really desired.

Profit-sharing compensation programs make individual compensation contingent upon such factors as market reception of a firm's products and general economic climate, which workers clearly cannot control. This can be discouraging—and sometimes confusing—for rank-and-file workers. A production team that performs brilliantly but is not rewarded because the company didn't show a profit is unlikely to perform brilliantly again. Merit-pay programs in which the rules for judging merit are unclear to workers also miss the opportunity to motivate workers by making pay contingent upon work accomplishments.

Finally, it should be remembered that the term *rewards* refers to more than just money. As we discussed in Chapter 12, the design of jobs substantially influences the nonmonetary rewards that accrue to workers, such as job satisfaction and feelings of belonging or accomplishment on the job. A dissatisfied staff might be unhappy about wages, but could just as easily be dissatisfied with a shortage of opportunities to express opinions and exercise independence on the job.

**Support Systems**   Elements in an organization that assist personnel in accomplishing their work tasks effectively are called **support systems.** AT&T ran a series of advertisements in 1987 emphasizing the importance of having a flexible and easy-to-use phone system, both for getting calls through and for projecting the correct corporate image. The phone system is one example of a support system that can dramatically help or hinder the efforts of a work force.

If projects are not getting finished on time or poor decisions are being made, problems may be arising in the support systems. An inadequate, outdated, or overloaded computer system can make life miserable for a production staff that depends upon computer output. An understaffed or poorly equipped maintenance department can turn minor problems into major roadblocks. If projects are continually being completed late, the clerical staff may be woefully undersupported. A shortage of information also can hinder performance. Putting in place performance feedback systems can improve performance by giving workers the information they need to know when their performance is off. As shown in the "Focus on: Support Systems," changes in feedback systems also can have tremendous symbolic value.

**Leadership**   In this model for change in organizations, the leadership role means coordinating and initiating action. Someone must monitor signals, decide when the change is required, and move the organization forward to accomplish the change effectively. Without adequate leadership, important signals may be missed, diagnosis may be poor, inappropriate actions may be planned, and even appropriate actions may never get implemented effectively. Someone has to run the show.

These six components of organizations—purpose, structure, relationships, rewards, support systems, and leadership—hardly comprise an exhaustive list of places to look for problems or solutions in organizations. They do, however, provide a framework for formulating plans for possible organizational change. There are also several ways to approach the *collection* of information about an organization during the diagnosis phase. The advantages and disadvantages of several common information collection procedures are summarized in Figure 17–5. Each of these techniques has particular strengths and weaknesses. Interviewing, for instance, provides opportunities to collect rich, probing information. Its value, however, is highly dependent upon the interviewer's skills and the awareness and forthrightness of the interviewee. Trustworthy diagnosis generally comes at the cost of combining multiple collection techniques. Once a problem has been diagnosed and a potential solution identified, the real business of change begins with unfreezing.

FOCUS ON:

Support Systems

**Giving Quality the Green Light**
When Don Kelley was brought in from another General Electric facility to manage GE's refrigeration plant, he found disillusioned line operators and defensive foremen. Whenever they attempted to communicate with one another, an explosion of previously pent-up anger occurred instead. Despite these entrenched problems, Kelley's strategy was to accentuate the positive.

Kelley set up a system that shut down the line if quality fell below a certain standard. That seemed like an outrageous thing to do. After all, wouldn't the union guys sabotage the line? The sabotage never occurred. Kelley says, "The hourly people were interested in building a quality product if given the chance. In truth, the greatest inhibition to doing that was coming from some of the managers and supervisors who were under the gun to get the product out the door."

Kelley had to do something radical to communicate to everyone his commitment to quality improvement. How did he go about it? "We went out and bought traffic lights, installing three lights out in the aisle of each assembly line. We do a quality check called an 'end-of-line' audit where we take about 2 percent of the product every hour, and then we turn on the green light if everything is acceptable. If we find a 'class one defect' (a defect that

would result in a service call 70 to 100 percent of the time), the end-of-line auditor switches on the red light, which stops the line." At first everyone thought Kelley was crazy. "For about the first six months, once the red light went on, nobody could start the assembly line again except me. I did that because the culture change we needed was so drastic."

Kelley did something else that is rare. "Our people are paid an incentive based on production. We made a decision that we were not going to penalize them from a pay standpoint when the line shut down. I recall having quite a go-around with a corporate auditor who wrote me up for costing the company something like $180,000. He felt that when the line was down we shouldn't continue to pay at the incentive rate. Our point was that we did not want to turn the quality around at the expense of the operators. We didn't want any negativity associated with improved quality. I was also told that people would make mistakes on purpose to stop the line, but that never happened, *even in the early days when there was a lot of animosity.*"

For Don Kelley, the solution to his problems was a simple support system—a stoplight that kept workers and managers abreast of quality—that had some complicated symbolic impact as well.

Source: Robert Waterman, *The Renewal Factor* (New York: Bantam Books, 1987), pp. 263–265.

UNFREEZING

**Unfreezing** is the process of getting an organization ready for change. Unfreezing is something akin to the pregame warm-ups for a major sporting event. Even if the coaches have a terrific game plan, it will never work if the players aren't told what the plan is and how to execute it. In the pregame warm-ups, the coaching staff has a chance to *prepare* everyone for the game, to get all the players loosened up and make sure

**FIGURE 17-5** A Comparison of Different Methods of Data Collection

Each of these four methods of data collection has both strengths and weaknesses. Questionnaires, for example, are easy to administer to large numbers of employees, but their predetermined format can bias the information that respondents supply. The best way to collect information is to use some combination of these different techniques.

| Method | Major Advantages | Major Potential Problems |
|---|---|---|
| Interviews | 1. Adaptive—allow data collection on a range of possible subjects<br>2. Source of "rich" data<br>3. Empathic<br>4. Process of interviewing can build rapport | 1. Expense<br>2. Bias in interviewer responses<br>3. Coding and interpretation difficulties<br>4. Self-report bias |
| Questionnaires | 1. Responses can be quantified and easily summarized<br>2. Easy to use with large samples<br>3. Relatively inexpensive<br>4. Can obtain large volume of data | 1. Nonempathic<br>2. Predetermined questions miss issues<br>3. Overinterpretation of data<br>4. Response bias |
| Observations | 1. Collect data on behavior rather than report behavior<br>2. Real time, not retrospective<br>3. Adaptive | 1. Coding and interpretation difficulties<br>2. Sampling inconsistencies<br>3. Observer bias and questionable reliability<br>4. Expense |
| Unobtrusive measures | 1. Nonreactive—no response bias<br>2. High face validity<br>3. Easily quantified | 1. Access and retrieval difficulties<br>2. Validity concerns<br>3. Coding and interpretation difficulties |

Source: D. Nadler, *Feedback and Organization Development: Using Data-Based Methods* (Reading, Mass.: Addison-Wesley, 1977), p. 119.

they understand their role in the game. The pregame warm-up is also a great time to put any conflicts on the table and get them settled.

Harkening back to the model of organizations presented in Chapter 1, uncertainty, complexity, and politics all present barriers to change efforts in organizations. Unfreezing is the process of lowering these barriers. It is the preparation phase, in which resistance can be broken down. The unfreezing phase has three objectives that correspond to the other three phases (diagnosis, movement, and refreezing) of the change process: selling the diagnosis, understanding the implementation, and preparing for the consequences.

**Selling the Diagnosis** It is easy to assume once you see why a change is necessary or even inevitable that everyone else will see it, too.

Unfortunately, that is a dangerous assumption. In fact, the only more dangerous assumption is that workers won't care about changes.

Unfreezing is the time to get everyone up to speed about an upcoming change. Once management has chosen a course of action, sharing with other organizational members insights about the problem, its probable causes, and the identified solution will help them understand the need for the change. This diagnosis sharing promotes ownership of the problem by the rest of the work force. Generating ownership even at the level of rank-and-file workers is critical if the conversion is to go smoothly, without hostility, resentment, or sabotage.

The importance of selling a diagnosis to the work force is illustrated by a story about a posh hotel resort in the Colorado Rockies. To cut costs, hotel management decided to install a video-surveillance security system rather than hire security guards to patrol the hotel. Unfortunately, top management failed to share its thoughts with any members of the hotel work force. When the first surveillance cameras appeared in the hotel kitchen, the kitchen staff was outraged. They assumed the cameras had been installed to police their behaviors. Their reaction was sabotage; the cameras were covered up with dish towels, and a minor blowup between the kitchen staff and hotel management quickly followed. Hostilities subsided as soon as management informed the staff of its real intent in installing the cameras. However, the entire conflict could have been avoided if management simply had shared its diagnosis with the hotel staff.[8]

Work-force participation in the diagnosis process provides a foundation of worker understanding of the necessity for change. As noted in our earlier discussions about participative management in Chapters 9 and 12, participation is two-way education. Participating workers provide management with a fresh and different perspective on problems, probable causes, and potential solutions. The participation process also allows workers to see more of the facts about a problem, to gain a broader, organizational perspective, and to learn management's thoughts and beliefs. As shown in the "FOCUS ON: Selling the Diagnosis," work-force participation in diagnosis can mean a much stronger sense of diagnosis ownership and consequently a stronger commitment to the changes when they occur.

**Understanding the Movement**   Even if all workers accept the need for a change, it is important that they realize their own role in the process. Unfreezing presents an opportunity to communicate the "game plan" to all relevant players in the upcoming conversion. Details should be provided about what will happen—for example, what days new equipment will arrive, what performance expectations are going to be

---

[8]Taken from a personal experience of one of the authors.

FOCUS ON:

Selling the
Diagnosis

**AT&T Answers the Call**   The date was Labor Day 1986, and the situation was grim. In the 33 months since a federal antitrust suit had forced American Telephone and Telegraph Co. to divest itself of three-quarters of its $150 billion in assets, the company that arguably had been the most consistently profitable, the most self-assured, and one of the best-managed corporations in the twentieth century had performed one belly flop after another. Although AT&T's leaders were trying to cut costs, expenses were still out of control. The company's computer business, one of the new ventures that was supposed to take up the slack after AT&T spun off its profitable local phone companies, was losing nearly $1 billion a year.

Work-force morale also was suffering. Thousands of employees were being laid off or shunted like pawns, destroying AT&T's fabled esprit. Employees who had chosen to stay with the parent company over going with a Baby Bell now wished openly that they had gone. "Some of them had no responsibilities," recalls one executive. "And they had nowhere to go. It was horrible." The worst part was that top management seemed stunned, too. That was why it took so long for AT&T to right itself. Robert Allen, now president, says it was "the first time in my career when I began to lose confidence in myself."

It was in this strained atmosphere that the company's new chairman, James Olson, gathered his 27 top executives at a Cape Cod golf resort called New Seabury. Olson brought with him a broad plan: He wanted to protect and improve AT&T's core businesses of long-distance service and phone equipment, get its com-

puter business into the black, and increase the 9 percent share of AT&T's $34 billion in revenues that came from overseas. But each strategy involved cooperation and trade-offs of a sort these executives seldom had to make while running fiefdoms in the old Bell System.

For five days, AT&T's leaders fought turf battles like congressmen arguing over budget cuts. How should they cut costs? What businesses should AT&T be in? Should it always rely on AT&T Bell Laboratories to design new products, or buy some from outside? They finally settled their differences, forging compromises for the common good. "Sure, some guys were trying to protect their businesses," recalls one attendee. "But there was a bigger feeling—that we had to do this now because we weren't going to get another chance."

To secure the commitments he'd won, Olson asked for an expression of loyalty. As chief operating officer, he had failed two years earlier to implement a more modest plan because "I hadn't gotten my managers to buy into it." This time, as chairman, "I wanted a buy-in." One by one, Olson invited each man to stand. "Are you with me?" he asked. "Yes, Jim, I'm with you," came the inevitable reply. "It was pretty dramatic," recalls Frank Blount, president of AT&T's Network Operations Group. "A powerful moment . . . a catharsis."

Within two years, the New Seabury summit began to show a big payoff. AT&T consolidated numerous back-office operations, cutting overall costs by 3 percent a year, and restructured its computer operations, slashing losses by 70 percent. By the end of 1987, improvements had pushed net income up nearly 50 percent, well

*(Continued)*

Sometimes important changes can best be accomplished off-site, away from the distractions and reminders of everyday organizational life. Outward Bound experiences offer work groups an opportunity to learn how to work together better. Outward Bound change efforts are conducted off-site to prevent the realities of the organizational environment from reinforcing old, dysfunctional habits.

during the conversion, and how business is going to continue (if it is) in the midst of the chaos.

Unfreezing is also the time to train workers to use new equipment or lay the foundations for new managerial habits. If a new compensation plan or a different phone system is going to be used, for instance, management will need to arrange information or training meetings so that everyone knows what to expect and what to do.

**Preparing for Consequences**   Unfreezing is also the time to prepare the work force for any foreseeable consequences of the change. Particularly sweeping changes in work-force size or organizational climate and culture may lead to the departures of some members. The offer of early-retirement programs or outplacement services may be appropriate to smooth the transition process. Overtime policies and extra temporary staff also may be desirable to get an organization through a particularly large changeover.

Management should make sure that one objective of the unfreezing phase is to reassure workers (if possible) that their jobs are not on the line. The uncertainty that arises in the work force concerning job security does more than distract employees and hurt short-term performance. Psychological studies have demonstrated that perceptions of job security are the number-one predictor of workers' *physical* health. The more permanent that employees perceive their jobs to be, the better their physical and mental well-being.[9] Since it is no secret that an organization suffers financially when the health of its employees suffers, both in lost productivity from sick days and rising health-care costs and insurance claims, it makes sense for management to use the unfreezing phase of organizational change to calm the fears of its work force about what is to come.

Unfreezing is also the time to put in place feedback systems to track the unforeseeable consequences of organizational changes. Management may find it advisable to set up temporary monitoring systems and

[9]M. Schanback, "Stress and Job Security," *Psychology Today,* May 1987, 16.

employee counseling programs. These procedures can not only help deal with unforeseen problems that arise as the implementation occurs, but also provide management with a watchful eye on the progress and problems of their change efforts.

## MOVEMENT

If the foundation for change has been laid effectively during unfreezing, the actual **movement**—implementation of the change plan—should be trivial. In fact, the ease of implementation should be a good gauge of how well the unfreezing process has broken down any potential pockets of resistance to the change. If unfreezing has been handled well, all employees will understand why the change is necessary and what their own role is in the change. However, it is important during movement that management make sure the channels of communication in the organization remain open and active. If implementation of the change plan creates confusion or unforeseen problems, early detection may be critical to the prevention of a groundswell of work-force resistance.

An important decision for management during the movement phase of an organizational change is whether to use external change agents. **External change agents** are expert consultants from outside an organization that management brings in specifically to execute a change. Their value lies in their experience and objectivity. Because they will have supervised similar changes in other organizations, change specialists will have the experience necessary to identify subtle sources of resistance to change and know what strategies will best deal with them. Because they are not part of the social fabric of the organization, the objectivity of external change agents puts them in a better position to act upon sources of resistance to change.

## REFREEZING

Finally, once the change has been fully implemented, **refreezing** is the process of institutionalizing the new changes—making the new changes into organizational habits. Institutionalization means monitoring the systems that have been put in place to track the consequences of implementing the change. Have any unforeseen problems developed? Have any members of the organization become disenfranchised or lost power or status? If so, how should these problems be handled? Did the change solve the problem it was intended to address? If not, should the change be scrapped and something different tried? Refreezing is a time to reflect on what has occurred in the change and get the work force settled into a new routine.

## ORGANIZATIONAL DEVELOPMENT

The four-phase model of change we have been discussing in this chapter epitomizes traditional approaches to managing change in organizations: Managers diagnose organizational problems, unfreeze the work force, implement the changes, and then refreeze the work force by institutionalizing the changes. **Organizational development (OD)** represents a different approach to managing the process of change in organizations. Organizational development can be formally defined as "a system-wide application of behavioral science knowledge to the planned development and reinforcement of organizational strategies, structures, and processes for improving an organization's effectiveness."[10]

Figure 17–6 lists the variety of interventions that typically might be undertaken as part of an organizational development effort. As shown in the above definition, organizational development differs from traditional approaches to organizational change in several important ways.

BEHAVIORAL
HEALTH

First, traditional organizational change efforts typically are *problem focused*. This means management identifies a problem that needs to be solved, and the focus of the change effort is on resolving the problem. A defining feature of organizational development, on the other hand, is its **process focus.** Organizational development focuses on the behavioral (interaction) patterns in an organization that produced or sustain problems. It assumes that an organization that is behaviorally healthy will anticipate and therefore prevent (or quickly resolve) problems.

A behaviorally healthy organization is more than just financially sound. AT&T's roller-coaster financial performance in the 1980s demonstrates that financial profitability can be short-lived. **A behaviorally healthy organization** is one whose internal interaction patterns put the organization in a position to become and remain financially sound. This kind of behavioral health arises from four other characteristics of organizations: communication, adaptation, innovation, and succession. Financial soundness is a partial reflection of these other sources of organizational health.

**Communication**    Andy Pearson, former president of corporate mega-conglomerate Pepsico, Inc., once noted, "We have 120,000 employees

[10]E. F. Huse and T. G. Cummings, *Organizational Development and Change* (St. Paul, Minn.: West, 1985), 2.

Finally, in traditional approaches to change, diagnosis is a management activity. This is known as **"top-down" problem solving.** The diagnosis (identification of the problem, probable causes, and potential solutions) is done by management—the top of the organization. The rest of the work force is informed about the change only when unfreezing begins. In the traditional approach to change, work-force involvement in diagnosis often represents little more than an attempt by management to promote ownership of the problem as defined by management. Organizational development instead is built on the assumption that work-force involvement is essential in all phases of change, especially diagnosis. This is known as **"bottom-up" problem solving:** the problem diagnosis comes up from the bottom of the organization.

Not surprisingly, there are not really two distinct approaches to change: the traditional approach and the organizational development approach. Rather, there is a spectrum of approaches to managing change in organizations. The process-focused, evolutionary, "bottom-up" orientation at the organizational development end of the spectrum represents a drastic departure from tradition for some managers. However, organizational development is an approach to change in organizations that is clearly in sync with the job design needs and desires of the current American work force, as discussed in Chapter 12.

Several organizational development techniques have been discussed in this book. Team building was discussed in Chapter 7, and quality circles were discussed in Chapters 9 and 12. Both are process-focused change efforts. The object of these activities is not to solve a particular problem. Team building and quality circles are both group processes that handle organizational problem solving naturally, by making the organization more communicative, adaptive, and innovative. Similarly, the time horizon for team building and quality circles is long term and dynamic. The object of these activities is not to solve one problem, but to create an organization that is behaviorally healthy for problem solving over the long haul. Finally, through both team building and quality circles, management puts in place "bottom-up" problem-solving processes that foster work-force participation in organizational problem diagnosis. In effect, organizational development is an approach to the diagnosis and unfreezing phases of organizational change that should make movement and refreezing considerably more effective.

The particular orientation of organizational development can be seen further by examining two other intervention techniques: survey-guided development and quality-of-work-life programs.

## SURVEY-GUIDED DEVELOPMENT

**Survey-guided development** (or survey feedback) is one of the most popular techniques of organizational development. It has been used in a wide variety of organizational settings including businesses, schools, hospitals, government operations, and even the military. The U.S. Navy alone has used this technique more than 500 times, collecting more than 150,000 individual survey responses.[14] The results of survey-guided development have been mixed. However, evidence suggests that it is the OD intervention technique most likely to produce both process and outcome benefits if only one OD technique is going to be used.[15]

As shown in Figure 17–7, survey-guided development uses questionnaires to construct a picture of an organization's internal processes and problems. Many organizations use employee surveys to assess the organization's climate and to identify sources of problems in organizational functioning. Survey-guided development differs from these traditional survey efforts in the amount of involvement it requires from rank-and-file workers. In a typical organization's employee survey, rank-and-file workers participate only by filling out the questionnaires. In survey-guided development, employees at all levels of the organization also play a role in *interpreting* the results. In some cases, survey-guided development techniques may even ask employees to identify issues that need to be addressed in the questionnaire.

The rationale behind encouraging employee participation in the development of the questionnaire is simple: The questions asked in a survey and the way they are worded play a large role in the picture of the organization painted by responses to the questionnaire. For example, if middle managers think that an organization's performance appraisal procedures are a central problem, their feelings are likely to surface only if the survey contains questions about the performance appraisal procedures. As demonstrated by the failures of one public school organizational survey effort, irrelevant questions or questions that are framed in values inconsistent with those of the organization can quickly render survey efforts futile.[16] When management encourages employee participation from all levels of an organization in the design of an employee survey, the discussions about which questions should be included and what issues should be addressed become as revealing as the questionnaire results. Participation in development of the survey itself becomes a forum for employees at all levels to discuss problems in the organization.

Employee participation in the interpretation of survey results is accomplished through a process called "**data handback.**" Once a completed survey-guided development questionnaire has been filled out by all employees and the results tabulated, these results are handed back

---

[14]Huse and Cummings, *Organizational Development and Change*, 133.

[15]J. Porras and P. O. Berg, "The Impact of Organizational Development," *Academy of Management Review* 3 (1978): 249–266.

[16]S. Mohrman, A. Mohrman, R. Cooke, and R. Duncan, "Survey Feedback and Problem-Solving Intervention in a School District: We'll Take the Survey but You Can Keep the Feedback," *Failures in Organizational Development and Change*, eds. P. Mirvis and D. Berg (New York: Wiley, 1977), 149–190.

**FIGURE 17-7** **Survey-Guided Development**

The key element of survey-guided development is the involvement of the work force not only in responding to the survey but also in interpreting the survey results. This problem-solving involvement helps "unfreeze" the work force for later changes suggested by the survey results.

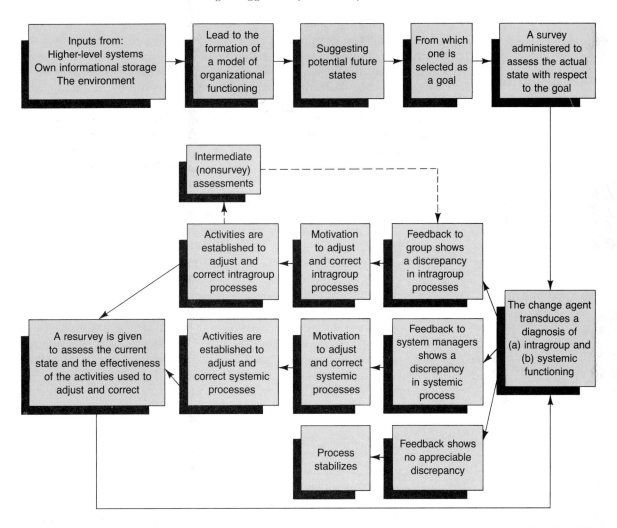

Source: David G. Bowers and Jerome L. Franklin, *Journal of Contemporary Business* 1(3), (Summer 1972): pp. 43–55; as appeared in Wendell L. French et al., *Organizational Development: Theory, Practice, Research*, 2/e (Plano, Tex.: Business Publications, Inc., 1983).

to the employees. In keeping with the spirit of organizational development, top management may see the results first, but in the end *all* members of the organization are encouraged to attend data handback sessions.

Data handback sessions have two purposes. Naturally, management can use these sessions to solicit suggestions from employees at all levels of the organization about implications of the survey results for organizational problem diagnosis. However, in survey-guided development, data handback also serves a more basic function. Employees also are asked to assess whether the picture of the organization painted by the survey results is accurate. If not, it may be advisable for top management to begin the questionnaire design process again. Even if a new questionnaire is not deemed necessary, employee discussion about the results and implications of the survey can help top management bring its perceptions of the organization into clearer focus. The benefit of survey-guided development, then, is that it gives top management *three* opportunities to solicit employee input about problems and processes in the organization—through their participation in survey design, survey completion, and survey results interpretation. Traditional organization survey attempts take advantage of only one of these opportunities.

In its ideal form, survey-guided development is not a one-shot attempt to understand organizational processes. In keeping with the dynamic orientation of organizational development, a central objective of survey-guided development is to put in place an organizationwide participative survey process. When used on a regular basis (such as annually or semiannually), survey-guided development provides an ongoing set of processes through which top management can track the development of the organization.

Often the questionnaire-development and results-compilation phases of survey-guided development prove to be beyond the skills of organization members. Questionnaire design and statistical analysis are, after all, rather technical skills, and (as noted earlier) incorrectly designed questionnaires or poorly analyzed or presented data can diminish the effectiveness of survey activities. Where necessary skills are lacking, top management should bring in outside assistance to guide the survey development process. How to manage survey-guided development activities without outside assistance then becomes part of the learning experience, and another large step toward behavioral health for the organization.

Because the intended output of survey-guided development is an accurate picture of the workings of the organization, it is primarily a form of problem and probable-cause identification. Survey-guided development is not a strong means for identifying potential courses of action, though it should aid this process by strengthening an organization's channels of communication. It is not surprising, then, that research has found survey-guided development to work best when combined with other techniques to form broader-scope OD programs.[17]

---

[17]Porras and Berg, "The Impact of Organizational Development"; also J. Nicholas, "The Comparative Impact of Organizational Development Interventions on Hard Criteria Measures," *Academy of Management Review* 7 (1982): 531–542.

**FIGURE 17–8**                 How Quality of Work Life Affects Productivity

Quality-of-work-life pro-
grams typically include a
combination of different
organizational-
development techniques,
and no two programs are
ever quite the same.
However, all QWL pro-
grams share the organiza-
tional development focus
on improving the quality
and effectiveness of em-
ployee interactions, on
the assumption that im-
proved organizational
outcomes such as
increased productivity will
no doubt follow.

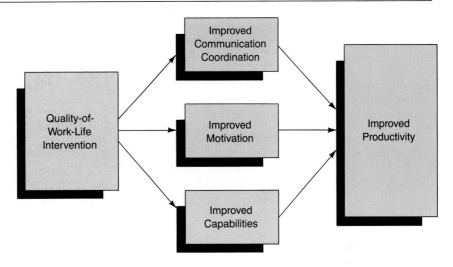

Source: E. Lawler III and G. Ledford, "Productivity and the Quality of Work Life,"
*National Productivity Review* 2 (Winter 1981–1982): p. 29.

QUALITY-OF-WORK-
LIFE PROGRAMS

**Quality-of-work-life (QWL) programs** are examples of broader-scope
organizational development programs. QWL programs are best characterized as systemwide attempts to simultaneously enhance organizational
effectiveness (usually defined in terms of productivity) and employee
well-being through a commitment to participative organizational decision making. Unlike survey-guided development, QWL does not refer to
a particular OD technique. Rather, QWL provides a framework for
pursuing organizational development goals, and may incorporate any
number of specific OD techniques.

QWL programs aim to enhance the work experience of the individual
worker. They typically have a strong flavor of worker rights and
industrial democracy, and many QWL programs have been designed as
cooperative ventures between unions and firm management. The typical
objectives of a QWL program would include fair compensation, a
conducive work environment, development of individual capacities,
social integration of the work force, protection of the dignity and rights
of each individual worker, and social relevance of the organization and
its activities for the organization's work force.[18]

The philosophy of the QWL framework is illustrated in Figure 17–8.
In virtually all QWL programs, joint management-union quality-of-work
committees are established to oversee QWL program development and
planning. QWL programs then may additionally include a team-building

[18]Huse and Cummings, *Organizational Development and Change*, Chapter 9.

GM's car assembly plant in Tarrytown, New York, was the scene of a major turnaround in work-force morale and productivity through organizational development. Serious problems in the plant led management and union representatives to work together to formulate a participative problem-solving program for the work force. The benefits realized from this initial program encouraged management to initiate a highly successful plant-wide quality-of-working-life effort.

or survey-guided development component. In the case of Shell Canada, one component was management-union cooperation in the design of a new plant and its jobs.[19]

In keeping with the overall philosophy of organizational development, the immediate focus of a QWL intervention is improving such organizational processes as communication, coordination, motivation, and personal development. The implicit assumption here is that improving these processes will enhance attainment of the individual objectives described above. Improved productivity and organizational effectiveness should follow.

The General Foods experiment in Topeka, Kansas (described in detail in Chapter 12), is considered to have been one of the pioneer QWL projects. In 1974, the U.S. Congress established the National Center for Productivity and Quality of Working Life to examine issues concerning the design of QWL programs and the enhancement of corporate effectiveness. In 1978, Congress decided that the Center's function belonged under the auspices of the Departments of Labor and Commerce, and it was abolished. The Center's work has continued, however, via the establishment of several university-sponsored research centers, including the Quality of Working Life Program at UCLA.[20]

QWL programs have had mixed success. The Ford Motor Company's QWL program at its Sharonville plant has claimed some dramatic successes. Customer complaints dropped by *70 percent* after QWL was instituted, and the proportion of employees in the plant rating quality as excellent rose from 54 to 72 percent. Ford also claimed annual cost improvements of almost 7.5 percent during the QWL program at

[19]Ibid., 209.

[20]Ibid., Chapter 9.

Sharonville—*three times* the average of other Ford plants during the same time period. Furthermore, 90 percent of Ford's surveyed employees said that Ford's QWL program was a good idea and should be continued.

General Motors has had similar successes with QWL. GM's Tarrytown plant—described in detail in the "FOCUS ON: Quality-of-Work-Life Programs"—went from 16th (out of 18 plants) to 1st, according to GM's internal measures. And GM management has directly attributed its success in negotiating union contracts to the presence of QWL programs in GM plants. On the other hand, only one of the eight QWL programs studied in depth by the University of Michigan QWL center lasted more than five years. Apparently QWL is not for everyone, and some important organizational factors—such as top management's commitment to QWL and the effectiveness of the labor-management steering committee—play a major role in determining the success of an organization's QWL effort.[21]

## CHANGE IN CORPORATE AMERICA

The American business environment in the 1980s could be charitably characterized as turbulent. Successful major assaults were made on American product markets by international business competitors, especially the Japanese. Closer to home, a staggering 138 U.S. banks failed during 1986, compared with only 10 in 1981. During all this, 30 million members of the American work force were dislocated by corporate restructuring efforts as Fortune 500 companies eliminated about 3 million jobs.[22]

Perhaps in response to the chaos—perhaps as *part* of the chaos—mergers, acquisitions, hostile takeovers, plant closings, and severe cutbacks in personnel all became commonplace during the 1980s. In effect, the 1980s provided more than just new heights of turbulence in the American business environment. The 1980s also set new standards for the severity of organizations' responses to the uncertainty and chaos around them. In a remarkable six-year stretch during the 1980s, General Electric alone acquired 325 businesses and sold off more than 225.[23] And at least one business analyst—Tom Peters, coauthor of the 1980s business best-seller, *In Search of Excellence*—thinks American companies had better start thinking in terms of even more change if they want to survive.[24] In the final few pages of this chapter, we will use the framework for change developed in the chapter to examine a few of the problems involved in managing major corporate reorganizations.

[21]Lawler, *High-Involvement Management*, 136.

[22]T. Peters, *Thriving on Chaos* (New York: Knopf, 1987), 3.

[23]Ibid.

[24]T. Peters, "There Are No Excellent Companies," *Fortune*, April 27, 1987, 341–352.

FOCUS ON:

Quality-of-Work-
Life Programs

**Learning from Tarrytown** This is the story of the General Motors car assembly plant at Tarrytown, New York. In 1970, the plant was known for having one of the poorest labor relations and production records in GM. In seven years, the plant turned around to become one of the company's better-run sites.

In the late 1960s and early 1970s, the Tarrytown plant suffered from much absenteeism and turnover. Operating costs were high. Frustration, fear, and mistrust characterized the relationship between management and labor. At times, as many as 2,000 labor grievances were pending. Union officers battled constantly with management. As one union officer described it, "We were always trying to solve yesterday's problems. There was no trust and everybody was putting out fires. The company's attitude was to employ a stupid robot with hands and no face." Workers were mad at everyone. They disliked the job itself and the inexorable movement of the high-speed line—56 cars per hour, a minute and a half per operation per defined space. Warnings, disciplinary layoffs, and firings were common.

In April 1971, the plant manager at Tarrytown, sensing the seriousness of the situation, approached some of the key union officers about a wholesale change in management philosophy.

The tough chairman of the grievance committee observed later that "this guy showed right off he had a quality-of-work-life attitude—we didn't call it that at that time—inside him. He was determined that this attitude should carry right down to the foremen, and allow the men on the line to be men."

The company decided to shuffle the entire layout around. At first, the changes were introduced in the usual manner, with manufacturing and industrial engineers and technical specialists presenting their proposals. Then two production supervisors, sensing that top management of the plant was looking for new approaches, asked a question that was to have a profound effect on events to follow: "Why not ask the workers themselves to get involved in the move?" The result was an impressive outpouring of ideas from the workers. "We found they did know a lot about their own operations. They made hundreds of suggestions and we adopted many of them."

Taking his cue from the successes of Tarrytown a year earlier, in 1972 Irving Bluestone, vice-president for the General Motors Department of the United Auto Workers Union (UAW), made the kickoff speech for the future of the quality-of-work-life movement:

Traditionally management has called upon labor to cooperate in

CORPORATE
REORGANIZATIONS

Mergers and acquisitions present very complete pictures of the spectrum of problems that major corporate change creates. As we discussed in Chapter 14, on paper many mergers and acquisitions look like good ways for organizations to combine complementary resources in the fight against a hostile and competitive business environment. Unfortunately, the combining of two companies' resources is not done just on paper. The marriage can go sour when one or more of a variety of behavioral problems occur.

increasing productivity and improving the quality of the product. My view of the other side of this coin is more appropriate; namely, that management should cooperate with the worker to find ways to enhance the dignity of labor and to tap the creative resources in each human being in developing a more satisfying work life, with emphasis on worker participation in the decision-making process.

In 1973, the UAW and GM negotiated a national agreement that included a "letter of agreement" in which both parties committed themselves to establishing formal mechanisms for exploring new ways of dealing with the quality of work life.

It was only natural that Tarrytown extend its ongoing efforts within the framework of the new agreement. Management and the union each selected a coordinator to work with a consultant, the supervisors, the union, and the workers. They proposed a series of problem-solving training sessions to be held on Saturdays, for eight hours each day. Thirty-four workers from two shifts volunteered for the training sessions; management agreed to pay for six hours of the

training. Again, top management was very impressed by the ideas generated from the sessions, and by the cooperation from the union.

By 1977, top management at Tarrytown had made the "big commitment" and launched a plantwide QWL effort involving 3,800 workers and supervisors. Each week, 50 different workers reported for 27 hours of training (three days for 9 hours each day). The sessions covered the QWL concept; plant, union, and management functions; and problem-solving skills necessary for effective worker involvement. The program cost GM $1.6 million, but the production manager at Tarrytown admits, "From a strictly production point of view—efficiency and costs—this entire experience has been absolutely positive, and we can't begin to measure the savings that have taken place because of the hundreds of small problems that were solved on the shop floor before they accumulated into big problems." Absenteeism dropped from 7.25 percent to between 2 and 3 percent, and by December 1978 there were only 32 pending grievances, compared with the 2,000 pending grievances before QWL began.

Source: R. H. Guest, "Quality of Work Life—Learning from Tarrytown," *Harvard Business Review,* July/August 1979, pp. 76–87.

While mergers and acquisitions represent the marriage of complementary resources, merging companies undoubtedly have some redundant functions. For example, the payroll offices of two merging companies each may be almost large enough to handle the entire payroll function for the new merged entity. This could necessitate cutbacks or transfers of staff to new functions where both companies previously were short in personnel. **Downsizing**—reducing the size of an organization's work force—also can occur as a reaction to a downturn in product demand. Finally, some mergers and acquisitions are quickly followed by a general "house cleaning"—replacement of key employees with newcomers not wedded to the old managerial habits of either company, or even the selling off or closing down of less profitable or outdated facilities and operations.

Such turmoil can prove extremely damaging to the morale of an organization's work force. Workers may become less productive because of uncertainty about life in the new organization (including job responsibilities and relationships with supervisors and coworkers), legitimate concerns about job security, and even feelings of betrayal if management was not particularly communicative about impending possibilities. Undesired turnover among key employees also can occur if they perceive the new corporate entity as too unstable or perceive an erosion of their influence or power, or if early retirement programs designed to thin the ranks are not managed properly. Maybe it is not surprising, then, that the success rate of mergers and acquisitions (as measured by appreciation in shareholder value) has been estimated to be only about 23 percent.[25] What can top management do to make sure its efforts become part of that successful 23 percent?

In the process of unfreezing for a merger or acquisition, it is critical that an organization's channels of communication be extremely open and active. Naturally, workers will want to know what's going on—who is buying whom, what the new name will be, who will be in charge now, and so on—even if their jobs are not going to change much. Federal legislation now requires employers to provide their work force advance notification of major plant closings. Meetings and memorandums can help diffuse a lot of hostility or concern that takes root in uncertainty. Many employees in the face of little or no information are likely to imagine the worst and react accordingly. Employees also should be provided opportunities to ask questions. The strategic concerns at the forefront of top management's minds during a major organizational change may have nothing to do with what is on the minds of the employees (their benefits package, for instance).

Included in the unfreezing stage for a major corporate reorganization should be an **outplacement program** to find new jobs for displaced employees, or those who choose not to stay on under a new regime. Good outplacement programs, like the one described in the "Focus on: Corporate Change in America," can do a lot more than just soothe a guilty corporate conscience. They also send the message to the *remaining* members of the work force that the organization is not going to abandon them. This message can play an important role in minimizing the psychological damage done to their feelings of job security. Some

[25]Peters, *Thriving on Chaos*, 3.

## FOCUS ON:
Corporate Change in America

**Easing the Pain** In early 1985, Stroh's Beer decided to close its Detroit brewery. For 71 years, this old brick plant had been a landmark, the symbol of a family brewing tradition. Closing the plant would permit Stroh's to operate the remaining plants at full capacity and, as a result, compete more effectively. In addition, the Detroit plant was very old, inconveniently located, and no longer competitive with modern facilities. This logic did not lessen the shock and concern of both city and state officials, the business community in general, and—most of all—the 1,159 plant employees whose jobs would be lost.

Needless to say, the loss of a job generates major changes in a person's life. It might mean new employment, part-time work, retirement, or a return to school. It also can generate emotional trauma and financial problems. To help its employees deal with these special needs, Stroh's management developed Stroh's Employee Transition Services, a program to deal with all the needs that employees might experience in transition, not just find them a job. To begin design of transition services, the human resource department analyzed the demographics of the brewery work force. Most of the hourly employees and more than half of the salaried employees were over 40 years old. Could they perform any jobs other than the ones they had at Stroh's? Were they too old to find new jobs? Even if they could find new employment, would the pay and benefits be equivalent to Stroh's?

First on the human resource department's list was a salary and benefits continuation program to provide workers a source of income after termination, to provide extended benefits to protect employees, and to recognize longer-service employees with special early retirement programs. Transition resource centers also were set up for both salaried and hourly employees—one at a cost of over $100,000 just for building renovations.

The transition program set up for the brewery employees included orientation meetings, job search skills workshops, job development and training activities, and ongoing counseling. Job skills workshops began with discussions about the closing and plain talk about future prospects. The remainder of the sessions dealt with assessing skills and creating individual development plans. One of the principal tools used in this work was the data processing system, which helped people develop high-quality resumes.

A major factor in the success of Stroh's program was the job development effort. The participants' own efforts to seek employment were supported by job developers, who made numerous inquiries and referrals to various employers. More than 4,000 employers were contacted and approximately 1,400 job possibilities were generated. Approximately 100 of the displaced workers also successfully completed some form of training that contributed to their placement.

The transition centers closed 13 months after the closing of the Detroit brewery. The program was very expensive: Stroh's spent more than $1.5 million, in addition to about $600,000 in government funding. However, the program also was very successful: overall placement for the brewery work force reached 98.3 percent. The program also had a positive effect on employees who were *not* affected by the plant closing. These employees, who were very much aware of how the affected employees were being treated, came to perceive Stroh's as more than just a good place to work. They see Stroh's as a company with a genuine concern for its employees.

Source: J.J. Fansem, "Easing the Pain," *Personnel Administrator*, February 1987, 50–55.

remaining workers are even likely to feel "survivor guilt"—guilt because they were allowed to remain while some of their coworkers were not.[26] Successful outplacement programs will help these workers turn their attention to the new work at hand, rather than becoming obsessed about their future in the new company. Good outplacement programs also help with community relations.

## SUMMARY

To respond effectively to the ever-changing demands around them, organizations must be prepared to change constantly. A key challenge for managers is maintaining a delicate balance between forces that encourage or demand change and forces within organizations that resist it. Managers must be able to recognize the need for change and identify and manage sources of resistance to change.

The change process entails four stages. During diagnosis, information that helps identify an organization's problems and isolate their causes is collected. Unfreezing lays the foundation for a change, and movement executes the change itself. Refreezing institutionalizes the change and checks to make sure the identified problem has been solved and no new problems created.

Organizational development is a different approach to change in organizations. Organizational development assumes that problems occur in organizations because they are not behaviorally healthy.

All organizational development change efforts therefore are aimed at improving organizational health —communication, adaptation, innovation, and succession. Survey-guided development uses work-force participation to develop, complete, and interpret questionnaires that construct a picture of an organization's internal processes and problems. Quality-of-work-life (QWL) programs are systemwide attempts to improve work-force effectiveness and morale through a commitment to formal work-force participation in organizational decision making.

The 1980s were an exceptionally turbulent time for businesses in America. Bankruptcies, hostile takeovers, mergers, and major reorganizations and work-force reductions all became commonplace. So much uncertainty plays havoc with an organization's ability to remain efficient and effective. Being able to manage the changes necessitated by such a turbulent business environment has become a key managerial challenge.

[26]J. Brockner et al., "Layoffs, Equity Theory, and Work Performance: Further Evidence of the Impact of Survivor Guilt," *Academy of Management Journal* 29 (2), (1986): 373–384.

KEY TERMS

**Behaviorally healthy organization**   One whose internal interaction patterns put it in a position to become and remain financially sound; arises from successful communication, adaptation, innovation, and succession.

**Bottom-up problem solving** Involving workers in all phases of the change process, beginning with diagnosis.

**Data handback**   Providing employees with the results of the questionnaires used in survey-guided development in order to assess whether the picture of the organization painted by the survey is accurate, and to solicit their suggestions about the implications of the survey results for problem diagnosis.

**Diagnosis**   First stage in the process of change; figuring out what actions to take in response to signals that change is needed; includes identifying the problem, causes, and an appropriate and effective solution.

**Downsizing**   Reducing the size of an organization's work force.

**External change agents**   Expert consultants from outside an organization that management brings in specifically to facilitate a change.

**Habit**   Tendency of a person or an organization to do things the same way, over and over again.

**Inertia**   Tendency of an object to continue in the same direction with the same velocity or intensity unless impacted by some force of change.

**Movement**   Third stage in the process of change; implementation of the change plan.

**Organizational development (OD)**   Systemwide application of behavior science knowledge to the planned development and reinforcement of organizational strategies, structures, and processes for improving an organization's effectiveness.

**Outplacement program**   Finding new jobs for displaced employees or those who choose not to stay on after a major corporate reorganization.

**Process focus**   Concentration of organizational development on the behavioral (interaction) patterns in an organization that produce or sustain problems.

**Quality-of-work-life (QWL) programs**   Systemwide attempts to simultaneously enhance organizational effectiveness (usually defined in terms of productivity) and employee well-being through a commitment to participative organizational decision making.

**Refreezing**   Final stage in the process of change; institutionalizing the change and monitoring the systems that have been put in place to track the consequences of implementing the change.

**Succession**   Turnover, retirement, or promotion of personnel.

**Support systems**   Elements in an organization that assist personnel in accomplishing their work tasks effectively, such as production technology.

**Survey-guided development** Use of questionnaires to construct a picture of an organization's internal processes and problems; also called *survey feedback*.

**Top-down problem solving** Diagnosis of a problem by management, with the rest of the work force being informed only during unfreezing.

**Unfreezing** Second stage in the process of change; lowering barriers to change by selling the diagnosis, understanding the implementation, and preparing for the consequences.

DISCUSSION
QUESTIONS

1. Considering what you have learned about participative approaches to managerial decision making, are there any circumstances in which "top-down" change efforts might be more appropriate than organizational development?

2. How does the progress of traditional change efforts and organizational development through the four phases of organizational change (diagnosis, unfreezing, movement, and refreezing) differ?

3. Why would survey-guided development probably be a useful first step in *any* organizational change or development program?

4. Refreezing is often a forgotten and neglected phase of organizational change efforts. Does this help explain why apparently successful change efforts often do not have lasting effects? Why is refreezing so important? What is likely to happen if it is *not* done?

5. What skills are likely to be required of a manager in a turbulent industry or during turbulent times?

6. Why is change likely to be easier to manage in a behaviorally healthy organization? Is change likely to be easier in a company like Ben & Jerry's because of its interest in the employees' welfare?

7. Are some sources of resistance to change more "rational" (that is, more justifiable) than others? Why might a little inertia (or even a lot) be a good thing?

8. Organizational development is a vehicle for change in organizations. For many organizations, however, organizational development itself represents a change. What kind of unfreezing might be needed to ensure success when an organization changes to the use of organizational development?

IF YOU
WANT TO
KNOW
MORE

Two recent popular-press books concerning the importance of managing change to corporate survival in today's turbulent business environment are by the authors of *In Search of Excellence:* Robert H. Waterman's *The Renewal Factor* (New York: Bantam Books, 1987) and Tom Peters's *Thriving on Chaos* (New York: Alfred Knopf, 1987). Rosabeth Moss Kanter's book, *The Changemasters: Innovation for Productivity in the American Corporation* (New York: Simon & Schuster, 1983) also examines the importance of managing change to remaining innovative on an ongoing basis. Kanter's book includes a particularly good chapter concerning the problems often encountered when organizations attempt to use participative approaches to weather the storms of major change.

A more theoretical treatment of the organizational change process is provided in Noel Tichy's *Managing Strategic Change: Technical, Political, and Cultural Dynamics* (New York: Wiley, 1983).

A classic article on sources of resistance to change in organizations is Coch and French's piece, "Overcoming Resistance to Change," in *Human Relations* (Winter 1948): pp. 512–532. Even today this article remains the foundation of our understanding of individual sources of resistance to change.

A classic article on organization diagnosis processes is William Pound's piece, "The Process of Problem-Finding," in *Industrial Management Review* 11 (1969): pp. 1–19. Marvin Weisbord's article, "Organizational Diagnosis: Six Places to Look for Trouble with or without a Theory," also provides some important insights into the diagnosis phase of change efforts.

An excellent sourcebook on organizational development is Huse and Cummings' text, *Organizational Development and Change* (St. Paul, Minn.: West, 1985). This book explains the theoretical underpinnings of the organizational development orientation and provides detailed descriptions of all major OD intervention strategies.

The February 1987 and January 1988 issues of *Personnel Administrator* have addressed the issue of managing corporate restructuring and its effects on an organization's work force. Included in these issues are articles on "Downsizing Strategies" (by J. Franzem, February 1987) and "When the Dust Settles" (by R. Korn, January 1988), which examine the effects of corporate restructuring on the survivors.

ON YOUR
OWN

**Likert's Profile of Organizational Characteristics: Short Form**  Are you in a work group that is ready for change? Keeping that group in mind, fill out the questionnaire below. For each question on the left-hand page, circle the phrase on the right-hand page that best describes your work group. Your instructor will give you scoring instructions that will tell you where your group stands, and if it might be ready for some changes.

Source: Rensis Likert, *The Human Organization* (New York: McGraw-Hill, 1975).

---

**Leadership**

1. How much confidence is shown in subordinates?
2. How free do they feel to talk to superiors about job?
3. Are subordinates' ideas sought and used, if worthy?

---

**Motivation**

1. Is predominant use made of (1) fear, (2) threats, (3) punishment, (4) rewards, (5) involvement?
2. Where is responsibility felt for achieving organization's goals?

---

**Communication**

1. How much communication is aimed at achieving organization's objectives?
2. What is the direction of information flow?

3. How is downward communication accepted?
4. How well do superiors know problems faced by subordinates?

---

**Decisions**

1. At what level are decisions formally made?

2. What is the origin of technical and professional knowledge used in decision making?
3. Are subordinates involved in decisions related to their work?
4. What does decision-making process contribute to motivation?

---

**Goals**

1. How are organizational goals established?

2. How much covert resistance to goals is present?

---

**Control**

1. How concentrated are review and control functions?

2. Is there an informal organization resisting the formal one?

3. What are cost, productivity, and other control data used for?

| System 1 | System 2 | System 3 | System 4 |
|---|---|---|---|
| None | Condescending | Substantial | Complete |
| Not at all | Not very | Rather free | Fully free |
| Seldom | Sometimes | Usually | Always |
| | | | |
| 1, 2, 3 occasionally | 4, some 3 | 4, some 3 and 5 | 5, 4, based on group-set goals |
| Mostly at top | Top and middle | Fairly general | At all levels |
| | | | |
| Very little | Little | Quite a bit | A great deal |
| Downward | Mostly downward | Down and up | Down, up, and sideways |
| With suspicion | Possibly with suspicion | With caution | With an open mind |
| Know little | Some knowledge | Quite well | Very well |
| | | | |
| Mostly at top | Policy at top | Broad policy at top, more delegation | Throughout but well integrated |
| Top management | Upper and middle | To a certain extent, throughout | To a great extent throughout |
| Not at all | Occasionally consulted | Generally consulted | Fully involved |
| Nothing, often weakens it | Relatively little | Some contribution | Substantial contribution |
| | | | |
| Orders issued | Orders, some comment invited | After discussion, by order | By group action (except in crisis) |
| Strong resistance | Moderate resistance | Some resistance at times | Little or none |
| | | | |
| Highly at top | Relatively highly at top | Moderate delegation to lower levels | Quite widely shared |
| Yes | Usually | Sometimes | No—same goals as formal |
| Policing, punishment | Reward and punishment | Reward—some self-guidance | Self-guidance problem solving |

CLOSING CASE
FOR CHAPTER 17

# THE MANAGER'S MEMO

FROM: J. Quigley, Vice-President

TO:     P. Winograd, Production Manager

RE:     Planning for Greater Productivity

As you know, our profits have suffered during the past year because our production facility has one of the lowest productivity levels in the industry. The Executive Committee has been exploring solutions to this problem, and we have come to the conclusion that we have a major need for greater automation and use of technology.

Therefore, we plan to introduce computer-aided design and manufacturing (CAD/CAM) to our production process. We intend to install the system next year.

CAD/CAM will enable us to offer greater service to our customers and will permit us to cut costs dramatically by eliminating 35 jobs. The remaining workers will have to learn to operate the computerized system, or we will need replacement workers who already have these skills.

I would like to meet with you on Tuesday to begin discussing the particulars of the CAD/CAM system. In the meantime, please send me suggestions for how we can introduce this system to the production work force. We would like to keep morale as high as possible, introducing the change as a positive move for the future of the company.

CASE DISCUSSION
QUESTIONS

Assume you are the production manager, and respond to the vice-president's memorandum. What sources of resistance to this change must you prepare for? What actions can the company take to make the change as beneficial as possible? What, if anything, should the company do for the workers whose positions will be eliminated?

# Emerging Trends:
# Managing in the Twenty-First Century

## 2002: A PERSONNEL ODYSSEY

"Good morning, 927431," my performance monitor (a supervisor in the old days) smiled as I walked into the sterile office of Universal Manufacturing where I would assume my new duties as human resources selector. It bugged me to be called by a number, but I guess it can't be helped since it came about due to federal regulations.

"If you're ready, we can get started on your new function. This is your new function station." He pointed to what used to be called a "reclining chair" back in the 1990s. As I sat down, it seemed that this station was a little more comfortable than the one I occupied in my old job with Universal, but it's probably only my imagination since all function stations are required by law to be designed to provide the same level of comfort.

"This is your communicator," he said as he handed me a small microphone wired directly into a small computer that rested in front of my function station. "Your

function is to select and hire applicants who apply for employment with Universal. Years ago, you would have been called an 'employment interviewer.' When the blue light on the computer lights, it will indicate that an applicant has entered one of our employment booths and is ready to be interviewed. You simply ask the applicant questions, and unless you find some valid reason for rejection, you hire the individual.

"There are a few other things you should know before you begin. Your computer has been programmed to supplement and monitor your performance and to educate you, with timely feedback, when your performance is not acceptable. You will quickly notice that all voice transmissions from the applicant are in the same monotone. The computer automatically eliminates any trace of accent or other intonations that might suggest the nationality, race, age, or sex of the applicant. In the event that the applicant speaks a foreign language, the computer automatically translates it into whatever language you understand best. It is currently programmed to operate in English because your personal data bank indicated that English would be the language you would select.

"The computer also protects you and Universal from any charges of inappropriate actions. It will instantly evaluate any question you ask to determine if it is a permissible preemployment question in accordance with the latest city, state, and federal regulations. When your question is a legal one, the green light on the computer will glow and you may proceed. When a question is illegal or a statement is inappropriate, the red light will glow and the computer will delete the communication so the applicant will never know that an illegal question was asked. As part of your indoctrination into your new function, the computer is programmed to explain any reasons for the deletions it makes."

"I think I understand. When can I get started?" I asked.

"Right now," he said. I'll return in a little while to see how you're doing; perhaps we can have lunch together—although I am required to advise you that you are under no obligation whatsoever to have lunch with me simply because I am your performance monitor."

I picked up my communicator, leaned back in my chair, and spoke, "927431, ready to function." Almost immediately the blue light glowed, indicating that an applicant was ready for interview-

ing. For lack of a better opening, I cleared my throat and said "Hello." The response came back in an indistinguishable voice: "Hello."

"How are you today?" I asked, and immediately the red light glowed brightly. Slowly, in an instructive tone, the computer said, "Your question has been intercepted and deleted. The question 'How are you?' carries with it the implication that you are trying to determine the physical condition of the applicant and the state employment commission ruled in 1989 that such questions are illegal as preemployment inquiries." Then, after a pause, it said, "Please proceed."

It took me a moment to recover, and I began again, "What kind of job are you looking for?" Again the red light and the voice. "Your question has been intercepted and deleted. The question is discriminatory since it penalizes the applicant who may not be aware of the types of jobs that are performed at the company, and it is not a permissible inquiry under the Positive Assurance [an offspring of the Affirmative Action] Guidelines. Please proceed."

Proceed? How the hell do I proceed? Everything I've asked has been intercepted and deleted. I tried once more. "Are you a human being?" I almost laughed when the green light glowed, followed shortly by the applicant's voice, "Yes, I am." Flushed with success, I asked, "Are you alive?" Again the green light glowed and the applicant's answer was yes. The computer, ever instructive, however, intervened. "I must advise you that the question you asked is the only one that is legal in this line of questioning. For example, the question, 'Are you dying?' as in 'Are you in good health?' is not permissible. Please proceed."

I hadn't noticed my performance monitor reentering the room. "How did it go?" he asked.

"Not too well," I responded. He moved to the computer and placed his hand on a small button. "When I push this button, the computer will give us a full evaluation of your first interview. Let's see if the computer agrees with your evaluation."

"This is the evaluation of the performance of 927431 interviewing 928563. The legal questions and responses were as follows:

Question: Hello.
Applicant Response: Hello.
Question: Are you a human being?

Applicant Response: Yes, I am.
Question: Are you alive?
Applicant Response: Yes.
Statement: You are hired.
Applicant Response: OK.

"While 927431 did propose some illegal inquiries, it is clear from the preceding transcript that the applicant was thoroughly interviewed and that virtually every legal line of questioning was pursued. The rating is highly satisfactory."

"Wait a minute. I never told the applicant that he or she was hired." I looked at my performance monitor. He smiled and said, "When it was clear to the computer that there was no justifiable reason for not employing the applicant, the computer added those words in your voice pattern. Congratulations! You've hired your first applicant."

Source: D. Zechar, "Beyond Affirmative Action: Personnel Odyssey 2002." Reprinted from the August 1977 issue of *Personnel Administrator*, copyright, 1977 The American Society for Personnel Administration, Alexandria, Va.

---

## INTRODUCTION

The preceding vignette is obviously a parody of the impact of the increasingly complex and restrictive regulation of the workplace. Although this parody exaggerates the effects of work-related legislation and regulation, fairness and justice in the workplace are becoming more important all the time. Organizational justice is one of three emerging trends we will be examining in this, the final chapter of the book. In addition, the following sections will examine the unique demands on managers of a global marketplace and the impact on organizations of the changing demographics of the work force.

## JUSTICE IN THE WORKPLACE

So often I am filled with so much rage and anger because of how I am treated . . . the broken promises and lies by my bosses, the undeserved recognition that others receive, or when I feel as manipulated as an accounting entry into our current fiscal year budget. . . .You know sometimes you want to grab them and shake them so hard that it hurts them as much as you feel hurt. . . . All I want here is a fair deal. . . . Yeah, I know there is no justice, but that makes it all the worse. With every day, it seems that revenge is becoming my only *real* option to gain some sense of justice.

—An assistant brand manager employed at a
*Fortune* 500 consumer products firm[1]

The employee quoted above is expressing outrage at the injustice he experiences at the hands of his employer. Examples of unfair practices and similar employee responses are common in organizations. Employee responses to perceived and real injustices can range from the trivial (gripe sessions when employees get together) to the critical (destruction of valuable company records by disgruntled employees) to the dangerous (employees who seek revenge on their employer through physical violence).

## INTERACTIVE JUSTICE

A number of researchers have identified important components of justice in the workplace. Employees may be concerned with **distributive justice** (the fairness of outcomes they receive)[2] or **procedural justice** (the process by which outcomes are allocated)[3] or **interactive** (or interpersonal) **justice** (the quality of the interpersonal treatment they receive).[4] While managers may have little to say about organizational rewards (distributive justice) or how they are allocated (procedural justice), they may have considerable discretion concerning how their employees are treated (interactive justice). For example, managers may be told that only a certain percentage of their employees may be given an outstanding rating and the concomitant salary increase. Thus, managers may be unable to reward employees equitably for their productivity. Or organizational policies may restrict managers' ability to gather input from the ratee when completing performance evaluations. Even when

[1]R. J. Bies, "The Predicament of Injustice: The Management of Moral Outrage," in *Research in Organizational Behavior*, vol. 9, eds. B. M. Staw and L. L. Cummings (Greenwich, Conn.: JAI Press, 1987), 290.

[2]See, for example, G. C. Homans, *Social Behavior: Its Elementary Forms* (New York: Harcourt Brace Jovanovich, 1961); and M. Deutsch, *Distributive Justice* (New Haven, Conn.: Yale University Press, 1985).

[3]See, for example, J. Thibaut and L. Walker, *Procedural Justice* (Hillsdale, N.J.: Erlbaum, 1975); and E. A. Lind and T. R. Tyler, *The Social Psychology of Procedural Justice* (New York: Plenum, 1988).

[4]See, for example, T. R. Tyler and R. J. Bies, "Beyond Formal Procedures: The Interpersonal Context of Procedural Justice," in *Advances in Applied Social Psychology: Business Settings* (New York: Erlbaum, 1988); and R. J. Bies and J. S. Moag, "Interactional Justice: Communication Criteria of Fairness," in *Research on Negotiations in Organizations*, vol. 1, eds. M. H. Bazerman, R. J. Lewicki, and B. Sheppard (Greenwich, Conn.: JAI Press, 1986), 43–55.

organizational impediments to fair treatment exist, whether or not employees *feel* justly treated will depend in large measure on the interpersonal treatment they receive from their managers *and* the managers' proper use of discretionary authority.[5]

**Interpersonal Treatment** In evaluating the quality of interpersonal treatment, individuals focus on whether they were treated politely and respectfully and whether the manager followed general principles of ethical conduct. In one study, students were asked whether they had been fairly or unfairly treated in job interviewing situations. Students believed they were fairly treated to the extent that the interviewer was candid and honest, provided timely feedback about whether they would be made a job offer, treated them with respect, focused on appropriate topics and avoided such inappropriate issues as gender, race, and marital status, and adequately justified the decision whether to hire them.[6]

**Use of Discretionary Power** A manager's use of discretionary power will also influence an employee's perception of justice. For example, when a manager allows employees more participation in making decisions that affect them, they will perceive the decisions as being more fair. Alternatively, employees will be outraged if they discover that their involvement is not seriously considered—that the participation is a sham. Employees will react more negatively to this false participation than they would if their views had never been solicited.[7]

The attribution of a manager's intent can also significantly influence an employee's perception of fairness. Even fair procedures will be discounted if managers use them for their own gain. For example, suppose a manager benefits personally from some procedure. If workers are given an opportunity to voice their objections about this procedure and their objections are ignored, they will view the procedure as even more unfair than they would if they never had the opportunity to complain.

Because the *perceived* fairness of an outcome or procedure may differ from its *objective* fairness, the attribution of intent is critical to the perception of organizational justice. Managers should be concerned not only with being fair but also with "looking fair." Managing impressions of organizational justice is critical to being perceived as just.[8]

---

[5]Tyler and Bies, "Beyond Formal Procedures."

[6]R. J. Bies, "Identifying Principles of Interactional Justice: The Case of Corporate Recruiting," in the symposium Moving Beyond Equity Theory: New Directions for Research on Justice in Organizations, Academy of Management, Chicago, Ill..

[7]R. Cohen, "Power and Justice in Intergroup Relations," in *Justice in Social Relations,* eds. H. Bierhoff, R. Cohen, and J. Greenberg (New York: Plenum, 1986).

[8]J. Greenberg, "Looking Fair Versus Being Fair: Managing Impressions of Organizational Justice," in *Research in Organizational Behavior,* vol. 12, eds. B. M. Staw and L. L. Cummings (Greenwich, Conn.: JAI Press, 1990).

FOCUS ON:
Looking Fair

**Cultivating an Image of Justice**   In a recent study, Jerald Greenberg asked 815 managers to describe the one thing they thought they could do to make their subordinates think they treated them fairly. The managers reported that they engaged in both *behavioral acts* (things done to look fair) and *social accounts* (things said to look fair) to create the perception that they were just.

Eighty-one percent of the managers reported that they could enhance their image of fairness by "publicly announcing all pay raises and promotions"—a behavioral act focused on outcomes. Fifty-one percent indicated that "allowing workers to participate in decision making"—a behavioral act

that focuses on process—would enhance the workers' perception of managerial fairness.

Forty-three percent of the managers said they could enhance their reputations for fairness by "explaining why certain work assignments were made" (a social account focusing on outcome). Giving social accounts about such processes as "how pay raises are determined" would increase their level of perceived fairness for 76 percent.

Greenberg suggests that one of the more interesting aspects of this survey was managers' awareness of entitlement tactics—tactics designed to increase their perceived responsibility for positive outcomes.

Source: J. Greenberg, "Cultivating an Image of Justice," *Academy of Management Executive* 2, (1988).

Managers may be perceived as more just or fair if they use tactics to reinforce the employees' perception of fairness. For example, managers can respond to threats to their fairness persona by using defensive tactics such as excuses ("Economic conditions necessitate my decision"), justifications ("I am punishing you for your own good!"), and apologies ("I am sorry I have to give you such a low rating"). These tactics distance managers from responsibility for their actions. In addition, managers may use more proactive tactics to portray themselves as fair and just. These include entitling and enhancement. **Entitling tactics,** the opposite of excuses, are attempts to gain responsibility for positive events and their consequences.[9] The "FOCUS ON: Looking Fair" illustrates a number of ways in which managers can increase their perceived responsibility for fair outcomes and, thus, their perception of being fair.

**Enhancements,** the opposite of justifications, are attempts to augment the positive consequences of one's behavior.[10] That is, managers may frame their behavior in such a way as to make it appear more fair or

[9]E. D'Arcy, *Human Acts: An Essay on Their Moral Evaluation* (New York: Oxford University Press, 1963).

[10]B. R. Schlenker, *Impression Management: The Self-Concept, Social Identity, and Interpersonal Relations* (Belmont, Calif.: Brooks/Cole, 1980).

positive than it objectively is. By presenting selective information about an ambiguous event, managers may socially construct the interpretation of that event as evidence of their fairness.[11] Individuals may manage their reputations for fairness by leaking information about their fair actions to opinion leaders or using informal communication channels to disperse specific interpretations or events.[12]

Both public and private benefits accrue to managers who appear fair. A reputation for fairness may enhance their self-esteem and self-concept. It also may aid in the development of their power base. The perception that managers are fair will encourage compliance on the part of subordinates. They may experience fewer challenges to their authority, and their credibility and trustworthiness will be enhanced.

Certain liabilities are associated with a reputation for fairness as well. If fairness is an integral part of a manager's identity, then hints of unfairness will be more damaging to that manager than to others for whom fairness is not an issue.[13]

Organizational justice is not limited to a manager's reputation or the perceptions of employees. The importance of fair treatment in the workplace is so critical that the U.S. government has intervened in the relationship between employer and employee to ensure it. The next two sections will examine both the trend toward regulating this relationship and the impact of discrimination in the workplace.

REGULATION

The last decade has seen competing views of regulation. The government has deregulated the airline, trucking, long-distance telephone, and railroad industries on the assumption that if regulations were removed, the free market would spur competition, increase productivity, and reduce prices. An opposite tack has been taken with regard to legislation and regulation aimed at organizations—specifically, their personnel practices. Consider, for example, some of the more recent rulings that regulate the personnel activities of many organizations:

- *Pregnancy Discrimination Act* (1978): Employers may no longer refuse to hire a woman because of her pregnancy, and pregnant employees must be treated just as any other employee for the purpose of benefits. Thus, pregnancy leaves are subject to the same conditions as medical or personal leaves.

- Unisex Pension Coverage (*Arizona Governing Committee* v. *Norris*, 1983): The court rejected the notion that because women on average live longer than men, they should receive a lower monthly

[11]Bies, "The Predicament of Injustice," 289–319.
[12]Greenberg, "Looking Fair versus Being Fair."
[13]Schlenker, *Impression Management.*

In 1973, the Vocational Rehabilitation Act prohibited discrimination against persons with physical or mental handicaps. The physically handicapped clothing salesman here is protected by law at the level of having access to a position in his organization. However, second-generation discrimination may still present him with considerable difficulty in advancing to the executive levels of management.

pension despite the fact that men and women contributed equally to the plan.

- *Discrimination against the Handicapped/Disabled*: Although the initial legislation on this issue was passed in 1973, the current controversy stems from the definition of *handicap.* An individual who has a "physical or mental impairment that substantially limits one or more major life activities, or has a record of, or is regarded as having such an impairment" is handicapped.[14] However, in recent years, the definition of the term *handicapped* has been expanded. Often included are those with contagious diseases such as tuberculosis and acquired immune deficiency syndrome and those with allergies and color blindness.

    The Supreme Court has ruled that the fear of contracting a disease is not sufficient justification for terminating an employee. Because the victims of such diseases as AIDS are protected under the law as handicapped individuals, employers have the burden of proof for justifying their actions against infected employees.

- *Discrimination on the Basis of Appearance*: The most well-known case of this genre is that of Christina Craft and KMBC (a television station in Kansas City). The issue here was that Craft was required to meet with clothing and cosmetic consultants—a demand not imposed upon her male coanchor. In the first trial, the jury awarded Craft $500,000 but the verdict was overturned by the judge. In a second trial, Craft won again and was awarded $325,000. The decision was appealed and overturned at a higher

---

[14]U.S. Code 24, Section 706 (7)(B)(Supp. IV, 1980).

court. Other individuals who have brought similar cases to trial have fared better. A woman weighing over 300 pounds was rejected for employment as a clerical worker for an electric utility, and an airline attendant was fired for being too unattractive and overweight. In both of these cases, the employers lost because they failed to prove that normal weight or attractiveness were "bona fide occupational requirements."

The regulation of organizations centers, for the most part, on attempts to prevent discrimination. Even with the myriad of laws and legal precedents, discrimination continues to be a problem. Organizations must confront two forms of discrimination.[15] First-generation discrimination is that which occurs at the decision to hire. Much of the previous legislation is directed towards ensuring that all qualified individuals, regardless of race, sex, religion, disability, and so on, have equal access to employment. Second-generation discrimination occurs at the decision to promote. This is the type of discrimination today's managers and employees must strive to end. In the following section, the issue of second-generation discrimination will be examined.

## DISCRIMINATION

It may be surprising that discrimination is included in a chapter on emerging trends. The general belief is that overt discrimination is a thing of the past. Legislation in the United States that has made discrimination illegal includes the 1963 Equal Pay Act, which prohibited unequal pay for males and females with equal skills and responsibilities and similar working conditions. The 1964 Civil Rights Act prevented discrimination based on color, race, religion, sex, or national origin. The 1972 Equal Employment Opportunity Act extended the jurisdiction of these anti-discrimination laws to include governmental and educational institutions. In 1973, the Vocational Rehabilitation Act prohibited discrimination against persons with physical or mental handicaps and created the office of Affirmative Action.

Changes *have* occurred as a result of this legislation—but primarily changes merely in the access that such protected groups have to positions in organizations. While many more minorities and women have found positions in organizations, they have experienced considerable difficulty in advancing to the executive levels of management. In 1979, for example, Fortune 1000 companies were surveyed. Within a sample of 1,708 senior executives, only 3 were black, 2 Asian, 2 Hispanic, and 8 female. The 1985 survey of 1,362 senior executives found 4 blacks, 6 Asians, 3 Hispanics, and 29 women.[16]

[15]J. Feagin, "Organizational Culture and Conflict: Issues of Gender and Race," paper presented at the conference on Theory and Practice in Organizational Conflict: Making the Connection, at the University of Minnesota, 1987.

[16]E. W. Jones, Jr., "Black Managers: The Dream Deferred," *Harvard Business Review*, May-June 1986, 84–93.

What has happened in the wake of this legislation is that overt (first-generation) discrimination against minorities, women, and the mentally and physically disabled has been replaced by a more covert and insidious form (second-generation discrimination). For blacks in corporate America, this second-generation discrimination may take the form of **colorism:** a predisposition to act in a certain manner because of a person's skin color.[17] While approximately 15 percent of white America may be extremely anti-black, 60 percent are more or less neutral about blacks. The managers and executives in this latter group are not overtly racist, but they are the people who for a number of reasons either see discrimination take place and do nothing about it or inhibit the advancement of black managers to avoid conflict within the organization.

For women in corporate circles, this subtle form of discrimination is called the "glass ceiling." The **glass ceiling** is not a barrier based upon an individual's inability to succeed at executive management; rather, it is a barrier that keeps women as a group from advancing higher simply because they are women.[18] Women have made strides in the business world; for example, women make up 33 percent of corporate middle management (compared to only 19 percent in 1972). However, the story is quite different in executive management positions. Only 1.7 percent of corporate officers are women. In addition, only 500 of the 6,700 managers at IBM are women; at AT&T, only 26 of the top 880 executives are women; and at BankAmerica, only 20 percent of the top 3,000 executives are women even though women comprise 64 percent of the company's officials and managers.[19]

Both colorism and the "glass ceiling" are insidious primarily because they are not obvious. Managers and organizations who fall prey to these tendencies may not even be aware that they are erecting these barriers for women and minorities.

## THE ENTITLEMENT MENTALITY

Determining what constitutes "fair" treatment in the workplace used to be the sole domain of management. But there has been an increasing erosion of management's rights. The **employment at will** issue provides a good example. In the past, the courts have upheld the notion that an employer may terminate an employee at any time for any reason, just as an employee may quit a firm at any time. The courts believed that the employment relationship should not be forced upon either the employer or the employee. In recent years, however, legislation and court rulings

---

[17]Ibid.

[18]A. M. Morrison, R. P. White, E. Van Velsor, and Center for Creative Leadership, *Breaking the Glass Ceiling: Can Women Reach the Top of America's Largest Corporations?* (Reading, Mass.: Addison-Wesley, 1987).

[19]See, for example, M. McComas, "Atop the Fortune 500: A Survey of the CEOs," *Fortune,* April 23, 1986, 31; K. Blumenthal, "Room at the Top," *Wall Street Journal,* March 24, 1986, 7d; and D. D. Bowen and R. D. Hisrich, "The Female Entrepreneur: A Career Development Perspective," *Academy of Management Review* (1986): 393.

have reversed this trend, suggesting that employees may, in some cases, be entitled to employment. The "Focus on: Employee Termination and Employment at Will," conveys a sense of the changes occurring in corporate America. In increasing numbers of situations, discharge is not an acceptable employer response. These situations include the following:

- Being a whistleblower (opposing company practices or policies that violate consumer protection, antitrust, and environmental protection laws)
- Having wages garnished for indebtedness
- Complaining or testifying about equal pay law violations
- Complaining or testifying about safety hazards or refusing an assignment because of a belief of unsafe working conditions
- Engaging in nonviolent, legal union activities
- Engaging in concerted activity to protest wages, working conditions, or safety hazards
- Filing a worker's compensation claim
- Filing unfair labor practice charges with the National Labor Relations Board or state agencies
- Filing discrimination charges with the Equal Employment Opportunity Commission or a state or municipal fair employment agency
- Cooperating in the investigation of a charge
- Reporting Occupational Safety and Health Administration (OSHA) violations.[20]

Fair treatment in the workplace does not only mean that all terminations be for just cause. Rather, organizational justice includes other considerations such as an employee's right to privacy and access to employment records. A number of states have recently enacted laws specifying under which conditions employees may have access to their personnel files. The privacy of these records is likely to become more of an issue because factors such as medical conditions (the most obvious being AIDS) may influence employee treatment in a variety of domains.

The final component of organizational justice that we will examine is *cooperative acceptance*—the expectation that employees will be treated with respect regardless of their race, sex, national origin, physical disability, age, or religion while applying for and performing a job. The most obvious violation of cooperative acceptance is sexual harassment.

## SEXUAL HARASSMENT

The definition of sexual harassment is fairly broad. What some employers or managers might view as good-natured joking may, in today's workplace, be considered sexual harassment. According to the

[20]"Firing," *FEP Guidelines,* No. 241(8), 3; and "Discrimination Denied," *Bulletin to Management,* June 13, 1985, 3.

**The Case for Due Process**   Trying to bring order out of the turmoil over privacy and other employee rights on the job is like trying to smother a hundred fires with one blanket. Each issue has a life of its own. But one common factor must be involved in any effort to standardize a good employment relationship: determining who will decide what constitutes fair treatment on the job.

For much of America's industrial history, employers made that judgment unilaterally. Unions won a voice in the decision-making process for unionized workers—some 33 percent of private-industry employees in the mid-fifties, but now only 14 percent. This leaves the vast majority of the 85 million–member work force without formal—and   binding—complaint procedure.

Under the old common-law doctrine of employment at will, workers had no recourse if they were fired without just cause. But since the late 1970s, state courts have entered the battle on the side of the employees, letting them sue for wrongful discharge under exceptions to the doctrine. Such suits are now permitted in 46 states. This occurred just as legions of nonunion employees in technical, professional, and managerial jobs were being swept aside in the workforce reductions of the 1980s.

These changes, along with a dramatic decline in corporate loyalty, led thousands of such workers to seek court-ordered redress. But litigation to resolve employment disputes represents the worst of all possible worlds,

according to William Gould IV, a labor law professor at Stanford University. Low- and middle-income employees seldom sue because of the high cost of going to trial. And lawyers operating on the contingency basis prefer executive clients seeking big awards.

Meanwhile, companies are subject to volatile and unpredictable juries that know little about the employer's business and sometimes ignore court instructions. Given such circumstances, some employers reluctantly favor a third option: laws to prevent firing without good cause. All other major industrial nations have them.

Gould and other academic analysts of unjust discharge believe legislation is needed to protect nonunion workers. But one expert wants employers to adopt complaint systems voluntarily, giving nonunion employees due process and a fair hearing.

Employers such as Federal Express, Citicorp, and IBM already have such systems, although none requires binding arbitration. Still, employees perceive them as fair. What seems to make these procedures work is that they are organized by companies dedicated to long-term employees, and there is a commitment to flexibility and change on the part of the workers.

About 10 percent of private employees have well-developed complaint systems. It is estimated that sometime in the mid-1990s the movement will hit the barrier of the final 30 percent of employers who always wait for the law to tell them what to do. Then, a law will be created for just that purpose.

Source: J. Hoerr, "It's Getting Harder to Pass Out Pink Slips," *Business Week,* March 28, 1988, p. 68.

1980 Equal Employment Opportunity Commission guidelines, **sexual harassment** is verbal or physical conduct of a sexual nature when any of the following apply:

- Submission to such conduct is made either explicitly or implicitly a term or condition of an individual's employment.
- Submission to or rejection of such conduct by an individual is used as the basis for employment decisions affecting the individual.
- Such conduct has the purpose or effect of substantially interfering with an individual's work performance or creating an intimidating, hostile, or offensive work environment.

The issue of sexual harassment in the workplace is likely to gain even more emphasis in the next decade because of a recent ruling by the courts that employers are responsible for the sexual harassing of or by their employees.[21] Employers need to develop strategies to prevent sexual harassment. The EEOC has suggested the following guidelines to help organizations solve this problem:

1. Develop a formal policy on sexual harassment and distribute a copy of the policy to all employees.
2. Identify mechanisms for those individuals who feel they have been or are harassed to report those behaviors without fear of incrimination *and* to ensure that such reports are thoroughly investigated.
3. Communicate to all employees (especially to those in supervisory positions) the importance of creating and maintaining an environment free of sexual harassment.
4. Discipline guilty parties with organizational sanctions that include terminating employees for cause.
5. Educate all employees about just what sexual harassment is, thereby alerting all employees to the issues and behaviors at the heart of this matter.

## MANAGING IN THE GLOBAL MARKETPLACE

Even as late as the 1960s, American companies and managers viewed foreign markets as "dumping grounds." That is, they made little attempt to design or customize products for non-American markets. Management of foreign ventures was also done within the comfort and security of U.S. borders. The expectation was that these markets would absorb whatever U.S. companies could not sell locally simply because it was made in America. Because selling to foreign markets was viewed as an ancillary activity, few organizational resources were directed towards

---

[21]M. S. Novit, "Employer Liability for Employee Misconduct: Two Common-Law Doctrines," *Personnel*, January-February, 1982, 11–18.

To work effectively in a foreign country, a manager must understand the culture of the host country. AT&T representatives at the company's first privately held exhibit in Tokyo were well prepared. They had learned not only language skills but also information about the shared knowledge, beliefs, and values of potential Japanese customers, as well as their behavioral scripts and ways of thinking and interacting.

cultivating and capitalizing on those markets. Obviously, times have changed and so have American companies' relationships with foreign markets.

In recent years, the importance of foreign markets to the profitability of U.S. firms has changed the complexion of organizational strategies. Rather than ignoring foreign markets, organizations are now creating new markets and developing products abroad, preparing employees to manage in different cultures, and providing increasing autonomy for organizational affiliates and divisions located in foreign countries. In the following section, we will examine some of the unique demands of managing in foreign markets.

## THE IMPORTANCE OF UNDERSTANDING FOREIGN CULTURES

To work effectively in a foreign country, a manager must understand the *culture* of the host country. As with corporate culture, a nation's culture is composed of the shared knowledge, beliefs, and values of the group, as well as behavioral scripts and ways of thinking and interacting. Research on thousands of employees in 40 countries suggests that national cultures differ in four ways:[22]

1. *Power distance:* the extent to which members of a society accept the unequal distribution of power in organizations and institutions. Countries in which there is a high power distance (that is, people

---

[22]G. Hofstede, "The Interaction between National and Organizational Value Systems," *Journal of Management Studies* 22 (1985): 347–357; and G. Hofstede, "The Cultural Relativity of the Quality of Life Concept," *Academy of Management Review* 9 (1985): 389–398.

accept the notion that power is unequally distributed) include Malaysia, the Philippines, and Panama. Countries that value low power distance are Israel, Denmark, and Austria.

2. *Uncertainty avoidance:* the extent to which a society is uncomfortable with uncertainty and ambiguity and takes measures to avoid them, as by providing career stability, establishing formal rules, not tolerating deviant behavior, and believing in expertise and absolute truths. High uncertainty avoidance countries include Greece, Portugal, and Uruguay. Countries with low uncertainty avoidance are Singapore and Jamaica.

3. *Individualism and collectivity:* the extent to which a society expects its members to take care of themselves and their immediate families only *or* expects its members to take care of one another and expects organizations to protect their employees' interests. Countries with the former individualistic orientation include the United States, Australia, and Canada. More collectivistic countries include Guatemala, Ecuador, and Panama.

4. *Masculinity/Femininity:* the extent to which the dominant values in the society reflect assertiveness, material success, achievement, and heroism (masculinity) *or* relationships, modesty, protection of the weak, and quality of life. Countries rated high on femininity include Sweden, Norway, Denmark, and Yugoslavia. Countries rated high on masculinity include Germany, Austria, and Mexico.

These four dimensions influence a number of factors important to successful management, such as managerial styles. Support for hierarchical management is much greater in countries whose cultures accept power differentials. Thus, bureaucracies are more common in Italy than in Germany. Indonesian managers believe that successful managers must know all the answers.[23]

Decision-making styles also differ across cultures. Managers in the United States view decisions as solutions to problems. In Thailand, Indonesia, and Malaysia, managers make decisions to adjust to existing situations. Negotiating styles differ across cultures as well. Ignoring cultural differences can produce agreements that are one-sided at best.

Many international companies have found themselves in very uncomfortable situations when they ignore the habits, religion, language, and common practices of another country. For example, when Coca-Cola was introduced into China, the company wanted to maintain the English pronunciation of the product. It had a translator develop a set of Chinese characters which, when pronounced, sounded like the English "Coca-Cola." Unfortunately, the characters had their own meaning to the

---

[23]A. Laurant, "The Cultural Diversity of Western Conceptions of Management," *International Studies of Management and Organization* 13 (1983): 75–96.

Chinese—sales were flat for the soft drink whose name translated as "bite the wax tadpole." Sales increased when the company changed to characters that translated as "happiness in the mouth." General Motors had a similar problem with language when it introduced its Chevy Nova into Puerto Rico. While "Nova" translates literally as "star," when it was spoken, it sounded like "no va," which means "it doesn't go." This name did little to boost sales of the car in Puerto Rico.[24]

An example of ignoring common practices occurred when Pepsodent used a promotion in Southeast Asia which stressed that the toothpaste would whiten the user's teeth. Because many locals deliberately chewed betel nut to achieve the prestige of darkly stained teeth, the promotion to whiten teeth was not very successful. In addition, Pepsodent's old slogan—"You'll wonder where the yellow went"—was viewed as a racial slur.

## SELECTION OF THE FOREIGN VENTURE MANAGER

These and hundreds of other examples provide ample warning about the potential pitfalls of managing in foreign markets. Decisions about who should manage and how they should manage are critical to the success of foreign ventures. Companies have three choices: (1) to select a member of the parent company—for example, to send an American to manage overseas, (2) to select a member of the host country, or (3) to select a member of a third country to directly manage the venture. Each of these choices has its advantages and disadvantages. For example, a member of the parent company is more likely to have the trust of other company employees and to understand the intentions and goals of the parent company. Alternatively, a member of the host country will bring a greater understanding of the culture and its unique weaknesses and strengths. The third choice—a manager associated with neither the parent nor the host country—is more likely to be an international manager skilled at adapting to different cultures, customs, and practices.

Regardless of national origin, the individual selected for an international management position should possess the following characteristics:[25]

1. An ability to get along well with people.
2. An awareness of cultural differences.
3. Open-mindedness.
4. Tolerance of foreign cultures.
5. Adaptability to new cultures, ideas, and challenges.
6. An ability to adjust quickly to new conditions.
7. An interest in facts, not stereotypes.
8. An aptitude for and interest in learning foreign languages.

[24]D. A. Ricks, *Big Business Blunders* (Homewood, Ill.: R. D. Irwin, 1983).
[25]Ibid.

If we examine these characteristics closely, we can see that they reflect a manager's ability to adapt to new situations—a critical skill in the rapidly changing environment of today's organizations.

Interestingly, the same factors that influence an American company's success in ventures outside of U.S. boundaries also hold for companies whose foreign ventures exploit the American marketplace. The American market is a major portion of total sales for companies such as Honda. The "INTERNATIONAL FOCUS ON: Managing on Foreign Soil" illustrates the problems of managing an international company that views America as a foreign country. It describes the problems the Japanese face in building cars in their U.S. plants and the difficulties of managing a company staffed by foreign nationals (in this case, Americans).

Mazda's preparation of managers to work in foreign countries includes special training to understand the subtleties of cultural differences between Japanese and American workers so that they can perform

---

INTERNATIONAL FOCUS ON:

Managing on Foreign Soil

**Japanese and American Managers Butt Up against Cultural Differences** In staffing its Ohio plant, Honda ran into considerable trouble with the federal government. When it set up shop in rural Ohio, it didn't seek minority employees. Ostensibly to build community ties, Honda hired employees who lived within a limited radius of its plant. It excluded the minority population of Columbus, which is only 40 miles away. Honda recently made a $6 million settlement with the Equal Employment Opportunity Commission and promised to boost minority hiring. Earlier, after complaints from the government, Honda agreed to provide more opportunities for women.

The difficulties that Honda management has experienced in trying to run the company in a foreign environment are similar, in many respects, to the problems confronting American recruits in Japanese subsidiaries located in the United States. Many Japanese companies have had difficulty integrating their Japanese and American staff. Turnover rates at such firms are high after the novelty of working for an international firm has worn off. The list of reasons for this turnover is headed by lack of career advancement. Many employees leave Japanese subsidiaries because climbing the career ladder can be slow and the path nebulous. Other reasons include language barriers, comparatively lower pay and longer working hours, and the demand to be a team member.

Newly minted MBAs often expect generous responsibilities early in their tenure with a firm and so often are disappointed in Japanese firms. Rather than work their way to the top, these graduates often believe their degree should guarantee them a shortcut. It is not so in Japanese firms. Furthermore, understanding and working within the culture and values of the host country are difficult for employees as well as managers and even entire organizations.

Sources: T. Lee, "Turning Japanese," *National Business Employment Weekly,* Spring 1988, pp. 4–5; and S. Toy, N. Gross, and J. Treece, "The Americanization of Honda," *Business Week,* April 25, 1988, pp. 90–96.

their leadership, decision-making, motivational, and control functions effectively. The traditional Japanese manager's preference for group decision making and nonconfrontational control and avoidance of individual competition must be overcome if the manager is to be successful in such foreign markets as the United States and Canada.

It is unclear what impact the movement towards a global economy will have on organizational behavior. Will American expertise and market know-how again take a leadership role in the world, or have they already been eclipsed? Will Gorbachev's *glasnost* revitalize the Soviet economy and strengthen Soviets' role as a world power? Will other countries have the impact on American manufacturing and marketplaces that the Japanese have had? In the next century, will we be as enamored of the Yugoslav quality control systems or New Zealand's skills at employee motivation as we now are of Japanese management techniques? The answers to these and other questions concerning the global economy are the domain of the managers of tomorrow.

## THE CHANGING DEMOGRAPHICS OF THE WORK FORCE

Beginning in the 1970s, organizational demographics such as age, sex, education, race, and experience began to change dramatically. The demographics of an organization are important because they often provide clues to how individuals in the organization relate to each other. For example, people with similar experiences and attitudes are more likely to interact with each other, like each other, and share a common bond.[26] In Figure 18–1, the relationship between various demographic characteristics and the amount of work-force integration and cohesion is presented. The model suggests that individuals who are similar are more likely to communicate with each other and form cohesive groups.

If social interaction, cohesion, and communication frequency are critical for organizational success, then organizations should select individuals who are as similar to one another as possible. However, research on creativity and innovation in organizations underscores the value of diversity. In fact, researchers of the creative process suggest that the most productive and creative individuals are those who have had a broad range of contacts and interacted with a variety of individuals from diverse backgrounds. Creativity may occur, then, only when basic beliefs or expectations are challenged. Over time, individuals working closely together tend to become more alike in their values and perspectives. As a result, creativity is stifled and people become insensitive to opportunities.[27]

[26]J. Pfeffer, "Organizational Demography: Implications for Management," *California Management Review* 28 (1985): 67–81.

[27]R. M. Kanter, "When a Thousand Flowers Bloom: Structural, Collective, and Social Conditions for Innovation in Organization," in *Research in Organizational Behavior*, vol. 10, eds. B. M. Staw and L. L. Cummings (Greenwich, Conn.: JAI Press, 1988): 169–211.

**FIGURE 18–1**     Similarity and the Integration and Cohesion of Cohorts

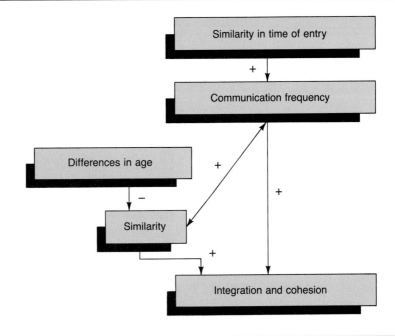

Source: J. Pfeffer, "Organizational Demography: Implications for Management," *California Management Review* 28, 1985, pp. 67–81.

HETEROGENEITY     The increasing heterogeneity of the work force has its advantages and disadvantages. While heterogeneity may increase the creativity and innovation potential of an organization, it reduces the likelihood of individual interaction and social cohesion. Nevertheless, heterogeneity is clearly a trend to which managers will have to adjust. By the year 2000, the demographic makeup of the work force will change substantially. While white, American males make up 47 percent of new entrants into the labor force in 1988, they will account for only 15 percent by the year 2000. Most of the 25 million new entrants into the labor force will be nonwhite, female, or immigrant workers.[28] By 1995, it is expected that 60.3 percent of women will be in the labor force. This means that dual-career couples will become the norm rather than the exception. The "Focus on: Dual-Career Couples" illustrates some of the problems that such couples face today.

[28]L. Silk, "Economic Scene: Changes in Labor by the Year 2000," *New York Times*, January 6, 1988, D2.

FOCUS ON:

Dual-Career
Couples

**Changing Expectations for Working Couples** According to government statistics, husband-and-wife wage earners now make up 56 percent of American marriages. Not surprisingly, some traditional expectations are giving way to new realities. It is now the dutiful husband who may find himself resisting the prospect of following his wife's career to a new city. Women, for their part, are no longer as willing to provide unquestioning—and unpaid—support for their husbands' career ambitions, a once-hallowed given of corporate, academic, and political life. Even the military can no longer count on blind obedience from officers' wives. Indeed, two women recently complained that brass at Grissom Air Force Base in Indiana warned them that their husbands' chances of promotion would be jeopardized unless they quit their civilian jobs. Following an investigation, Defense Secretary Casper Weinberger forbade commanders to intrude in the careers of military spouses.

Another long-held assumption that is fading fast is that women are ever ready to pack up and travel for a husband's advancement. Now men are often doing the moving. Russ Ringl is giving up his position as vice-president of human resources for Playboy in Chicago to follow his wife,

Karen, to Los Angeles, where she has become vice-president for nursing services at the Hospital of the Good Samaritan. Finding a satisfying job is proving a slow process, he says, though he remains optimistic.

Some couples solve the problem by living and working apart and seeing each other on weekends. About 700,000 U.S. couples have such commuter marriages, says Fairlee Winfield, a professor of business at Northern Arizona University. Another alternative is for employers to consider hiring both spouses. Indeed, antinepotism rules are slowly being lifted at companies across the nation. O'Melveny & Myers, one of the nation's largest law firms, has engaged several married couples. Martin Marietta, a giant aerospace and defense contractor, actually has an affirmative hire-a-couple policy. The company believes it is a sound strategy to lure and retain top people. Its Denver division now adds about 100 couples a year. And there is no charity involved. "Eight out of ten times, the recruited person is married to someone with skills we can use," says Personnel Administrator Joseph Weiner. There are a few rules, however: Partners, for example, cannot supervise each other.

Source: A. Toufexis, A. Sachs, and D. S. Wilson, "Dual Careers, Doleful Dilemmas," *Time*, November 16, 1987, p. 90.

DUAL-CAREER
COUPLES

Organizations will have to develop strategies for coping with dual careers. There are at least ten ways in which dual-career couples can influence the personnel activities of a corporation:[29]

[29]F. S. Hall and D. T. Hall, "Dual Careers—How Do Couples and Companies Cope with the Problems?" *Organizational Dynamics* (Spring 1978): 57–77. The quote is from page 71.

By 1995 it is expected that 60.3 percent of women will be in the labor force, meaning that dual-career couples will be the norm rather than the exception. Organizations will have to develop strategies for coping with dual careers in the areas of recruitment, scheduling, promotions, travel, benefits, and career development, among others.

1. *Recruitment.* Recruiters are becoming increasingly sensitive to the role of the spouse in career decisions.
2. *Scheduling.* The need for flexibility has made scheduling more of a problem. The scheduling of vacation time and work hours is affected by the growing number of employees who seek time off to coincide with children's school schedules and day-care center hours.
3. *Transfers and relocation.* This area probably poses the biggest problem for large companies. Refusal to relocate may mean the company must send less-qualified people into a new assignment. Those who refuse to relocate may quit or be fired, leading to high replacement and training costs.
4. *Promotions.* Many couples are less eager for promotion opportunities, regardless of whether they involve a geographic move. Many two-career couples have aspirations for more free time, less work pressure, and fewer responsibilities. With two incomes, the pay differential may not compensate sufficiently to make promotions worthwhile.
5. *Travel.* Two-career couples with many family demands are less willing or able to travel. Such people seem to "burn out" faster in high-travel occupations such as public accounting, sales, and consulting.
6. *Benefits.* The need for benefit program revision is growing. Both men and women are seeking maternity or paternity leaves or leaves without pay to accommodate spouse and family demands. Life insurance has become more important as people adapt to a standard of living based on two incomes. "Personal days" are another benefit that couples seek and use with greater frequency.
7. *Conflict of interest.* Employees whose spouses work in the same profession or for competing firms may represent a potential liability or security risk. In the same firm, one spouse may have information not normally available to the part of the organization in which the other spouse works.
8. *Career development.* The most significant change that couples have had on career development programs is in the design of career ladders. Many firms are finding they need to redesign training programs with limited geographic mobility in mind.
9. *Deadwood.* The combination of resistance to relocation, lower aspirations, unwillingness to travel, and other drawbacks of this kind presents a potential problem of deadwood among high-potential recruits who would otherwise develop and advance.
10. *Career bargaining.* A newly emerging trend is for couples to bargain for considerations that result directly from the career of a spouse. Examples are assurances of being sent to a particular location, assistance in finding a new position for the spouse, and subsidies until the spouse obtains a position.

Thus, organizations will have to find new ways of recruiting an increasingly scarce resource and one with growing demands.

Not only will the race, gender, and spousal limitations of the typical worker change, so will age and educational level. In the 1970s, about 3 million people entered the work force each year at age 18; by 1990, that number will drop to 1.3 million and by 1995, there will be 7.5 million fewer workers in the 18-to-24 age group.[30] The proportion of the labor force that has completed four years of college grew from 14.7 percent to 24.2 percent between 1970 and 1983. While the number of college-educated workers grows, so does the number of entry-level applicants who lack basic reading and math skills.[31]

**BABY BOOM/ BABY BUST**

One reason for this swing in demographics is the occurrence of the "baby boom" and the "baby bust." As the large number of individuals born in the late 1940s and early 1950s age, they produce the bulge illustrated in Figure 18–2. Notice that in the mid-1970s, the greatest bulge occurred in the group aged under 25; ten years later, the greatest bulge occurred in the 25-to-34 age group. The baby bust of the late sixties was the product of both the personal decision of many working women to postpone childbearing and the introduction of effective birth-control methods that put reproduction more under an individual's control.[32] The results of the baby bust were first felt in the declining enrollment in elementary schools and are currently being experienced at the university and college level. One symptom is the proliferation of marketing directors hired by institutions of higher education to increase their visibility and sell more places in incoming classes to the decreasing number of potential consumers.

One major result of the baby boom/ baby bust demographic pattern is that younger workers—those born just after the prime baby boom years—will find their progress up the organizational ladder impeded by the glut of older workers. Given the increase in life expectancy and the removal of mandatory retirement laws, a real problem is brewing. Not only will young workers find their climb impeded, but there will also be fewer of them to support the increasingly large population receiving social security benefits. Second, as older workers become a larger and more politically powerful group, it is likely that they will demand more job security, employee rights, and programs designed to meet their specific needs. For example, a recent employee survey by Travelers

---

[30]G. S. Odiorne, "The Crystal Ball of HR Strategy," *Personnel Administrator* (December 1986): 103–106.

[31]D. Arthur, "The Human Resources Function and the Growing Company," *Personnel* (November 1987): 18–24.

[32]Odiorne, "The Crystal Ball of HR Strategy."

**FIGURE 18–2**  Age Composition of the Adult Population: Baby Booms and Baby Busts

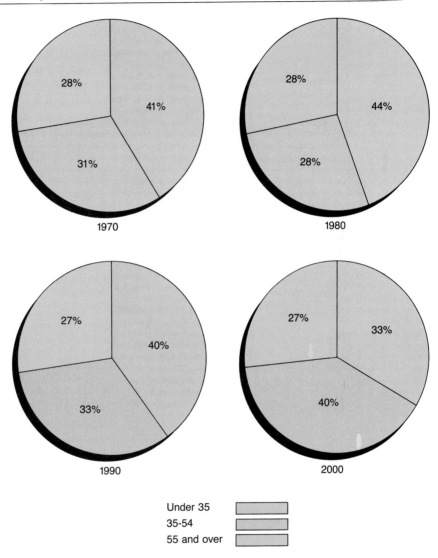

1970

1980

1990

2000

Under 35
35-54
55 and over

Source: Dennis A. Ahlburg and Lucinda Kimmel, "Human Resource Management Implications of the Changing Age Structure of the U.S. Labor Force" (Working paper, Industrial Relations Center, University of Minnesota, 1985).

Insurance found that 8 percent spend an average of 35 hours per week providing care to elderly family members. Given these findings, the trend toward the creation of on-site child-care centers in the 1980s may give way to the creation of parent-care centers in the twenty-first century.

## THE RISE OF THE SERVICE SECTOR

Not only will new workers be stuck in lower-level positions in the typical organization, they will also find that the fastest-growing segment of the economy is likely to be the service sector. As we move into the twenty-first century, the number of manufacturing jobs as a share of gross national product will decline. In 1955, for example, manufacturing accounted for 30 percent of all goods produced; in 1985, it accounted for 21 percent of all goods produced. Around the year 2000, it is expected that manufacturing will account for only 17 percent of goods and services produced.[33] The loss of manufacturing jobs and the increase in jobs in the service sector (such as health care, education, retailing, and government) will also have an impact on the distribution of wages. In the service industry, wages tend to be bimodal—high or low, with fewer wage levels in between.

Because of the dearth of teenagers and new entrants into the job market, the hardest-hit sector of the service economy will likely be the minimum-wage employer. Hiring older employees, especially women, and newly arrived immigrants is one way to combat the lack of young entrants. However, the needs of the older workers and immigrants who will be filling these jobs are very different from the needs of the teenagers who now occupy them. Employers will have to incorporate these new demands in their personnel plans.

## PART-TIME EMPLOYEES

The last trend we will examine is the increasing number of skilled and professional employees who are working fewer than 40 hours per week. Such employees may be self-employed or independent contractors or consultants; they may be part of a temporary agency's staff or hired permanently by one employer.[34] The beginning of this trend can be observed in today's work force. Almost one in five individuals in the United States works part time. Most do so voluntarily. The typical part-time worker is a female at either end of the age spectrum, and her job is in either the service or the retail sector.

In 1985, the average number of employees on the payrolls of temporary-help firms was 696,000, of which at least 20 percent were professionals. A recent survey of members of the American Management Association found that permanent part-time employees were widely used by private- and public-sector firms, but very few of these positions were professional, technical, or managerial. Only 29 percent of the firms responding offered a part-time option to professional and technical personnel, and only 12 percent permitted supervisors and managerial personnel to work part time.[35]

[33]Silk, "Economic Scene."

[34]D. S. Rothberg, "Part-Time Professionals: The Flexible Work Force," *Personnel Administrator* (August 1986): 28–32, 104–106.

[35]Ibid.

In 1985, the average number of employees on the payrolls of temporary employment firms was 696,000, of which 20 percent were professionals. Use of temporary employees provides an organization with benefits such as allowing it to keep valuable employees by adjusting their work schedules, flexibility for heavy and slow operating periods, and avoiding paying overtime to regular employees.

The advantages of using part-time employees neatly match some of the emerging trends we have discussed previously. For example, part-time employment may allow the organization to keep valuable employees by adjusting their work schedules. This avoids the new parent's all-or-nothing decision when faced with what appears to be the choice between family and career. As the current crop of workers ages, employers may have to be more creative in using older workers profitably. Rather than retiring a valuable employee, an organization may implement a phased retirement program in which the individual is allowed to move from full-time to part-time employment.

A work force that includes part-time employees can also provide employers with greater flexibility in work assignments. Part-time employees may build their work schedules around the needs of the organization, which can reduce the pressure on full-time personnel and eliminate payment of overtime. With part-time employees, managers can staff peak business hours better and extend their service hours.

The dark side of this trend concerns the 8 percent of part-time employees who are not voluntary. Employers may use part-time employees to avoid paying costly benefit packages. An alternative to no-benefits part-time employment is the use of *leased* employees. Employee-leasing firms assign their own employees, on contract, to other firms for work ranging from a few hours to a few months. Although the client supervises the workers, the contractor pays, hires, and fires them.

Employee leasing can provide all or some of the individuals needed to run a small business. The leasing company can act as the personnel department for such small firms, handling their hiring, firing, and payment of benefits and salaries. The small business would still have control over the daily activity of its leased workers and could make recommendations about promotions and raises, but such tasks—often viewed as extremely unpleasant by management—would be left up to the leasing company.[36]

The importance of a flexible work force to the competitiveness of U.S. corporations will become increasingly critical by the twenty-first century. But it is just one problem—or opportunity—that the next generation of managers will have to face. The ability to foster creativity and innovation among employees, meet the new needs of the changing work force, and create organizations that uphold the rights of the employee and employer are the managerial challenges that lie ahead. These and other issues will determine whether managers can meet the challenges of tomorrow's business world.

## SUMMARY

The purpose of this chapter was to highlight some of the emerging trends in organizational behavior. Three such trends were highlighted: the increasing demand for justice in the workplace, the growing emphasis on managing in the global marketplace, and the changing demographics of the work force.

Traditional studies of organizational justice have focused on the fairness of the distribution of outcomes. In the future, however, interactional justice—the quality of interpersonal treatment in organizations—will come to the forefront. The perception of interactional justice depends on whether employees feel they have been treated courteously and respectfully and whether they believe their managers use their discretionary power fairly.

Because interactive justice is grounded in the perception of justice, the way in which a manager is perceived is critical. As concerns with interactive justice increase, there is likely to be a simultaneous increase in managerial concern about *appearing* fair. Managers can enhance employee perception of their fairness through defensive

[36]M. Chestnut, "Workable Solutions," *Women in Business*, March-April 1986, 15.

and proactive tactics. Defensive tactics include the use of excuses, justifications, and apologies. These tactics are designed to distance managers (and their actions) from the responsibility for harmful outcomes. Proactive tactics are designed to increase the manager's association with positive events. They include entitling and enhancement tactics. Entitling tactics posit the manager's behavior as responsible for some positive event. Enhancements attempt to frame a manager's behavior as more positive than it objectively may be. Successfully managing a fair persona may increase the manager's power base and level of subordinate trust. The cost of *appearing* fair but not *being* fair is that the fall from grace can be precipitous.

Interactive justice depends upon the behavior of a manager towards subordinates. However, the scope of organizational justice extends beyond this dyadic level of interaction. While the government continues to reduce its regulation of industry, it is stepping up its control of the employer-employee relationship. As recent legislation such as the Pregnancy Discrimination Act and rulings involving comparable worth, unisex pension coverage, and other discrimination-related issues suggest, there is an increasing attempt on the part of government to ensure the fair treatment of employees.

Unfortunately, even with past legislation, the issue of discrimination is one that will continue to haunt management in the twenty-first century. The discrimination

of the present and the near future is not the radical racism or sexism of the past. Rather, this second-generation discrimination functions to deprive women and minorities of the opportunity to advance up the corporate ladder into executive management. Known as the "glass ceiling" for women and "colorism" for minorities, it represents a much more insidious form of discrimination because those who practice it may be unaware of its existence.

The final organizational justice issue discussed in the chapter is the entitlement mentality. Over the years, the expectations of employees have changed. What may have been perceived as fair treatment of employees 25 years ago is not considered fair by today's standards. The most vivid example of this is in the employment-at-will doctrine. In the past, it was widely accepted that management had the right to fire an employee for any cause. Just as employees were free to discontinue a relationship with an employer, the employer had the right to end its relationship with an employee. Recently, however, a number of court cases have challenged this employment-at-will doctrine. The trend here is clearly in the direction of employers' proving a just cause for dismissal.

Other examples of this entitlement perspective include the employee's right to privacy, right of access to personnel records, and right to cooperative acceptance. Cooperative acceptance refers to the expectation that employees will be treated with respect regardless of their race, sex, age, religion, or other demographic characteristics. Sexual harassment in the workplace is probably the most salient violation of the right to cooperative acceptance.

The second major trend we discussed is the growing emphasis on managing in a global marketplace. In recent years, there has been a very definite trend towards viewing management as a global rather than a local activity. To be effective in a foreign country, a manager must understand the culture. Cultures differ along four dimensions: (1) power distance, or the extent to which members of society accept unequal distribution of power; (2) uncertainty avoidance, or the extent to which a society believes in expertise and absolute truths; (3) individualism or collectivism, or the extent to which a society expects its members to care for themselves or to care for one another; and (4) masculinity or femininity, or the extent to which the dominant values of society are more aggressive or more social.

Failing to take into consideration the unique culture of the host country can cause considerable problems for a foreign venture. The ability of a manager to adapt to the demands, expectations, and mores of the host country is therefore critical. Recent research has identified a set of characteristics associated with successful international managers, such as good interpersonal skills, awareness of cultural differences, the ability to adapt, and tolerance of differences.

The third and final trend examined in this chapter was the chang-

ing demographics of the work force. The aging of the work force, the increasing participation of women and minorities, and the problems of dual-career couples are all factors with which the organizations of tomorrow will have to cope. Coupled with the trend towards service-sector employment and the associated demand for entry-level, minimum-wage employees, the dearth of such employees caused by the aging of the work force may precipitate major changes in these industries. These dramatic changes in the composition of the work force will require a radical rethinking of benefits, recruiting strategies, and incentive structures to attract these new groups of employees.

Not only will there be fewer entrants into the job market of the future, but there will also be an increasing number of professionals and nonprofessionals who choose to work in a part-time or temporary position. The rise of temporary and permanent part-time employees may benefit employers by providing a more flexible work force. However, to accommodate such a novel form of employee, organizations will have to relinquish certain forms of control such as the right to hire, fire, promote, and reward employees to other groups and agencies. The long-term impact of these changing demographics on organizational productivity and on managers' ability to manage effectively may well be the basis of the organizational behavior textbooks of the future.

KEY TERMS

**Colorism**   Predisposition to act in a certain manner because of a person's skin color.

**Distributive justice**   Fair treatment of employees in awarding organizational rewards or in administering organizational punishment.

**Employment at will**   Freedom of an employer to terminate an employee at any time for any reason, now being eroded in the courts.

**Enhancement**   Attempt to augment the positive consequences of one's behavior to increase the perception of fairness among employees; the opposite of justification.

**Entitling tactic**   Attempt to gain responsibility for positive events and their consequences in order to increase the perception of fairness among employees; the opposite of *excuse*.

**Glass ceiling**   Barrier that keeps women as a group from advancing to executive management simply because they are women and not because of their individual ability.

**Interactive justice**   Equitable treatment of employees in interpersonal treatment by managers.

**Procedural justice**   Equitable treatment of employees in the processes by which organizational rewards are allocated and punishments are administered.

**Sexual harassment**   Verbal or physical conduct of a sexual nature when submission to such conduct is made either explicitly or implicitly a term or condition of an individual's employment, influences employment decisions affecting the individual, or substantially interferes with the individual's work performance or work environment.

DISCUSSION QUESTIONS

1. Why is a heterogeneous work force critical for maintaining high levels of organizational creativity and innovation? What problems are likely to result from having a great deal of diversity in a work force?

2. Why may it be as important to *look* fair as it is to *be* fair? What purposes do apologies, excuses, and justifications serve in making a manager appear fair?

3. Why is interactive justice particularly important to the practicing manager?

4. What is the basic intent of government's increasing regulation of the workplace? How has it succeeded in that intent? How has it failed? What are some of the indicators of its failure and success?

5. What are the important characteristics of an international manager? What type of manager is most likely to succeed in an international assignment?

6. What are the major implications for organizational staffing of the baby-bust years? What are some strate-

gies management might implement to be more successful in future recruiting?

7.  What are the costs and benefits of part-time employees for the organization? For the individual?

8.  If a rise in service-sector employment does occur, what are the implications for employees of the bimodal distribution of salaries?

**IF YOU WANT TO KNOW MORE**

A number of texts examine emerging organizational and societal trends. One of the most well-known is *Future Shock,* by Alvin Toffler (Random House, 1970). When it was published, it caused quite a sensation and seemed to readjust America's view to the future. Toffler's book represents the beginning of an increasing emphasis on the future of management and organizations. In recent years, such books as John Naisbitt's *Megatrends,* published by Warner Books in 1984, have underscored the importance of planning for the future. While not all of Naisbitt's predictions may be accurate, he does focus on the future importance of the global economy, information technology, and computer-mediated interaction, among other topics.

Other books that examine current and future trends include Tom Peters and Nancy Austin's 1987 *The Renewal Factor: How to Best Get and Keep the Competitive Edge,* published by Bantam Books; and the 1986 *Frontiers of Management* (Dutton/Truman Talley Books), written by Peter Drucker, a well-known management-practice specialist. The members of the consulting group Goodmeasure, Inc., have collaborated on a book titled *The Changing American Workplace: Work Alternatives in the '80s,* published by the American Management Association, 1985.

The preceding books examine overall trends in management. Readers specifically interested in the future of executive management for women and minority members should examine the new book *Breaking the Glass Ceiling: Can Women Reach the Top in America's Largest Corporations?* by A. Morrison, R. White, E. Van Velsor, and the Center for Creative Leadership (Addison-Wesley, 1987). An older, more general, book on the topic is John Fernandez's 1981 *Racism and Sexism in Corporate Life,* published by Lexington Books. The invisible ceiling for blacks is highlighted in Anne B. Fisher's article, "Good News, Bad News, and an Invisible Ceiling," in the September 16, 1985, issue of *Fortune.* The June 22, 1987, issue of *Business Week* contains an excellent article on corporate women entitled "Corporate Women: They're about to Break Through to the Top."

An excellent overview of organizational justice can be found in the recent book by Allan Lind and Tom Tyler, *The Social Psychology of Procedural Justice,* published in 1988 by Plenum Press. A good review article on interactional justice has been written by Tom Tyler and Robert Bies. Entitled "Beyond Formal Procedures: The Interpersonal Context of Procedural Justice," it appears in a 1988 volume edited by John Carroll, *Advances in Applied Social Psychology: Business Settings* (Erlbaum).

To explore further the issues facing dual-career couples, see Francine S. Hall and Douglas T. Hall's *The Two-Career Couple*, published by Addison-Wesley in 1979. Another possibility in this area is Helen Axel's 1985 *Corporations and Families: Changing Practices and Perspectives*, published by The Conference Board. Long-distance marriages are the subject of Fairlee Winfield's 1985 *Commuter Marriages*, published by Columbia University. Additional information on the male response to dual-career families may be found in L. A. Gilbert's 1985 book, *Men in Dual-Career Families* (Erlbaum). Joan Aldous edited a book in which a variety of issues facing the dual-income family are addressed. Entitled *Two Paychecks*, it was published in 1982 by Sage Publishing Co.

ON YOUR
OWN

**Balancing Roles: Managing Multiple Perspectives** On a sheet of paper, draw a large circle. After reflecting on how you have spent your time in the preceding week, divide the circle as if it were a pie into sections representing the different roles in which you spent your time (include work, family, home, and all other roles). The size of each section should be proportional to the amount of time and energy you invest in that particular role. Labels for these sections might include *student, employee, friend, spouse,* and so on.

Now consider what sections of your role pie are most important to your sense of identity. Number the sections from most important (1) to least important. Note that the numbers frequently do not correspond to the size of the sections.

Consider which of the sections in your role pie tend to contribute to role overload—that is, what activities and roles infringe upon other, more important activities and roles? Identify those sections of your role pie.

In light of the conflict you have identified above, answer the "Role Management Inventory" below. When you have answered all the questions, score the inventory according to the instructions that follow the questionnaire. Which is/are your most important coping style(s)? Is this optimal for you?

Source: Francine S. Hall and Douglas T. Hall, *The Two-Career Couple* (Reading, Mass.: Addison-Wesley, 1979), 76–79.

## Role Management Inventory

How do you deal with these conflicts or issues? How often do you do each of the following?

| | Nearly All the Time 5 | Often 4 | Sometimes 3 | Rarely 2 | Never 1 |
|---|---|---|---|---|---|
| 1. Decide not to do certain activities that conflict with other activities. | _____ | _____ | _____ | _____ | _____ |
| 2. Get help from someone outside the family (e.g., home maintenance help or child care). | _____ | _____ | _____ | _____ | _____ |
| 3. Get help from a member of the family. | _____ | _____ | _____ | _____ | _____ |
| 4. Get help from someone at work. | _____ | _____ | _____ | _____ | _____ |
| 5. Engage in problem solving with family members to resolve conflicts. | _____ | _____ | _____ | _____ | _____ |
| 6. Engage in problem solving with someone at work. | _____ | _____ | _____ | _____ | _____ |
| 7. Get moral support from a member of the family. | _____ | _____ | _____ | _____ | _____ |
| 8. Get moral support from someone at work. | _____ | _____ | _____ | _____ | _____ |
| 9. Integrate or combine roles (for example, involve family members in work activity or combine work and family in same way). | _____ | _____ | _____ | _____ | _____ |
| 10. Attempt to change societal definition of sex roles, work roles, or family roles. | _____ | _____ | _____ | _____ | _____ |
| 11. Negotiate or plan with someone at work, so their expectations of you are more in line with your own needs or requirements. | _____ | _____ | _____ | _____ | _____ |
| 12. Negotiate or plan with members of your family, so their expectations of you are more in line with your own needs or requirements. | _____ | _____ | _____ | _____ | _____ |
| 13. Establish priorities among your different roles, so that you are sure the most important activities are done. | _____ | _____ | _____ | _____ | _____ |
| 14. Partition and separate your roles. Devote full attention to each role when you are in it. | _____ | _____ | _____ | _____ | _____ |
| 15. Overlook or relax certain standards for how you do certain activities. (Let less important things slide a bit sometimes, such as dusting and lawn care.) | _____ | _____ | _____ | _____ | _____ |
| 16. Modify your attitudes toward certain roles or activities (e.g., coming to the conclusion that the *quality* of time spent with spouse or children is more important than the *quantity* of time spent). | _____ | _____ | _____ | _____ | _____ |
| 17. Eliminate certain roles (e.g., deciding to stop working). | _____ | _____ | _____ | _____ | _____ |
| 18. Rotate attention from one role to another. Handle each role in turn as it comes up. | _____ | _____ | _____ | _____ | _____ |
| 19. Develop self and own interests (e.g., spend time on leisure or self-development). | _____ | _____ | _____ | _____ | _____ |
| 20. Plan, schedule, and organize carefully. | _____ | _____ | _____ | _____ | _____ |

21. Work hard to meet all role demands. Devote more time and energy, so you can do everything that is expected of you.    _____ _____ _____ _____ _____

22. Do not attempt to cope with role demands and conflicts. Let role conflicts take care of themselves.    _____ _____ _____ _____ _____

---

### Scoring

- Add up the values you entered for items 1 to 12. Divide by 12. This is your *role-redefinition score:*_____
- Add up the values you entered for 13 to 17. Divide by 5. This is your *personal-reorientation score:*_____
- Add up the values you entered for 18 to 22. Divide by 5. This is your *reactive coping score:*_____

**Interpreting Your Scores**   These three scores give you some indication of the extent to which you use each of the three strategies. The scores can range from a *high* of 5 to a *low* of 1. If you score *over 3* on a scale, you score relatively high, meaning that you make frequent use of this coping strategy. A score of *less than 3* indicates relatively infrequent use of this coping strategy. Here are some problems that may be indicated by your scores on the three scales:

*Low Role-Redefinition Scores*   You often let others place demands on you, often unrealistic demands. You need to negotiate with these people, your role senders, to make certain that the roles they impose on you are compatible with other responsibilities and interests. Some ways of doing this include:

- Simply agree with role senders that you will not be able to engage in certain activities. (For example, in our community, a hotbed of volunteerism, we are both known as "spot-jobbers." We will accept specific one-shot volunteer jobs, but we will not accept continuing positions.)
- Enlist assistance in role activities from other family members or from people outside the family (for example, cleaning or baby-sitting help).
- Sit down with role senders (boss, spouse, children) and discuss the problem. Together, work out an acceptable solution.
- Integrate conflicting careers by working with your spouse or working in related fields (so that the two careers become more like one). This method of coping has been described as "linking up."

If you can successfully reduce role conflicts by practicing some of these proactive negotiations, you will be stopping them at the source, and chances are you'll be very happy with the results—*you* will be managing the situation.

*Low Personal-Reorientation Scores*   Your problem is that you don't distinguish between the roles assigned to you; you lack a clear vision of what roles are truly important. You need to reevaluate your attitudes about various roles and take on only those heading the list. Some hints to help you achieve this are:

- Establish priorities ("A child with a high fever takes precedence over school obligations. A child with sniffles does not. A very important social engagement—especially one that is business related—precedes tennis.")
- Divide and separate roles. Devote full attention to a given role when in it, and don't think about other roles. ("I leave my work at the office. Home is for the family and their needs.")
- Try to ignore or overlook less important role expectations. ("The dusting can wait.")
- Rotate attention from one role to another as demands arise. Let one role slide a bit if another needs more attention at the time. ("Susan needs help now. I'll pay those bills later.")
- Remember that self-fulfillment and personal interests are a valid source of role demands. ("Piano and organ playing are a release for me while the children are small and need me at home.")

This style of coping means changing yourself rather than the family or work environment, although personal reorientation may be a necessary step to take before you can accomplish real role redefinition. Before you can change other people's expectations of you, you have to be clear about what you expect of yourself. Personal reorientation alone is not significantly related to satisfaction and happiness.

*High Reactive Coping Scores*   You try to take on every role that happens your way. You cope with conflict by working harder and sleeping less. Your style of coping includes:

- Planning, scheduling, and organizing better.
- Working harder to meet all role demands. (As one expert on women's roles and role conflict said in frustration, "After years of research, I've concluded that the only answer to a career and a family is to learn to get by on less sleep!")
- Using no conscious strategy. Let problems take care of themselves. This reactive behavior, in contrast to role redefinition, is a passive response to role conflict. Not surprisingly, people who use this style report very low levels of satisfaction and happiness (passive coping).

Reactive coping is not a very effective way of dealing with your roles. Rather than managing them, you are letting them manage you. If your goal is to eliminate conflict, then you need to reorient your own perceptions as a first step toward negotiating with others to restructure the roles in your life.

# THE MANAGER'S MEMO

FROM: J. Reynolds, Manager, Human Resources

TO:      P. Copeland, President

RE:      Staffing the European Sales Office

With the opening up of the European market as those countries lower their trade barriers, we will need a creative and energetic team for our new European sales office. Because we'll want to be ready with the best people possible, I have spent considerable time reviewing the resumés we have on file. I recommend that you consider making your selections from the following people:

- David J. McDonald is the top salesperson at our major competitor, Biggs Consumer Products. I think he feels he has reached his potential there and would bite at an offer that would open new opportunities.
- Dan Peachtree has been a reliable member of our sales force for ten years, often among the company's top five sellers. He has already relocated for us six times.
- Thomas Dodd received his MBA from State University three years ago and has been selling for us ever since. His performance appraisals consistently rate him Outstanding.
- Bill Phillips started with us when he received his engineering degree two years ago, and he switched to sales one year later. He hasn't been selling long, but with his engineering background, he'll know the product inside and out.
- Robert Peterson will be receiving his bachelor's degree in marketing this May. He has a remarkable track record as an Amway salesperson while in school. Last year he sold $1 million of their products.

A few other names have come up. There's Marybeth Peters, our top-performing salesperson of the past two years, and Felicia Jones, who has been on the sales force for four years and who was mentioned because she received her degree in German language and culture. I doubt either would want to move and disrupt her family. Paul Yamamoto developed the new selling system that seems to be increasing our sales so much this year, but I can't imagine he'd feel very comfortable in our Frankfurt office.

I hope I have given you enough ideas for selecting a sales manager and two other representatives. Please let me know who you'd like to interview.

CASE DISCUSSION
QUESTIONS

Assume you are the president, and respond to the memo from the manager of the human resources division. Select who you would like to interview to staff a new, three-person sales office that will launch an important company expansion overseas. Drawing on the considerations raised in the chapter, briefly state your reasons for your selections.

EXERCISE FOR
PART 5:
Sears vs. K mart

Here is a field exercise you can do the next time you go shopping. It is designed to help you explore the significance of various aspects of organization structure on effectiveness and goal accomplishment.

You will be asked to analyze two different establishments in the same line of business. You will compare and contrast these firms as carefully as you can to see what makes them really work. Since you've probably visited one or both of these stores, you already know something about them. But try to place yourself in a position of seeing them for the first time. Then try to integrate what you have learned in this chapter and from other experiences in this book about how firms are managed.

Form into groups of about four and read your assignment. As a group, visit each store (preferably in the same general location). You might want to evaluate service, quality, price, and so on.

YOUR ASSIGNMENT

Your group, Fastalk Consultants, is known as the shrewdest, most insightful, and most overpaid management consulting firm in the country. You have been hired by the president of Sears to make recommendations for improving the motivation and performance of personnel in their operations. Let us assume that the key job activity in store operations is dealing with customers.

Recently, the president of Sears has come to suspect that his company's competitor, K mart, is making heavy inroads into Sears's market. He has also hired a market research firm to investigate and compare the relative merits of products and prices in the two establishments, and has asked the market research firm to assess the advertising campaigns of the two organizations. Hence, you will not need to be concerned with marketing issues, except as they may have an impact on employee behavior. The president wants you to look into the organization of the two stores to determine the strengths and weaknesses of each.

The president has established an unusual contract with you. He wants you to make your recommendations based upon your observations *as a customer*. He does not want you to do a complete diagnosis with interviews, surveys, or behind-the-scenes observations. He wants your report in two parts.

1.  Given his organization's goals of profitability, sales volume, and fast and courteous service, he wants an analysis that will compare and contrast Sears and K mart in terms of the following concepts:

- **Organizational Goals**
  Conflict?
  Clarity?

- **Environment**
  Stable/changing?
  Simple/complex?
  Certain/uncertain?

Source: Lawrence R. Jauch, Sally A. Coltrin, Arthur G. Bedeian, and William F. Glueck, *The Managerial Experience: Cases, Exercises, and Readings*, 5th ed. (Hinsdale, Ill.: Dryden, 1989), pp. 165–166.

- **Size**
  Large?
  Medium?
  Small?
- **Personnel**
  Knowledgeable?
  Well-trained?
- **Horizontal Division of Labor**
  Formalized policies?
  Departmentalization?
  Standardization of rules?
- **Vertical Division of Labor**
  Number of levels?
  Span of control?
  Centralization?
- **Communication**
  Direction?
  Openness?

- **Leadership Style**
  Task oriented?
  People oriented?
- **Jobs**
  Variety?
  Wholeness?
  Interaction?
  Freedom?
  Time of work?
  Location of work?
- **Employee Motivation**
  Type?
  Intrinsic/extrinsic?
  Rewards?
  Support?
  Coordination?
  Decision making?

How do Sears and K mart differ in these aspects? Which company has the best approach?

2.  Given the corporate goals listed under point 1, what specific actions might Sears's management take in the following areas to achieve these goals (profitability, sales volume, fast and courteous service)?

- Job design and work flow
- Organization structure (at the individual store level)
- Employee incentives
- Leadership
- Employee selection

3.  Having completed your contract with the president of Sears, prepare a report for presentation to the class. This should include:

   a.  Specific recommendations you have considered in 2 above.
   b.  Reasons for these suggestions based on your knowledge of leadership, motivation, job design, organization, and so on.

CASE FOR
PART 5:
Dashman Company

The Dashman Company was a large concern making many types of equipment for the armed forces of the United States. It had over 20 plants, located in the central part of the country, whose purchasing procedures had never been completely coordinated. In fact, the head office of the company had encouraged each of the plant managers to operate with their staffs as separate independent units in most matters. Late in 1940, when it began to appear that the company would face increasing difficulty in securing certain essential raw materials, Mr. Manson, the company's president, appointed an experienced purchasing executive, Mr. Post, as vice-president in charge of purchasing, a position especially created for him. Mr. Manson gave Mr. Post wide latitude in organizing his job, and he assigned Mr. Larson as Mr. Post's assistant. Mr. Larson had served the company in a variety of capacities for many years, and knew most of the plant executives personally. Mr. Post's appointment was announced through the formal channels usual in the company, including a notice in the house newsletter published by the company.

One of Mr. Post's first decisions was to begin immediately to centralize the company's purchasing procedure. As a first step he decided that he would require each of the executives who handled purchasing in the individual plants to clear with the head office all purchase contracts which they made in excess of $10,000. He felt that if the head office was to do any coordinating in a way that would be helpful to each plant and to the company as a whole, he must be notified that the contracts were being prepared at least a week before they were to be signed. He talked his proposal over with Mr. Manson, who presented it to his board of directors. They approved the plan.

Although the company made purchases throughout the year, the beginning of its peak buying season was only three weeks away at the time this new plan was adopted. Mr. Post prepared a letter to be sent to the 20 purchasing executives of the company. The letter follows:

Dear _____,

The board of directors of our company has recently authorized a change in our purchasing procedures. Hereafter, each of the purchasing executives in the several plants of the company will notify the vice president in charge of purchasing of all contracts in excess of $10,000 which they are negotiating at least a week in advance of the date on which they are to be signed.

I am sure that you will understand that this step is necessary to coordinate the purchasing requirements of the company in these times when we are facing increasing difficulty in securing essential supplies. This procedure should give us in the central office the information we need to see that each plant secures the optimum supply of materials. In this way the interests of each plant and of the company as a whole will best be served.

Yours very truly,

Mr. Post showed the letter to Mr. Larson and invited his comments. Mr. Larson thought the letter an excellent one, but suggested that, since Mr. Post had not met more than a few of the purchasing executives, he might like to visit all of them and take the matter up with each of them personally. Mr. Post dismissed the idea at once because, as he said, he had so many things to do at the head office that he could not get away for a trip. Consequently he had the letters sent out over his signature.

During the two following weeks replies came in from all except a few plants. Although a few executives wrote at great length, the following reply was typical:

Dear Mr. Post,

Your recent communication in regard to notifying the head office a week in advance of our intention to sign contracts has been received. This suggestion seems a most practical one. We want to assure you that you can count on our cooperation.

Yours very truly,

During the next six weeks the head office received no notices from any plant that contracts were being negotiated. Executives in other departments who made frequent trips to the plants reported that the plants were busy, and the usual routines for that time of year were being followed.

## Questions for Discussion

1. Was the centralization of purchasing at Dashman necessary?
2. Was the letter from Mr. Post sufficient to implement the new procedure?
3. Why did the head office not receive any notices of contracts being negotiated?

# APPENDIX

# The Scientific Method

The study of organizational behavior is aimed at explaining, understanding, and predicting how people behave in organizations. To do this, information that is collected about behavior in organizations must be accurate and trustworthy. How can that be ensured? The best way to collect accurate and trustworthy information is by using the **scientific method.** As shown in Figure A–1, the scientific method is a systematic set of procedures for objectively collecting and evaluating information.

If a consultant offered you a "highly successful" new training program, how would you know whether to trust the consultant's claim? The consultant's belief that the program is highly successful could be a function of the high quality of the program. But the program also could only appear to be "highly successful" because of the way success was measured, the person who did the measuring, or the group of people who were trained. To trust information, you need to be able to evaluate its quality and meaning.

The scientific method allows you to evaluate the quality and meaning of information. As noted in Figure A–1, the scientific method requires that the procedures for information collection be *public* and *precise*. If the consultant told you that the training program was evaluated by participants through an attitude questionnaire (rather than by an objective measurement of participants' learning or subsequent performance) and showed you the questionnaire, you would have a better understanding of the label "highly successful." Therefore you would better understand the limits of the information.

It is also the aim of scientific information collection to be *objective,* so that collected information reflects reality rather than the opinions of the information collector. Public and precise methods for information collection help ensure that personal opinions do not significantly

## FIGURE A–1                    The Scientific Method

1. *The procedures are public.* A scientific report includes a complete description of the procedures used to collect information, so that readers could attempt to reproduce the findings or decide for themselves the limitations of the information collection procedures.

2. *The definitions are precise.* When describing the procedures used, it is critical that the wording be clear, with all terms defined. If performance is the outcome of interest, how was performance measured?

3. *The information collection is objective.* The information collection procedures should not allow the information collector to inject his or her subjective opinions into the information. The scientific observer should be collecting or recording information, *not* interpreting it.

4. *The findings must be replicable.* Despite a scientist's best intentions to maintain objectivity, personal feelings can influence scientific findings. Scientific findings become truly trustworthy only when they have been reproduced by other scientists.

5. *The approach is systematic and cumulative.* The object of scientific inquiry is not to produce isolated findings but to combine those findings progressively into more and more complete theories of human behavior.

6. *The purposes of scientific inquiry are explanation, understanding, and prediction.* The reason for having theories in organizational behavior is to use those theories to improve and enhance life in organizations. For this to occur, our theories must do a good job of explaining why behavior occurs, thereby allowing us to predict and control it.

Source: B. Berelson and G. Steiner, *Human Behavior: An Inventory of Scientific Findings* (New York: Harcourt Brace Jovanovich, 1964), pp. 16–18.

influence information collection processes. The scientific requirement that results be *replicated*—reproduced by other scientists—before being accepted as fact also helps. You should feel better about a training program that has been successfully implemented by a variety of trainers in several different companies. It is then unlikely that the program's success was a function of any single trainer or company setting.

Finally, scientific information collection is *systematic* and *cumulative*. If this training program is successful, what features does it share with other successful programs? Are there common threads that differentiate among many successful and unsuccessful programs? The systematic accumulation of knowledge demanded by the scientific method provides another check on the trustworthiness of information. Trustworthy information should be consistent with past scientific findings.

These characteristics of the scientific method do not suggest that there is only one correct way to gather information or acquire knowledge. In fact, the scientific method encompasses many acceptable ways of gathering information about behavior in organizations. These various approaches differ in the extent to which they trade off control and realism in collecting information. Think back to the new training program. You are considering using the program, but first you need to know: Will the program improve employee performance? How could you answer this question *scientifically*?

THE CASE STUDY     One way of assessing the value of a proposed training program is to do a **case study.** The case study is the method of scientific information collection most like the way we typically learn from experience. A case study would involve collecting information about the experiences of one organization that had used the training program. The scientific observer would look at how well the program had worked in that organization, then try to figure out what characteristics of the training program or the organization might have predicted success or failure.

There are several important differences between a scientific case study and more informal ways of learning from experience in organizations. First, in a scientific case study information collection is systematic. All employees are asked the same questions. This ensures that different employees do not report different impressions of the training program just because they were asked different questions.

Second, a case study differs from informal observation in terms of the depth of inquiry. You might informally notice that the new training program worked out when it was tried. In a scientific case study, the scientific observer would look harder and deeper. In what ways was the training program successful? For how many of the trained employees was the training helpful? Were there any characteristics shared by all the employees who profited from the training? These questions go beyond simply knowing whether the program succeeded or failed and help generate an understanding of *why* success or failure occurred.

Finally, a scientific case study differs from informal "learning from experience" because the information collected is carefully recorded. Often learning from experience is unreliable because our memory for past experiences is poor. We may completely forget important aspects of past experiences or remember events that never occurred. The scientific case study includes careful recording of information so that all aspects of an experience (and only those which in fact occurred) are retained for later consideration.

In a case study, observations and speculations often occur "after the fact": in this example, after the training program already has been tried. The hallmark of a scientific case study is that the scientific observer of the experience is only that, an observer. The scientific observer makes no attempt to control important factors, such as characteristics of the training program or which employees are selected to be trained.

FIELD RESEARCH     If you wanted to exercise more control in collecting information about the effects of the training program, you might conduct some **field research.** Typically, in field research the scientific observer carefully measures what workers are thinking and doing (sometimes even *while* they are thinking and doing!) through the use of questionnaires, surveys, and observational techniques. The scientific observer also *controls* which organization (or which part of it) tries the training program and when. In a case study, this control is beyond the reach of the scientific observer.

Often it is difficult to pinpoint the cause of an effect. Did the training program succeed because it is a good program? Or was the trainer particularly good? Or were the trainees particularly motivated? Sorting out the answers to these questions is crucial to understanding whether the training program *or something else* is improving worker performance. To address this problem, researchers use multiple groups of subjects in a study. In our example, some of the groups could be trained by one trainer and others by a different trainer, both using the same training program. Some groups might not receive training or be given a different training program. This would give us lots of useful comparisons that would help us *isolate* the effects of our training program. If performance for the trained groups improved and performance for the untrained groups did not, that would be good evidence that training improves performance. What if performance for both trained and untrained groups improved equally? That would be good evidence that something *other than* training improves performance.

Notice that without the multiple groups (called *control* groups), there would be no way to know whether performance would have improved even without the training program. The control groups help us separate the effects on performance of factors that we are not interested in (such as rumors about layoffs that may make everyone's performance improve) from the effects of factors we are interested in (the training program).

## Laboratory Research

If you wanted to exercise even more control in assessing the effects of the proposed training program, you might conduct some **laboratory research.** In laboratory research, the employees to be trained would be taken out of the organizational context for training and observation. Many laboratory studies are not really done in scientific laboratories, merely away from the normal organizational setting. This is desirable because the information collected through case studies and field studies suffers from a certain amount of "noise"—things going on in the work setting that have nothing to do with the training program and cannot be controlled but which do influence performance. The laboratory study offers the best opportunity to isolate the effects of the training program on performance from the effects of other factors that we are not interested in. Thus, the laboratory study offers the clearest view of the effects of the training program.

On the other hand, the "noise" factors in work settings (such as the relationships between workers, the culture of a particular organization, and even production crises that arise) are part and parcel of the work setting. They will influence the effects of the training program when it is used in an actual organizational setting. Therefore, while the controlled environment of the laboratory might be best for finding out how the training program works in some ideal sense, only field and case studies will reveal how the training program works in an actual organizational setting.

All three of these methods for collecting information about behavior in organizations—case studies, field research, and laboratory research—share the central scientific orientation noted in Figure A–1 of careful, controlled, objective collection of information. This scientific orientation toward information collection is what differentiates organizational behavior as a scientific endeavor from other, more informal ways of learning about behavior in organizations, such as casual observation or intuition. In practice, these different techniques for collecting information scientifically would be used together. A case study could be used to generate potential insights about what makes a training program a success or failure. These insights then could be refined through the use of laboratory studies. Finally, the successfully refined training program could be put to the test using a field study. The field study would demonstrate whether the successes of the training program in the laboratory (that is, isolated from many of the realities of organizations) could be reproduced in actual organizational settings. The field study results may suggest more fine-tuning of the training program (through more laboratory studies) or may push the researcher back to observing organizations (case studies) for new insights.

Research on group decision making (which was discussed in Chapter 9) provides a good example of the complementary nature of case studies and laboratory and field research. Case studies have documented both good and bad group decision making at the White House prior to the "Bay of Pigs" invasion of Cuba and the Cuban Missile Crisis. These case studies raised important concerns about influence processes in group decision making and also demonstrated their consequences.[1] No doubt these concerns also will be raised in trying to explain and understand the Challenger disaster.

These same influence processes also have been examined in the laboratory, where a variety of studies have identified social comparison processes (discussed in Chapter 7) as an important source of influence in group decision making.[2] Finally, the importance of social comparison processes in decision making has been validated with field experiments examining bystander apathy in emergency situations.[3] In group decision-making research, case studies have stimulated systematic and controlled research in the field and the laboratory. Laboratory research has isolated important cause-and-effect relationships, and field research has verified the importance of these cause-and-effect relationships in real-world settings.

---

[1]G. T. Allison, *Essence of Decision* (Boston: Little, Brown, 1971).

[2]S. E. Asch, "Effects of Group Pressure on the Modification and Distortion of Judgments," in *Groups, Leadership, and Men,* ed. H. Guetzkow (Pittsburgh: Carnegie Press, 1951), 177–190.

[3]J. M. Darley and B. Latane, "When Will People Help in a Crisis?" *Psychology Today* 2 (1968): 54–57, 70–71.

SUMMARY

The scientific method is used to ensure that information collected about behavior in organizations is trustworthy and accurate. The scientific method is a systematic set of procedures for objectively collecting and evaluating information. The scientific method encompasses several different approaches to collecting information, including case studies, field research, and laboratory research. These approaches differ in the extent to which they trade off control and realism in collecting information. In practice, these different approaches would be used in combination, in order to construct an accurate representation of the realities of organizational behavior.

KEY TERMS

**Case study**  Careful and systematic observation and recording of the experiences of a single organization.

**Field research**  Using questionnaires, surveys, and observational techniques in controlled study of actual organizations.

**Laboratory research**  Carefully controlled experimentation and observation outside of traditional organizational settings in order to identify and isolate important cause-and-effect relationships.

**Scientific method**  Systematic set of procedures for objectively collecting and evaluating information.

 IF YOU
WANT TO
KNOW
MORE

A general discussion of the process of scientific inquiry is provided in Thomas Kuhn's *The Structure of Scientific Revolutions* (Chicago: University of Chicago Press, 1962). Specific methods and techniques for conducting scientific research studies in organizational behavior can be found in *Research Methods in Organizational Behavior*, by Eugene Stone (Glenview, Ill.: Scott-Foresman, 1978) and *Methods of Social Research*, by K. E. Bailey (New York: Free Press, 1978).

CONTINUING ON

By the second month of the training period, trouble developed. The painters learned more slowly than had been anticipated, and it began to look as though their production would stabilize far below what was planned. Many of the hooks were going by empty. The painters complained that the hooks moved too fast, and that the engineer had set the rates wrong. A few painters quit and had to be replaced with new ones. This further aggravated the learning problem. The team spirit that the management had expected to develop through the group bonus was not in evidence except as an expression of what the engineers called "resistance." One painter, whom the group regarded as its leader (and the management regarded as the ringleader), was outspoken in taking the complaints of the group to the supervisor. These complaints were that the job was messy, the hooks moved too fast, the incentive pay was not correctly calculated, and it was too hot working so close to the drying oven.

**Question**

1. What would you recommend that the responsible manager do now? Why?

CONTINUING ON

A consultant was hired to work with the supervisor. She recommended that the painters be brought together for a general discussion of the working conditions. Although hesitant, the supervisor agreed to this plan.

The first meeting was held immediately after the shift was over at 4:00 in the afternoon. It was attended by all eight painters. They voiced the same complaints again: the hooks went by too fast, the job was too dirty, and the room was hot and poorly ventilated. For some reason, it was this last item that seemed to bother them most. The supervisor promised to discuss the problems of ventilation and temperature with the engineers, and a second meeting was scheduled. In the next few days the supervisor had several talks with the engineers. They, along with the plant superintendent, felt that this was really a trumped-up complaint, and that the expense of corrective measures would be prohibitively high.

The supervisor came to the second meeting with some apprehensions. The painters, however, did not seem to be much put out. Rather, they had a proposal of their own to make. They felt that if several large fans were set up to circulate the air around their feet, they would be much more comfortable. After some discussion, the supervisor agreed to pursue the idea. The supervisor and the consultant discussed the idea of fans with the superintendent. Three large propeller-type fans were purchased and installed.

The painters were jubilant. For several days the fans were moved about in various positions until they were placed to the satisfaction of the group. The painters seemed completely satisfied with the results, and the relations between them and the supervisor improved visibly.

The supervisor, after this encouraging episode, decided that further meetings might also prove profitable. The painters were asked if they would like to meet and discuss other aspects of the work situation. They were eager to do this. Another meeting was held, and the discussion quickly centered on the speed of the hooks. The painters maintained that the engineer had set them at an unreasonably fast speed and that they would never be able to fill enough of them to make a bonus.

The discussion reached a turning point when the group's leader explained that it wasn't that the painters couldn't work fast enough to keep up with the hooks, but that they couldn't work at that pace all day long. The supervisor explored the point. The painters were unanimous in their opinion that they could keep up with the belt for short periods if they wanted to. But they didn't want to because if they showed they could do this for short periods then they would be expected to do it all day long. The meeting ended with an unprecedented request by the painters: "Let us adjust the speed of the belt faster or slower depending on how we feel." The supervisor agreed to discuss this with the superintendent and the engineers.

The engineers reacted negatively to the suggestion. However, after several meetings it was granted that there was some latitude within which variations in the speed of the hooks would not affect the finished product. After considerable argument with the engineers, it was agreed to try out the painters' idea.

With misgivings, the supervisor had a control with a dial marked "low, medium, fast" installed at the booth of the group leader. The speed of the belt could now be adjusted anywhere between the lower and upper limits that the engineers had set.

## Questions

1. What changes do you now expect in the level of output of the painters? Why?
2. What changes do you expect in the feelings of the painters toward their work situation? Why?
3. What other predictions do you make about the behavior of the painters?

CONTINUING ON          The painters were delighted, and spent many lunch hours deciding how the speed of the belt should be varied from hour to hour throughout the day. Within a week the pattern had settled down to one in which the first half hour of the shift was run on a medium speed (a dial setting slightly above the point marked "medium"). The next two-and-a-half hours were run at high speed, and the half hour before lunch and the half hour after lunch were run at low speed. The rest of the afternoon was run at high speed with the exception of the last 45 minutes of the shift, which was run at medium.

The constant speed at which the engineers had originally set the belt was actually slightly below the "medium" mark on the control dial. The average speed at which the painters were running the belt was on the high side of the dial. Few, if any, empty hooks entered the oven, and inspection showed no increase of rejects from the paint room.

Production increased, and within three weeks (some two months before the scheduled ending of the learning bonus) the painters were operating at 30 to 50 percent above the level that had been expected under the original arrangement. Naturally, their earnings were correspondingly higher than anticipated. They were collecting their base pay, earning a considerable piece-rate bonus, and still benefiting from the learning bonus. They were earning more now than many skilled workers in other parts of the plant.

**Questions**

1. How do you feel about the situation at this point?
2. Suppose you were the supervisor. What would you expect to happen next? Why?

CONTINUING ON

Management was besieged by demands that the inequity between the earnings of the painters and those of other workers in the plant be taken care of. With growing irritation between the superintendent and the supervisor, the engineers and supervisor, and the superintendent and engineers, the situation came to a head when the superintendent revoked the learning bonus and returned the painting operation to its original status: the hooks moved again at their constant, time-studied, designated speed. Production dropped again, and within a month all but two of the eight painters had quit. The supervisor stayed on for several months, but feeling aggrieved, then left for another job.

# Glossary

**Accommodating** Strategy for interpersonal conflict that maximizes the other party's concerns or outcomes.

**Active listening** Receiver accepting responsibility for ensuring proper transmission of the intended message.

**Administrative intensity** Proportion of administrators and managers in an organization's total work force.

**Alternative dispute resolution (ADR)** Series of techniques for avoiding litigation between organizations, usually by encouraging the disputants to arrive at a mutually agreeable solution through the use of specific techniques such as mock juries, minitrials, and so on.

**Alternative sources** Other ways to fulfill a resource dependency, thereby reducing an individual's dependence on any one source; a form of slack.

**Anchoring-and-adjustment effect** Tendency of individual perceptions or judgments to be similar to a reference point even when the reference point is arbitrary or irrelevant.

**Anticipation** Making internal changes in the organization to respond to the environment's demands.

**Approach-approach conflict** Occurs when an individual must choose between two equally attractive options, both with positive outcomes.

**Approach-avoidance conflict** Occurs when an individual must choose among options with both positive and negative outcomes.

**Arbitration** Resolution of a conflict by a neutral third party who, after hearing both sides of a dispute, determines a final, binding outcome.

**Attention** Individuals' choice of where to direct and how to ration their limited sensory input system.

**Attribution** Process of perceiving the causes of actions and outcomes; provides models of how other people function, what their motives are, and what determines their behaviors.

**Automation** Using machines to replace (or assist) workers.

**Availability bias** Assessing the frequency or likelihood of an event's occurrence by how easily it is remembered, even though memory recall is influenced by factors unrelated to the frequency of an event.

**Avoidance-avoidance conflict** Occurs when an individual must choose between two equally unattractive options, both with negative outcomes.

**Avoiding** Strategy for interpersonal conflict that is suitable when the positions of both parties are trivial or when one party is seriously outmatched by the other party.

**Behaviorally anchored rating scale (BARS)**  Employee evaluation format in which the organization analyzes a particular job to determine what types of behavior reflect varying degrees of performance, using actual descriptions of behavior to define the ratings.

**Behaviorally healthy organization**  One whose internal interaction patterns put it in a position to become and remain financially sound; arises from successful communication, adaptation, innovation, and succession.

**Behaviorism**  View of human motivation that all behavior can be understood by examining only contingencies and consequences.

**Beneficence**  Generosity, leniency, and helpfulness of the environment concerning needed resources.

**Bottom-up problem solving**  Involving workers in all phases of the change process, beginning with diagnosis.

**Boundary spanners**  Individuals such as liaisons who represent an organization in interactions with the forces in its environment.

**Bounded rationality**  Model of individual decision making that diverges from the rational ideal in being based on a limited perspective, the sequential evaluation of alternatives, satisficing, and the use of judgmental heuristics.

**Brainstorming**  Group creativity technique facilitating free discussion and exchange of ideas by withholding criticism of ideas, encouraging unusual ideas, generating as many ideas as possible, and piggybacking ideas.

**Buffer**  Mechanism that reduces the environmental shocks or interdepartmental conflict to allow an organizational unit to complete its task more smoothly.

**Bureaucracy**  Form of organization in which there are clearly defined lines of authority and responsibility for members, and behavior is tightly controlled by rules, policies, and job assignments.

**Bystander apathy**  Failure of observers to lend assistance in emergency situations; an example of the results of social anchoring effects on judgment.

**Career ladder**  Specific series of jobs or experiences necessary to advance in an organization.

**Case study**  Careful and systematic observation and recording of the experiences of a single organization.

**Cautious shift**  Tendency of a group as a whole and each member to be less willing to accept risk after a group discussion than prior to it.

**Centralization**  Resting decision-making power with one or a few individuals, based on the competing needs of coordination and division of labor.

**Charisma**  Persuasiveness derived from personal characteristics desired or admired by a reference group.

**Charismatic leadership** Process used by transformational leaders to develop a common vision of what could be, discover or create opportunities, and strengthen organizational members' control of their own destinies.

**Closed system** Completely self-contained organization that functions apart from and is unaffected by what goes on around it.

**Coalition** Collection of individuals who band together to combine their individual sources of power.

**Code of ethics** Mechanism for institutionalizing ethics within an organization that describes the general value system of the organization, its purpose, and guidelines for decision making consistent with these principles.

**Codetermination** Policy of allowing workers a say in major organizational decisions, not just minor operational decisions.

**Coercion** Threat of punishment for not engaging in appropriate behaviors.

**Cognitions** Beliefs and thoughts; the information processing that goes on inside an individual's head.

**Collaborating** Strategy for interpersonal conflict that is suitable when both your own and the other party's concerns are equally important, when the issue is too important to compromise, when trying to engender commitment among the parties, or when trying to gain insight.

**Collectivity stage** Second phase of the organizational life cycle, in which management concentrates on human resource issues such as cooperation, employee commitment, and morale, and in which the beginnings of formal systems such as structured departments, job assignments, and a hierarchy of authority are seen.

**Colorism** Predisposition to act in a certain manner because of a person's skin color.

**Communication** Transmission of information and understanding from one organization member to another through the use of symbols.

**Comparable worth discrimination** Discrimination in which men are paid more than women for jobs that are substantially equal in terms of skill, ability, and effort required.

**Compensation system** A major way an organization conveys to its employees what it wants done and how they should behave, consisting of wages or salaries, benefits, nonrecurring financial rewards, and noneconomic rewards.

**Competing** Strategy for interpersonal conflict that is suitable when the individual is concerned about his or her own needs, issues, or outcomes, such as when in an emergency or critical situation, when the other party is untrustworthy, or when the individual or group is sure of the correct solution.

**Complexity** Overabundance of inputs that managers must keep track of, consider, and manage.

**Complex learning** Form of learning requiring acquisition of new behaviors not yet available in a worker's behavioral repertoire.

**Compromise coalition** Coalition in which all members are interested in the same issues but each is flexible enough about specifics to make sure that the coalition gets its way.

**Compromising** Strategy for interpersonal conflict that is suitable when both sets of goals are important but not worth the potential disruption of more aggressive strategies.

**Computer-integrated manufacturing (CIM)** Manufacturing technologies that combine task mechanization with computerized information processing about the task.

**Concurrence seeking** Suppression of conflict by group members to seek agreement.

**Conditioning** The use of reinforcement and punishment to create habits.

**Conflict** Differences among the perceptions, beliefs, and goals of organization members.

**Conformity** Form of social inhibition in which a group member engages in a behavior or professes a belief that is encouraged by the group even though the member believes it is incorrect or inappropriate.

**Consequences** A central concept of the law of effect: the good or bad results following from a behavior.

**Construction** Process of perceiver organizing and editing sensory inputs in a way that makes them potentially meaningful; subject to both input source and perceiver influences.

**Content theories of motivation** Theories that focus on the factors within people that motivate them to perform; for example, the theories of Maslow, Herzberg, and McClelland.

**Contingency** A central concept of the law of effect; the relationship between actions and their outcomes.

**Contingency model of leadership** Theory suggesting that leadership effectiveness is determined both by the characteristics of the leader and by the level of situational favorableness that exists.

**Contingency theory** Approach to organizational behavior stating that choice of appropriate management technique is dependent on the particular situation.

**Contract** Control strategy of managing environmental demands using a legally binding document that guarantees an organization delivery of and terms for a particular resource.

**Contrast effect** Tendency of individual perceptions or judgments to be seen as very different from an extreme reference point.

**Contributions** The productive capacity toward achieving an organization's purpose offered by an individual who is entering into a psychological contract.

**Control** Molding the environment to fit the organization's needs.

**Controlling** Management function of directing and motivating the work force, often by generating direction and enthusiasm for work through leadership.

**Controversy** When one person's (or group's) ideas, information, perspective, or opinions are in conflict with another's and the two seek to understand and resolve these differences.

**Corporate responsibility** Need for an organization to take or avoid actions in order to measure up to society's moral and ethical standards.

**Covariation** Central principle of attribution theory, stating that behaviors are attributed to causes that are present when the behaviors are present and absent when the behaviors are absent; covariation is judged by distinctiveness, consensus, and consistency.

**Creativity** Individualistic, novel, idea-generating process.

**Critical incidence file** A memory aid containing examples of an employee's behavior to help managers prepare for performance appraisals.

**Critical incidents** Particularly successful or disastrous new behaviors that lead to the establishment of new group policies or norms.

**Cross-training** Encouraging workers to learn their coworkers' jobs; provides challenges for workers and flexibility for management.

**Custodial leadership** Process used by transactional leaders to improve working conditions, compensation, and fringe benefits.

**Data handback** Providing employees with the results of the questionnaires used in survey-guided development in order to assess whether the picture of the organization painted by the survey is accurate, and to solicit their suggestions about the implications of the survey results for problem diagnosis.

**Debate** Involves two individuals or groups who argue for incompatible alternatives and a judge who makes a decision based on the relative merits of both sides' arguments.

**Decision analysis** Separating the decision to be made into its components before making a decision.

**Decision tree** A common type of decision aid using four types of information: possible courses of action, events that might follow from these actions, likelihood of each event, and value of each event.

**Decoding** Attempts by receivers to extract meaning from messages.

**Deindividuation** Submersion of personal identities and personal responsibility of group members in the identity of the group.

**Delphi technique** Group decision-making technique that minimizes interaction among members; members complete mailed questionnaires and a coordinator summarizes results.

**Departmentalization** Grouping tasks into organizational units according to the knowledge and skills required or based on similar levels of skills and abilities.

**Diagnosis** First stage in the process of change; figuring out what actions to take in response to signals that change is needed; includes identifying the problem, its causes, and an appropriate and effective solution.

**Differentiation** Second stage of group development, in which the group decides what its goals and priorities will be and structures its interaction to ensure effective group functioning.

**Diffusion of responsibility** Sharing the credit or blame for the outcomes of a group's actions over the entire group.

**Distributive justice** Fair treatment of employees in awarding organizational rewards or in administering organizational punishment.

**Distributive negotiation** Common negotiation strategy in which parties decide only how to allocate a fixed amount of resources.

**Downsizing** Reducing the size of an organization's work force.

**Effectiveness** Ability of an organization to accomplish an important goal, purpose, or mission.

**Efficiency** Amount of effort required to deliver a promised good or service; can be increased through specialization and economies of scale.

**Elaboration stage** Fourth and last phase of the organizational life cycle, in which management redirects the organization's emphasis from bureaucracy to a renewed interest in cooperation and teamwork, and in which decentralization often occurs and innovation and creativity are once again valued.

**Empathy** Ability of one individual to appreciate another's perspective.

**Employee assistance programs** Typically in-house or contractual programs that diagnose and treat a variety of stress-related problems, such as drug and alcohol abuse and other emotional and psychological problems.

**Employee (socioemotional)-oriented leadership** Process used by leaders that emphasizes the individual worker's needs in managing group performance; also called *initiating consideration.*

**Employee stock ownership plan (ESOP)** Group-based incentive plan in which an organization contributes to a trust fund to buy stock, which is allocated to employees based on seniority.

**Employment at will** Freedom of an employer to terminate an employee at any time for any reason, now being eroded in the courts.

**Encoding** Three-part process of creating a message for the receiver to receive: selecting contents of the intended meaning, selecting a communication medium and channel, and translating the contents into symbols.

**Enhancement** Attempt to augment the positive consequences of one's behavior to increase the perception of fairness among employees; the opposite of justification.

**Entitling tactic** Attempt to gain responsibility for positive events and their consequences in order to increase the perception of fairness among employees; the opposite of excuse.

**Entrepreneurial stage** First phase of the organizational life cycle in which the organization comes into existence and the founders concentrate on creating the product or service and surviving as an organization.

**Environmental scanning** Process of anticipation in which the organization collects information from the environment.

**Equity** Workers' judgments of fairness based on the ratio of work inputs to work outputs.

**Escalation** Committing additional resources to failing causes based on the slim hope that there will be a dramatic change.

**Expectancies** Workers' cognitions concerning the likely consequences of their actions.

**Expectancy theory** Theory stating that worker behaviors are a function of workers' *beliefs* about consequences and contingencies.

**Expected value** Value of an option, determined by summing the value assigned to each possible consequence of an action, multiplied by the probabilities that each of these possible consequences will occur.

**Expert power** Individual power based on the possession of special information, knowledge, or ability.

**Expert systems** Computer programs that mimic the thought processes of an expert decision maker or problem solver.

**Explicitness** Extent to which individuals cannot deny that a behavior occurred, serving to commit individuals to their actions.

**External change agents** Expert consultants from outside an organization that management brings in specifically to facilitate a change.

**Externalities** Causes of a worker's behaviors or the consequences of those behaviors that are beyond the worker's control.

**Extrinsic rewards** Rewards like money or praise provided in exchange for appropriate behaviors.

**Factfinding** Form of third-party intervention in which a neutral third party determines a reasonable solution based on evidence presented by the parties, who are not bound to follow the recommendation.

**Field research** Using questionnaires, surveys, and observational techniques in controlled study of actual organizations.

**Flextime work scheduling** Method of context enrichment in which management gives workers limited discretion in arranging their work hours.

**Forecasting** Process of environmental anticipation in which the organization uses mathematical models to predict future environmental demands.

**Formalization stage**  Third phase of the organizational life cycle, in which management values stability, efficiency, rules and procedures, and other bureaucratic trends.

**Formation**  First stage of group development, in which group members decide whether membership is necessary, learn the traits and strengths of other members, and identify a leader.

**Framing**  Judgmental heuristic that decision makers use to deal with risk in which they become increasingly likely to take risks when confronting potential losses and increasingly likely to avoid risks when confronting possible gains.

**Free rider**  People who accept the benefits of being a member of a group but are unwilling to contribute to the larger good of that group.

**Fundamental attribution error** Tendency of individuals to perceive others' behaviors as caused primarily by stable, internal characteristics (such as personality) and to perceive their own behavior as primarily a response to environmental characteristics.

**Glass ceiling**  Barrier that keeps women as a group from advancing to executive management simply because they are women and not because of their individual ability.

**Goal**  A specific direction for action and a specific quantity of work to be accomplished.

**Goal commitment**  Extension of effort, over time, toward the accomplishment of a goal and an unwillingness to give up or lower the goal.

**Gold-collar managers**  Managers who combine business know-how with technical expertise in how to get people and machines to work together (rather than fight each other) in the workplace.

**Group**  Organized system of two or more individuals who are interrelated so that the system performs some function, has a standard set of role relationships among its members, and has a set of norms that regulate the function of the group and each of its members.

**Group development**  Process of identifying and resolving present and future group interaction problems.

**Group objectives**  Goals, purposes, and functions that a group is trying to achieve.

**Groupthink**  Tendency in highly cohesive groups for members to seek consensus so strongly that they lose the willingness and ability to evaluate one another's ideas critically.

**Growth need strength**  Interest of a worker in growing and developing on the job.

**Habit**  Tendency of a person or an organization to do things the same way, over and over again.

**Halo effect** Tendency for an individual's perception of an input on one dimension to influence his or her perceptions of that input on other dimensions.

**Hierarchy of human needs** Abraham Maslow's theory of five distinct classes of human needs—physiological, safety, social, esteem, and self-actualization—some of which ("higher" needs) become important to a worker only after "lower" needs have been fulfilled.

**Horizontal conflict** Conflict between people at similar organizational levels.

**Horizontal integration** Involvement of an organization in several different activities (e.g., product lines) in order to distribute its resource dependence risks across a variety of activities.

**Human resources** View of workers' mental capabilities as key resources in organizational efficiency and effectiveness; emphasizes worker participation for more informed organizational planning and decision making.

**Hygiene factors** In two-factor theory, workers' basic needs of pay, safety on the job, quality of supervision, and social environment, fulfillment of which prevents dissatisfaction.

**Idiosyncrasy credits** Allowances given to group members to violate group rules and norms because of consistent past adherence to those rules and norms.

**Image advertising** Attempts to influence the environment's overall perception of an organization.

**Individualistic decision making** Each member of the group independently selects his or her most preferred alternative without interacting with other group members.

**Inducements** The compensations of steady employment and payment offered to an individual by an organization that is entering into a psychological contract.

**Inertia** Tendency of an object to continue in the same direction with the same velocity or intensity unless impacted by some force of change.

**Informal organization** Interpersonal realities of an organization, such as employees' personal goals, perceptions, and beliefs, that are not part of the organization's formal goals and plans but that must be taken into account to achieve organizational efficiency and effectiveness.

**Information overload** State of perceivers when their sensory input systems are overwhelmed with new, unusual, attention-grabbing inputs.

**Ingratiation** Doing nice things for someone in the hope of creating a sense of obligation in the individual to return the favor.

**Input source influences** Characteristics of a source object or event that affect perceivers' attempts to direct their attention, including motion, distinctiveness, novelty, vividness, contrast effect, anchoring-and-adjustment effect, and halo effect.

**Inquisitor** Informal third-party role in a dispute in which a manager exerts a high degree of control over both the outcome and the process of conflict resolution.

**Instability**   Rate of change in an organization's environment.

**Instrumentality**   Worker's belief that attaining the required levels of performance will produce desired personal outcomes.

**Integrating device**   Strategy of conflict management aimed at enhancing communication across groups and maintaining appropriate levels of interaction.

**Integration**   Third stage of group development, in which group members define a set of rules and roles to coordinate group interaction and make pursuit of the goals effective.

**Integration**   Role of management defined by D. McGregor as the creation of conditions such that members of the organization can best achieve their own goals by directing their efforts toward the success of the enterprise.

**Integrative bargaining**   A more cooperative negotiation strategy that assumes there can be an expanding amount of resources for the parties to divide.

**Interactive justice**   Equitable treatment of employees in interpersonal treatment by managers.

**Interlocking directorates**   Negotiation strategy for managing environmental demands in which a corporation appoints to its board of directors representatives from a variety of organizations on which it is dependent.

**Interpretation**   In perception, the process of assigning meaning to a constructed representation of an object or event.

**Intrinsic rewards**   Rewards that occur naturally as the product of engaging in a behavior.

**Irreversibility**   Extent to which behavior cannot easily be revoked or undone, serving to commit individuals to their actions.

**Jargon**   Special words or common words used with special meaning that summarize a group's common experiences and history and allow simple communication of complex meanings.

**Job analysis**   Gathering of information about a job in an organization, including a description of tasks and activities, results (products or services), and the equipment, materials, and working conditions that characterize the job.

**Job characteristics model**   Theory of job enrichment in which the presence of five job characteristics (skill variety, task identity, task significance, autonomy, and feedback) leads to critical psychological states (meaningfulness of work, responsibility for work outcomes, and knowledge of work activity results) that in turn result in positive work-related outcomes such as productivity and worker satisfaction.

**Job description**   Written document that specifies an individual's role in a work organization: duties to be performed, to whom the person must report, and the goals he or she must attain.

**Job enlargement** Redesign of work tasks that increases the number of tasks in a job to make it more interesting and involving.

**Job enrichment** Redesign of work tasks that makes a job more interesting and involving by allowing workers to fulfill higher-order needs such as achievement and control.

**Job rotation** Method of increasing workers' skill variety by allowing them to switch jobs occasionally.

**Job specialization** Division of the overall mission of an organization into various smaller tasks.

**Joint venture** Two or more unrelated organizations that pool their resources to collaborate on projects.

**Judge** Informal third-party role in a dispute in which a manager exerts a high degree of control over the outcome of a dispute but not the process by which it is resolved.

**Judgmental heuristics** Rules of thumb, or shortcuts, that reduce the information-processing demands on decision makers.

**Laboratory research** Carefully controlled experimentation and observation outside of traditional organizational settings in order to identify and isolate important cause-and-effect relationships.

**Leadership** Increment of influence over and above an employee's mechanical compliance with routine directives of the organization.

**Learned helplessness** Workers' beliefs that they are incapable of producing a required performance or that the required performance, even if produced, would not lead to desired consequences; causes the worker to stop trying.

**Learned needs** Content theory of motivation proposing that three categories of needs—affiliation, power, and achievement—are learned, not innate, desires.

**Least-preferred coworker (LPC) scale** Questionnaire that measures how respondents characterize their feelings about a person with whom they work least effectively. A high LPC score (favoring the least preferred coworker) suggests that the leader derives satisfaction and a sense of accomplishment from relationships with others; a low LPC score suggests that the leader emphasizes completing tasks, even at the expense of interpersonal relationships.

**Legitimate power** Individual power based on an individual's authority to control the behavior of others for their own good and for the good of a social system.

**Line-staff conflict** Conflict between employees involved directly in some aspect of producing the organization's product and employees who provide technical and advisory assistance to the line.

**Lobbying** Negotiation strategy for managing environmental demands in which a representative of an organization convinces a source of resource dependence in the environment of the correctness of the organization's perspective.

**Logrolling**   Form of coalition in which participants lend each other power so that each can pursue interests not shared by other coalition members.

**Loose coupling**   Relationship of an organization and its environment in which what happens in the environment may or may not be reflected by immediate changes in the organization.

**Machine bureaucracy**   Organizational structure using highly specialized and routine tasks, formalized procedures for the transformation process, a proliferation of rules and communication channels, a functional departmentalization structure, a large span of control, and an elaborate administrative and technical structure.

**Managerial functions**   Activities that must be performed for organizations to outperform individuals, including planning, organizing, staffing, and controlling.

**Managerial grid**   Leadership training program conducted by Robert Blake and Jane Mouton that reflects two dimensions of leader behavior: concern for production (task-oriented leadership) and concern for people (socioemotional leadership).

**Managerial leadership**   Process used by transactional leaders to provide subordinates work that is less routine and more challenging, build cohesive work teams,

and give employees more say in decisions that affect them directly.

**Maturity**   Final stage of group development, in which group members work within its structure to pursue its goals.

**Mechanization**   Programming a machine to execute the component actions of a work task faster, more precisely, and more consistently than any human.

**Mediation**   Resolution of a conflict by a neutral third party who can control the interaction between the disputants but has no authority to force a solution on them.

**Mentoring**   Process of senior employees instructing younger, less-experienced protégés.

**Milgram study**   Stanley Milgram's classic experiments at Yale University in the early 1960s that examined the extent to which volunteer participants would obey, even if the demands of authority violated their moral responsibilities.

**Motivators**   In two-factor theory, factors that provide the work satisfaction, such as the opportunity for achievement, responsibility, and recognition through work.

**Movement**   Third stage in the process of change; implementation of the change plan.

**Need for power**   Desire to control or to have an impact on others; David McClelland's research revealed that it is high in individuals who are competitive and aggressive, who desire the outward trappings of power such as prestige possessions, who prefer action situations, and who join a number of groups.

**Negotiation** The process whereby two or more parties decide what each will give and take in an exchange between them.

**Neutralizers of leadership** Factors that paralyze, destroy, or counteract the effectiveness of leader behaviors, making it difficult for them to have an impact.

**Nominal group technique (NGT)** Group decision-making technique that focuses on generating alternatives and selecting among them by asking group members to independently write down ideas, present them in turn, clarify them for the group, and rank them by voting privately.

**Nonverbal communication** Use of any communication channel other than formal language, such as facial expressions, eye contact, body language, and the use of physical objects and space.

**Norm** Informal, unstated rule that governs and regulates group behavior.

**Objective self-awareness** Individuals' perceptions of their own roles in causing behaviors and their consequences.

**Open system** Organization whose activities are inescapably influenced by its environment.

**Open systems theory** Management theory proposed by D. Katz and R. L. Kahn, which focuses on the assumptions that organizations are (1) social systems in which changes in one part are reflected by changes in other parts, and (2) open to influence from the environment.

**Organic structure** Flexible organizational structure that can respond efficiently and effectively to new demands placed on it.

**Organization** Form of human association for the attainment of a common purpose by combining the talents and efforts of its members.

**Organizational atrophy** Organization's use of a particular response to a situation long after the situation has changed.

**Organizational behavior and modification (OB-Mod)** Systematic application of simple conditioning and reinforcement theory principles to the management of organizational behavior.

**Organizational commitment** Relative strength of an individual's identification with and involvement in a particular organization.

**Organizational culture** Expectations and practices of the organization, including shared philosophy, attitude toward employees, leaders and heroes, rituals and ceremonies, and belief about the direction of the organization.

**Organizational decline** (1) Cutback in the size of an organization's work force, budget, resources, clients, and so on. (2) Mature organization's inability to stay in touch with changing markets, technologies, and client preferences, leading to stagnation, bureaucracy, and passivity.

**Organizational development (OD)**   Systemwide application of behavior science knowledge to the planned development and reinforcement of organizational strategies, structures, and processes for improving an organization's effectiveness.

**Organizational life cycle**   Predictable pattern of evolution of organizations' structure, leadership style, and administrative systems.

**Organizational ombudsman**   Individual whose responsibility it is to interpret policy, counsel disputing parties, resolve disputes, and provide feedback and identify potential problem areas for senior management.

**Organizational socialization**   Process of conveying the organization's goals, norms, and preferred ways of doing things to new employees.

**Organizational structure**   Skeleton of an organization based on the relationship among its positions or roles.

**Organization design**   Process of actively creating a structure composed of groups of activities, roles, or positions to coordinate the interdependencies among organizational actors effectively.

**Organizing**   Management function of creating a structure through which members can produce the organization's central goods or services.

**Orientation training**   Process of introducing newcomers to organizational procedures that is conducted jointly by the training staff and the new employee's supervisor.

**Outplacement program**   Finding new jobs for displaced employees or those who choose not to stay on after a major corporate reorganization.

**Output customization**   Extent to which an organization's products or services are influenced by customer needs.

**Paralysis of analysis**   When timely and decisive decision making fails to occur because too much irrelevant, detailed, obsolete, or poorly organized information is readily available.

**Partial reinforcement**   Rewarding an appropriate behavior in a noncontinuous or variable manner, serving to develop desirable work habits that are more resistant to extinction than those acquired under continuous reinforcement.

**Perception**   Process by which individuals receive and interpret sensations from the environment so they may act upon it.

**Perceptual grouping**   Tendency of the perceiver to organize sensory inputs into familiar and potentially meaningful patterns by the principles of closure and continuity.

**Perceptual set**   Expectations that a perceiver brings to the perception task, based on suggestions, beliefs, or previous experiences.

**Piece-rate plan**   Incentive plan in which employees are paid a given rate for each unit produced.

**Planning** Management thought processes that precede action in an organization.

**Political conflict** Occurs when different members of an organization pursue conflicting *personal* (rather than organizational) agendas.

**Political system** Collection of individuals or groups that must work together and speak with one voice even though each has a private agenda to pursue.

**Pooled interdependence** Exists when each department or unit contributes to the larger good but is not dependent on the others.

**Power** Ability to influence the attitudes or behavior of others, usually through the control of resources.

**Procedural justice** Equitable treatment of employees in the processes by which organizational rewards are allocated and punishments are administered.

**Process focus** Concentration of organizational development on the behavioral (interaction) patterns in an organization that produce or sustain problems.

**Process theories of motivation** Theories that focus on the process by which rewards direct behavior; for example, expectancy, equity, and reinforcement theories.

**Production (task)-oriented leadership** Process used by leaders to direct activities related specifically to the task; also called *initiating structure*.

**Psychological contract** Set of unwritten, reciprocal expectations between an employee and an organization.

**Public relations** Negotiation strategy for managing environmental demands in which an organization actively controls its interactions with the environment using activities such as image advertising.

**Punishment** Administering an unpleasant consequence (for example, docking a worker's pay) in response to inappropriate work behaviors.

**Quality circle (QC)** Voluntary group of approximately ten people from the same work group who meet periodically to discuss and develop solutions to problems related to quality, productivity, or product cost.

**Quality-of-work-life (QWL) programs** Systemwide attempts to simultaneously enhance organizational effectiveness (usually defined in terms of productivity) and employee well-being through a commitment to participative organizational decision making.

**Rationality** Basing a decision on careful and calculated action alternatives and their consequences.

**Realistic job preview** Mechanism used by organizations to present both the desirable and undesirable aspects of the job and the organization, to provide the potential employee with more complete and accurate information about the position.

**Reciprocal interdependence**  Exists when the outputs of one department become the inputs of a second, and the outputs of that second unit become the inputs for the first.

**Referent power**  Individual power based on a high level of identification with, admiration of, or respect for the power holder.

**Refreezing**  Final stage in the process of change; institutionalizing the change and monitoring the systems that have been put in place to track the consequences of implementing the change.

**Regulation**  Legal restriction of behaviors in or by organizations.

**Reinforcement**  Reward for a behavior that increases the probability that the behavior will be repeated.

**Representativeness**  Decision heuristic based on the belief that an outcome should resemble its cause.

**Resource conflict**  Individuals having separate and incompatible interests.

**Resource dependence**  Individual's need for resources, which exposes the individual to influence.

**Resource pooling**  An advantage groups have over individuals by combining the perspectives, ideas, suggestions, and information of all members.

**Resource redundancy**  Preventing the lack of a particular resource by maintaining relationships with several suppliers.

**Resource scarcity**  Not having enough of a particular commodity (for example, food, love, attention, cars, clothes, opportunities, etc.) for all to accomplish their goals.

**Reward power**  Individual power based on the control of resources valued by another; the opposite of coercive power.

**Risk**  Amount of uncertainty associated with a particular decision alternative or choice.

**Risk averse**  Willingness of a decision maker to pay a premium to avoid risk, ignoring the expected value solution.

**Risk neutral**  Indifference of a decision maker between risky and certain outcomes if they have the same expected value.

**Risk seeking**  Willingness of a decision maker to pay a premium to experience risk.

**Risky shift**  Tendency of a group as a whole and each member to be more willing to accept greater levels of risk after a group discussion than prior to it.

**Robot**  Machine guided by automatic controls to perform various complex functions like a human being.

**Role**  Formal or informal definition of the set of behaviors appropriate to a particular position occupied by a member of a group.

**Role conflict**  Occurs when two or more role-specific activities, or expectations of other organizational members, are incompatible.

**Role differentiation** Establishment of clear concepts for group members of their specific duties and responsibilities to the group, based on their individual strengths and weaknesses, and how these duties and responsibilities contribute to the realization of the group's goals.

**Role therapy** Training technique in which someone from outside the group comes in temporarily to act as a catalyst to improve the effectiveness of group interaction by ensuring that role differentiation has been accomplished appropriately.

**Rule** Formal policy or informal norm that defines the boundaries of acceptable and expected behavior in the group.

**Satisficing** Foregoing the optimal solution in favor of one that is acceptable or reasonable in order to save the time and effort needed for extended comparisons.

**Scientific management** Frederick Taylor's theory of careful and systematic observations and prescriptive techniques for designing jobs and incentive pay schemes for rank-and-file factory workers.

**Scientific method** Systematic set of procedures for objectively collecting and evaluating information.

**Selection** Process of collecting and evaluating information about an individual in order to extend an offer of employment.

**Self-efficacy** Workers' beliefs that they can produce required levels of performance by engaging in appropriate work behaviors.

**Self-fulfilling prophecy** Expectation about how someone is likely to act that actually causes the person to meet the expectation.

**Self-serving bias** Tendency of perceivers to attribute the causes of actions or their outcomes in a way that reflects well on the perceivers or absolves the perceivers from responsibility for poor outcomes.

**Semiautonomous work group** Team of workers given full responsibility for a series of tasks (including arrangement and assignment of the work).

**Sensation** Process of nerve endings sending inputs to the brain with no meaning attached.

**Sequential interdependence** Exists when the outputs of one unit become the inputs of another unit.

**Sexual harassment** Verbal or physical conduct of a sexual nature when submission to such conduct is made either explicitly or implicitly a term or condition of an individual's employment, influences employment decisions affecting the individual, or substantially interferes with the individual's work performance or work environment.

**Similar-to-me bias** Rating bias in which raters tend to rate more positively those individuals whose background and experience are similar to their own.

**Simple structure** Organizational structure common in young or small organizations in which coordination is largely a function of direct supervision, the top manager or entrepreneur has significant control, employees have very little discretionary decision-making power, and there is little formal policy or procedure.

**Slack** Excess resources that can minimize conflict because they reduce the amount of necessary interaction.

**Social adjustment** Changes the organization must make in response to environmental changes that are unrelated to its actions.

**Social anchoring** Forming perceptions or judgments in an extremely uncertain situation by relying on the opinions of others.

**Social audit** Mechanism organizations use to see where they stand with respect to corporate-responsibility demands by identifying important issues in the social environment, cataloging the actions the organization is presently taking, and assessing their effectiveness.

**Social comparison** Process of having one's perceptions influenced by the comments and perceptions of others.

**Social covenant** Set of rules that constrains and structures group interaction.

**Social evidence** Using the opinions of other people as an input to individual beliefs.

**Social facilitation** Tendency for the presence of others to enhance an individual's energy level.

**Social information processing** Framework of job design that emphasizes the importance of perception and social cues from co-workers and supervisors in understanding how workers react to their jobs.

**Social inhibition** Tendency for the presence of others to impair an individual's performance, including social loafing, self-handicapping, and conformity.

**Sociotechnical systems** Approach to job redesign that moves beyond semiautonomous work groups by making technology a central concern in making jobs more interesting, involving, and motivating for workers.

**Span of control** Number of people reporting to a manager.

**Staffing** Management function of supplying a work force (people) to fill the organization's designed structures.

**Standard hour rate** Payment rate per hour based on the amount of time, determined by industrial engineering standards, that it should take to produce each unit.

**Status** Position of a role in the social hierarchy.

**Stereotype** Complex set of expectations and beliefs associated with specific personal characteristics, such as sex, race, or occupation.

**Stockpile** Resource set aside for future use, such as money put into savings for a "rainy day"; a form of slack.

**Stress quotient**   The amount of stress a job is likely to generate in the job holder.

**Substitutes for leadership**   Individual, organizational, and task characteristics that have the capacity to serve the same purposes as leader behaviors.

**Succession**   Turnover, retirement, or promotion of personnel.

**Successive approximation**   Reinforcing increasingly better attempts at a final desired behavior; may include shaping or chaining.

**Superstitious behavior**   Belief that a behavior will be rewarded even though the behavior is in fact irrelevant.

**Support systems**   Elements in an organization that assist personnel in accomplishing their work tasks effectively, such as production technology.

**Survey-guided development**   Use of questionnaires to construct a picture of an organization's internal processes and problems; also called survey feedback.

**Synergy**   Mutual influence process of stimulation and encouragement among members of a group.

**System 4**   Management theory of Rensis Likert proposing that in superior work units management has an optimistic, supportive, and humanistic view of workers, and every worker belongs to a highly cohesive and participative work group with high performance goals and expectations.

**Task identity**   Sense of completion and achievement that occurs when a set of assigned tasks allows the worker to see a process through from start to finish.

**Task interdependence**   Power accruing to a particular job or group of jobs in an organization when two or more employees must depend on each other to complete assigned tasks.

**Task significance**   Worker's sense that a good or poor performance on the job makes a difference to someone.

**Team development**   An inward look by the team at its own performance, behavior, and culture for the purposes of correcting dysfunctional behaviors and strengthening functional ones.

**Technological determinism**   Perspective that the way a firm is organized (how it makes decisions or how much training its line workers receive, for example) depends on the technology the firm uses to transform its inputs into outputs.

**Technological type**   Joan Woodward's classifications of ways an organization can transform inputs into outputs, which determine behavior in the organization: (A) unit or small-batch production, (B) large-batch production, and (C) mass production or process manufacturing.

**Technology**   The knowledge, tools, and techniques available to an organization to transform inputs into outputs.

**Telecommuting**   Employees completing their duties outside the office using home computers that double as information storage and retrieval systems and electronic mail receipt and transmission stations.

**Telecourse systems**   Training workers using television programs or computer links in the workers' homes.

**Theory of social exchange** Theory suggesting that social behavior is an exchange of material and nonmaterial goods (such as approval and prestige), and that in relationships people continually monitor the rewards and costs to work out balanced exchanges.

**Theory X**   Management's traditional view of workers, including the assumptions that workers are naturally lazy, self-centered, and resistant to change and will avoid responsibility, and management must direct, motivate, and control them.

**Theory Y**   View of workers as naturally motivated to work as much as to rest or play; workers will exercise self-direction and self-control in the service of objectives to which they are committed.

**Third-party intervention**   Involvement in a conflict of someone not directly concerned, such as arbitration, mediation, and fact finding.

**Time-and-motion studies**   Scientific management technique of timed observations and experiments to identify the most efficient means for accomplishing a task.

**Top-down problem solving** Diagnosis of a problem by management, with the rest of the work force being informed only during unfreezing.

**Total job situation**   Seven characteristics of a job derived by C. R. Walker and R. H. Guest, including the worker's immediate job, relation to fellow workers, relation to supervisors, relation to the union, pay and job security, promotion and transfer prospects, and working conditions in the plant.

**Trait-rating scale**   Employee evaluation format that asks the rater to evaluate the ratee on such factors as dependability, cooperation, leadership, obedience, and loyalty.

**Transactional leader**   Leader who motivates followers by exchanging rewards for services.

**Transformational leader** Leader who arouses intense feeling and generates turbulent one-to-one relationships with followers and is inspirational and concerned with ideas rather than processes.

**Two-factor theory**   Content theory of motivation framed in terms of factors that affect work dissatisfaction and satisfaction: hygiene factors and motivators.

**Two-way communication**   Communication in which receivers can return messages to senders.

**Type A personality**   Set of personality characteristics found in many stress-prone people, such as impatience, competitiveness, and the drive to succeed.

**Type B personality**  Classification of behaviors found in less stress-prone people, such as a relaxed, easy-going, noncompetitive attitude toward work and life.

**Uncertainty**  Not knowing for sure; may include future actions or events, or the relationships between actions and their consequences.

**Unfreezing**  Second stage in the process of change; lowering barriers to change by selling the diagnosis, understanding the implementation, and preparing for the consequences.

**Union**  Group of workers who have banded together to give themselves more bargaining power with their employer.

**Valence**  The perceived value of a behavior's consequences.

**Vertical conflict**  Conflict between people at different levels in an organization.

**Vertical dyad linkage model**  Model based on the exchange theory that stresses the importance of individual relationships between leader and subordinates. Each relationship is termed a vertical dyad.

**Vertical integration**  Acquisition of one organization by another with the goal of controlling resource dependencies that are important in its production process.

**Vicarious learning**  Acquiring desirable behaviors by observing the behaviors of other people; also called *social learning*.

**Visibility**  The observability of behaviors serving to commit individuals to organizations by making their association with it public knowledge.

**Volition**  Extent to which individuals believe they have a choice in their behaviors, serving to commit them to their actions.

**Work simplification**  Design of work tasks to be simple and easily mastered so each worker can become expert at some very small number of tasks and learn to do them repeatedly with lightning speed and no mistakes.

**Work standards**  Scientific-management technique of providing specific instructions to workers for doing a task, including expected time for completion and expected volume of output.

# Photo Credits

# Name Index

# Subject Index

Note: Page numbers in bold type indicate pages where key terms are discussed.